A SOCIAL AND RELIGIOUS
HISTORY OF THE JEWS

Ancient Times: Volumes I–II

VOLUME I

TO THE BEGINNING OF THE CHRISTIAN ERA

A SOCIAL
AND RELIGIOUS
HISTORY OF
THE JEWS

By SALO WITTMAYER BARON

Second Edition, Revised and Enlarged

Ancient Times: Volumes I–II
VOLUME I
TO THE BEGINNING OF THE CHRISTIAN ERA

Columbia University Press
New York
The Jewish Publication Society of America
Philadelphia

ISBN 0-231-08838-8

SECOND EDITION 1952

PRINTED IN THE UNITED STATES OF AMERICA

15   14   13   12

To My Wife

PREFACE

THAT EVERY GENERATION rewrites all history has become almost a truism. In some respects more than a generation has passed since the preparation of the first edition of the present work. Mankind as a whole has gone through the catastrophe of the Second World War, and seems to be heading toward an even greater crisis. The Jewish people, inured though it has been to tragedies, has lived through the greatest tragedy of all its history. At the same time it witnessed the fulfillment of a millennial hope, the rebirth of its nation on its ancestral soil.

From this perspective the whole historic career of the Jewish people appears in a new light. Even the First or Second Jewish Commonwealth looks different from the vantage point of a third commonwealth. The story of the Jewish dispersion, the friendly or unfriendly relations between Jews and their neighbors, economic and social transformations, even the development of the Jewish religion—all assume new aspects when viewed from the standpoint of the tragic decline of European Jewry, the Nazi and Communist onslaught on the foundations of the Judeo-Christian civilization, and the newer world-wide economic and cultural trends.

Moreover, the last fifteen years belong to the most fruitful years in the discovery of new vestiges of ancient life and the reappraisal in their light of all previously known records. During the preparation of the first edition the Ras Shamra epics had just begun to be deciphered. Now Ugaritic has become a significant discipline in the field of Semitic studies. Lachish, Mari, 'Ain Fashkha were hardly more than geographic names. Apart from the archaeological discoveries, however, there has been going on a steady process of reorientation of biblical scholarship in both the Old and the N.w Testament fields. By throwing off the shackles of the then still regnant Wellhausenian theory, scholarship has split up, to be sure, into a number of schools. But, however controversial and often chaotic in its disparity this reassessment of the past has been, it has reopened the vast and ever growing factual records to new and independent reëxamination.

Under these circumstances a mere revision of the work done fifteen years ago no longer seemed feasible. In the process of rewriting, some of the older views had to be abandoned, but many others had to be amplified and newly documented in such a way as to make the present edition to all intents and purposes a new work. As in the first edition, the respective chapters do not adhere to a strict chronological order. On the whole, however, Chapters II–V deal with the Old Testament period until Alexander. Chapters VI–X discuss the crucial developments during the four centuries from the Greek conquest of the Near East to the second fall of Jerusalem, while the concluding five chapters (XI–XV) bring the story up to the conclusion of the talmudic period about 500 C.E.

Remarkably, it was the first introductory chapter which underwent the least change. The fundamental aspects of Jewish history have changed somewhat less than the approach to and appreciation of individual links in that millennial evolution. By far the greatest changes occurred, naturally enough, in the bibliographical documentation. Not only have many older references been replaced by newer literature but, in view of the increased size, an effort was made to quote more fully the primary sources as well, so as to acquaint the reader with the nature of the available evidence. Not to multiply the number of notes, however, brief references to sources were often given in the text itself, while more extensive source material was frequently combined in longer annotations at the end of the respective paragraphs. As in the first edition more detailed discussions were relegated to the notes, some of which have therefore assumed the character of regular excursuses.

While the notes are now printed at the end of each volume, fuller bibliographical data had to be postponed to the concluding volume of the series. For the time being, the reader will find the bibliographical entries sufficiently identifiable. But all subtitles, places and years of publication and other relevant but secondary data will be given in that final bibliography. A genuine effort was made to assure up-to-dateness of these references. Although far from exhaustive, the notes are likely to mention all the more important publications in any language which had come to the writer's attention until about April 1, 1951. A small fraction of these entries (approximately one percent of the total) was not available for consultation and verification. But, if otherwise more or less reliably recorded, these references were included for the benefit of readers who might have access to them. If, at the time of publication of the Bibliography they should still remain unavailable, they will, as in the first edition, be indicated by a dagger.

Without making a fetish of it, we have genuinely endeavored to be consistent. In some cases a rather artificial decision had to be made. For example, the adjective "Judean" is consistently used to describe developments relating either to ancient Judah or to Judaism. We speak therefore, for example, of Judean prophets or the Judeo-Christian heritage. But in all matters referring to post-exilic Judaea, we have preferred the designation, "Judaean." Similarly authors whose names were changed or are differently spelled in different publications (for instance, Torczyner—Tur-Sinai; Bickerman—Bickermann—Bikerman; Tcherikover—Tscherikower; and Edmund—Menahem Stein) are cited, as a rule, in the form given in their respective books or articles. But these studies will, of course, be listed together in the Bibliography.

In conclusion, it is a genuine pleasure to acknowledge indebtedness to several coworkers. My colleague and former pupil, Dr. Philip Friedman, proved very helpful in verifying some references in the notes to Chapter VI–XV. My secretary, Mrs. Miriam Antler Brownstone, had complete charge of the technical preparation of the manuscript. She and Mrs. Ida B. Perlmann have also assisted me in reading the proofs. Miss Matilda L. Berg of Columbia University Press has edited the entire manuscript. I am deeply grateful to all of them. Most of all, I am indebted to my wife for her untiring encouragement and collaboration.

S.W.B

Yifat Shalom
Canaan, Conn.
June 29, 1951

CONTENTS

I JEWISH SOCIETY AND RELIGION   3
INTERDEPENDENCE OF JEWS AND JUDAISM; HISTORI-
CAL MONOTHEISM; ETHICS OF A CHOSEN PEOPLE;
EMANCIPATION FROM STATE AND TERRITORY; HISTORI-
CAL LITERATURE; MENACE OF A NEW SCHISM; NATION-
ALISM AND UNIVERSALISM

II ISRAEL'S ORIGINS   32
AMIDST ADVANCED CIVILIZATIONS; ISRAEL'S SOJOURN
IN EGYPT; ETHNIC UNITY; MONOTHEISTIC ANTECED-
ENTS; THE WORK OF MOSES; INFLUENCE OF PALES-
TINE; RESOLUTION OF ANTITHESES

III KINGS AND PROPHETS   63
MONARCHICAL POWER AND ITS DRAWBACKS; ECO-
NOMIC DECLINE AND SOCIAL UNREST; GOVERNMENTAL
DIFFUSION; RELIGION AND LAW; PROPHECY AND SO-
CIAL REVOLUTION; ANTIMONARCHICAL TRENDS; NA-
TIONALITY AND STATE; RELIGIOUS UNIVERSALISM AND
PARTICULARISM; IDEALIZATION OF THE PAST; DIVINE
INSTRUMENT

IV CRUCIAL TEST   102
SIGNIFICANT SIXTH CENTURY; GROWING DISPERSION;
ECONOMIC PROGRESS; WOMAN'S ENHANCED STATUS;
LEGAL PROTECTION; ASSIMILATION OR PRESERVATION;
DIASPORA COMMUNITY; STIMULI OF PERSIAN IMPERI-
ALISM; PIONEER COMMUNITY

V RETHINKING FUNDAMENTALS   134
NEW TIDINGS; IMPACT OF THE LAW; HIERARCHY;
ETHNIC EXCLUSIVISM AND HUMANITARIANISM; TERRI-
TORIAL RESTORATION; DEFIANCE OF NATURE

VI EXPANSION OF JUDAISM 165
NUMERICAL AND GEOGRAPHICAL EXPANSION; NATURAL
INCREASE AND CONVERSIONS; CHANGING ATTITUDES;
CULTURAL EXCHANGES; CLASSICAL ANTISEMITISM;
JEWISH APOLOGIAS; PHILO JUDAEUS; DIVERGENT
ESCHATOLOGIES; WEAKNESS OF EXPANSION

VII PALESTINIAN CENTER 212
JEWISH METROPOLIS; POLITICAL AND CULTURAL RELA-
TIONS; THEOCRATIC REGIME; POLITICS AND MARTYR-
DOM; POLITICAL CONFLICTS; IMPERIAL STATUS; IN-
TERDEPENDENCE OF FATE

VIII SOCIAL TURMOIL 250
AGRICULTURE; TRADE AND INDUSTRY; DIASPORA ECON-
OMY; RICH AND POOR; SLAVES AND FREE WORKERS;
SOCIAL STRATIFICATION; POPULAR UNREST; WEAK-
NESS OF CONFUSION

ABBREVIATIONS 289

NOTES 293
I, 293–97; II, 298–319; III, 320–40; IV, 341–55; V,
356–68; VI, 369–91; VII, 392–405; VIII, 406–415

A SOCIAL AND RELIGIOUS HISTORY
OF THE JEWS

Ancient Times

Volume I TO THE BEGINNING OF THE CHRISTIAN ERA
      I   JEWISH SOCIETY AND RELIGION
      II   ISRAEL'S ORIGINS
      III   KINGS AND PROPHETS
      IV   CRUCIAL TEST
      V   RETHINKING FUNDAMENTALS
      VI   EXPANSION OF JUDAISM
      VII   PALESTINIAN CENTER
      VIII   SOCIAL TURMOIL
Volume II CHRISTIAN ERA: THE FIRST FIVE CENTURIES
      IX   NEW HORIZONS
      X   THE GREAT SCHISM
      XI   BREAKDOWN AND RECONSTRUCTION
      XII   CLOSING THE RANKS
      XIII   INCIPIENT MEDIEVALISM
      XIV   WORLD OF THE TALMUD
      XV   TALMUDIC LAW AND RELIGION

High Middle Ages

Volume III HEIRS OF ROME AND PERSIA
      XVI   THE PREISLAMIC WORLD
      XVII   MOHAMMED AND THE CALIPHATE
      XVIII   PROTECTED MINORITY
      XIX   EASTERN EUROPE
Volume IV MEETING OF EAST AND WEST
      XX   WESTERN CHRISTENDOM
      XXI   AGE OF CRUSADES
      XXII   ECONOMIC TRANSFORMATIONS
Volume V RELIGIOUS CONTROLS AND DISSENSIONS
      XXIII   COMMUNAL CONTROLS
      XXIV   SOCIORELIGIOUS CONTROVERSIES
      XXV   MESSIANISM AND SECTARIAN TRENDS
      XXVI   KARAITE SCHISM
Volume VI LAWS, HOMILIES, AND THE BIBLE
      XXVII   REIGN OF LAW
      XXVIII   HOMILIES AND HISTORIES
      XXIX   RESTUDY OF THE BIBLE
Volume VII HEBREW LANGUAGE AND LETTERS
      XXX   LINGUISTIC RENASCENCE
      XXXI   WORSHIP: UNITY AMIDST DIVERSITY
      XXXII   POETRY AND BELLES-LETTRES
Volume VIII PHILOSOPHY AND SCIENCE
      XXXIII   MAGIC AND MYSTICISM
      XXXIV   FAITH AND REASON
      XXXV   SCIENTIFIC EXPLORATION
      XXXVI   MEDICAL SCIENCE AND PRACTICE
INDEX TO VOLUMES I–VIII

TO THE BEGINNING OF THE
CHRISTIAN ERA

I

JEWISH SOCIETY AND RELIGION

THAT there is no direct correlation between the *fate* of Jews and that of Judaism has often been observed. Particularly in the last century and a half, developments favorable to individual Jews have frequently proved detrimental to Jewish group life, and consequently to Judaism. The "Emancipation" itself, which raised the economic and social status of millions of Jews by removing legal disabilities and special burdens, was attended by the destruction of Jewish self-government, the material limitation of the applicability of Jewish law, and a partial disintegration of traditional religious and cultural patterns. From another angle, Russian Communism, while relieving the Jewish masses of the severe oppression suffered under the czars, has become a serious menace to the survival of traditional, perhaps of all Judaism. More recently, the projected separation of state and church in the new state of Israel would formally divorce the destinies of the people from those of its religion.

INTERDEPENDENCE OF JEWS AND JUDAISM

The contrast between Jews and Judaism is, nevertheless, apparent rather than real; and not only in the obvious sense that Judaism cannot exist, for any length of time, without Jews, nor Jews without Judaism. Besides this inherent correlation which obtains between every creed and its believers, every culture and its bearers, there is a certain specific, and even more significant connection between Judaism as a creed and as a culture. To Judaism the existence of the Jewish people is essential and indispensable, not only for its realization in life, but for its very idea; not only for its actuality, but for its potentiality. The Jewish religion without the "chosen people" is unthinkable. Neither could it, like the other religions, be transplanted from the Jewish to another people. No matter how many adherents it might gain in the outside world, the physical extinction of the Jewish people would sound the death knell of Judaism. For the Jews, as such, their religio-cultural heritage is all the more vital, because they have so long lacked the other basic elements of human group life—territory, state, and language. Next to the blood ties of common descent, it is primarily this heritage that makes Jews Jewish; more Jewish, indeed, when they affirm Judaism with their conscious and voluntary allegiance than when they accept it as a sheer accident of birth. The unity of Jews and Judaism thus has a deep meaning, and the interrelation between the two, the interplay of the social and religious forces throughout the entire course of Jewish history, appears to be of controlling significance.[1]

This interpenetration need not apply to all individual members of the Jewish people. In a sense, Judaism is independent of the number of those who profess it. Theoretically there might remain only a few hundred Jews in the world and Judaism would still be a living religion. Consequently we speak of a prolonged struggle between Judaism, or the "essential" Mosaic religion, and the so-called "popular religion" of ancient Israel. Regardless of how few the votaries of the former, how many the adherents of the latter, Judaism in its Mosaic formulation remained the main stream in Jewish history. Similarly, in later times the many schismatic movements among Jews usually broke off from the main body of Jewry and, sooner or later, the people and its religion were once again coextensive.

On the other hand, numbers are by no means negligible, even in the religious sense. Whether the total number of Jews amounts to thousands or to millions makes a calculable difference in their social and hence in their religious life. Their distribution in many lands their economic and political status, their contacts with other cultures, are all deeply affected by their numbers. Quantity here often becomes quality, affecting the religious life and even the religious thought of the people.

HISTORICAL MONOTHEISM

To understand fully this intrinsic interdependence of Jewish social and religious life, we are forced to consider at greater length the distinctive nature of the Jewish religion. To put it summarily at the start: the Jewish religion has been from the very beginning, and in the progress of time has increasingly become, an *historical* religion, in permanent contrast to all *natural* religions. This distinction was long felt by Jewish thinkers and found its best formulation in the philosophy of Yehudah Halevi. To the present generation, however, the contrast between history and nature is becoming clearer. From the outset the historical element was so predominant in the religious ideas of the Jewish people that historical (or historico-ethical) monotheism may be regarded as the essential contribution of Israel's religion to the history of human creeds.

Many examples may be cited. It is well known, for instance, that the ancient Israelitic festivals were taken over from the earlier oriental cultures of Canaan and Babylonia. But in each case ancient Judaism changed the fundamental meaning of the festival first by adding to it, then by substituting for its natural an historical interpretation. Thus the *shalosh regalim*, the three great holidays of the year, originally natural holidays of agricultural production, became, for the Jews, holidays commemorating great historical events. Passover, the ancient spring festival, became and remained the festival of the Exodus from Egypt, or of the origin of the Jewish nation. The very name *Pesah* may not have been derived, as the Bible's popular etymology has it, from the Hebrew equivalent of "pass over," but rather, as Fritz Hommel suggested, from the Egyptian equivalent of remembrance. "And this day shall be unto you for a memorial," reads the crucial injunction (Exod. 12:13–14). Pentecost, still "the day of the first-fruits" in the Old Testament, was transformed by the early Pharisees into a memorial chiefly of the giving of the Torah, that is, of the foundation of the Jewish religion. The Feast of Tabernacles celebrates chiefly the migration through the desert, that traditional formative period of both Jewish nationality and Jewish religion. New Year's Day is essentially a memento of the world's creation. Having the choice between two Babylonian New Years, Judaism selected the Autumnal date, although the one in spring, reflecting nature's annual rebirth, was more "natural." Together with the Day of Atonement, the Jewish New Year also became the day of judgment for all mankind, obviously an historical event of primary importance in its annual repetition.

Not yet satisfied, however, the rabbis tried to lend to both festivals a specifically Jewish historical character in commemoration of certain biblical events whose dates had not been recorded. The exclusively historical sanctions attached during the Second Commonwealth to Hanukkah and Purim (the deliverance from Syrian oppression and the schemes of Haman) have so thoroughly suc-

ceeded in obscuring the original natural background of these ancient oriental holidays that modern scholars have experienced great
difficulty in their attempts at identification. Finally, Sirach saw in
the very celestial bodies nothing but implements of the Jewish
calendar. Exaggerating the biblical reasoning, he stated: "Moreover
the Moon He made for its due season, to rule over periods and for
an everlasting sign. By her (are determined) the feasts and the times
prescribed." [2]

Even the Jewish Sabbath, whose main origin is in Babylonian
astronomy (the lunar month with its four quarters and, in part, the
seven planets), received quite a novel and profound sanctification
by virtue of its connection with the beginnings of all history—the
day chosen by God for rest after his labors of creation. Nowhere
else, except in Judaism and its daughter religion, has the Sabbath
received this character of holy and absolute rest. Prophesying in
Babylonia itself, Ezekiel by a curious irony drew the distinction between Jews and Gentiles on precisely this basis of Sabbath observance: "Moreover also I gave them My Sabbaths, to be a sign between Me and them, that they might know that I am the Lord that
sanctify them" (20:12). So significant did the day become that, as
we shall see, "Shabbetai" was the most familiar of the new Hebrew
names adopted by the Jews during the Babylonian Exile. To the
Graeco-Roman world this institution of a day of rest appeared so
foreign, even after the Romans had taken over the oriental seven-
day week, that the Jews were accused of "laziness." So little was the
Sabbath understood and so much was it resented that many a Greek
city, and once apparently a Roman emperor himself, prohibited its
observance. But the Jews resisted, and now the majority of mankind regards every seventh day, at least, as a day of rest.

On the other hand, the one natural holiday of the New Moon,
long celebrated even in ancient Israel, gradually lost its importance,
because it was not reinterpreted historically. The quasi revival of
that forgotten holiday by modern Hasidism is simply another back-
to-nature aspect of that movement.

The other fundamental ceremony of Judaism, circumcision, provides another capital illustration. This custom, widespread among
primitive nations all over the world, had been practiced from time
immemorial in Egypt and Canaan-Phoenicia. But here again, Israel's
lawgivers divested it of its original natural meaning and gave it a
new and unheard-of historical significance: they advanced the time
of performance from the age of thirteen to the early days of in-

fancy, severing its intrinsic connection with male pubescence, and making of it an eternal symbol of God's covenant with the Jewish people. Under this guise, the ceremony survived all the opposition which from time to time arose against it within and outside Jewry. It withstood the rigid prohibition (with capital punishment as the penalty of violation) of the powerful Roman Emperor Hadrian; it survived the hatred of some medieval Church leaders for the "Cain's sign" of the wandering Jew; it outlasted even the antagonism of Holdheim and other nineteenth-century Jewish reformers. Today, as always, practically all Jews adhere to it as the symbol of the unity between Israel's creed and Israel's people and not merely negatively, as is sometimes believed by unfriendly observers, *ut diversitate noscantur* (Tacitus, *Hist.*, V, 5).

Such examples could easily be multiplied. In most Jewish religious institutions, rituals, and doctrines, this historical reinterpretation of old customs is so obvious as to require no emphasis. History is the all-pervading dominant sanction for the most fundamental ideas, including the concepts of messianism, the chosen people, the covenant with God, and the Torah. God created the world at a certain time; later He created man; still later He selected Israel as his nation of priests; led them out of Egypt; gave them their law; commanded them to observe that law for their inner sanctification—and all this in the interest of an ideal goal in the messianic future. In that age, "history" will finally vanquish "nature," even changing its very course, for in that day "the wolf shall dwell with the lamb" (Isa. 11:6), and, in general, nature will be transformed into a community.

At this point it may be well to distinguish between what we have designated the religious conception of history's victory over nature and the scientific conception of man's increasing dominion over nature. While, according to the latter, man gradually masters the forces of nature and makes its laws subservient to his own equally natural needs, Isaiah's messianism preaches the final transformation of the immutable laws of nature themselves. In the meantime, the Jew's ideal should be, not mastery over nature, but independence of it, the achievement of supremacy over it by refusing to recognize its superior powers. This attitude, however, does not involve extreme asceticism. The evil is not nature as such, but its power over man. As long as the Jew fully complies with the Law of God, and thus serves God's inscrutable aims as they realize themselves through the progress of time, he may and even should satisfy all his natural needs, because then they are of no intrinsic significance. But whenever there is a conflict between nature and the Law, the latter is to be recognized as supreme. The Jew, in some instances, must sacrifice his life in order to obey the Law. Emancipation from nature, then, rather than nature's suppression, is the cardinal goal: for the time being limited and well defined legally, it will be thoroughgoing in the messianic age.

Nor will the course of developments, until that age be reached, resemble the pattern depicted by modern theories of evolution. History will vanquish nature, not by a gradual progression toward the final goal, but by a sudden more or less miraculous realization at some point now undetermined. The fact that Judaism believed not only in the golden age of the first days of mankind, however, but also in the more enduring age of uninterrupted peace in nature to come at the end of days, tended to make of the Jewish religion an essentially optimistic creed. In this very world of ours, the full realization of the great aims of religion will come through processes in history, however difficult it may be to comprehend their final developments. These processes of history are neither the processes of political victory and conquest, the vicissitudes of power—the prevalent conception of commonplace history—nor those of successive defeat and ultimate failure of every human achievement, as visualized by pessimistic surveyors of the ups and downs of mankind. History thus seen is neither the open arena, where consecutive generations of gladiators meet in their perennial struggle for power, nor a mass of smoldering ruins and abandoned débris testifying to the grandeur of extinct civilizations. It is a progression of conspicuous and hidden human and Jewish achievements, of conspicuous and hidden frustrations guided by the inscrutable will of God. Manifest victory is often really defeat, and apparent surrender the mark of actual conquest. The impotence of man as an instrument of an Almighty Power to achieve the ultimate, truly decisive victory over nature—this is the core of "historical" Judaism.

With this outlook Judaism could easily become a religion based upon life on this earth. In the perspective of history, this globe and man upon it has a much more central position than in the relativity of nature. Although ancient geocentric and anthropocentric conceptions of the natural world have been entirely discarded by modern natural science, in the realm of history, even in the history of the universe, man occupies a peculiar position. Here individuals and nations, as well as mankind as a whole, are not mere infinitesimal particles of the cosmos, but their fate is, in each case, specific, peculiar, unique, and consequently of central importance, at least to that particular individual or nation or to mankind.

Judaism has sometimes been called a this-worldly religion. This description is true in so far as its central emphasis is laid upon the destinies of mankind and, within mankind, of the Jewish people, *in this world*. In contradistinction to many other religions, and in particular to that of the great southern neighbor Egypt, Judaism (especially in the earlier periods) cared comparatively little about death. The paucity of biblical references to the idea of individual life after death or resurrection, is well known. Indeed, these references are found only in later writings, such as the Book of Daniel. When Judaism, for reasons which will be explained in another chapter, ultimately stressed the belief in resurrection, the rabbis of the Mishnah were at a loss to find clear support for it in the Pentateuch or Prophets. Both early and later Judaism, however, continuously emphasized a firm belief in the survival of the group and in the "eternal" life of the Jewish people down to, and beyond, the messianic age.

Along with the emphasis on history, then, went an affirmation of life as it realizes itself through history. In contrast to the teachings of the early Church Fathers and the religious thinkers of India, and even of extreme wings which appeared time and again in Judaism itself, the main stream of the Law sanctified daily pursuits performed in the spirit of service to the family or nation. It has been well pointed out that the Hebrew term *melakhah* (connected with *malakh*), as well as the corresponding English and German expressions (used by the Protestant translators Cranmer and Luther) "calling" and "Beruf," combines with the idea of vocation or mission that of an economic occupation. Indeed, this approval, and not mere tolerance of economic activity, finds numerous formulations in the teachings of the rabbis. A well-known legend best characterizes the two opposed views in Judaism. Rabbi Simon ben Yoḥai and his son, the Talmud tells us, had been confined in a cave for twelve years in order to escape the wrath of the Romans. They spent the time divorced from the normal pursuits of life, engaging in mystic speculations. When they finally left the cave and emerged into the world at large, they saw some farmers tilling the soil. "They neglect the eternal life," Simon exclaimed, "and busy themselves with the life of a moment." So great was their anger that wherever they cast their eyes, the fields withered under their gaze. The legend concludes, however, with a voice from heaven calling to them: "Have you come to destroy my world? Go back to the cave!" (Shabbat 33b). In another connection the rabbis positively reversed the meaning of the ancient curse which biblical mythology still associated with Adam's downfall. They represented the first man as gravely perturbed over the prospect of eating thorns and thistles with his donkey, but fully pacified when he heard that he was to eat bread in the sweat of his brow (Pesaḥim 118a). Official Judaism has ever since peremptorily rejected the deprecation of manual labor.

ETHICS OF A CHOSEN PEOPLE

This affirmation of life is far from an acceptance of things as they are, however. On the contrary, in the great conflict between history and nature, man is gradually to overcome nature. The Law often demands this struggle of man against both external nature and undisciplined human nature, and in this struggle morality emerges. Thus morality becomes man's chief means of realizing the aims of history. In this sense the historical monotheism of Judaism is also ethical monotheism. But only in this sense! A monotheism primarily ethical would be expected to set up definite moral aims and to appeal to the individual by placing before him his own ethical goal, and his own ethical means of achieving that goal. Judaism, however, stresses the general aims of the Jewish people and, in a way, of mankind, to be realized in some unknown future by unknown miraculous means. This failure to relate the moral life of the individual to the ultimate and unknowable goal, which is therefore in a sense non-moral and attainable only through the career of the nation, is intelligible only from the point of view of an *historical* monotheism. Individual righteousness has so little direct bearing on the advent of the Messiah that according to one version he may come in a generation consisting exclusively of sinners. To this day orthodox Jewish ethics has remained in its essence national rather than individual, and this accounts, incidentally, for the otherwise incomprehensible legal theorem of the common responsibility of *all* Jews for the deeds of each.[3]

Here, too, lies the root of the Law's supreme power over the individual, who must comply with it whether he understands its reasons or not. Its great aims transcending the individual, the Law has underlying motives which may remain hidden to him. He may, like Maimonides and others, try to rationalize it, but he must not change it in the least. This may have appeared to philosophers of the school of Hegel as an expression of spiritual bondage, this may have induced a Wellhausen to accuse the Pharisees, the representative teachers of Judaism, of lack of individualism and extreme subjection to the rule of law, but it is the necessary consequence and intrinsically consistent form of an historical monotheism. True, there were not lacking in Jewish history men who dared to question the very foundations of the system. From Abraham's query, "Shall not the Judge of all the earth do justly?" (Gen. 18:25), through Moses and Job down to the last Ḥasidic rabbis and Berditshevski, grave questions have been raised from generation to generation. But the main current proceeded unperturbed in the bed carved out for it by history.

This spiritual servitude, however, was never intended to be a forcible subjection. The purposes of the Law, as an instrument of history, would have been totally defeated, had not the compliance with it been a matter of spontaneous, indeed, enthusiastic affirmation. The ancient adage *timor facit deos* has often served to expound the supposedly gloomy surrender of the Semite to the will of the deity. But in fact the affirmative "fear of the Lord," one of the corner stones of Old Testament piety, became to such a degree a sublimation of this negative fear, to say the least, that it unquestionably belongs to another category. It found its highest expression in the *teshubah,* that is, in something more than "repentance," in the sinner's complete voluntary *return,* in his unequivocal retracing of his steps toward a reunion with God. After the rebirth of his personality, he carries the "burden of the law" with even greater ease than the pious man inured to it through constant practice.[4] In either case, however, man, being a weak though godlike creature, needs divine grace to sustain him. Individual merit is, indeed, a combination of personal effort and unfathomable divine support. "Sanctify yourselves, therefore, and be ye holy. . . . And keep ye My statutes, and do them: I am the Lord who sanctify you" (Lev. 20:7–8). Voluntary moral conduct in accordance with the divine law, as an act of self-assertion, but combined with wholehearted self-resignation as an instrument of God's will for the fulfillment of his unknown and unknowable aims—this is the essence of ancient Jewish ethics.

We can now understand the deeper meaning of the concept of the "chosen people" in Israel's religion. Not only is the nation the chief vehicle of history itself, but in this conquest of nature by history a selected *group* of men is indispensable. Nature's resistance to history is enormous. Only a chosen few are qualified to overcome it, even in the limited sense understood by the Jewish religion for the period preceding the advent of the Messiah. If these chosen few retain their individual life independent of one another, then religion remains an individual, not a group phenomenon. This would prevent it from ever becoming the religion of mankind, the largest of groups, and consequently the aim of history to vanquish nature *through mankind* would never be accomplished. A group religion, therefore, needs a *selected body* of men; this is the core of the idea of a "chosen people."

Furthermore, history's processes are not eternally recurrent like those of nature. They are unique and unrepeatable. Consequently, in order to be realized through history a religion needs, not general standards, but a chosen few who, through a life independent of nature, come to exemplify religion for all. Others, again, will not merely imitate this unparalleled example, but will receive the teaching for a new, equally inimitable conduct of their own. Hence this insistence upon the chosen nation, a nation chosen for the special purpose of living the hard life of an exemplar! Hence also, the distinction between the 613 laws regulating the behavior of the Jew and the 6 or 7 fundamental duties enjoined upon all the sons of Noah! The uniform belief even of the most "universalistic" of the Jewish prophets was that before the messianic age there is little chance for mankind as a whole to overcome nature. Consequently, until that age shall come segregation is necessary to preserve at least one exemplary group from mixing with the masses of others over whom, they assumed, nature's power was prevailing. In this sense the Jews had to be Jews "contrary to all men," to quote Paul (I Thess. 2:15). At the same time, they were being Jews *for all men.*

The nation overshadows the individual in other respects as well. What really matters in the Jewish religion is not the immortality of the individual Jew, but that of the Jewish people. Even when later Judaism adopted the belief in the immortality of the soul and physical resurrection, the central point remained the eternal life of the nation. Hence the extraordinary attachment to life manifested by orthodox Jews. Life on earth, the care of the sick and the poor, the duty of marriage and increase in family—all these are repeatedly stressed that the race and the people may be maintained until the end of days. Concerning what this "end of days" will actually bring, opinions vary. Some think that even in the messianic age the Jewish people will retain its identity, as will the other nations, the only difference being that all will profess the same creed. Some, whom we may call religious cosmopolitans, dream of the mingling of all nations into one uniform mankind, likewise under the domination of one creed, the Jewish. Then the Jewish people will disappear, because it will have accomplished its duty and also because, in a sense, all men will have become Jews.

The prohibition of *imagery* in the Jewish religion is a necessary part of such teachings. Because this religion was detached from nature, it had also to be divorced from the soil and from every kind of concreteness. Imagery is concrete; it is localized. It tends to focus worship in a certain place. Imagery makes the local sanctuary supreme, and with it a special attachment to a particular territory. The Jewish religion was forced to contend against such allegiance. Here was more than a mere means of suppressing the advanced anthropomorphism of Israel's neighbors. In commenting on the persistent adherence of Judaism to the two metaphors, *Abinu Malkenu* (our Father, our King), Claude G. Montefiore asks: "Do they show that the Jewish conception of God if, by its rejection of the Incarnation dogma, not anthropomorphic enough on the one hand, is yet, by its insistence upon the divine Kingship and Fatherhood, too anthropomorphic upon the other?" (in Bevan and Singer's *Legacy of Israel*, p. 519). The answer is obviously that the Jewish religion rejected both the localized Baal and Incarnation as anthropomorphisms of a natural order, but tenaciously clung to the historical anthropomorphisms of God the Father and King.

If one were to indulge in metaphysical speculation, one might argue that historical monotheism is adumbrated in the very first great Mosaic theophany. God revealed his name to Moses as *Ehyeh asher Ehyeh* (Exod. 3:14, inadequately rendered by "I am that I am"). These words, however difficult their construction, not only connote, as in a related Egyptian phrase, God's irresistible might, but certainly mean to express also his continuity of being, of existence in past, present, and future. Even the usual ineffable name of Israel's God—the name which since the thirteenth century has been frequently misread Jehovah and which, by a kind of common consent, is now often pronounced *Yahweh*—has essentially the same significance. Although Jewish philosophers since the Middle Ages, with their increasing emphasis on the transcendent character of God, would have disputed this interpretation and declared that time itself, having been created by God, is finite, they would have

to admit that at least God's realization in this universe as reflected
in our mind comes through the endless flow of time. This process
one might call history in the widest sense. In this long historical
process God may assume different shapes in the minds of men. He
may divest himself of one historical form and take on another to
suit the new conceptions of the age. So profoundly imageless is God
in Judaism, however, that these transformations have no effect whatever upon his eternally uniform substance.[5]

It was, then, no lack of artistic ability which prevented the Jews
from creating plastic representations of their deity. Other Semites,
not to speak of the nearly Semitic Egyptians, expressed their religion in notable art creations. The ancient Israelites, too, glorified
their creative artists, often placing them on a par with their inspired
prophets. Bezalel, for example, appeared to them as filled "with the
spirit of God, in wisdom, in understanding, and in knowledge, and
in all manner of workmanship" (Exod. 35:31). The more recently
excavated third-century synagogue of Dura-Europos has overthrown
all the preconceived notions concerning the artistic insufficiency of
the Jews even in the talmudic era. Conscious restraint rather than
native inability appears to have been the determining factor.

According to tradition, the Jewish religion could get along for a
time with no sanctuary at all, then, in the days of Moses and the
Judges, with a migrating sanctuary, until, after centuries, the Jewish kings built the central Temple in Jerusalem. (Why this became
necessary at that time will be explained in a later chapter.) But
even this Temple was rivaled, for a long time, by sanctuaries not
only in Northern Israel but in the land of Judah itself. It reigned
supreme in Jewish life only for a very brief period, probably only
during the three and a half decades from the time of Josiah to its
destruction. Furthermore, even before the destruction, prophets
(such as Isa. 19:19) could foretell the erection of a Jewish sanctuary
in a foreign land, in Egypt. This dream was to be realized later both
by the Elephantine soldiers and by the high priest Onias. Onias,
himself the legitimate heir of the high priest of Jerusalem, apparently found no difficulty in obtaining the permission of the Palestinian authorities for the construction of his temple in Leontopolis.
This temple was later closed, not on account of Jewish opposition,
but by a decree of a foreign monarch three years after the destruction of the Second Temple in Jerusalem.

All these sanctuaries, however, soon found a substitute in an
institution even more detached from any particular locality. The

synagogue could be erected wherever Jews happened to live. Indeed synagogues sprang up everywhere in and outside of Palestine, even while the Temple was still in existence. One was erected on the Temple mountain itself, and its liturgies chanted by any odd assortment of voices must have strangely blended with the levitical hymns accompanying the sacrificial rites. In the synagogue Judaism evolved a form of religious gathering most in accord with its own spirit and created an institution of the deepest significance in the history of religious worship. The synagogue, together with its daughters the church and the mosque, has, for scores of generations, been among the most important vehicles of history's progress against nature.[6]

Little wonder that again and again the Bible draws a sharp distinction between the nations who worship nature in some form or other and the Jewish people whose chief concern is its central position in history. We need cite only the following two verses from Deuteronomy:

And lest thou lift up thine eyes unto heaven, and when thou seest the sun and the moon and the stars, even all the host of heaven, thou be drawn away and worship them, and serve them, which the Lord thy God hath allotted (*halaq*) unto all the peoples under the whole heaven. But *you* hath the Lord taken (*laqah*) and brought forth out of the iron furnace, out of Egypt, to be unto Him a people of inheritance, as ye are this day [4:19–20].

Here we have it succinctly: Exodus versus astral powers!

It might be objected that this concept of historical monotheism introduces too much historical relativity into a field which claims to reflect the absolute, eternal truth. We are, however, now chiefly concerned with the religion of men, religion as seen and realized by men. This religion may have fundamental eternal ideas, as eternal as man himself. At the same time there must be other less eternal aspects which change with the changes in man, their bearer. Whether these changes are great or insignificant, sudden or slow, depends on the transformations in man. The history of human civilization is very short, indeed, in comparison with the history of man, which, in turn, is no more than a brief chapter in the so much longer history of the universe. Correspondingly, the changes in fundamentals, even in the realm of ideas, may require geological ages, while only comparatively minor matters may change with the changing history of civilization. But even these minor matters are of greatest importance. It is their totality which gives life to the "eternal" elements. Only that religion can last "forever" which, while retaining its "eternal" elements, is able to adapt itself to the changing needs and outlooks of man. Judaism has obviously been such a religion. The often-heard question: "Will Judaism survive?" is anything but disquieting to those interested in its survival. Often it means only: "Will this or that form of Judaism survive?" Moreover, the very fact that an anxious soul is demanding the settlement of doubts, is only another expression of the essential, persistent, historical feeling. It is perhaps one of Spengler's finest insights to have pointed out how "care" (*Sorge*) is fundamental to all historical feeling. And for the Jews, care as well as its opposite, firm hope (*bittaḥon*), has always played a most prominent part. Even the troubled query as to extinction is a symptom of the will to live.

EMANCIPATION FROM STATE AND TERRITORY

To this peculiar position of the Jewish people within the framework of the Jewish religion, corresponds the peculiar history of that people itself. The history of every people is unique, and some value this uniqueness as an extraordinary distinction. Hence the many "chosen peoples" of mankind. But Israel emphasized the importance of its history for its religion and vice versa, as has no other nation. The Exodus from Egypt was apparently a minor occurrence in the history of that time, so minor, indeed, that the nation most concerned in it next to the Jews themselves, the Egyptians, never took the trouble to record it. "One merely has to bear in mind," says Hugo Winckler, "what this event meant, or rather, what it did not mean to Egypt" (*Kritische Schriften,* I, 27). But it was precisely this event that was made by Moses and the prophets the corner stone of a new development, the point of departure for a new era in mankind. Time and again lawgivers and poets, priests and prophets, referred back to the deliverance from Egypt, because in it they saw the origin of the Jewish people, and the final conclusion of the covenant between the people and its God.

Since that time this *people* has had an unusual history. In the period of the conquest and settlement in Canaan, under its own kings, and to an even greater degree in the two and a half millennia of the dispersion, the career of this people represents a remarkable interplay of the history of an individual nation and of that of many nations or of mankind at large. Situated between two of the greatest trade routes of antiquity, ancient Israel watched the endless procession of Egyptian and Assyrian soldiers, Babylonian priests, Phoenician merchants, and Arabian Bedouins. It saw itself constantly and irresistibly drawn into the whirl of world politics and commerce. Other ethnic and religious groups lived for long in the very heart of ancient Israel, just as, from the eighth century onward, the Jews began again to live in other lands among varied alien majorities. This cannot be a mere accident of history. To insist that "peculiar" destinies of individuals and nations "happen" precisely to those individuals and nations with an innate disposition for them, may seem to be reaching out too perilously into the realm of metaphysics. Under the same circumstances, however, many other peoples would certainly have perished and disappeared from history. That the Jews survived is largely due to the fact that they were prepared for their subsequent destinies by their early history.

The most striking corollary to the contrast between history and nature in the Jewish religion appears to be the contrast between nationality and state in Jewish history. For a relatively short time the Jews had a state or states of their own. Gradually the nation emancipated itself from state and territory. As the Jewish religion developed away from any particular locality, the Jewish people— and this certainly was a contributory cause of the former development—also detached itself more and more from the soil. Common descent, common destiny and culture—including religion—became the uniting forces. Fustel de Coulanges declared that "true patriotism is not love of the soil, but love of the past, reverence for the generations which have preceded us" (*Questions historiques,* p. 6). If a Frenchman, whose nation has been rooted in its soil for millennia, can regard history and not the soil as essential to his own national feeling, how much more deeply ingrained is this conviction in the mental make-up of Jews, for whom it was no mere theoretical abstraction, but a matter of life and death! This development away from the soil has, of course, been attended by tragedies: after fifteen and more centuries of sojourn in a country the Jews can be regarded as strangers to its soil even by peoples (for example, the Bulgarians) who settled there long after them.

This tragedy is a necessary consequence of the revolt of nature against history. Despite all that Judaism stands for and all that the Jewish people has lived through, it cannot be denied that, at least until the day of the Messiah, which can come only in a miraculous way, history will not have vanquished nature. Until then, nature is the necessary substratum for history, as is the soil for the life of a nation. This eternal conflict marks the *tragic* history of the Jews. Time and again the Jews have reverted to nature, time and again they were obliged to create their territory. Fichte once said, reflecting on the conditions of the then divided German nationality, that his nation, without territory and state, without even (political) history, must create all these out of its own national existence, that is, evolve out of its *Denken* its actual *Sein*. How much more true of the Jews, in whom "existence without state and beyond state, their purely spiritual development" (Fichte, *Sämmtliche Werke*, VII, 572) are such conspicuous features of their national history. Indeed the Jews several times succeeded in creating such an actual *Sein* out of their ethnic and religious heritage. The slaves in Egyptian bondage conquered Canaan, the refugees in the Babylonian Exile soon established a new self-governing state, and settlers from all over the world are now building up, against tremendous odds, the new state of Israel. In the two millennia of the Diaspora the quasi-political aspirations of the people have never ceased to be a living force. The very failures of all the messianic movements throughout the ages were, in their tragic grandeur, nothing but the continuous reaffirmation of that yearning for the return to the soil. The people's half-conscious wish to become again rooted in a territory and state also found repeated expression in the various substitutes it devised. We shall see how throughout the ages the Jewish community organization partly replaced the missing state and how the Jewish quarters of ancient Alexandria or under the Caliphate, in North Africa or in medieval and modern Europe, were a surrogate, however poor, for Israel's territory.

These are not inconsistencies, they are rather necessary compromises in life. History in its realization needs nature, as any given moment in time is realized in space. This is a tragic conflict and in its attempts to resolve it the Jewish people has often suffered severely. We have just witnessed the greatest tragedy in Jewish history which accompanied the onslaught of a "blood and soil" ideology on the fundamentals of history-made Western civilization. It was scarcely surprising that Nazism's concentrated fury hit the people whose entire career had longer and more persistently than any other embodied these historic fundamentals. But this tragic destiny is, perhaps, the most magnificent feature of the history of the Jews! As Martin Buber once remarked,

The Jewish people has become the eternal people not because it was allowed to live, but because it was not allowed to live. Just because it was asked to give more than life, it won life [*Kampf um Israel*, p. 297].

Such persistence in living *in despite of nature* has often amazed and repelled external observers. Even in recent years keen and liberal-minded historians of the rank of Mommsen and Nöldeke could not conceal their impatience with and disapproval of the "unnatural perseverance" of the Jews after the loss of their political independence. Much gratuitous advice has been proffered to them throughout the ages, bidding them give up their stubborn resistance to the "normal" ways of life, mingle with the nations and thus simplify a perplexing situation. In almost every generation, indeed, Jewish individuals and minor groups tread this road to easygoing regularity. Now, however, the people as a whole could not embark upon it, even if it wanted to do so. Apart from the powerful "Aryan" opposition to assimilation, a simultaneous mass conversion of all Jewry to Christianity and Islam, if it were at all feasible, would clearly lead to the immediate constitution of a Judeo-Christian and Judeo-Muslim group which would continue living the segregated "unnatural" life of present-day Jewry. This unnaturalness would be inordinately aggravated through the removal of what has thus far been the most constructive force: the common religious heritage.

The life of the Jews contrary to nature has also led to their characteristic polarity in action and in thought. The acknowledgment of the "Exile" as a temporary sojourn under foreign oppression might have been in former days the necessary complement to the belief in Israel's "selection." Beyond the need for psychological compensation for the feeling of inferiority connected with the *Galut* by a sense of superiority as a "chosen people," exilic existence was frequently hailed as a necessary instrument of the divine government of the world. Only as a dispersed people could the Jews serve as "the light" of many nations. In modern times the attempt to combine full political amalgamation with the maintenance of a separate ethnic existence has become more complex and has resulted in a "dual allegiance" so frequently assailed and still more frequently misunderstood. The necessity, through two millennia, of cultivating at least two languages (as Hebrew and Greek, Arabic, or English; or even Hebrew, Aramaic, and Greek; or Hebrew, Yiddish, and Polish) for daily routine and synagogue prayer, for business correspondence and literary pursuits, demonstrated to every Jewish youth the abnormality of his national existence. The great poet Yehudah Halevi was not altogether wrong when he placed bilingualism into the very cradle of Israel's history and stated that Abraham himself spoke Aramaic in his daily intercourse, but resorted to Hebrew for sacred uses (*Kitab al-Khazari*, II, 68). We need but vary this statement, in accordance with our historical knowledge, and say that Abraham and his family probably long continued using their Accadian dialect from Haran, while learning to converse with their Canaanite neighbors in the latter's Hebraic tongue. To clinch it all came the gradual elimination of the Jews from the soil of medieval Europe and their increasing concentration upon trade and money lending. The pious expounders of the biblical prohibitions of usury and the talmudic disparagement of all interest (even if charged to Gentile borrowers) were thus forced into a position of leadership as the chief "usurers" of the Western world. Later, too, the often sincere protagonists of "ethical monotheism" saw themselves inescapably involved in some of the most nefarious practices of modern economic exploitation.

Similary, Jewish national character and religious thought became full of contradictions. The eyes even of casual onlookers have been caught by the contrast between the practical sense of the Jew and his unrestrained idealism; between his adherence to tradition and his proneness to innovations; between his quick, intuitive grasp and endless, arid casuistry; between his commercial avidity and unlimited charitableness. In Jewish religion, since the days of the prophets, universalism and particularism have been logical antitheses persistently linked in a living unity. "For Judaism," says Leo Baeck, "there exists no creed without moral teaching, no mystery without commandment, no distance without proximity, no recognition of the Hereafter without a recognition of this world" (*Wesen des Judentums*, 5th ed., p. 207). Did not ancient Pharisaism accept determinism and free will, and the medieval Jewish philosophers, God's transcendence and immanence as coexisting realities in defiance of all logical consistency? All life is a compromise between irreconcilable logical contradictions, and every train of thought reflecting reality will end in unbridgeable antinomies. But the Jewish mind, following the logic of its extraordinary destinies, appears as an uninterrupted chain of antinomies and paradoxes.

The greater the discrepancy between theory and reality, the

more tragic became the inner conflicts in the Jewish personality. The steady equanimity and cheerfulness of the ghetto days (hidden to the uninitiated behind a drab and gloomy appearance) vanished in the modern period, especially when the Jews became more conscious of this glaring discrepancy. Mankind as a whole was constantly losing faith in eudaemonistic progress. Gone, for the most part, was the enthusiastic belief of the Enlightenment that the pursuit of happiness would proceed untrammeled, if only a few political obstacles were removed. From the days of Rousseau and Kant to those of Dostoievski and Nietzsche, Spengler and Russell, the most representative thinkers of the West recognized that the progress of civilization "has created more and deeper sufferings than it has eliminated through its growingly successful struggle against many of their underlying causes" (Scheler, *Moralia*, pp. 64 f.). As a Jew and as a European, the emancipated Jew suffered doubly from the shattering of his high hopes. Messianic expectations attached to the new era of freedom and equality in the early period of Emancipation had to be toned down in the face of ever-new complications. The tiny but solid bridge of the ghetto having broken down, a chasm between Jewry's exalted mission and sordid reality opened, abysmal and terrifying.

Many Jews, steeped in their cultural and ethnic heritage, have gazed without perturbation into the precipice and searched for new paths on which to continue their historic march. Others, less free from dizziness, have completely lost their balance. Some have become the harshest Jew haters of modern times. The Jew's proclivity to self-criticism, even self-irony, was strengthened by a long and venerable tradition, going back to the ancient prophets. The struggle with nature and reality had produced a "negativism," a denial of the existing modes of social and individual life, whose edge was pointedly aimed at Jewish realities and at the Jewish forces which supported them. Sometimes this negativism was wholly constructive, preaching the subjugation of the present to the superior aim of molding the future. In many instances, however, it became negativism pure and simple, barren and unproductive, delighting in contradiction for contradiction's sake. Self-accusation has been magnified to satanic self-hatred, with which few men have ever been so deeply afflicted as some unbalanced modern Jews. Theodor Lessing, in describing several such Jews who had become an abomination unto themselves to the point of self-destruction (notably Weininger, Trebitsch), has rightly sensed that even these aberrations were merely distortions of the legitimate consequences of Judaism's historic emphases (*Der jüdische Selbsthass*). Were not the Jews, even in their most constructive representatives, the "yeast" among the nations? Their undermining of existing institutions, although a wholesome and often absolutely necessary function, irritated not only those interested in the preservation of these institutions, but also the more neutral bystanders. As Mommsen rightly remarked, every process of decomposition spreads a bad odor, and the Jewish "element of decomposition" had no right to complain when even its salutary and often indispensable labors aroused widespread resentment.

With the Jewish denial of existing realities went the refusal to recognize the powers of the day. Power itself often became the cause of suspicion and resentment rather than of admiration and acquiescence. The exaltation of powerlessness in the Jewish religion found its counterpart in the evolution of a people without political power. It has been observed that, from the very beginning, most biblical leaders were not born into power, but were said to have been endowed with it by a special act of divine grace. While biblical law, following widespread oriental prototypes, acknowledged the natural superiority of the first-born son, biblical legend and history attached a higher importance to those younger sons whom God had called to perform a service. In the long series of biblical heroes, Abel, Isaac and Jacob, Moses, David and Solomon were all younger members of their respective families who became qualified for membership in defiance of natural succession. In the ultimate supremacy of the defenseless, persecuted, suffering prophets over the mighty kings of Israel and Judah, the recognition that there exists a higher power than sheer political force found definite acceptance. In Deutero-Isaiah's poems of the suffering "servant of the Lord," in the prototype of a suffering "powerless" people which none the less comes out victorious in the end, was reflected not only the actuality of the Babylonian Exile, but also the gradual emancipation from the natural category of power as equivalent to political expansion and state domination.

Jewish messianic humanitarianism and internationalism spring from the same root. There have been many German thinkers who, glorifying power as do the spokesmen of no other nation (the British and Americans, for example, quietly take it for granted that power is and should be theirs, but do not theorize about it), reiterated that humanitarianism is "a ruse of the weak," invented by the weak (especially the Jews) for their self-protection. The inherent fallacy of this contention in the face of powerful cosmopolitan currents within mighty empires (Seneca and *Emperor* Marcus Aurelius at the climax of Roman puissance or Voltaire at the height of French "glory") is of less consequence here. The Jewish people doubtless rationalized the lack of its political power in the face of vast empires. But it must have felt then that it possessed powers other than political, which were their full equivalent. Will not even those power worshipers who view human history only from the standpoint of success, and equate "right" with ultimate acceptance by those in power, admit that the Jewish people has manifested an extraordinary "power" to endure beyond all the mighty empires of antiquity? Early recognizing the ultimate futility of even the greatest human power, ancient Judaism exalted the omnipotence of God alone, appearing "not by might, nor by power but by My spirit, saith the Lord of hosts" (Zech. 4:6). The religious and ethnic power of perseverance, rather than the political power of expansion and conquest, became the corner stone of Jewish belief and practice. Such "power" was naturally defensive and passive, and mutual non-aggression was one of its major safeguards. Thus Jewish universalism and pacifism may have been the rationale of Jewish political impotence, but at the same time they flowed from the vast stream of a real, although nonpolitical, potency.

It is necessary at this point to correct an even more widespread fallacy. Political powerlessness has often been mistaken by foe and friend alike as the equivalent of the Jews' utter despondency and misery throughout the history of the dispersion. In recent years one has heard more and more frequently of the age-old "pariah" existence of the Jews. This concept, based on a false analogy with the Indian "untouchables," is wholly misleading. It is, indeed, flatly contradicted by all known historical facts, both objective and subjective. Neither under the Hellenistic, Roman and Persian Empires nor under Islam and Byzantium, as will be seen, nor even in the worst years of medieval persecution, did the status of the Jews warrant any such comparison. The Jews doubtless suffered a great deal in their millennial procession. Scores of thousands of their martyrs have "sanctified the Name" (of the Lord) in untold sufferings, and daily and hourly ordinary Jews have borne the brunt of arrogance and ill will in passive, but none the less heroic fashion. They had, however, the great compensations which accompany every truly religious sacrifice. And were they the only people of the earth to suffer? Has not the lot of all men, especially in those dark and cruel ages of scarcity and horror, been to suffer indescribable agonies for, or what is much worse, without a just cause? Who would dare weigh one suffering against another and prove that the scale of one group of men has, over a long period, dipped lower than that of other groups? It is quite likely, moreover, that even the average medieval Jew, compared with his average Christian contemporary, man by man, woman by woman, child by child, was the less unhappy and destitute creature—less unhappy and destitute not only in his own consciousness, but even if measured by such objective criteria as standards of living, cultural amenities, and protection against individual starvation and disease. And subjectively, as long as the Jewish religion was at all intact, the people never conceded final defeat nor acknowledged its own inferiority in any ultimate category!

The wide assumption of a pariah status of pre-Emancipation Jewry could never have arisen, were it not for the prevalent view of Jewish history in the dispersion as one of incessant suffering and persecution. This view has an old and venerable tradition, with such diverse roots as the opinions of Graeco-Roman Jew-baiters, patristic polemists against Judaism and talmudic sages. The arrogance of medieval ecclesiastics and nobles gave definite shape to the picture of the Jew as a harassed and universally despised creature. In a more realistic retrospect, however, one must never forget that these were the same people who heaped contempt and oppression, equally boundless and cruel, upon the majority of their fellow Christians, peasant serfs and villains. Even among them, the more serious-minded pondered over the historic riddle of Jewish survival and, like the Muslim sages, composed endless treatises in defense of their own creed against the claims of Judaism. Certainly no such relationship can be conceived between pure-blooded Brahmins and pariahs in India as would permit of religious disputations. However fateful their consequences to the Jewish participants, these and the perennial attempts to induce the Jews by suasion and force to abandon their faith and to join the majority on a highly respected footing were essentially an admission of the basic equality of the synagogue with the church and mosque.

Moreover, unlike genuine pariahs, Jews could, severally and collectively, leave their group and, at their own discretion, join the dominant majority. At least until the rise of modern "racial" antisemitism nothing was formally easier for a Jew than, by an act of simple conversion, to become a respected, sometimes leading member of the Christian or Muslim community. We shall see that, according to a sixteenth-century Lithuanian law, baptism made the convert immediately eligible for the rank of nobleman. The fact that so many Jews throughout the ages repudiated this easy escape, indeed furiously resisted all blandishments and force, testifies to their deep conviction that they would lose, rather than gain, from severing their ties with the "chosen people." [7]

HISTORICAL LITERATURE

The intimate relation between the Jewish people and its religion was felt at the very threshold of the history of both. It is no accident that among the oldest literary documents of the people are not only war songs, legends, and tales such as are found in other civilizations, but, primarily perhaps, laws and religious and moral teachings. Probably one of the oldest parts of the Bible is the so-called Book of the Covenant, containing essentially civil and criminal laws. The ancient, most probably Mosaic, Decalogue itself deals with fundamentals of creed only in the first two or three commandments, devoting all the rest to laws concerning the conduct of daily life. The first of the writing prophets, Amos, is chiefly concerned with the problem of justice, the main principle of overcoming nature by history, of controlling the innate powers of the strong by the power of an organized historical group. Justice, and especially social justice, remained throughout the ages the corner stone of Jewish public life and theology.

Neither is it an accident that this people was also the first to *write* great history. Historical narratives, songs, and the like existed among all nations. But a consecutive historical literature with that fine combination of factual statement, pragmatic interpretation, and charming presentation, as composed by the Hebrew writers and compilers between the tenth and eighth centuries, finds no parallel whatever in other ancient literatures before the Greeks. Even the otherwise most distinguished Greek historians, such as Herodotus and Thucydides, lacked something of the historical perspective of the Israelitic historians. Deuteronomy is able to reproach the Jews of ingratitude towards God because they have failed to "remember the days of old, consider the years of many generations" (32:7). The historical novels such as Ruth, Esther,

Tobit, and Judith, referring to historical rather than to mythological events, played in Judaism a role unparalleled in the ancient world. Extraordinary events in the Jewish past, moreover, were interpreted in the light of their total significance for the destinies of all nations. Hence the universal aspect and also, in a sense, the universal treatment of history by these early writers. They start out with the admission that twenty generations preceded Abraham, and that many other peoples may regard themselves as direct descendants of the Jewish patriarchs. This catholicity was in sharp contrast to the assumptions of the Babylonians and the Egyptians that they were the first to be created by their gods. Nowhere else, at that time or before, was such a sympathetic treatment of "world history" possible as is found in Chapter 10 of the first book of Moses.

In view of this early historical bent, the fact that, during the dispersion until about a hundred years ago, the Jewish people seems to have lost interest in writing even its own history, might appear doubly astonishing. That this cannot be fully ascribed to the influence of the peoples among whom the Jews lived, is obvious; the medieval Arabs and the modern European nations displayed a vivid interest in history and produced many able historians. There were many other reasons at work; among them the lack of "political" history in the ordinary sense, the supreme power of the Law which suffered no rivals, and the continuous migrations which steadily interrupted historical continuity and made increasingly difficult the preservation of historical records. But, even in those ages, the essential orientation of the Jewish people toward its past and future cannot be subject to doubt.

MENACE OF A NEW SCHISM

The intrinsic unity of Jews and Judaism has been somewhat obscured in recent generations. On the one hand, Reform Judaism, at least in its earliest formulations, tried to emphasize more and more strongly the universal element in the Jewish religion. In consequence, the Jewish people as a whole lost its essential standing within the Jewish creed, and became rather an outward means toward the realization of a universal religion in the whole world. He who, as a matter of principle, thinks that the fundamental teachings of Judaism are reserved for the Jewish people "denies the One and Only God of messianic humanity," said Hermann Cohen, undoubtedly the greatest Jewish thinker of the last generation, in trying to demolish the nationalist movement. Even more significantly, he and many of his confreres bowed their heads in reverence before the supremacy of the state. Abandoning the general liberalistic aloofness toward the state ideal, many of these religious "liberals" paradoxically proclaimed:

However central religion appears to us modern men within the general compass of history, it is none the less merely a concentric specialty within the unity of ethical culture. It is the state which occupies, for us, the focal position in human civilization [H. Cohen, *Jüdische Schriften*, II, 323, 331].

Even Cohen's qualification, that the state realizes the moral aims of mankind "as the symbol of a league of states," could not conceal the radical departure of Jewish liberalism from traditional nonpolitical, more truly universalist Judaism. While this attitude, and even more general assimilationist tendencies, led toward a denial of the Jewish national entity, Zionism and other Jewish national movements laid increasing stress upon the secular aspects of the Jewish people, often trying to detach the national being of the Jews from their religion. In their own way they also emphasized the state idea or political action to safeguard the rights of the Jewish minority.

All these movements in their extreme tendencies appear to be based largely upon the application of certain general formulations to a specific case which they do not fit. According to the widest accepted definition of nationalism, a nation (in the ethnic, not the political sense) is a group of men linked together by common ties of destiny and culture (*Schicksals- und Kulturgemeinschaft*). Even on the basis of this formula, the common Jewish fate and culture includes the past generations of primarily religious Jews and the past history of Jewish culture which, at least until recently, was mainly a religious culture. We know how deeply rooted are modern Jewish cultural movements in one or another religious experience of bygone days. Hebrew, the language adopted by a large part of secular Jewish nationalism, is permeated with religious content. Neither will Yiddish, it appears, be wholly purified from its religious ingredients in the near future. This evolution has not yet run its course and we certainly lack the perspective to judge what will be the ultimate resultant of the strong conflicting forces in contemporary Jewish life. In the opinion of numerous observers, however, it is very likely that, just as Jewish nationality represented a vital element in the Jewish religion of former days, so the Jewish religious heritage will soon be more generally recognized, under one shape or another, as an integral part of Jewish nationalism.

In the past as well as in the present, the existence of the Jews has always been a peculiar one (whether this peculiarity is a reason for pride and a feeling of chosenness is, of course, a matter of individual judgment), and all attempts to explain this phenomenon in general terms without paying attention to specific elements must necessarily fail. The hasty usage of analogous terms borrowed from the general situation to define Jewish developments has, in fact, often been seriously misleading. "Political Zionism," for example, is, strictly speaking, a misnomer, inasmuch as its controlling trend is dominated by an humanitarian ideal. To be sure, the events of the last twenty years went far in disproving A. Grabowsky's contention that neither the Indians nor the Jews knew anything of "the essence of power and the struggle for power" (*Zeitschrift für Politik*, XIX, 530 f.). Nevertheless both peoples do carry with them the indelible imprint of their nonpolitical religious heritage. It has thus come to pass that, through a perverse irony of history, the Jewish nationality, the first nationality (in the modern ethnic rather than political sense) to appear on the historical scene, was long denied the right to be classified as a national entity altogether. That this happened in the period of modern nationalism, at a time when, one might say, the ancient Jewish conception of nationality was finally accepted by the world at large, makes this paradox even more poignant.

At any rate the middle course seems, at present, to be victorious in countries where the Jews constitute a comparatively small section of the population. Such are all the countries of central and western Europe, and of America, including the United States. The Jewish Reform movement, extremely antinationalist, anti-Zionist, and anti-Hebraic in its earlier history, is now more and more on the road to reconciliation with these traditional forces. On the other hand, Zionism and nationalism have failed in these countries to secularize Jewish life to any considerable extent. Even among the five millions of American Jewry all attempts to revitalize Judaism as "the Jewish way of life become necessarily secular, humanist, scientific, conditioned on the industrial economy, without having ceased to be livingly Jewish" (H. M. Kallen, *Judaism at Bay*, p. 5) have thus far not progressed beyond the stage of wish dreams. Quite different, of course, was, until the recent tragedy, the situation in such countries of Jewish mass settlement as Russia and Poland. Should secular Jewish nationalism really prevail there in the end and for the first time in history divorce the Jewish people from its religion, the possibility of a deep schism in Jewry would become real.

Such a menace is perhaps enhanced by the relatively large number of Jews now living and the vast extent of their settlements. Twelve million Jews are an unwieldy mass, difficult to control and still more difficult to unify under the most favorable circumstances. Scattered all over the globe, participating in the economic struggles and cultural evolution of almost every nation, they can hardly achieve uniformity or unity of a positive nature.

Extreme Jewish individualism and the impossibility of any mass of Jews agreeing on almost any single course of action, on the other hand, in themselves partly the result of these historical and geographic divisions, may be regarded as obstacles rather than aids to serious schismatic ventures. However great the readiness on the part of many modern Jews to deviate from the road of official Judaism (if such a term still has any meaning today), they spend most of their energies in mutually combating one another's newly chosen road to salvation. The various schismatic trends, one might say, are so heavily charged with electricity, positive as well as negative, that they are likely to neutralize one another for a long time to come. The growth of the new Israel center, aided by the unprecedented technological facilities for mutual communication, should also strengthen the centripetal forces. Jewish solidarity, moreover, at least in the face of a common enemy, may likewise for a while counteract the disintegrating forces of individualism—another living Jewish antinomy which has baffled outsiders and easily lent itself to exaggeration and misunderstanding.

Despite all these retarding influences, the deep divergences in Jewish outlook, the numerical and geographic expansion of the people, seem to indicate the proximity of a climactic break and the falling off of many sections now loosely connected with the main body. The Jewish people has on several occasions experienced such a violent upheaval after a period of rapid growth. The separation of Northern Israel and Judah after the great expansion under David and Solomon might perhaps have been avoided. The formation of numerous sects and the separation of Christianity, however, at a time when the Jewish Diaspora spread over many lands, and most likely included some eight million members, was doubtless an historical necessity. When Judaism, recovering from this eruption under the Caliphate of Bagdad, again rallied under its flag millions of prosperous and self-reliant adherents, forces of disintegration again arose, threatening to disrupt the national body into warring sects. Only with supreme effort and at the price of losing some of its most advanced and influential sections, did official Judaism repel the onslaught of Karaism and other sects. Despite the newer ties of solidarity forged in the heat of a world-wide antisemitic onslaught and of the Palestine struggle, many distinct symptoms in our time appear to point toward some ultimate violent separations, perhaps of a magnitude unprecedented in Jewish experience.

Most remarkably, the Jewish people seems to view these prospects with perfect equanimity. Not only those who prefer the easygoing road of delusion and try to minimize the dangers, but also those who courageously face them, appear sublimely unconcerned. Did not the prophets of old indoctrinate the people with the belief that it is not the masses that count, but a "saving remnant"? As far back as Amos this term apparently carried a widely accepted popular connotation. Soon after, Isaiah called one of his sons by the symbolic name *She'ar Yashub* (the remnant will return). Since Amos and Isaiah, Judaism has learned more and more to stress quality above quantity. Increasingly realizing the necessity of a chosen people as an example, and the intricacies of its own nonpolitical power of self-preservation, it placed the true vital inner power of the chosen few above the fictitious and externally glamorous force of the many. It is little wonder that down to our own days many a Zionist has professed disinterestedness in the ultimate destinies of the Diaspora and many a radical orthodox has prayed for the total secession of the internal "enemy." Even the suicidal dream of some extreme assimilationists and communists that the Jewish people will soon disappear from the stage of history is nothing but a truly Jewish "negativistic" inversion of the positive doctrine of the "remnant."

By another paradox, however, Judaism has always been deeply interested in the preservation of its followers. In ancient times the economic and military importance of numbers was fully recognized. Like the other oriental nations, Israel gloried in the host of its conationals and the size of its blessed families. To become "as the dust of the earth" or "as the sand of the sea" (Gen. 13:16, 32:13) was long a dream of the people. To have many children was the deepest yearning of the Israelitic mother. Psalms 127 and 128, although apparently of postexilic origin, still reflect the religious inclination toward aggrandizement of family and nation. With the loss of political independence, emphasis was shifted to ethnic preservation, but the goal remained the same. Orthodox Judaism is still most insistent, in theory and practice, upon procreation and the maintenance of the biological strength of the people.[8]

However large or small may be their number at the conclusion of the present turbulent period of their history and whatever should be the outcome of these inner conflicts, few Jews are concerned about the prospects for the survival of their people because of these internal difficulties. The preponderant instinct among the majority, in any case, still perceptibly tells them that the Jewish religion, buttressed by the Jewish nationality, and the Jewish nationality, supernationally rooted in the Jewish religion, will weather the forthcoming storms, too, and that together they will continue their historic march into the unfathomable future.

NATIONALISM AND UNIVERSALISM

Let us summarize briefly the various points discussed in this chapter. We have seen that, apart from the general interrelation between the social and religious histories of any group, there is a special nexus in which the history of the Jews and that of Judaism meet. Peculiar circumstances have led to a gradual alienation of the Jewish people from its soil and to the emancipation of the Jewish nationality from state and territory. Correspondingly, Jewish "historical" monotheism has set up the ideal goal of man's emancipation from nature and, in the meantime, detached religious worship from its territorial ties and divorced the main religious institutions from their original, "natural" background. Jewish history has increasingly become a rare combination of national and world history. The Jewish faith also represents a peculiar synthesis of a national and a universal religion. Developments of this kind, often against the "nature" of things, cannot but harbor eternal conflicts. Their final solution is expected by both the religious and the national Jew only with the realization of some messianic hope, which both cherish in one guise or another.

II

ISRAEL'S ORIGINS

THIS singular product of millennia of slow growth was adumbrated upon Israel's first appearance in history. The origins both of the people of Israel and its religion are still obscure, as are those of all organic life. A few general laws may be known about individual plants and animals, if not about whole species, but every nation and religion arises in a unique fashion. Thus it is that, although Israel was, so to say, born in the full light of history (unlike Egypt and Babylonia), and although invaluable work has been done by archaeologists, historians, and philologists, much remains and probably will always remain problematic.[1]

A fresh reworking of the whole science of Jewish history seems to be in the offing. A few basic lines of development may, however, be regarded as more generally accepted by contemporary scholars. The tendency now prevailing among Old Testament critics is to give ever greater credence to biblical records, including those of the early period. Partly as a result of a general reaction against the extremely radical, almost antibiblical, higher criticism of a few decades ago, and partly because of our increased knowledge of the ancient Near East, the present generation, on the whole, accepts the historicity of the fundamental facts underlying early biblical narratives. In accordance therewith the period of Israel's origins is divided into three successive phases: "the period of the Patriarchs" —the appearance of the first Hebrew groups in Palestine, some of them penetrating down into Egypt; the "Mosaic period"—their Exodus from Egypt and migration through the desert under Moses; and the period of the final conquest of Canaan and settlement under the "Judges."

AMIDST ADVANCED CIVILIZATIONS

In this period of origins, covering at least the whole second half of the second millennium, we already find a situation in many ways extraordinary. Israel crossed the threshold of its history not in a primitive environment, but in countries where previous civilized history covered two millennia, or—if one may draw such a parallel

—almost as long a period as that of Europe north of the Alps down to the present time.[2] Into these ripened civilizations there gradually drifted seminomadic tribes. Transplanted into this already fertile soil, they burgeoned into a civilized nation much more rapidly than would have been the case had they relied solely on their inner growth. The first phases of Israel's history present, therefore, the picture of a more or less primitive group assuming the variegated hues of the neighboring civilizations. Thus in a way peculiar to itself Israel skipped many stages of normal development. It was as if a group of present-day Bedouins, whose life, on the whole, is less "civilized" than was that of the earliest Hebrews on record, were suddenly transported to Tel Aviv or Jerusalem.[3]

So precocious a maturation, so facile an assumption of surrounding mores was stimulated by natural factors. In the geography of Palestine, if we include Transjordan, the desert and its winds seem eternally to be warring against the sea and its breezes. When the latter finds an accomplice in man, in a period of progress, the desert recedes, yielding several miles of its territory to human habitation. When man's hold weakens, however, the winds sweep over the border line and soon vast stretches of land are again covered by desert sands and lost to civilized life. In few of the world's areas do we possess evidence for such frequent historic "intermissions," usually extending over half a millennium or longer, as in Transjordan. Similarly, there has been throughout the ages a persistent struggle between the children of the desert and the settled agricultural population. One Semitic migration after another swept Palestine; between them a steady, more or less peaceful, penetration took place.

The previous history of the Hebrew groups, however, lent their conquest of Canaan many extraordinary features. Before their arrival in Palestine, some of them had apparently been connected with the mature civilization of Babylonia. The biblical tradition, though overlaid with legendary motifs, preserved the distinct recollection that Israel's patriarchs had stemmed from Chaldaea and more particularly from the cities of Ur and Haran. Ur, as we know from British excavations during the last two decades, had been an ancient center of Sumero-Accadian civilization. Whether or not Abraham's father, Terah, and his brother, Nahor, had any connection with like-sounding raiders in Syria and Palestine allegedly mentioned in two Ugaritic poems, their names have been plausibly deduced from Mesopotamian localities. Of course, personal names have often been derived from place names and vice versa. Certainly the invention of such coincidental names by a later Palestinian poet or historian, an hypothesis long accepted by biblical critics, would require much more arduous explanations than the now prevalent assumption of a solid kernel of authentic historic tradition in the biblical narratives. The lifelike description of the human strengths and weaknesses of Abraham, Isaac, Jacob, and Joseph in the book of Genesis is also more likely to reflect actual historical personalities than mere personifications of later Hebrew tribes. Few biblical historians would still profess to be shocked even by the extreme statement that "it is no longer a matter of argument that behind the biblical Abraham an eminent historical personality is manifest, a prophetic leader equal in stature to Mohammed, as the prophet of Islam." [4]

The available extrabiblical evidence does not yet justify, however, any definite conclusions concerning the chronological setting of the patriarchal careers or their specific connection with any of the turbulent ethnic and religious movements throughout the Near East. As Hebrews ('ibrim) they seem to have been intimately connected with some of those stray groups of condottieri who, under the name of Ḥabiru, Ḥapiru or Apiru (also Ša-Gaz), suddenly appear in the course of more than a millennium in such diverse places as Accadian Mesopotamia, Hittite Anatolia, Canaanite Syria and Palestine, or Pharaonic Egypt. Sometimes these shadowy tribesmen may be identified as alien raiders attacking well-established sedentary populations. At times they serve as mercenaries in the petty wars waged by neighboring city rulers. In the Amarna letters, particularly, they often become targets of mutual recrimination by Canaanite princes. Abdiḥipa of Jerusalem actually threatens his Egyptian overlord that, unless he receives speedy military aid, "the king's land would be lost to the Ḥabiru" (J. A. Knudtzon's El-Amarna-Tafeln, II, 877, No. 290). On occasion the latter appear as unfree laborers who had forfeited their freedom under economic stress, reminding us of the "Hebrew slaves" of biblical legislation.

None of these records controverts, however, the general impression of a slow, usually pacific penetration of Palestine's sparsely inhabited hill country by small outside clans as depicted in the somewhat oversimplified idyllic stories of Genesis. Most native villages had clustered around the few known wells, leaving between them vast stretches of "no man's land" for ready occupancy. Only here and there do we learn of such military exploits as are reflected in the sagas concerning Abraham's victory over the four powerful invaders or Simeon and Levi's treacherous conquest of Shechem.[5]

ISRAEL'S SOJOURN IN EGYPT

No less perplexing are the problems relating to the crucial period of Israel's life in Egypt, so graphically depicted in the biblical narratives. Although Egyptian sources are singularly inarticulate on this phase of their country's history (the record certainly offered the Egyptian rulers little opportunity for their customary self-glorification), few scholars now doubt that some Hebrew clans had at one time descended into the Nile valley and, after a period of great hardship, left it abruptly under the guidance of an inspired leader.

Relations between Egypt and Palestine reach back into the earliest periods of their civilized history. Already under the fifth and sixth Egyptian dynasties (in the middle of the third millennium) Egyptian troops repeatedly invaded Palestine and Syria. Time and again Asiatics, driven by famine, traversed the frontier in the opposite direction. At one time some warlike tribes, later known under the name of Hyksos (the Egyptian rendering of "shepherd kings," originally perhaps of "rulers of foreign countries"), entered Egypt in force and overpowered it "without difficulty or even a battle" (Manethon cited by Josephus in *Ag. Ap.* I, 14.75). For some 108 years (about 1675–1567) they ruled over large parts of Egypt with an iron hand, until a successful native revolt overthrew their regime. The reversal was so complete that the victorious rebels are said to have followed the Hyksos remnants back into Asia.[6]

The connection between the rise and decline of the Hyksos and the changing destinies of the Hebrews in Egypt and Palestine, first asserted by Josephus, was long repudiated by the overcritical, and hence in some respects uncritical, last generation of scholars. It has been reasserted, however, by some leading Egyptologists and biblical critics today. It appears that after the Hyksos debacle, the remnants of the Asiatic population residing around Tanis, the destroyed Hyksos capital formerly called Avaris, were placed in bondage and treated with utmost cruelty. The hardships inflicted on an enslaved population by Egyptian taskmasters may soon be fully documented by a more reliable decipherment of the Proto-Sinaitic inscriptions, in so far as these stem from slave laborers in

Egyptian mines located on the Sinaitic Peninsula. We do not know whether these mineworkers had any direct kinship, racial, linguistic or religious, with the Israelites in Egypt. By grossly overdrawing the picture and trying to find there traces of Yahwistic worship and even of the career of Moses, A. Hubert Grimme came close to discrediting all attempts at historically in any way linking the two groups. He may prove right, however, in contending that the deep sufferings and apparent yearnings for deliverance of the Sinaitic slaves offer a remarkable parallel to the fate of the royal villeins in Goshen.[7]

These villeins did not belong to a single racial group. The Hyksos infiltration into Egypt, archaeologically documented as early as the nineteenth century, was part and parcel of large ethnic movements throughout the Near East. While the "shepherd kings" themselves undoubtedly spoke a West-Semitic dialect akin to Hebrew (most of their recorded names are typically Western Semitic, including such good Hebraic names as *Hur* or *Ya'aqob-har* reminiscent of the Hebrew patriarch, Jacob), they seem to have brought with them a conglomeration of footloose migrants, including Hurrians and even Indo-Europeans. It is not impossible, however, that apart from their common Asiatic origin and Egyptian hostility there was some unifying religious bond which held together this heterogeneous mass. They not only worshiped the general Semitic deity *El*, and gave him the fairly common attribute *har* (mountain or rather mountain-god), but, according to Manethon, they began their reign by razing "the temples of the gods to the ground." More significantly, Queen Ḥatshepsut of the victorious Eighteenth Dynasty boasted in an inscription,

I have restored what was ruined, and have raised up what was neglected previously (?), (at the time) when '*A*' '*amu* [Asiatics] were in the midst of Avaris of the Northland, and strangers in the midst of them overturned what had been made. They ruled without Re', no one (?) acting according to the divine command, down to My Majesty.[8]

To be sure, the Hyksos ruling classes were subjected to speedy assimilation by Egyptian culture and, before long, many of them adopted Egyptian names and ways of life. But they, and particularly the mass of their followers, seem to have persisted in their religious disparity. Unfortunately we know very little about the events which led to the overthrow of the Hyksos regime and their expulsion to Asia. Manethon (or some of his Hellenistic para-

phrasts) probably confused this evacuation, which he pictur-
esquely described, with the exodus of the Israelites a long time
thereafter, about which he may have heard a great deal from his
Hellenistic Jewish neighbors. His story that the Hyksos were first
expelled from all the rest of Egypt and "confined in a place called
Avaris," which they surrendered only after a protracted siege, and
that ultimately the victorious Egyptian monarch had to consent to
their "unmolested" evacuation, dovetails the more closely with
the biblical tradition, as Avaris was indeed located in the area of
the present Wadi Tumilat to which the Bible gives the Western
Semitic name of Goshen. This area was also dotted with such other
Semitic localities as Succoth, Migdol, and Baal-zephon. It is small
wonder that as late as the twelfth century Egyptian papyri casually
mention *Apiru* (Hebrew) settlers in this region.[9]

Certainly not all the "Hyksos," nor even all the "Hebrews"
among them, who remained behind after the overthrow of their
regime, belonged to that particular religious and ethnic group
which soon came to be called "Israel." Many Hebraic settlers undoubtedly were later arrivals, swept into Egypt by that perennial
mainspring of international migration, the lack of nurture in their
native land. Once in Egypt these newcomers would naturally join
the related Asiatic groups with whom they also shared the common
Semitic worship of *El*, although they may already have developed
some religious and ritualistic peculiarities of their own. Such successive waves of immigration are clearly reflected in the biblical
narratives concerning Abraham and Isaac's "visits" to the Nile
valley, Joseph's sale into slavery and subsequent rise to power, and
the final settlement there of the seventy souls belonging to the
family of Jacob.

The Egyptians paid little heed to these internal differences
among their Asiatic neighbors which must have been, however, a
source of constant friction among these Asiatics themselves.
Through one of the shifts characteristic of the checkered dynastic
history of Egypt, Raamses II (1301–1234), himself of Hyksos ancestry, ascended the Pharaonic throne and began restoring the
worship of Seth, the Canaanite Baal's Egyptian counterpart. Understandably he turned upon that persistently alien group which,
apparently on conscientious grounds, had resisted complete amalgamation. As often in history, this internecine struggle proved
more venomous than a conflict among strangers. No wonder then
that, when Raamses decided to rebuild the long deserted and out-

lawed Hyksos capital of Avaris (Tanis) and to rename it Per- or
Pi-Ra'amses (the House of Raamses), he utilized the enforced labor of those *Apiru* among the city's neighbors who had resisted his
religious fiats. He thus became that much-blamed "Pharaoh of the
oppression" who, though unnamed by the biblical narrators, has
betrayed himself by the new name he gave to Avaris. The name
Pi-Ra'amses, so identified in Egyptian records only during the relatively short period of two centuries (1300–1100 B.C.E.) could not
possibly have been known to a later biblical writer in Palestine,
unless he based his story on some oral or written tradition going
back to the twelfth century or earlier.[10]

Throughout these centuries of their sojourn in Egypt, whether
living in a state of comparative well-being or in one of severe oppression, these Israelites seem to have maintained close relations
with other Hebrews who remained in Palestine. Commercial and
cultural relations between the two countries, always strong, were
reinforced by political ties both under the Hyksos regime and
under the subsequent, more or less continuous, Egyptian supremacy over Palestine. Immediately after the expulsion of the Hyksos
from their country, the ambitious rulers of the victorious Eighteenth Dynasty reëstablished Egyptian overlordship over the neighboring Asiatic province. While their control was not always fully
effective and Thutmes III alone had to buttress it by seventeen
military campaigns, it offered much opportunity for the widely
scattered Hebrew settlers on both sides of the border to exchange
ideas and to maintain direct personal relations. The family of
Moses, for example, seems to have had connections with both Nu-
bia and Northern Arabia, as is illustrated by his "Ethiopian" wife,
the Midianite and Kenite background of his father-in-law, Jethro-
Hobeb, and the Nubian-Egyptian name of his grandnephew,
Phineas.[11]

These far-flung interterritorial contacts merely reflected the profoundly international character of the Near Eastern civilizations in
the Late Bronze Age. Their major focus was in the centrally located
land of Canaan, to which the destinies of the Hebrew settlers were
increasingly tied. Long before the Hebrew conquest, Palestine and
the rest of Canaan had been the battle ground of many races and
ideas, and Babylonian, Egyptian, and Hittite influences continued
powerful. The new arrivals mixed freely with the natives. Abraham's injunction to his servant, "that thou shalt not take a wife for
my son of the daughters of the Canaanites, among whom I dwell,"

if not altogether an invention of later, less tolerant generations, evidently sprang from the patriarch's desire not to sever all his connections with his Mesopotamian family. In fact, he himself did not hesitate to marry Keturah and to beget sons with her and his native concubines. Simon, Judah, Joseph, and Moses are also expressly recorded as having married native women. Political assimilation and religious conversion, at that time often interchangeable processes, accelerated the pace of these racial mixtures. At the very threshold of their history the Israelitic tribes thus obviously absorbed a multitude of racial ingredients.[12]

Moreover, the development of ancient Phoenicia, a part of ancient Canaan, soon afterwards brought the country into contact with a colonial empire reaching through the whole Mediterranean region.[13] The Exodus from Egypt, the most momentous of the early events, was part of a great commotion among the peoples of the Near East. Shortly thereafter the appearance of the Philistines on the west coast of Palestine, diverting the energies of the Canaanite population, created conditions favorable for a time at least to the expansion of the Hebrews along the eastern and southern frontiers.

Whatever chronology we adopt and whatever historical truth we ascribe to the legends about the patriarchs, the Exodus, and the settlement, one thing appears certain: between the first appearance of the Hebrew patriarchs, the assaults on the Canaanite city states in the El-Amarna period and the final conquest during the period of Judges, many centuries elapsed.[14] During this epoch some of these newcomers settled and learned advanced ways of life from the local population, while others lingered on the border as seminomadic cattle raisers.

ETHNIC UNITY

It was during these seething and turbulent centuries that Israel's nation and creed were born. How these diverse tribes from different parts of the country, settling at different periods, were able to retain a memory of their unity and to continue to feel themselves members of one nation remains one of history's great enigmas. Not even the fact of foreign pressure fully explains how they were finally united under a single monarch. It is, moreover, not known that the successors of Moses encountered any serious difficulty in convincing the tribes which had been in Palestine before them that Yahweh, the God brought by the newcomers, was the very god

worshiped by their own ancestors. Even in Egypt Moses had to communicate to his coreligionists the divine message, "I appeared unto
Abraham, unto Isaac and unto Jacob, as God Almighty [*El Shaddai*], but by My name YHWH I made Me not known to them."
Moses' extraordinary success in persuading the Israelites that they
worshiped the God of their forefathers is explainable only through
the great facility with which divine names were transferred from
one Near Eastern people to another or, if newly introduced, speedily replaced the older names without any change of function. This
general acceptance laid the foundation for that emergent consciousness of unity which alone made possible the subsequent national
evolution. In the end all Israel came to believe that it had participated in the Exodus.[15]

One reason for this remarkable sense of solidarity may be found
in the general political situation. The first Hebrew tribes, unable
to overcome the well-accoutered Canaanites of the valley, won
some less populous mountain districts. After a time their hold on
these isolated settlements became rather precarious. Many became
subservient to their more powerful neighbors. Under these circumstances they more than welcomed the assistance of brotherly frontier tribes. Even the Canaanite city kings had made extensive use
of those fighters for their petty internecine struggles. In fact, we
owe most of our information about the Ḥabiru of that age to the
aforementioned recriminatory letters on this score, addressed to
the Egyptian overlord and preserved in the archives of Tell el-
Amarna.[16] The Gibeonites, too, the book of Joshua relates, once
asked the Hebrews to help them repel an alliance of five other
Palestinian city kings. The earlier Hebrew settlers had still better
reasons to appeal to the invaders, who may have readily conciliated
settled members of their own stock in order the more successfully
to attack other tribes.

In any case, in this formative period the Israelites who remained
in Palestine were for a long time outnumbered by the "seven"
Canaanite peoples. The tribes that went to Egypt were obviously a
scant minority in the midst of a powerful nation. In Goshen they
apparently lived a segregated and ethnically sheltered life despite,
perhaps because of, outside oppression. The ritualistic rigidity of
the Egyptians would have created some social segregation even if
the Israelities had not sunk into villeinage. In the period of greatest friendship and conviviality under Joseph's regime, we are told,

"the Egyptians might not eat bread with the Hebrews; for that is an abomination unto the Egyptians." [17] In fact, one wonders whether this pre-Mosaic Egyptian ghetto did not already cast its shadows over all the future history of the people. Nevertheless, it is remarkable that there and during their migrations through the desert the Israelitic tribes retained a vivid memory of their previous dwelling in Palestine and of their blood relation with the Palestinian Hebrews whom they were soon to join.

Here we already encounter the special genius of Israel's religion, the bent it received for all future time. Neither the territory of Palestine, nor the desert, nor Egypt is regarded as significant, but the memory of unity, a consciousness of a common history apart from that of other peoples. "They went about from nation to nation, from one kingdom to another people," sang a later poet (Ps. 105:13). By choosing the peculiar name "Israel," or rather *Bene Yisrael* (children of Israel), as their ethnic designation and attributing it to their patriarch, Jacob, they emphasized this historic connection. Curiously at its very first historic appearance (on the Merneptah stele of 1229) "Israel" already designates a people and not, like the other names in that inscription, a conquered area.[18] Only in this way can we explain the retention of their identity in Egypt and their return to a country which, while not that of their primeval origin, was the land of some of their brethren and, they felt, the scene of their destiny.

It was, then, to a group of migrating tribes loosely organized by a sense of relationship, a common past, and common destiny, and aiming at a specific country where alone they could build their life, that Moses had to submit the early formulation of Israel's religion. One may doubt whether that religion would have been born and would have sufficed so admirably without the towering mentality of Moses. But certainly no such drastic religious proclamation could have had so enthusiastic a response or could have remained intact in essence, however obscured by later developments, had it not been suited to the people's objective conditions of life. To compare the time of Mohammed with that of Moses may be suggestive, but the differences are more significant than the similarities. Mohammed dealt with Arabian tribes well established in agricultural and even commercial settlements and having states of their own, Moses with straggling seminomadic tribes. He had to strive to organize them suitably for travel and at the same time to lay a basis for a future settled life in Canaan. To accomplish this he had to endow with vivid appeal an imaginary, unseen territory, the "promised land."

The Hebrew tribes were not entirely unprepared for such an experience. They had been anything but typical Bedouins even during their desert migrations. The beautiful legends of Genesis, depicting the life of the patriarchs, are chiefly responsible for the view, still prevalent in some circles, that Israel's career started in Palestine as that of a typical nomadic tribe or group of tribes. Indeed, the school of Wellhausen tried on this basis to establish a gradual evolution from nomadic beginnings to the life of a civilized nation. Such an inner evolution obviously needed several centuries to mature. Hence representatives of this school have been generally inclined to postdate as far as possible the biblical sources, the main argument being that such and such a complex social phenomenon or advanced religious idea could not possibly find its place in the earlier stages which they had classified as primitive. They have not only overlooked the fact, mentioned before, that immediately after their settlement the Israelites were implanted in an age-old civilization, but also that behind those biblical narratives lay a conscious historical construction. The historian of the tenth or ninth century, the "Yahwist," as well as his successor, the "Elohist," were both men of great culture, and both were prone at least partially to accept the view, so vivid in prophetic, Nazirite and Rechabite circles, that the civilization of their own day was merely a sinful degeneration from the good old times of unspoiled primitive life. To attach too literal significance to these narratives would be like judging the conditions of medieval Europe on the basis of the poetic descriptions of nineteenth-century Romanticism.[19]

Nor could the Hebrews' past experiences in Egypt, where, however alien and oppressed, they had led a "civilized" life, be quickly wiped out. They doubtless remembered of the Nile valley much more than its "fleshpots." During their lengthy sojourn at Kadesh (now Ain Qudeis, fifty miles southwest of Beersheba), an oasis then more fertile than now and abundant in wheat and barley, some of them lived more as an agricultural community than as wandering herdsmen. But this could not satisfy their craving for all Palestine. Stimulated by the perennial drive of nomadic races toward settled regions whose wealth appears to be fabulous, the memory of their sojourn in the country in bygone days glowed even more brightly under the inspiring words of their prophet. Two great, though not quite successful, attempts were made to break through in the south under the guidance of Moses. These were followed by a half-pacific, half-bellicose penetration there and in the north during the following generations.

Thus evolved the imposing religious concept which, transcending the needs of migrating herdsmen and future farmers and townsmen, affirmed the "eternal" behind the transitory, the essential beyond the accidental. Shall we not believe that a leader of vision, confronted by a challenging social situation, found a memorable formula of belief and action?

One must not regard, however, the Mosaic conception of God as a radical break with the previous tribal religious history of the Hebrews. Some of its essential elements grew directly out of the life of a people still organized on the basis of clans and families. Although there is no evidence of ancestor worship among the early Hebrews, religion was, nevertheless, largely a clan affair. There were communal religious ceremonies and festivals, conducted by elders who were also priests. God himself was, in a sense and under certain aspects, related to his clan or clans as a kind of god-parent. Moses built upon these ethnic principles of the clan society and upon this relation of God to the people as a whole. Despite his reputed query, "Is not He [the Lord] thy father that hath gotten thee?" (Deut. 32:6), he conceived this parenthood in the moral sense only. None the less, since the Hebrews had evolved a patriarchal, rather than a matriarchal, society probably even before their emergence as a separate identifiable group, God's parenthood appeared more and more in the light of fatherhood. Hence also the lack of a female deity, a Ba'alah, the "great mother," as the closely related Carthaginians called her.[20]

MONOTHEISTIC ANTECEDENTS

Although the sources at our disposal are all of a later, consciously monotheistic age, we may nevertheless deduce that Moses had before him the example of the patriarchs even in the worship of a single God. It is immaterial in this connection, whether we regard the God of the three patriarchs as one and the same deity, or whether we see in "the God of Abraham and the Fear [Kinsman] of Isaac" (Gen. 31:42) as well as in "the Mighty One of Jacob" (Gen. 49:24) three distinctive regional *numina* worshiped by different Hebrew tribes in different sections of Palestine. The religion of the early Hebrew settlers had already prepared the ground for later Yahwism, in so far as, in contrast to Canaanite creeds, it was a religion with a preponderant emphasis on the relation between God and man, especially on that of God and human society, without close attachment to any particular place. That is why it was so well adapted to all the changes in the destinies of its adherents.[21]

More than thirty years ago Andrew Lang opened the still unconcluded discussion of the "high gods" of primitive tribes; it has constantly become clearer that the early Semites had the idea of a single original "maker" of all things, one supreme "El." Though this *Urgott* idea, this "primitive monotheism," was far removed from the advanced monotheism of Moses and the prophets, it might well have served as a starting point from which, under favorable circumstances, a much higher form could and did develop. Indeed, the later biblical historians in sketching the piety of Enoch and Noah seem to lend expression to a dim recollection of such an early monotheistic heritage.[22]

There is no reason why these ancient Semitic ideas should not have continued among the early Hebrews. They might easily have become modified into "monarchical polytheism," particularly among those Ḥabiru who had come in contact with the Babylonian cities of Ur and Haran, where the Moon god was worshiped above all others. Indeed the Hebrew saga reflects that the ancestors of the Abrahamites had "served foreign gods" in the two moon-worshiping centers. The striking association between some of the names of Abraham's family (Laban, Sarah, Milcah, Terah, and possibly even Abram) and the Moon cult can hardly be a mere coincidence. Whatever revolutionary changes might have been brought about by Abraham's new religious attitude, his economic status as a cattle raiser in Palestine could not but enhance the importance of the moon, as a celestial body, in the eyes of his clan. By no means altogether a nomad, this "mighty prince" (Gen. 23:6) somewhat resembled contemporary Canaanite city rulers. Yet as an owner of flocks he often traveled and, because of the heat of the day, he did this by night. He was therefore more dependent on the lunar month than on the solar year. That is probably why the New Moon was retained as an important holiday in ancient Israel and why the lunar calendar had been accepted by Jews. According to some scholars the shadows of the Babylonian moon deity, Sin, fell even on the Mosaic

age. The names of Mt. Sinai, the desert of Sin, and the bush of the
first Mosaic theophany (*sneh*) are said to have sprung from this root.
In Jericho, it may be noted, the Canaanites had a moon city of their
own.[23]

Canaan's Moon god was reinforced by Babylonian influences,
but it found a powerful rival in the cult of the Sun, so important
to agricultural peoples. The northern Canaanites of Ugarit (Ras-
Shamra) worshiped both a male and a female Sun deity (Ym and
Shpsh). At the height of Egyptian political influence, especially,
some such obsequious vassals of Akhenaton (ab. 1387–66), as the
petty kings of Tyre and Jerusalem, professed a deep reverence for
their overlord's Sun god. Even though we find no traces of sun
worship among the patriarchal Hebrew settlers, some faint notion
of the Egyptian universal monarchy and universal deity, cherished
for long centuries in priestly traditions on the Nile, must have
penetrated into the most distant Jordan villages, all of which had
long been under Egypt's military and commercial control. In the
subsequent rejection of these polytheistic cults, at any rate, the
Sun and the Moon appear invariably linked in the imagination
of the biblical writers.[24]

The religious ideas of the Hittites, of the Aegean and of some
peoples of Indo-European speech also filtered into the country with
the stream of soldiers and merchants. The ethical deity Varuna, in
particular, whether of Indian origin or not, was known to the
Mitanni and the Hittites of Asia Minor as early as the fourteenth
century. It may well have found worshipers among Hittite warriors
in Syria. In Palestine of the Canaanite age, at any rate, there was,
according to one Hebrew source which had no particular reason to
be friendly to the natives, a king of Salem (Jerusalem) who was the
priest of "God the most High" (the *El Elyon*, Gen. 14:18). This
means, of course, that one god must have been worshiped above all
others. The name of this king, Melchizedek (my king is Zedek)
and of his successor in the days of Joshua, Adonizedek (my lord is
Zedek), may indicate that this highest of gods was called Zedek
(righteousness), incidentally a divine name known also from Phoenician sources. In this case ethical attributes must also have been
attached to the deity.

One need not be astonished by this great emphasis on the idea of
"justice"; it is easily explicable by the general heritage from primitive Semitic conceptions of God as a kind of heavenly sheikh and
source of all law. In this sense, the later rabbinic theology was right

in attaching to the divine name *Elohim,* a derivative of the generally Semitic "El," the attribute of justice, while *YHWH,* the more specific Israelitic name, represented the idea of "mercy." [25]

In addition to these Babylonian and native Canaanite influences upon the tribes which remained in Palestine, the Hebrews who left Egypt must have had a more or less vivid recollection of Akhenaton's unodeistic (if one may call it so) reform of the preceding century. Even if we should accept an earlier dating for the Exodus, we must admit that strong monotheistic tendencies had existed among the Egyptian priests for centuries before Akhenaton. Moses, at any rate, might have been familiar with these teachings. The Kenites and Midianites, desert tribes with whom the Israelites associated during their migration, but concerning whose religion we can formulate only hypotheses, may also have influenced the religious thought of the great lawgiver. Even the Hebrew legend, however colored by later attitudes, depicts in glowing colors Balaam, a native prophet "who heareth the words of God and knoweth the knowledge of the Most High." [26]

THE WORK OF MOSES

In the last analysis, however, the God of Moses differed essentially from all these gods. After the great feat of creation, the "maker" of the primitives becomes an inactive god without further relation to the world or man. Not even the Egyptian Aton, the pervasive sun ray which is the source of all life, has a direct interest in human actions. The God of Moses, however, was anything but a *deus otiosus,* anything but a morally indifferent natural entity. The chief task facing the Hebrews was immediate action—motion forward, struggle, the storming of Canaan; and their God, as one might expect, became a God of action, a God who had led his people out of Egypt and who was engaged in guiding them safely through the desert and to the ultimate conquest of the promised land. The extraordinary occurrences of the Exodus recorded by all later traditions were apparently of volcanic origin and left a permanent imprint upon later conceptions of God. The mild and pacific God of the patriarchs became the "Man of War," a God of storm and conquest.[27]

Such a God of action, however, might easily and perhaps more logically have become divided up into many deities, each representing a specific phase of action, a specific function. That this Hebrew

God remained a single God was due to the combined influences of a weighty tradition, of the singular needs of the day and of Moses' creative personality. Renan explained Mosaic monotheism as simply that "minimum of religion" natural to desert nomads. This once famous theory has fallen into just disrepute in recent years. In so far, however, as the intricacies of civilized life naturally tend correspondingly to increase the number of functional deities in a polytheistic religion, it has a kernel of truth. The more primitive a nation, the less numerous ought to be its gods, unless we call each spirit a god. In Moses' time, in any case, there was apparently no difficulty in persuading the Hebrew tribes of the sole existence of a single God. Indeed, the traditionally supreme God of the patriarchs was now an urgent necessity for the unification of all the tribes.

Moses, conscious of the demands of tradition and the hour, had also a vision of the future. He linked God with the fate of Israel in history in an inseparable way. His is not only the God who created the world and who continuously supports life, but One who realizes himself in past, present, and future through the process of history, the history of this world and of man's place in it. Israel occupies the central position within mankind. In contrast to the Babylonian mythology, the early biblical narratives pay far less attention to cosmogony and anthropogeny than to the subsequent human destinies. The history of man serves as a background for the still more significant history of Israel. Thus through the efforts of Moses, the creation was displaced by the Exodus as the *leitmotif* of all ancient Hebrew literature and theology. Such a God, related to human life past and present, must be affiliated with man. He can and should be worshiped. Whatever man does, concerns God; consequently moral behavior is essential.

Of course, no one will dare minimize the importance of Gen. 1–11 for Israel's general outlook on the world. The differences between the biblical and the Babylonian stories of creation are, in many respects, more significant than the parallels. The creation of the world by one God uttering words, rather than using external means, and crowning his work by bringing forth man in his own image, instead of creating him from the blood of an evil deity, is ethically so far superior that many critics have tried to ascribe this biblical "refinement" to a much later, more advanced age. Considering, however, the equally basic differences between the biblical notions of the world's origins and the ramified Canaanite mythology now so familiar to us from the Ugaritic poems, it seems likely that the biblical cosmogony goes back to some even more remote sources.[28]

Additional sanction was given the relationship between this God and the people of Israel by the idea of the Covenant. Whether or not God's name was taken over from one of the desert tribes, the Israelites certainly concluded a covenant with a deity outside themselves, a God, the terms read, who of his free will and for his own purposes had miraculously redeemed them from Egypt and who would now expect complete loyalty. To serve other gods became a grave offense against the Covenant. The desertion of one for another god was a new, until then unheard-of, religious crime. The Covenant was also the first appeal for wholehearted devotion, for relentless sacrifice of life to religious conviction—the first urge to religious martyrdom in history. On the other hand, by concluding the Covenant, God, too, subjected himself to its terms, thus becoming a sort of heavenly constitutional monarch exercising his reign over the people under the provisions of a self-imposed law. This unprecedented idea was itself the offshoot of, and became in turn a source of great strength for, both the law-mindedness and the "democratic" urge of Israelitic society.[29]

This monotheism was necessarily detached from the soil. Even for worship one may not be allowed recourse to a "Baal," the lord of a specific district. Beyond all local habitations, there is only one God to be worshiped. For the same reason plastic representations of the deity are taboo. Every image tends in its concreteness to localize the deity and finally to create an attachment to one place or another. Since, however, it would have been impossible to abstract God so abruptly from all locality, he remained the God of the desert long after Israel's settlement in Canaan. From the days of Deborah to those of the writing prophets, God appears in poetic vision as having his seat on Mt. Sinai, or Mt. Seir, in the desert of Paran, or in other places—all outside Palestine. Not even the combined efforts of the kings and priests in Jerusalem to associate the divine presence with the Temple on Zion could succeed until the destruction of the Temple itself. Israel's God thus became definitely dissociated from exclusive residence on Israel's soil.

In so far as God was primitively represented by any object, the object could be fortuitous. The patriarchs, like other early Semites, sacrificed upon a simple unhewn stone. Such a stone, a rock altar, later served as an altar for divine service. The insistence in later laws upon unhewn stones or altars of earth becomes significant when we realize that an unhewn stone is, after all, an accidental stone. One can be found and erected anywhere in the world. The old biblical source itself gives this motivation: "In every place where I cause My Name to be mentioned [*azkir*, according to the Syriac version even more pointedly: *tazkir*] I will come unto thee and bless thee" (Exod. 20:21). Indeed, the principal sanctuary in the Mosaic age and much later was the Tabernacle, an easily movable tent. Likewise, the mobile Ark of the Covenant, probably a simple wooden box containing at most two inscribed stones, became the shrine which represented God, wherever it happened to be. The oracular lots, the *Urim* and *Tummim*, were no less portable.[30]

Neither the prohibition of imagery nor the movable shrine was peculiar to Israel. General Semitic and other races followed "portable shrines" into battle. Although the recent excavations of the necropolis of Minet el-Beida and elsewhere have brought to light a number of statuettes of Reshep and Astarte, what we know of the religion of the Canaanites indicates that in divine worship at their temples they made little if any use of plastic images. The imageless cult purposively established by Moses was of a decidedly different order, however.

Not that he or any of his early successors tried to steer clear of ascribing to God human qualities and to view Him in man's image as they viewed man in God's image. At this stage of Israel's religion, anti-anthropomorphism which, as we shall see, was to play such a great role in the thinking of leaders of the Greek and Arabic speaking Jews, though perhaps a perfectly reasonable deduction from the radical opposition to images, would have been totally meaningless and hence harmful to the religion of the masses. Certainly the emphasis on the dignity of man, of *any* man, as created in God's image, was far more important than some philosophic abstraction about the incorporeality of God.[31]

It does not matter at what period the Decalogue received its present wording. There is no better document of Mosaic monotheism than this "catechism of the Hebrews in the Mosaic age," as Gressmann calls it. It begins with the principle of monotheism and monolatry, prohibiting any graven image or other likeness of God. God's claim upon the Jews is justified since he brought them "out of the land of Egypt, out of the house of bondage." Added point is given to his sovereignty by the threat to punish evildoers and the promise to reward the obedient, not only in their own lifetime but by "visiting the iniquity of the fathers upon the children until the third and fourth generation," while "showing mercy unto the thousandth generation" (Exod. 20:2, 5–6). For the attainment of this objective in the course of history, society and its basis, the family, must be organized on a moral foundation, laid down in the remaining commandments. None of these speaks of a sanctuary or of sacrifices as essential. That in its essence the Decalogue transcends all localized worship is only what one would expect of a code framed in the desert for a wandering folk. It may not be authentic word by word as an historical document, but it renders a poetic truth, in so far as it embodies a set of ideas which should have been voiced in precisely this way by a person like Moses in the period of Moses.

Fewer and fewer scholars are now prepared to stake their reputation on the defense of the supposed priority of the so-called "ritual Decalogue" (Exod. 34) over the "ethical Decalogue" (Exod. 20 and Deut. 5). This once widely held theory sprang from the assumption that the former, being more "primitive," must have been formulated in Israel's earlier stage of evolution, whereas the lofty ethical commandments could not possibly antedate the intellectual advances of the ninth century. The entire underlying assumption has been undermined, however, by the general reorientation of biblical scholarship with respect to the supposedly slow and unilinear evolution of ancient Israel. Today many students are inclined to accept the contrary argument that, since the "ritual Decalogue" presupposes settled agricultural conditions, its social background postulates a decidedly later dating than do the "timeless" ethical demands of Exod. 20. The latter almost directly point to an author of great vision confronted by an unprecedented, unsettled and, in many ways, unforeseeable social situation. Moreover, its historic authenticity as an essentially Mosaic proclamation has found increasing support in extrabiblical sources. The similarity of some of its ethical teachings with Chapter 125 of the Egyptian "Book of the Dead," the oldest manuscript of which dates from the fifteenth century, and with the second tablet of the Babylonian magical series *Shurpu*, written some time between 1500 and 1100, by no means detracts from the originality of Moses' work. It does, however, remove the objection to his teaching, so to say, in a vacuum.[32]

None of the Ten Commandments mentions sacrifices, but the

Mosaic religion was by no means opposed to them. Such a proscription would have been inconceivable to a Semite of the time. The sacrificial element is, indeed, consistent with both the patriarchal and the Mosaic religion. In so dry a country there would naturally be, as Bertholet has pointed out, a high estimate of blood as a liquid source of life. Moreover, blood was the cohesive fluid of social life. The family and clan were based entirely on blood relationship. A stranger who wanted to become a member of a primitive Semitic clan had to undergo a blood ritual. Therefore, how could the union between the clan and its god be better expressed than by a blood ceremony? Among some primitive tribes, children and household animals which, in a sense, also belong to the family, had to be sacrificed to God as a symbol of that union; unclean animals could never be sacrificed. Naturally, such sacrifice was costly to a cattle-raising tribe. Even in Israel's later, agricultural period, the killing of a household animal for food was a luxury in Palestine, where meat never became a staple commodity. It was entirely proper to offer God the most precious of one's possessions. In the semi-nomadic stage, moreover, herds were communally owned, and every sacrifice was a common renunciation of common property, and thus a sanctification for the community as a whole.

To be sure, the opinion that both Abraham and Moses organized a religious league rather than a clan or a people, contains a degree of truth. The emphasis upon religious beliefs and actions made it easier for persons of foreign stock to join the Israelite community. But in those comparatively primitive conditions there were few foreigners at hand. Apart from the small number of slaves whom the Hebrew tribesmen might have carried with them in their migrations, there was little opportunity for an outsider to profess a creed other than that of his own tribal group. To renounce one's native religion then meant to forsake one's nationality. The invaders undoubtedly assimilated whole groups of natives, a process which involved considerable absorption of foreign blood. But the voluntary acceptance of Israel's religion by individual foreigners is rarely mentioned, even as late as the period of the kings. The few newcomers were quickly absorbed by the national body. In such a community ancestry and blood kinship and consequently blood sacrifice, were inevitably of great importance.[33]

A question which can receive no adequate answer today is whether Mosaic monotheism was universal and absolute or national and relative. Moses appears to have stressed the primacy of the Israelitic people. This tendency is surely understandable for that formative period, when the nation was still to be welded together. Whether Moses expected that finally all men would worship the one and only God, as later prophets speaking in his name alleged, cannot be ascertained; but it is not impossible. Some kind of universal monotheism had been thought of even before Moses. The more we learn about the history of mankind in general, the further back can we trace all fundamental ideas. In any case, these ideas are older than any traceable sources. Indeed, it would not be altogether whimsical to believe that all our basic viewpoints were seen obscurely as through a glass by the first race of men, perhaps those who lived in caves. The beautiful Jewish legend that all human souls for all generations were attached to Adam's body explains how all men can participate in the original sin and consequently suffer punishment; it may also be construed as symbolizing the adumbration in Adam's mind of all future ideas. From this point of view the development of ideas may be considered as a sequence of formulations. Thus Moses, by personal experiences and still more by his people's experiences, was led to formulate his historical monotheism, centering chiefly in Israel. Subsequent vicissitudes of the people induced other men, whose personal equipment was equally rich, to restate that historical monotheism with a much greater emphasis on the universal aspect. Its essence, however, remained the same.

Of course, neither Moses nor the prophets were philosophers interested in a sharp and unequivocal definition of terms. While one can draw obvious distinctions between their type of monotheism and that of medieval Jewish, Christian, or Muslim scholastics, there is absolutely no evidence for an essential difference between the monotheism of Moses and that of the prophets. One must never forget that Moses lived in a more internationally minded civilization than any of its successors until the Persian Empire. In his days commercial, political, and cultural relations among the various ethnic groups were so intimate that translations of major literary works from one language to another were rather common. The single school of scribes established at Ugarit has yielded tablets inscribed in six different languages. It was perfectly natural for such a civilization to produce sweeping assertions about the cosmic nature of the divine power like "Thou art the only one who created what there is," included in the ancient Egyptian Amun hymns antedating the fifteenth century, and to culminate in the philosophic, almost overspeculative "unodeism" of Akhenaton. The latter's influence on certain Israelitic psalms (104, 139) and on Moses himself is at least likely.

Under these circumstances the intrinsically dubious phrase, "Thou shalt have no other gods *before* Me" (Exod. 20:3), is no more cogently "henotheistic," or implies that other gods may legitimately be worshiped by other nations, than do similar exclamations in Deut. 29:25; 32:8-9; 33:26, probably written at the height of prophetic monotheism, according to some scholars, as late as the fifth century. Similarly the psalmist sees no contradiction in asserting, "There is none like unto Thee among the gods, O Lord," and then emphatically adding, "All nations whom Thou hast made shall come and prostrate themselves before Thee, O Lord" (Ps. 86:8-9). Nor did the author of II Chr. 2:4, though writing long after the Second Isaiah, evince any compunctions in ascribing to King Solomon the exclamation, "For great is our God above all gods." [34]

In short, Moses, reflecting the varied experiences of the people in the period between the Egyptian bondage and the conquest of Canaan, set up and exalted the Jewish people as against a Jewish territory, their movement through time as against their occupancy of space, the course of history rather than the contours of nature. The idea was somewhat hazy and equivocal; God, eternal and therefore indifferent to time, brooded over history and waited, as it were, for a clearer articulation, when circumstances should favor or demand it.

INFLUENCE OF PALESTINE

This history-centered religion of Moses and the desert tribes was soon to face an acid test. Scarcely had the tribes, led by Joshua, settled in Palestine, when nature began to reassert itself. Under the rule of Israel's judges the country partly relapsed into semiprimitive conditions. The political disaster which overtook Canaan as a result of the loss of territory to both the Israelites and the Philistines was accompanied by a sudden decline in material civilization. Archaeological excavations have shown that the Early Iron Age witnessed a speedy deterioration in the quality of both pottery and masonry and that houses, as well as fortifications, became less sturdy and elaborate. Some of these changes were occasioned by such technological improvements as the introduction of iron or the use of bonded masonry in lieu of more massive fortresses. But others seem to reflect the country's temporary relapse into more primitive ways of life.

In the long run, however, this relapse proved a blessing in disguise. The previous great wealth of the country, illustrated by the large amounts of booty carried away by the Egyptian conquerors, had long benefited only the upper classes. Under the sharp feudal cleavages, apparently established under the Hyksos regime, the lords filled their palaces with ornate gold and silver utensils, some of which now stand out in the excavations of Jericho, Lachish, and Megiddo. But these palaces were usually surrounded by a great many shacks of poverty-stricken villeins whose forced labor had built them. The egalitarian structure of the Israelitic clans, on the contrary, long prevented excessive accumulation of wealth and, without necessarily lowering the average standard of life, militated against any form of conspicuous consumption.

Similarly the weakening of Egyptian control over the country (except for a brief period after 1195) doubtless removed a significant cultural factor and contributed to the country's relative isolation from the mainstream of Near Eastern evolution. But by making possible the Israelitic conquest and the self-assertion of Israel's new religious culture, it opened the gate to the influx of those memorable new ideas which were soon to be formulated by Israel's prophets and priests. Israelitic, Philistine, and Aramaic conquests, moreover, by narrowing Phoenician domination to a few coastal cities, forced their dense population into the open seas and laid the foundation for one of the greatest colonizing ventures in history. It is no exaggeration, therefore, when Millar Burrows asserts that:

In several respects the Israelite invasion of Palestine was like the barbarian invasions of the Roman empire and the Arab invasion of the Byzantine empire in later centuries. For the student of the Bible this is perhaps the most striking and surprising of all the results of archaeological research in Palestine, but it is also one of the most certain.[35]

No sooner, however, did the Israelites settle permanently in the land when they became bound to the soil, and with this attachment the history-conscious ethnic unity began to founder. Nature was abetted by geographical features. Palestine, though a small country, presents an extraordinary range of geographical differences. From the perennial snow of Hermon to the subtropical regions of the South which never have snow, from the heights of

Lebanon to the lowest lying land found anywhere in the world, is but a short distance. The Jordan does not serve, like the Nile or the Euphrates, as a unifying element, but, precipitous and unnavigable, it is a barrier between Transjordan and western Palestine. It has been estimated that not less than forty different climatic and geographic units may be counted within the area of this country, whose more hospitable western section is no larger than the state of Vermont. Thus the inhabitants were broken into groups. Hence arose the numerous city states of the El-Amarna age and thereafter the permanent partition of the country among many ethnic groups such as Ammonites, Moabites, Edomites, and Philistines, apart from some Phoenicians and Aramaeans, all of whom shared the tiny area with the Israelites. Hence also the tendency toward tribal divisions among the Israelites themselves.

Apart from the conflict between ethnic unity and territorial section, social life as a whole began to develop along natural and territorial rather than along historic and ethnic lines. Hitherto the social structure had been based upon the family and clan; now it was divided into units of towns, each with its environs. Instead of a bond of common ancestry and a common cult, inherited from generation to generation, there now arose the territorial unity natural to a people occupying the same area and employed in the same economic pursuits. They were dominated, not by the elder of a clan, but by the ruler of a district. Of course the change did not occur suddenly nor without interruption. Traditional institutions did not disappear in a day, but often synthesized with newly rising forces. Clan and family religious festivals continued down to the period of the kings. Politically, too, the clan elders often continued to rule under the guise of city councilors or royal advisers and military lieutenants. But the controlling natural forces tended to transform the Israelite clan society into a territorial society.[36]

There was a concomitant economic evolution from nomadic or seminomadic cattle raising to settled agriculture. Again territory was the controlling factor. In distinction to the nomad who lightheartedly leaves his land in search of more profitable pasturage, the farmer is attached to a particular bit of soil. The more advanced the agriculture, the deeper do the roots of the peasant population sink. This was especially so in Palestine where intensive cultivation, including devices for irrigation, had already existed in the Canaanite period. Often land had to be redeemed from the desert or the numerous swamps, or restored after an earthquake. Fruit growing, which sometimes exceeded even grain growing, demanded long cultivation before yielding a return. The love of the soil grew in proportion to the toil of tilling it.

The native inhabitants had not disappeared, moreover. For generations the newcomers had to live side by side with diverse races divided among warring city states. These peoples further intensified the internal division of Israel, since, regardless of their racial origin, they too had grown to love the local fatherlands. They were superior in civilization to the new arrivals. Even in districts where the Israelites permanently obtained the upper hand, they had to learn the natives' art of cultivating the soil, the city life, and, to a certain extent, their language and culture. Here no more than elsewhere did mere conquest prevent the assimilation of the conquering group to the superior culture of the conquered population.

Moreover, the Hebrew settlers themselves were not quite homogeneous. There were differences between the tribes which had been in Egypt and those which had been left behind. Other differences arose from the time and manner of each tribe's penetration into the land. There seems also to have been another important division. Inferences drawn from the biblical texts and confirmed by other evidence seem to indicate that there lived in Palestine along with the Israelites another group of Hebrews who were not Israelites. The Bible itself regards many nations as descendants of *Eber,* including those whose ancestors were connected with the family of Israel's patriarchs. Such were the Ammonites, Moabites, and Edomites. In Egypt there must have been Ḥabiru other than the Israelites, although the Egyptians did not distinguish between them. It is probably for that reason that Moses, speaking to Pharaoh, refers, with one uncertain exception, to the *Hebrews* —of whom the Pharaoh might be expected to have heard—but, when speaking to his own people, addresses them as *Israel,* thus distinguishing them from other Hebrews (cf. Exod. 5:1–3).

Later Jewish legends concerning those "evildoers" who refused to join the Exodus may allude to such non-Israelitic Hebrews. Indeed, we find Egyptian references to *Apiru,* the Egyptian equivalent for Hebrew, even under Raamses III and Raamses IV in the twelfth century, at least several decades after the Exodus. The other legend of the "mixed multitude" ('*ereb rab,* Exod. 12:38) which accompanied the Israelites on their way from Egypt, and which on account of its creedal dissidence proved a disturbing factor, may be but a confused recollection of the fact that such a group of non-Israelitic Hebrews did join the refugees. The division probably persisted for many generations and possibly found legal reflection in the distinction between the "Hebrew" slave and the "Israelite" who may never become a slave. Certainly those distinctions had not been wiped out in the period of settlement in Canaan.

To all this must be added the influence, lasting for centuries, of the pressure of other tribes on the frontier. Palestine's ethnological make-up must have been chequered and in constant flux. After the settlement, Israel engaged in wars with the Amalekites and the Midianites, the latter appearing even in the northern districts. These invasions were one passage in that eternal Bedouin assault on Palestine which was followed by the steady spread of the North Arabian tribes. The Nabatæans, in particular, throughout the following centuries, were drifting into the Edomite, Moabite, and Ammonite territories, and finally reached distant Mesopotamia. Later historical development was to decide which of these alien groups were to be incorporated into the Israelitic-Judean nation (Kenites, Kenizzites, Yerahmeëlites, Calebites) and which were to be outside. Economically, too, outlying districts, such as southern Judah and Transjordan, whether Israelitic or not, remained until the end cattle-raising rather than agricultural regions.[37]

Such bewildering complexity found its apposite religious expression. In agricultural sections there were moves to reintroduce the local deities, the various "Baalim." The idea of a god-father gradually was supplanted by the conception of a god-lord of a territory, a "Baal." For the first time, too, some Israelites began to worship a female deity, Astarte, the goddess of fertility and generation, and consequently also of love. We have seen that the patriarchal society of their seminomadic ancestors had no room for such a mother goddess. The seminomadic southern Arabs, to be sure, took *Ishtar* into their pantheon of gods, but they and, probably following them, the Moabites, transformed her into a masculine god, *Athtar*. Characteristically enough, both Arabs and Hebrews called the planet Venus, named by the Greeks and Romans after the Babylonian Ishtar, by a masculine name. Now, however, as the Israelitic settlers became more and more absorbed in agriculture, they began to be increasingly impressed by the importance of natural regenerative forces. For them Astarte was no longer the "mother" of clan or people, but "mother earth," her bosom filled with blessings for the farmer. Thus Israelites began to worship "the lady of vigor and joy," as she is called in an ancient Babylonian dedication, in the orgiastic manner of a youthful and exuberant peasant population.

The increasingly important role played by women in orchard and field labor stimulated the worship of a female deity. The status of the Israelitic woman must have been fairly auspicious from the beginning, if we are to place any credence in the legends of the patriarchs' lives. Certainly, the story of Sarah, so rich in local color, seems to contain authentic material, revealing how, even in the earliest times, the woman had many rights, including property rights. Later legislation further increased these. Hence it is not surprising that the Israelite farmer should have been susceptible to belief in a goddess enjoying a standing more or less equal to that of his Lord.[38]

Needless to say that the favorable social position of women was merely a contributory cause, not the reason, for the Astarte worship. Many nations whose women occupied a markedly inferior status worshiped female deities, as did the Romans in the early centuries. On the other hand, the later Mosaic religion, while insisting upon the singleness of God, tried at the same time to improve in many ways the woman's position within the family and in society at large.

In general we know that, among the cultural influences of the native population upon the Israelites, were those affecting religion. We have seen how the complexity of political and social life gradually weakened the people's ethnic unity and with it their common creed and worship. Along with the dissolution of the clan went many ancestral rites. For them were substituted modes of worship found ready to hand among Canaanite neighbors. Each little district had its own immemorial legends and holy places. The newcomers, becoming attached to the soil, accepted these legends naturally, incorporating them into their own sagas and gradually coming to regard the local shrines as sacred. In the agricultural districts, particularly, nature came into its own. Its forces, so decisive for the farmer, now overawed the Israelites. They succumbed to the ancient festivals connected with the seasons of the year, or other recurring events in nature, which now became the pervading feature of religious life. Local sanctuaries, each with its own form of worship, became the chief religious centers for each district. Thus there grew up that "popular religion" of ancient Israel which was so obnoxious to all true believers in the genuine Mosaic religion.

The religion of Moses by this time, however, had gathered sufficient momentum to become a social force itself, capable of reciprocally influencing the life of the time and adapting itself to the new society. A small but influential group throughout the country stood firmly on the teachings of Moses. Most levitical priests remained faithful adherents of the Mosaic religion as they understood it. They officiated in the new sanctuaries but, whenever they sacrificed to the Baalim, it was in the name of the one supreme God of Israel.[39] There were also bands of ecstatic visionaries, so-called *nebiim*, who traversed the land from one end to the other, preaching in the name of the one common God. Some sanctuaries, like that of Shiloh, gained prominence and obtained at least regional importance. The Ark, inherited from Mosaic times, gave preëminence to whatever place it happened to be in.

This was, of course, not pure Mosaism but a syncretistic creed in which the already mixed native religion fused with the predominant conception of Israel. "Yahweh" became "Baal," a name which also had the connotation "Lord." The proper names *Yobel* (preserved by the Septuagint but eliminated from the official Masoretic text) and *Bealiah*, both of which can mean only that "Yah" is "Baal," are excellent illustrations of this syncretism. Gideon's father, himself bearing the Yahwistic name Joash (YHWH has given) did not hesitate to name his son Jerubbaal (probably meaning, May Baal give increase). Nor did Saul evince any compunctions about calling one son Jonathan (Y. has given) and another Ishbaal or Eshbaal (Man of Baal or Baal exists). Even in the later ostraca excavated in Samaria, we find numerous names of Israelites compounded with Baal and others combined with Yahweh. Apparently the bearers of these names saw no distinction between the two; both regarded themselves as true worshipers of the one God of Israel.[40]

Apparently even the prohibition of graven images was partly adhered to, at least for public worship. True, excavations have brought to light many figurines of Astarte of the Israelitic period, but their size indicates that they were used chiefly as household ornaments or, as has been suggested, for magical and healing purposes. In any case, few if any seem to have been produced within the country. They were imported by foreign merchants, perhaps not at all for the use of Israelites.

Other social forces contributed to maintain Yahwistic elements. There always were numerous cattle raisers in the wide plains on the eastern border and in the south. After the breakdown following the invasions, the towns were rehabilitated. An increasing section of the population took up handicrafts and commerce. Metal workers in particular were a necessity both in war and in peace. The Kenites, the southern tribe with which Israel was so closely associated during the desert migration, were mostly smiths, metal working being a craft common among nomads. This tribe was soon incorporated in the larger tribe of Judah. In fact, Cain means "smith" in Aramaic and Arabic, though not in Hebrew, and the book of Genesis names Tubal-Cain as the first "forger of every cutting instrument of brass and iron" (4:22). Even before the Iron Age, which began in Palestine more or less in the period of the Judges, a class of metal workers in bronze must have been an economic necessity. The recent excavations in the southern districts have, in fact, brought to light many metallic objects apparently produced by local craftsmen. Moreover, Horsfield's, Albright's, and Glueck's investigations have revealed that southern Palestine (Moab-Edom) was a copper-producing area of great importance throughout the Bronze Age. If "there was no smith found throughout all the land of Israel" in the days of Samuel (I Sam. 13:19) this was merely the effect of enforced disarmament imposed upon Israel by the Philistines. The latter's extreme prohibition even to repair agricultural implements (unlike, for example, that of Porsenna, *ne ferro nisi in agricultura uterentur*, according to Pliny's *Historia naturalis*, XXXIV, 39) is conclusive proof that the Palestinian smiths must have been sufficiently numerous to inspire real fear in the excellently equipped conquerors.

Commercial caravans incessantly traversed the country. Commerce declined after the El-Amarna age, of course, but some continuity of economic life was doubtless preserved. Money never disappeared as the primary means of exchange. An economic system in which money played a prominent part naturally operated to bring about social differentiation.[41]

Nor did the cattle raisers, craftsmen, or traders show the characteristic features of the agricultural population in religious matters. For them nature and territory did not play the same crucial, immediate role. But while merchants and artisans were influenced in other directions by their predecessors and masters among the

Canaanites and Phoenicians, the shepherds on the frontiers retained many of the attitudes of their desert ancestors. They continued to adhere to what Budde rather sweepingly called "nomadic ideals," and repeatedly, down to the age of the writing prophets, their messengers cried for the restoration of the pure Mosaic religion. It was no accident that Elijah, for example, came from Gilead, a backward district of Transjordan.

The feeling of ethnic and religious unity persisted, manifesting itself especially whenever a foreign enemy threatened. Occasionally several tribes joined under one "judge" to resist a foreign oppressor in their Lord's name. Israel's God, who had now, perforce, become primarily the God of War and the Lord of Hosts, remained always in times of crisis the only God of these Israelitic tribes. There appears even to have been a permanent *amphictyony* of the northern tribes long before the period of the kings. Judah, which headed another such confederacy of the still somewhat independent southern tribes, seems occasionally to have joined the northern league. At regular intervals all twelve tribes gathered at Shechem to pay homage to their common "amphictyonic" God, the *El berit* (Judg. 9:46). It has often been pointed out how different was their attitude from that of the ancient Hellenic tribes toward their confederate deity, Apollo, in addition to whom each tribe retained the cult of its own local gods.[42]

Finally came the great decision. Under the pressure of the Philistines with their superior armaments and political organization, the Israelitic tribes were forced to unite. Unity was promoted by the great Yahwistic "seer," Samuel, and made permanent by David, the Judean shepherd. Monarchy arose, and with it the outward unity of the Israelitic *Eidgenossenschaft*. Monarchy, although in some ways a hindrance, in others paved the way for the timely reassertion of pure Yahwism against eclectic Yahwism, of historical monotheism against natural syncretism; it made possible the deepened restatement of the Mosaic religion by the prophets.

RESOLUTION OF ANTITHESES

Recapitulating, we observe an extraordinary chain of circumstances bringing about the formation of the Israelitic people and its religion. Appearing in the midst of one of the great Semitic migrations, the Hebrew tribes settled in Canaan after a process of penetration, partly martial and partly pacific, extending over several centuries. In the meantime the respective tribes reflected striking antitheses: semiprimitives touched by the age-old civilizations of Babylonia, Egypt, or Canaan; seminomadic herdsmen, whose eyes were turned toward the rich agricultural settlement of Palestine; clans and tribes held together by strong blood ties but surrounded by often hostile aliens; finally, a people without state or territory which wanted both but could not regard either as essential. A politically wise consciousness of unity, indispensable for survival, encountered strong disintegrating forces.

At that critical juncture arose a man who, through his supreme genius in statesmanship and religion, resolved these conflicts into a new religious expression, an historical monotheism centering in the history of God's own, the chosen, people. Through his religious adeptness he created a unifying social force, with the capacity of developing beyond the desert or Palestine, beyond all natural boundaries, beyond state and territory. The question whether this religious formulation would survive the settlement in Canaan or be submerged through nature's revolt in the syncretistic "popular religion" was left to be answered in the following period by Israel's kings and prophets.

III

KINGS AND PROPHETS

THE establishment of monarchy in ancient Israel followed a national catastrophe and was part of a great national revival. For a time the Philistines threatened to conquer all Palestine and to subdue the dismembered Israelitic tribes. Of Lycian-Carian origin, they probably were of "white dark" racial stock and resembled in many ways the Greeks of Asia Minor and Hellas who had also assimilated many Cretan ingredients. They suddenly appeared in history as part of a mysterious commotion of "sea peoples" in the eastern Mediterranean. Turned back by Egypt about 1187 B.C.E., they settled in western Palestine during the last Hebrew conquests in the east and south. Ironically, the whole country still bears their name, merely because the coastal plain first came to the attention of the Greek world.

Before long the Philistines adopted the Canaanite language and religion, in particular worshiping Dagon, the god of corn and fertility. The Ugaritic epics attest also the Canaanite antecedents of their god of heaven, Baalzebul, whom the Israelites derisively renamed Baalzebub (lord of the fly). Even most of their personal names were Canaanite, although some of their leaders bore non-Semitic names as late as the eighth century. They retained their own political organization, however. Each of their five city states was under a separate *seren,* a title which, since the appearance of the Syriac and Aramaic versions, has often been identified with the Greek city ruler *tyrannos.* A single alliance of more or less permanence united them all. They also retained their own methods of warfare, far superior to those of the local tribes.[1]

Contact with these invaders was fateful for Israel. The very existence of the people long hung in the balance, and the Israelites had to forget their tribal differences for the sake of the common cause. In some ways, it may be said, the encounter foreshadowed the future clash with the Greek world.

Under the pressure of the enemy, and led by such men as Samuel, Saul, and David, the Israelites merged into a united nation. These wars of liberation left further permanent imprints on their history, and, indeed, helped to shape those elementary forces which were to operate in subsequent centuries. Thenceforth a foreign enemy constantly menaced Israel, which, precisely in moments of gravest emergency, became most profoundly conscious of its ethnic-religious oneness. Despite its corruption, Yahwism remained a vital social force and its priests and "seers" could supply the needed leadership. The first king himself had some characteristics of an ecstatic, occasionally appearing "among the prophets."

MONARCHICAL POWER AND ITS DRAWBACKS

There followed the development of a uniform monarchy constantly growing in strength. The period of the Israelitic kings before Solomon was marked by a rapid extension of the royal power both territorially and internally. The population grew immensely and seems to have reached a density of about two hundred and fifty inhabitants to the square mile, not much less than that of New York State.[2] Towns and cities, already numerous in the Canaanite age, grew in size and wealth, and new ones were founded. All the neighboring tribes, from the Red Sea in the south to the Lebanon in the north and beyond, perhaps as far as the Euphrates, were made tributary. The alliance between the Phoenician city of Tyre, with its maritime resources, and Solomon, master of the gateway to the Red Sea, opened to Phoenician and Israelitic merchant-adventurers a safe route to Yemen, East Africa, and India. It made Israel's king a partner in the world's greatest commercial organization of the day. Israel's sailors, who had occasionally enlisted on Phoenician ships before (this seems to be the meaning of Deborah's allusion to Dan's "sojourn by the ships," Judg. 5:17), now began sailing the Mediterranean Sea in Tyre's "refinery" fleets which brought copper from the Phoenician mines in Sardinia and Spain. Domestic commerce and industry likewise flourished during the long-uninterrupted peace.

True, Solomon had to pay for Hiram I's assistance by ceding him twenty cities in Galilee. He also had to allow Gezer to fall prey to Egypt's revived imperial appetites, although he soon secured its return as a wedding gift to his Egyptian wife (I Kings 9:11, 16). But he was able to utilize the prevailing winds in Ezion Geber on the Red Sea for the exploitation of a large-scale copper refinery which, when unearthed, astonished a world wholly unprepared for it by any biblical hint.[3] In general, Solomon and his successors were large entrepreneurs; they established factories and employed numerous "king's merchants" and artisans. Agriculture became more intensive and more profitable. Jar handles of that period, found in various mounds, still bear mute witness to the speed-up of industrial output and commercial exchanges. A new degree of well-being was experienced throughout the country.

Israel's monarchy thus started to develop normally in the direction of a peaceful autocracy, with all the corresponding drawbacks, particularly tax burdens and compulsory labor. Taken as a whole, it seemed as though Israel might fall in line with the general practices of the ancient Orient in becoming an imperialistic, ambitious, conquering, worldly nation, devoting all its forces to political and economic expansion.

Such a state of affairs could not fail seriously to affect religious life. Traditional Mosaic religion had been threatened with extinction by the Philistine conquest and the loss of the needed minimum of political independence. The same danger now loomed from a superfluity of political power and economic prosperity. State interests now appeared to transcend all others. The youth David had at least declined to serve other gods even in exile (I Sam. 26:19), and all through his life he remained a devoted adherent of the religion of Moses, as he understood it. "So he shepherded them [Jacob and Israel]," the Psalmist praises him, "according to the integrity of his heart; and led them by the skilfulness of his hands" (Ps. 78:72). King Solomon, however, married foreign princesses as a political stratagem and, in line with the custom of the age, established altars for his wives' deities.

Even David's selection of Jerusalem as the royal capital was entirely a political move to counteract centrifugal tribal tendencies. After taking the city from the Jebusites and incorporating it into Benjamin-Judah, the two tribes of whose fidelity he was surest, he had to rebuild it to serve as the fortified capital of the whole kingdom. The site was particularly auspicious, since it was only twelve miles distant from Ephraim, where lived the richest and most advanced sector of the population. The building of a temple as the sole or central national sanctuary would logically have been the immediate sequel, but David realized that to associate divine worship permanently with a particular place was to abandon Mosaic tradition. Although he introduced minor innovations, he dared not go so far as to defy the prophet Nathan, through whom God said, "For I have not dwelt in a house since the day that I brought up the children of Israel out of Egypt, even to this day, but have walked [*mithalekh*] in a tent and in a tabernacle." But by the time of Solomon, monarchy and state were so glorified as to be able to silence all opposition. The Temple was built in Jerusalem; the territorial principle had won![4]

Constructed as one of the customary "royal chapels," the Temple revealed even in its external design and equipment the spread of Canaanite-Phoenician influence.[5] The biblical record itself mentions the employment of Phoenician architects, in contrast to the native Israelitic builders of the desert tabernacle. Perhaps even the imageless cult of the previous antiterritorial period was largely abandoned in the early days of the monarchy down to Hezekiah. Characteristically neither Elijah nor Elisha protests against images in Northern Israel, although the bulls erected by Jeroboam I in Bethel and Dan certainly represented a serious departure from the prohibition of imagery. Jeroboam's "sin" was far-reaching, indeed, even if we accept Obbink's somewhat tenuous theory that these bulls were merely pedestals upon which stood the invisible God. Nor was the Temple in Jerusalem itself without blemish. We learn not only of Maacah's "image" (*mifleset*) soon after Solomon, but also of Hezekiah's belated breaking "in pieces the brazen serpent that Moses had made; for unto those days the children of Israel did offer to it; and it was called Nehushtan." If, as has been suggested, this snake symbol was taken over by David from the Jebusite temple in Jerusalem and subsequently traced back to Moses for purposes of self-justification, so far-reaching an appeasement of a defeated enemy would merely underscore the irresistible force of the territorial principle upon the minds of such empire builders as David and Solomon.[6]

It was a curious revenge that history took over nature when Jerusalem and the Temple later gained an historical prominence which by far exceeded whatever natural importance they had ever commanded. In contradistinction to almost all large cities in the world, Jerusalem was situated neither on the coast nor on a large river, nor was it easily accessible by water or by any important land route. Nevertheless, it later became the "metropolis," as Philo and King Agrippa called it, of widely scattered Jewish settlements, and still later the "holy city" of a large section of mankind. As for the Temple, never, even during the short reigns of Josiah and the early Maccabees, did it exert such influence on national history as after its destruction, when it had become merely a memory and an ideal.

ECONOMIC DECLINE AND SOCIAL UNREST

Soon after Solomon, however, great changes occurred. His reign betrayed manifest marks of decline in foreign relations. After him Egypt's interference helped separate the northern from the southern kingdom. From the beginning of Asa's reign until the time of Josiah, a weakened Egypt had to cease sending armies into Palestine. Another influential factor—the Aramaeans—appeared now in western Asia. Hitherto divided among many small states and partly dominated by Israel's kings, they now succeeded in organizing a powerful monarchy around Damascus. For centuries to come Israel had a hard uphill fight for independence, often being a tributary of Aram.[7] Judah, still weaker, was not powerful enough to resist the northern brethren.

All these developments were soon overshadowed by the stupendous expansion of the Assyrian hosts. For a century before Tiglath-pileser reached Palestine, Assyria cast its shadow over the shores of the Mediterranean. In fact, the first definitely datable event in Israelitic history was Ahab's participation in the battle of Karkara (853–852). According to a contemporary Assyrian inscription, Ahab served as an ally of the king of Damascus, commanding the relatively large contingent of 2,000 chariots and 10,000 infantrymen. This battle seems to have ended in a deadlock or perhaps even in Assyria's defeat, but it underscored Israel's subordinate position. From that time on Israel and Judah, irresistibly drawn into the whirl of western Asiatic affairs, were impotent to direct their own destinies.

These international developments found corresponding expression in domestic social and economic conditions. After a long peace, continuous warfare prevailed. Such respites as were enjoyed under the powerful Jeroboam II (793–753) cast into higher relief the general weakness of the nation and merely afforded opportunity for inner conflicts to ripen and take clear form. Instead of receiving tribute, Israel and Judah had to send, from time to time, heavy loads of precious metals to foreign overlords. Sometimes foreign invaders ransacked the country and its central treasuries and carried off rich spoils. The economic situation became worse and worse. The population which, under vigorous leadership in times of peace, with foreign indemnities pouring in, had achieved a measure of well-being, was increasingly impoverished.

General economic decline was accompanied by a steady process of differentiation. Some of the rich grew richer at the expense of their fellows under the prevalent precapitalistic forms of exploitation. Each catastrophe, national or international, affected largely the poor peasant. Foreign invasions, earthquakes, alternating droughts and floods or, worst of all agricultural plagues, the locust, repeatedly destroyed the accumulated fruits of years of labor. Such domestic or foreign upheavals frequently resulted in the transfer of property from one family to another. Expropriation of real or alleged traitors and the bestowal of land upon loyal adherents (I Sam. 22:7; II Sam. 16:4, 19:30–31) must have accompanied every one of the numerous dynastic crises in Northern Israel.

Once some families had secured more than their due share, the trend became irresistible for the poorer farmers sooner or later to lose their land, while a group of comparatively few rich landowners accumulated large estates. Isaiah's passionate exclamation, "Woe unto them that join house to house, that lay field to field, till there be no room and ye be made to dwell alone in the midst of the land" (5:8; cf. also Hos. 5:10; Micah 2:1–2) shows how clearly intellectual leaders saw the system's inherent dangers. The story of King Ahab and Naboth (I Kings 21) illustrates the less legal form of expropriation, probably often exercised by more powerful aristocrats in Israel, as elsewhere. The frequent prophetic denunciation of abuses in the administration of justice are in part directed against just such proceedings as these.

Naboth's persistent refusal to part with his inheritance indicates the psychological effects of the threat of expropriation. Whether or not the loss of a farm involved exclusion from the clan and total forfeiture of political rights (this depends on how we interpret the background of the protective laws in Lev. 25:25, 35, 39–40), the position of a landless man in ancient Israel was legally and socially far from enviable. In Babylonia and Egypt this process of property accumulation by a small minority had gone on in historically obscure periods; Israel experienced it at an advanced stage, so that mass dissatisfaction was able to find effective forms of expression. The more so, as the Israelitic farmers seem to have been far more literate than most of their neighbors.[8]

The force of tradition helped to increase social unrest, since there lingered on a realization that in the period of the conquest the country had been divided up into equal family shares. Land had never been a simple commodity in Israel, transfer ordinarily taking place only when an insolvent debtor had to forego his rights in favor of creditors, or when a thief had to sacrifice his land to pay a fine. Even then, legal theory reflected ancient clan laws by insisting that the first option to purchase the property of an impoverished farmer go to a relative; the latter was morally obligated to "redeem" it for the family. How bitterly must such a clan have resented it, when no member was able to do this, and an inheritance of generations had to go to a stranger!

Other features of the prevailing precapitalistic system tended to intensify difficulties. Money, although not yet in coined form, became a dominant factor. Economically exhausted (through the frequent wars and payments of regular or irregular tributes), the country must have suffered a severe capital shortage. If in contemporary Assyria, with all the vast resources of a great empire, the average rate of interest exceeded 25 per cent, credit must have been much more expensive in this impoverished country.[9] The poorer peasants were often permanently ruined by their debts, since the income from their agricultural production could not long stand the strain of such high interest rates. Israelitic law, like that of the other ancient oriental and western nations, gave the creditor the right to exact payment in the form of prolonged involuntary service. Thus many "Hebrews" became, at least for a time, "slaves" of more well-to-do brethren. When the term of bondage of such debtors was over, they could only join the increasing mass of landless workers.

Nor were the conditions of industry and commerce good. True, increasing social differentiation stimulated new economic needs, and skilled workers could be employed to meet diverse new demands, such as that of the rich ladies of Jerusalem for fashionable attire, so vividly described by Isaiah (3:18-23). Situated in the midst of the most advanced industrial civilizations of the time, however, this small country was flooded with foreign products, and because of political weakness it often had to admit foreign merchants against its will. Of course, there always were enough craftsmen in Palestine to satisfy daily needs in excess of each family's own production. At times their number was sufficiently large to form regular guilds which, because of the hereditary nature of ancient crafts and their frequent concentration in special villages or quarters, had many earmarks of clan organization. These clan ties, however, made it doubly difficult for a farmer deprived of his land to secure industrial employment.[10]

Under these circumstances comparatively few landless peasants could be absorbed by industry and commerce. Most of them became hired agricultural laborers on large estates. Although the general population remained almost as large as in the days of affluence, the number of free landless workers constantly grew. Inevitably they had to accept low wages and often could find no work at all. There are some records of annual employment contracts (Isa. 16:14; 21:16), but the majority of these wage earners seem to have worked on a day-to-day basis without security of tenure. Seasonal unemployment must have been considerable at all times, but the country seems not to have escaped the evil of permanent unemployment. For this, among other reasons, the "Hebrew" slave sometimes chose to remain with his master even after he had completed his six-year term.

Of prime importance is the fact that—at least according to the present author's estimates—the number of regular, that is, Gentile, slaves was always rather small. At the very height of Israel's prosperity under King Solomon, the available slaves did not suffice for public works, and he had to draft tens of thousands of free subjects to build the Temple and the royal residence.[11] With the steady decline in military power, few prisoners of war were brought in. As elsewhere, slaves showed no natural generative powers and many new slaves had to be purchased. The Phoenician merchants, the main slave traders of the ancient Orient, charged high prices for their merchandise. The thirty silver shekels recorded as the average value of a male or female slave in the early days of the Book of the Covenant (Exod. 21:32) represented a considerable sum in view of the low standard of life. Only a few wealthy Israelites could therefore afford slaves, whom they largely employed in domestic occupations and for purposes of "conspicuous consumption." Even on the large estates, it must have been much more profitable to employ hired labor for production, since the free wage earner received no more than a minimum subsistence wage. Even if we take literally the loaded praise of the Hebrew slave in Deuteronomy, "for to the double of the hire of a hireling hath he served thee six years" (15:18), the purchase of a Gentile slave must have appeared of dubious value. Capital being scarce, to invest a large sum and undertake an obligation to maintain the slave in all seasons and in old age involved a considerable burden.

There were legal deterrents as well. Hebrew legislation protected even the Gentile slave against extreme mistreatment, inflicting a severe penalty upon a lord who killed his slave, and liberating any slave irremediably injured. The Sabbath laws guaranteed man and beast a weekly day of rest. When serving as concubines, as was usual, female slaves were not disposable merchandise. They could be divorced, but not sold. When life became intolerable, the slave could flee, and at least Deuteronomic legislation expressly forbade the return of a fugitive slave to his owner (Deut. 23:16). In view of all these risks, entrepreneurs preferred to hire the plentiful free Israelites who were ready to work on a clearly stipulated contractual basis.[12]

If judged by purely economic standards, therefore, the position of the free laborer was not necessarily superior to that of a slave. In fact, his rights were much more vague and ill-defined. Perhaps on account of his formal contractual freedom, he enjoyed only the general legal protection granted every free Israelite. It has long been doubted whether the very word *sakhir* (Exod. 22:14) refers to a hired man or a hired animal. Even later the main concern of the Deuteronomic and Priestly jurists was to secure to the daily laborer, the "poor and needy," the payment of his wages on the same day (Deut. 24:14–15; Lev. 19:13). Hence, although some preëxilic passages are quite relevant, comes that paucity of biblical references to hired workers which has so greatly obscured their undoubted significance in ancient Israel.[13]

From the point of view of social life, however, the hired laborer was a full-fledged member of society, a copartner in Israel's covenant with God. Of course, he resented the invidious economic distinctions. For this reason, the relative lack of Gentile slaves brought a considerable sharpening of conflicts or, to use modern terminology, an intensification of the class struggle.

Another factor of crucial significance in the whole history of ancient Israel is the development of the Israelitic town. Today there is a more or less clear distinction between the urban population, engaged primarily in industry and commerce, and the rural population. The inhabitants of the ancient Palestinian towns, however, included a large number of farmers. This was, and still is to a certain extent, true of all oriental countries. In ancient Palestine, especially, the peasants sought the security of town walls on account of the frequent Bedouin raids. Many small towns with a population of a few hundred or at most a few thousand were essential, in order that farmers might live safely in the vicinity of their places of work, leaving their town homes each morning and returning there in the evening. Only at harvest time did they stay overnight in tents, a custom which may, by the way, explain the Canaanite origins of the Feast of Tabernacles.[14]

In Israel and Judah, for the most part covering only about seven thousand square miles, there were not less than four hundred settlements classifiable as towns. That the country did not break up into many city states as in the Canaanite age was due to the new religious and national unity made secure during the century of the early kings. The continual pressure of foreign armies also counteracted centrifugal tendencies. The development of the two capitals, which soon surpassed all the other cities in size, economic power, and lure of life, contributed materially toward preserving unity. Samaria, a comparatively young city (between its artificial founding and its destruction by Assyria there elapsed only a century and a half) never succeeded in focalizing all North Israelitic life, but Jerusalem gradually became the real heart of the country. Having been an important city of the Jebusites long before David's conquest, it shared the glory of his and Solomon's reigns and, despite the subsequent decline in the power of Judah, it held its own as a real center of national, religious, and intellectual life. Even addressing a northern populace in Bethel, Amos could announce that "the Lord roareth from Zion, and uttereth His voice from Jerusalem" (1:2).

The effect of this partial urbanization of both the Israelitic and the Judean population was tremendous. The deep social antagonisms were intensified. Serving at the royal courts or in the central administrations or else attracted by the glamor of metropolitan life, many of the greatest landowners settled permanently in Jerusalem or Samaria, probably leaving the administration of their distant estates in the hands of strangers. As is usual under absenteeism, there resulted mismanagement and oppression. Moreover, in every town, and particularly in the two capitals, there gathered many impoverished peasants, seeking employment and gradually acquiring the characteristics of an urban working class.

Economic and social conflicts were further aggravated by the fact that whole communities of shepherds and cattle raisers still persisted in outlying districts, particularly in Judah and Transjordan. There, too, the clan organization had to give way more and more to the new territorial organization, but in many other respects age-old customs and attitudes persisted. Their life and ideals were worlds apart from the life and ideals of either Samaria or Jerusalem!

GOVERNMENTAL DIFFUSION

Political conflicts arising from the clash of interests and traditions added to the social instability. Neither in Israel nor in Judah after Solomon, was there a strong government for any length of time. To be sure, the monarchy was hereditary and if it lasted for several centuries, as it did in Judah, it greatly contributed to the stability of the existing order. In Northern Israel, however, which because of its size and wealth was the more direct continuation of Solomon's kingdom, the royal power started with a rebellion and continued to fall prey to ambitious generals and adventurers. Of the ten dynasties which ruled the country in its two centuries of political independence (931–722 B.C.E.) all but two were replaced after the reign of one or two kings. The first more enduring regime, which lasted through four kings reigning forty years, was founded by Omri (Israel was long known to the Assyrians only as the "House of Omri"), a man of obscure origin and bearer of a non-Israelitic name.

Theoretically the people as a whole retained its "sovereignty" but, since the size of the country precluded an assemblage of the whole people, its direct exercise of power became almost impossible. Even the democratic injunction of the Deuteronomist (31:10–12) that, at least every seventh year during the feast of tabernacles, the whole people—"the men and the women and the little ones, and thy stranger that is within thy gates"—should be assembled at the sanctuary, was never fully enforced. The people, or at least many of them, intervened directly only in such periods of crisis as during the revolutions preceding the accession of Jehu in Northern Israel or of Joash and Josiah in Judah; also when covenants were concluded between ruler and people, as under these two Judean kings and later under Nehemiah. In ordinary years, however, there was no direct democracy, the people usually being represented by "elders" recruited from the leading families. Representation became so much the rule that the biblical narrator sometimes uses the term "elders" when he means the entire people.[15]

The aristocracy of elders itself was split into many groups. The heads of the traditional clan units retained influence because of their large landholdings, and the elders of the cities were often recruited from among them. However, many merchants and industrialists and even persons of Canaanite or other foreign stock also became elders. Another "aristocratic" group gradually arose from the bureaucracy. The kings employed officials, often in high posts, without regard to descent or family connections. It was obviously in the interest of centralized monarchy to counterbalance the power of the groups by appointing its own faithful servants to high civil and military positions. The kings often endowed such officials with landed property. Others accumulated riches by abuse of power in the usual manner of oriental pashas. The unpopularity of these extortionist officials is exemplified by Rehoboam's tax collector, Adoram, who was stoned by "all Israel" (I Kings 12:18). No sharply drawn lines ever existed between the aristocracies of birth, wealth, and office, but certain distinctions must have prevailed at least for a time. There was one more distinguished aristocratic group: the influence of the priests must have been considerable even in preëxilic times, although far from what it was during the Second ("theocratic") Commonwealth.

Royal power was insufficient to maintain an equilibrium among all these forces. Theoretically the king was not even a lawgiver. The legislative power remained wholly in the domain of God himself; and God acted either through the people as a whole or through the teachers of the Torah. Whenever great legislative reforms were to be enacted, the kings had to conclude public covenants with the people. The levitical teachers expounded whatever laws tradition accepted, as revealed by God to Moses. The king could issue ordinances, but these had validity only in so far as they were reconcilable with the "divine" laws and thus acceptable to public opinion. In Northern Israel, particularly, aristocratic conspiracies or popular upheavals often put a bloody end to the reign of a hated king. Four of the last six occupants of the throne in Samaria were assassinated.

The lack of a well-defined constitution added to the confusion. There was no actual division between the legislative and the executive or between the administrative, the judiciary, and the military powers. To be sure, as early as the reign of David, there were high court officials with special functions. He and Solomon followed therein, directly or by imitating their more immediate neighbors, long-established patterns of Egypt's central administration, down to the distinction between a royal "scribe" and "recorder." Neither of them ventured, however, to replace the individual or clan ownership of land by royal and temple domains along Egyptian models which, sooner or later, would have resulted in a vast tenant army run by a more or less corrupt bureaucracy displacing Israel's free peasantry. Only by instituting an extensive *corvée* and an oppressive fiscal system Solomon began laying the foundations for overwhelming centralized controls. But his efforts were checked by Jeroboam's successful revolt, notwithstanding Jeroboam's as well as his Judean rival's attempt to continue along the same lines. Neither of them seems to have succeeded in fully exploiting the administrative and fiscal efficiency created by Solomon's division of the country into twelve districts, apart from Jerusalem which was apparently governed directly by a viceroy.[16]

Solomon's administrative units seem to have been retained in both kingdoms and greatly helped to break up the traditional tribal divisions. But the progressive weakening of the royal power removed the props from under his bureaucratic system. Most administrative functions, particularly on the local level, had to be entrusted to the municipal elders not subject to royal appointment. The administration of justice was so entirely in local hands that we hear nothing about a royal judiciary in the provinces until the Chronicler's report about Jehoshaphat's reform (II, 19:5–11) which has all the earmarks of a later "theocratic" self-justification. It is even dubious whether a supreme judge (mentioned in Deut. 17:9, 12) ever really functioned in Jerusalem or Samaria.

As everyone else, the Israelites paid a price for this type of "democracy," and Abimelech's query, "Which is better for you, that . . . threescore and ten persons rule over you, or that one rule over you?" (Judg. 9:2), carried considerable conviction not only with his fellow Schechemites. The provincial governors, on their part, tried to control whatever state power there remained. Directly responsible only to their superiors, they probably displayed the usual oriental characteristics of servility toward those higher up and tyranny over those beneath them. Uncertain of their tenure, dependent on the whimsies of the kings or the faction in power, they must have tried to accumulate, through legal or illegal means, as much wealth as they could in the briefest possible time. The restraint put upon tribal chiefs by custom or blood relationship was gone, now that the clans had broken up.

Might often replaced right. In legal theory there were no class distinctions in Israel. In contrast to the other oriental codes, such as the Babylonian, the Assyrian, and the Hittite, Israelitic laws, starting with the Book of the Covenant, recognized no separate estates, no special privileges. All Israelites, with the exception of the *gerim* (strangers) and perhaps the landless proletarians, were supposed to enjoy perfect equality before the law. In fact, however, the exercise of rights in the lower strata was often curtailed by the superior power of the upper classes. In periods of affluence the kings arrogated to themselves rights denied them in most other periods. The stronger kings, the military commanders, and the leading priests often ignored legal obstacles encountered on the way to power. The very existence of a large landless proletariat, which often degenerated into what the Germans call *Lumpenproletariat*, enabled ambitious adventurers to organize armed groups of desperadoes. It was not only Jephthah and Abimelech, but also David, who assembled around him "every one that was in distress, and every one that was in debt, and every one that was discontented" (I Sam. 22:2). This proceeding must have been repeated frequently by successful, or unsuccessful, and therefore unrecorded, challengers of the ruling power. In fact, the divergence between theoretical right and actual power was so striking that most laws were enacted by classes which had the right to do so, but had no power to carry them out. Hence the extremely idealistic and doctrinaire slant of the biblical laws which have come down to us. The Deuteronomic legislator, for instance, must have been aware of his own weakness, when he set up as law so many ideal prescriptions without regard to their practical applicability.

The powers of the state were poorly defined. Israel inherited from the clan society and Canaanite city state an extensive local self-government which, down to the end of the two kingdoms, had to be respected even by the most autocratic monarchs. The affairs of the individual were affected more by local than by national developments. Even in the religious life of the people, at least down to the Deuteronomic reformation, the local sanctuary and the local priest played the most important role.

Apart from commanding the military forces, the king's main prerogative was the collection of taxes, which scarcely added to his popularity. Time and again public opinion, nourished by the inextinguishable memories of the seminomadic age, objected to such interference with the private life and property of the individual citizen. Even though it is not quite clear how the fiscal system operated, we may assume that much was left to arbitrary decisions of the moment. The only tax clearly indicated in the records was an extraordinary levy of 50 shekels "exacted" from each of the

60,000 "mighty men of wealth" (*gibbore ha-ḥayil*) by King Menahem to meet a national emergency (II Kings 15:20). However, excavations in Samaria have brought to light a number of tax receipts adjacent to stamped jar handles, showing that more or less
regular payments of wine and oil in jars of standard size were made
by the Palestinian farmers. Very likely such other staple commodi-
ties as dates and barley were also subject to taxes in kind.

Combined with income from royal monopolies, foreign trade,
"gifts" from seekers of royal favors, and the like, these taxes enabled the kings and higher officials to live in comparative luxury.
But the splendor of Solomon's court could never be duplicated by
any of his successors. The biblical descriptions of the wise king's
fabulous wealth and luxurious living also bear the earmarks of
popular exaggeration. Despite the rich booty accumulated by his
father from extensive conquests, his alleged annual revenue of
666 talents of gold (the equivalent of some $220,000,000 according
to the present gold standard, but of many times that amount in pur-
chasing power) would have seemed excessive, even if the biblical
narrator had not added "that which came of the merchants, and of
the traffic of the traders, and of all the kings of the mingled people
and of the governors of the country" (I Kings 10:14–15). Ahab and
his successors were, nevertheless, able to surround themselves with
the luxuries of a royal palace which, though not as large as, for
instance, the palace of Mari built a millennium earlier, was
adorned with exquisitely carved ivory panels. Elephants were still
roaming Palestine and Syria at that time (apparently excessive exploitation alone brought about their extinction there before the
fall of Jerusalem), but the price of ivory must have been extremely
high. Such luxuries, however, only increased the malaise of farsighted rulers who doubtless realized their own inadequacy in rem-
edying the existing economic anomalies.[17]

RELIGION AND LAW

This abnormal social situation inevitably found its religious cor-
relative in ancient Israel, where national and religious life were so
closely interwoven. It evoked those lofty and intense prophetic utterances which have since exerted a profound influence on the
religious thought of the Jewish people and of mankind at large. In
the religious field, too, there were many conflicting forces at work.
Kings and great landowners wanted to adapt religion to changing

social and political needs even to the point of surrendering some of the fundamentals of the traditional faith. Some of the levitical priests scattered throughout the country, being economically dependent on these leaders, followed them blindly. Some others, however, appeared as the natural guardians of the Mosaic tradition, feeling that their own claim to an exclusive sacerdotal charisma was based only upon the validity of this tradition. On the other hand, there emerged all sorts of independent movements directed against the established order. The Nazirites and the Rechabites looked for salvation from a nonsocial, primitive life. From the erstwhile bands of ecstatics now arose the free religious preachers, the new *nebi'im*. Some were in the royal employ, interpreting the future and God's wish in cases of important actions in war or peace. Others, however, were free to speak their minds, and sometimes felt obliged to speak, even against their own will. It was no accident that a few of them reached pinnacles of religious thought as lofty as any known to man.

Yahwism, in the meantime, took deeper and deeper root. In the course of time everyone declared himself a votary of the one God of Israel. Even Ahab, who under the influence of a Phoenician wife, promoted the worship of Baal, regarded himself a true worshiper of Yahweh. The recorded names of his children, as was mentioned, are all compounded with Yah. Similarly Amon (642–40), who continued Manasseh's crudely paganizing regime, worshiped the graven image of Asherah erected by his father at the Temple, cultivated the foreign astral religion and generally "walked in all the way that his father walked in" (II Kings 21:21), nevertheless named his own son "Josiah." The royal stewards mentioned in the Samarian ostraca bore five names compounded with Yahu and only two compounded with Baal, although the latter compound seems to have been more popular among such average citizens as the consigners of wine and oil. Here the ratio rose to eight Baal against six Yahu names.[18] Of the seventeen kings of Judah, from Jehoshaphat on, there were only three whose names did not contain this element.

Furthermore, practically all the kings of Israel and Judah had a deep reverence for the men of God, even when they bore ill tidings for the country or for the royal house. Such was the force of public opinion (since neither the kings nor any single class had concentrated power) that attempts to punish prophets, however subversive their preaching, were rare. Jezebel's threats against Elijah, the expulsion of Amos from Northern Israel, Jehoiakim's execution of Uriah, the sufferings of Jeremiah, and the enforced silence of Judean prophecy during the reign of Manasseh (the unnatural death of Isaiah is mentioned only in a late talmudic source) are merely exceptions. From time to time the kings undertook an adjustment of the official religion to the demands of these men of God. In Judah, particularly after the destruction of Samaria, Kings Hezekiah and Josiah became the leaders of Yahwistic religious reformations. It was only natural, however, that they should try to reconcile state needs with religious demands, and therefore emphasize the practical aspects of religion, its law and worship.

The ensuing developments, particularly in law, were of great moment for the people and their religion. The Mosaic law gradually developed, nourished by the vital common law which had grown up in Palestine during two millennia and by common oriental, especially Babylonian, legal concepts and mores; but it was also influenced by the highly complex social situation. The famous biblical insistence on "life for life, eye for eye, tooth for tooth" (Exod. 21:23-24; Lev. 24:20), underscored by the Deuteronomic injunction possibly aimed at some opposing faction, "And thine eye shall not pity" (Deut. 19:21), represents the well-nigh universal law of retaliation. But when compared, for example, with the varying scale of penalties according to the rank of the injured party and the offender in the Code of Hammurabi, it stands out by its strictly egalitarian emphases.

Similarly the responsibility of a whole town for unsolved crimes committed in its vicinity is but a facet of communal solidarity widely accepted in Asiatic lands and practiced by the colonial governments to the present day. But the substitution for a collective fine of a sacrificial ceremony during which the town elders must solemnly recite, "Our hands have not shed this blood, neither have our eyes seen it. Forgive, O Lord, Thy people Israel, whom Thou hast redeemed, and suffer not innocent blood to remain in the midst of Thy people Israel" (Deut. 21:7-8), invested the whole punitive proceedings with deep expiatory meaning far beyond the immediate occasion. Whatever may have been the general oriental origin of "levirate marriage," Hebrew law moved away gradually, but unmistakably, from the idea of mere inheritance of a brother's widow to that of perpetuating the dead brother's memory. These examples, which could readily be multiplied, show that if Israel took over legal concepts and practices from its immediate or more

distant neighbors, from Canaan, Mesopotamia, or Egypt, it completely readjusted them to its own peculiar social needs and novel
outlook on life.[19]

We may thus speak of an Israelitic legal system, not in the Roman sense of a systematic arrangement of general concepts in logical order, but rather in that of a large collection of typical cases
from which judges and students could draw analogies. Apart from
such "casuistic" laws, however, usually introduced by a conditional
"if," Albrecht Alt has detected, particularly in the ancient Book of
the Covenant, a large number of "apodictic" commandments, positive or negative ("thou shalt" or "shalt not") which he considers a
genuine Hebrew innovation.[20]

Whether or not Alt is right in assuming the Canaanite origin of
the "casuistic" laws, there is little doubt that, from the outset, the
new masters of Palestine had at their disposal a substantial body of
legal doctrines and usages. These were constantly enriched by ever
new legal precedents established in the various law courts and transmitted from one locality and generation to another. With increasing literacy many new decisions were written down, at times evoking prophetic fulminations against "them that decree unrighteous
decrees, and . . . the writers that write iniquity" (Isa. 10:1). Ultimately legislators and authoritative redactors compiled collections of such older laws and more recent precedents in written
form, thereby securing for them a wider audience and making them
more definitive.

At the same time no expert knowledge of the law was required
in most cases, and almost any intelligent layman could learn the
necessary rudiments of legal thought. The administration of justice lay mostly in the hands of the local elders, the lay representatives of the people. Whether they spoke in the name of their own,
the small-town aristocratic class, or in the interest of the people at
large (particularly the provincials), their voice was certainly not
that of the king or the higher judges in Jerusalem and Samaria. If
the Deuteronomic injunction that the main administrators of justice should be judges elected *by the people* (Deut. 16:18, seemingly
addressed to the whole people) was carried out, the people's direct
contributions to the growth of law must have been even more
decisive. In any case, most judicial proceedings, contentious or voluntary, took place at the city gates in public view, and the crowds,
usually watching them, doubtless shouted their approval or disapproval. Such active participation in the dispensation of judicial

authority must have constantly stimulated the interest of the average Israelite in legal matters.[21]

As in other hierocratic states the Israelitic lawgivers, and all the expounders and codifiers of Jewish law who followed, drew no distinction between *jus* and *fas*, between strictly legal prescription and general moral commandment. From the very beginning ritualistic laws were an integral part of the legal structure. But as they became more and more intricate, experts were needed to expound and apply them. Many, originating in long-forgotten primitive conditions, puzzled the ordinary man by their apparent irrationality. Certainly after the disappearance of his Canaanite neighbors, he did not know how many of these "taboos" had sprung from his ancestors' mere opposition to an existing pagan practice. He must have wondered, for example, over the prohibition of seething a kid in its mother's milk (Exod. 23:19, etc.), which, we now know, was but an early reaction to an existing Canaanite ritual. Moreover, in ritualistic laws the form counted as well as the substance. A ceremonial duty must be performed correctly to the minutest detail.[22]

Hence the supreme authority of the priest in the realm of ceremonial and, to a large extent, in that of moral law. Not the exclusive right to offer sacrifices gave the priest his preëminence in sacrificial worship—no such exclusiveness was as yet established in law—but his expert knowledge of the prescribed ritual. This meant, primarily a knowledge of the law. Such expert familiarity was required particularly in the treatment of all sorts of physical impurities, an elaborate system of which had sprung up in pre-exilic days. Only the priest knew enough to detect and isolate a leper or to treat a house stricken by a "plague." He alone was also competent to administer whatever vestigial ordeals were still included in Hebrew legal procedure, such as the bitter water given to a woman suspected of marital infidelity.[23]

In the domain of Temple and sacrifices, the priest enjoyed still greater, though not yet exclusive, authority. Even after the victory of the royal power in the contest between Samuel and Saul the priest continued to exercise a variety of sacerdotal functions. We may, with J. Morgenstern, deny the existence of a high priest under whatever title in preëxilic Jerusalem, and yet concede the presence of high ecclesiastical officers at the royal courts of both Jerusalem and Samaria to whom the king often delegated his own priestly functions and who served as chief royal counselors and executives in ritualistic matters. Certainly the more elaborate the worship at the Temple became, the more it required a professional class of priests, endowed with various skills including the use of musical instruments. But professional training was not enough. To exercise these functions, which often required direct communication with the Deity, one had to be endowed also with some supernatural charisma.[24]

Only members of the tribe to which Moses had belonged enjoyed such hereditary sanctity, but no magic powers were ascribed to them. The Israelitic *kohen* was never the same as an Arabic *kahin*, a soothsayer. From the outset, ancient Israel, perhaps in conscious opposition to Egyptian practice, rejected all forms of magic. Capital punishment was the penalty for common forms of sorcery and communication with the dead. Even the highly revered oracles, the *Urim* and *Tummim*, seem in time to have fallen into desuetude as a means of ascertaining God's wish. They are hardly mentioned in the later centuries of the Israelitic and Judean monarchies.[25] Their place was taken by knowledge of the law, the Torah, in which, it was increasingly felt, God's will was sufficiently revealed. Particularly in the southern kingdom proficiency in the law secured for the priests not only a privileged position in adjudicating ceremonial matters, but also a comparatively large share in the administration of civil justice. Even disestablished priests of extinct sanctuaries retained influence as teachers of the Torah and as judges. In both capacities they contributed materially to the growth of Israelitic law. They were the main bearers of continuity as against the constantly changing interests of lay judges and kings.[26]

Since, however, kings, judges and priests all held responsible positions, they had to take account of realities. The laws they formulated and expounded had, therefore, all the weakness and strength of compromise with actual social conditions. The less satisfactory social life as a whole was, the more dissatisfaction could be expressed by the relatively large educated class which did not have to consider the responsibilities of office. Backed by the popular masses, who were deeply disaffected with economic inequalities, they did not hesitate to criticize the overemphasis upon the fulfillment of the ritualistic commandments. Of course the more discriminating leaders, and particularly the prophets, knew that no matter how antagonistic they were to the existing order, no matter how much they preached the inwardness of religious piety, they must insist upon the full validity of the remotest detail of Mosaic law. No Israelite, they taught, however pious and righteous intrinsically, may escape the fulfillment of God's commandments as embodied in the traditional legislation.

The masses and their prophetic leaders, however, interpreted existing law differently from the ruling classes, especially as concerned social life. They wished to see the law expanded so as to mitigate the prevalent social evils. Under their combined influence there arose at a propitious moment that unique system of laws incorporated in Deuteronomy. It is not altogether an exaggeration when its author boasts, "And what great nation is there, that hath statutes and ordinances so righteous as all this law, which I set before you this day?" (4:8.) To be sure, at many cardinal points this law ignores hard realities and often is altogether utopian. The Deuteronomist, conscious of the artificiality of his precepts, can find no other justification than the unique historical position of Israel. Since the miraculous Exodus from Egypt, he argues, God has imposed upon Israel an absolute obligation of righteous living "for our own good always, that He might preserve us alive." [27] This strained Deuteronomic reformation had, nevertheless, a larger share in reshaping conditions for subsequent generations than most "realistic" legal systems have ever had.

The growth of Jerusalem aided the religious reformation. Unlike Samaria, whose Yahwistic sanctuary, if it existed at all (the only biblical reference is to a "house of Baal" destroyed during the Jehu revolt, II Kings 10:21–27), was far overshadowed by the ancient temples of Dan and Bethel, restored to their glory by the first Northern king, Jerusalem became more and more the center of all Judean public life and lent increasing preëminence to the Temple of Solomon. Sooner or later conflict had to break out between this central sanctuary and the many local holy places. The more the popular religion of ancient Israel, or syncretistic Yahwism, gave way to the monotheism of the prophets, the easier it became to argue that the one God must be worshiped only in this one place. This monotheistic basis and Josiah's reform, which put much of the prophetic teaching into legal form, concealed for a time the fact that the Temple itself had been a victory for the territorial principle. The opponents of the latter could find comfort in the fact that at least the provincial sanctuaries, with their even more localized worship, were suppressed. Nevertheless, Jeremiah, though at first apparently a warm supporter of Josiah's legislative measures, did not hesitate to stress, even more than his predecessors, the supremacy of worship in the heart over the sacrificial ceremonies in the Temple. Temple services are not wrong in themselves, he taught, but become wrong when they replace inner duties.[28] Thus it was that Jeremiah was led to emphasize more than anyone else in the ancient Near East the element of individual conscience in religion.

PROPHECY AND SOCIAL REVOLUTION

As a rule the kings did not quite approve the existing social conditions, because they must have perceived that social injustice, causing widespread pauperization and dissatisfaction, must in the end weaken the state. This assumption is not based only upon analogy with modern times. It is known, for example, that the kings of Assyria actually tried to protect by law the masses, because they regarded their excessive exploitation as a danger to national military strength. In Israel, too, it is not at all certain that the so-called *gibbore ha-ḥayil*, the backbone of the Israelitic army, consisted exclusively of wealthier landowners who provided their own costly armaments. And in any case the kings must have realized the value of the poorer peasants and artisans for defense against foreign invasion and for minor military tasks. David's census, though allegedly undertaken against the advice of his commander-in-chief, doubtless pursued military as well as fiscal objectives. Nor was Solomon's *corvée* necessarily limited to public works. He certainly needed a large mass of soldiers to man his thousands of chariots. While, like his father, he undoubtedly employed foreign mercenaries, many Israelites served as his "men of war, and his servants, and his princes, and his captains, and rulers of his chariots and of his horsemen" (I Kings 9:22). Very likely his successors continued this practice. Josiah, in particular, seems to have made a special effort to revive the Israelitic militia for his ambitious scheme of reconquering all former Israelitic territories.[29]

These as well as fiscal considerations afforded plenty of reason for the kings to try to remedy some social wrongs by legislation or, more correctly, by interpretation of the God-given laws. On the other hand, the kings were often powerless against the alliance of those diverse mighty groups who were interested in preserving the social *status quo*.

Only King Josiah went so far as to accept the Deuteronomic legislation as binding upon himself. And this legislation, although partly of prophetic origin, could not cure all social evils. It prohibited usury, the main source of the growing social inequality, as earlier laws had done. But with respect to Hebrew slavery, the other result of excessive indebtedness, Deuteronomy gives but a few halfhearted regulations, insisting, for example, that when a Hebrew slave is liberated after his six-year term, his master must provide him with means sufficient for a new start in life so that freedom may not become a curse. A female Hebrew slave was also to be freed after six years, while previously the Book of the Covenant had taken it for granted that the chief aim in the acquisition of such a slave was sexual and not economic. The Deuteronomic lawgiver, we recall, also forbade the return of any fugitive slave to his master, thus threatening ruthless slaveowners with the permanent loss of their property. But he did not venture to go as far as the author of Leviticus, who proclaimed the principle that Israelites should never be enslaved, "for they are My servants [slaves], whom I brought forth out of the land of Egypt; they shall not be sold as bondmen" (Lev. 25:42).

Nor do we hear of any such attempts at general price fixing for the benefit of the consumer as are attested for Babylonia and Assyria at various times from the third millennium down to the seventh century. Certainly the weak Israelitic states lying athwart, or close to, major trade routes and economically dependent on their mightier neighbors could not dream of imposing effective controls. They had to be satisfied with prohibiting flagrant misrepresentation and moral injunctions concerning just weights and measures.

The greatest social evil of the age, the expropriation of the land of destitute peasants, is met by the Deuteronomic law merely with a general moral prohibition of the removal of a neighbor's landmarks. Although this prohibition is repeatedly stressed and even put under the sanction of the "curses" proclaimed by Moses from Mount Ebal (Deut. 27:17), there is no indication that such expropriations became illegal. As heretofore, an insolvent debtor lost his property to his creditor. Here, too, the later legislation goes far beyond this effort at protection by introducing the general *restitutio in integrum* at each Jubilee year. The fact that this institution may never have become fully effective and that the social evils recurred repeatedly in the days of Nehemiah and later, only throws into sharper relief the intentions of the "levitical" lawgiver who was by no means blind to economic realities. Taking cognizance, for instance, of the extensive urbanization of preëxilic Palestine, he drew a sharp distinction between rural property, including houses in places "which have no wall round about them" and dwelling houses in "walled cities." Only the former were to be subjected to the restitution of the Jubilee year.[30]

Nor was the recurrent emphasis upon charity of all kinds, especially toward widows, orphans and *gerim* (a class including all sorts of strangers and, perhaps, landless Israelitic laborers) more than a well-intentioned, but hardly effective, remedy for economic inequalities. One remarkable law, however, prevented actual starvation.

When thou comest into thy neighbour's vineyard, then thou mayest eat grapes until thou have enough at thine own pleasure; but thou shalt not put any into thy vessel. When thou comest into thy neighbour's standing corn, then thou mayest pluck ears with thy hand; but thou shalt not move a sickle unto thy neighbour's standing corn [Deut. 23:25–26].

There is every reason to assume that public opinion enforced this law and hence we never hear of actual starvation in times of peace. Religious opposition to usury apparently also had some permanent effects. The Yahwistic sanctuaries seem always to have refrained from lending out money for commercial or military purposes, then a common practice throughout the Mediterranean world. The only biblical reference to such a transaction is in connection with a Baal temple in the period of the Judges.[31]

If even the best and most farsighted kings had, because of the power of the landed aristocracy, to limit themselves to halfhearted measures, men were not lacking who demanded more. Out of the social unrest emerged revolutionary leaders, whose denunciation of the existing order has left a strong imprint upon the career of mankind. Some of them belonged to the oppressed classes; others, like Isaiah and Zephaniah, were members of the highest aristocracy, or, like Jeremiah, belonged to a financially independent family of provincial priests. This espousal by the more thoughtful members of the privileged classes of the cause of the disinherited, forecast, as often afterwards, the downfall of the existing order.

Whether wealthy or poor all these preachers safeguarded their independence by refusing to benefit financially from the performance of their duties. They spoke with contempt of colleagues who, being employed by the kings or satisfying popular "superstitions" by supernatural means, made the announcement of God's will a profitable calling. Amaziah, the priest of Bethel, added insult to injury when he expelled Amos from his temple and told him to go back to Judah "and there eat bread, and prophesy [or rather: by prophesying] there." Amos retorted proudly, "I was no prophet, neither was I a prophet's son; but I was a herdman, and a dresser of sycomore-trees." Micah cursed the "prophets that make my people to err; that cry: 'Peace,' when their teeth have anything to bite; and whoso putteth not into their mouths, they even prepare war against him." No harsher words can be found in the Bible than those used by Jeremiah against the soothsayers of Samaria and Jerusalem. Thus the great leaders castigated "false" and venal prophets, who were bringing disgrace upon their calling. Ashamed to belong to the same group, these men often rejected the name of "prophet" or "spokesman." [32]

These leaders depended on the people. The effectiveness of their message was determined by its reception by the masses to whom they preached on the streets and in the temples. Unlike the priests, these messengers of God were not "established." They had no territorial ties. In this sense, too, they were true heirs of the Mosaic tradition, with its detached, movable sanctuary. The prophets went wherever they felt their mission would be best fulfilled. Sometimes they spoke to the kings and the high officials, sometimes directly to the "sovereign" people, out of whom had arisen the influential and not inconsiderable "intelligentsia." To make their words as widely known as possible, they began to write their preachments and distribute them throughout the country. Thus originated, to use Weber's phrasing, "the earliest known pamphlet literature of immediate political actuality." [33] The direct relation of prophet and people helps to explain how, with no real financial or military backing, these messengers of God wielded such influence.

Before this sympathetic audience the prophets could cry out against religious and social wrongs. Unburdened by office and responsibilities of office and by nature and tradition perfectionists in both form and substance, they condemned any compromise with sin on a par with sin itself. No more dramatic story appears in the Bible than that of Elijah's struggle against the priests of Baal on the Carmel, although it appears that the latter merely tried to synthesize their own belief in the God of Israel with the deeply ingrained local worship of the Baal of Carmel and that of the cosmic deity Baalshamem in neighboring Tyre. For the most part religious ecstatics themselves, these prophets sharply repudiated all forms of magic and fertility cults, which they rightly considered dangerous alien borrowings, doubly dangerous because of their appeal to the masses; instead they called for more and more *knowl·*

edge of the Lord. No matter how much they deprecated religious externals and how frequently they thundered against the average citizens' excessive absorption in the ceremonial aspects of their law, they were even more impatient with the syncretistic rites practiced at the various "altars" and the "wicked abominations" worshiped at the very Temple of Jerusalem.[34]

With equal vehemence they castigated the oppression of the poor, the exploitation of free labor, the expropriation of small landholders, and the political, administrative, and judicial system which sanctioned these crimes. The content of their complaints was, in many respects, like that of social reformers of every land in which existed such conditions, inherent in an overcrowded country under a precapitalistic system. But here it was far more directly associated with the fundamentals of religion.

In fact, these preachers regarded themselves as primarily religious rather than social reformers. If asked, they would probably have objected violently to the distinction: their view was precisely that social life is part of religious life, that social crimes become religious sins. Had not God freely chosen Israel as his people, led it forth from Egypt, and brought it to Palestine, to which it had no prior claim? God therefore was surely the real lord of all the land of Palestine. Time and again, Israel's prophets and historians reiterated, "And I gave you a land whereon thou hadst not labored, and cities which ye built not, and ye dwell therein, of vineyards and olive-yards which ye planted not, do ye eat." [35] Hence ownership of any parcel of Palestinian land was not a right, but a privilege conferred by God upon favored Israelites for a higher reason known only to Him. The lamentable social situation must be an abomination unto God.

Therefore the Israelites must not resign themselves to existing economic conditions, but must raise the banner of justice against the natural flux of uncontrolled economic cause and effect. Furthermore, all members of the *chosen nation* are parties on an equal basis to the Covenant concluded with God. As in all ancient society, slaves were not full members of the nation, but free laborers were; and a system based upon the exploitation of those who were equal partners in the contract with God was certainly contrary to its intent. Hence social justice came to be regarded as one of the root essentials of the religion of Israel.

Out of the cattle-raising south and east came even more extreme denunciations of the economic system. Memories of clan-owned property, kept alive by the slow rhythm of economic evolution, made some of the leaders archopponents of private ownership and disdainful of the individual's interest in personal economic gain per se. The Rechabites demanded that property be held communally and that cattle raising be favored over industry, commerce, or even agriculture, thus harking back to their conception of what had been the ideal conditions in the period of the patriarchs and the first settlers.

The prophets, on the whole, did not share these extremist "nomadic ideals." Elijah and Hosea, themselves offshoots of the cattle-raising fringe in Transjordan, may have blamed the evil ways of contemporary society on Israel's addiction to Canaanite prototypes in agricultural and urban life. But the prophetic party led by Elisha readily supported Jehu's rebellion against the Omride dynasty, which was essentially an uprising of the provincial peasantry against the "metropolitan" life of Samaria. Amos spoke with pride of his petty sycomore growing. Another eighth-century prophet, the "aristocratic" Isaiah, was neither a champion of the peasantry nor an exponent of nomadic ideals. He merely envisaged a much-reformed Davidic dynasty governing the country from Jerusalem "through justice and through righteousness." Jeremiah, too, evinced no admiration for the Rechabite ideals as such, but set the group up as a shining example to the recalcitrant people of Judah and Jerusalem, "because the sons of Jonadab the son of Rechab have performed the commandment of their father which he commanded them, but this people has not hearkened unto Me." Similarly the Deuteronomist knew of no more dire threats for Judah's disobedience than "cursed shalt thou be in the city, and cursed shalt thou be in the field," considering the destruction of the existing urban and agricultural civilization as an extreme punishment. These prophets and lawgivers were united only in singing the praises of an idealized past not necessarily nomadic, and in invoking history's judgment on the achievements and shortcomings of their people.[36]

As a result of this radical arraignment, prompted by widespread popular suffering and political helplessness, the covenant between God and his people was invested with new meaning. Dissatisfaction was so persistent that there grew steadily a belief that God himself was appalled by existing conditions, and that he would not countenance such a society simply because of the covenant. For the first time the validity of the covenant was seen to be conditional. Israel's

God was not to be expected, like gods of other nations, to help his people under any and all circumstances. He came to be regarded as an exacting partner, meticulously insisting on the execution of the terms of the contract. "You only have I known of all the familes of the earth; therefore I will visit upon you all your iniquities" (Amos 3:2). Since the existing order clearly involved a breach of the contract on Israel's part, God's wrath must be aroused, he must wish to punish his recreant people, if necessary, through the instrumentality of a foreign enemy. This novel conception is understandable only in view of the intensity of the opposition to the existing order, to destroy which, even though it might mean the political extermination of both Israel and Judah, was the fixed resolve of the prophets. Hence the unpatriotic, or perhaps ultrapatriotic conception that God himself had chosen Assyria as the tangible "rod of his anger," wherewith to punish Israel for its social and religious sins.

The novelty of this concept even within leading Yahwistic circles is vividly illustrated by Num. 14:11–29, which, even if attributed, as it often is, to the "Jehovistic" compiler of the eighth century, clearly reflects the older view. Here Moses is able to persuade God to desist from his intended annihilation of Israel by saying that the Egyptians might argue that "because the Lord was not able to bring this people into the land which He swore unto them, therefore He hath slain them in the wilderness." The great prophets would have seen in such destruction but another sign of God's omnipotence. To be sure, the idea that gods inflict punishment upon their own people for the transgression of their commandments is to be found among many nations. Not only do early Hellenic writers and Plato often stress this point, but a close neighbor of Israel, Mesha, king of Moab, goes to the extreme of declaring in his famous inscription that the Israelitic invasion was due to the god Kemosh's anger at the sins of his people. From this admission, however, to the conviction that, except for a saving "remnant," the whole state may be destroyed and the nation wiped out was an enormous step. The prophets of Israel, beginning with Amos, introduced this radical concept by causing survival to be dependent upon the fulfillment of the covenant and by divorcing the divine presence in the world from the empirical existence of any significant number of worshipers.[37]

Extreme punishment always appeared to the prophets to be impending, and finally they saw it come in the succession of national catastrophes. God, they none the less believed, does not really want to destroy his people but only to chasten it so that it will mend its ways. The Deuteronomist spoke in terms of the age-old conception, "And thou shalt consider in thy heart, that, as a man chasteneth his son, so the Lord thy God chasteneth thee" (8:5). Hosea drew out of his personal experience another eloquent analogy. The covenant between God and Israel resembles the union between husband and wife. The husband who really loves his wife, loves her even though she be fickle. He punishes her and sends her away because of his love for her, but finally, when she is destitute and forlorn, he is prepared to take her back. Let Israel but learn new ways out of the chastisement and wholeheartedly return to the pure religion of Moses, and it will once again become the beloved of God.[38]

ANTIMONARCHICAL TRENDS

The attitude of the historical and prophetic writers toward the political system was also most significant. The institution of monarchy appeared to them to be the basis of the degraded social order. Such opposition was especially articulate in the northern kingdom where dynasties followed each other in rapid succession through court intrigues and usurpation. Later authors even rewrote the previous history of the nation in conformity with the increasing antimonarchical spirit. The events leading to the establishment of monarchy in the period of Saul lent themselves especially to tendential reinterpretation. For instance, the remarkable warning put into Samuel's mouth (I Sam. 8:11–18) is obviously an accentuated description of later conditions written from a decidedly antimonarchical point of view. The opposition argued that the king had broken two covenants, that of Israel with God and that of the ruler with his people. The conception prevailed that the people had voluntarily elected kings to reign in accordance with the popular will. It must have been buttressed by the actually concluded public covenants of Joash and Josiah. The reverse conclusion was thus ready to hand that the people might also reject royal rule at will. Indeed opponents of monarchy in modern Europe could cite many Old Testament passages in support of the idea of the social contract and the sovereignty of the people.

This basic sovereignty of the people, or of God acting through the people, was fortified by the fact that the kings were never supreme autocrats, but always remained *under* the law. This limitation, true in part of all oriental monarchs, was emphasized here by the fact that neither the king's person nor his office had any religious sanctity to speak of. Except in poetic metaphor without legal significance (for example, Ps. 2:7), neither Israel's nor Judah's kings were regarded as gods or as the sons of a god. Not only did this conception, then prevailing throughout the Near East and carried from Egypt through the Alexandrian and Hellenistic empires into ancient Rome, fail to take hold in Israel, but here even obsequious subjects did not venture beyond such verbal homage as that of the woman of Tekoa, "As an angel of God so is my lord the king to discern good and bad," or of the Lachish soldier, "How can thy servant benefit or injure the king?" Conversely, we have no record of the existence in any period of Israelitic monarchy of a statutory crime of *lèse majesté* at all comparable with blasphemy against God, or even with the offense against a local Canaanite ruler discovered in a cuneiform tablet from fourteenth-century Lachish.[39]

More, the king was not even a prominent "charismatic" priest. Of course, during a long period he could perform sacrifices, but every Israelitic layman appears to have had that prerogative. The king could appoint or depose priests, but so could many monarchs in later Christian countries without claiming a special clerical sanctity. At any rate, Israel's king was not a *born* priest. He was not, for example, entrusted with the oracles.[40] The greatest claim of the adherents of monarchy was that the king was "the Lord's anointed," and that to kill him was both a civil crime and a religious sin, more grievous than the murder of an ordinary man (I Sam. 24:7).

Even such monarchists, then and later, emphasized the obligations of the king. "Thou hast loved righteousness, and hated wickedness; *therefore* God, thy God, hath anointed thee with the oil of gladness above thy fellows," sings a later psalmist. Another prays in typical oriental fashion that the king may "have dominion also from sea to sea, and from the River unto the ends of the earth," but at the same time he emphasizes, more than any other oriental court poet, righteousness and the protection of the poor as the king's primary duty. Although we have no reason to doubt the monarch's usual legislative prerogatives, it is curious to see that the only time the Bible mentions a king issuing "a statute and an ordinance for Israel unto this day" is in connection with David's distribution of booty, an essentially administrative act. The king was actually held accountable for his acts, at least in the early days of the monarchy, as is clearly intimated in Samuel's speech "unto all Israel" and Rehoboam's negotiations with "all Israel." In short, justice being the basis of his government, his elevated position is conditional on a strict application of God's law. "The essence of the royal office was that the king was the *nomos empsychos,* the incarnation of the spirit of Yahweh's legalism." [41] Abuses of the law by the king were, therefore, a doubly flagrant breach of contract. Hence the significance of the Naboth episode in Ahab's reign, regarded by subsequent generations as a remarkable example of royal desertion of duty under the instigations of a foreign-born queen.

It was only a step to the denunciation of monarchy per se as a foreign institution and as a desertion of God, who alone is the lawful king of the Israelitic people (I Sam. 8:5; Deut. 17:14; and elsewhere). From the days of Isaiah on, God's royal character was ever more stressed. Of course the conception of divinity as a royal power was common to all Orientals, but beginning in the eighth century Israel's prophets and teachers were arguing not only for the kingship of Yahweh as against that of Marduk or any other god, but also for Yahweh's reign over the people of Israel as against that of earthly kings. Finally came the famous parable of Jotham, attributed to premonarchy days: the worthy trees, such as the olive and the fig, and also the vine, successively declined to rule the tree world; finally the wild bramble accepted the responsibility of royal office. The more the royal authority declined under the last kings, the more widespread became such views. It was therefore easy to come to regard monarchy as, under certain circumstances, an instrument of evil and a breach of the covenant.[42]

True, this generally antagonistic position did not prevent the ancient writers from assuming a more favorable attitude toward the house of David, which had reigned legitimately and without interruption for centuries from the one capital, Jerusalem. As David's person was increasingly exalted by subsequent generations, the Davidic line was invested with superior qualities. His descendants received praise and support, however, only when instrumental in carrying out God's covenant and establishing a social, political and religious order fully consonant therewith.

NATIONALITY AND STATE

Along with this evolution, nationality became separated from state in a sense far more profound than was involved in the question of monarchy or republic. A wholly new conception of nationality arose. Historically the division into two kingdoms came first.

Two and no more. A dissolution into numerous city states, as in the El-Amarna age and in contemporary Greece, might have seriously weakened the conception of unity. Even in the period of tribal division, the idea of a single common God gave rise to a community much superior to that of the Hellenic world. After about a century of real unification and general prosperity, national and religious unity was so firmly rooted that division into two political bodies merely emphasized it.

Notwithstanding political quarrels, Israelites and Judeans seem always to have visited each other's sanctuaries. In the eighth century Northern Israelites made pilgrimages to Beersheba in southern Judah (Amos 5:5; 8:14), while Amos, hailing from the southern kingdom, preached in the northern royal sanctuary at Bethel. It has even been suggested [43] that the northern kings themselves encouraged these Beersheba pilgrimages, in order to ween away their subjects' loyalty from Davidic Jerusalem toward the patriarchal town whose cultic significance had been hallowed by the much older pre-Davidic tradition. Religious unity went far beyond the worship of one common God, and many characteristic religious conceptions were shared by Israelites and Judeans alike. The expectation of a forthcoming "Day of the Lord" was so widespread that prophets in both the north and the south could use the term, investing it with whatever meaning conditions of the age and their own religious experience suggested. Its metamorphosis from a day of triumph and victory to one of doom and judgment was not limited to any one realm. The common geographic designation, "from Dan to Beersheba," still marked the essential ethnic boundaries, whereas at no time can the political borderline between Israel and Judah be traced without difficulty.

Perhaps even more amazing is the attitude of the great contemporary historians. Neither the Judean Yahwist nor the Israelitic Elohist seems to pay the slightest attention to the political separation. For both, the people of Israel and Judah are an indivisible unity. This failure to take cognizance of the state was further emphasized by the weakness of the state and the growing opposition to monarchy, its chief organ. In the ancient Orient, with its identification of monarchy, or even of the individual king, with the state, deprecation of the king's power could easily pass over to denunciation of the very idea of statehood.

Equally important were world developments. Some Israelites began to settle abroad even before the fall of Samaria (722–721). To a large extent these were prisoners of war carried off by a foreign invader and sold abroad as slaves and remaining abroad even when liberated. The oriental practice of selling subjects as soldiers to serve in foreign lands in exchange for military aid or war material must also have caused the translocation of many Jews. The injunction of the Deuteronomist that the king should not "cause the people to return to Egypt, to the end that he should multiply horses" (17:16) is generally assumed to be aimed at such proceedings, which undoubtedly were more frequent in the periods of strong monarchy in Israel (for example under Jeroboam II) than in the revolutionary age of the Deuteronomic reformer. Intermittent revolts in Northern Israel were another source of, at most, semivoluntary expatriation. Many an unsuccessful rebel doubtless emulated the example of Jeroboam in the days of Solomon and took refuge abroad. Later the incessant strife of the Egyptian and Assyrian parties in Judah forced many influential partisans to flee the fatherland. At the same time a measure of voluntary emigration must have been going on. Such was recorded in the case of the Danites who hired themselves out to Phoenician shipowners in the early period of Deborah. Some Israelites engaged in commercial pursuits settled abroad (for example, those for whom King Ahab obtained special streets in Damascus, I Kings 20:34).

All these movements were accelerated when, in 733 and 722–721, the great national catastrophe of the northern kingdom was followed by the deportation of at least tens of thousands of Israelites into distant regions in the northeast. The 27,290 deported from Samaria in 721, mentioned in the well-known inscription of Sargon, represent only a fraction of the Israelitic exiles. We must add not only a number of women and children who accompanied them but, in all probability, unrecorded further groups deported in 734–733, and perhaps in 720. Similarly Sennacherib's boast about the effects of his campaign against Judah in 701, "200,150 people, small and great, male and female, horses, mules, asses, camels, oxen and sheep without number I brought out of their midst and counted as booty," whether or not absolutely accurate, reflects a large-scale involuntary expatriation.[44]

These victims of Assyrian imperialism were not entirely forgotten by their brethren in Palestine. They must have maintained their identity for a time even in alien lands, and some may have joined the exiles in Babylonia after 586. News of their struggle for survival often reached the Palestinian remnant in subsequent generations down to Ezra and Nehemiah. Other groups of Israelites and Judeans trickled into Egypt between the eighth and sixth centuries.

Theory had to follow reality. No longer was settlement on the soil of Palestine or life under a Jewish government essential to Jewishness. Even in the dispersion, far from their own country and under a foreign monarch, Jews remained Jews ethnically. Of course, this dismemberment of the Jewish nation was regarded as an anomaly, and the exiles hoped it would be temporary. But rational hopes of return must have appeared foolish in view of the world situation. For a long time Assyria, and afterwards Babylonia, appeared indomitable; an Israelitic military victory over them was out of the question. In this fashion the belief spread that no military victory, no ordinary victory can avail. It is by a miracle that God will open a new age, an age of eternal peace between man and man and even in nature, an age in which by universal concurrence the Jewish people will again be gathered unto the Holy Land.

Events abroad must also have impressed the thoughtful with the impermanence and relative inconsequentiality of the state. Egypt, in steady contact with Palestine for millennia, had seemed as eternal as history. Now Egypt was conquered by Asarhaddon and by Ashurbanipal. Assyria, too, soon fell to pieces. It is hard to imagine what impression the fall of Nineveh (612), for so long the cosmopolitan metropolis of the Orient, must have made upon the minds of men. A Greek thinker of Asia Minor drew from it the apothegm, "Better is a small town on a rock in orderly condition than Ninos gone mad." All this occurred during the great sweep of the Scythians to the very borders of Syria.[45] Such events must have reinforced the Palestinian prophets' deprecation of political power. In the turmoil, all political organisms seemed to be sinking, and the prophets could see only the approaching day of the Lord.

RELIGIOUS UNIVERSALISM AND PARTICULARISM

Thus was proclaimed a religious concept destined to have great influence on succeeding generations. As long as they continue to worship God in their hearts, the prophets concluded, Jews are Jews even though detached from the soil, even though unable to worship in a temple. This they may easily do, since their God, although He may not be acknowledged as such by the majority of inhabitants, is also the God of each country where they happen to live.

"Are ye not as the children of the Ethiopians unto Me, O children of Israel? saith the Lord. Have not I brought up Israel out of the land of Egypt, and the Philistines from Caphtor, and Aram from Kir?" (Amos 9:7.) For this reason, too, not even political and military defeat is proof—as it would have been anywhere else in the Orient—that Israel's God has been defeated by the god of a foreign people. As there is no other God but Yahweh, He must have himself selected the foreign nation as a means of punishing His obstinate people. Israel's defeat itself proves the power rather than the impotence of Israel's God as the God of all mankind.

This universalism of the prophets did not imply that the Jewish people may now be exterminated. Were it to disappear totally, there would be nobody to carry on the commands of God and maintain the true religion until the end of days. Israel is still the "chosen nation"; chosen, however, not for the imperialistic aim of glory through political conquests—the "messianic" view of the more powerful oriental nations—but for the inscrutable aims of history. In the words of the Deuteronomist,

The Lord did not set His love upon you, nor choose you, because ye were more in number than any people—for ye were the fewest of all peoples—but because the Lord loves you, and because He would keep the oath which He swore unto your fathers, hath the Lord brought you out with a mighty hand, and redeemed you out of the house of bondage, from the hand of Pharaoh king of Egypt [7:7–8].

The common descent from Abraham, Isaac and Jacob is the main element securing Israel's exalted position within the family of nations, wherever and under whatever conditions it may happen to live.[46] The Jews may live and worship their God in foreign lands for a time, but when they shall have merited it, God will gather them again from the four corners of the earth.

Such doctrines of the nature of Israel's chosenness were voiced by different "spokesmen" under varying circumstances with poetic fervor rather than terminological precision. Although not yet as refined as in the postexilic age, these teachings were nevertheless sufficiently articulate to show that they had neither been the outgrowth of sheer racial haughtiness (the prophets' deep concern for the fate of foreign nations and their missionary zeal served as sufficient correctives) nor presented a claim to special privilege. In fact, any expectation of Israel's glory was overshadowed by deep forebodings of immediate doom, which might leave behind it but a small "saving remnant" of the people.[47]

The singular synthesis of universalism and nationalism in the prophetic religion involves no inner contradiction. The prophets grasped the meaning of an abnormal world situation in their own way. They saw states vanish and reappear. They saw state power in Israel and Judah used by dominant classes as a means of oppressing the masses. They saw myriads of Jews remaining Jews in foreign lands. They drew the conclusion that there is a unity more indefeasible than that of state and territory. They had also seen, both in their own country and in the successive empires above them, many different ethnic groups living together in comparative peace and retaining their respective identities for a long time. It was natural to assume that, with the final disappearance of all states and the establishment of universal peace, there would prevail the same conditions, in the ethnic sense, on a much larger scale. Unlike the idea of the state, the pure ethnic principle is not directed *against* anybody. It is a positive principle, without intrinsic negation. Unlike the territorial element implying limited space and a consequent scrimmage for it, the *ethnos* offers prospects for the coexistence forever of different racial stocks, with full coöperation of the various cultural forces. It can easily be made to identify the wholeness of mankind with its own frictionless and coördinating parts. Such a reconciliation could take place all the more easily after the miraculous advent of the Messiah visualized by the prophets!

The messianic hope thus became a corner stone of prophecy. The idea of a Golden Age to come may not have been entirely new. The vexed question of oriental, in particular Egyptian and Babylonian messianism has been widely but inconclusively discussed. It can, however, hardly be denied that, whatever messianic ideas crept into the Canaanite religion from the two neighboring civilizations, and whatever their effect on the popular religion of ancient Israel, the prophets reinterpreted them so exhaustively as to constitute a novel and unique type of messianic expectation.[48]

The central figure in messianism, the "anointed of the Lord" or the "redeeemer," clearly shows the interdependence of social and religious features. More than one vigorous imperialistic king of mighty Egypt and Babylonia flattered himself, and was often told by obsequious courtiers, that he would extend the boundaries of his realm to the ends of the known world and thereby restore the Golden Age. Israel could not hope for world conquest in these centuries of decline. God himself was to accomplish this feat in a superhuman way. Experience, however, had taught that God performs miracles only through men, for example, Moses and Elijah.

The new miracle would also have to be accomplished through some one man. The levitical priests probably looked for a return of Moses. The prophets of the north seem to have been so much impressed by the vivid memories, embellished by legends, of the striking demeanor and personality of Elijah that they hoped for his miraculous return in the same manner as when he "went up by a whirlwind into heaven." [49] For the Judean prophets it was natural to expect that the Messiah would be a scion of David, whose house had ruled the country for centuries and in its early years had been blessed by God with power and prosperity. Despite the dynasty's later corruption, there was still a hope that the exalted poet-king would reappear and establish an age of unrivaled glory. The priests of that age left little, if any, writings, and Samaria had vanished as an independent state at the very beginnings of written prophecy. The ideology of the southern prophets, therefore, soon overshadowed all others. The Davidic Messiah became the apotheosized figure on which all later Jewish eschatology centered. Moses, Elijah, even the Messiah of the house of Joseph so prominent in later times, were relegated to secondary positions.

Different conceptions of the final goal of Israel's restoration betray their different social backgrounds. We need but compare the statements of the prophets of the eighth century to see the principal line of demarcation. Hosea, whether a "Bedouin" or not, was certainly the only Northern Israelite among them. He saw no hope for the corrupt civilization of Samaria, which must be entirely annihilated. "Back to the desert," "Restoration of the Mosaic age," even a completely fresh beginning, are his watchwords. Amos from Tekoa and Micah from Moreshet also denounced the evils of city life in both Israel and Judah but looked for the Golden Age as a rejuvenation of the Judean countryside. Finally Isaiah, the prophet of Jerusalem, looked forward to the day when "Zion shall be redeemed with justice" and when Jerusalem, which "had become a harlot," shall again "be called the city of righteousness." [50] Quite naturally, when Jerusalem was destroyed and its Temple lay in ashes, the whole people idealized the city, more even than Isaiah did.

IDEALIZATION OF THE PAST

This idealization of the past was a general characteristic of the age. In a sense it eclipsed the messianic hope. Eschatological passages, strange as it may seem, are not foremost in the prophetic writings. Some prophets never refer to the end of days. Those who do, speak of it as of a well-known popular idea and limit themselves to cryptic allusions. It is the glorification of bygone days which fills their writings and the other poetical and legal works of the Old Testament. No wonder that there arose a collection of historical writings the equal of any literary achievement of the Hebrew Bible.

No other oriental nation [writes Eduard Meyer] was able to create such an historical literature. Even the Greeks succeeded in producing one only at a much later stage of their development, in the fifth century.[51]

This riddle also finds its key in the extraordinary national situation. Thoughtful Israelites were growing more and more disgusted with the conditions of the day; they naturally turned increasingly to the past. There was so much vitality left in the Israelitic, and even more in the Judean people, that they refused simply to throw up their hands in despair of resolving the social conflicts and the unending national frustrations. They turned to ancestral lore not only for comfort but for a way out of difficulties. The Judean Yahwist, with his consummate artistry and detachment tinged with irony; the Israelitic theologian and antimonarchist, the Elohist; indeed, all the contributors to the Pentateuch and Former Prophets conveyed a moral through historical narrative. Degeneration of political and social status did not come about without cause. There is a hand that guides all history, punishing the evildoer and rewarding the deserving. Beyond this common philosophy of history, these ancient historians greatly differed in method, attitudes to life, and artistic skill and style. But they were all aware that not extravagant exaltation, but a discriminating glorification of the past could teach a lesson to the overcivilized, sophisticated citizens of Jerusalem and Samaria. Thus the glorified past was to combine with an exalted future to serve as a psychological buoy for a drowning people which refused to die.

DIVINE INSTRUMENT

History thus became more than an escape. It became the dominating principle in the national and religious life. The present may appear to be desperately bad—the people became accustomed to hearing—but it is only a moment in history, a transitory link between an ideal past and a still more perfect future. There seems to be no natural solution of pressing problems, but the supernatural force pervading all history will eventually provide one in a supernatural way. Social inequalities, pauperization, and mass enslavement have natural economic justification, but they will give way to a reign of justice and equal rights, established, as in the days of old, by God. Judges, administrators, even kings, may now abuse their power and engage in worldly pursuits. They will soon be replaced by a scion of the house of David who will reëstablish on a higher plane the order which prevailed under the ideal shepherd king. The political independence of Jewish nationality may gradually vanish, the Jews may be more and more forced to abandon the country for foreign lands. Yet the people had had no state or territory in the days of Moses, and none the less it was so much happier then. Not territorial basis, not even the highest religious expression of territorial anchorage, the Temple and its sacrifices, really matter; to obey the commands of the Lord in all places is what matters to the Jew. Indeed Palestine, once received from the hands of God as his spontaneous gift after a series of miraculous happenings, will again be restored to the people through another such series. Israel is inferior in military power to Assyria, Egypt, or Babylonia, but militarism will soon vanish altogether, and "nation shall not lift up sword against nation" (Isa. 2:4).

At that time, Israel's God can abolish all states, because He and He alone is Lord of all states and nations. He is Lord of the whole world because there is no God beside him. He chastises his people at the hands of other nations, which are likewise creatures of his will. But He does not forget this people of his, with whom He concluded his covenant in the wonderful days of its youth. When Israel shall have changed its ways and fully complied with the terms of this pact, God will send his redeemer to establish another Golden Age. Then all conflicts will find their final solution, and under the direct rule of the one God revered by all mankind, there will take place a complete reconciliation of all social classes, of the urban, rural, and nomadic populations, of the Jewish nationality and its state, of the Jews and all other nations.

Thus in days of great suffering and, in a profound sense, out of them, was born the idea of a Jewish people beyond state and territory, a divine instrument in man's overcoming of "nature" through a supernatural process in the course of "history."

IV

CRUCIAL TEST

THE destruction of the First Temple and the loss of national independence in 586 provided the first decisive test of the vitality of these ideas of a Jewish people living beyond state and territory, God's chief instrument in man's overcoming of "nature." Would the Jews remain Jews even in exile and under a foreign monarch? Could a nationality exist without state or territory? Could the Jewish religion preserve its distinctive feature, that subtle amalgam of universalism and nationalism; or must it surrender the national element and, stressing universalism, be submerged in its first uninsulated contact with the outside world?

SIGNIFICANT SIXTH CENTURY

Unusual developments of the next century or two gave the answers to these questions. The sixth century was one of the great historic centuries. The Neo-Babylonian Empire, apparently solidly founded on the ruins of imperial Assyria, had fallen an easy prey to Cyrus, who had also subdued Media and Lydia. The boundaries of the Persian Empire were soon extended from India and Central Asia to Egypt and the Balkan Peninsula. Within a single empire the Indo-Iranian cultures thus confronted the ancient civilizations of the Fertile Crescent, Egypt and Phoenicia and the Greek culture of Asia Minor. In all the history of religious thought no century can boast of a more distinguished galaxy of names, to mention only Confucius, Lao-tse, Buddha, Pythagoras. And, even if Parsee traditions that the founder of their faith, Zoroaster, lived in the sixth century be—unjustifiably—rejected in favor of an earlier dating, certainly his teachings played a significant role only after the rise of Persia.

It is not difficult to imagine what an overwhelming impression these sudden and turbulent movements must have made upon clear-sighted men in the Asiatic world. Certainly the almost simultaneous expansion of both Parsiism and Judaism from Egypt to Iran brought about as deep a spiritual upheaval in the minds of all western Asiatic peoples as did Persia's military victories in the political sphere. "A race which did not acknowledge a plurality of gods," writes Sidney Smith, "the men of Israel and Judah had been scattered over many provinces by the Assyrians and Nebuchadrezzar. Peoples who would not worship figures of gods in human shape, the Medes and Persians, were impinging on the civilized peoples of western Asia from the east. . . . Some effort at reform and clarification of the polytheistic chaos was necessary." [1]

Conversely, the Jews themselves were confronted with these epochal changes in the outside world at a crucial period of their own national history. The deportations, life during the Exile, the partial restorations under Zerubbabel and Ezra-Nehemiah, the change in the status of the Jews under Persia in and outside of Palestine, created unprecedented situations. Again there arose such able leaders as Ezekiel and Deutero-Isaiah, comparable to the noblest of the prophets before them, to make a new intellectual advance in explaining new perplexities.

Unfortunately information about these basic developments is slight. It was in these centuries, according to the prevailing judgment, that many books of the Old Testament were written, while older ones received a more definite formulation. But it is open to conjecture how much of these writings in their present form was novel, and how much the heritage of former generations adapted to new demands. The incisive and often stimulating discussions of biblical critics have, if anything, added to our uncertainty and reinforced the demand for a total reëvaluation of the postexilic period. True, only a small minority denies the very historicity of a large-scale exile and restoration. But many scholars have expressed sharply divergent views about the authorship of most oracles attributed to Ezekiel, as well as about the date or location of those which they considered authentic.[2]

Similar, though somewhat less insistent, doubts have been voiced concerning the life and work of Deutero-Isaiah. If but relatively few ventured to defend the fundamentalist view of the unity and common authorship of the whole book, many have carried on an unceasing debate about the literary and historical details of Chapters 40–66. Often distinguished by great ingenuity and learning, this debate has shown little progress toward genuine agreement. Trito-Isaiah, in particular, that phantom author of the last eleven chapters, still serves as a convenient springboard for the confusion of many issues. The recent dramatic discovery of the Isaiah scroll, however significant from other angles, has not resolved any of these

major historical problems. It is, of course, of superlative importance to have the testimony of a good text written in the Maccabean age or soon after. Millar Burrows was right in early pointing
out "the remarkable fact that there is nothing [in it] which can be
called a major addition or omission, comparable to the additions
and omissions to be found in the Septuagint, for example. There
is no important dislocation or disarrangement of the text." This
discovery has pushed back our documentary evidence of this prophetic work by more than a millennium. Yet it has not answered
decisively any of the vital questions concerning the nature of that
very text and its authorship at the time of its final composition
some three or four centuries before.[3]

Neither is there any greater agreement today, than there was a
quarter century ago, concerning the work of Ezra the Scribe. Even
those who accept his indubitable historic achievements, continue
debating whether he lived under Artaxerxes I, and hence preceded
by a decade his fellow Babylonian, Nehemiah (whose activity about
445 is one of the few bedrocks of postexilic chronology), or under
Artaxerxes II, and hence about 397. Few scholars, however, still
doubt the early composition of the two biblical books bearing their
names. According to the majority view today, they as well as the
two books of Chronicles, were composed by a school of historians
during the Persian period. Whether dating from the early fourth
or, possibly, late fifth century, they seem rather reliably to record
major historical developments soon after the events.[4]

Whatever decision we may reach about these perplexing problems, we shall readily admit that the generation which survived the
fall of Jerusalem had to make some immediate, fateful decisions.
The all-pervading question was: Would all or most Jews accept the
prophetic teaching and reconcile themselves to the Exile, while
retaining the belief that it was *their* God and none other who had
inflicted the punishment? Would they not rather feel that the victorious gods of the conquering nation had been responsible and,
hence, refuse to live as Jews in a foreign land? For a time the answer was not clear. Apparently the refugees who fled to Egypt after
the death of Gedaliah, carrying along the old prophet Jeremiah,
were among the staunchest patriots. And yet they, or at least their
women, had ascribed their misery not to the all-powerful God of
Israel but to the anger of the Queen of Heaven whom they thought
they had offended. In Palestine the influences of foreign religions
and cultures were likewise marked. Here the old "popular religion"

again raised its head, now influenced not only by many Canaanite elements, but more than ever by the Babylonian cults maintained for the benefit of Babylonian officials. Some new mysterious and awe-inspiring rites also got hold of people "that sit among the graves, and lodge in the vaults; that eat swine's flesh, and broth of abominable things is in their vessels" (Isa. 65:4).

In Babylonia proper the danger of assimilation and complete extinction of the Jewish nationality was, of course, even greater. The glittering cosmopolitan civilization, with its medley of races and cultures, must at once have repelled and attracted, fascinated and bewildered, the provincials from Palestine. The external grandeur of the fifty-five temples devoted to the worship of the great gods and of many lesser sanctuaries in the capital alone, the elaborate and picturesque services before the colossal gilded statue of Marduk, and the vast masses of worshipers of every tongue and costume doubtless infused many a Judean onlooker with a sense of inferiority and shame. None the less, Jewish survival owes itself, paradoxically enough, not to those who remained at home but to the nationalistic vitality of those living so precariously in Exile.

GROWING DISPERSION

The assumption of many modern scholars that only a small number of Jews had been deported, while almost the whole peasant population remained in Palestine, needs serious qualification. That this assumption directly contradicts biblical statements is not significant, since the latter may have been colored by later partisan opinion. General historical and archaeological considerations, however, force us to assume that the local population was seriously depleted by successive deportations in the years 597–586 (602–582), and by the numerous wars and semivoluntary migrations. It appears, indeed, that fully one-third of the total pre-war population of Judah was forcibly removed by the conqueror, while many thousands fell by the sword or died of hunger and destitution. Thousands of others, particularly in the provinces, fled the country before the approaching Chaldaean armies, and only a part of them returned after peace was restored. The contrary assertion that, after Gedaliah's appointment, "all the Jews returned out of all places whither they were driven" (Jer. 40:11–12) need not be taken any more literally than the even more emphatic statement that, after the assassination of Gedaliah, "all the people, both small and great" escaped to Egypt (II Kings 25:26). The archaeological evidence of widespread destruction and depopulation after 587 is so overwhelming that not until the 1934 excavations of Bethel has there been any sign of slow revival during the sixth century.[5]

In any case, Judah, although not quite waste, became so depopulated that the neighboring tribes, particularly the Edomites, began, or rather continued, to spread northward, gradually displacing the Jewish inhabitants in the southern districts as far up as Hebron. Under the pressure of Arab tribes, which later succeeded in dislodging them entirely from their ancient settlements in Seir (or what the Romans were to call their province of "Arabia"), the Edomites began expanding more and more into southern Palestine. This movement, apparently set in motion already by Sennacherib's invasion and deportations, which had left behind a demographic vacuum, now gained great momentum. Ultimately the entire southern district of Palestine came to be known as "Idumaea," a name already recorded in the Zenon papyri about 258 B.C.E.[6]

At the same time, the Jews in the Diaspora, especially in Babylonia and Egypt, must have constituted a considerable mass. It is not altogether unlikely that the Judean exiles settling in Babylonia received reinforcements from the previously deported Israelites, a remnant of whom must have survived into that age. One may view with extreme skepticism the perennial attempts of imaginative writers, especially popular two or three centuries ago, to retrace the history of the northern tribes since their deportation by Sargon. But it cannot be denied that in the Chronicler's rewriting of Israel's history the total disappearance of the Northern Israelites soon after their deportation finds no mention at all. On the contrary, in Ezra's list of those who participated in the first return under Zerubbabel, there are recorded among "the men of the people of Israel" many descendants of exiles from localities which formerly belonged to the northern kingdom.[7]

On the other hand, those sections of the "remnant" which remained in their original habitation throughout Media and Mesopotamia were swelled in numbers and upheld in their religious allegiance by more recent arrivals.

In general, the forces making for migrations before the fall of Jerusalem operated with increased vigor now that the people as a whole had lost its territorial moorings. The widening of the boundaries in the Chaldaean Empire and the still greater extension of the Persian Empire gave a new impetus to migratory movements among all the subject races, whether Babylonian, Greek, or Jewish. The whole habitable world known to the Palestinian prophets opened its gates to Jewish settlers. So many and so specific are the references by the later prophets to a really world-wide Diaspora, that they cannot be explained away as lavish interpolations. Consider the consolation of Deutero-Isaiah:

I will bring thy seed from the east, and gather thee from the west. I will say to the north: "Give up" and to the south: "Keep not back, bring My sons from far and My daughters from the end of the earth."

Such utterances were no mere propaganda or eschatological wish dreams. They must have had some relation to actual facts. Even the "back-to-Palestine" movement, which began with the downfall of Chaldaea, could not check this steady, inevitable growth of the Diaspora. Thus even before the end of the Persian rule a Jewish author could put into the mouth of a hostile courtier in Susa that famous denunciation still echoed by antisemites, "There is a certain people scattered abroad and dispersed among the peoples in all the provinces of thy kingdom; and their laws are diverse from those of every people." And Achaemenid Persia was the vastest of all ancient empires.[8]

From the outset, however, we are confronted with a very difficult problem. Babylonia had for thousands of years been a highly developed, relatively prosperous and densely populated country. Why then should Nebukadrezzar have chosen for settlement by the Jews "the most proper places of Babylonia," [9] such as the region around Nippur on the important "river Chebar," one of the largest cities in the Chaldaean Empire? That some of these Jews should soon settle in the city of Babel itself was, since the rapidly expanding metropolis threw her gates wide open to immigrants from all lands, natural enough.

Perhaps some Jewish, or rather Israelitic, settlements had been established in these regions before the deportations of 597 and 586. Under Assyria, the cities of Babylon and Nippur were less focal centers, and foreign mass settlements might have been welcomed by the government. The most important group of aliens in Northern Israel after Samaria's fall, came from Kuta. If those scholars who identify this place as a district one day's journey from Babylon be correct, it is entirely possible that the Assyrian monarchs, pursuing their ancient policy, settled there, in exchange, some of the Israelites deported in 721 and after. With the rise of Chaldaea, this district, because of its proximity to the new capital, became one of the central regions of the empire. Many of the Israelitic exiles as well as some voluntary immigrants who perhaps had joined them during the seventh century, may have spread through all Babylonia while it was still under Assyrian domination. Thus later deportees could settle in established Israelitic centers. This concatenation of circumstances would also explain in part the equally astonishing fact that as early as the first third of the sixth century, when Ezekiel prophesied, the Jews had achieved an advantageous economic position. Although in general the policy of Assyrian and Babylonian monarchs toward deported nations was favorable, such a prodigious development in the course of a few decades would otherwise be an almost insoluble riddle.[10]

ECONOMIC PROGRESS

Detachment from Palestinian soil had lasting effects upon the economic life of the Jews. The deported had belonged almost exclusively to the "urban" population in Palestine. Some of them had been artisans whose deportation in many ways resembled the forced disarmament of a vanquished country today. Many others had been administrative officials or had served in the standing army, more especially the royal bodyguard in Jerusalem. Among the landowners many were absentee landlords accustomed to spending their lives in urban occupations or in idleness and pleasure in the capital. All these, when transferred to the Babylonian countryside, had considerable difficulty in adjusting themselves. To till the foreign soil was a great change, and it is no wonder that many poured into the larger cities, such as Nippur, whenever they were free to do so.

Here they entered the active industrial and commercial life of the country. It appears to be an old sociological law that, on account of their knowledge of at least two languages and their lack of attachment to any particular parcel of land, aliens are more likely to become merchants than farmers. The Jewish exiles must have been doubly attracted to commerce in that "city of merchants" and "land of traffic" which their temperamental prophet was soon to denounce with such vehemence (Ez. 16:29; 17:4).

Perhaps not by mere coincidence large-scale private banking replaced temple credit in the Assyrian empire in the latter part of the seventh century, some three generations after the arrival of the first deportees from Samaria. This was one of the most notable transformations in economic history. The fact that the founder of the house of Egibi, the greatest of these private firms, bore the unmistakably Hebrew name, Jacob, and that most of the early loans are recorded to have been granted without interest may, indeed, reflect one of the earliest Jewish contributions to mankind's material civilization. Other bankers charged the customary 20 per cent per annum attested from the days of the Eshnunna code, through that of Hammurabi, down to the Neo-Babylonian and Persian empires. "Loan sharks," like the Murashshu Sons, a leading pagan banking and warehouse firm in the city of Nippur, some of whose business records dating from the fifth and fourth centuries have survived, did not hesitate to charge on occasion double that rate.

Jews, however, seem to have acted under the twofold religious compulsion of abhorring dealings with pagan temple treasuries and of considering all interest as "usury." At the same time they, too, faced the need of speeding up the monetary circulation and utilizing credit for their advanced and rapidly expanding business transactions. They may have pioneered, therefore, in the development of a banking system based on loans granted on the security of real-estate mortgages and pawns which, while minimizing risks to the lenders, enabled borrowers to obtain cash quickly. That these bankers were not simon-pure philanthropists goes without saying. Very likely they made use of the slaves or cattle and collected the revenue from fields or houses entrusted to them for the duration of the loans. They often also stipulated for, and exacted, a substantial "penalty" from debtors who failed to meet their obligations on time. In the hands of ruthless individuals these new methods could become another source of exploitation of the masses. But they were a significant factor in accelerating the "progress" of Babylonia's and Persia's semicapitalist economies.

The majority of Israelitic and Judean exiles, however, formerly engaged in farming at home, doubtless went to work on Assyro-Babylonian estates, whether of their own or of foreign masters. To these men above all others was addressed Jeremiah's famous injunction to build houses and plant gardens. In Babylonia, where renting a house was far more frequent than in Palestine, such construction of one's own dwelling must have doubly given the impression of intended permanence. Half a century later the exiles had become so deeply rooted in their new environment that, when the call came to return to their homeland, only "a fixed number from each family" departed.[11]

Economic activities of the exiled Jews thus were even more varied than in the fatherland. Many extant records of the house of Murashshu show that, at least a century after the Exile, many men bearing Hebrew names had become landowners, merchants, contractors, and rent collectors. Understandably, such business records would lend a commercial tinge even to purely agricultural pursuits. If, for example, the administrator of a large estate entrusted several Jews with the raising of his master's sheep and goats in return for a specified annual delivery of cattle, butter, wool, and hides, he dealt with farmers rather than tradesmen. Similarly, the five Jews who requested the Murashshu Sons to equip them with five nets and a permit to fish in the firm's waters, promising to deliver in return five hundred good fish within twenty days, were professional fishermen.

On the whole, there hardly was any important vocation, including public office, in which Jews and other non-Chaldaeans were not represented. The absence of Jewish "scribes" in the Murashshu records is probably accidental. At the most it may suggest that the Jews of Nippur even in the fifth century had not yet become so familiar with the Babylonian language and the cuneiform script as to rival their native competitors for this position. Although in the sixth century relatively few Jews could as yet have amassed large fortunes, those who returned to Palestine under Zerubbabel, certainly not the wealthiest of their group, owned 7,337 slaves as well as thousands of heads of cattle (Neh. 7:67–69; Ezra 2:65–67). Soon after their arrival in the country they were also able to take up a collection for "the treasury of work" (for the reconstruction of the Temple), which yielded, according to Eduard Meyer's computation, a sum equal to $400,000 in present American money and having many times its purchasing power.

In Egypt, too, the economic position of the refugees seems not to have been altogether bad. Under the conditions of relative prosperity prevailing after the seventh century, even strangers could find suitable employment. Foreign mercenaries were much sought after, the Egyptian kings often preferring them to native soldiers because of the latter's frequent mutinies. That Jews, too, were so employed has long been known from the records of a Jewish military colony in the Elephantine in Upper Egypt settled by Psammetichus I or II or by Apries in the seventh or sixth century to protect the country against Ethiopian invasions. The Elephantine Jews were, for the most part, soldiers and farmers, although we also have records of commercial transactions among them. That the amounts involved were quite small—there are few references to talents or even minas—is hardly astonishing in the case of a military settlement far from the country's mercantile centers.[12]

We possess far less information about the economic life of the Jews in other parts of Egypt in this period. But we may assume that their social and economic position was not inferior to that of other strangers. From the days of Cambyses on, there existed a still more perceptible predilection on the part of the Persian government for Hebrew and other foreign elements. While an extant Aramaic deed dated 515 B.C.E. merely records a share-cropping transaction between a Jewish landlord, Pedaiah (?), and a tenant Aḥa in another rural district in Egypt, in the larger cities Jews must have entered other occupations as well. Most of Jeremiah's contemporaries, for example, who lived at Migdol, Taḥpanḥes, or Noph (44:1), must have been employed in some branch of industry or commerce. It is immaterial whether the reference to these three cities, usually identified with Magdalos, Daphne, and Memphis in Lower Egypt, belongs to the days of Jeremiah or to those of a somewhat later glossator, as is presumed by certain critics. In either case it reflects the existence of noteworthy Egyptian Jewish settlements in the exilic or early postexilic period. Of these three towns, Daphne alone was a frontier stronghold of the type of Elephantine. But it was situated much nearer the important arteries of commerce running through the empire. In cosmopolitan Memphis, Jews doubtless joined other western Asiatic settlers among the workers in the royal arsenal (*bet sefinata* = house of ships), importers of Syrian wine, and so on. In fact, one fifth-century papyrus seems to have preserved the names of a Jewish arsenal worker named Ḥiyyah and of another whose father's name was Yehoram.[18]

WOMAN'S ENHANCED STATUS

Of unusual interest is the economic and legal position of the Jewish woman of the period. The official records, preserved in the Pentateuchal laws, do not indicate the full extent of the change which had occurred. The law, while giving the woman great protection within the family, assigned to her a minor role outside it. According to the Priestly Code, she remained fully dependent upon her father or husband, having practically no property rights of her own, except when there happened to be no male heir. She could be divorced arbitrarily, her only protection being the old custom, taken for granted by the Deuteronomist as a basis for further legislation, that the husband had to give her a formal writ of divorce. The "sending off" of a wife meant the loss of one working family member and, as long as the Israelitic people was preponderantly agricultural, this loss of a cheap and devoted laborer was an adequate safeguard against arbitrary divorce. With the growing urbanization and the increase of the proletarian class in ancient Israel, however, the protection extended to women by the traditional law must have become less and less effective.

Growing class differentiation must also have enabled a larger percentage of the wealthy to practice polygamy. Apparently marriage of more than one wife was never widespread in ancient Israel for the simple reason that there were not enough women in a society which seems to have had no word for bachelor and which, after Solomon's reign, never had a plethora of foreign slaves. But now the ratio of non-Jewish slave girls may well have increased. Wherever indulged in, polygamy tended to lower the status of the nonfavorite wives and, indirectly, of all women.[14]

Life in the Diaspora and even in Palestine after the deportations brought about many marked changes hardly reflected in legal documents. Babylonian influence is clear. In Babylonian law from the days of Hammurabi, the woman had extensive property rights as well as a certain amount of protection against the disadvantages of a polygamous system in which one wife was recognized as the main consort. These legal principles necessarily exercised upon the Jewish minority in the Euphrates Valley a much greater influence than they had previously upon the more or less independent nations of Palestine. Demotic papyri of the age also reveal an increase in the rights of Egyptian women which must have affected Jewish practice. When Jeremiah arrived in Egypt, it seemed to him that women were leaders of the Jewish communities. This gynarchy found expression in the worship of "the Queen of Heaven," which seems to have relegated male cults to the background. The aged prophet addressed one of his most violent harangues, the last that has come down to us, "unto all the people and to all the women." [15]

Even more basic than these environmental adjustments were the social transformations which accompanied the Exile. Although many women and children voluntarily accompanied the heads of their families, there was undoubtedly a large surplus of men in the new Jewish communities. The subsequent stream of voluntary Jewish immigrants must have maintained this surplus, since enterprising young men are always readiest to face the risks of expatriation. As is usual where women are relatively few, they experienced here a rise in social status.

In the Elephantine military colony, at least in its first period, the preponderance of men over women must have been still more marked. Women acquired there a degree of independence known nowhere else in that period. They succeeded in maintaining this position even when an equable numerical balance between the sexes had been restored. In the papyri many women appear as parties in civil litigations and independent business transactions even with their own husbands and fathers. It is also possible that commercial pursuits were left largely to women because the men were engaged mainly in military service. Women, moreover, seem to have acquired the right to divorce their husbands at will by making a public declaration "in the congregation" (ba-'edah). The husband, it is true, still had the power of divorce by an even less formal procedure; he, apparently, could "drive out" his wife by merely handing her a writ of divorce. Marriage contracts, however, usually stipulated a heavy fine to be paid by the husband in such cases, and he faced public disapprobation as well. The career of Mibtaḥiah, a well-to-do girl of the fifth century, is particularly instructive. Having obtained two large dowries from her father, she later lent him money in her own name. Upon his failure to repay the cash, she received a house. She married at least three times. With one husband, an Egyptian, who had perhaps adopted Judaism, she concluded a marriage contract minutely safeguarding her rights. No better illustration of the economic independence of the Elephantine woman can be adduced than the list of contributors to the religious chest of the community in 419. Among the 124 members, recorded as having contributed two shekels each, we can identify 37 women and 60 men.[16]

Nor can we consider certain customs, recorded in Mibtaḥiah's marriage contract with Aṣḥor (Cowley, No. 15), as anything but symbolic survivals of woman's former status of dependence. If the bridegroom, for example, pledged himself to pay a sum of money to the father of the bride, although she was at that time thirty years old and had been married before, this was merely a vestige of the ancient *mohar*, as is the wedding ring of today. Both are ceremonies sanctified by tradition and often demanded by law as external symbols. That is why Aṣhor paid only 5 shekels to his father-in-law (whether this was the legal minimum, or a higher amount on account of the bride's wealth, we do not know), while his gifts to the bride amounted to 65½ shekels in value. On the other hand, he promised to pay three times as much (200 shekels), should he at any time proceed to "drive her out of his home." It is probably but an accident that this sum corresponded to the legal minimum demanded by the Mishnah (Ketubot I, 2) for each marriage contract with a virgin. In fact, Mibtaḥiah was then a widow or divorcée whom later talmudic law was to provide with a minimum settlement of only half that amount.

These exceptional rights for women probably were limited to such a "Jewish army camp" as that in Elephantine. Elsewhere among the Jews the supremacy of the husband was doubtless retained, although even in Palestine there was a certain elevation of woman's social status. Again the surplus of men among those who returned from the Exile made itself felt. There seem to have been some 30,000 men and only 12,000 women among the new arrivals. Hence the divergence between the figure of 42,360 Jews, besides servants, in the "whole congregation" of the returning exiles and the itemized list of "the men of the people of Israel" totaling roughly 30,000 (Ezra 2:2–65).

Since the intellectual leaders harshly condemned marriage with foreign women, which had thus become necessary, numerical inferiority could only benefit the Jewish woman. Even before the final repudiation of mixed marriages by Ezra and Nehemiah, Malachi proclaimed that, while to divorce one's first (usually Jewish) wife was legal, it was an abomination unto God. Deutero-Isaiah, too, put the rhetorical question: "And a wife of youth, can she be rejected?" (54:6). From this period on, the movement against divorce and for extensive protection of woman's rights was a strong force in the Jewish society of the Second Commonwealth. It finally reached its climax in the Shammaite school's restriction of divorce to cases of a wife's sexual infidelity (M. Giṭṭin IX, 10) and the analogous anti-divorce laws of early Christianity. Both in the full freedom of divorce found in the Elephantine colony and in the rejection of divorce by Malachi, the woman's position in Judaism became one of a peer. The high praise of the "woman of valor," which concludes the collection of biblical proverbs, reflects the popular recognition of this improved status.

LEGAL PROTECTION

As far as our records reveal, legislation during the Babylonian Exile was by no means unfavorable to the Jews. During the first few years the Jews, naturally enough, felt oppressed by their new rulers. The barbarous ill-treatment during the deportation, particularly, burned itself deeply into the souls of the sufferers. Afterwards, however, the government's behavior corresponded to the Jews' improved economic standing. In Babylonian society there were three main classes: the privileged nobility, the nonprivileged half-free subjects, and the slaves. The Jews apparently belonged to the large middle class comprising almost all inhabitants of the cities and their environs, with the exception of slaves. Within this class, it seems, the Jews lived on the basis of perfect equality. Those who had accumulated great wealth or who possessed some personal merit, achieved prominence at the king's court in Babylon, and to an even greater extent in Susa, the Persian capital.

Such favorable treatment may have begun with the very first royal prisoner, Jehoiachin, carried into Babylonian captivity in 597. Recent evidence has shown that, rather than being held technically "in prison," the youthful king was allowed to live with his family as one of many royal pensioners. The traditional picture of his sufferings in Exile, drawn from the references to "prison" and "prison garments" in the concluding passages of the book of Kings, received a severe jolt when the excavations in Tell Beit Mirsim (Debir) yielded a seal reading "To Eliakim, Steward of Jokin." Apparently dated in the reign of Zedekiah, it indicated that the exiled Jehoiachin was still considered the legitimate king in his country. Two other Hebrew seals bore out this suggestion. Even more conclusive was the discovery of the name Yaukin, king of Judah, together with those of five royal princes and other Judeans, among the regular recipients of oil, barley, and other royal gifts, in Babylonian tablets dated between 595 and 570. These data have served to confirm the biblical historian's other emphatic assertion that Jehoiachin was the Babylonian king's pensioner "all the days of his life" (II Kings 25:29–30) which could hardly refer to Amel-Marduk's (Evil Merodach's) brief two-year reign alone.[17]

Nebukadrezzar himself, it appears, after having replaced Jehoiachin by Zedekiah on the royal throne of Judah, toyed with the idea of restoring him some day to a position of an obsequious vassal. Perhaps only the excess of irredentist fidelity toward their former king shown by such Judean patriots as the prophet Hananiah (594 B.C.E.; cf. Jer. 28:1–4), interfered with the execution of these plans. Nebukadrezzar's son, Amel-Marduk, however, upon ascending the throne in 561, considered the rebellious province sufficiently pacified formally to "lift up the head" of Jehoiachin, and to "set his throne above the throne of the kings that were with him in Babylon" (II Kings 25:27–28). Whether or not Amel-Marduk conceived this elevation as a step toward Jehoiachin's restoration to Jerusalem —this plan may have been frustrated only by his death in 559—he thereby gave the Jewish communities throughout the empire a recognized leader of the house of David who could serve as their official spokesman before the Babylonian authorities.

Other Jewish citizens of standing in the administration often intervened even more effectively in behalf of their coreligionists. Such services as Ezra and Nehemiah were able to render their people by virtue of their influence in Susa doubtless were emulated by other influential Jews. These frequently regarded their own brilliant achievements as serving a divine purpose in the deliverance of their people. Many of them must have thought along the lines of Mordecai's reply to Esther: "And who knoweth whether thou art not come to royal estate for such a time as this?" (Esther 4:14.) Neither are the legends concerning Daniel, Hananiah, Mishael, and Azariah without historical merit, in so far as they reflect the people's general expectation of complete loyalty on the part of Jewish courtiers.[18] Conversely, the enhanced position of the Palestinian center after the Restoration accrued also to the advantage of the Diaspora leaders.

The political status of Egyptian Jewry was somewhat less favorable. While the Persian government doubtless treated the Jews equally well or better in that province where it needed their help against the recreant population, this governmental favoritism brought about a natural resentment in the native majority. Even in Elephantine the Jews did not get along well with the mass of Egyptians. To be sure, they maintained business relations with them, and both intermarriage and proselytism seem not to have been infrequent. But the antagonism of the population to the Persian rulers necessarily was also directed against their Jewish satellites. Indeed, a few years before the successful revolt of 404, which brought the country temporary independence, serious anti-Jewish riots resulted in the destruction of the Jewish temple. The perennial misunderstandings arising from the differences in national and religious mores also kept the two groups apart. In the Elephantine colony "the Jewish force" thus lived the sheltered life of imperial clients apart from the natives. Whether Jews elsewhere in Egypt also lived this sort of ghetto life we do not know, but it seems that Egypt was at all times an excellent place for the development of group segregation.

Neither the Babylonian nor the Persian government seems to have hostilely interfered with the inner life of the Jewish community. In general, the vast empires of antiquity (except Assyria) learned to be tolerant of religious differences. Polytheistic themselves, their rulers had no real difficulty in acknowledging the existence of other gods whenever political reasons made that expedient. It was only with the rigid interpretation by Israel's prophets of the covenant with God that it became a religious crime to serve a god other than that worshiped by one's own national group. Only at a later stage of its evolution was Parsiism to emulate Judaism's and Christianity's religious exclusiveness. Moreover, there was little reason, in the imperial policy of an ancient conqueror, to convert a vanquished nation forcefully. As most vanquished nations would be inclined to see defeat as proof of the superior power of the foreign god, deportation was fair guarantee of eventual religious assimilation.

Since religious tolerance was so deeply ingrained, it is not surprising that, soon after the conquest of Babylon, Cyrus, not yet a Zoroastrian and hence not affected even by dualist convictions, freely worshiped the local deities. Immediately upon Babylonia's surrender he inscribed on his cylinder, "Marduk, the great lord, moved the understanding heart of the people of Babylon to me, while I daily sought his worship." Indeed, he did this so commonly that, were we to follow Babylonian records only, we might conclude that he adopted the Babylonian religion. Similarly in addressing Jews he did not hesitate to assert that "all the kingdoms of the earth hath the Lord [Yahweh], the God of heaven, given me." It mattered little whether Cyrus sincerely meant what he said or merely made such public declarations for the benefit of conquered populations. Even if designed for propagandistic purposes on a par with the rumors, whose spread he doubtless fostered, about his alleged clemency to vanquished rulers, these professions of toleration greatly aided in the enduring pacification of the vast empire. Under these circumstances the Jewish religion easily remained, to use the Roman term, a *religio licita*, a religion permitted by law.[19]

ASSIMILATION OR PRESERVATION

It is clear, therefore, that to answer our question concerning the survival of the Jews as a separate entity in the Diaspora we must turn to the Jews themselves. The decision was one which they were free to make.

Conflicting forces were influencing this decision not only during the period of the Exile proper but throughout the following centuries. They continued to operate on the masses of Jews in Babylonia and Egypt, even after the return of the small group to Palestine. The necessary, thorough remodeling of inherited ways of life, as well as the epochal transformations going on in the outside world, influenced the Jews toward complete assimilation. The national catastrophe itself and the subsequent years of poignant suffering must have brought weaker refugees to utter despair. Many may have accepted the idea that Babylonia's gods had really been victorious over the God of Israel. Others, going to the opposite extreme, must have expected imminent fulfillment of God's promise, made through the prophets, of a messianic age. Indeed, there often appeared among them men who, pretending to be messengers of the Lord, announced the coming of the Redeemer to be at hand.

Even Jews of sanguine temperament on finding these forecasts time and again to be false, must have grown thoroughly disillusioned; along with their messianic hopes they were inclined to throw over their whole Jewish heritage. There were also people of the type of "the men that are settled on their lees, that say in their heart: 'The Lord will not do good, neither will He do evil,' " against whom Zephaniah had stormed in the days of Josiah (1:12). Although the number of these lukewarm Jews must have diminished under the severe strain of religious reformation and national catastrophe, some persisted into the days of the Exile. They, too, fell an easy prey to the changed environment. A large number, however, chose a middle course. While remaining Jews in belief and habit, they gradually adopted Babylonian speech, folk ways, and other cultural elements. For instance, the Babylonian month names, although originally strongly religious in connotation, were gradually adopted by all Jews. Even the nationalist Nehemiah used them consistently, as has all Jewry ever since.

An external sign of such assimilation, partial or complete, seems to have been the adoption of Babylonian names. To cite the Murashshu records again, we find a number of Jewish businessmen mentioned in these contracts, whose fathers had Hebrew names while they themselves were called by some names current in Babylonia. As a matter of fact, these documents may have many more names of Jews which we cannot distinguish owing to the fact that their fathers before them had taken Babylonian or Persian names. That this kind of assimilation did not begin during the middle of the fifth century, when these business documents were written, but coincidentally with the Exile, is shown by the names borne by the two most important leaders of the Jewish communities who headed the first return to Palestine in 538. Sheshbazzar and Zerubbabel are both Babylonian names; indeed, pagan theophorous names. If Sheshbazzar is to be identified with Shenazzar (I Chron. 3:18), the son of the former king Jehoiachin bore a name meaning "The Sun god Shamash [or the Moon god Sin] may protect the son." His nephew, Zerubbabel, had the rather common Babylonian name, "scion of Babel."

Of course, the Jews may have been at that time as little aware of the forgotten meaning of common names as is an East-European orthodox Jew today, when he selects for his son what he thinks the specifically Jewish name, "Feivish" derived from Phoebus Apollo. Nor does the author of the ardently nationalistic book of Daniel evince any concern about the Babylonian names of his four noble youths, including the obviously theophorus Belteshazzar and Abed-nego (1:6–7). But the fact that Sheshbazzar was given that name in the early years of his father's captivity (five of Jehoiachin's seven sons are mentioned in the Babylonian tablets of 592) and that he possibly changed his name to Shenazzar under Nabonidus to flatter that king's enthusiasm for Sin, the Moon god of his native Haran, is the more significant, the less opposition it seems to have evoked in Jewish circles.[20]

There is a bare possibility that these two scions of the house of David had Hebrew names in addition, as did all of Shenazzar's brothers and Zerubbabel's brother and children. If so, they appeared under their Babylonian names only because of their outstanding position at court, where they evidently lived even before the elevation of Jehoiachin. However, it would be difficult to explain in this case the Chronicler's total silence about their Hebrew names despite his excellent familiarity with the genealogy of the Davidic family down to the seven sons of Elioenai, who apparently were his own contemporaries. Neither do we know of any Hebrew names for Mordecai, Bilshan, and Bigvai three of Zerubbabel's lieutenants during the return to Palestine (Ezra 2:2). They, too, must have been fairly advanced in years to be leaders of that first Restoration. Nevertheless their families had lived long enough in Babylonia for them to be known by non-Jewish names only.[21]

While some Jewish names of the period reveal signs of assimilation, others reflect a pronounced nationalistic consciousness. Although we do not hear of any protests, then or later, against the adoption of Babylonian names, the stricter Jews preferred Hebrew names for their children. Even Jehoiachin's other sons are known to us under Hebrew names only. Both the Old Testament and the external sources give many cases of Jewish fathers who, themselves known under Babylonian names, used the Hebrew or Aramaic nomenclature for their children. Here apparently is a sign of nationalist reaction against incipient disintegration.

Babylonian Jews now even invented some new Hebrew names or revived some forgotten ones, so that their children might be constantly reminded of important Jewish customs. It has been pointed out that among the seventy-odd persons whom we can identify as Jews in the Murashshu letters, not less than five had the unusual and previously unrecorded name "Shabbetai." Two were called Agga or Haga (Haggai), a name which had fallen into desuetude since the early days of Israel, but which had been made famous shortly before by a leading prophet of the late prophetic age. These two names obviously commemorated festivals of Jewry, the Sabbath and the holidays, "holiday" without an adjective referring usually to the Feast of Tabernacles. This is not to deny that, in consonance with a widespread ancient custom, birth on a holiday may have been regarded as a propitious omen for the newborn child and that parents may merely have seized the opportunity of increasing the infant's happy prospects by whatever magic powers they ascribed to a name expressing this connection. Nevertheless, the sudden introduction of "Shabbetai" during the Exile, as well as the frequency of its use (if the proportion of 5:70 is more than accidental, it would indicate that every other Jewish boy born on a Sabbath was so named) reveals at least strong parental convictions that a constant reminder of this birthday would prove advantageous to their child. This practice was, moreover, in sharp contrast to the Babylonians, whom the birth of the child on the seventh, the "evil day," must have filled with dismal forebodings. Thus by a curious historical irony, the Jews who originally, though indirectly, had derived the idea of a seven-day week from Babylonia, now singled out the Sabbath as the chief distinction between themselves and their Babylonian neighbors.[22]

In Egypt the name Haggai seems to have been most popular. In the Elephantine papyri we find no less than eleven Haggais, sons of different fathers, in addition to several Haggais without a patronymic. There were also four different Shabbetais and a woman Shabbetit.[23] It appears in general that the Jews in Elephantine, living in greater seclusion than their Babylonian coreligionists, retained to a much greater extent both their Aramaic names and the Aramaic language. True, we also find some Egyptian, Babylonian, and Persian names among the Elephantine soldiers, especially in the higher ranks. But apart from the possibility that the Jewish soldiers had some non-Jewish commanders, we may assume that they were joined, from time to time, by outsiders, by Jews coming from other parts of Egypt or the empire. For instance, one of the soldiers, Dargman by name, came from the extreme northeast, from Khivar. On conversion to Judaism, Egyptians may have retained their Egyptian names, although giving Hebrew names to their children. This would explain the reference in these records to men with Hebrew names and Egyptian patronymics.

It is characteristic, however, that this whole question of names found no expression whatever in the literary documents of the age. As in previous centuries, Israelites and Jews seem to have been much more open to influence from Babylonia, kindred in race and tongue, than from Egypt. It is truly amazing how comparatively slight Egyptian influence was, even in the period of Egypt's domination over Palestine, or when the Jews actually lived in the blessed "garden of the Lord." [24]

DIASPORA COMMUNITY

This onomastic problem is, of course, of derivative and heuristic rather than fundamental importance, although it illustrates the extent to which at the very threshold of the Jewish dispersion, as in all subsequent centuries, names offer a most significant key to the ascertainment of basic historic facts.[25] Much graver questions arose when the Jews began to adjust themselves to the new environmental conditions. A most interesting program for this adjustment was framed at home by the great Palestinian prophet who was continually announcing the approaching downfall. In the period between the deportation of Jehoiachin and that of Zedekiah,

Jeremiah, who maintained close contacts with the developments abroad, had sent to the captives in Babylon his famous letter containing a remarkable expression of his ideas of universalism and peace:

Build ye houses, and dwell in them; and plant gardens, and eat the fruit of them; take ye wives, and beget sons and daughters; and take wives for your sons, and give your daughters to husbands, that they may bear sons and daughters; and· multiply ye there, and be not diminished. And seek the peace of the city [the Septuagint reads: "of the land"] whither I have caused you to be carried away captive, and pray unto the Lord for it; for in the peace thereof shall ye have peace" [Jer. 29:5–7].

Followed literally, such a line of conduct might have led to utter extinction. Something more constructive had to be evolved to put into practice the old theories of the national survival of the Jews without territory. There arose among them another great prophet, Ezekiel, also a Palestinian, who was carried off as a prisoner in one of these deportations, or possibly even emigrated voluntarily about 592. Under his intellectual leadership the elders of the Jewish people in Babylonia tried to establish an entirely new system of life whereby they might retain their identity in the foreign land. While Jewish nationality might have survived, emancipated from the ordinary type of state, it could not last for any length of time without some substitute. Thoughtful leaders saw that an artificial state must be created, an organization to embrace all Jews, to keep them united, to supply specific forms of national and religious expression and to furnish guidance in emergencies.

Erection of new temples where Jews could perform sacrifices to their God in the Palestinian form of worship must have seemed the most natural solution. Indeed, the exiles could invoke the prophecy that "in that day shall there be an altar to the Lord in the midst of the land of Egypt." Ezekiel objected, however. He who so fondly remembered every detail of Solomon's Temple that, in one of his prophecies, he was able to describe its gates from memory in a most graphic manner (40:6 ff.; they evidently bore close resemblance to other gates erected by that king and recently unearthed at Megiddo), could not endure the idea of its duplication in the land of exile.[26]

When it came to the test, therefore, Babylonian Jewry decided against the building of a new temple. Cattle raised in a foreign land, crops sprung from foreign soil, could scarcely appear an agreeable sacrifice to the Lord. Moreover, the sacrificial temple should, whatever the circumstances, be restricted to Jerusalem. This limitation did not arise out of the traditional prophetic minimizing of the Temple and sacrifices, in comparison to the duties of the heart. It was rather an echo of the Deuteronomic desecration of the Palestinian *bamot* and centralization of the worship in Jerusalem. The longer the Jews were separated from their country, the more they idealized Jerusalem and its Temple, and precisely therefore they rejected the practice of sacrificial worship on any other earthly spot.

On the other hand, there was felt the necessity of some sort of divine worship. The leaders of Babylonian Jewry found an answer in prayer. This was no artificial substitute, no radical departure from previous institutions. Prayer as a mode of worship is found among all early religions, and it played a great part during Israel's sojourn in Palestine. While not competing with the sacrifices, it effectively supplemented them. The language of the prayer of Hannah may be of much later date than its setting; there is no historical difficulty in assuming that she, or any other woman of her position and time, might seek to offer prayers at the entrance of the Lord's sanctuary. The existence of a considerable number of preëxilic psalms is another proof that hymns accompanied sacrificial worship in the Temple itself. Whether or not many psalms (for example, 93–100) served as ritual enthronement hymns highlighting the New Year's celebrations at the Temple, they well illustrate the use of the spoken word in the priestly ceremonial. The existence of Temple musicians in Israelitic as well as Canaanite Palestine also presupposes extensive use of hymns and prayers set to music. If as far back as the nineteenth century B.C.E. Semitic craftsmen arriving in Egypt are depicted as carrying with them musical instruments and if, according to Sennacherib's boast, "male and female musicians he [Hezekiah] sent after me to Nineveh," we must assume extensive nonsacrificial worship in preëxilic Palestine.[27]

Frequent fast days in national or local emergencies served as occasions for communal gatherings, of which the keynote seems to have been not sacrifices but prayers for rain, the extermination of locusts, the abatement of a pestilence, the warding off of a threatened invasion, or any other general need of the moment. Deeply religious men among the priests, prophets, and laymen—and in a country and period which could produce the great preëxilic prophets these must have been fairly numerous—undoubtedly communed with their God through some kind of devout utterances. The occasional condemnation, by such prophets as Hosea or Isaiah, of these convocations on new moons and Sabbaths was directed against prayer even less than against animal sacrifices. They merely denounced their insincerity and lack of inwardness. "And when ye spread forth your hands," Isaiah thundered, "I will hide Mine eyes from you; yea, when ye make many prayers, I will not hear; your hands are full of blood" (1:15; cf. Hosea 7:14; Jer. 14:11–12).

Of course, these prayers had not yet been standardized. Each said what was in his or her heart, in words flowing freely from the lips or perhaps not even spoken aloud. Under conditions of Exile, however, prayer came to the fore as the substitute for sacrifice. "So will we render for bullocks the offering of our lips" became the watchword of the age. The first wave of returning exiles included a professional group of "two hundred singing men and singing women." It is characteristic that here again language followed the new practice. The Arabic word 'atar means "to offer." In the Hebrew of the period, when it seems to be occurring more frequently, it received the meaning of "prayer." [28]

In connection with prayer arose another, perhaps even more important institution. If the Jews, far from their native towns and villages, were to have any communal life, it was imperative, everyone felt, that they organize communities of a new order. That unique organism, the Jewish community, thus came into being as the germ of all future communal life in the dispersion. First there were simply periodic gatherings of all the members of a community. On the Sabbath and Jewish festivals, particularly, the exiles assembled to voice longings for the homeland, to offer prayers, to discuss the problems of life in strange surroundings, and sometimes to take up political and social questions of general interest.[29]

The new Jewish community necessarily embodied in general the ethnic rather than the territorial principle. Of course, there were exceptions. As in later ages, some groups organized on the basis of common Palestinian territorial origin. The tendency of such groups to maintain their original allegiance was so strong that half a century later, in the days of Zerubbabel, almost all of them remained distinguishable. Those 642 participants in the return who could not be thus classified were under suspicion as to "whether they were of Israel" (Neh. 7:61 and Ezra 2:59), or were proselytes or descendants of proselytes who had joined the Jewish community in Babylonia.

Scattered widely throughout the Diaspora, however, and increasingly involved in economic and social intercourse with Jews of other regional origin, these *Landsmannschaften* gradually lost their hold. There came to the fore another principle, more essentially ethnic in nature, and hence appropriate for a deterritorialized people. The family and the clan again became the prime cohesive force in Jewish life. Because of their determination to maintain their Jewishness, families and even whole clans were inclined to cling together. After all, the chief boast was their common descent from Abraham, Isaac, and Jacob. Quite naturally each group also took pride in its distinction as the offspring of this or that outstanding priest or leader in ancient Israel. That is why the clan units returning with Zerubbabel were already numerically far stronger than the local units. Several generations later the contingent under Ezra seems to have completely forgotten its diverse local origins, but it staunchly cultivated its family traditions.[30]

These tendencies were strengthened under Persian domination, since the ruling Persian nationality, both under the Achaemenids and under the Sassanians, attached much importance to family distinction. Purity of family was valued in Babylonia as never in Palestine before or after. For centuries the Babylonian Jews kept careful records of all significant family events so that they might be able to prove at any time pure descent from priestly or other distinguished stock. As late as the talmudic age, genealogical accounts (*megillot yuḥasin*) are frequently referred to. They must have been composed on the basis of records often covering a whole millennium. At that late date, at least, Palestine itself acknowledged Babylonia's superiority in this matter.

Out of these family groups came the elders of the community at large, under whose guidance all gathered for religious and communal purposes. Prayers were doubtless said, commemorating those historical events with which Jewish festivals were being increasingly associated, until religious reinterpretation emptied them of their ancient meaning. Psalms, hymns, and other poems may have been sung by the whole community. Those portions of the ancient law which had by that time been, to some extent, canonized, may have been read and discussed (cf. Neh. 8:8). In fact, such congregational needs may have added zest to the collection of older writings which, reflecting the general antiquarian interests of the other contemporary Near Eastern peoples, had found royal promoters in Hezekiah and Josiah. All statements about these public gatherings are made here with considerable diffidence, since little is known about what went on. But it seems certain that they soon gave rise to the institution which became the foundation of Jewish life in the Diaspora—the synagogue.[31]

Everyone felt, however, that this kind of divine worship was only a substitute. Now that the Temple was destroyed and Jerusalem in ruins, the sins and abuses of the dominant classes, to which, indeed, most deportees belonged, were gradually forgotten. And while, it is true, some aristocrats had deprecated the decadence and social inequity of urban civilization with as much fervor as the oppressed themselves, the class as a whole was inclined to condone its own transgressions, easily persuading itself that, however great its or its forefathers' sins, ample expiation had already been made by the suffering of the wars and the Exile. Now the aristocrats began to hope that the wrath of God would soon subside. The people would soon be restored to Palestine. The Temple would be rebuilt and sacrifices would again become the principal means of divine worship. The institution of sacrifice had been frowned upon by the leading prophets of the preëxilic period, not so much as an evil in itself but because it diverted the Israelites from the more essential ethical elements in their religion. But now that it was no longer practiced, sacrifice was praised and exalted. All opposition was silenced in this interval when the Temple and its sacrifices stood as the symbol of independence and freedom, of power and wealth and glory. Finally a prophet himself scolded the returning exiles for being concerned about their homes much more than about the Temple. Although evincing little interest in the type of sacrifices to be offered, he exhorted his countrymen, "Go up to the hill-country, and bring wood, and build the house; and I will take pleasure in it, and I will be glorified, saith the Lord" (Haggai 1:4, 8).

Not that the memory of the old prophetic denunciations was completely lost. A vocal minority, at least among those who grew up in Palestine itself, seems to have persisted in rejecting the entire traditional system of sacrifices. Extremists like the Second Isaiah could denounce the very erection of the Temple and declare that "he that killeth an ox is as if he slew a man; he that sacrifices a lamb, as if he broke a dog's neck; he that offereth a meal-offering as if he offered swine's blood; he that maketh a memorial-offering of frankincense, as if he blessed an idol." Whether or not the reference to the dog's neck betrays, as has been suggested, the impact of the Parsees' high regard for dogs and their general rejection of sacrifices, it is remarkable that even the meal-offering (minḥah) is specifically repudiated here on a par with all other sacrifices. The same prophet, however, or some one of his followers, predicted the return of all Jews to the holy mountain "as the children of Israel bring their offering in a clean vessel [hence no animals] into the house of the Lord." More emphatically, Malachi, facing a reconstructed temple, and also deprecating the "dung of your sacrifices," delighted in the "pure oblations" (minḥah ṭehorah) offered by believers in many lands, as well as in their prayers of repentance. Opposition to animal sacrifices, however moderate, may also account for the increased use of incense in the Jewish sanctuary. Another echo of the inner struggles and mixed feelings generated by this conflict is still preserved in Psalm 51, if indeed its last verses are not a later interpolation. Ascribing his beautiful prayer to David after the affair with Bathsheba, the author made the repentant king pray, "O Lord, open Thou my lips; and my mouth shall declare Thy praise. For Thou delightest not in sacrifice. . . . The sacrifices of God are a broken spirit. . . ." But he immediately added: "Build Thou the walls of Jerusalem. Then wilt Thou delight in the sacrifices of righteousness, in burnt-offering and whole offering." It is this concluding passage, rather than the preceding peroration, which mirrors accurately the prevailing attitude among the returning exiles.[32]

Even without this yearning for the restoration of an idealized past, however, animal sacrifices would have been the logical outcome of the religious needs of the exilic society. We have seen that the sacrifices in the nomadic age were not so much the remnant of prehistoric ancestor worship as an appropriate expression of the religious needs of a clan society, symbolizing the ideal blood relationship between the members of the various clans, or the people and their God. As the family in the Babylonian Exile became again the basic social element, it naturally tended, in accordance with the religious ways of the age, to restore the apposite symbol. And what could appeal more to a crushed generation, living under the shadow of sin and longing for repentance, than the expiatory sacrifice, now stressed above all others, a sacrifice which even warded off the consequences of sins committed unawares?

Such was the force of tradition, however, strengthened by the extravagant sanctification of Jerusalem, that this supreme symbol of the communion between Israel and God was reserved for the Holy City. Thus their imagination forever linked the "ethnic" practice of animal sacrifice with the "territorial" characteristics of the Temple in what was, fundamentally considered, an artificial synthesis. But after all, did not the extremely pro-Palestinian Deuteronomic school itself put into King Solomon's prayer at the dedication of the Temple the utterance, "Behold, heaven and the heaven of heavens cannot contain Thee; how much less this house that I have builded" (I Kings 8:27)? How much more imaginary had this territory now become during the long sojourn in Babylonia!

Elephantine Jewry knew no such restraints. Perhaps it consisted mainly of descendants of emigrants who had left Palestine before the Deuteronomic reformation. Perhaps it interpreted the prohibition of altars outside of Jerusalem as referring to Palestine's countryside only. Did not a Palestinian prophet himself soon glory in the universal worship of the Jewish God among the nations and without compunctions emphasize that "in every place offerings are presented unto My name, even pure oblations" (Mal. 1:11)? In any case, these soldiers erected a large and costly temple modeled on the sanctuary at Jerusalem.

The more rooted the colonists became in their new environment, the more strongly there germinated within them the seeds of the ancient "popular religion." This revival signified itself not only in their localized worship, but in the belief in several deities secondary to, or more probably identical with, their Jewish God. Anticipating their Hellenistic successors, who unhesitatingly identified their own "Lord of hosts" (ṣaba'ot), with the Near Eastern deity Sabbazius, the Elephantine soldiers apparently did not resist the equation of their own divine name with such widespread divine appellations as 'Anat and Bethel. As soldiers they understandably appealed frequently to their "Lord of Hosts," although for some reason they usually replaced the Tetragrammaton by the shorter form, spelled YHW or YHH. But they also readily invoked the old Canaanite goddess, 'Anat, known to us from many Ugaritic poems, and called her 'Anati or even 'Anat-Yahu, meaning 'Anat is (rather than belongs to) Yahu. More frequently they referred to the deity Bethel which, perhaps mentioned already by Amos, seems to have found worshipful followers in many countries of western Asia from the seventh to the fourth centuries. Stimulated also by the sudden revival in the early sixth century of the Palestinian city of Bethel, which is attested by recent excavations, they invoked the name of that deity in such noteworthy syncretistic combinations as Harambethel, Ashimbethel, and even 'Anatbethel.[33]

Not for a moment, however, did the Elephantine Jews consider themselves worshipers of more than one God. Like their predecessors among the followers of the Israelitic "popular religion" and their Hellenistic successors they seem to have seen no harm in such a play on names. For the most part connected with West Asiatic, rather than Egyptian divine appellations, these combinations did not even endanger their ritualistic segregation from their Egyptian neighbors. The latter had long been living examples of how one could effectively combine great latitude in theophorus nomenclature with extreme ritualistic isolationism.[34]

When Cambyses conquered Egypt in 525, the Jewish temple had already been in Elephantine for some time and it now shared the protection he extended to all non-Egyptian creeds. It was only natural that animal sacrifices, along with other offerings, should be the signal element of worship. The Elephantine priests were so ignorant of their deviation from the prevailing Babylonian and Palestinian principles that, when their temple was destroyed by the Egyptians in 411, they turned for help to the high priest in Jerusalem. The Palestinian authorities left their petition unanswered. Even three years later when the southern colonists, supported by the Samaritans, obtained from Judaea's Persian governor Bagohi permission to rebuild their temple, only the right to "offer the meal-offering and incense" was included. No mention is made of animal sacrifices. This conscious omission doubtless was, in part, the result of the Judaean insistence that this worship be limited to Jerusalem only.[35]

STIMULI OF PERSIAN IMPERIALISM

Persia's imperial policy was favorable inasmuch as it encouraged preservation of the national mores amongst all subject peoples. From the outset the Persian chancery willingly corresponded in Aramaic with the various provinces of western Asia. These friendly relations went so far as to make an outsider believe that "of all men the Persians most welcome foreign customs" (Herodotus I, 135). With respect to Judaism amicable understanding was further facilitated by the superficial similarity in religious approaches. No wonder the theocracy in Jerusalem was given more liberty of action than were, for instance, the chief priests in the sanctuaries of Asia Minor in regard to the inner life of their respective coreligionists.

Within a decade of his conquest Cyrus ordered the rebuilding of the Temple at government expense and the restoration to it of the treasures removed by Nebukadrezzar. Darius I and Artaxerxes I or II enjoined the provincial governors of Syria to defray part of the expenses of the sacrificial worship. The latter king also ordained "that touching any of the priests and Levites, the singers, porters, Nethinim, or servants of this house of God, it shall not be lawful to impose tribute, impost, or toll, upon them." The high priests were given the right of independently taxing Palestinian Jewry and even of coining their own money. Several Hebrew coins of the fourth century bearing the legend *Yahud* (Judaea) and one fifth-century Hebrew shekel are still extant to testify to this semi-sovereign right of the Jewish hierarchy. Even the temporary resistance of the Persian authorities to the erection of a wall around Jerusalem arose only from the intrigues of Judaea's neighbors and from the fact that the Persians did not surround their own cities by walls, contenting themselves with strong citadels.[36]

Jewish leaders gladly reciprocated with tokens of friendliness. In addressing Persian officials, they readily designated their own God as the "God of Heavens," making him appear almost identical with the Persian Ahuramazda. In Palestine, Elephantine and, in all probability, all over the empire the Jews introduced special prayers for the "life of the king and of his sons." Many new king's psalms were composed in adoration of the monarch of Susa. Deutero-Isaiah must have shocked even some of his contemporaries when he exalted Cyrus as "My shepherd" and the Lord's "anointed . . . whose right hand I have holden." [37]

Not all Jews reacted with equal enthusiasm. Many dreamed of the restoration of the Davidic monarchy and looked forward to some major international disturbance which would offer them the opportunity of shaking off Persian overlordship. Such an opportunity seemed to offer itself when, after Cambyses' death, revolts broke out throughout the empire. When the new king, Darius I, emerged victorious in 522, Haggai and Zechariah toned down their revolutionary preachment, but insurrectionary movements persisted underground. They reappeared on the surface whenever conditions seemed more auspicious. Characteristically even official Jewish leadership down to Nehemiah continued to compute its chronology not on the basis of the regular year beginning on Nisan 1, but on that of the regnal years of the former kings of Judah.[38]

The great personal interest taken by the Persian kings in the affairs of the Jewish people would therefore be doubly hard to understand, had not the ever-growing Jewish Diaspora been a really influential segment of the population. Darius II's memorable decree of 419 which, apparently addressed to all the Jewish communities in the empire, ordered them to observe strictly the Feast of Unleavened Bread, cannot be explained merely as the result of a successful intrigue on the part of a Jewish courtier. Much rather we have here the first clear manifestation of a basic phenomenon in the entire history of the Jewish people. We shall see later that Diaspora Jewry almost invariably prospered most in heterogeneous empires, whereas ethnically and religiously homogeneous nations often proved extremely intolerant to it. Even in Achaemenid Persia the progressive assimilation of the various racial and religious groups endowed with some measure of realism Haman's purported denunciations of Jewish separatism. Perhaps in connection with certain rebellious movements among the Jews, this deterioration of Persian-Jewish relations found telling expression when, about 350 B.C.E. on the eve of the empire's downfall, Artaxerxes III Ochus forcibly deported many Jews to the inhospitable region of Hyrcania, on the Caspian Sea.[39]

Persia's earlier friendly policy facilitated the task of the Jewish teachers in adjusting the religious life of the Diaspora to the new environment. But one must not exaggerate, as Meyer did, by asserting, on this score, that postexilic Judaism was altogether created "in the name of the Persian king and on the strength of the authority of his empire. The effects of the Achaemenid Empire thus extend directly to our day with a power equalled by few contemporary phenomena." [40] This generalization is analogous to assuming that German neo-orthodoxy of the nineteenth century was the creation of the Prussian or Frankfort governments which, for a time, actually tried to discourage all reforming tendencies among their Jewish subjects. Many other local theocracies in Asia Minor, Egypt, and even Babylonia were allowed by Cyrus or Darius to flourish under the strong arm of the "king of kings." But how easily were they, and most of what they stood for, swept away by the onslaughts of Hellenism! In fact, all the main lines of development in Jewry under the domination of Persia are clearly discernible in the preceding period. Judaism was by that time too strong and self-assertive an entity to be totally suppressed, even if a Persian king had attempted to do so, as reported in the book of Esther. Persian tolerance, indeed, only opened the road for a peaceful and undisturbed concentration on their religious problems for those Jews who chose to be loyal to their heritage of centuries.

PIONEER COMMUNITY

On the whole, the Jewish people may be said to have very well stood the test of Exile, the most momentous and critical in its entire history. Its prophetic religion had itself become a tremendous social force and, coupled with a living ethnic organism, not only influenced Jewish society in its turn, but in fact saved it from threatened extinction. Its persistence in the face of adversity must have impressed even the conquerors. That is why Amel-Marduk embarked upon a policy of pacifying it and perhaps even thought of restoring it to its mother country. This design, possibly entertained also by Nabonidus from his imperial residence in neighboring Teima, was soon carried into effect by the great empire builders of Persia.

Persistence was combined with great open-mindedness and pliability, however. This semirural population, hailing from hundreds of little towns and villages, adjusted itself rapidly to the ever-quickening tempo of life in the Near East's leading metropolises. A people of farmers and petty artisans entered the highest echelons of Babylonia's trade and commerce. Perhaps because of their strong religious biases the exiles may have helped secularize banking and thus pioneered on the uncharted seas of private monetary transactions. In this way they may have helped increase many times over the circulation of the limited cash resources of the successive empires. Before long some of their leaders also partook of the ramified political activities at the royal court of Susa.

Although thus well integrated in the imperial fabric, the Jews nevertheless retained their cultural and religious identity to such an extent as to arouse the ire of such "hundred percenters" as Haman. Facing an unprecedented situation, they also took unprecedented heroic measures. Their decision, particularly, not to build a temple on foreign soil, forced them to establish a new, revolutionary institution: a house of worship dedicated to prayer without sacrificial offerings. Today when worshipers in the Western world attend churches or mosques as well as synagogues, it is difficult for us to imagine how deeply upsetting the abandonment of sacrifices everywhere outside a single specified locality must have been to Ezekiel's Gentile as well as Jewish contemporaries. Precisely because this innovation was introduced by persons of known religious piety and rigid adherence to ritualistic practice, and because it sprang, almost unwittingly, from highest appreciation, indeed idealization of sacrificial worship, it seems to have been accepted without too much resistance by generations which did not quite realize the synagogue's revolutionary implications. Around the synagogue began to be grouped other communal institutions which, individually resembling similar establishments among other more or less temporary, "foreign" groupings, in their totality formed the nuclei for the new Diaspora community, equally unprecedented in both quality and endurance.

Such new forms of communal coöperation also called for a new rationale. Combined with the general perplexities of life on foreign soil and the ensuing deep menace to Jewish survival, they forced the exilic and postexilic leaders to delve deeper and deeper into the mysteries of Jewish and human destinies. For sheer self-preservation hearkening back to the experiences and traditions of the ancestors in the Holy Land, they had to submit them to careful review and readjustment in the light of novel conditions. Out of this painful striving and searching of the soul emerged the more definitive formulation of biblical Judaism.

V

RETHINKING FUNDAMENTALS

SUFFERINGS during the first years of Exile and unrelenting external pressures ever after forged the unity of the people. Gone were the deep inner dissensions which had characterized the public life of both Samaria and Jerusalem before their downfall. No longer did the farmer resent the landlord, the small craftsman the city patrician, and all of them the king and his entourage. No longer did messenger after messenger of the Lord appear condemning the shortcomings of Jewish civilization, since most of the vices which had to be denounced were obviously not of Jewish making. On the contrary, "Comfort ye, comfort ye, My people" (Isa. 40:1) became the watchword of the age.

The new sense of unity permeated particularly the exilic community around Babel and Nippur. Recruited to a large extent from the previously dominant classes of landowners and priests, this community was not only prone to ponder over the instability of all human affairs and its religious meaning, but also to hope that its sins had been entirely forgiven. Its leaders were quick to realize that preaching courage and upholding the morale of the people were needed now far more than chastening. They did everything they could to instill confidence in Israel's survival against all rational odds and its ultimate victory at the "end of days."

In the first years after the destruction, the authors of Lamentations still joined the old prophetic chorus in blaming that calamity on Israel's guilt alone. However, these traditional self-accusations soon went out of fashion. Ezekiel, especially, eventually abandoned the idea that God's vengeance (*neqamah*) was directed principally against the people of his covenant. On the contrary, the mighty vengeance, which this extremist among the prophets fanatically discerned in God, was to be spent upon the heathen nations. In visions of tremendous intensity often hovering on the brink of madness, which earned him the designation of "father of apocalyptic," Ezekiel prophesied the revival of the dry bones of "the whole house of Israel" and proclaimed the Lord's determination, "Behold, I will open your graves and cause you to come up out of your graves, O My people; and I will bring you into the land of Israel." [1]

NEW TIDINGS

From these premises evolved other fundamental teachings. Stimulated by the momentous international transformations concomitant with the rise of Persia, Deutero-Isaiah, in particular, had deep premonitions of an emergent new order. "I have announced unto thee new things from this time" became a keynote of many of his prophetic messages. "For behold," he exultantly proclaimed in the name of the Lord, "I create new heavens and a new earth; and the former things will not be remembered, nor come into mind." At the same time, he insisted upon historic continuity. The things to come, he declared time and again, were to be but the realization of "former things," long foretold by God's genuine messengers. "I have declared the former things from of old . . . and they came to pass." In fact, he constantly taunted the heathen nations for their inability to learn in advance the shape of things to come. That is why he constantly exhorted resurrected Israel to sing a "new song" unto the Lord. But this song was to be only a new elaboration and expansion of truths long accepted by the chosen few among their sinful ancestors.[2]

Many minds among the Jews of the Babylonian dispersion, however, were deeply perturbed over this evil heritage of ages. Inured for centuries to the idea of communal responsibility, they not only believed that their exile as such was merely a punishment for the sins of their forefathers, but also feared that they and their descendants were going to suffer the consequences for yet untold generations. Beginning with Ezekiel, therefore, exilic leadership considered it incumbent upon itself to allay these fears. While constantly reminding his compatriots, as in the prophecy cited above, that their own welfare was tied up with the revival of the dry bones of the whole nation, Ezekiel nevertheless reassured them that God would not avenge the sins of the fathers on the sons and grandsons, as they had been accustomed to believe. Only "the soul that sinneth, it shall die" (Ez. 18:20).

Decline of corporate responsibility did not involve, however, the elimination of the sense of corporate personality (to use Henry Wheeler Robinson's felicitous term). In fact, until the present day Orthodox Jewry believes that "Israelites are responsible for one another." It also constantly invokes the "merit of the fathers" (*zekhut abot*) in its pleas for divine mercy and, on a more popular level, lends credence to the anonymous existence in each generation of thirty-six pious men whose unpublicized good deeds redeem their less deserving contemporaries. This conviction of mutual responsibility, deeply ingrained by all previous historic experience, was reinforced by the realities of exilic life, when Jews must often have suffered from the general penchant for blaming a whole minority for the misdeeds of any member. Was not a typical Jew-baiter like Haman supposed to have refused to take revenge on Mordecai alone, but rather to have "sought to destroy all the Jews . . . the people of Mordecai" (Esther, 3:6)? Such generalization must have been particularly common under the Persians who, according to F. von Spiegel, inflicted punishments on the whole family of a convicted criminal. But the people's conscience now rebelled against attributing such injustice to God himself.[3]

Individual retribution, however, had little to do with the individual's nearness to his Creator—the basic thought in the prophecy of Jeremiah. Both emphases obviously have a common origin in the disintegration of the clan under the kings and the ensuing decline of corporate responsibility. Ezekiel's individualism is surely a theological extension of the legal principle that every person should be himself responsible for his actions, a principle already enunciated in Deuteronomy, "The fathers shall not be put to death for the children, neither shall the children be put to death for the fathers; every man shall be put to death for his own sin" (24:16). In its logical fulfillment, this exaltation of personal responsibility, far from bringing the individual nearer to God, as with Jeremiah, involved a decided detachment of God from the world of man.

Certainly, the correlation between the individual's sin and his punishment was daily contradicted by the facts of life. How many truly pious irreproachable Jews, devoutly adhering to every word of God's commandments, were carried off into the Exile and "punished" direly? As in other periods of great crisis the problem of theodicy deeply agitated the minds of men. The ancient narrator of the destruction of Sodom and Gomorrah had already attributed to Abraham the characteristic query, "Shall not the Judge of all the earth do justly?" (Gen. 18:25.) Among the exilic and postexilic Jews the combination of the national catastrophe and the decline in corporate responsibility created an insistent quest for some newer, more satisfactory answers. The classic debate between Job's new outlook on the nexus between sin and retribution and his friends' defense of the traditional view of corporate responsibility has remained the unsurpassed expression of this perennial conflict.[4]

Remarkably, not even the author of Job suggests the existence of a world to come or future resurrection as a solution for the agonizing perplexities of his hero. At the same time, there were enough eschatological ingredients in the belief and ritual of even the pre-Israelitic population of Palestine to prepare the ground out of which, under the new conditions of the Hellenistic period, was to arise the ramified doctrine of the Hereafter. While living in Egypt the early Hebrews must have become acquainted with the Egyptian teachings of continued existence after death. They must have seen such mortuary art as was erected in Beth-shan under the nineteenth dynasty and the Phoenician sarcophagi imitating these Egyptian prototypes. There may even have been some connection between the Canaanite fertility cults, with their annual rebirth of various nature deities, and the belief in human resurrection. But these very conceptions underlying the despised heathen rituals may have induced the Old Testament writers, without rejecting the Hereafter altogether, to stress this-worldly rewards, at least so long as Egypto-Canaanite influences were considered dangerous. Egyptian examples had shown, however, that such an emphasis upon this-worldly retribution was not inconsistent with a belief in reward and punishment after death as well. For this reason the various biblical passages of uncertain date hinting at a Hebrew belief in immortality or resurrection need not all be later interpolations. This is particularly true in the case of the much-debated prophecy, "Thy dead shall live, my dead bodies shall arise" (Isa. 26:19). Not until the new crisis of the Maccabean age, however, were the Jewish theologians prepared to state clearly their belief in resurrection and to connect it with the doctrine of rewards for the sufferings of the just in this world.[5]

As Judaism thus was not yet ready to emphasize reward and punishment after death, only one explanation remained: God's wish is inscrutable, his ways unknown, too different from those of men. "For my thoughts are not your thoughts, neither are your ways My ways, saith the Lord." Such a belief, reiterated by Deutero-Isaiah, led straightway to God's transcendence, now emphatically reaffirmed in a degree far beyond the intent of the older prophets. True, in remarkable visions pregnant with fateful consequences for the entire history of mystic thought, Ezekiel himself elaborated the old concept of "the Lord of hosts, who sitteth upon the cherubim" and described in detail the divine "chariot." Nevertheless, his and Deutero-Isaiah's God had become so remote from the grasp of human reason that everything He does is for a higher purpose beyond the possibility of human understanding. God does nothing simply for the benefit of man or of the Jewish people. Everything is an assertion of God's own glory, that His name should be made known to all mankind.[6]

This conviction necessarily gave rise to other changes in theological fundamentals. Earlier prophets had repeatedly stated that the selection of Israel as a "chosen people" multiplied rather than lessened its duties. But nowhere had so vigorous a rejection of Israel's claim to special treatment been made as in Chapter 20 of Ezekiel. No other Israelitic prophet so deeply despised all men, not excluding his own people, as to insist that

because they had not executed Mine ordinances, but had rejected My statutes and had profaned My sabbaths and their eyes were after their fathers' idols. Wherefore I gave them also statutes that were not good, and ordinances whereby they should not live. And I polluted them in their own gifts, in that they set apart all that openeth the womb, that I might destroy them to the end, that they might know that I am the Lord [20:24–26].

After having reached the idea of individual responsibility with that of the complementary transcendence of God, it was manifestly imperative that this seeming antinomy should find resolution in increased exaltation of God's holiness. Not every transcendent God necessarily assumes the quality of holiness, that *mysterium tremendum et fascinosum*. This attribute could arise only from the juxtaposition in God of transcendence with a moral character. Being holy in an absolute sense, such a God naturally demands holiness in the people which he chose to be holy. The holiness of God, first discerned by Isaiah, now became, through Ezekiel and Deutero-Isaiah, the corner stone of Jewish theology.[7]

Belief in God's transcendence and absolute holiness raised many problems other than that of theodicy. The name Yahweh itself, the holy Tetragrammaton, began to inspire awe. The postexilic writers increasingly refrained from using it, preferring substitute designations. The thinkers of this age were, on the whole, not concerned with the problem which later occupied some of the best minds, namely: Why did this holy and perfect God create so imperfect a world? But a sense of its insistence can be seen, for example, in the story of creation, as narrated by the priestly redactor. For him it was "the spirit of God" that had hovered over the face of the waters.

and when he was through, "God saw everything that He had made, and behold, it was very good." This optimistic approval of existing realities was immediately combined, however, with speculations about the interrelated origins of sin and death. Forever after, and particularly after the revelation on Sinai, added the forceful Deuteronomic writer, God had set before them the alternatives of "life and good, and death and evil. . . . Therefore choose life." [8]

In these biblical speculations on the ultimate meaning of life and good, in this new intensity of interest in the origins of the world, death, and evil, one may detect the new, broadened outlook. It is evident also in Deutero-Isaiah's reflections on God's power over nature and the cosmic meaning of Israel's deliverance. But there was another, even more immediate question: How can such a transcendent God communicate his will to man? Reluctantly a theory of intermediaries was adopted. Old Israelitic myths about God's angels, as messengers of his will, were utilized. Ancient Canaanite, Chaldaean, and later Persian, influences were also present. Finally Satan appeared, still merely an instrument in God's hand, but, already in the world outlook of Zechariah, the Chronicler and the redactor of Job, the great antagonist of man in the court of their common Creator. No more characteristic example could be adduced than the report of the same event, namely, the census taken by David as given by the naïve narrator of the second book of Samuel and by the theological doctrinaire in the book of Chronicles. The former says, "And again the anger of the Lord was kindled against Israel, and he moved David against them, saying: 'Go number Israel and Judah' " (II Sam. 24:1); while the Chronicler has it, "And Satan stood up against Israel, and moved David to number Israel" (I Chron. 21:1). Spirits of all sorts, angels and demons, soon began to fill the world of the ever more theologically and mystically minded Jew.

Because of the traditional opposition to magic and sorcery there is no evidence that early postexilic Jews tried to manipulate these demonic powers for their private purposes. Mowinckel's long-popular interpretation of many psalms directed against "workers of iniquity" as magic texts whose recitation was intended to cast off spells of wicked sorcerers is shared by few scholars today. Whatever incantations and other magical texts have come down to us from that region and period were evidently written by non-Jews, speaking either Aramaic or a Phoenician-Hebrew dialect. But to the ordinary Jew, and increasingly also to his leaders, God's intervention often appeared necessary to counteract the menace of these powers of darkness and of those wicked men who made use of their services. Of course God, who was also their master and ultimate creator, would usually intervene through his other intermediaries, the angels of light and goodness.[9]

A transcendent God is also to be regarded, to an even greater degree, as the one God of all mankind. In inscrutable ways, He alone created this imperfect world filled with evil and misery. Evidently controverting Zoroastrian dualism, Deutero-Isaiah taught, "I form the light and create darkness; I make peace and create evil, I am the Lord that doeth all these things." This one God of the whole universe has, for his own good reasons, selected Israel to be, like himself, holy. But as Israel cannot expect to understand the aims of God, so it cannot choose its own mode of holiness. Therefore, it must render implicit obedience to the commands which the "Holy Spirit" (or the transcendent God himself) had revealed to Moses in the days of old.[10]

IMPACT OF THE LAW

Thus all forces united to direct the Jewish people toward the observance of its law. A people in Exile, away from its own country, needs the law even more than a people dwelling on its own soil. If the Jews were not to give up their religious identity as a minority among the other nations, they must have laid out for them a definite line of conduct, for each one of them and for all together, which would regulate their life beyond personal whims. Only divine law could be thus supreme. At the same time, they reasoned, it is possible that God revealed only a few fundamentals, leaving the detailed application to those especially qualified to serve him.

Even before the destruction of the Temple, the Torah had started to become more than mere priestly counsel based on oracles offered to individuals in a sanctuary. It became the whole ancestral wisdom in its application to life. More and more in times of the later prophets we hear of some who knew the Torah better than others and taught it to their fellow men. The centralization of worship in Jerusalem after Josiah's reform forced the provincial priests to look for services they might render the community in lieu of the performing of sacrifices and other functions at the now-desecrated sanctuaries. Thus they concentrated, more than ever before, on advising their people concerning the commands of the Law. The further progress of the urbanization and the commercialization of the people after 586 enabled more and more Jews to take an interest in the world of letters. Thus the lay intelligentsia also steadily increased in numbers.

It seems that even before the destruction of the Temple there were in Palestine, and particularly in Jerusalem, regular schools of wisdom. Although law was not the exclusive subject of such instruction, it was given a prominent place along with the philosophical attitudes to life and practical wisdom, so necessary for a successful career in the growingly complex world. The great proverbial literature, apparently the literary crystallization of the teaching in these schools, clearly reflects the great reverence of these wise schoolmen for the Torah. Law and Wisdom also became a source of great pride to patriotic Jews. They seemed to offer the best answer to the ridicule heaped by the Gentiles upon the Jewish people because of its political weakness. Deutero-Isaiah was not alone in exhorting his compatriots, "Hearken unto Me, ye that know righteousness, the people in whose heart is My law; fear ye not the taunt of men, neither be ye dismayed at their revilings," for, unlike the temporary glory of other nations, "My favour shall be for ever" (51:7–8).

Popularization of the Torah, making the widest possible circles of Jews conscious of their religious heritage and familiar with its ritualistic as well as ethical and historical contents, became a major national preoccupation. The Torah, and often indistinguishably blended with it, the more secular aspects of Wisdom, now went out into the streets to appeal to the masses. Even in the ancient days of the Song of Deborah, bards used to circulate among the people, rehearsing "the righteous acts of the Lord." Increasingly, however, during the monarchical and postexilic periods songs and narratives were combined with pearls of practical wisdom and legal maxims. Now Wisdom "calleth at the head of the noisy streets, at the entrances of the gates, in the city, she uttereth her words." Although attributing that far-reaching reform to Jehoshaphat, the Chronicler doubtless also had the conditions of his own day in mind, when he spoke of priests who "having the book of the Law of the Lord with them . . . went about throughout all the cities of Judah and taught among the people." [11]

The transformations accompanying the Exile added stimulus to the study of the law. Legal matter itself expanded in all its ramifications. The example of the Chaldaeans and the Persian Magi, with their elaborate ceremonial law, encouraged extensive regulations concerning the ritual, especially in regard to purity and impurity. Not only did the new conditions produce a more complex system of laws, but the interest of the people as a whole in such matters grew immensely. If the nation was really to become "a nation of priests," then everyone, and not only the priest, had to be an expert in law.

Many branches of the ancient jurisprudence, particularly the ritual and ceremonial, which had for centuries been the exclusive domain of priests, had to be made accessible to secular men of learning. New compilations of law, amplified especially in these sections hitherto esoteric, had to be written down and made available to the public. If ceremonial law was now allotted so much space in the Priestly Code, this was less the effect of the new "legalistic" orientation than of the need for popularization of knowledge, formerly confined to the priestly class. Ezra, whom the Chronicler praises for having "set his heart to seek the law of the Lord, and to do it, and to teach in Israel statutes and ordinances," did not become the "ready scribe in the Law of Moses" *because* he happened to be a priest. In the progress of time the majority of "scribes" belonged to the non-priestly class, finally even becoming (in the struggle between Pharisaism and Sadduceeism) the leaders of the anticlerical group.[12]

Law in its wide ramifications was so necessary in the life of the day that nobody seemed to resent its "yoke." Environmental factors, too, fostered the extension of the religio-legal system into every corner of life, since Babylonians and Persians likewise developed imposing legal structures. Judaism, while pursuing its own ways, effectively intrenched itself within the walls of its law. Even individual Jews felt their own life safer and more sheltered within such walls. Hence the incessant praise showered upon the Torah, which runs through the whole exilic and postexilic literature whether written by ecclesiastics or laymen, psalmists or teachers of wisdom:

The law of the Lord is perfect, restoring the soul; the testimony of the Lord is sure, making wise the simple. The precepts of the Lord are right, rejoicing the heart; the commandment of the Lord is pure, enlightening the eyes. The fear of the Lord is clean, enduring forever; the ordinances of the Lord are true, they are righteous altogether; more to be desired are they, than gold, yea, than much fine gold; sweeter also than honey and the honeycomb. Moreover by them is Thy servant warned; in keeping of them there is great reward [Ps. 19:8–12].

Did the mention of the Law even at this time remind everyone of the great "shepherd" Moses? It is not impossible. At any rate, Deutero-Isaiah seems to refer to Moses more frequently than to any other prophet. But he was not the only one whose mind reverted to the founder. Did not the Exile resemble in so many ways the age of Moses? The people had again become a nation without state and territory. Their life once more combined features of "Egyptian" bondage and "desert" migrations. Again a law was needed by which to live in the Exile, but which would last beyond the Exile into the days of resettlement in the Holy Land. This was not an easy task, nor one destined to be accomplished by one man. Even Ezekiel, trying to establish a law for the anticipated restoration, succeeded in drawing up only a paper constitution. Moses' great achievement of bridging over two epochs by finding a law for both, but also beyond both, had to be repeated now, in greater detail, by a slow evolution and the patient coöperation of many. Still the figure of Moses stood behind the whole work, not only as the originator of the tradition which had come down the ages to serve now as the foundation for further development, but as a direct inspiration and an example for his people, confronted by difficulties essentially similar to his own.

Of course, there were also new regulations or new emphases upon old laws. The Sabbath, for instance, now gained a prominence which it never had had before. To be sure, the institution as such seems to belong to the most ancient of Israel. Its inclusion in the Decalogue, as the only festival, immediately after the commandments pertaining to the unity of God, makes it probable that it reaches back to the Mosaic, if not pre-Mosaic age. The very name "Shabbat," whose etymology has puzzled generations of scholars (even its equation with *shabattu,* the unlucky day of the Babylonians, is more than dubious), betrays its great antiquity. It is possibly older than the Hebrew language itself. The different formulations of the biblical injunctions relating to its observance also seem to indicate its pre-Mosaic origin.[18]

In the progress of Israelitic life under the kings the Sabbath gained rather than lost in vitality. From the beginning, its social element, the idea of rest for the worker, was preëminent. Under the revolutionary currents of the later centuries, with the growth of cities and a free working class, compulsory rest for all hired labor gained the support of the progressive forces. After the national disaster, however, the evanescent social conflict gave way to the national tendency toward segregation and holiness. Instead of a day of rest for recreation, the Sabbath became a day of absolute inactivity, or rather a half-ascetic, half-jocund abstention from work.

Previously the day could be used for making a journey, or occasionally to visit a public market in Jerusalem which was patronized by Gentile traders as well as by Jewish peasants in the neighborhood who were free from work. Now Nehemiah violently objected to such a profanation of the sacred day, the sanctity of which had been extolled with Deutero-Isaiah's inimitable eloquence, "If thou turn away thy foot because of the Sabbath, from pursuing thy business on My holy day; and call the Sabbath a delight, and the holy of the Lord honourable; and shalt honour it, not doing thy wonted ways, nor pursuing thy business, nor speaking thereof, then shalt thou delight thyself in the Lord, and I will make thee to ride upon the high places of the earth." [14]

Of great interest is the motivation given to the Sabbath commandment in the sources, according to the different stages of Jewish social and religious life. In the early Book of the Covenant it is a social institution pure and simple. The Deuteronomist, applying his general philosophy of history, gives it a national-historical slant by putting the Exodus from Egypt into his version of the Decalogue, as the reason for this commandment. The priestly redactor of the exilic age regards it as the symbol of God's own day of rest after his work of creation: "and [the Lord] rested on the seventh day; wherefore the Lord blessed the sabbath day and hallowed it." But whether primarily social or religious, whether rooted in national or cosmic history, the day became the paramount national institution, especially for those in the dispersion. So firmly convinced was Babylonian Jewry of its Sabbath's unique distinction that it refused to accept any designation of the days of the week from its neighbors, while offering little objection to the adoption of the Babylonian names of the months. It continued its resistance under the domination of Persians who soon had names to differentiate each day of the month. Even today, Hebrew-speaking Jews designate the week days only by numbers indicating their relative proximity to the Sabbath. [15]

Legally, too, the Sabbath's sanctity exceeded that of every other holiday except the Day of Atonement, the "Sabbath of Sabbaths." Not even the awe-inspiring features of the New Year's festival, which was soon celebrated as the great annual day of judgment, placed it on a par with the Sabbath in regard to total abstention from work. Nor is this supreme exaltation of the Sabbath altogether surprising. While the other festivals had first to be purged of their "natural" ingredients and vested with a new "historical" meaning, the recurring seventh day of the week was much more artificial, without sufficient justification through either the solar or the lunar calendar. The seven-day week, flowing through the months and years in utter disregard of their natural seasonal variations, thus became the support of Israel's place in history, a symbol around which the scattered members of a vast Diaspora could rally. It was an institution so fundamental that, even in the eyes of the most universalistic prophet, it must first be adopted by the Gentile nations, before God's house "shall be called a house of prayer for all peoples" (Isa. 56:6–7).

This prophecy, incidentally, pointed up another fundamental function of the Sabbath developed by the exilic community, namely, its association with congregational worship. Deutero-Isaiah stressed this association even more strongly in another messianic vision, placed by the redactor as a climactic finale to all his oracles: "And it shall come to pass, that from one new moon to another, and from one sabbath to another, shall all flesh come to worship before Me, saith the Lord" (66:23). Evidently in exilic times the Sabbath had already become the great weekly day for regular prayerful assemblies which it has, ever since, been for Judaism, as well as for Christianity and Islam.

Just as Sabbath observance sharply differentiated between the Jewish people and its pagan neighbors, minute regulation of family life assisted it in the endeavor to concentrate on the ethnic principle, while all around acids of disintegration were attacking its unity. Minority status, steady migrations, apostasy of individuals—all necessitated the erection of dams to stem the tide. Although family legislation dated from preëxilic times, it was now imperative to adapt it to the individual's new social independence. What Jeremiah, Deuteronomy, and Ezekiel had taught about the individual's close relationship to God, or his personal responsibility before God, was supplemented and reinforced in the Wisdom literature and the Psalms.

Restoration of a pure clan society was neither possible nor desirable from the point of view of those who had in mind the unity of all Israel. That is why the Levitical lawgiver retained, at least in theory, the institution of asylum, where a homicide could find protection from the legitimate demands of the dead man's clan. On the other hand, the Deuteronomist felt himself obliged to inflict capital punishment upon a rebellious son, and the legislators of the later period had to go even further in protecting the family against the forces of dissolution. After the Return the leaders encouraged, in particular, the reëstablishment of the allegedly Davidic "priest cities" for the better preservation of the priestly families. While essentially continuing the preëxilic legislation concerning the inheritance of daughters, they also emphasized that all such heiresses must marry into their father's tribe, so that "no inheritance of the children of Israel [should] remove from tribe to tribe." [16]

Here we may also find the reason why legal recognition of the new social status of the Jewish woman was withheld. Apart from their justified suspicions of feminine orthodoxy, the leaders of the community deliberately tried to maintain the supremacy of the husband as a means of strengthening the family bonds. They attempted also to discourage divorce, if not by legal obstacles, at least by moral suasion. Although the old life with its corporate responsibility was gone forever, the new leaders tried at least to maintain the wholeness of the nation, the ideal of the responsibility of all Jews for one another. To effect such social control, the wholeness of the basic unit, the family, had to be preserved intact. Moreover, as Pedersen has pointed out, *shalom* (meaning peace) could psychologically be achieved by a Hebrew only when he lived *shalem*, that is, within such an integrated wholeness.

With this aim in mind the old laws of restraint on sex life were elaborated. In recoil from the orgiastic cults of Baal and Astarte worship, Israelitic law had even in preëxilic times put the generative forces of man under the control of law. More than among other folk, sexual life became regulated, deviations being considered egregious religious sins. This was a contention against nature, but in no other domain have religious conceptions had a more lasting effect upon subsequent generations than in that of Israel's sex morality and in the ensuing sex casuistry. From the beginning the sanctification given to the various forms of religious prostitution was eschewed. The hierodules (*qedeshim* and *qedeshot*), the priestly practitioners of such rites, were totally eliminated from the Temple. Women seem to have found a place in the sanctuaries as musicians and perhaps even as Vestal priestesses of a sort; these functions, however, had nothing to do with sex life as such. In time they gradually disappeared and, it seems, were later even consciously omitted from historical records.[17]

Laws of incest and prohibited degrees in marriage were likewise expanded from period to period. Incestuous marriage, widespread among Egyptians and Hittites, early provoked even more violent attacks by Israel's lawgivers than it did among the Babylonians. These prohibitions not only strengthened national unity by forcing members to marry outside the immediate family group, but also kept out foreign admixtures by insisting upon tribal endogamy, in order to exclude most of the surrounding nations. Prohibitions against intermarriage, occasionally recorded and apparently fairly well enforced before the Exile—it is noteworthy that, except for Solomon and Ahab, even the kings of both Israel and Judah seem to have married only Israelitic women—became an urgent necessity for the preservation of the Jewish people in Exile and, for a while, also of the struggling community restored to Palestine. Only thus can we understand Ezra and Nehemiah's racialist extremism, unparalleled in either the earlier or later laws. The fears of the reëstablished community that mixed marriages would open the gates to the incursion of alien religious practices are well reflected in the accusation of its prophetic leader, "For Judah hath profaned the holiness of the Lord which He loveth, and hath married the daughter of a strange god." [18]

In the course of the Second Commonwealth, religious issues increasingly overshadowed those of a purely tribal endogamy. Even preëxilic laws expressly prohibiting the admission of any member of four neighboring nations (the Ammonites, Moabites, Edomites, and Egyptians) were, as we shall see, somewhat liberalized in application. The general exclusion of a *mamzer* unto the tenth generation (Deut. 23:3) was retained, but its meaning changed from the offspring of mixed marriages (*me 'am zar*) to one of adulterous and incestuous unions. With the renewed emphasis upon the people's holiness, on the other hand, grew also the public concern for all aspects of the laws of purity. Family life in so far came to be regarded as a particular sphere for their application, as here pure or impure living was clearly exhibited. Hence the many regulations concerning the menstruating and pregnant women as well as those afflicted with diseases, all of whom were declared impure.

Other laws were promulgated lest overemphasis upon the family undermine the interests of the nation as a whole, lest family rites stimulate separatist tendencies and interfere with the religious worship of the entire people. Just as control of sexual impulses did not lead to curtailment of the nation's reproductive capacity (in fact increased it by sharply outlawing castration, which was widely practiced in other Near Eastern lands), so the reinforcement of the family must not prejudice the religious unity of the nation.

How easily that reconciliation was effected is best seen in the example of Passover. Originally a family festival, with the Paschal lamb slaughtered at a local sanctuary, it tended more and more to assume the character of a national holiday commemorating the Exodus. The Deuteronomist, in his attempt to centralize all sacrificial worship in Jerusalem, excused many families unable to come to the capital. Unleavened bread, previously a minor feature, now took the place of the lamb at the family feast. With the destruction of the Temple and the increasing dispersion, the Paschal lamb grew still less important. After the Restoration, the priestly lawgiver apparently attempted to restore its use in the Diaspora by allowing each family a private nonsacrificial slaughtering (Exod. 12:3 ff.). His objective must have been the strengthening of the family where it was most needed, in foreign lands. But the nation refused to avail itself of that permission. The Paschal lamb remained an exclusive prerogative of the Temple as long as it lasted: the individual family was satisfied with the celebration of the national holiday as a Feast of Unleavened Bread. This is, indeed, the tenor of Darius II's famous decree, issued in 419 at the instigation of Jewish leaders. Through his Egyptian governor, Arsham (Arsames), the king ordered the Jewish colony in Elephantine,

Let there be a Passover for the Jewish garrison. Now you accordingly count fourteen days of the month Nisan, and keep the Passover, and from the 15th day to the 21st day of Nisan (are) seven days of Unleavened Bread. Be clean and take heed. Do not work on the 15th day and on the 21st day. Also drink no beer and anything at all in which there is leaven do not eat from the 15th day from sunset till the 21st day of Nisan, seven days, let it not be seen among you; do not bring (it) unto your dwellings, but seal (it) up during those days.[19]

Until the present day, Passover presents a remarkable combination of a national and family festival.

Family rituals more reminiscent of pagan rites and not reconcilable with the national religion had long been suppressed, however. Exilic and later laws needed merely to maintain and amplify older maxims, to remove the threat of ritual family separations. For example, if there remained any vestige of ancestor worship or the cult of the dead, so strongly developed in neighboring Egypt, Israel's law not only excluded its magic applications, but entirely cut the ground from under its feet by declaring a corpse to be the supreme embodiment of impurity. As the later rabbis phrased it, the dead man became the grandfather (abi abot) of impure things.

HIERARCHY

All these laws in their ever-growing complexity enhanced the importance of the ritual expert, the priest. In fact, after the destruction of the Temple the priestly class gained rather than lost prestige in the eyes of the people. It is true, the *Kohanim* could no. longer perform sacrifices, pronounce oracles, or participate in any of the sacerdotal functions, but, with the idealization of the Temple, those who had administered its services shone in reflected glory. As the importance of purity in family life increased during the Exile and under the domination of Persia, a claim to greater esteem could easily be made by the group whose peculiar position (priestly rights being based altogether upon noble descent dating back to the great lawgiver) made it especially careful to guard its genealogical purity. Even the kings who had the right to appoint and depose priests had recognized the hereditary principle. When Solomon ousted his father's chief priest, Abiathar, and appointed Zadok in his place, this breach in the law of succession was resented for centuries. The Zadokite family had to resort to an historical reconstruction to justify it, claiming that the sins of the sons of Eli caused "a man of God" to announce the future removal of Eli's line, to which Abiathar belonged (I Sam. 2:27 ff.). But even in the last decades of the monarchy it needed the character of a Jeremiah, himself the descendant of Abiathar, to lend support to the Deuteronomic reformation destined to strengthen the hold of the sons of Zadok upon the people. In view of these circumstances, perhaps only the descendants of the royal house of David among the exiles could claim a nobler parentage than did the priests.

Moreover, the tremendous power of the Egyptian priesthood restored by Darius I, and that of the Babylonians after the death of Nebukadrezzar, invited emulation. The idea of the holiness, too, both of God and of the people naturally elevated those whose professional duty it was to observe higher standards of purity. In his blueprint for the restoration of the Temple, Ezekiel or one of his successors emphasized the ritualistic segregation of the priests from the ordinary Jews. A special place was to be assigned to the priests, for instance, for the boiling of various offerings, "that they bring them not forth into the outer court, to sanctify the people." In the eyes of an ever more ritualistically minded people such segregation, rather than creating resentment, became a claim to distinction.[20]

From the same state of mind sprang also the detailed regulations concerning priestly behavior included in the third Book of Moses, which not unjustifiedly came to be known later as the *torat koha-nim* (the Priestly Law). The apparent attempt to force laymen to slaughter any animal intended for consumption as a peace offering at the sanctuary, running counter to the Deuteronomist's express permission of lay slaughtering, is likewise explainable only in the light of changed historic circumstances. Under the expansive .regime of Josiah, the majority of the population lived too far away from Jerusalem to be able to offer there each and every animal used for household consumption. Since all local altars had been outlawed, private slaughtering had to be permitted. Now, however, the tiny settlement around the capital could repair to the central sanctuary without undue hardship. No sooner, however, did the Jewish settlement extend over most of Palestine in the Maccabean age, than these restrictions were again relaxed in favor of lay slaughtering, which must have been widely practiced in any case in all countries of the dispersion.[21]

Priestly functions also underwent considerable change. For a long time instruction in the *Law* of Moses remained largely in the hands of the priestly teachers. But the progressive participation of the whole people in Jewish learning and the continued growth of a secular class of scribes gradually removed the field of education from the exclusive jurisdiction of the official hierarchy. Nevertheless, the latter's contributions to intellectual life, although less spectacular than those of the great prophets, and always covered with the screen of anonymity, were among the fundamental creations of the Jewish mind. Not only did the priests, more than anyone else, help erect the monumental edifice of Mosaic law, but they were also the leading poets, musicians, thinkers, and scientists of ancient Jewry. Whether the Psalms are preponderantly preëxilic or postexilic, there is no doubt that they were composed principally to be recited to the accompaniment of music in the Temple or at other religious gatherings. The poets who wrote these immortal lyrics, the composers of the accompanying music, which unfortunately has not been preserved, and the virtuosi who recited both were almost exclusively members of the priestly class.[22]

Who knows how great a share is to be ascribed to the priests in the creation of that literature of Wisdom of which the book of Job is the greatest extant specimen? The Proverbs particularly seem to contain many pearls of wisdom, epitomizing the results of the perennial pondering in the schools of priestly sages. The older the origin of this literature—and it is the tendency of present-day scholarship to date it ever earlier—the larger is likely to be the share of priestly authors.

Of course, laymen, too, actively participated in the development of such worldly wisdom, which often reflected their daily experiences in the world of affairs. Some of it was doubtless acquired in extended journeys, like that of the husband of the mysterious "strange woman" of the book of Proverbs, and hence clearly betrays its foreign provenance. Chiefly appealing to the upper classes, it was often so quietist and even eudaemonistic as to provoke the Lord's ire, according to the author of Job. Notwithstanding its far-reaching secularization, however, the biblical Wisdom literature is permeated with the Jewish religious and national heritage and, in more than one connection, betrays vestiges of priestly influence. Although generally steering clear of ritualistic problems, the compiler of the book of Proverbs nevertheless enjoins the reader, "Honour the Lord with thy substance, and with the first fruits of thine increase." Ecclesiastes demands at least, "Pay that which thou vowest." These injunctions may, indeed, reflect the anxiety of the priestly class over the slowness in the collection of tithes, of which Malachi complained and which Nehemiah tried to remedy by a special compact with the people.[23]

Priests and lay schoolmen (among them apparently the two Isaiahs, cf. 8:16; 50:4–6; 54:13) thus coöperated in teaching Israelitic and Judean youth matters of practical wisdom which they regarded as conducive to happier life. With the stimuli of a vast dispersion and the growing contact with the outside world, this literary genre became ever more popular. Its complete impotence, however, to penetrate the deeper mysteries of existence was soon realized by one of these same littérateurs, the great creator of "Job." Simultaneously its inadequacy in solving the perplexities of the difficult Jewish situation caused the official leaders of the school of Ezra to withdraw behind the walls of the Law. Nevertheless the composition of new "proverbs" went on undisturbedly, and Jesus Sirach (a *priest* according to a later tradition) issued another collection about 200 B.C.E. Not much older, it appears, is the book of Ecclesiastes, whose pessimistic speculations have long been associated with the mental climate of the Hellenistic world.

All this creativeness, however, never obscured the main, sacerdotal, function of the Jewish priesthood. As soon as the Temple was rebuilt in Jerusalem, the priest resumed his position in the sacrificial worship. The oracles, even before the destruction of the first Temple, long in disuse, were now altogether abandoned. Their place was taken by the exposition of the Law, especially in those branches in which lay the priests' main strength, the ceremonies, the laws of purity and impurity and those concerning ritual food. For all these reasons the Jewish priesthood gained unprecedented prominence in the Exile and after. Some writers of the period began calling the head of the priesthood *ha-kohen ha-mashiah* (the anointed priest), reminiscent of the "anointed" kings of Israel. Enjoying the full coöperation of Persian authorities, which thus hoped to stem movements toward political liberation, this chief official of autonomous Judaea was soon generally known as "high priest." He thus initiated a regime for which Josephus was to coin later the designation of "theocracy." [24]

Prophets, on the other hand, gradually became less influential. Even accepting the assumption, still widely disputed, that Deutero-Isaiah, "le grand Inconnu" as Renan called him, lived in Babylonia when he wrote his prophecies, he might have been born on Palestinian soil, like Ezekiel. At any rate, the longer the Jews were alienated from their country, the more their source of inspiration appeared to be drying up. For a while, national misery, like social injustice and religious aberration earlier, was an incentive to prophecy. Again as in the case of the Sabbath, social ideologies were translated into national and religious concepts. Just as in the social struggle of the age of independence, the class of the disinherited, the "poor" and the "humble" (*'aniim* and *'anavim,* often interchanged in Hebrew) was exalted by its prophetic spokesmen, so now, when the whole nation lived in shackles, this title of distinction was conferred upon the people as a whole. From a class term it became a national term of religious significance with increasingly eulogistic connotations, and gradually all eyes turned toward the coming of the Messiah, "lowly [*'ani*] and riding upon an ass." [25]

Soon the status of the Jews was sufficiently improved to reconcile the majority of the people to its fate, especially in the absence of the old economic abuses which could not yet have crept into this rather anaemic society. While many still called themselves "prophets," the new conditions were not conducive to great literary originality. The majority of "prophets" had been lowly even in the most glorious days of prophecy, and now that the redeeming few were missing they sank ever lower. Their complete extinction was finally announced, with great relief, by one of their own leaders,

"And it shall come to pass that, when any shall yet prophesy, then his father and his mother that begot him shall say unto him: 'Thou shalt not live for thou speakest lies in the name of the Lord'; and his father and his mother that begot him shall thrust him through when he prophesieth." This decline was further accelerated when the increasing dispersion of the Jews eliminated the previous intimate contact between the prophet and his people. As the written message became the chief medium of communication, prophecy became more and more bookish. No wonder that inspiration gradually gave way altogether to learning. Out of the book-prophet was born the apocalyptic writer and, more important, the scribe.[26]

The usual depreciation of both priest and scribe in comparison with the prophet has, however, little justice. True, we do not find personalities among the priests and the early scribes who sustain comparison with the great prophets. But is not such an array of religious thinkers and preachers as that of the prophets from Amos to Deutero-Isaiah a rare, if not unique, phenomenon in the history of all religions? Furthermore, the strength of prophecy lay in the individuality of the man, that of priesthood and the early sages in the group. We would know few priests or scribes by name were it not for their accidental appearance in the political arena, but their anonymous contributions, however slow and imperceptible, were as vital and lasting as the more spectacular contributions of the others. There is no means of measuring human greatness. Would one venture to decide who was greater, the anonymous author of Deuteronomy, or Jeremiah, the prophet, the tragic grandeur of whose life has been so rich a source of inspiration? As it happened, both these men were priests.

We are often prone to exaggerate the very distinction between prophet and priest, whose invidiousness becomes particularly clear in the case of so-called "cultic prophets" serving in the employ of sanctuaries and rulers. The Chronicler was not unjustified in speaking of families of singers set aside by David to "*prophesy* with harps, with psalteries, and with cymbals." Evidence has, indeed, been accumulating in recent years that regular "bands of prophets," like those mentioned in the book of Samuel, performed a variety of ceremonial functions throughout western Asia. So overpowering was, in fact, the impact of law and ritual even on secular prophets that, for example, Jeremiah felt the need of spelling out the prohibition of carrying burdens on the Sabbath in a manner unrecorded in any contemporary legal compilation. Elisha's insistence upon the felling of "every good tree" in hostile Moab and particularly Ezekiel's numerous ritualistic injunctions were so obviously at variance with the more widely accepted legal requirements as to cause serious embarrassment to the later rabbis (the Talmud records the protracted efforts of Ḥananiah ben Hezekiah to harmonize Ezekiel's law with that of the Torah and thus make possible the inclusion of his book in the canon). Perhaps responding to the new need of concentrated legal authority, Malachi himself enjoined his listeners that "the priest's lips should keep knowledge, and they should seek the law at his mouth; for he is the messenger of the Lord of Hosts." The same schools, moreover, including many priests, which in the early postexilic period busied themselves with the compilation and editing of the Law, were also active in assembling and revising prophetic oracles and incorporating them into their collections of sacred writings.[27]

Certainly the priestly caste, too, had its ups and downs. Like every human group, it could count among its members only a few real idealists or really creative thinkers. The indictment of the ruling priests, so frequent among the preëxilic prophets, although exaggerated with polemical intent is doubtless not without basis in fact. But even in these indictments, there lurks the tacit expectation that the priest should be better than the ordinary man. In fact, it may be said that the average priest was superior both in culture and character not only to the average man in the street, but to most so-called prophets. True in the period of the kings, this is even truer after the loss of national independence.

What is more, when the prophets preached in Israel before and immediately after the destruction of the Temple, they were only a small minority. Against them stood the majority of the people, addicted to a creed and mode of life which seemed sheer idolatry. But now the people were physically decimated and socially run down, threatened with national extinction, living, so to speak, without firm ground under their feet. Nevertheless, in this condition they actually came nearer the goal set by the prophets than ever before. The leading groups in the Babylonian Exile gradually developed the characteristics of holiness on a national scale, rather than in a few representative men. The faith of the prophets became a democratic possession; it spread and encompassed the whole ethnic group. It was at this time that Joel proclaimed the ideal,

And it shall come to pass afterward, that I will pour out My spirit upon all flesh; and your sons and your daughters shall prophesy, your old men shall dream dreams, your young men shall see visions. And also upon the servants and upon the handmaids in those days will I pour out My spirit [3:1–2].

It seems to be one of the drawbacks of all democratic societies that they are conducive less to the rise of a few outstanding men of genius than to the raising of the general cultural level. In the complicated social conditions existing after 586, daily counsel and advice were more essential to the good life than vigorous protestation. This was no longer a time for revolutionary agitation against the established order. The real need of the age was reconstruction, guidance not by impulsive geniuses, but by moderate and sober statesmen, priests, and sages.

ETHNIC EXCLUSIVISM AND HUMANITARIANISM

A most momentous problem facing the Jewish people and their leaders was, of course, their relation to the surrounding Gentile nations. The entire future of the people depended on a satisfactory solution. Exilic Jewry was not altogether unprepared, since its ancestors had been living amidst various racial and religious groups during the early centuries of their national existence. Even under the kings they had come in contact with many foreign nations, and a large number of foreign merchants were always to be found in their commercial cities. Characteristically, the Deuteronomist, speaking of the election of the king, thought it necessary to issue a formal warning, "Thou mayest not put a foreigner over thee, who is not thy brother" (17:15). That these fears were not completely groundless, may be seen in the stratagem of Pekah of Northern Israel who, in alliance with Rezin of Aram, attempted to place Ben Tabal (the son of Tabeel), an Aramaean, on the throne of Judah (Isa. 7:6). Some such tendencies seem to have made themselves felt in Judah itself after the assassination of Amon shortly before the Deuteronomic reformation.

From the period of the conquest there had also come down a large number of former natives who lived as metics in the service of the Israelitic kings and sanctuaries. They probably constituted the majority of the so-called *gerim,* a word correctly rendered in the Septuagint by the Greek legal term *proselytoi.* In their original meaning, both words refer to strangers who live permanently in a country not their own and suffer legal disabilities as a consequence. The Deuteronomic law as well as the preëxilic prophets frequently refer to this half-foreign element in the population. They stress, as a rule, the moral if not the legal obligation of the Israelites to protect these strangers against oppression, to assign them a share in the distribution of charity: in short, to treat them almost as brethren. Characteristically enough, "history" is invoked to support all these injunctions, the Israelites being reminded time and again that they also had been strangers in the land of Egypt.

The Deuteronomist is favorably inclined even toward full-fledged foreigners. Of the four references to these *nokhrim* in the book (14:21; 15:3; 17:15; 23:21), one states, as has been mentioned, that the Israelites should not elect a foreigner as their king. Another insists that an animal which dies of natural causes, and which therefore cannot be eaten by an Israelite, should be given to a *ger* or sold to a *nokhri*. The remaining two draw the well-known distinction between the Israelite and the foreigner in regard to usury and the cancellation of debts in the sabbatical year. This last discrimination was hardly the result of special animosity, for which a much more adequate expression could have been found, but reflected prevailing economic conditions in the country. The foreigner was usually a businessman, who borrowed money for use in profitable commercial transactions, while the Israelitic farmer borrowed to satisfy personal needs. The results in his case were often disastrous and led to that expropriation and enslavement which so violently shook the whole national body. Since, moreover, the Israelites could not forbid foreigners to lend them money on interest, it would have been unreasonable to let a Gentile obtain a cheap loan from one Israelite in order to lend it at a profit to another.

Animosity toward neighboring nations, such as the Edomites, Moabites, and Ammonites, were exceptions to the rule that Israel was not hostile to most foreigners in the period of national independence. The Israelitic people, secure in its home, could well afford relative tolerance. But what about the people in exile? Can a minority be tolerant and yet resist the cumulative power of assimilationist tendencies?

The answer to this difficult question was immediately given by Ezekiel and his successors. While there was to be no hostility toward foreign nations, there was to be definite segregation from them. In his utopia, the ideal constitution which he or one of his disciples drafted for use after the return to Palestine, this most zealous of prophets insisted that the resident alien in the new state be assigned an inheritance of his own. The author of the Priestly Code likewise missed no opportunity to emphasize, "Ye shall have one manner of law as well for the stranger, as for the home-born; for I am the Lord your God." On the other hand, he and Ezekiel both demanded that no foreigner be permitted to approach the Temple. This exclusion of the Gentile from the sanctity of Israel was typical of the entire new legislation. Even the most universalistic of Israel's prophets envisaged the Temple of Jerusalem as "a house of prayer for all peoples" only after "the aliens that join themselves to the Lord" keep the Sabbath and hold fast by the covenant. Circumcision was stressed more than ever, because the Jew was now living among uncircumcized nations. The more the laws of diet, purity, and other external expressions of inner holiness were emphasized, the wider grew the gulf between the life of the Jew and that of the Gentile.[28]

Notwithstanding all this, universalism remained a strong religious force. The great broadening of outlook which came in the wider world of Babylonia and Persia could not but strengthen the conviction that beyond differences of nationality and state there is one mankind. The recognition of one transcendent God worked in the same direction. No wonder, then, that prophetic universalism found its most remarkable representative in Deutero-Isaiah, half a century *after* the destruction of Jerusalem. Whether or not his mind had been sharpened by religious disputations with Babylonian priests (41:21–24 may be a sample of such perorations), his penetrating poetic vision discerned deeper truths behind apparent realities; he saw reconciliation where only differences seemed to prevail. Since the universal God is simultaneously the Holy One of Israel, he felt, the unity of mankind and the holiness of the Jewish people are complementary aims. The Jew must live a different life from that of the other nations, not so much for his own sake as for theirs.

In this way arose the prophet's wonderful vision of the Messiah: The Jewish people is the "Servant of the Lord" who, despised and forsaken of men, "by his knowledge did justify the Righteous One to the many and their iniquities he did bear." This was the prophet's consolation to those who asked why Israel must suffer more than the other nations, though itself no worse. But this answer, like that of Ezekiel, led directly to the recognition of God's transcendence and holiness, of the holiness of Israel and of its life according to the commands of the Torah.[29]

Nor was the universalist idea abandoned after the Restoration.

Ezra and Nehemiah, both zealous nationalists, stressed the national element above all others—and thereby rendered an important service to their people and ultimately, one might say, by salvaging it, also to mankind at large. But there were others, in less responsible positions, who preached universalism as vigorously as ever. Although the author of the book of Ruth, for example, must have known of the endogamous exclusion of Moabites from the Jewish fold, he depicted with apparent naïveté a Moabite woman as the ancestress of the house of David, the exalted dynasty of the past and future.[30]

Similarly, the book of Jonah is nothing but a veiled appeal to loving-kindness toward all men. It ends with the severe rebuke given to the recalcitrant prophet by God, "And should not I have pity on Nineveh, that great city, wherein are more than six score thousand persons that cannot discern between their right hand and their left hand, and also much cattle?" The last prophets, Zechariah and Malachi, are no less emphatic. Malachi's query, "Have we not all one father? Hath not one God created us?" may have been addressed to his fellow Jews, but it clearly implied the brotherhood of all men. In fact, the prophet foresaw almost immediate fulfillment of his ultimate vision, that God's name would be "great among the nations." The author of Job debated with his friends the fundamental problems of ethics and theology in such an humanitarian vein that (except once in a possibly interpolated passage), he even failed to mention the name of Yahweh, and preferred such general Semitic designations as El or Eloah or the then indubitably archaic Shaddai.[31]

Perhaps even more remarkable is the book of Proverbs. The reconciliation of nationalism and universalism seems to be no problem in these aphorisms, many of which must have been the product of the exilic period. The words of wisdom reflect the experience of all men and are addressed to all men. The cosmopolitan tone is so pronounced that, as we have seen, passage after passage from a strikingly similar Egyptian collection could be taken over verbatim without creating resentment.

TERRITORIAL RESTORATION

Nevertheless, throughout the entire period of the Babylonian Exile, as in the mind of Moses during the desert migrations, the feeling persisted: "This cannot last." No matter how prosperous or affluent, learned or law-abiding some members of the scattered Jewish communities were, there was a pervasive sense of insecurity. Nature, hitherto suppressed and covered with an artificial screen of holiness and law, was bound to revolt. The more observant patriots among the descendants of the Babylonian exiles witnessed with deep sorrow the signs of incipient disintegration. Chaldaean religious propaganda and the force of Parsiism which, though not a state religion in the technical sense, enjoyed a good deal of protection from the central and provincial authorities, were a grave menace. To be sure, Parsiism of the Achaemenid age is, in itself, far from a known entity. It has largely been reconstructed by modern scholarship from sources compiled centuries later under Sassanian rule. There is, therefore, much arbitrary interpretation as to which religious idea or institution may claim priority in Parsiism and which in Judaism. Each the more readily influenced the other, as the Persian authorities increasingly used Aramaic in their relations with the peoples of the western part of the empire. It seems, nevertheless, a reasonable assumption that at least in eschatology, demonology, the doctrine of reward and punishment, and the laws of purity Judaism must have received particularly strong stimuli from the great Aryan religion.[32]

Apart from these external religious influences economic and social success itself foreboded danger. There was too much smug contentment and too much intercourse with the Gentile population. It became questionable whether the artificial wall of the Law, the exaggerated emphasis on segregation and holiness, would suffice to save Jewry and Judaism from strong assimilationist forces pressing from the outside, or whether a majority of those deported from Jerusalem, following in the footsteps of their predecessors from Samaria, would succumb.

Dreamers and visionaries among the people pinned all their hopes on God's pledge through the mouth of his prophets to send his Messiah, who would miraculously gather them from the four corners of the earth. But there were among them enough realists, merchants, statesmen and priests who, without giving up their faith in miraculous redemption, wished a more tangible abatement of pressing immediate difficulties. They realized that a return of even a minority to its own country would supply to the whole people that minimal natural basis without which, they feared, it might not survive. Both visionaries and realists, however, were united in the desire to make use of the shifting political alignments to help lay foundations for such a return, and to rebuild the Temple, the paramount ideal in the darkest days.

It is astonishing to note with what tenacity the leaders of Babylonian Jewry marched toward their goal through a century of uninterrupted effort. They utilized every favorable turn in the international and national situation. They supplied the resources of man power and money necessary to construct a Jewish self-governing community in and around Jerusalem. We know from the writings of Ezra and Nehemiah, themselves Babylonian Jewish leaders, under what trying circumstances this work proceeded. They had against them not only all the forces of inertia and the unpredictable policies of the central and provincial governments in Persia, but also the desolation of Palestine itself and the petty jealousies, often open hostility, of their neighbors. Obviously it was too much to expect that any larger portion of the people would leave the great commercial centers where they had led a rather sheltered and prosperous life, in order to settle in a backward country. Furthermore, on account of its closeness to Egypt, Palestine was exposed to the plundering and abuses of Persian armies traversing it from one end to another, to conquer or to pacify this continually revolting African province. The old social inequalities, expropriation and enslavement of the poor by the (relatively) rich soon crept into the young society again while still in the progress of reconstruction.

Relations between the returning exiles and the Judeans who had been left in Palestine by the Babylonian conqueror also represented a serious problem. As is natural, the former must have claimed the return of their families' estates abandoned during the deportations. They could buttress their claims by excellent genealogical records, whose careful preservation may actually have been owing, in part, to such expected restitution. Just as naturally the newer occupants were reluctant to relinquish property which their fathers and perhaps grandfathers had held for several decades under untold hardships. Heavy taxation, aggravated by the rapacity of the Babylonian and Persian bureaucracies, caused royal service to be "heavy upon this people" (Neh. 5:18). Nehemiah himself was justly proud of his exceptional behavior in not demanding "the bread of the governor."

Even those who were allowed to retain their land sooner or later had to borrow heavily in order to meet these governmental exactions or emergencies arising from crop failures. Since the returning exiles evidently were in possession of funds either of their own or given them by their Babylonian coreligionists in accordance with Cyrus' decree (Ezra 1:4), the preëxilic vices of unproductive and expensive loans, followed by foreclosures and personal bondage came back with a vengeance. A covenant concluded, under Nehemiah's instigation, by a public assembly, though reinforced by solemn abjurations (5:1–13), must have given but temporary respite to the much-harassed peasants. The economic conditions in the capital, on the other hand, were so bad that Nehemiah had to take stringent measures to stem the mass flight to the country, especially of the Temple personnel (13:10).

The religious situation was equally unsatisfactory. Although, like their neighbors in Samaria, prepared to collaborate with the returning exiles in the restoration of the Temple, these local farmers had, for too long, been deprived of the leadership of their priests and prophets and had lapsed again into the beliefs and habits naturally emanating from their soil. Again, as in the days of the early Israelitic settlers, the popular religion of Canaan asserted itself. It was made even more repugnant to the zealous exiles by some such awesome rituals as "eating swine's flesh and the detestable thing, and the mouse" which the Palestinians seem to have adopted during the interval. Now, however, this popular syncretism was confronted by a highly developed Mosaic religion intensified by a period of estrangement from the Palestinian soil.[33]

Babylonian Jewry persisted and won. Only a minority returned to the homeland: during the first Restoration, under Zerubbabel, about 50,000 (including more than 7,000 slaves); during the second, under Ezra, approximately 5,000. The whole Diaspora must have numbered hundreds of thousands by that time. The returning exiles did not make light of the difficulties. Unlike his Deuteronomic predecessor, the Priestly narrator, for instance, does not depict Palestine glowingly as a country "flowing with milk and honey." It is the Holy Land, assigned to the Jews by God, and there they must go. Those who come back to report that it "is a land that eateth up the inhabitants thereof" (Num. 13:32) are wrong and will be punished for their lack of faith. It is true, the original hopes had to be toned down. Haggai's prophecy in the first rush of enthusiasm during the early years of the Restoration—"the glory of this latter house shall be greater than that of the former" (2:9)—was to come true only centuries thereafter.

Even in the depressing conditions of generations immediately following, however, the Temple and the little district around it, enjoying a large measure of self-government, were the focus of all Jewish intellectual life. To be sure, the new Jewish Commonwealth was very small. King Eshmunazar of Sidon let it be inscribed on his Egyptian sarcophagus, "And the lord of Kings gave me also Dur and Jaffa [and] the magnificent corn lands of the valley of Sharon. . . . And we added them to the area of the country so that they be the property of the Sidonians for ever." Tyre controlled the rest of the coast line, in so far as it had not been occupied by the Edomite push northwards. The Jews shared the interior with Samaritans, Ammonites, and others and exercised control only over some 1,200 square miles in the immediate vicinity of Jerusalem.[34]

Theirs was but a tiny segment of the vast Persian Empire which at its height embraced more territory than did Rome in the period of its grandeur. The relative position of all Palestine within the empire may perhaps best be gauged from its contribution to the imperial Treasury. The figures given by Herodotus show that Palestine (Jewish, Samaritan and Gentile), together with Cyprus and the rich Phoenician cities, was assessed 350 silver talents, or about $680,000 (present gold value) annually—an amount representing only some 2 per cent of the Treasury's total revenue in specie. Moreover, Palestine seems to have been free from contributions in kind which, in many other satrapies, equaled or exceeded the monetary payments. The Indian provinces, for instance, are said to have furnished every year gold dust worth 40,680 talents of silver, or about $80,000,000. Nevertheless, the semisovereign authority of the high priest, soon assisted by the more or less permanent council of the "Men of the Great Synagogue," became a visible sign of Israel's unity throughout the lands of the dispersion.[35]

Unlike the First Commonwealth which had owed its origin to military conquest, the Second was built principally by the combined forces of Jewish statesmenship and priestly learning. This was possible, because the new form of religion corresponded so well to the new situation. A most remarkable thing happened. Just as in the days of the Judges, the people in Palestine now had to live by a law formulated outside their own country. It is immaterial whether it was the whole Pentateuch in its then known form, or only the so-called Priestly Code that Ezra submitted to the people gathered in Jerusalem. It was apparently brought with him from Babylonia. To be sure, it drew on the rich, centuries-old mines of

Palestinian judicial and priestly lore. It was also, in many ways, a child of the spirit of the Palestinian prophets. But the emphasis, the lights and the shadows, the whole tone, as well as many detailed extensions, were Babylonian. The elevation of the Law to a supreme position in the Jewish religion, the extreme accentuations of the ritual, the laws of purity and those concerning food, and even the exalted appreciation of priesthood and sacrifices reflected mainly exilic conditions and ideals.

Ideal holiness of the people through segregation found its counterpart in both Ezra's and Nehemiah's insistence upon ethnic purity and their prohibition of intermarriage. This principle of ethnic exclusiveness was for centuries to come a necessity for the preservation of the Jewish people even in Palestine. But in its essence it is the main safeguard of a people in dispersion against national extinction. Ethnic purity was here in a remarkable way combined with the idea of a universal, transcendent, and holy God. The chief task of the Jewish people thus became that of a "nation of priests" living a holy life apart from the others "before the coming of the great and terrible day of the Lord" (Mal. 3:23). Such a nation of priests does not depend on the number of its members, but on its quality of holiness and purity. Therefore, a select group of such sacerdotal or lay "priests," even though it be an insignificant minority of the Jewish people itself, living in the Holy Land, would be able to exercise a significant influence on all Israel in the dispersion, and through it on the whole world. Thus originated that anomalous Jewish "theocracy" in a corner of the Persian Empire, small and neither politically nor economically significant. Through its vital influence on the whole Jewish people in many lands, however, this little province soon became a factor of consequence to the world at large.

DEFIANCE OF NATURE

In building the Second Jewish Commonwealth exilic and post-exilic leadership embarked upon another unprecedented venture. Never before had a people, dispersed through foreign lands, created out of its spiritual and material resources a homeland and ultimately a state. This was, however, but a logical consequence of its leaders' conscious determination from the outset to go on living as a national entity in defiance of all precedents. Building upon the foundations of their historic heritage, their faith reinforced by their belief in the imminence of a messianic future, they reconstructed the communal life of their people and reformulated its basic ideologies with the view toward a perplexing present and an unpredictable future. In order to achieve this end they often had to tone down some of the traditional emphases and, more frequently, stress certain elements with unprecedented vehemence.

One of the most amazing characteristics of that entire exilic and early postexilic experience was the astounding rapidity with which the Jewish minority groups in Babylonia, and apparently also in Egypt, recovered from the shock of the loss of national independence and the miseries of deportation. While adjusting themselves to the new environments, however, often achieving wealth and influence, they retained their national and religious identity. New leaders arose. Instead of denouncing a social structure no longer their own, instead of preaching comfort and consolation to a people most of whom no longer were suffering individual distress, they evolved a whole new system of law and theology. While fully maintaining continuity with the previous intellectual evolution, they found new theoretical and practical implications for a nation without state and territory. A transcendent and holy God, they taught, has selected the people of Israel as his holy nation, for reasons known only to Him. Through a life of holiness and, if necessary, of great suffering this people will continue to make known the name of God until the end of days, when all nations shall recognize their error and worship this one God. In the meantime, Israel must keep aloof from these other nations, in order not to be contaminated by their errors and their unholy life. Such an aim can only be achieved by a full, specific, and peculiar law in all its ramifications. The life thus demanded is necessarily artificial and contrary to nature in many ways. Therefore the Jew has to live, if necessary, in defiance of nature.

On the other hand, the leaders of the age were not blind to the dangers threatening such an artificial structure. They also must have seen that large sections of the people were as yet unprepared to live without territorial anchorage. Hence their attempt to reconquer that minimum of territory and political independence which they felt was indispensable even for the life of such a nation. It was a minimum of territory and only a surrogate for a state, but sufficient to give a foothold to a colossal body which might otherwise have tumbled over. In fact, however, Palestine soon turned out to be much more than merely a foothold for the Jewish people.

VI

EXPANSION OF JUDAISM

WHEN Babylonian Jewry, through Zerubbabel, Ezra, and Nehemiah, had accomplished the feat of founding the little theocratic state in Palestine, it builded better than it knew. In this way alone it saved itself as well as Jewry at large from threatened extinction. The corrosive forces at work would doubtless have proved fatal to an organism so delicate and so newly shaped had it been deprived of an isolated corner in which to enjoy untrammeled growth. Egypt with its heterogeneous Jewish groups, the Palestinians who had been addicted to the resuscitated popular religion, and even Babylonian Jewry, long the most steadfast, would hardly have been able to survive in separation from one another. The far-flung settlements in other lands were even more exposed to forces of decay. Palestine, however, by becoming the recognized center for all Jewish communities, profoundly altered the situation.

The centuries following the restoration of the Jews to Palestine are among the least well known in Jewish history. Whether or not the result of destruction wrought by Maccabean zealots on monuments and writings considered pagan or heterodox, sources for the period between Nehemiah and the Maccabean revolt are so limited and of such slight historical value that even the essential lines of development appear ambiguous. While we have some glimpses of Palestinian and Egyptian life, almost nothing is known of other Jewries in the Diaspora. The sparse and scattered references to the Jewish masses left behind in Babylonia prove little more than that there was an unbroken continuity until the Jews reappear in history in large and well-organized settlements about the beginning of the Christian era.

Even Egyptian Jewry, outside the Elephantine colony, remains a sealed tomb until after the conquest of Alexander the Great. Then, under the domination of Hellenism, there developed that peculiar compound known as Hellenistic Jewish culture. But the intervening centuries are of the greatest moment as an era of consolidation. After the violent convulsions incident to the decline of the monarchy, the Exile, and the Restoration, there came an age of comparative quiet. The people were left to shape their internal life in accordance with the far-reaching program laid down by the founders of the new community in Palestine.

The general condition of Palestinian and world Jewry underwent no significant change, when, a century after Nehemiah, Persian rule was replaced by that of the Macedonian, Ptolemaic, and Seleucid dynasties. The broad self-determination given the people by the Achaemenid rulers remained unimpaired until the days of Antiochus IV Epiphanes. Only the right of the high priests to issue their own coins, a right which they seem to have enjoyed in the Persian period, was curtailed for a time. It was not regained until the recapture of full political sovereignty by Simon the Maccabean.[1]

Under the surface, however, an enormous mass of inflammatory material accumulated in that period of profound transformation of all Mediterranean nations. The ever-imminent clash between the new Hellenistic cultures and Judaism could be long postponed, but not avoided. Palestine solved the conflict by the Maccabean [2] revolt; Egyptian Jewry, in a more pacific way. In both countries, however, the Jewish people revealed a vitality undreamed of by superficial contemporaries. These vital forces were further enhanced by the short and often unpopular, but at least outwardly impressive, rule of the Maccabean family.

Not even the far-reaching developments within the country and outside after the conquest of western Asia and Egypt by the Roman legions were at first inimical to the position of the Jewish people in the world. On the contrary, during the century and a third before the destruction of the Second Temple (63 B.C.E.–70 C.E.) the vitality of Palestinian Jewry could more easily be communicated to the Jewries outside, since most Jews were now united within the great Roman Empire. At least these last phases following the Maccabean upheaval took shape in the full light of history. Our knowledge of that period is relatively satisfactory, owing both to the large number of extant contemporaneous sources, some of which possess exceptional historical value, and to centuries of untiring research. Through the coöperation of Christian and Jewish theologians, historians, and philologists, all deeply interested in the origins of Christianity, the rise of Pharisaic and talmudic Judaism, and the extraordinary story of the Roman Empire in the period of its greatest glory, there has arisen a vast literature of real distinction.[3]

NUMERICAL AND GEOGRAPHICAL EXPANSION

The vital energies of the Jewish people were revealed by their continued expansion throughout the eastern Mediterranean basin. In Palestine the settlement which from Zerubbabel down to the first Maccabees had been restricted to an area of less than twelve hundred square miles in the environs of Jerusalem, extended its boundaries, during the century of the Maccabean domination, over practically all Palestine and Transjordan. Of course, many Jews lived outside the confines of the theocratic state even before the Maccabean revolt. There are early records of settlement in the vicinity of Beersheba and along the coast, later also in Galilee and Transjordan. But these constituted a relatively defenseless minority. The leaders of the Maccabean revolt, fearing reprisals against their coreligionists by the Syrian authorities and the local populace of these regions, took most Jewish residents "in Galilee and Arbatta with [their] wives and children, and brought them into Judaea with great gladness." Here they were protected by the army.[4]

After peace was reëstablished Jews again drifted into these districts. Within a few decades, John Hyrcanus and Alexander Jannaeus, the great conquerors of the age, annexed in quick succession Samaria, Galilee, Transjordan, Idumaea, and some of the coastal plain. In all regions supposed to have been previously Israelitic the inhabitants were forced to accept the Jewish creed so that idolatry would not contaminate the traditional holiness of the land. Only the Samaritans, regarded as half-Jews, were allowed to retain their creed. The successors of Jannaeus, to be sure, proved incapable of maintaining all these gains, and Jewish domination over many districts along the coast and east of the Jordan came to an end under the pressure of the Nabataean Arabs and the first Roman invaders under Pompey. Nevertheless, rapid progress was made in the process of assimilating and integrating the disparate elements in the territories which remained Jewish.

Herod's considerable kingdom had, in any case, a vast Jewish majority, although the principal cities along the coast and in Transjordan remained more or less self-governing Hellenistic municipalities. These cities, too, had large groups of Jews, but their municipal governments were in the hands of the Greek majority which sometimes dared maltreat Jewish inhabitants on Palestinian soil. The Samaritans, living in close settlements in the province of Samaria and forming a distinct religious as well as ethnic group, presented another obstacle to national and religious uniformity. Indeed, next to the Jews they were the only group in Palestine's heterogeneous population to merit the designation *ethnos* in Josephus' *Antiquities* (XVII, 1, 3.20; XVIII, 4, 1.85).

None the less, the country as a whole was by that time thoroughly judaized. As illustrated by the narratives concerning Jesus and the Galilean apostles, the province of Galilee, which not long before had been a *gelil ha-goyim* (a district of foreign nations), was fully Jewish at the beginning of the first century. If estimates, derived by the present author from scattered and not altogether reliable sources, are correct, Palestine before the destruction of the Temple had a population of about 2,500,000 including some 500,000 Samaritans, "Greeks," and Nabataeans. The capital, too, had grown considerably. Jerusalem's residents before the destruction of the First Temple probably never exceeded 30,000 in number. Shortly before the end of the Second Commonwealth the city must have counted more than the 120,000 inhabitants ascribed to it by Hecataeus of Abdera three centuries earlier.[5]

Different in character, but no less vigorous, was the expansion in the countries of the dispersion. The Jewish settlements of Babylonia and Egypt continued to grow from generation to generation. For Babylonia the information is scanty, but that Jews dared resist the orders of Alexander the Great to rebuild the Temple of Bel, and that a large district around Nehardea was in the first century dominated by two Jewish brothers, Asinaeus and Anilaeus, are facts which substantiate Josephus' insistent claim that the Jews beyond the Euphrates were "countless myriads whose number cannot be ascertained" (*Antt.* XI, 5, 2.133). It is also corroborated by the developments in the small neighboring kingdom of Adiabene, where they must have considerably increased in numbers after the conversion of the royal house. While, at first, King Izates was advised even by his Jewish counselor to refrain from circumcision lest this act arouse popular indignation, such restraint was no longer necessary after his decisive victories over his opponents. It may readily be assumed that his example found imitators among loyal subjects. Together with the Jewish immigrants, these proselytes must have constituted a sufficiently populous Jewish settlement for Josephus to record it among those regions where the original version of his "War" was widely read (*War* I, 1, 2.6).

The growth of Egyptian Jewry astonished even contemporaries. Josephus took pains to explain it by numerous deportations from

Palestine, which he relates in such detail as to arouse suspicion among modern critics. But other literary sources, papyri and potsherds of several regions, fully confirm the picture of strong, affluent communities throughout Egypt down "to the boundaries of Ethiopia" (Philo, *In Flaccum*, VI, 43). Syria, the nearest neighbor, was even more densely populated by Jews. Many reached the coastal cities of Asia Minor, which were thoroughly hellenized. In smaller groups they penetrated even the interior, where, for centuries to come, the native population retained its racial and religious identity.

Apart from these, the four largest centers of Diaspora Jewry, masses of Jews lived in Cyrenaica adjoining Egypt, in the European Balkans, and on the islands of the eastern Mediterranean. Jewish settlements of the first century, established by more or less reliable records, extended from Italy and Carthage in the west to Mesopotamia and Babylonia in the east, from Upper Egypt in the south to Crimea and the Sea of Azov in the north. Furthermore, it is more than likely that some Jews had at an early age settled in Armenia, lying between such important Jewish aggregations as those of Babylonia, Syria, and Asia Minor. Local tradition, recorded by Faustus of Byzantium, had it that King Tigranes had brought back from Syria a large number of Jewish settlers (*Geschichte Armeniens*, p. 138). The rule of Herodian princes over Armenia must have strengthened, at least for a time, both Jewish immigration and religious propaganda. In fact, many a noble Armenian family boasted of its Jewish descent. The well-informed chronicler, Moses of Khorene, ascribes Jewish ancestry even to the Bagratuni family, which beginning in 66 c.e. occupied the highest office below that of the king.

Other Jews continued to penetrate east into Persia, south into Arabia and Abyssinia, west to Mauretania-Morocco, Spain, and possibly France. In Abyssinia, Judaism must have been firmly established during the Second Commonwealth, or else the Falasha Jews could not have remained until today ignorant of the festivals of Ḥanukkah and Purim. Neither their Bible nor that of the Coptic Christians (in the Talmud the latter's language is several times referred to as *gipṭit*) includes the book of Esther—an obvious sign of their separation from the main body before the final canonization of the Old Testament. The long list, in Acts, of Jews living in Jerusalem "out of every nation under heaven" clearly indicates the places of Jewish settlement.

Parthians, and Medes and Elamites [thus St. Luke describes the dramatic scene], and the dwellers in Mesopotamia and in Judea, and Cappadocia, in Pontus and Asia, Phrygia, and Pamphylia, in Egypt, and in the parts of Libya about Cyrene, and strangers of Rome, Jews and proselytes, Cretes and Arabians, we do hear them speak in our tongues the wonderful works of God [2:9–11].

This list is, nevertheless, incomplete, particularly with respect to western countries. For example, Spain, destined to play such a great part in later Jewish history, is not mentioned here or in any other reliable source prior to the third century. But the fact that Paul contemplated a missionary journey thither is a sure sign of the existence of considerable Jewish communities, from whom alone (as we know from his other travels) this "apostle of the Gentiles" expected to attract immediately a sufficiently responsive audience.[6]

In the concentrated Jewish settlement, the Jewish belt as it were, extending from Persia to Rome and from Upper Egypt to the Black Sea, the number of Jews must have been conspicuously large. In all probability Syria, Egypt, Babylonia, and Asia Minor harbored a Jewish population of 1,000,000 or more each. There is every reason for assuming that, although of comparatively late date, the statement of Bar-Hebraeus (a thirteenth-century Christian Syrian writer of Jewish extraction) concerning Claudius' census of all his Jewish subjects represents a fair historical reminiscence. Nor is the figure of 6,944,000, given by him for the total Jewish population, impossible or even improbable. On this basis we must assume that over 4,000,000 Jews lived within the boundaries of the Roman Empire outside Palestine. There must have been at least 1,000,000 more in Babylonia and other countries of dispersion not subjected to Roman rule. A Jewish world population of more than 8,000,000 is, therefore, fully within the range of probability.[7]

Jewry's numerical weight was accentuated by its preponderantly urban character. Although thousands were swept by the storms of national or individual life into the remotest hamlets and villages, the large majority doubtless inhabited the big commercial and cultural centers. Accustomed to much urban life through the centuries of Babylonian and Persian rule, many Diaspora Jews were doubly attracted to the newly founded Hellenistic cities, as the latter invited settlers of all races and creeds and extended to them generous privileges. Thus arose in all countries of Jewish mass settlement considerable communities which left a permanent imprint upon the physiognomy of almost every large city in the Hellenistic Near East. For instance, it seems possible that in the first century Alexandrian Jews constituted nearly two-fifths of the city's population, variously estimated between 500,000 and 1,000,000. Since the non-Jewish majority consisted of a cosmopolitan medley of races, one can easily see to what extent this commercial and intellectual metropolis of the Mediterranean world was, as Mommsen said, "almost as much a city of the Jews as of the Greeks." [8]

Under these circumstances, we are bound to assume that Diaspora Jewry by far outnumbered that of Palestine even before the destruction of the Second Temple. During the Persian period the district around Jerusalem could harbor only a relatively small part of world Jewry, and even after the great conquests of the Maccabeans the balance in favor of the Diaspora was speedily restored. If the figures here given are approximately correct, Diaspora Jewry in the first century was about three times as numerous as that of all Palestine. Indeed, Alexandria contained a larger Jewish community than did the "holy" capital of the Holy Land.

As a result of this stupendous expansion, every tenth Roman was a Jew. Inasmuch as the overwhelming majority of Jews lived east of Italy, that part of the empire, including the most advanced regions, had almost 20 per cent Jews. In other words, every fifth "Hellenistic" inhabitant of the eastern Mediterranean world was a Jew. So impressed by these masses of his coreligionists was the philosopher Philo, that he spoke of "one half of the human race," whose knowledge of Jewish law was a source of annoyance to the other half (*De vita Mosis*, II, 5, 27; cf. also *Legatio ad Caium,* 31), a statement which was approximately correct in respect to his native city, Alexandria. To indicate the meaning of this Jewish expansion, one need but note that, even before the recent tragedy of European Jewry, neither Poland nor any other country outside Palestine had such a large Jewish population and that the average proportion in the East European mass settlement, extending from Austria to the Ukraine, did not surpass 6 per cent of the total.

NATURAL INCREASE AND CONVERSIONS

The reasons for this unusual phenomenon have continued to arouse the curiosity of scholars. By the time of Josephus there already existed a whole literature devoted to explanations. All of these can, now as then, be reduced in principle to two: the natural increase of a highly prolific race, and gains through proselytism, while losses through apostasy were comparatively slight.

Extremely complex forces operated to bring about a steady distribution of the Jewish masses throughout the different countries. The expatriation of numerous captives after each invasion of Palestine or any other region densely populated by Jews, and the forced deportation of entire groups under the rule of Egypt and Syria, frequently assumed considerable proportions. The author of the *Letter of Aristeas* (12–14) may have exaggerated when he reported the removal of 100,000 Jews from Palestine by Ptolemy I, of whom 30,000 able-bodied men were distributed among the various garrisons in Egypt. He seems, nevertheless, to have preserved the sound historical recollection of a sudden influx into his country of a mass of involuntary Jewish expatriates. In no respect, however, was the quickening of pace more evident than in the continual voluntary emigration from congested areas in Palestine. Of course, some emigrants returned home after a prolonged sojourn abroad. Many reëmigrations, even of whole groups, from Babylonia and other countries are recorded. Josephus, for example, mentions without any amazement Herod's settlement of 600 Babylonian Jews in turbulent Trachonitis (*Antt.* XVII, 2, 1–3.23–31). But the total number of those that returned could hardly have outweighed the heavy emigration in any period.

Migratory movements from one Diaspora country to another likewise assumed ever vaster proportions. At times they might have outrivaled the flow to and from Palestine. Rome laid throughout the Mediterranean world a system of splendid roads and afforded comparative security of maritime communications. The opportunities for Jewish wanderers were thus greatly enhanced. Indeed, if a Phrygian tombstone inscription could refer without much ado to seventy-two journeys of the deceased (Flavius Zeuxis) from Asia Minor to Rome, and if often in Alexandria foreign students outnumbered the natives from all over Egypt, one can easily see that nothing need have hindered the Jewish trader or preacher who wished to migrate in whatsoever direction. Taken as a whole, the establishment of the great empires as well as the intensification of commercial relations caused more thoroughgoing changes in the ethnic composition of the eastern Mediterranean countries than had the enforced deportations of the ancient Assyrians.[9]

Proselytism, too, must have been a tremendous force in Jewish life. Although there were no professional missionaries, uninterrupted religious propaganda seems to have gone on throughout the dispersion. There must have been Jews among the numerous itinerant preachers and rhetoricians who voyaged from city to city, propagandizing for one or another idea.[10] To this extent the well-known denunciation of the Pharisees by Jesus—"Woe unto you, scribes and Pharisees, hypocrites! for ye compass sea and land to make one proselyte; and when he is made, ye make him twofold more the child of hell than yourselves" (Matt. 23:15)—reflects reality. To be sure, there is not the slightest evidence that the official Pharisaic leaders ever made an organized attempt to spread Judaism among the nations, but at least in that period they did not discourage individual efforts. Many converts must have become propagandists even more zealous than their teachers. The extensive travels of Jewish merchants, a steadily increasing factor in international commerce, helped familiarize even distant peoples with the main tenets of Judaism. Ananias, the Jewish merchant-missionary who converted the royal house of Adiabene, may indeed have been prompted no more by religious zeal than by a wish to enlist royal support for his commercial transactions.

The world situation was propitious, indeed. The spread of Hellenism had torn down many barriers separating peoples from one another and had corroded all traditional beliefs and modes of life. Positively, it had developed its own tremendous religious propaganda. Utterly unhistorical, the conquering Greeks were impressed by superficial similarities and inclined to disregard deep differences in cultures and creeds, arising through centuries of varied evolution. From the days of Herodotus they often thought that merely by giving their own names to deities or ceremonies, they made them identical with their own. For a while the expansive forces of Hellenism operated effectively in the religious field, but soon the Orient reasserted itself. The reawakening of the ancient oriental cultures was first expressed in creedal and ritual elements. Soon everything oriental became fashionable, even in western Mediterranean countries. Thus opened the greatest syncretistic age in history.

In these widespread currents, in which popular religious philosophies mingled with one another, Judaism found a great opportunity. It appealed strongly to generations in which the craving for the supernatural was coupled with a wish for a rational understanding of life, and dominated by a desire for moral rules which, while simple and easily grasped, were firmly rooted in the realm of the infinite. What Judaism brought to a religiously minded Hellenist was in some way less, in others more than mere philosophy.

It was faith and revealed truth [says Wilhelm Bousset], a certainty without the eternal contradictions and the perennial doubts of schools, it was religion. At the same time it was an impregnable community, much more vigorous than the fluctuating conventicles of the philosophic schools and at least just as important and powerful as the other greatly revered oriental mystery religions.

The very stability of the Jewish way of life, as the rabbis realized, even the spectacle of a large community eating and abstaining from the same foods, often impressed sensitive pagans. Disturbed by the anarchical diversity of modes of living and worship, many of the latter found escape in the inner security of the Jews' strictly regulated behavior. The inhabitants of the ever-growing metropolitan centers, in particular, the more readily succumbed to the Jewish example as their uprootedness from ancestral soils had rendered meaningless their old shrines and territorially bound forms of worship.[11]

At the same time the new philosophic ideas of the Supreme Being were no effective substitute for the loss of the deep attachment to ancestral faiths. That they exerted little influence upon the daily life of even their ardent protagonists is clearly demonstrated in the case of the Ciceronian circle. Cicero certainly mentions the "gods" on every occasion. Nevertheless, observes W. W. Fowler, "in the whole mass . . . of the Ciceronian correspondence, there is hardly anything to show that Cicero and his friends, and therefore, as we may presume, the average educated man of the day, were affected in their thinking or in their conduct by any sense of dependence on, or responsibility to, a Supreme Being." Even in theory there was an obvious cleavage between the Cosmic Intellect of Plato's *Timaeus* and *Laws* or the first exoteric writings of Aristotle, and the respective city cults. Nevertheless, the masters themselves adhered to the latter even in the purely theoretical discussions in the *Republic* and *Politics*. Hence Josephus and other Jewish apologists found considerable approval for the contention that "our earliest imitators were the Greek philosophers, who, though ostensibly observing the laws of their own countries, yet in their conduct and philosophy were Moses' disciples, holding similar views about God." [12]

Economic and social forces added momentum to purely religious propaganda. To become a Jew appeared at that time an advantage rather than an obstacle to many an economic career. The far-flung Diaspora with its complex contacts, the solidarity of the Jewish people, the protection extended by its communal organization, the support of its charitable institutions—all these contributed to counterbalance whatever minor disabilities were connected with Jewishness. One could publicly profess Judaism without the loss of any worthwhile right except perhaps that of holding public office. Poverty-stricken masses were frequently better off as Jews enjoying the benefits of both municipal and Jewish relief. The practical application of the religious duty of loving-kindness and almsgiving, coupled with the generally democratic trends within Pharisaic Judaism, doubtless enhanced the effectiveness of the Jewish mission within the urban proletariat. It is not surprising, therefore, that such opponents of the Jewish mission as Tacitus viewed with considerable alarm the solidarity and the considerable financial resources of the Jewish communities.

On the other hand, even wealthy merchants doubtless found it profitable to join a widespread creed which offered them brotherly reception wherever a community of their coreligionists existed. To be sure, at least at a later date, the rabbis tried to discourage conversions for worldly reasons. "One shall not accept," they declared, "converts for the sake of love, a man for the sake of woman, a woman for the sake of man, converts [seeking advancement] at a royal court, or [like the Samaritans] afraid of lions, or [like those] joining Mordecai and Esther" (j. Qiddushin IV, 1, 65b; variant in b. Yebamot 24b). But they also realized the complexity of human motivations and, with Abba Arikha (Rab), decided that even such persons, once admitted, should be treated as full-fledged proselytes.

Certainly economic considerations of this kind accounted for the existence and long-term preservation of many foreign commercial colonies throughout antiquity. For instance, as early as the fourth century B.C.E. Athens was forced to recognize the religious worship of her strong Egyptian community. In the Hellenistic-Roman period the Phoenician colonies, in particular, not only persisted all over the Mediterranean but perhaps even grew in size and affluence after the loss of all political power by their mother country. It becomes more and more evident that along with the commercial activities the religious life of these Semitic settlers, wherever found, deeply influenced their European or African environment.

These outposts of the ancient Canaanite race constitute more than a parallel, however. The Phoenician colonies and especially

Carthage, the largest among them, with her dependencies offered a vast field of activity to Jewish propagandists. Even after the Punic Wars, Carthage was not such a deserted region as would appear from Roman literary records. Excavations make it ever clearer that a flourishing Semitic civilization persisted in North Africa for centuries after the destruction of the capital by Scipio. There the Jews began to play a prominent part. The families of the Phoenician slave traders, often permanent or temporary owners of Jewish captives, may have been exposed to Jewish habits and ideologies more than any other group of the population. Being of a closely related racial and linguistic stock, conversion to Judaism would have transformed them almost instantly into full-fledged Jews. Greeks and Romans often would not become full proselytes because of the necessity for circumcision, followed, as it was, by open derision of the protagonists at every subsequent gymnastic performance by them in the stadium. The Phoenicians, however, had practised circumcision for ages.

Most decisive seems to have been the social situation confronting these colonists after the loss of national independence of their mother cities of Tyre, Sidon, and Carthage. While tenaciously clinging to their ethnic and economic peculiarities, these Phoenician ghettos in Rome and Alexandria, in Persia and in Spain, gradually developed the characteristics of a nationality without state and territory. Hard pressed, this race could quite naturally have adopted the patterns of belief and behavior developed by a related people through centuries of similar experience. Thus it came about that, in the centuries following the annihilation of Phoenician and Carthaginian political power, these Semites, carrying with them a considerable admixture of native (in North Africa especially Berber) blood, swelled the ranks of Jewish converts with a related type of people. That is why there are extant Jewish records from an early period, only of those western districts previously under Carthaginian rule. Nor was Rab's choice of localities purely accidental when he declared that "from Tyre to Carthage they know Israel and their Father in Heaven." In short, a vanishing world factor, the Phoenician, disappeared within the new world factor, the Diaspora Jew.[13]

The Jewish mission must have been equally effective among the other relatives, the Syrians. The very violence of anti-Jewish feeling pervading all classes of Syrian society is indicative of that mission's extraordinary success. Women, particularly, seem to have adopted Judaism in large numbers, as frequently happens in all religious conversions, but especially in this case, because they were not confronted with the major obstacle. In Damascus, Josephus tells us, the Jew-baiters, preparing for a general massacre of Jews, distrusted "their own wives who, with few exceptions, had all become converts to the Jewish religion" (*War* II, 20, 2.560).

Success served as a stimulus to ever-increasing efforts, as is abundantly revealed by the literature of the age, Jewish as well as Gentile. At first primarily apologetic, trying to present Judaism in a most favorable light to ruling Gentile groups, Hellenistic Jewish letters soon became the most effective vehicle of propaganda. In fact, many pursued directly missionary as well as defensive aims. This is true not only of outright apologias, but also of many philosophic, historical, and even literary works.

Perhaps it was subconsciously felt that the best means of defense was attack. Jewish preachers in the dispersion not only assailed the prevailing polytheistic beliefs and idolatrous practices, but also made effective use of the historic record preserved in their Scriptures to prove to a sympathetic and historically naïve Gentile world the antiquity and venerability of the Jewish tradition. Certainly the story narrated by the biblical historians carried greater conviction than the confused concoction of sagas blended by Herodotus with his own keen observations.

Jews also made good use of the universalistic appeal of their prophets and the humanitarian counsels of their teachers of Wisdom. "Unto you, O men, I call," they repeated after Wisdom personified in the book of Proverbs, "and my voice is unto the sons of men." Their task was greatly facilitated by the gradual permutation of the term *ger* in the Old Testament. Originally designating an ethnic and political stranger, it had long assumed the meaning of a religious convert. The Greek translators of the Bible, confronted by this double meaning, seem to have invented the term *proselytos,* and further underscored the humanitarian treatment of both categories of strangers enjoined by the biblical legislation.[14]

Hellenistic apologists of Judaism also followed in the footsteps of the Old Testament writers by refraining as much as possible from direct polemics against specific gods or customs of the surrounding nations. They preferred to speak generally of the weaknesses of idolatry and heathen mores, while dwelling at length on the superiority of Judaism. The finest specimen of that literature is Josephus' "Against Apion." The few extant fragments of Philo's

"Apology for the Jews" (probably identical with his *Hypothetika*) and of other Alexandrian writers, show throughout the same remarkable reserve.

Even in literary creations aimed primarily at Jewish readers apologetic and propagandist elements always broke through. Philo, though undoubtedly aware of the great need of Greek Scriptures for Egyptian Jewry, asserted that the Septuagint translation was made in order to enlighten the Gentile world (*De vita Mosis*, II, 6.36). The oldest of the so-called Sibylline poets, writing in Egypt or Asia Minor in the second century B.C.E., was firmly convinced of his role in his nation's mission to "be to all mortals the guide of life" (III, 195). For more popular consumption there were calendars of virtues and vices in which Jewish attitudes usually appeared as virtues and those of heathen nations as vices. This type of literature served as a model for early Christian catechisms, such as that in the first six chapters of the *Didache*. "When one turns," says C. Clemen, "to the magical papyri containing Jewish names of God or angels one may indeed say that no other religion of that age produced an equally extensive literature." No wonder many a Jew felt as Philo did when he contrasted the particularism of the laws of the different countries with the universalism of the laws of Moses. "They attract and win the attention of all," he concluded in praise of the latter, "of barbarians, of Greeks, of dwellers on the mainland and islands, of nations of the east and west, of Europe and Asia, of the whole inhabited world [*oikoumene*] from end to end" (*De vita Mosis*, II, 4.20).

While there certainly were numerous proselytes in the full sense, who became integrated members of Jewish society, there must have been throughout the empire larger groups which adopted some of the main tenets of Judaism and observed one or another Jewish religious custom, but were not counted as fully Jewish. The delightful story, reported by Suetonius, about the Rhodian grammarian Diogenes, who refused to see Tiberius the Emperor before the seventh day because he "used to lecture every Sabbath only," may serve as an illustration. It was not merely a flight of fancy on the part of Josephus when he asserted that

the masses have long since shown a keen desire to adopt our religious observances; and there is not one city, Greek or barbarian, nor a single nation, to which our custom of abstaining from work on the seventh day has not spread, and where the fasts and the lighting of lamps and many of our prohibitions in the matter of food are not observed.

The rigid rule adopted by the talmudic sages that "a proselyte willing to accept all commandments of the law but one shall not be admitted," later sharpened to include all minutiae of rabbinic law, seems to reflect their hardening attitude after the fall of Jerusalem. In fact, R. Eliezer and R. Joshua, the leading rabbis at the turn of the first century, still debated the question as to whether circumcision without baptism or baptism without circumcision sufficed to make one a full-fledged convert. The third initiatory rite, a burnt-offering, was from the outset required only for the partaking of sacrificial meals and must have gone into disuse in the Diaspora long before the fatal torch of a Roman legionnaire put an end to the entire Jewish sacrificial practice. In any case, the Jewries of the dispersion doubtless treated with great friendliness those Gentile neighbors who adopted but a few of their beliefs and ceremonies. More readily than the Palestinians they applied to these half-proselytes the friendly Mosaic provisions in favor of the *ger toshab* (resident alien) which term, too, underwent the usual change from a political to an ethnic-religious category.[15]

Such "god-fearing" men (*sebomenoi* or *metuentes*) were often kept from full conversion to Judaism only by legal difficulties. A grave obstacle was the conflict between the duty of every citizen of a pagan municipality and member of a pagan family to worship a local deity, and the extreme condemnation of all idolatry by Jewish law. Born Jews might have been exempted, but for converted Greeks or Romans the failure to attend the local ceremony constituted the crime of "atheism." Indeed, many a devoted Jewish (or Christian) proselyte was prosecuted by the state as an *atheos*. Hellenistic and Roman laws never seriously interfered with the worship of an additional god, however, and quite frequently the first generation remained in a semiproselyte stage, the second becoming fully Jewish. Thus Juvenal in one of his satires (XIV, 96 ff.) pokes fun at the Roman father who eats no pork, observes the Sabbath and worships only the heavenly God, but whose son undergoes circumcision, despises the Roman laws, and studies the Torah of the Jews.

CHANGING ATTITUDES

Through this highly effective religious propaganda, religion naturally exercised a tremendous influence on Jewish society. The Jewish masses in western Asia and Egypt with their appendage of *sebomenoi,* were also social agglomerations, altogether different from what they would have been had they remained sparse and scattered communities. Indeed, no less an observer than the geographer Strabo, writing about the condition of the Jews more than a century and a half before the destruction of the Temple could not refrain from remarking that "it is not easy to find any place in the habitable world that has not yet received this nation and in which it has not made its power felt." [16]

Reciprocally, the Jewish religion was deeply affected by these developments. One could even question whether this opening of the gates did not constitute a serious break in the line of tradition, the abandonment of the principle of ethnic purity so vigorously proclaimed by both Ezra and Nehemiah. Jewry, once firmly established with a widely accepted and clearly defined system of belief and behavior, could be much more liberal in admitting outside elements than could the weak group of Judaeans in fifth-century Jerusalem, struggling against so many adversities. The enthusiasm over growing political and religious successes had, in fact, implanted in the hearts of even the most nationalistic Jews the belief that the old messianic prophecies were soon to be fulfilled. The flocks of Gentiles joining the Jewish communities appeared to be evidence of the onset of that long-foretold age when all mankind would revere the one God of Israel.

No doubt Palestinian leaders, then and later, differed widely from one another in their attitude toward proselytism. We shall see how the far-reaching divergence in social philosophy between the Sadducees and the Pharisees deeply affected their respective positions as to the principles and methods of religious propaganda. But even the representative Pharisees did not pursue a uniform policy. Hillel, author of the well-known apothegm, "Be of the disciples of Aaron; one that loves peace and pursues peace, that loves mankind and brings them nigh to the Torah," was always ready to apply this principle practically. Shammai, however, was proverbially impatient with Gentiles who wished to embrace Judaism. Almost coincidentally with Jesus' purported denunciation of Pharisaic propaganda, there were enacted the "eighteen laws" which segregated Jews from Gentiles more peremptorily than ever before. Somewhat later came R. Eleazar ben Pedat's famous pronunciamento of the mission of the Jewish people, "The Holy One, blessed be He, sent Israel into the Exile among the nations only for the purpose of acquiring converts; as it is written 'and I will sow her unto Me in the land' no one sows a *se'ah* unless he expects to reap many *korin*" (one *kor* contains thirty *se'ahs*). On the other hand, R. Eliezer ben Hyrcanus interpreted the repeated scriptural emphasis upon the good treatment of the *gerim* as motivated by recognition of the intrinsic evil of their nature and their proneness to fall back into idolatry. In short, opinions varied with variation in individual temper and personal experience, or with the changing conditions of each successive generation.[17]

As a whole, however, this difference of opinion had no great effect on the important reality: the admission into the fold of a large number of proselytes. The religious principles concerning admission accommodated themselves to the new demands, but paradoxically, the principle of ethnic purity was maintained. If anywhere, the Jewish law has here shown itself capable of bridging an apparently irreconcilable contradiction. Through a conscious process of assimilation, the proselyte was expected to divest himself of all former racial and ethnic characteristics and gradually to become ethnically a Jew. It is more than an historic coincidence that Jews, Greeks, and Persians, the same three ancient peoples which more than any others had developed some modern characteristics of ethnic-cultural nationalism independent of statehood, also made religious conversion an immediate preliminary to national assimilation. Upon initiation in the Eleusian mysteries foreigners instantly became members of the Hellenic nation. By undergoing the initiatory rituals of Mithraism they became generally known as "Persians." Similarly, converts to Judaism joined, according to Philo, a "new and godly commonwealth [*politeia*]." [18]

By a curious legal fiction, a proselyte was classified as a child newly born into the community of Israel. His family was no longer his family, his children previously born were no longer his children, and they lost the right to his inheritance, even if they had adopted Judaism together with him. If the laws of his own community had allowed him to marry his aunt, he could, the majority ruled, remain married to her after their conversion without being guilty of incest. These rigid laws, which came down from a somewhat later age, surely represent in essence the program of the Pharisees. Even the less rigid Philo described the proselytes as men who "have left their country, their kinsfolk and their friends and their relations for the sake of virtue and holiness" (*De spec. legibus*, I, 9.52). Tacitus, with his anti-Jewish bias, complained that no sooner did these converts accept the teachings of Jewish preceptors than they began "to despise the gods, to disown their country and to regard their parents, children and brothers as of little account" (*Hist.*, V, 5). To borrow a phrase from Canon Law, conversion was held to possess a *character indelebilis*, and even subsequent relapse did not release the convert from any of the obligations of a born Jew. Conversely, the proselyte enjoyed full legal equality. Attempts to create for liturgical purposes a separate group of proselytes, fourth in rank after the "priests," levites, and "Israelites," succeeded only among the sectarians of Damascus. Socially, however, a convert was not treated as a full-fledged Jew before the second or third generation. In some respects, for example in case of marriage with a priest, birth from a purely Jewish father or mother or at least, according to some rabbis, from converted parents was a prerequisite. The latter fact was stressed, for instance, on that curious Roman inscription which recorded the decease of three-year-old Irene, *Eiovdea Isdraelites* (Israelite Jewess). The more rigid among the rabbis insisted that the proselyte be reminded of the distinction in his daily prayers. "If he is praying alone," they stated, "he says: 'the God of *Israel's* fathers,' if he is in the synagogue he says: 'the God of *your* fathers,' but if his mother is of Israel he says: 'the God of *our* fathers.' " Only after a prolonged process of adaptation to the new environment could a newcomer expect to be regarded as a bodily descendant of the Israelitic patriarchs. Many a proselyte symbolically assumed the name of Abraham or Sarah (for example, Beturia Paula or Paulina "nomine Sara," recorded on a Roman inscription). It is truly amazing that, regardless of all these obstacles, many became full Jews and that some of the most distinguished intellectual leaders of subsequent generations were said to be among their descendants.[19]

Of course, these rigid laws were not always strictly adhered to. In the countries of the dispersion, particularly, interpretation and practice were more lenient. Philo's famous definition of the name "Israel" as "the man who sees God" was more than the private opinion of an individual thinker. In fact, its etymology from the Hebrew *ish ro' eh* [or *ra'ah*] *el* (man who sees, or saw, God), seems to have antedated Philo. It is found in the interesting apocryphon, "Joseph's Prayer," unfortunately known to us only from two brief quotations by Origen. Needless to say that neither Philo nor the author of this apocryphon wished to deny Israel's chosenness. On the contrary, the latter hastens to make clear that Israel is "the first-born among all living beings created by God." Philo, too, reiteratedly emphasized that it was the people of Israel which was particularly endowed with the faculty of "seeing God." But both writers doubtless considered proselytes as full-fledged Israelites, whose very decision to join the community of the Lord attested to their ability to "see" the divine truth.[20]

The less meticulously orthodox and ethnically pure some foreign Jews were, the more inclined were they to let their religious zeal or ambition overcome legal scruples and to admit converts with less discrimination. Both trends are to be seen in the story of the conversion of the royal house of Adiabene as told by Josephus (*Antt.* XX, 2, 4.38–49). Eleazar is the representative of the more rigid Palestinian halakhah. The chief missionary, Ananias, however, is satisfied with a conversion without circumcision, usually the outstanding ceremony of admission to Judaism. Notwithstanding these differences, the Jewish communities in the Diaspora must have represented a more or less homogeneous ethnic group, even outside Syria and Carthage where the majority of the native proselytes belonged to a closely related racial stock. The steady influx from Palestine, combined with the extraordinary fecundity of the earlier Jewish settlers, helped overcome all racial admixtures and preserve a measure of ethnic unity.

CULTURAL EXCHANGES

Jewish population increase, migrations, and propaganda naturally enough attracted general attention. The Jewish question began seriously to occupy the best minds of the Graeco-Roman world and to arouse the passionate interest of the masses. The Jewish people and its religion became topics of heated controversy. Sympathizers often went to the extreme of adopting Judaism themselves, while opponents denounced it as the most debased and unworthy of religions. *Taeterrima gens* or *despectissima pars servientium* are the epithets heaped on Jews by so balanced a writer as Tacitus. No harsher expressions could be desired by a vulgar Jewhater on the street.

The first significant cultural encounter of the Greek and Jewish worlds was very friendly. Discounting the more accidental clash under Pharaoh Necho whose mailclad Greek hirelings helped defeat King Josiah at Megiddo in 609 B.C.E., we must assume that points of contact were established as far back as the sixth century before the Christian era. Greek inscriptions found in Lachish date from that period. Perhaps typical of some other Greeks of the sixth century, the poet Alcaeus seems to have become acquainted with a prophecy of Isaiah (5:1–6) through the mediation of his brother who, as one of the Greek mercenaries in Nebukadrezzar's army, had participated in the siege of Jerusalem. The Greeks of Daphne, Egypt, mentioned by Herodotus (II, 30), lived side by side with the Jewish community established there, as we recall, before the days of Jeremiah. Later, under Persian domination, Greek and Jewish detachments frequently fought side by side. Jewish merchants met Greek patrons or competitors on their travels, the coasts of the entire Near East being dotted with numerous Greek trading emporia. Coins found in Beth-Zur reveal that even before the end of the Persian period the Attic drachma had become the basic currency of Palestine, thus confirming the statements in Ezra and Nehemiah. Relations must have been closest in regions where the Jewish Diaspora touched Greek mass settlements, such as northern Syria and the eastern Mediterranean islands. Although most of the native population was evidently ignorant of their life and history, it is very probable that some Jews penetrated even into Asia Minor before the time of Alexander, since Phocylides and Hecataeus, both of Miletus, betray considerable familiarity with Jews and Judaism.[21]

Early Greek thinkers, to whom the Macedonian conquest of Persia suddenly opened new horizons, saw in the Jews representatives of a higher philosophy and morality. In their innocence of history they declared the Jews to be descendants of the Indian sages. The first to advance this theory apparently was Clearchus of Soli who thus tried to explain to his readers the astonishing wisdom of a Jew of Coele-Syria whom his master, Aristotle, had met. This Jew, Clearchus reports Aristotle as saying, "not only spoke Greek, but had the soul of a Greek. During my stay in Asia, he . . . came to converse with me and some other scholars, to test our learning. But as one who had been intimate with many cultivated persons, it was rather he who imparted to us something of his own." This narrative, quoted by Josephus and Clement of Alexandria, may be regarded as substantially authentic. The subsequent friendly reception of Alexander's armies by the Jews of Palestine, who, like their neighbors, had become disgruntled over the progressive deterioration of the Achaemenid administration, must have greatly fostered these amicable relations. Even if stripped of the many legendary features with which popular imagination later overlaid every act and utterance of the celebrated conqueror, Josephus' report of Alexander's friendly treatment of Palestinian Jewry has a solid kernel of historic truth. Nor have we any reason to doubt Alexander's invitation to Jews to settle, under favorable conditions, in the newly founded Egyptian capital bearing his name.[22]

Spartans, in particular, soon discovered affinities with the Jews. Even in her period of decline, Sparta preserved great traditions of law and of communal spirit, mores to which Judaism was congenial. The Jews apparently began to settle in the city a few decades after Alexander, perhaps at the invitation of King Areus (309–265 B.C.E.), whose letter reminding the Jews of Palestine "that the Spartans and Jews . . . are brethren, and that they are of the stock of Abraham" cannot be dismissed as a common forgery. It is significant that, when conditions in Palestine became unbearable under Antiochus IV, the high priest Jason fled to Sparta (168 B.C.E.), expecting to find asylum in a Jewish community under the rule of a friendly government.[23]

Rapid Hellenization of Jewry strengthened the ties of friendship. Jews, especially in the dispersion, more and more tended to adopt Greek as their native tongue. Even after the Maccabean reaction, Greek was generally understood in the Jewish sections of Palestine. When Paul addressed a Jerusalem crowd after his arrest, the listeners were pleased that he chose the "Hebrew" language (Acts 22:2), but apparently would have been able to understand Greek. At no time do we hear of a Hellenistic or Roman official who needed an interpreter while addressing Jews. The author of the *Letter of Aristeas* (39) took it for granted that there were in Palestine six elders of each of the twelve tribes who were "men of noble life and skilled in your law and able to interpret it" who would have no difficulty in translating it into Greek. Certainly Lysimachus of Jerusalem who, according to an extant manuscript colophon, translated the book of Esther, and Sirach's grandson who rendered his grandfather's work into Greek were Greek-writing Palestinians.

That the knowledge of Greek was superficial is self-evident. Even in Antioch, the center of Hellenism, the majority of the people spoke primarily Aramaic. In Palestine, even the historian Eupolemus, though apparently a diplomat dispatched by Judah Maccabee to Rome in 161 and hence evidently conversant with spoken Greek (his father had already served as an envoy to an Hellenistic court), had little command of the literary language. "No secular book," says J. Freudenthal, "composed outside Palestine during the sec-

ond half of the second century is written in such faulty Greek."
Two centuries later Josephus, a well-to-do and educated young
man, knew so little Greek that, after years of steady conversation at
the court of the Flavian emperors, he had to admit that he could
not pronounce Greek with sufficient exactness. Throughout his
literary work runs, as Thackeray has shown, a thread of corrections
by his various Greek assistants to whom Josephus himself made a
belated acknowledgment in his *Contra Apionem*. Some of these assistants were greater purists than others. Nevertheless, knowledge
of the language was sufficiently disseminated to open the road to
mutual understanding between Greeks and Jews.[24]

Linguistic assimilation of Diaspora Jewry went much deeper.
The Jews of Egypt, after a century or two, had so far lost command
of the Hebrew language that a translation of their Scriptures into
Greek became imperative even for use in synagogues. In the first
pre-Christian century they still seem to have prayed in Hebrew, if
we may take a clue from the Nash papyrus which contained the
Decalogue and the *Shema'* (Deut. 5:6–21; 6:4–5) and which was
evidently intended for liturgical use. But later on the rabbis were
forced to acknowledge the validity of a Greek recitation of *Shema'*
because of its widespread use in the dispersion. In the *Apostolic
Constitutions* of the fourth century we find, in christianized form,
some of the original benedictions of the silent prayer, *'Amidah,* as
read in Greek-speaking synagogues, a small fragment of which has
also been detected in a Greek papyrus. Philo, extremely pious and
patriotic, indeed a foremost champion of Judaism in the Greek
world, spoke and wrote only in Greek (which he called "our own
tongue") and gave Hebrew little place in his extensive studies. He
frequently adopted most peculiar etymologies because he was apparently unwilling to check the Septuagint with the Hebrew original.[25]

That the masses of the Jews did not speak pure Greek is obvious.
The language of the Septuagint and of some books of the New
Testament bears so many marks of Semitism that for a few decades
Viteau's theory that the Jews of that time spoke a language of their
own, a sort of Judeo-Greek, was widely adopted. Analogies were
frequently drawn between modern Yiddish or Ladino and some
clearly unclassical terms in the ancient versions or in the Palestinian Greek literature. A contemporary, Cleomedes, derided synagogue Greek in a manner common to modern assailants of the
Jewish "jargons" (Reinach's *Textes,* No. 121). This theory has been

exploded by recent investigations based upon a better knowledge of the vernacular Egyptian and Palestinian Greek, the *koiné*. A. Deissmann has proved that Semitic influences were equally strong in the numerous papyri and inscriptions written at the time by non-Jewish Orientals. In fact, since the Palestinian Jews themselves already spoke Aramaic rather than Hebrew, their linguistic mixtures and regional dialects could not differ widely from those of their Gentile neighbors.

If the Septuagint shows a more marked Hebrew influence, it was primarily because of the reverence of translators toward every word of Scripture, which they tried to render as literally as possible. Even the King James version, written after centuries of experience in translating, contains innumerable Hebraisms. How much more must this have been the case with translators whose knowledge of Hebrew was not always adequate! According to a much-debated theory, some of them were so little conversant with Hebrew that they had to use Hebrew texts transliterated into the Greek alphabet, such transliterations having long been in use by Egyptian Jews. This theory, however erroneous in itself, reveals the low esteem in which the linguistic equipment of some of these ancient translators is held by modern scholars. Neither is their Greek vocabulary particularly rich. As was pointed out, they had to use the stereotyped verb *poiein* (do) to render 118 different Hebrew terms. Had they been creative artists of the caliber of Buber and Rosenzweig, they might have produced an aesthetically impressive, but consciously artificial Hebraic Greek, which would never be suspected of having been their spoken tongue.

It must be said in their favor, however, that they were pioneers in their gigantic attempt to translate an entire literature into another tongue. In comparison with their work, all previous examples of translations in world literature, such as the Aḥiqar story, shrink to insignificance. Like the King James version the Septuagint, with all its deficiencies, also made linguistic history. Jewish and Christian writers, inured to it by daily readings and public recitations in synagogues and churches, unconsciously emulated its lexicographical and syntactic peculiarities, especially in their discussion of religious subjects. In this sense we may accept A. D. Nock's assertion that "in the vulgar Greek of the Levant there was nothing corresponding to the Semitic flavor of the early Christian writers. . . . Paul is not writing peasant Greek or soldier Greek, he is writing the Greek of a man who has the Septuagint in his blood." [26]

CLASSICAL ANTISEMITISM

This Hellenization of the Jewish masses, at first pleasing to Greek expansive ambitions, later turned out to be the chief aid to Jewish propaganda. As such, it was a most effective check on the spread of truly Hellenic conceptions and institutions. The rapid growth of the Diaspora thus evoked a protracted anti-Jewish reaction, which gave rise to widespread ancient "antisemitism" (an expression to be taken with more than a grain of salt since most Jew-haters were themselves of Semitic extraction) which bears comparison with the various shades of modern Jew-baiting.[27]

Jew-hatred was profound among the masses in the Hellenistic East. In a city like Alexandria or Antioch, the Jews were regarded as aliens who sought to dominate the rest of the population by virtue of their numbers, affluence, and solidarity. Even in republican Rome the great forensic orator, Cicero, facing the difficult task of pleading for the obviously guilty defendant, Lucius Valerius Flaccus, resorted to the usual trick of attacking the Jewish plaintiffs, whose sacred money had been appropriated by this erstwhile Roman governor. "You know," he whispered to the court with reference to the numerous Jews in the audience, "what a big crowd it is, how they stick together, how influential they are in assemblies."[28]

The ever-noisy and quarrelsome citizenry of a Graeco-Oriental municipality resented, in particular, the peculiarities of the Jewish way of life. The segregated life of the Jewish communities injected further venom into the strained relationship. Already the Jews had a sort of ghetto. At least in Alexandria, Sardes, and Apollinopolis Magna (Edfu), perhaps also in Rome, Oxyrhynchus, Hermopolis, and Halicarnassus, there existed predominantly Jewish quarters. That, apart from the general oriental predilection for topographical segregation of ethnic and religious groups, the Jews themselves were coresponsible, is best seen from Josephus. Speaking about Alexandria, the Jewish historian regards it as a privilege that Alexander (or his successors) "assigned them [the Jews] a quarter of their own, in order that, through mixing less with aliens, they might be free to observe their rules more strictly."[29]

Life within these quarters, proceeding in strange and incomprehensible ways, filled the superficial Gentile observer with awe and suspicion, or with abhorrence and contempt. The few who, attracted by this strange world, developed closer relations with the Jews, often left their own group altogether and joined the Jewish community. Instead of serving as intermediaries for reconciliation, they helped increase prevailing suspicions. A patriotic Jewish poet viewing the situation as early as 140 B.C.E. sadly sang, "And every land shall be full of thee and every sea; and every one shall be incensed at thy customs" (*Sibylline Oracles* III, 271–72). The strong Jewish communal organization was declared to be a government within the government. Emperor Claudius, generally friendly to the Jews, wrote in his letter to Alexandria,

I bid the Jews not to busy themselves about anything beyond what they have held hitherto, and not henceforth as if you and they lived in two cities to send two embassies—a thing such as never occurred before now—nor to strive in gymnasiarchic and cosmetic games, but to profit by what they possess, and enjoy in a city not their own an abundance of all good things [H. I. Bell's *Jews and Christians in Egypt*, p. 29].

In Egypt, particularly, the ancient animosities were further aggravated by the equivocal position of the Jews between the successive conquering minorities and the oppressed native majority. The great emphasis placed by the Bible on the Exodus from Egypt and the glorification of this event in the Passover Haggadah and Greek dramas, like the *Exagogé* by the Jewish playwright Ezechielos, wounded the national susceptibilities of the Egyptians and, before long, also of their Hellenistic overlords. Although somewhat toned down in Alexandrian Jewish historiography and, apparently, also in the Palestinian liturgy under Ptolemaic rule, the story of the ten plagues, the drowning of the Egyptian hosts in the Red Sea, and so on, was told in full by the Septuagint translators to the chagrin of many patriotic Egyptians. The latter countered by accepting the basic ingredients of the story, but explaining its details in a different light. Already Hecataeus was familiar with the Egyptian counternarrative which, ever more embroidered in subsequent generations, reinterpreted the Exodus of the ancient Israelites into a forcible expulsion.

Ritualistic segregation of Jews and Egyptians in the consumption of food was also more severe than elsewhere because of mutual exclusion by religious taboos. The endogamous prohibitions carried over from early biblical tribalism further envenomed the intimacy of social relationships and even played havoc with the conversion of individual Egyptians. Of the four nations singled out by the biblical lawgiver against entry "into the assembly of the Lord" (Deut. 23:4–9), the majority of Edomites (now Idumaeans) were forcibly incorporated into the Jewish body politic by John Hyr-

canus. The Ammonites and Moabites had been so thoroughly overrun by Nabataean Arabs that Josephus no longer distinguished
clearly between them. The Egyptians alone remained more or less
intact. As late as the second century an Egyptian proselyte among
R. 'Aqiba's disciples speculated on having his son marry (the daughter of) an Egyptian woman proselyte, thus securing for his grand-
children the "third generation" status required for full admission
to the Jewish fold.[30]

These socioreligious controversies had been far overshadowed,
ever since the Persian period, by the alliance between the Jews and
the imperial power. The support extended by the Elephantine colony to the Persian rulers against their rebellious Egyptian subjects
embroiled it, we recall, in many a conflict with the local population. After Alexander's conquest numerous Jews were again found
among the civil and military supporters of the Ptolemaic regime.
Whatever one thinks about the Ptolemies' general solicitude for
the welfare of their subjects, many Jews unquestionably aided and
abetted the oppression of the long-suffering native majority subjected to the so-called *laographia*. Certainly the Jewish tax farmers,
occasionally recorded in the papyri, did not enhance the popularity of the Jewish group among these hard-driven taxpayers.

At the same time the Hellenized citizens of the "Greek" municipalities of Alexandria, Naukratis, and Ptolemais (after Hadrian,
also Antinoupolis) resented the Jewish drive for full civil and political equality with them. Particularly after the Roman conquest
these "Greeks" and "Macedonians," having themselves become a
subject population, doubly wished to differentiate between their
own and the Jewish groups then still growing by leaps and bounds.
Hostility against Rome thus could readily be combined with attacks on Jews, as is shown in the so-called "Acts of the Heathen
Martyrs." In fact, one of the recurrent themes in these remarkable
martyrologies is the alleged favoritism shown by the emperors to
the Egyptian Jews. In one of them the hero, Isidorus, is said to have
accused Emperor Claudius to his face of being the son of a Jewess.[31]

Not surprisingly, however, Rome's own ruling classes often bitterly objected to the Jewish attachment to their emperors. In the
early period of the Principate the older patrician groups doubtless
viewed with alarm the unequivocal Jewish allegiance to such imperial "upstarts" as Caesar or Augustus. On its part, the Jewish
minority in the dispersion always had to establish some *modus vi-
vendi* with the powers that were, even at the price of alienating

powerful opposition groups. In the case of the first Caesars such Jewish loyalties were reinforced by a genuine feeling of gratitude for the imperial benefactions.

No less, moreover, than the provincial, the conservative groups in Rome frequently felt endangered by the progressive dissolution of accepted morals and the evident success of Jewish religious propaganda. Writing some thirty years after the fall of Jerusalem, Tacitus realized with deep misgivings that the victory of Roman arms had not decided the issue. Just as he was prepared to justify Nero's persecution of Christians *utilitate publica* (cf. his *Annales,* XV, 44), so he considered the Jews a menace to the established order, subverting, especially, its three main pillars of religion, country, and family. Certainly a comparison with the favorable status of Jewish women must have increased the restiveness of Roman wives under the extreme authority over life and death still theoretically exercised by their husbands by virtue of the traditional *patria potestas.* In view of Christianity's ultimate conquest of Rome one cannot altogether condemn this Roman patriot for giving vent, although perhaps in too harsh a language, to his keen anxiety over the survival of his deeply cherished civilization.

Above all, however, here and throughout the empire there was widespread resentment of the "alien" character of Jews, raised to a high pitch by the growth of Jewish population, both native and converted. Populace and intellectuals went arm in arm, and almost simultaneously with the mob assaults upon Jews in Alexandria in 88 B.C.E., historical and philosophical literature began to inspire increasing hostility. When popular animosity in the Egyptian metropolis later found an outlet in the first real "pogrom" in 38 C.E., it was a contemporary thinker, the usually reticent Stoic Seneca, who gave the most passionate expression to the inveterate grievance, "The customs of that most accursed nation [more exactly: most criminal nation, *sceleratissimae gentis*] have gained such strength that they have been now received in all lands; the conquered have given laws to the conquerors" (quoted from *De superstitione* by Augustine in his *City of God,* VI, 11). Seneca's phrase, *Victi victoribus leges dederunt,* which in its context sharply contrasted with the well-known more benevolent adage concerning captive Greece having conquered victorious Rome, became the keynote for many subsequent pagan and Christian anti-Jewish writers.

At the same time other Jew-baiters echoed the opposing argument of ancient conquerors that the Jews' political weakness was proof of their religious inferiority as well. Four years after Pompey's occupation of Palestine Cicero argued,

Even while Jerusalem was standing and the Jews were at peace with us, the practice of their sacred rites was at variance with the glory of our empire, the dignity of our name, the customs of our ancestors. But now it is even more so, when that nation by its armed resistance has shown what it thinks of our rule; how dear it was to the immortal gods is shown by the fact that it has been conquered, reduced to a subject province, made a slave [*Pro Flacco*, XXVIII, 69].

Apion, too, saw "clear proof" against the truth of Judaism in the fact that the Jews "are not masters of an empire, but rather the slaves, first of one nation, then of another" (*Ag. Ap.* II, 11. 125). This argument was to be repeated, with much more telling effect, by Christian as well as pagan assailants of Judaism after the political defeats of 70 and 135. Tacitus who, like nearly all his Judeophobe contemporaries, was ignorant of Israel's preëxilic history, even contended that the Jews had never had a significant state of their own nor distinguished themselves on the field of battle. Did not even the better-informed Hecataeus believe that the Jews had never had a king?

Seneca's irate exclamation was not entirely unjustified, however. Even in the days of Augustus, when the western part of the empire was but slightly affected by Jewish proselytism, the Jewish seven-day week assumed ever-increasing importance. The Jewish Sabbath, however, that crowning point and indeed profound justification of such a week, was rejected and generally ridiculed as a day devoted to idleness. Seneca himself sharply censured its observers for the ensuing loss of one-seventh of man's labor—an accusation which would have more fittingly come from an efficiency-obsessed Roman administrator than from this distinguished expounder of Stoic philosophy.[32]

Much of the inflammatory material in vogue in anti-Jewish propaganda evidently was the product of conscious fabrication. When Antiochus Epiphanes desecrated the Temple in Jerusalem, the Jews' outburst of indignation found a ready response in the whole Hellenistic world, in which sacrilege committed even in a foreign sanctuary was regarded as an unpardonable crime. To defend the actions of their king, the Antiochian "publicity agents" initiated a campaign of vilification of the Jewish people and their religion. It was then that the myth of the "ritual murder" originated. Combining several current folkloristic and ritualistic motifs, the Seleucid fabulists composed a dramatic story of how Antiochus, on entering the Jerusalem sanctuary, found a Greek captive awaiting immolation to the Jewish God. The king learned to his amazement that the prospective victim had been informed by Temple servants that it was an established practice of the Jews that "they would kidnap a Greek foreigner, fatten him up for a year, and then convey him to a wood, where they slew him, sacrificed his body with their customary ritual, partook of his flesh, and, while immolating the Greek, swore an oath of hostility to the Greeks." So unprepared was the Graeco-Roman world for monotheism and imageless worship that it found in such tales, combined with Antiochus' other contention that he had found a donkey in the holy of holies, a means of grasping rationally what it thought was the real object of worship of Jews, and later Christians, namely, the donkey. If Tacitus, knowing that Pompey on entering the Temple found no divine statue there, implied that the image of the donkey had merely served as a votive offering rather than an object of worship, his formulation was so equivocal as to mislead Tertullian and most modern writers. Certainly the unsophisticated masses never drew such fine distinctions but believed in outright Jewish donkey worship. In this way the Hellenistic party of Jerusalem, which partly because of fear that Jewish persistence in the traditional way of life would increase anti-Jewish feeling had invoked the aid of Antiochus and thus embroiled him in a protracted war with the loyal Jews, unwittingly contributed to the spread of that most vicious form of ancient antisemitism.[33]

In the following centuries the ritual murder accusation was not frequently made against the Jews, but rather against Christians whose use of the Eucharist seemed to lend it a measure of verisimilitude. The Christians, in turn, began to accuse their own gnostics and other sectarians of such rites. Beginning in the twelfth century, however, the Jews again became the main sufferers. Their segregation and purported solidarity led the classical world to nurture lingering suspicions that all Jews were imbued with indiscriminate hostility toward Gentiles. *Odium generis humani* became the constant refrain in singling out the Jewish and later the Christian "enemies of mankind."

Since the Jewish refusal to share in Gentile meals served as a constant irritant and reminder of that "enmity," many perhaps otherwise open-minded persons gullibly accepted the most ridiculous strictures. They could cite as authorities such distinguished philosophers as the leader of the middle Stoa, Poseidonius, and such influential rhetoricians as Apollonius Molon, teacher of Cicero and Caesar. Juvenal later in all seriousness asserted that a Jew never would show the way to a Gentile or lead him to a fountain. Tacitus pointed out as the culmination of Jewish hatred that, "although as a race, they are prone to lust [*proiectissima ad libidinem gens*], they abstain from intercourse with foreign women." As is usual in antisemitic letters these complaints did not prevent another writer, Meleager of Gadara, from voicing the opposite grievance that a Jewish rival had taken away his mistress. "White-cheeked Demo," he lamented, "some one hath thee naked next him and is taking his delight, but my own heart groans within me. If thy lover is a Sabbath-keeper, no great wonder. Love burns hot even on cold Sabbaths." [34]

To general denunciations of Jewish aloofness were added many attacks on Jewish customs and beliefs, some of which have a modern sound. From the disparagement of Jewish "contributions to civilization" to the discovery of an offensive odor emanating from Jewish bodies; from cheap witticisms about circumcision and abstention from pork to allegations of "atheism," almost every note in the cacophony of medieval and modern antisemitism was sounded by the chorus of ancient writers. Josephus refers to Apollonius who has scattered his accusations "here and there all over his work, reviling us in one place as atheists and misanthropes, in another reproaching us as cowards, whereas elsewhere, on the contrary, he accuses us of temerity and reckless madness" (*Ag. Ap.* II, 14. 148).

Occasionally there is a taunt of Jewish "cunning," and one Alexandrian merchant warned a friend involved in debt "to beware of the Jews." As a rule, however, Greeks and Romans were equally efficient businessmen, employing the same methods as Jews. Nowhere are the Jews accused of "usury." On the contrary, Jewish poverty rather than wealth attracted the attention of most satirists of stage and literature. It is difficult, indeed, to detect here any of those strong economic motivations which were to color so much of the Jew-hatred in the later periods of greater Jewish concentration on a few fields of economic endeavor.[35]

Vituperation of contemporary Jews was not deemed sufficient. In view of the "classical" reverence for tradition, with its undistinguishable maze of mythology, folklore, and actual history, it was necessary to prove that Judaism had been corrupt from the beginning. Hence the oriental Hellenists proceeded to retell the history of the Jews in an unfavorable light. They dwelt especially upon the period of Israel's origin, the personality and the age of Moses. Seizing upon the story told about half a century after Alexander by Manethon, an Egyptian priest-historian, concerning the expulsion of the Hyksos from Egypt, they interpreted the biblical Exodus as an expulsion motivated by the fear that the Jews would contaminate the people of the country with leprosy. Thus Manethon's fairly innocuous statement grew into a legend, repeated and amplified by one writer after another. It was finally adopted as an historical truth by most Graeco-Roman historians.[36]

It goes without saying that anti-Jewish feeling was not everywhere equally strong and steady. Structural changes in Jewish and general society, complex transformations in the social and political status of the Jews, naturally exercised a decisive influence upon the spread and intensity of anti-Jewish sentiment. In Rome, for instance, down to the age of Augustus, the pro-Jewish policies of the government rendered literary antisemitism relatively inexpedient. With the reversal of imperial policy, the crudest type of Jew-baiting was quickly echoed by intellectual leaders. After a momentary effervescence during the time of the Jewish "rebellions," passion subsided in the third century, soon to be succeeded by most vehement anti-Jewish denunciations of the increasingly powerful Christian heirs of ancient society.

JEWISH APOLOGIAS

Against such an accumulation of prejudice and hatred Jewish apologists might try to rewrite biblical stories in a manner more palatable to contemporary readers or even to "embellish" them with more "modern" features. But they hardly ever reached the truly Gentile public. Not even those who wrote on Jewish subjects read Jewish apologetical literature. Appollonius Molon, who early in the first century B.C.E. wrote a *Diatribe against the Jews,* was exceptional in that he showed some desire to acquaint himself with the few Hellenistic Jewish writings then available. Later antisemites usually were satisfied with copying one another without any attempt at verification through Jewish letters. Many were notoriously superficial, for example, Apion, a hellenized Egyptian demagogue of Alexandria, whose irresponsible attacks on Jews and others earned him from Emperor Tiberius the epithet *cymbalum mundi*. Then as later, most Jewish apologists soliloquized sadly in a sort of collective monologue to a sympathetic audience of Jews or half-Jews who had asked for no apologies.

Unfortunately, our knowledge of the intellectual life of Diaspora Jewry is almost entirely derived from Hellenistic Egypt. Apart from Philo's works, moreover, little more than the Septuagint and parts of the apocryphal literature are in a more or less satisfactory state of preservation. These writings, because of their subject matter, are permeated with the spirit of the Old Testament and of Palestine. Biblical anthropomorphisms, though less pronounced than those of Homeric mythology, often evoked disparaging comments from "enlightened" heathens. Nevertheless the Greek translators of the Bible ventured but rarely to deviate from the Hebrew text. While one translator was more successful than another in avoiding the numerous pitfalls, they were all less consistent and radical in circumscribing overt anthropomorphisms than even the Palestinian author of the Aramaic Targum. For one example, the passage, "God is not a man" (Num. 23:19) is rendered by the Septuagint by "God is not like man," while the Targum uses the circumlocution of "Not like the words of man is the Word [*memra*] of God." In this sense, the "Hellenization of Semitic monotheism," to use Adolf Deissmann's much-debated phrase, was formal rather than integral.[37]

Otherwise only minor fragments of independent historical, apologetical, poetic, and philosophic writings have come down, permitting a few glimpses into their apologetical and theological outlook, but hardly a reconstruction of a whole credo or system of defense. We learn, for example, from Eusebius that Aristobulus, the oldest known Jewish philosopher (second century B.C.E.), tried to persuade King Ptolemy VI that the anthropomorphic expressions in the Bible were not to be taken literally and that Homer and Hesiod had already accepted the allegorical meaning of a divinely instituted weekly day of rest. But we neither know whether he borrowed or himself fabricated the Greek poets' evidently spurious verses, nor are we even certain of the genuineness of his own statements. Whether or not wholly authentic, however, his views seem to be typical of a wide circle of Alexandrian Jewish apologists. Similarly, from the standpoint of characteristic attitudes, it makes little difference how we view the much-debated authenticity and date of the *Letter of Aristeas*. The spiritualization of Jewish ceremonial

law, attributed by it to high priest Eleazar addressing the visiting
Egyptian dignitaries, and the pearls of religious and mundane wisdom cited by it from the alleged table talks of the seventy-two Palestinian translators entertained at the court of Alexandria, were ideas
which many Diaspora Jews wished their neighbors to consider pe-
culiarly Jewish.[38]

Even the poetic license of Ezechielos did not allow him to follow
too closely the biblical narrative, where it conflicted with his own
and his environment's theological views. He described the slaying
of Egypt's first-born as having been accomplished by an angel of
God, rather than God himself—a view of the Exodus with which
the Palestinian Passover Haggadah takes specific issue. Other ro-
mancers, like the author of *Tobit*, idealized the moral conduct and
piety of their heroes. Still others extolled the Jewish people as such.
Although generally following the pattern of Greek romances, the
author of the Third Book of Maccabees diverged "in the absence
of two elements essential to Greek romance, the erotic factor and
the personal hero. The hero is patently all Israel." [39]

Some writers preferred to criticize directly other religions. The
author of the apocryphal *Epistle of Jeremy*, expatiating on Jer. 28,
advised the Babylonian exiles to adhere staunchly to their faith
and not to surrender to Babylonian idolatry. He was so scathingly
familiar with the intricacies of the Babylonian religion as to evoke
doubts in modern scholars whether his message had originally been
written in Greek. As if an Egyptian or Syrian Jewish writer could
not, in order to lend greater credence to his pseudepigraphon, familiarize himself with the Babylonian beliefs and rituals! He could
have learned all he wished from any itinerant Babylonian priest.
Certainly those predominantly Alexandrian Jewish, and later
Christian, poets, who borrowed from Berossos the Babylonian
Sibylla called Sambethis and converted her into a Jewish prophetess, did not hesitate to utter through her memorable words of doom
for all existing pagan civilizations and to go on predicting the
downfall of Rome's imperial power at the very height of its grandeur.[40]

Exalted predictions of this kind were evidently aimed less at the
Gentile world than at the much-confused Hellenistic Jews themselves. Jewish leaders must have felt that building up the morale of
their people was as important as antidefamation, in fact the most
eminent means of fortifying their own people against accepting
standards of values set by its antisemitic detractors. In 132 (or 110),

Sirach's grandson translated his grandfather's words of wisdom for the benefit of those who "in the land of their sojourning desire to be lovers of learning, being already prepared in respect of their moral culture to live by the Law" (Prologue). About the same time Jason of Cyrene described, with much embellishment, the heroic struggle of the Maccabeans against their Syrian oppressors. Later writers not only vastly amplified the story of the seven "Maccabean" martyrs, making it the subject of a special book (IV Maccabees), but also told the story of a miraculous redemption of Alexandrian Jewry from a monarch's evil designs in the so-called Third Book of Maccabees. The parallel older Palestinian story of Esther, on the other hand, found an effective propagandist in Dositheus and his son, who brought a Greek translation of the book to Egypt a decade after the first outbreak of anti-Jewish riots in Alexandria. All these writings clearly aimed at combating internal defeatist attitudes, much more than at countering anti-Jewish arguments.[41]

In contradistinction to their modern successors, however, these ancient apologists did not constantly invoke the prophets. Like their opponents they, too, treated extensively only the period of the patriarchs and, more especially, that of Moses. In his epic poem, *Peri ta Hierosolyma*, Philo the Elder sang the praises of Jerusalem which, as he must have known, had become Jewish only in the days of King David. None the less he principally glorified Abraham's covenant with God and Joseph's rule over Egypt. This is at least the content of two of his three extant fragments. Similarly, the Alexandrian author of the Wisdom of Solomon, though invoking the shades of the wise king, merely told the story of his people from Adam to Moses which, allegorically amplified, was to serve as an object lesson of the divine guidance of the universe through the instrumentality of the chosen people.[42]

Utilizing the indisputable historic priority of Moses over the Greek thinkers, these defenders of their ancestral faith followed a good Greek custom in synthesizing the most diverse strains in cultural history and declaring that all Greek wisdom was derived from Mosaic antecedents. They eventually went so far as to claim Israel as the fountainhead of all human knowledge. Josephus' *Antiquities* were largely written in order to make clear "the extreme antiquity of our Jewish race, the purity of the original stock, and the manner in which it established itself in the country which we occupy today. That history embraces a period of five thousand years" (*Ag. Ap.* I, 1.1; cf. *Antt.* I, 1, 3. 13).

While Josephus merely exaggerated the age of his people, Arta-panus, apparently a scion of Persian-Jewish settlers in Egypt, did not hesitate to make Moses the main teacher of the ancient Egyptian religion, although, like other Jews of the time, he certainly deeply detested Egyptian animal worship. Even to Philo, the Pentateuch is the section in the Bible that really matters. For him as for his predecessors prophetic teaching is only one element of Judaism, in which ceremonial law is equally, if not more, important. The actions of men counted more than their convictions in the ancient world. Philo's statement concerning Moses "that there are four adjuncts in the truly perfect ruler[:] he must have kingship, the faculty of legislation, priesthood and prophecy" is truly representative of what, he thought, would appeal to a Hellenistic reader, whether Jew or Gentile. Philo's arguments sounded so persuasive that more than a century later a non-Jewish Platonist, Numenius, is reported to have called Plato "a Moses speaking in the Attic idiom." [43]

This exclusive treatment of the origins of the people accounts for the increasing oblivion into which subsequent epochs of Jewish history gradually fell. When the professional historians showed so little interest in what happened after Moses, nothing was to be expected from the masses. Certainly, it was primarily owing to the negligence of the Hellenistic age that so few reliable records have come down to us from the preceding Persian period. The later rabbis so completely forgot the significant developments during that crucial age that they reduced its duration from more than two centuries to thirty-four years, notwithstanding the difficulties they encountered in explaining the succession of kings and events recorded in Ezra and Nehemiah. [44] In this fashion, the people of "history," whose career was an historical mission, whose religion celebrated its historical crisis, whose fathers wrote memorable history, tended completely to forget, under the influence of the Greek mind, the sequel to its birth and the succession of its own experiences.

PHILO JUDAEUS

There were, of course, many diverse trends among the millions of Jews. On the one hand, Palestine, especially after its successful Maccabean revolt, could never reconcile itself fully to the fact of the dispersion. For Palestinian Jewry the Diaspora always remained the *galut*, the exile, a curse inflicted by God upon a sinful people.

On the other hand, thinkers of the Diaspora rationalized their situation. Philo offered a most memorable, though somewhat apologetic, rationale,

So populous are the Jews that no one country can hold them, and therefore they settle in very many of the most prosperous countries in Europe and Asia both in the islands and on the mainland, and while they hold the Holy City where stands the sacred Temple of the most high God to be their mother city [metropolin], yet those which are theirs by inheritance from their fathers, grandfathers, and ancestors even farther back, are in each case accounted by them to be their fatherland [patridas nomizontes] in which they were born and reared, while to some of them they have come at the time of their foundation as immigrants to the satisfaction of their founders [In Flaccum, VII, 45–46].

Here we have an adumbration of the Balfour Declaration of 1917, which stressed the Palestinian homeland while safeguarding the rights of the Jews as natives of other countries.

In the different lands, however, different habits and religious observances arose. With the passage of time the Jews increasingly "modified their ancient institutions because of their mixing with strangers," as noted already by Hecataeus. The conflicts arising from such ritualistic divergences seem to have furnished Onias one of his main arguments for the need of a central sanctuary for Egyptian Jewry. Certainly, the religious customs of Alexandria as recorded by Philo, differed considerably from what we may reconstruct of the official law of contemporary Palestine.[45] While there were here germs of future conflict, what then mattered was that Philo himself was but slightly aware of any serious deviations. He certainly considered himself an observant Jew even from the Palestinian standpoint.

Going back to the fundamental principles underlying Jewish law, Philo was able to construe a basically new and comprehensive theological system. Preserved for posterity and eagerly studied by subsequent generations of Christian thinkers, his numerous writings (to a large extent still extant) marked an epochal departure in human thought, by their combination of Greek philosophical thinking with Jewish traditional content and the interadaptation of both. Outwardly, they were little more than an explanation, in the light of philosophy, of events and laws recorded in the Pentateuch.

The Alexandrian philosopher may have resented the circumstance which for a while imposed upon him a diplomatic mission in defense of his coreligionists. His involved literary style, with its frequent mystic allusions comprehensible only to a chosen few, may have been a conscious stratagem to discourage the uninitiated. Bousset and Gressmann go too far, however, in asserting that "Philo's writings convey with all desirable clarity the impression of his solitary life and his consciousness of writing only for a small and intimate circle." Philo may, indeed, have been influenced by the age-old debate among Greek thinkers as to whether social life or that of a recluse was most suitable to a philosopher. In his mind this problem undoubtedly was connected with the more general question as to the relative merits of contemplative and practical life. Whatever his personal inclinations, however, as a pious Jew interested in moral conduct he had to emphasize both. He declared that "while virtue involves theory and practice, it is of surpassing excellence in each respect; for indeed the theory of virtue is perfect in beauty, and the practice and exercise of it is a prize to be striven for." No matter, therefore, what his private life and predilections may have been, Philo became a true spokesman of the most typical currents in Egyptian-Jewish Hellenism.[46]

Of course, Philo was far removed from the ideals of the Hellenizers in the pre-Maccabean age, who wished to substitute Hellenism for Judaism. He undoubtedly was endeavoring to do no more than implement his inherited creed with Hellenistic elements of his own choice. Under the influence of Greek philosophy and facing entirely different social conditions in Jewry, however, his theological outlook is naturally different from anything known in Palestine. Alexandrian Jewry was part and parcel of a developed early capitalistic system. The well-to-do and cultivated members of the community tended to find theoretical formulae for their religious heritage. As in other prosperous societies both rationalistic philosophy and mysticism offered more satisfactory solutions than did the naïve creed of forefathers with its main emphasis upon practical behavior.

Transgressors of traditional law understandably enough were far more numerous among the Hellenistic Jews than in Palestine. Here the conscious attempt of the early Hellenizers, "Let us go and make a covenant with the nations that are round about us; for since we separated ourselves from them many evils have come upon us" (I Macc. 1:11), was terminated by the successful Maccabean revolt. But in the dispersion, forces of amalgamation were merely slowed down by the new influences emanating from Jerusalem. Among Philo's compatriots there were many who, in the philosopher's words, "cherish a dislike of the institutions of our fathers and make it their constant study to denounce and decry the Laws" (*De confusione linguarum*, II, 2).

Philo himself sharply condemned such views. Although transgressions of the law were not enough in his eyes to cause exclusion from the body of Israel, he himself was quite pious in observing religious rites. To him, ceremonies had in themselves higher meaning. In many a passage he showed himself adverse to the extreme spiritualization of religious rites and urged the reader "to let go nothing that is part of the customs fixed by divinely empowered men greater than those of our time." At the same time he stressed here the law's validity merely as a body; the soul of Jewish life is those other "things" which the law symbolizes. He was still more explicit in numerous passages sharply attacking the literal interpretation of Scriptures, an interpretation which was not unknown even in the countries of the dispersion. Indeed, the main objective of a major part of his writings was to detect the moral significance underlying each general and "special" law.[47]

The highest goal in these ceremonies is mystic communion with God. Such communion can be achieved only through highest ecstasy, "enthusiasm," and "sober ebriety." Although in describing prophecy Philo contends that "the mind is evicted at the arrival of the divine Spirit," the tenor of his main line of thought consistently was that the gap between man and his transcendent Creator would be bridged not by self-effacement, but by ecstatic rapture to be derived from deeper and deeper contemplation and knowledge of God. In Philo's philosophic speculation, God, while retaining his immanence inescapably postulated by Jewish ethics, became even more transcendent than in the prophetic and apocalyptic visions. The Alexandrian sage, therefore, explained God's relation to this imperfect world only through the intervention of a mediator, the *logos*, a concept of great fruitfulness in the thought of the following generations.[48]

A God of this kind is, of necessity, the One and Only God, which shows, in Philo's opinion, the utter foolishness of "the propounders of polytheism, who do not blush to transfer from earth to heaven mob-rule, that worst of evil polities." He condemned as equally erroneous the view, propagated by some Greek philosophers, of the plurality of universes which, as we shall see, was to find an echo even in a later rabbi's doctrine of God's successive creation and destruction of various worlds before the emergence of the present universe. At the same time Philo's God himself is not only incorporeal—such biblical passages as those referring to God's "image" in the creation of man merely indicate that the latter's spiritual past was "an idea or type or seal, an object of thought, incorporeal, neither male nor female, by nature incorruptible"— but also entirely divested of all qualities which human reason may ascribe to him. "We must first become God, which is impossible," Philo is supposed to have said, "in order to be able to comprehend God." God is *apoios*, without quality. Only deep contemplation of his works, particularly the constant pondering over the divine government of the world and the story of creation as described in the book of Genesis, will enable man to penetrate some of the mysteries of existence and, what is more, lead to a rich and contented life.

He that has begun [reads the conclusion of Philo's cosmological treatise] by learning these things with his understanding rather than with his hearing, and has stamped on his soul impressions of truths so marvellous and priceless, both that God is and is from eternity, and that He that really is is One, and that He has made the world and has made it one world, unique as Himself is unique, and that He ever exercises forethought for His creation, will lead a life of bliss and blessedness, because he has a character moulded by the truths that piety and holiness enforce.[49]

Such a God is necessarily universal, embracing all mankind. The "chosen people" must appear to this spokesman of an intellectualized missionary group as a spiritual, and not a purely ethnic unity. Nevertheless, Philo cannot altogether free himself from the concept of "selection." In his opinion not even the physical descent from Abraham should be underestimated. In one remarkable passage he glorified the great patriarch as the progenitor of "a whole nation, and that the nation dearest of all to God, which, as I hold, has received the gift of priesthood and prophecy on behalf of all mankind" (*De Abrahamo*, XIX, 98). Therefore, only such are welcome as proselytes as are ready not only to accept the main beliefs but also to live Jewish life fully. Disregarding what already in his day must have become a keynote of classical antisemitism, Philo insisted, as we have seen, that, spiritually at least, converts must forsake their country, relatives, and friends for the sake of virtue.

In return, proselytes were, according to Philo's interpretation of Jewish law, to be treated as full-fledged members of the Jewish community with all the rights and duties of native-born Jews. If in need (doubtless often resulting from their severance of ties with their former communities) they had a valid claim on communal support. Disregarding the biblical context, Philo actually sought to extend to them the protective laws of Deut. 10:18, on a par with orphans and widows. For—and we perceive here an echo of Diaspora Jewry's general rationalization of its political inferiority reiterated by the Sibylline poets for two centuries before Philo—God the omnipotent "holds their low estate worthy of his providential care, while of kings and despots and great potentates He takes no account." Except for such specially reserved areas as royal office or the peculiar treatment of a "Hebrew" slave, the biblical phrase, "Thy brother," applied to proselytes as much as to any physical descendants of the Israelitic patriarchs. In fact, if they accepted Judaism for its own sake and lived up to the high demands of Jewish law and ethics, they might well be appreciated by God more highly than "nobly born" Jewish sinners. In short, as a true spokesman of missionary Hellenistic Jewry, Philo marshaled all possible arguments in order to facilitate that "journey to a better home, from idle fables to the clear vision of truth." [50]

Just as the proselyte is at once subjected to the whole range of Jewish law, so is, in Philo's opinion, that law's demonstrable attraction for thoughtful persons from all nations in itself proof of its universality and superiority to all other, locally delimited, legal systems. "Moses himself," he exclaimed in his homiletical biography of the lawgiver (II, 3.12), "was the best of all lawgivers in all countries, better in fact than any that have ever arisen among either the Greeks or the barbarians, and his laws are most excellent and truly come from God." Already Aristobulus and the author of the Wisdom of Solomon had identified Mosaic law with Wisdom, that "breath of the power of God," which "was present when Thou wast making the World" (Wisdom 7:25; 9:9). Tacitly accepting these high-strung praises of the Law (whether or not he knew their peculiar background in the Hebrew term, torah), Philo stressed somewhat paradoxically both its eternal validity and its suitability for all conditions of men, however diverse.

Confronted by the equally law-minded Graeco-Roman civilization, the Jewish apologist did not have to argue the general merits of strictly regulated behavior or even the need of dietary laws. Although doubtless aware of the frequent Gentile objections to those special requirements which tended to segregate the Jews from their neighbors, he merely lauded their excellence in steering a middle course between Spartan austerity and Sybarite voluptuousness (De *spec. leg.*, IV, 17.102). Once he thus acknowledged law, including every ritualistic commandment, as the basis of Jewish living, he had to find for each of its details some proper rationale. To do so, and to explain other passages in the Pentateuch which might appear obnoxious to a sophisticated Alexandrian Jew, he resorted to his well-known method of allegorical interpretation.

Under these circumstances, it is no surprise that Philo's philosophy was based upon an essentially static view of the world. Although not entirely denying their historic reality, his allegories transformed the unique historical personalities and events recorded in Scripture into personifications of abstract ideas and virtues. The element of history, so fundamental in the Jewish religion, evaporated here into the eternal, static categories of the philosophers of the Academy or Stoa.

In this respect Philo was the most extreme even among Hellenistic Jewish writers. The author of the Wisdom of Solomon, for instance, utilized the allegorical method of interpretation quite extensively. But his allegory was mostly like that of the Aggadah, which gave historical connotations even to those passages in the Bible unrelated to any real historical events. Even when he followed Greek allegorists in deriving moral teachings from an historical event—as when he deduced from the victory of Jacob over the angel that "godliness is more powerful" than supernatural force (10:12)—he did not nullify the real historical importance of the event. The second part of his work, in which he surveyed the forces operative in the history of Israel down to the Exodus, was written entirely in this vein. The last sentence, "For in all things, O Lord, thou didst magnify thy people, and thou didst glorify them and not lightly esteem them; standing by their side in every time and place" (19:22) was as historically minded and nationalistic an utterance as anything found in Palestinian letters.

For Philo, however, the repeated statements of the prophets that Israel should not claim for itself the credit of having conquered Canaan, merely indicated that no man should claim credit for his own virtues. In a way he felt apologetic about the entire historical section of the Pentateuch. In his opinion, Moses

did not, like any historian, make it his business to leave behind for posterity records of ancient deeds for the pleasant but unimproving entertainment which they give; but, in relating the history of early times, and going for its beginnings right to the creation of the universe, he wished to shew two most essential things: first that the Father and

Maker of the world was in the truest sense also its Lawgiver, secondly that he who would observe the laws will accept gladly the duty of following nature and live in accordance with the ordering of the universe, so that his deeds are attuned to harmony with his words and his words with his deeds.

This attitude is the more striking as Philo, following the example of his predecessors in Hellenistic Jewish letters, was sincerely an apologist. Like others he wanted to show that all the wisdom of Hellas had its origin in the teachings of Moses. But otherwise he knew very little of a development in history, at times even less than Paul was ready to admit. In brief, to cite Siegfried's apt characterization, "the history of his people, though literally believed to be true, became in his treatment essentially a didactic and symbolic poem." [51]

Philo thus stood at the crossroads between Judaism and Hellenism. He tried to reconcile the historical and the static. That he did not quite succeed and seemed to be in an almost inevitable discord with the world and himself is due to the ultimate impossibility of such an attempt. Historical monotheism, operating endlessly in time, could not be subsumed under such entirely different categories of the eternally changeless and infinitely extended. For this reason, the rigidly orthodox, observant, patriotic, essentially Pharisaic Philo was, if viewed from the Palestinian standpoint, really less of a Jew than the most violently denounced Sadducean sectarian. And it was Palestinian ideology which ultimately determined the course of Judaism.

That is why so few traces of Philo's thinking have been detected in subsequent Jewish literature. His writings may have been extant among Jews as late as the geonic period, but they were little studied and rarely, if ever, cited.[52] The ultimate indebtedness of medieval Jewish philosophy to the Alexandrian sage was mediated through Christian and Muslim thinkers. Ever since Clement and Origen (Alexandrians also), the Church faced, to an even greater extent, the problem of reconciling its Jewish with its Hellenistic heritage. For it, as for Hellenistic Jewry before it, Philo was the revolutionary pathfinder who not only raised some of the most fundamental problems of the dichotomy between Revelation embodied in Scripture, and Reason as propounded by the Greek schools of philosophy, but also pointed a way toward their reconciliation via the allegorical interpretation of Scripture. If, in the process, some of the philosophic doctrines had to be controverted or discarded and most scriptural passages given a strangely twisted meaning, the supremacy of Scripture and of all the vital ingredients of an age-long oral tradition superimposed upon it seemed nevertheless permanently assured.

DIVERGENT ESCHATOLOGIES

Philo was by no means alone. One can witness the decomposition of Palestinian Jewish concepts under the corrosive forces of Egyptian Hellenism even more pronouncedly in Philo's immediate predecessors, Aristobulus and Artapanus. All the shortcomings of Philonian allegory and apology, as well as the unsuccessful juxtaposition of natural and historical categories, are even more clearly discernible in the few extant fragments of these lesser lights of Egyptian Jewry.

In one focal point the contrast between Palestinian and Egyptian Judaism reaches its peak, in Jewish eschatology. No matter who the authors are, none of them, not even such pious preachers as the authors of Wisdom and the Fourth Book of Maccabees, profess the belief in bodily resurrection. This is the more remarkable, as IV Maccabees largely depends on II Maccabees which stresses the belief in resurrection more than any other treatise of the age. We need but remember the great speech of the mother of the seven martyrs, " 'Twas not I who gave you the breath of life or fashioned the elements of each! 'Twas the Creator of the world who fashioneth men and deviseth the generating of all things, and He it is who in mercy will restore to you the breath of life." Such enthusiasm for physical rebirth, understandable not only from the ancient Palestinian antecedents of biblical eschatology, but also as a reflection of a deeply felt need during the Maccabean revolt, makes it highly probable that these passages stemmed from the Palestinian epitomizer rather than from his Hellenistic source, Jason of Cyrene.[53]

This problem of immortality seems to have greatly agitated the minds of Alexandrian Jews. The heritage of the ancient Egyptian beliefs in the Hereafter, still cultivated by Egyptian priests, combined with the newer philosophic debates on life after death to produce no less than three different philosophic doctrines of immortality (not resurrection) which, according to Philo, his Jewish contemporaries interpreted into the biblical phrase, "Thou shalt go to thy fathers in peace." Philo rejected them all in favor of his own theory. Nor were there lacking Jews who, influenced by either

Sadducean or Epicurean doctrines, completely repudiated the belief in life after death. The views of these "ungodly" men were summarized and sharply combated by the author of Wisdom. This identification of the Epicureans with the "impious" generally, shared also by the Neo-Pythagoreans of the first century B.C.E., incidentally helps explain its prevalence also in the talmudic literature, where "Epicuros" is used as a generic term. The majority, however, seems to have resolved the conflict between the growing Palestinian belief in resurrection and the rationalistic denial of all eschatological expectations by subscribing to the survival of the soul alone.[54]

Once again we see here the profound cleavage between the Hellenistic and Palestinian Jewries on the score of "history." After all, resurrection in its full complexity can only be accepted by one whose eschatological hope is turned toward an historical event of prime significance. That is why Palestine stressed resurrection above immortality. For a typical Hellenistic Jew immortality of the soul was the only acceptable affirmation. He need not go the whole distance with those Greek thinkers who saw in the soul of man a part of the "fifth" element in the superlunar world, whereto the soul retires for eternity after its separation from the body. Even if he rejected, with Philo, the Stoic conception of the ethereal, and consequently material, essence of the rational soul, he clung to the immutability and eternality of the spiritual world as a part of the natural world. Thus the profound divergence in the conception of the Hereafter between the "historical" dogma of immortality culminating in resurrection and the Hellenistic "naturalistic" belief in immortality without resurrection illustrates more strikingly than anything else the conflicting Jewish views of life in this world.

All these emphases, however, are but variations of one fundamental theme—monotheism, carried on by a chosen group within mankind. Not even Philo can free himself of the historical element in Judaism sufficiently to deny the messianic ideal, although the dynamic personality of a Messiah has no proper place in such a serene, eternally ordered world. To be sure, restricting his comments largely to passages from the Pentateuch, he was not forced to refer directly to the scion of the house of David. Moreover, as a patriotic Jew viewing the contemporary Palestinian realities under the rule of Herodian princes and high priests claiming, at best, Aaronide descent, he had no occasion to insist upon the Davidic messiah. He may well have been aware of the fact that this had become a partisan issue in Palestinian politics. Clearly, from his perspective, the misrule of later Maccabeans could not dim the glory of the priestly saviors of their people in the great crisis.

Nevertheless, it was quite in keeping with Philo's entire outlook to tone down that celebrated individual irruption into the destinies of man, and rather to emphasize that, as a result of the growing success of the Jewish people, "each nation would abandon its peculiar ways, and, throwing overboard their ancestral customs, turn to honoring our laws alone." Though retaining their national identity, all peoples would then live under one law and thus become parts of a world which would be "as a single state enjoying that best of constitutions, democracy." Like the overwhelming majority of his coreligionists, Philo thus remained a staunch believer in a future Golden Age unrivaled in glory, when all peoples will abandon idolatrous practices and join the Jews in the worship of the one God in Jerusalem. To him as well as to any other Diaspora Jew applied, indeed, Paul's reproachful observation, "And art confident that thou thyself art a guide of the blind, a light of them which are in darkness." [55]

WEAKNESS OF EXPANSION

The unshakable belief in the eternality of the Jewish people and in its great mission, the assertions, reserved or arrogant according to individual tempers, that the final success of that mission was close at hand, reflected only one indubitable fact: the vast expansion of Judaism. Many had been the vicissitudes in the national life of the Jews, the foreign invasions of the mother country, and the foreign domination in the lands of the Diaspora. In spite of all these, the people as a whole continued to wax in numbers and grow in influence. Even in the victories of the Roman legions a sanguine Jew saw milestones in the road on which phalanxes of Jews would march toward a more conclusive victory.

To be sure, grave danger signs were not wanting. The success of Jewish propaganda provoked bitter reaction. The larger the masses of Jews were in any one region and the more pronounced their confidence and assertiveness became, the deeper was the resentment of the Gentile peoples. For a while the security of the Jews, as of everybody else, was guaranteed by the Roman sword. But the Romans might not indefinitely protect against almost everybody's attack a national group whose hostility they often felt and whose claim to exclusive possession of final truth appeared to them impudent, if not positively dangerous.

A perspicacious onlooker must have considered the internal conditions of Jewry even more disquieting. Would the colossal body maintain its cohesion for any length of time, or would the forces of decomposition sooner or later prevail? The profound differences between Hellenistic Jewry and the Palestinian and Babylonian centers and the far-reaching social and economic differentiation among the masses in the various lands harbored germs of deep, perhaps irreconcilable, conflicts.

No simple lack of vision was the reason why even the less sanguine Jews overlooked threatening perils. The messianic expectation of the approaching downfall of the Roman world-empire reflected the actual awakening of the Orient. More and more the Hellenistic veneer was rubbed off by resuscitated oriental, especially Semitic, cultures. Coming at the crest of a new Semitic cultural wave, Jewish expansion had untold possibilities. The evolution of the Roman Empire, the scattering of large masses of Semites over the whole Mediterranean basin, the very destruction by Greek and Roman arms of the territorial and political basis of the Semitic nations, enhanced the position of Jews. Instead of Assyria, Babylonia, or Phoenicia, the nonpolitical Jewish people assumed the leadership of the Semitic world, now deprived of state and territory.

Conversion of the royal house of Adiabene which, ruling over *Nineveh* and the adjacent districts, was the closest successor to the ancient Assyrian conquerors, was more than a symbol. Patriotic Jews could see therein an historic revenge for the conquest of ancient Israel by Assyrian hosts. They could flatter themselves with the hope that soon this feat would be duplicated, and that Roman imperialism would likewise succumb to the spirit of Judah. They could acknowledge the great feat of bringing together the whole civilized world (*oikoumene*) under one rule, achieved by the sword of the nation which, in the words of Pliny, claimed to be *numine deum electa* (chosen by the providence of the gods), and yet hope that this was but a preliminary step to its real unification under the laws of the truly chosen, the "holy nation." Some more worldly and warlike Jewish patriots felt that even an outright military victory was not beyond reach. At the outbreak of the Great War an alleged oracle found widespread credence: "that at that time one from their country would become ruler of the world." [56]

This undeniably was the great "chance" of the Jewish people, as Renan has suggested. However, the use it would make of its new opportunity depended as much on the inner Jewish evolution as on external developments.

PALESTINIAN CENTER

THE high hope of Jewish patriots was not to be realized. Rome and the West were still too vigorous to be overcome by the oriental renaissance led by Jews. Several centuries were to elapse before the oriental (at that time Arab) wave could submerge the weakened empire. In the first and second centuries all such attempts were premature, and in the military clash between Rome and the Jewish people, Rome won the upper hand.

Western resistance in culture and religion was equally powerful. Anti-oriental (especially anti-Jewish) sentiment increased and even made inroads within Judaism itself. The Hellenization of large masses of Diaspora Jewry, accompanied by political, economic, and social transformations, eventually disrupted the unity of the Jewish people. What is more, the Palestinian homeland itself revealed many intrinsic weaknesses which ultimately undermined this main pillar of the world Jewish structure.

From the outset the overemphasis on the power of the Jewish religion, the sublime conviction that Judaism must finally conquer all other creeds and cultures, would have been unthinkable without a vigorous Jewish center in Palestine. However much the Jews in the Diaspora outnumbered those in the homeland, however deep the dissensions among Palestinian leaders, Palestine remained the focus of all Jewish life as such. Even in the period before the Maccabees, the self-governing theocracy of Jerusalem had begun thus to reinterpret the whole system of Judaism that it might be validated for life in the Diaspora. At the same time, a Palestinian psalmist extolled the dispersed brethren of "Rahab" and Babylonia, of Philistia, Tyre, and Ethiopia, but insisted nevertheless that "the Lord loveth the gates of Zion more than all the dwellings of Jacob" (Ps. 87:2–4). Later, in both its gain and its loss of national independence, it was primarily Palestinian Jewry which made Jewish history.

JEWISH METROPOLIS

Such a conclusion is based not merely upon the records which happen to have been preserved. Were we to follow them only, we should think that Babylonian Jewish history between the fourth and the first centuries B.C.E. was slight, and that of Syria and Asia Minor negligible. Historical records are sufficient to let us know that vast masses of Jews lived in these three countries, but we can only guess about their concrete political, social, and religious life. Only Egypt, because of its famous Hellenistic Jewish literature and a dry climate which preserved innumerable papyri, appears correlated with Palestine. Among the papyri and ostraca published thus far, some four hundred have been conservatively identified as elucidating one or another phase of Jewish life between Alexander and Mohammed. Further publication of Greek and, particularly, non-Greek papyri is likely to enhance our knowledge in geometric progression.[1]

Egypt itself, however, was steadily nourished from the inexhaustible source of Jewish life in Palestine. The Temple of Jerusalem, to which they turned in their prayers, was regarded by all Jews as the "navel" of their world far more than that of Delphi was by Euripides and other Greeks. Already the author of Daniel made his hero pray from an upper chamber with windows open "toward Jerusalem." The rabbis later made it clear that "those who pray abroad shall direct their hearts toward Palestine, those who pray in Palestine shall turn their hearts toward Jerusalem . . . so that all Israel will be found praying toward the same spot." [2]

The Temple, particularly the magnificent structure which Herod built and to which even the rabbis could not refuse grudging recognition, also attracted regular pilgrimages from all countries. When the distance was not too great, pilgrims walked to Jerusalem. From more remote regions they traveled by ship or on camels and donkeys, usually in large caravans to repel attacks of robbers. Babylonian Jewry, in particular, sent out annually large companies of pilgrims on the well-kept roads linking the Euphrates to the Jordan by a fortnight's trip. Fulfilling a great religious duty, whether or not they considered it legally binding, they traveled in a mood of song and merrymaking. Even when relations between the Parthian and Roman empires were very strained, the Babylonians persisted in complying with a duty from which in Palestine proper, according to rabbinic law, only old, sick, and abnormal men as well as women, small boys, and slaves were exempted. Women often participated voluntarily. The Talmud has preserved the obscure recollection of a time when the pilgrimage was prohibited by the authorities, and when, nevertheless, many of the pious travelers succeeded by subterfuge in reaching their goal.[3]

Philo was not exaggerating, therefore, when he wrote, "Countless multitudes [*myrioi apo myrion*] from countless cities come, some over land, others over sea, from east and west and north and south at every feast." That the Alexandrian sage had himself been among the pilgrims is attested by his incidental remark concerning his observations at Ascalon, "when I was journeying to the Temple of my fathers to offer prayers and sacrifices." These masses of·pilgrims made such an overwhelming impression on onlookers, that Josephus stated, without fear of contradiction by his contemporaries, that on one occasion the visitors had numbered about 3,000,000. The Talmud later raised the figure to more than 12,000,000. Needless to say, these figures are exaggerated, but they convey the distinct idea that pilgrims must often have far outnumbered the permanent residents of the "holy city." [4]

Of course, the Jewish rulers of Palestine did everything to foster the movement. Even Herod saw it to his advantage to keep open the road from Babylonia. This seems to have been the main purpose of his settling a large colony of warlike Babylonian Jews in the wilds of Batanaea, east of Lake Tiberias. By pacifying this turbulent district and extirpating brigandage, the newcomers were to help secure the safety of travel for their former compatriots. Passover, in particular, by virtue of its national significance, the opportunity it offered for bringing a family sacrifice, and its coincidence with favorable climatic conditions, attracted vast masses of pilgrims. To facilitate the exchange of money in a period when every autonomous city had the right to issue its own coinage, bankers opened establishments on the fifteenth of Adar in the provinces of Palestine, and on the twenty-fifth in Jerusalem, in anticipation of the rush of tourists. In Jerusalem these foreign Jews found legal protection against exploitation by local innkeepers. All fees for shelter, except hides of the sacrificial animals, were prohibited. Generally the reception was extremely amicable and new arrivals often had the opportunity to join a congregation of coreligionists from their own country. Indeed, such synagogues of "Cyrenians and Alexandrians and of them of Cilicia and of Asia" were permanent centers around which a large mass of visitors assembled during the holidays. A synagogue, erected by an Italian Jew Theodotos, son of Vettenos, probably under Agrippa I, included, according to its inscription, "the Hospice and the Chambers; and the water installation for the lodging of needy strangers." [5]

A unifying bond of equal importance was the *didrachmon,* or the annual half shekel, paid by every male Jew over the age of twenty. Hence the great wealth of the Temple treasury which aroused the cupidity of conquerors. Explaining the large amounts carried away by Crassus, which may be estimated at some $18,000,-000 in gold, Josephus remarked that "no one need wonder that there was so much wealth in our temple for all the Jews throughout the habitable world, and those who worshipped God [*sebomenon ton theon*], even those from Asia and Europe, had been contributing to it for a very long time." This temple tax was collected regularly by local Jewish authorities throughout the world, Philo intimating that the leading citizens of each community vied for the honor of being entrusted with its personal delivery to Jerusalem.[6]

In this matter the Jews disregarded all political boundaries. The *cause célèbre* of the Roman governor L. Valerius Flaccus in Asia Minor illumines the whole proceeding. He tried to appropriate some such large collection from Apamaea and three other cities under the pretense of prohibiting the export of gold. Only the skill of Cicero, who sidetracked the issue into extralegal channels, won from the Roman Senate his acquittal from the charge of "sacrilege." The Roman administration settled all remaining doubts, however, when through Marcus Agrippa, Augustus' viceroy in the East, it formally placed these temple funds under the sanctions long imposed by Graeco-Roman law on temple robbery. Although Agrippa's decree applied directly to Asia Minor or even Ephesus alone (he issued another decree for Cyrenaica), it doubtless was invoked with telling effect by other Diaspora communities as well.[7]

POLITICAL AND CULTURAL RELATIONS

Apart from the financial gains accruing to the country from the tourist trade and the temple tax, Palestine's political position in the Mediterranean world was greatly enhanced by her vast "colonies." When Cleopatra invaded Palestine and the fate of Alexander Jannaeus hung in the balance, Ananias, the Egyptian Jewish general, uttered this significant warning to his queen, "An injustice to this man will make all us Jews your enemies" (*Antt.* XIII, 13, 2.354). This warning of the influential commander, chagrined by the preceding devastation of Palestine by the queen's son and enemy, Ptolemy Lathyrus, and the ensuing threat to Judaea's newly won independence, sufficed to save the Jewish king. Ananias must have known that he was not only risking his own life in the case of victory of Lathyrus' expansionist party, but that his action would increase the virulence of the aspersions cast upon Egyptian Jewry's loyalties to the Crown. It is quite possible that the first anti-Jewish riots recorded in Alexandria (88–87 B.C.E.) were the outcome of passions thus aroused. Nevertheless most Egyptian Jews doubtless felt justified in supporting the peace party.

Diaspora Jewry's participation in Palestinian affairs even extended to meddling in local factional strife. When, for instance, the Palestinian Pharisees approached the rulers in Rome with the peculiar request that the existing Jewish government be abolished, they were accompanied by many Roman Jewish followers. When Herod, on the other hand, wished to make sure that the high priest's office would not serve as a focus of popular disaffection but rather as an instrument of his dictatorial policies, he turned with preference to foreign priests. His first choice was Ananel, a Babylonian of low birth, while during the last two decades of his life he entrusted the office to Simon, son of Boethos of an Alexandrian Jewish family.[8]

Conversely, the Diaspora was indebted to Palestine for extensive moral and political backing. When Antiochus III conquered Palestine from the Ptolemies he tried to wean away the Palestinian Jews from their former overlords by extending to them a memorable "charter" safeguarding their cultural and religious autonomy. The provisions of this charter doubtless accrued to the benefit of all Jewish subjects of the far-flung Seleucid Empire, including Babylonia and Asia Minor. Antiochus himself had settled two thousand Babylonian Jewish families in Asia Minor to help him keep in submission the restless population of Lydia and Phrygia. The capital, Antioch, "partly owing to [its] greatness," had by that time likewise attracted a large Jewish community. These Jewries were obviously included now in the "charter's" guarantees to "all members of the nation [ethnous]" who were to live "in accordance with the laws of their forefathers." To be sure, the Palestinian controversy between the Orthodox and the Hellenizers soon apparently embroiled all Jews in a sharp conflict with Antiochus IV Epiphanes. But the victory of the Maccabean arms evidently brought about the restoration of their liberty of conscience and their other rights, by Antiochus V in 163, and by Demetrius I and II in 152 and 142. If we are to believe Josephus, Antiochus IV's successors "granted them citizen rights on an equality with the Greeks" and returned to the community of Antioch some of the holy vessels looted by him from the Temple in Jerusalem.[9]

Curiously, much as their own future depended on the outcome of the Maccabean struggle, neither Syrian Jewry nor any other segment of the Diaspora seems to have taken an active part in the revolt. Few foreign Jews immediately perceived its deeper significance. To most of them it undoubtedly appeared at first as but an internal conflict between the Palestinian Hellenizers and conservatives—which it indeed was in its initial phases—and their private sympathies may well have been predominantly on the side of the protagonists of Hellenistic culture. Only when Antiochus IV desecrated the Temple and wished to impose complete apostasy, must Jewish opinion in all countries have rallied behind the Maccabees.

One need not place too much credence in speeches inserted by ancient historians, but there may be more than sheer rhetoric in the statement attributed by Josephus to the Syrian commander Lysias. Explaining to his soldiers the sudden lifting of his siege of Jerusalem early in 162, Lysias said that it was "much better to make a treaty with the besieged and seek the friendship of the whole nation [ethnos] by permitting them to observe their fathers' laws." By that time the rebellious mood of Jews living in the other provinces of the Seleucid Empire and, possibly, some anti-Syrian agitation in other countries (the Maccabean contacts with Rome and Sparta were probably mediated by some foreign Jews) may well have given pause to the Syrian high command and induced it to pacify the "whole nation." Jason of Cyrene, very likely writing soon after the events described by him (II Macc. ends with Judah's victory over Nicanor in 161), collected the information transmitted to North Africa by Palestinian refugees and travelers. But he also voiced, with characteristic vigor, the elation of the majority of Diaspora Jewry over the military successes of their Palestinian coreligionists.[10]

As soon as the danger of complete suppression of the Jewish faith had passed, however, Diaspora Jewry seems to have relapsed into political inactivity. Certainly the constant internal conflicts under the Maccabean and Herodian rulers, often degenerating into family intrigues and cruel atrocities, must have proved perplexing to Jews of other lands. Only when the fate of the Jewish commonwealth was at stake, as in Cleopatra's designs, did Jewish solidarity reassert itself. When Demetrius III invaded Palestine (about 88), he doubtless brought with him some Jewish soldiers from Syria in addition to employing Palestinian members of the Jewish faction militantly opposed to Alexander Jannaeus. The Jewish king, on the other hand, at first relied more on his Greek mercenaries than on his Jewish subjects. Nevertheless, according to Josephus, "there was much activity in both camps, the one side attempting to cause Alexander's mercenaries to desert because they were Greeks, while the other made the same appeal to the Jews who were with Demetrius." After Alexander's decisive defeat this agitation proved successful enough for 6,000 Jews to desert the Syrian army and to save the Jewish king (*Antt.* XIII, 14, 1–2.378 ff.; *War* I, 4, 5.93 ff.).

In any case, as long as the Maccabean rulers represented a power in western Asia of which the expanding Roman republic had to take account, Jewry in the dispersion derived direct benefit. In almost every treaty of alliance concluded by Rome with Judaea during that period was a clause placing upon Rome the obligation to protect the rights of Jews not only in the countries under her direct domination, but also in those of her "allies." Indeed, in the eyes of Julius Caesar, Hyrcanus, the high priest of Jerusalem, was not only the ethnarch of "Judaea" but of the "Jews" generally. During his stay in Egypt (in 48–47) the Roman dictator had himself received Palestine's armed support at a crucial moment and observed Hyrcanus' influence on the Egyptian Jewish soldiers. In his subsequent decree he spoke, therefore, of Hyrcanus as the high priest who, "being also ethnarch, shall be the protector of those Jews who are unjustly treated" (*Antt.* XIV, 10, 3.196). He thus formally recognized the political and spiritual leader of Palestinian Jewry as the spokesman for Jews of all lands.

That this right was not merely nominal is seen in the example of Herod who dispatched his counselor, Nicolaus of Damascus, to Asia Minor to plead before Marcus Agrippa the cause of the Jews of that province. It appears that the Roman governor saw nothing improper in this intervention of the Jewish king and lent a willing ear to the arguments advanced by his representative. Even later King Agrippa I, overtly acting as the political head of world Jewry, addressed his famous letter to Caius Caligula in which he emphasized the importance of Jerusalem as the mother city of vast Jewish settlements. With this argument he tried to persuade the emperor to desist from his intended enforcement of the imperial worship among Jews.

Caligula's attempt highlighted at the same time Palestine's precarious position in the face of the antisemitic movements in other lands. Despite Agrippa's childhood friendship with, and continued personal influence on, the emperor, the country might have become involved in a life and death struggle with the Roman Empire because of a controversy which was started by Alexandrian Jew-baiters with the connivance of a Roman official. The Alexandrian example was soon emulated by the Greek-speaking populace of Jamnia in Judaea which now saw "an admirable opportunity of attacking," under the cloak of patriotism, its Jewish neighbors (Philo's *Legatio*, XXX, 200–201). Before long, Caligula himself, become aware of Jewish resistance, ordered Petronius, his newly appointed legate of Syria, to erect a statue to himself at the very Temple of Jerusalem. Only Petronius' recognition that the execution of this order would require a long and sanguinary campaign, his readiness to suffer death for disobedience and, ultimately, Caligula's assassination averted this grave emergency.

These economic and political interrelations between Palestine and the Diaspora Jews were overshadowed by the religious and cultural influences steadily emanating from the holy city and permeating all Jewish life in and outside Palestine. Of course, the cultural influences of Hellenistic Jewry even in Palestine were not slight. In more than one respect Alexandria was, in the words of a leading Palestinian rabbi (Simon ben Shetah), a "sister" of Jerusalem. In the last two centuries of the Temple's existence, however, the religious hegemony of Jerusalem was unchallenged.

No better proof could be adduced than the virtually total disappearance of those Canaanite-Babylonian elements of the Israelitic popular religion previously predominant in the creed and worship of the Elephantine Jews or of those who fled to Egypt with Jeremiah. Even the temple, newly erected in Leontopolis (Tell al-Yahudia) by the refugee high priest Onias IV during the early years of the Maccabean revolt (about 160), was from the beginning a mere imitation of that in Jerusalem, which served as a model for its whole system of sacrificial worship. There is little reason to assume that any effective challenge to the superiority of the Jerusalem Temple over that in Tell al-Yahudia was made later when Palestine became more powerful. According to the laws of the Mishnah, enacted it is true by Palestinian rabbis, sacrifices destined for the temple of Onias could be offered in Jerusalem, but not vice versa, and Onias priests, though legitimately functioning in Egypt, were forbidden to officiate in Palestine. Like priests with a blemish, however, they were allowed to partake of the priestly portions at the Temple.[11]

The moderation of the Jerusalem leaders, who with all their insistence upon the superiority of Jerusalem did not alienate the worshipers of the Egyptian temple as they had those at Mt. Gerizim, was met more than halfway by the priests of Leontopolis. Although descendants of the legitimate high priests, the latter did not denounce the Maccabeans as usurpers. Notwithstanding certain misgivings as to the legitimacy of some Palestinian priests, such as are hinted at by the Greek translator of the Book of Esther (in his remark about Dositheus "who said that he was a priest and levite"), the Egyptian priests acknowledged the supremacy of the Jerusalem Temple. Laymen were even more enthusiastic. Whatever patriotic interests may have originally animated them in trying to secure religious independence from a sanctuary controlled by hostile Seleucids (this anti-Syrian purpose doubtless motivated their king, Ptolemy VI Philometor, in abetting the scheme of the Palestinian refugee priests), lost their significance as soon as the Syrian regime was replaced by that of the Maccabeans. Even under ambitious Herod, Egypt never felt threatened in the way it had when Antiochus IV had occupied it and been forced to abandon it only by the intervention of a Roman legate. Characteristically, Philo, who time and again exalted the Temple of Jerusalem as the sanctuary of the whole nation, did not mention at all that of Leontopolis. "At the same time," rightly observed A. Schlatter, "the proselyte from Ethiopia passed by the city of Onias on his pilgrimage to Jerusalem." [12]

Palestinian hegemony in matters of calendar and festivals (including the newly introduced feasts of *Purim* and *Hanukkah*) was uncontested. In 143 when the Palestinian leaders under Simon felt assured of the permanence of their victory, they requested, or rather courteously ordered, the Egyptian communities to join them in the annual commemoration of the Temple's "rededication" twenty-one years before. When Egyptian Jewry, however, after an alleged escape from imminent danger, introduced its own annual Purim-like festivals in Alexandria and Ptolemais, or when it decided to commemorate the Greek translation of Scripture in an annual celebration on the island of Pharos (graphically described by Philo), it entertained no hope whatever that these holidays would be observed outside its own country. They may not have been observed in Egypt itself outside the two communities.[13]

Scriptures were adopted by Diaspora Jewry at the dictation of Palestine. Books composed in the motherland after the translation of the earlier writings (which had made Jewry abroad somewhat more independent) were speedily canonized and translated. Palestinian law reigned supreme and Jewish communities abroad frequently addressed legal inquiries to Palestinian authorities. Of course, at a time when Jewish law even in Palestine was still much in flux, local variations could readily develop. We shall see how much the Babylonian observances were to be, for centuries to come, an independent source of the *halakhah*. Alexandria, too, must have developed a legal structure of its own, which is partly reflected in Philo's works. Nevertheless, a most characteristic question was put by the Alexandrians themselves to R. Joshua concerning a point in the Temple ritual a few decades *after* the destruction of the Temple! As early as Alexander Jannaeus, distinguished "Persian" Jewish visitors (*bene nash rabrebin*) requested the king to invite to the dinner table the elder (Simon ben Shetaḥ) whose fame as a man of learning had come to them. Rome, in particular, a much younger community, seems to have followed closely the patterns gradually evolving in the Palestinian homeland of most of its settlers. Even here a local elder, like Theudas, versed in rabbinic lore, ventured to introduce such a ritualistic innovation as the consumption, on Passover nights, of "helmeted" lambs (roasted in their entirety with legs, entrails, and the rest). But the Palestinian leaders reprimanded him for this overt emulation of the Passover sacrifice. They gave him an unmistakable warning, "If you were not Theudas [the rabbis explain later that he had been a scholar and patron of learning], we would have excommunicated you." [14]

In any case, the main teachings of Pharisaism spread unchecked by geographic boundaries. Hillel of Babylonia, Nahum of Media, Saul of Tarsus, felt its impact. Once in Palestine, the first became the principal leader of the movement, the second one of its representatives at a crucial historical moment, the third its greatest enemy. The Alexandrian Jew, Boethos, became the founder of a special sectarian group of Sadducees.

THEOCRATIC REGIME

The expansion of Jewry in Palestine and abroad, however, forced a religious reorientation. As long as Jerusalem was a capital of a small autonomous district, it had all the characteristics of a city state. The whole population could actively participate in political and religious life. As late as 142 it was still possible for Simon the Hasmonean to convoke "a great congregation of priests and people and princes of the nation, and of the elders of the country," somewhat reminiscent of the popular assemblies in the days of Josiah and Ezra. This gathering made Simon "their leader and high priest . . . because of the justice and the faith which he kept to his nation, and because he sought by all means to exalt his people." But already Simon, though elected with the qualification, "until a faithful prophet should arise" and hence not even for life, made the provision that none of the people or priests should ever "gather an assembly in the country without him." [15] The moment, moreover, the boundaries were extended to the Dead Sea and the Lebanon, the frame of the city state was shattered.

Although the new government of the country increasingly resembled an autocracy, the people continued none the less remarkably active in public affairs. Direct representation in a national parliament was still unknown, but there was a supreme council and tribunal, soon styled the Sanhedrin, whose members, although not elected, were appointed with some popular sanction. True, the Sanhedrin's claim to supreme legislative, judicial, educational, and even executive authority was never respected by the Ptolemaic, Seleucid, and Roman governors, and even less so by the Maccabean and Herodian rulers. It is still a moot question whether, after the Maccabean age, the high priest, a more or less pliable appointee of the Herodian dynasts and Roman procurators, or a Pharisaic teacher was presiding officer. Nor can we tell for certain whether there was only one such body or two with mutually agreed, or conflicting, prerogatives. One must always bear in mind that our main information concerning this institution is derived not from the casual references in the New Testament or Josephus, but from the extensive documentation in talmudic literature. Obviously the talmudic rabbis often transferred features of their contemporary institution, which served principally as an academy of learning and supreme court and only secondarily as a legislative and administrative body, to the royal council under the same name which had functioned in Jerusalem before 70. Nevertheless, it appears that, if supported by the extremely vocal populace of Jerusalem which, on one occasion, dared to pelt Alexander Jannaeus and his counselors with citrons it had brought along to the Temple services on the

Feast of Tabernacles, this council offered a serious check on the extremes of royal tyranny.[16]

At any rate neither the Maccabees nor even the Herodians could reign as despots of the oriental or Hellenistic type. Because the growth of the country rendered balloting impractical and reverence for the hereditary principle made it appear superfluous, Simon's election by a popular assembly may not have been repeated by any of his successors. None the less, even the great conquerors John Hyrcanus and Alexander Jannaeus had to struggle incessantly not against other pretenders, but against the growing popular faction, the Pharisees. On his death-bed Jannaeus, undefeated, counseled his wife and successor, Salome-Alexandra, to make peace with these indefatigable enemies. The very fact of Salome's succession seems to have been an attempt at compromise. The Pharisees had long demanded the separation between the royal and the ecclesiastical powers, which now were divided between the queen and her son, the high priest.

Salome generally followed her husband's advice and reigned for nine years with relative peace and prosperity. But she no sooner closed her eyes (in 67), when her two sons started a memorable struggle which ended in Pompey's occupation of Palestine four years later. Pompey appeared not only as an arbiter between the quarreling brothers, but also between them and "the nation," or rather its Pharisaic leadership (*Antt.* XIV, 3, 2.41). Despite Herod's tyrannical excesses, in part explainable by his tenuous hold on the people and his constant fear of conspiracies, it would seem vain to seek for analogies to the Jewish legend, repeatedly recorded in talmudic literature (M. Soṭah VII, 8, and elsewhere), concerning king Agrippa's tearful public avowal that, racially an alien, he had no right to be king of Judaea.

Such a political situation found no parallel in the ancient world, and Josephus had to coin a new word to describe the Jewish form of government.

Some peoples [he wrote in a famous passage] have entrusted the supreme political power to monarchies, others to oligarchies, yet others to the masses. Our lawgiver, however, was attracted by none of these forms of polity, but gave to his constitution the form of what— if a forced expression be permitted—may be termed a "theocracy," placing all sovereignty and authority in the hands of God [*Ag. Ap.* II, 16.164–65].

The word has since had a strange career, having been widely—perhaps too widely—adopted by modern scholars in their characterization of the Second Commonwealth. But its meaning was not uniform even then. At first it was a theocracy on a democratic basis, then it became an oligarchic and even a monarchical theocracy, until finally, under the domination of Rome, its monarchical, aristocratic and democratic constituents came into open and insoluble conflict.

The rapid conquest of the various provinces by the early Maccabean rulers also affected the social status of their population. Galilee, the most fertile region in the country, was the scene of sharp social conflicts. The Judaean aristocracy, partly dominating the country from Jerusalem, looked with contempt on the masses, a large part of which had been converted to Judaism but a short while before. Whether or not that conversion had been enforced by Judah-Aristobulus in 104–103 (even in the case of the former Ituraean part of Galilee Josephus' report is somewhat dubious), there is no question that significant differences in background, outlook, and observance were long to distinguish the Galileans from their southern compatriots. The South itself was far from homogeneous, since newly annexed Idumaea injected a strong alien ingredient into the population. True, S. Klein has made it plausible that John Hyrcanus' conquest and conversion of "all the Idumaeans" (alleged by Josephus) was, in fact, limited to the inhabitants of Adora and Marisa specifically mentioned in this connection. These cities were located in a district which had been part of Judah during the First Commonwealth and was overrun by the Edomites as a result of the decline of the local Judaean population after Nebukadrezzar (or Sennacherib). Essentially, Hyrcanus and Jannaeus thus forcibly judaized only territories to which the Jews had made historic claims. However, the slower, and more voluntary absorption of the rest of the Idumaeans must merely have increased the internal frictions.[17]

Conflicts were further accentuated by the fact that many important towns, including some relatively young cities in Transjordan and Galilee, were in the hands of Greeks. While the Ptolemies evinced little interest in colonizing these areas, their friendly rule stimulated the formation of Greek-speaking and Greek-governed municipalities. The latter grew in number and affluence under the still greater favoritism of the Seleucids. This process was slowed down, but not completely halted, during the brief period of Maccabean sovereignty. In the days of Jannaeus, Pella preferred extinction to the adoption of Judaism. After Pompey's invasion, all these cities recaptured municipal autonomy under the direct sovereignty of Rome. Nine cities of Transjordan were joined by Scythopolis (Beth-shan) in Samaria to form an alliance of Ten Cities (the Decapolis) which, later enlarged, played an important political role, coördinate with, rather than subordinate to, that of the Herodians. Similar self-determination was exercised by the coastal Greek cities from Ptolemais (Acre) in the north to Gaza in the south. Indeed, Herod himself rebuilt Samaria, destroyed by John Hyrcanus in 107, as a regular *polis* and dedicated it to Augustus under the name of Sebaste. He also established Caesarea as Palestine's foremost harbor and fortified several other Greek-speaking towns as bastions against his own recalcitrant people. In all these cities, although on Palestinian soil, the Jews lived only on sufferance.[18]

In these respects we already see a great difference between this period and that of Israel's kings, who held the whole Israelitic settlement under their domination. The distinctions between the older and more recently assimiliated Hebrews (the latter having long retained their economic and cultural superiority) had been gradually blotted out by the complete absorption of the conquered Canaanites. The Maccabean rulers bore the same royal title and sought to regain the same ancient territories, reëstablishing there full religious uniformity, and to revive the same ancient language and script. The numerous surviving Maccabean coins still bear mute witness to their consciously archaizing efforts. They nevertheless wielded much less authority, willingly accepted by their subjects, than even the much-abused monarchs of ancient Israel. Except during a few decades before Pompey's invasion, the country was altogether dominated by a foreign power. The ambitious and munificent gestures of Herod and his successors ultimately depended on the good will of Rome. Even in the periods of Assyrian overlordship of Judaea during the seventh century there had been no resident official comparable to the Roman procurator. Indeed, the Herodian kings themselves, being of Idumaean stock though Jews in religion, were open to denunciation as a foreign element. To some nationalistic Jews, Palestine must have appeared as under a double foreign domination.[19]

The main exponents of the national-religious ideology, the Pharisaic scribes.[20] thus faced a situation much changed since the days of the prophets whose function they now performed in many ways. Territorially unattached, they, too, were more purely in line with the Mosaic tradition than the priests. Wherever they happened to be, they could teach and adjudicate matters in the name of the Torah. They, too, succeeded in maintaining financial independence by refusing to accept monetary reward for their teaching and by choosing a trade, often simple manual labor, as a source of livelihood.

Objectives and methods, however, had to be adapted to new needs. Unlike the ancient leaders, they could not direct denunciations against the dominant Jewish classes. Those most responsible for existing conditions could not be accused of breaking the covenant with God, as they were foreigners. In form, too, the Pharisees neither could nor needed to appeal to the people in the name of the great religious principle of justice. Their opponents claimed to agree with them on the transcending importance of this principle. Even the foreign oppressor pretended to rule in the name of justice.

What mattered now were details, cases of concrete application or disregard of the great ethical principles. Again unlike the prophets, the scribes could refer to an elaborate and binding set of laws easily applicable to every particular occurrence. Thus legalistic accusations took the place of inspired denunciations. Perhaps, also, the size of the task was conducive to coöperative endeavors rather than to the rise of great individuals. In ancient Palestine, even before the destruction of Samaria, a great and revered prophet could count upon a hearing from the whole people. But little could be accomplished individually in a Jewish world consisting of millions scattered over many lands. Even early Christianity could become successful only after it had evolved a church, an organization carried on collectively. This was doubly true in the case of those who remained within the fold of a traditional creed and a living national organism.

Many modern observers, unaware of these vital forces behind the legalistic veneer, have been struck by the apparently incongruous position held by law in the life of the people. Moreover, since the days of Paul, it had been customary to denounce the preponderance of ceremonial over ethical elements in Pharisaism. Leaving out of consideration all polemical and apologetical arguments, indeed the whole question of values, it should be stated that the element of law certainly is one of the basic constituents of Judaism in all periods. The same holds true of all ancient religions, and especially of Parsiism, that other ancient creed of universal significance.

Law does not mean, however, ceremonial law exclusively. In fact, it may easily be proved that in Judaism morality, however dependent on specific social attitudes, was the source of law, while the reverse is true in the case of Rome. No authoritative Jew ever declared that to comply with the letter of the law was sufficient. Judaism, and all its official spokesmen, always taught its children that the first and greatest revelation of God was the pronouncement of the Ten Commandments, the ethical rather than the ritual Decalogue. The vast space allotted to all aspects of the ceremonial law in the Pentateuch, the Mishnah, and the Jewish codes, is misleading. To conclude on statistical grounds that in the eyes of the lawgiver the ceremonial was more important than the moral law is somewhat like assuming that modern legislative assemblies evince almost exclusive interest in crimes against property. In no modern penal code do the paragraphs pertaining to murder occupy one-tenth the space given to those directed against theft and fraudulent actions. Only extremely prejudiced opinion, even among communists, would conclude that the capitalist lawgivers put property rights high above the right to live.

Any number of examples could be adduced, showing how serious political and social conflicts were translated into a struggle over the import and meaning of certain laws. A legalistic controversy during the reign of John Hyrcanus was the prelude to a civil war which was to rage for two generations. Some Pharisaic opponents of the combination of royal and high-priestly prerogatives in one person are said to have denounced the legitimacy of Hyrcanus' high priesthood on the ground that his mother had been a captive during the revolutionary years. According to their interpretation he was, therefore, permanently disqualified from serving as a high priest at the Temple. Of course, behind this, as behind many similar controversies in that period and later, lurked deep political antagonisms.[21]

POLITICS AND MARTYRDOM

Judaism itself thus comprised many contrary movements. Here lies the root of some of the most momentous religious developments of the age. In the periods of Persian and early Hellenistic domination we hear very little about internal quarrels or disputes over religious principles and views. But from the days of the Maccabean revolt, religious and nationalist conflicts came to overshadow all other matters of national and international policy.

One need not search far for the reasons of the new upsurge. For a long time after Ezra and Nehemiah, the Jews enjoyed full self-government in religious and national affairs and lived secluded from the rest of the world under the domination of their own religious leaders. Although Persian influences imperceptibly penetrated, this occurred so slowly and with so little outward pressure that Judaism could easily assimilate them and make them fully Jewish. With the conquest of western Asia by Alexander the Great, however, the cultural life of the Jews was irresistibly drawn into the whirl of the Hellenistic synthesis of east and west. Like all other Near Eastern countries the people of Palestine, especially the upper classes, began to be Hellenized, some deeply, some more superficially. As in Syria and Egypt, the wealthier, educated, ruling groups could not resist the lure of Hellas, the magnificence of its culture, enhanced by the political and economic forces of the new empires.

Some Jews soon began to forget the ancestral mode of life and to despise their Jewish heritage. Sirach, writing in the generation preceding the Maccabean upheaval, felt bound to warn his readers not to be ashamed "of the Law of the Most High and the statute." From such shame to the preachment of complete assimilation was only a step. Indeed, there did evolve a decidedly radical movement, which Meyer somewhat confusingly called "Reform Judaism." Beyond even the most radical wings of modern Reform, its leaders wished to conclude "a covenant with the nations." Their emulation of the Greek ways of life reached a climax when "they built a gymnasium in Jerusalem according to the manner of the Gentiles. They also submitted themselves to uncircumcision and repudiated the holy covenant." The building of a gymnasium was the height of adulation of "Greek fashions" in so far as this institution, which speedily caught the imagination of all conquered peoples, combined political and intellectual with purely athletic exercises and often was under the patronage of the Greek pantheon, especially Heracles or Hermes. Its importance to the Greeks was well expressed in the facetious remark of Anacharsis, the Scythian, who, after visiting Greece, reported that "in each city of the Greeks there is a place set apart in which they act insanely day after day." [22]

Politically, too, as elsewhere in Syria, the Jewish religion was to become a state religion with the priests serving as state officers and fulfilling the duties prescribed by public law. A hereditary, charismatic priesthood could then easily be replaced by lay officers, as in Hellas or Rome. It was quite logical, therefore, that Menelaus, apparently of the lay house of Tobias, should supplant Jason, the Aaronide leader of the new movement, as a high priest in Jerusalem. Even Jason sent an offering of three hundred drachmas of silver to the quinquennial festival of Heracles in Tyre. In short, Jerusalem under the Seleucids was to become a Greek municipality pure and simple, with a government modeled after that of the imperial capital, Antioch. There is even reason to assume that the name Jerusalem, like that of several other Asiatic cities, including Transjordan's Gerasa, was to be changed to Antiocheia.[23]

Before long the very Temple hitherto dedicated to a God with an ineffable name (to the Greeks the equivalent of "without a name") was to be renamed, like its rival sanctuary at Mount Gerizim, the temple of Zeus. In this case it would have become the object of Antiochus IV's generosity toward Greek sanctuaries, so greatly extolled in contemporary inscriptions and by Polybius. Did not the Samaritans, like most other subjects, address the king as *theos epiphanes* (the manifest god) close to Zeus himself? Loyal Jews were, of course, deeply shocked. They viewed the king, in the words of the visionary author of Daniel, as one who "shall do according to his will; and he shall exalt himself, and magnify himself above every god, and shall speak strange things against the God of gods." [24]

Hellenistic influences among the poorer classes in Palestine were even less manifest, however, than in Egypt and Syria. These humbler folk continued to speak the old language and live the accustomed life, quietly but effectively resisting the combined influences of foreign settlers and their own Hellenized groups. This evolution was brought to an abrupt end by Antiochus IV who, misled by the leaders of the Hellenistic party, forgot all prudence. Out of opposition to his oppressive measures arose that patriotic movement which, uniting all forces of preservation, freed the country from foreign domination and along with it ostensibly shook off all Hellenistic culture patterns.

We need not retell here the familiar story of the Maccabean insurrection and its vicissitudes from Mattathias' raising of the flag of revolt to his youngest son Simon's proclamation of a fully independent kingdom of Judaea (140 B.C.E.). In all essentials modern historians have had to follow the sequence of events as described in the first two books of Maccabees, merely clarifying one or another detail. Neither Josephus and the rabbinic letters, nor the few pertinent Graeco-Roman sources nor any significant archaeological discoveries have shed any substantially new light on what has long been known about that vital quarter century of Palestinian history. They have merely helped us better to understand the general international background, as well as the internal conditions of the Seleucid Empire which, in part, accounted for both Antiochus' early intransigeance and his relatively speedy defeat. Psychologically, however, this struggle appeared to many Jewish contemporaries not as a mere conflict between the powerful empire and a small segment of its unruly subjects, but as a sign of direct divine intervention in the course of history.

In those crucial days was, indeed, born that great exaltation of religious martyrdom which was to dominate the minds of Jews and Christians for countless generations. The people was prepared for it by the age-old glorification of prophets who, against tremendous odds and at great personal sacrifice, had proclaimed the word of God. Popular legend now embellished these biblical narratives with ever new details and superimposed upon them ever new motifs from its own fertile imagination. The conviction spread that, ever since Abraham, true Jews were ready to suffer endless tortures and death in behalf of their faith. Before long the terms "prophet" and "martyr" became indistinguishably blended in the popular mind, which now saw that combination personified in Abel, the first victim of religious persecution at the very dawn of history. We get a glimpse of that new indoctrination of youth in the alleged speech of the mother of the seven Maccabean martyrs. Describing the instruction given them by their late father, she reminisced,

He read to us of Abel who was slain by Cain, and of Isaac who was offered as a burnt-offering, and of Joseph in the prison. And he spake to us of Phineas, the zealous priest, and he taught you *the song* of Ananias, Azarias and Mishael in the fire. . . . He sang to us the words of David the psalmist, "Many are the afflictions of the just."

More, through Deutero-Isaiah the people became inured to the idea of the whole nation enduring untold hardships for the sake of its beliefs and of serving as mankind's suffering "Servant of the Lord." [25]

When the test came, the author of Daniel comforted his people with the story of the four martyrs and an apocalyptic vision of the approaching end of days. In fact, a considerable number of Jews rallied around Mattathias of Modein who, setting the example for many future witnesses for their faith, destroyed the altar of the foreign god in his town regardless of consequences. Sacrificing all in the defense of their religion, his sons and followers engaged in a mortal struggle against impossible odds. They persevered long enough, however, until, under changing constellations of international politics, they not only salvaged their faith but also reëstablished their fully self-governing community.

In this state of mind it is not astonishing that, despite the availability of such unequivocal records as the two first books of Maccabees, the people remembered Mattathias rather than their great military heroes, Judah Maccabee and his brothers. Judah is not even mentioned in the talmudic literature. (Only through *Yosippon,* the medieval paraphrase of Josephus, his name became known more widely among Jews, to be extolled above all other Maccabeans in the period of modern Jewish nationalism.) Similarly, of the later wars against the Romans, the people remembered best the apocryphal story of the Ten Martyrs, although it was not altogether sure of their individual identity. Certainly the memory of R. 'Aqiba and Eleazar of Modein was cherished far more than that of Simon son of Giyoras or Bar Kocheba. This readiness for martyrdom, often reaching the state of mass psychosis, was exemplified also in the resistance of Jews to Emperor Caligula's demand that they sacrifice to him in the accustomed ways of the imperial worship. A large crowd of Jews, including women and children, we are told by Josephus, appeared in Ptolemais before Petronius, Roman governor of Syria, and urged him to desist from placing Caligula's statue in the Temple. While reiterating their professions of loyalty and pacific intentions, they insisted that "if he wished to set up these statues, he must first sacrifice the entire Jewish nation." They meant what they said and actually "presented themselves, their wives and their children, ready for the slaughter." [26]

Diaspora Jewry was even more prone to overlook the secular factors in the Maccabean uprising. To it that revolt became the most illuminating example of an intrinsically rewarding religious martyrdom. Was not Deutero-Isaiah's "Servant of the Lord" himself born out of the travail of the Babylonian Exile, if not altogether on Babylonian soil? Long before the Maccabean revolt the Diaspora had produced, in the book of Esther, the record of a threatening massacre of all Jews and their salvation through the religious steadfastness of Mordecai. Now in the Greek translation the ingredients of court intrigue, which in the original version had somewhat obscured the religious issues, were toned down in favor of divine and earthly rewards for unflinching religious loyalty.

Jason of Cyrene went further. He not only inserted into his otherwise matter-of-fact description of the Maccabean revolt a long speech by the aged scribe-martyr Eleazar and the subsequently famous story of the martyred seven "Maccabean" boys and their mother, but also rationalized his entire account,

Now I beseech the readers of this book not to be discouraged by such calamities, but to reflect that our people were being punished by way of chastening and not for their destruction. . . . In the case of other nations, the Sovereign Lord in his forbearance refrains from punishing them till they have filled up their sins to the full, but in our case He has determined otherwise, that His vengeance may not fall on us in after-days when our sins have reached their height. Wherefore He never withdraweth His mercy from us [II Macc. 6:12–16].

A later Hellenistic author made this theme the subject of a lengthy semiphilosophic dissertation on the virtues of martyrdom and called it the Fourth Book of Maccabees.

Following the same general outline, although departing completely from the historical background of the Maccabean revolt, an Alexandrian Jewish writer described in the so-called Third Book of Maccabees a sudden emergency affecting the entire Egyptian Jewish community in the days of Ptolemy Philopator, half a century *before* that revolt. Here, too, salvation came as the result of the religious steadfastness of the majority who resisted the royal order to serve idols, even under the promise of enjoying "equal rights with the citizens of Alexandria." At the moment of greatest danger they beseeched God "to deliver them by a glorious manifestation from the fate yawning ready before them." That, incidentally, a century or more before the fall of Jerusalem an Egyptian writer should invent a story, or at least retell with gusto one previously invented, about extreme anti-Jewish persecutions in his country some two centuries earlier, is noteworthy, but not wholly unexpected. Even his deriving therefrom the lesson of untenability of Jewish life in the *galut* (*apoikia*), is not surprising since the equally "assimilated" Jew, Philo, voiced what doubtless was a prevailing sentiment among his coreligionists. "For even though they dwell," he wrote, "in the uttermost parts of the earth, in slavery to those who led them away captive, one signal, as it were, one day will bring liberty to all." [27]

This idea of religious martyrdom was doubtless reinforced by the growing emphasis in the entire Graeco-Roman civilization upon self-sacrifice for the common good. There was, however, a basic distinction. To Greek and Roman patriots, the ideal hero was the man who sacrificed his life for his country, and death on the battlefield was extolled as a supreme virtue. Even Alexandria's so-called "heathen martyrs" suffered death principally in behalf of a political cause, although their spokesman, Apion, tried to intermingle with it the cause of their faith, when he asked, "Why, then, if they [the Jews] are citizens, do they not worship the same gods as the Alexandrians?" Only self-sacrifice in behalf of one's convictions even against the state's wishes, as exemplified in such widely venerated philosophers as Pythagoras and Socrates, bore some resemblance to the Jewish idea of martyrdom. But there still was a difference between such individual intellectual heroism and a whole people's readiness to suffer martyrdom for a nonpolitical cause. To all intents and purposes the Maccabean revolt was the first "war of religion" in history. Even in his description of the heroism of Essenes during the *war* with the Romans, though evidently intended to impress the Graeco-Roman world, Josephus emphasized not their bravery in battle but the fact that "racked and twisted, burnt and broken, and made to pass through every instrument of torture, in order to induce them to blaspheme their lawgiver or to eat some forbidden thing, they refused to yield to either demand, nor ever once did they cringe to their persecutors or shed a tear." [28]

Such exaltation of martyrdom and indoctrination of the people in its ultimate rewards became one of the mainsprings of Jewish survival in the dispersion. It alone could help maintain the people's morale in the recurrent periods of crisis. It also enabled Jewish leadership to maintain the internal controls needed to steer Judaism's historic course in defiance of all external and internal pressures.[29]

POLITICAL CONFLICTS

No sooner, however, was victory won over the common enemy than the solid patriotic front was broken. In ensuing party struggles it became clear that a great many Hellenistic ideas had been unconsciously absorbed. By a curious irony of history, the leadership of the revolt was taken over by the most deeply Hellenized classes, which now were in no position to eschew completely an experience of generations. Those who, like Eupolemus the historian, utilized their Greek training and manners to serve in the new regime's diplomatic missions, did not abandon overnight their cherished ways of living and thinking. At the same time others, less thoroughly Hellenized, saw in the great crisis a visible warning that they better return to the old folkways and traditions of their people.

These deep conflicts took the form of a combat between the two principal religious sects, the Sadducees and Pharisees. The Sadducees were undoubtedly as patriotic as the Pharisees, but even their patriotism was permeated with Hellenism. Mostly of the upper classes of priests and great landowners, they had undergone a degree of assimilation before the anti-Hellenistic reaction set in. Not until the foreign hand struck at the roots of Judaism and threatened extinction did they awaken. Then they became the real leaders of the anti-Syrian revolt and the subsequent reconstruction.

It is significant, however, that they fought the enemy with his own weapons. It must be born in mind that in the Hellenistic empires, as later in Rome, the *state* was the paramount life principle. The city state or the empire arrogated to itself the right to regulate the life of its citizens in the light of its own, supreme interests. Religion and nationality were recognized only in so far as they were instruments of the state. Religion and religious worship, in the form prescribed by the state, was a civic duty. So was, in particular, in many countries the worship of king or emperor as personification of the state. On the other hand, atheism, chiefly the refusal to participate in state worship, was a civic crime.

Beyond that the state was not interested in religious beliefs or observances. As long as a man complied with religious duties prescribed by the state for its own, mainly political, good, he was free to add to his pantheon any number of other gods, to introduce into his family rites whatever forms of worship he might choose. Nationality had been of relatively small consequence even in the Hellenic age. With the expansion of the Macedonian power, the new vast empires, embracing so many disparate ethnic components, emphasized still more the supremacy of the state over the nationality, of the *politeia* over the *ethnos*. The Sadducean leaders unconsciously adopted this principle. They fought the Syrian state on its own ground, erecting against it the power of the Judaean state. Statehood thus became far more significant than it had ever been under the most powerful monarchs of ancient Israel. To its glory ethnic purity might readily be sacrificed. It was, therefore, only a logical consequence that Hyrcanus and Jannaeus, conquering one Palestinian province after another, should circumcise many natives, if need be forcibly, and incorporate them into the national body. Along with the glorification of the state, naturally went the glorification of Palestine. To restore to its ancient purity the territory of ancient Israel was one of the chief aims of the new policy. It must not be defiled by idolatry, nor even by a sectarian temple such as the Samaritan sanctuary on Mt. Gerizim. Outside the boundaries of ancient Israel, however, all could remain Gentiles, and the populations of former Moabite and Ammonite territories were not subjected to circumcision. Hence, too, Hyrcanus, seeking territorial and political aggrandizement, had to become a Sadducee, although he is reported to have been, in his youth, an active adherent of Pharisaism.

This transition is noticeable also on coins and other implements. The early Maccabeans seem to have adopted the lamp as an outward symbol of their newly proclaimed festival of Ḥanukkah. It is probable that they merely wished to imitate thereby the ancient illumination of the Feast of Tabernacles, under which name the new festival appears as late as 124 in the second letter of the Jerusalem leaders to Egypt on this subject. In consonance with the popular victory and the ensuing democratic basis of their regime, the Maccabeans apparently made that illumination obligatory upon every household. Moreover, to judge from recent archaeological finds, they even consciously changed the shape of the lamp in order to make it a distinctly Jewish instrument even in daily life. This fervor soon evaporated, however, and most of the lamps found in younger layers represent more run-of-the-mill specimens.[30]

While these reforms must, in part, be conjectured from the meager evidence available, there is no question that, when Simon Maccabee began striking his own coins, he chose such specifically Jewish symbols as the *ethrog* and *lulab* (citron and palm branch) and provided some of them with the nationalistic legend, "For the Redemption of Zion." But his immediate successor, John Hyrcanus, had already reverted to the standard Hellenistic wreaths of laurel and double cornucopiae. Both inscribed their coins in the archaic Hebrew script, completely disregarding these coins' greater usefulness as commercial media in the country and abroad, if provided also with Greek identifications. Even John Hyrcanus seems to have issued only coins bearing the simple Hebrew legend, "Yehohanan [Johanan] the high priest and the Jewish Community [*ḥeber*]." Jannaeus, however, soon began striking bilingual coins. Under Herod the Hebrew inscriptions were abandoned altogether. His coins were still at least largely aniconic; only a few bear the representation of an eagle. But Agrippa I, though generally more restrained in regard to Jewish religious sensitivities, did not hesitate to circulate in his non-Jewish domains coins bearing his own or the emperor's likeness.[31]

Nor did the Herodian monarchs hesitate to erect Greek structures, which to pious Jews must have appeared as stark symbols of paganism. Herod I's building mania led him far afield. He not only completely rebuilt as beautiful Greek cities Caesarea and Sebaste (both called in honor of the Roman rulers, Sebastes being the Greek equivalent of Augustus), but also erected large structures in the foreign cities of Berytus (Beirut), Tyre, Sidon, Damascus, Byblus, Ptolemais, and Tripolis. For the first time he also paved with marble blocks the two and a half miles of the main thoroughfare of Antioch and adorned it "with a colonnade of equal length." In Rhodes he subsidized shipbuilding and restored the local Pythian temple "on a grander scale."

Many cities [Josephus adds], as though they had been associated with his realm, received from him grants of land; others, like Cos, were endowed with revenues to maintain the annual office of gymnasiarch to perpetuity. . . . Corn he supplied to all applicants. . . . Need I allude to his donations to the people of Lycia or Samos, or to his liberality, extended to every district of Ionia, to meet its needs? Nay, are not Athenians and Lacedaemonians, the inhabitants of Nicopolis and of Pergamum in Mysia, laden with Herod's offerings? [War I, 21, 11.423-25.]

No wonder that, on one of his visits to Greece, Herod became president of the Olympic games, as much a pagan as a sportive festival.

It is possible that these munificent gifts, as well as Herod's rich festive offerings to the Olympic games were intended to help allay the tension between the Jews and Greeks, particularly with respect to the refusal of the Jews to participate in local worship and their collection of funds for the Temple of Jerusalem. None the less,

such disposition of revenue, largely derived from Palestinian taxation, for alien and idolatrous purposes must have doubly irked
Herod's orthodox subjects. Even the gratitude which they owed
him for rebuilding their Temple on a magnificent scale and with
due regard to the provisions of Jewish law was largely dissipated by
his erection of a theater, amphitheater, and hippodrome in the
capital but a short distance from that very sanctuary.[32]

To the Pharisees such proceedings must have appeared as abrupt
deviations from tradition. They, the intellectual leaders of the vast
middle class, had been much less affected by the Greek spirit than
their opponents. For a time, to be sure, they or their predecessors,
known as *hasidim,* joined forces with the richer classes to defend
their national and religious existence against foreign oppression
and internal denationalization. Indeed, these *Assidaioi,* as Josephus
calls them, furnished the rank and file of the warriors, and their
enthusiasm helped carry the revolt through many reverses to final
victory. As soon as the new state was more or less solidly established,
however, these two groups had to separate. The Pharisees would
not abandon that signal achievement of previous Jewish history,
the emancipation of nationality and religion from political power.
They expressed their ideas in other words, but this was their meaning. When the new rulers, following in the footsteps of the enemy,
exalted the state above all else, the Pharisees denounced them as
enemies of Judaism.

As long as the Jewish state remained powerful and continued to
expand, the Sadducees retained their hold over the country. But
the moment their political power weakened, their antagonists grew
in strength. No wonder the Sadducees steadily lost ground after the
conquest of the country by Pompey. It is also characteristic that the
Pharisees did not resent foreign domination so long as it did not
interfere with their inner way of life. In their excessive zeal, they
occasionally welcomed foreign rule as a lesser evil. When Pompey
invaded Palestine, we recall, Pharisee representatives of the "nation" opposed both Maccabean rivals "and asked not to be ruled by
a king, saying that it was the custom of their country to obey the
priests of the God who was venerated by them, but that these two,
who were descended from the priests, were seeking to change their
form of government in order that they might become a nation of
slaves." Twenty years later, in the early days of Herod, three successive delegations urged Antonius, then in Syria, to remove the
semi-independent Jewish government. These delegations grew

larger, more representative, and more insistent each time, until Antonius had to use military force to eject them. After the death of Herod, a Pharisaic delegation went as far as Rome to submit a similar request to Augustus. The fact that each member of these delegations knew that bloody revenge would be the penalty for failure reveals how deep was the desire of the Pharisees to rid themselves of their own, religiously more and more obnoxious, rulers. This consistently "unpatriotic" attitude shows that the scribes were the genuine heirs of the prophets in regarding the state not as evil per se, but as an instrument of evil when it subverted the interests of religion and nationality.[33]

IMPERIAL STATUS

Pharisaic and other opponents of the Herodian regime were encouraged by Roman administrators to look to Rome for their salvation. As in other provinces of the empire, classes and factions were often played against one another in accordance with the imperial policy's fundamental maxim "to divide and rule." Moreover, even when their procurators directly managed the country's affairs, the emperors long tried to assuage their fiscal pressure by extreme delicacy in religious and cultural matters. It was not easy for them to understand why the Jews should object to Herod's placing a golden eagle, the Roman emblem, over the Temple's great gate. They must have been doubly incensed if they knew that the ancestors of these Jews had for centuries acquiesced in the displaying of the picture of Susa, the Persian capital, at the eastern entry to the Temple of Zerubbabel "in order to impress upon them the fear of the Kingdom." Nevertheless the Roman officials now as a rule respected these and other Jewish religious sensitivities.[34]

In a famous episode (of 26 c.e. or soon after) the newly appointed procurator, Pontius Pilate, an otherwise imperious and stubborn man, witnessed an amazing Jewish display of "intense religious zeal" and ordered the removal from Jerusalem of Roman standards bearing the effigies of Caesar. A decade later, L. Vitellius, governor of Syria, detoured Roman detachments carrying such standards from Jerusalem. He may have been influenced by his personal unfriendliness toward Herod Antipas, whom he had been ordered to aid and, hence, may have rejoiced over the ensuing delay. But he doubtless also sensed the significance of the previous incident to pious Jews and the then prevailing feeling of impending crisis.

Vitellius also went out of his way in relinquishing control over the vestments of the high priest. Theretofore these vestments had been held in the fortress of Antonia and delivered to the high priest each year only for the solemn services on the three major holidays and on the Day of Atonement. Jews generally attached tremendous importance to the latter services and considered their successful performance a significant augury for the following year. We may understand, therefore, their great anxiety over the possibility that any unfriendly Roman captain might arbitrarily withhold from them these essential implements of their worship. When, after the death of Agrippa I, the new procurator Cuspius Fadus wished to restore the vestments to Antonia, the Jews went all the way to Rome and persuaded Claudius himself to rescind this order.[35]

Nor did the Romans object to the perpetuation on Herod's Temple of inscriptions (two physical specimens are still extant today, one of them on a stone 20 inches high and 12 inches thick) forbidding all aliens, including the Roman officials themselves, to enter the sacred precincts. "Whoever is caught, shall himself bear the blame for the death which will ensue." Considering that transgressions of this type elsewhere in the Graeco-Roman world were at worst punishable by a fine and that only this lesser penalty had been sanctioned in Antiochus III's privilege for Jerusalem, the Roman administrators must have been aghast at such threat of capital punishment. Whether it was to be inflicted after trial by a Jewish court or, what is more likely, by immediate legalized lynching, this sanction must have doubly repelled the Romans, as by that time they themselves and other pagans were wont to visit more or less freely one another's sanctuaries. But they acquiesced in it to the very end of the Temple.[36]

The great self-control of Roman officials is also well illustrated by an incident in the days of procurator Ventidius Cumanus (48–52). In the midst of a punitive expedition against some villagers, a Roman soldier found a scroll of the Torah, tore it to bits and threw it into the fire. "At that the Jews were roused," Josephus records, "as though it were their whole country which had been consumed in the flames." They did not rest until Cumanus ordered the culprit's execution.[37]

Early Roman legislation concerning Jews and Judaism in the other provinces of the empire was even more favorable, inasmuch as the imperial masters did not have to contend here with ambitious and unreliable princes and often overtly rebellious masses. Rarely in the history of the Diaspora have Jews enjoyed such a high degree of both equality of rights and self-government, under the protection of public law, as in the early Roman Empire. Responsible exponents of Roman rule repeatedly stressed the principle that the Jews were to be treated in all legal, administrative, fiscal and, to a certain extent, political questions on an equal footing with other citizens. This policy found expression in various decrees of Julius Caesar, Augustus, and Claudius, partly proclaimed in the name of the Roman Senate as a perpetual privilege to all Jews throughout the empire. Josephus claimed that at the time of his writing (93 c.e.) many of these decrees were "still to be found engraved on bronze tablets in the Capitol." In passing judgment on the highly complex problems of Jewish rights in Alexandria, Claudius also wrote in his edict of 41 c.e.,

Whereas the Jews of Alexandria who are called Alexandrians have for a long time been joint residents of the city ever since its beginning along with the Alexandrians themselves, and have received from the kings equality of rights with the latter, as is attested by their records and decrees. . . . Now therefore I wish that the insanity of Gaius [Caligula] shall not deprive the Jewish population of these rights and that they continue to enjoy the same privileges as formerly, remaining faithful to their own customs.

In another edict the emperor extended these safeguards to the Jews of the Empire as a whole. "It is only just," he wrote, "that in the entire civilized world subject to Our authority, the Jews should likewise preserve their ancestral customs without infringement." Former doubts concerning the authenticity of most of these decrees are no longer entertained by leading experts on Roman law.[38]

Not all Jews were Roman citizens, of course. In the complicated political structure in the provinces of the early Roman Empire, each individual belonged to a group with a citizenship peculiar to itself. The Jews, as a rule, seem to have constituted a group apart; but some individuals, for special reasons, enjoyed the advantages of Roman citizenship, indeed, of more than one citizenship. Civic allegiance was not deemed to be exclusive in those days as it had been under the Republic. For example, in Alexandria, Jews now could theoretically enjoy simultaneously the privileges of Roman, Macedonian, Persian, and local Alexandrian citizenship—if such privileges had been extended to them or to their ancestors by the successive governments. How many were also found among the native Egyptian majority with its subjection to a special poll tax, the *lao-*

graphia, is uncertain. No foreign-born Jew would have voluntarily accepted such a lowering of his status, but Egyptian converts to Judaism probably remained, for a time at least, within their hereditary group. All Jews, however, simultaneously belonged to the Jewish community (*politeuma*), thus having a special kind of citizenship with a certain half-religious and half-political allegiance to Palestine.

This was no clearly defined legal status, to be sure. Against their very nature, Roman emperors and jurists preferred to leave the legal position of Jews obscure during the first century, as their successors failed to define the status of Christians a century later. Some were deterred by the complexity of the problem, others respected the heritage of centuries of Egyptian-Syrian rule. On the one hand, the emperors not only remembered the Jews' original "worthy deeds on our behalf and their goodwill toward us," but also still regarded the Jews as the cohesive cosmopolitan element whose "fidelity and friendship to the Romans" (*Antt.* XIV, 10, 8.216; XIX, 5, 3.289) would help keep together the disparate and unruly peoples. On the other hand, every liberal step in favor of Jews increased the animosity of the natives in those eastern Greek municipalities where the Jews most needed protection.

No wonder, then, that even in antiquity the content of these elusive privileges was a matter of dispute, and that Jews and Greeks quarreled for generations about their form and meaning. On matters of such complexity and endless local variations, modern courts would have accumulated hundreds of lengthy and fully documented briefs written by competent lawyers. After spending months, even years, in listening to the testimony and pointed cross-examination of witnesses they would weigh the available evidence and pronounce a sentence, with all the necessary qualifications. Under some circumstances, various courts might reach contradictory decisions, a lower court might be overruled by a superior tribunal, and even a supreme court itself might in the course of years reverse its earlier sentence.

Nothing of the kind is available for the ancient Judeo-Greek legal controversy. Even Roman emperors and magistrates decided each particular issue on political, more than on strictly juridical grounds. The spokesmen on either side were communal leaders, publicists, historians, or philosophers, rather than legally trained persons. Philo, for example, who headed the Jewish delegation to Caligula, had but a superficial understanding of the legal aspects of his case. Certainly a statement like that inserted by him into his philosophic biography of Moses was rather apt to confuse the issue. "For strangers," he wrote, "in my judgement, must be regarded as suppliants of those who receive them, and not only suppliants but settlers [*metoikoi*] and friends, who are anxious to obtain equal rights with the burgesses [*aston*] and are near to being citizens [*politais*], because they differ but little from the original inhabitants [*autochtonon*]." Since the last term was usually applied to Egypt's least privileged group subjected to the poll tax (the *laoi*), one can see how hopelessly muddled is this sentimental outpouring. Nor was Philo much more precise in his two treatises directly bearing on the case, the very preservation of which we owe principally to their theological objectives and didactic formulation. On the Greek side, Apion was a bombastic demagogue, whose arguments, even if preserved, would doubtless have proved no more accurate and precise than are the purported discourses of the Alexandrian "heathen martyrs." [39]

It is not astonishing, however, that the Roman decrees have come down to us almost entirely in their pro-Jewish formulation, as preserved by Josephus. Obviously the Jews found it advantageous to collect only such edicts and ordinances of the central governments —Ptolemaic, Seleucid, and Roman—as safeguarded their rights. Moreover, most of these decrees were issued *ad hoc,* when a Jewish minority appealed for protection. Since the majority rarely needed the assistance of the central government, ordinances setting precedents favorable to the Jews easily outnumbered the unfavorable ones. Favorable decisions, as a rule, were based upon imperial or regional privileges previously granted to Jews and, hence, could readily be invoked by Jews in other localities. Most unfavorable decisions, on the other hand, were likely to stem from local ordinances and usages which could not establish full-fledged precedents for differing local situations. A collection of pro-Jewish decisions, therefore, probably was already in the hands of Nicolaus of Damascus when he pleaded in behalf of the Jews of Asia Minor. In the course of time these compilations must have consisted of an impressive array of official documents confirming over and over again the Jewish privileges.

Under these circumstances, the very terms *isopoliteia* and *isonomia,* as applied to Jews, seem to have received an exceptional twist, because the whole position of Jewry was twisted and exceptional. They no longer meant "equality of rights" pure and simple, but an equality only in specific rights, which the legislator, however, failed to enumerate. The distinction might perhaps best be understood in the light of the struggle for emancipation in central Europe during the nineteenth century. Frequently the Jews themselves did not wish full equality, knowing that equality of political rights involved an equality of political duties, particularly the abandonment of Jewish autonomy. They insisted, therefore, only upon limited equality, on what the Germans called *privatbürgerliche Gleichberechtigung*, or equality in civil and not in political matters. Some such limited, though largely undefined, equality was indeed granted the Jews in the whole Graeco-Roman world. In principle, the Jews remained eligible even for public offices of any kind until the days of the Christian emperors. In practice, there were serious obstacles. If we discount some obvious exaggerations, Tertullian's later statement about Christian officials applied, in essence, to Jews also.

We concede [wrote this legally well-trained Christian apologist] that a Christian may [without endangering salvation] assume the honor and title of public functions if he does not offer sacrifices nor authorize sacrifices, if he does not furnish victims, if he does not entrust anybody with the upkeep of the temples, if he does not take part in the management of their income, if he does not give games either at his own or at the public expense, if he does not preside at them, if he does not announce or arrange any festival, if he avoids all kinds of oath and abstains, while exercising power, from giving sentence in regard to the life or the honor of men, decisions as to money matters being excepted; if he does not proclaim edicts, nor act as a judge, nor put people into prison or inflict torture on them. But is all this possible? [40]

As a matter of record few Jews seem to have served in the earlier Roman civil service. Even in Egypt where the prevailing state control over the economy had, in Ptolemaic times, forced numerous Jews into semipublic occupations, particularly in the fields of state banking, tax farming, grain collection and shipping, the number of Jewish officials seems to have greatly diminished under Rome's more direct collection of taxes and greater economic freedom. The honors and titles conferred upon the Herodian family are naturally in a category by themselves. So is the retention of their respective positions by proselytes, such as (perhaps) Sergius Paulus, the governor of Cyprus. Otherwise a few individuals, especially proselytes, may have compromised with their conscience, but the bulk of the people was practically excluded from Roman or Hellenistic officialdom, with the exception of the aforementioned semicommercial positions.

The evolution of the empire in the direction of absolute monarchy made political rights less significant, while such equality of opportunity in economic and social life as the law could guarantee, mattered more and more. That is why *isopoliteia* in civil law gave the Jews all the rights they really wanted, and exempted them from those duties which they most detested.

In the first place, throughout the empire the Jews were relieved of one civic duty of primary importance: participation in the state and municipal divine worship. Since the Jewish religion insisted that a Jew sacrifice his life rather than commit idolatry, the Hellenistic rulers early recognized that enforced participation in the performance of this civic duty was tantamount to a suppression of the Jewish creed. Having no other alternative to utter intolerance, the Ptolemies and Seleucids granted exemption to their Jewish subjects. On the other hand, the local citizenry begrudged the Jews this more than any other privilege, because every such exemption necessarily increased the proportional financial burden of the rest of the population. The attempt of Antiochus Epiphanes, and the alleged less spectacular one of Ptolemy IV Philopator, to force the Jews to accept this patriotic-religious obligation, proved futile in the face of the stout resistance of the Jewish masses.

Roman legislation, whether or not its emperor-worship was essentially a development of these Hellenistic-oriental antecedents, followed in the footsteps of Rome's predecessors in establishing a general exemption of Jewry. While it was natural to a Roman to deify the deceased "bearer of the empire's omnipotence" as the benefactor and guarantor of peace and prosperity, such an idea must have horrified a pious Jew. No Jew could treat his God with that extreme levity, often characteristic of the emperors themselves in imperial worship. Witticisms such as Vespasian's, who on his deathbed exclaimed, "Alas! I think that I am going to become a god!" or that of Caracalla, who, having instigated the assassination of his brother, consented to the latter's deification, *sit divus, dum non sit vivus* (Let him be a god, as long as he is not alive), would have seemed execrable blasphemies to a Jew. By that time the Jews were even refraining from the common use of *Adonai*, the Lord, as a substitute for the "ineffable" name.

Jews could, however, instead of sacrificing to the emperor, offer a daily sacrifice *in the name* of the emperor to their God in Jerusalem. Augustus, in accordance with his conciliatory policy, seems to have renewed the ancient Persian usage established by Artaxerxes during the construction of the Second Temple, and granted an imperial subsidy for the upkeep of this daily sacrifice. His successors in office and divine honors acquiesced in this arrangement. Only the megalomaniac Caius Caligula objected, reproaching the Alexandrian Jewish deputation thus: "You sacrificed to another god, and not for my sake; and then what good did you do me? Moreover you did not sacrifice to me." His aggressive policy to force conformity would have brought about serious complications had not the hand of an assassin cut short his ambitious venture. After the destruction of the Temple, the Jews were unable to offer sacrifices, even in the name of the emperor. The emperors seemed contented with the offering of prayers for them, which was all that remained. Ever since, Jews, mindful of Jeremiah's injunction, have prayed for the welfare of the land in which they dwelt and of its ruler.[41]

Jewish self-government, as will be seen, was equally respected, and even protected by imperial legislation. Jews lived a full Jewish life among themselves without outside interference. They were governed by Palestinian law, and inner quarrels were adjusted exclusively by their own judges. Their communities not only were "artificial persons" in regard to ownership of property, but could levy compulsory taxes, collected, when necessary, with the help of the Roman authorities. Jewish houses of worship, like those of the Romans, were, under the law, institutions endowed with a sacred character. Every violation of a synagogue was classified by Roman law as a sacrilege. So also were cases of embezzlement of the sacred money collected in the Diaspora for the Temple in Jerusalem, whether consisting of the half-shekel contributions or of additional voluntary gifts. In his benevolence toward the Jews Augustus went so far as to order the Roman courts not to call Jewish parties or witnesses on the Sabbath. Such needy Roman Jews as took advantage of the distribution of grain and oil were given a double portion on Friday to avoid complications on the Sabbath. Since some Palestinian authorities prohibited the dietary use of heathen oil, they could demand money instead of oil. Thus Augustus decided a question of Jewish law in a stricter sense than the final Palestinian Halakhah itself.[42]

Incipient signs of reaction, however, were visible as early as the first century. While the central government so effectively protected the Jews against their Gentile neighbors in the provinces, the antagonisms in Roman society could not remain without influence, at least on the Roman municipal government. That is why, in 19 C.E., Emperor Tiberius' counselor, Sejanus, took measures, according to Eusebius' exaggerating report, "completely to destroy the whole [Jewish] race." The Jews were expelled from Rome and perhaps from all of Italy, and 4,000 young Jews were condemned to forced labor in Sardinia. Tiberius soon reconsidered, however, and twelve years later formally readmitted the Jews to the city, from which many of them had probably never departed. If we may rely on a clue from three contradictory sources, Claudius later lost patience with Jewish religious propaganda and prohibited public gatherings of Jews in Rome. In fact, already in his letter to Alexandria, Claudius allowed himself a threat toward the Jews in case of noncompliance, which showed how much he was impressed by the stock argument of ancient Jew-baiters. If the Alexandrian Jews were to continue, he wrote, to invite other Jews from Syria or Egypt, he would conceive the greater suspicion and "I will by all means take vengeance on them as fomenting a general plague for the whole world." [43]

Claudius' unfriendly remark need not indicate his real antagonism to the Jews, but rather his growing impatience with this ever troublesome group of subjects. Certainly the reports which he received from Palestine, *after* the issuance of his friendly edict earlier in 41, did not indicate any real relaxation of existing tensions. To appease the Jews further Claudius handed over to easygoing Agrippa I an even larger area than had been held by Herod—an evidently hazardous step from the standpoint of imperial policy. Now the Alexandrian controversy flared up again, this time occasioned by riots in which the Jews appeared as the aggressors. Finally, the Jewish religious propaganda in Rome itself, which had antagonized Tiberius, also ran counter to Claudius' own attempt at reviving the conservatory religious policies of Augustus. In such a state of mind the anti-Jewish pleadings of the Alexandrian delegation must have made a certain impression, without converting the emperor into a real Jew-baiter or making him alter the basic Roman policy toward Jews. In any case, both he and Tiberius continued to protect the Jews in the provinces. Nevertheless such intemperate words and actions, reflecting the growing anti-Jewish feelings and suspicions in Roman society at large, boded ill for the Jews' continued enjoyment of unrestricted religious freedom.

INTERDEPENDENCE OF FATE

Political struggles of this kind underscored the community of destiny linking the Jews of the various countries of the dispersion with those in Palestine and with one another. It was, for example, a great blow to all Jews in the Graeco-Roman world that Judaea lost her sovereignty in 63 B.C.E. Instead of being treated as an ally whose dispersed "colonies" Rome repeatedly promised to protect in her own domains, as well as in other allied countries, Palestine now became one of Rome's most turbulent provinces. Those Pharisaic and other anti-Maccabeans who repeatedly petitioned Rome to remove their existing leadership may have acted in accordance with their much-cherished nonpolitical tradition. But unwittingly they thereby gravely jeopardized the position of Jewish minorities in other lands; in the long run their people certainly was to pay an enormous price for whatever immediate religious and cultural gains had been secured by the overthrow of a rapidly degenerating regime.

Nor was Diaspora Jewry free of responsibility. As soon as the emergency of the Syrian persecutions had passed, it abdicated its part in shaping the policies affecting world Jewry. Palestinian rabbis, or even such Egyptian delegates as Philo, were given brotherly reception by the Jewish communities on their political missions. The Roman community, in particular, seems to have vigorously supported whatever cause these messengers happened to espouse in the imperial capital. But there neither existed any regular forum for the exchange of ideas and the airing of mutually advantageous proposals, nor any permanent agency whereby Diaspora Jewry could make its weight felt before decisions affecting all Jews were reached in Jerusalem. By delegating all responsibility for world Jewish affairs to the Palestinian leaders alone, and taking care (not always in the best possible manner) only of their local or regional struggles, the communities of Egypt, Syria, and other lands became largely passive bystanders in the great drama of Jewish history which unfolded in the later Maccabean and Herodian age. This political stupor, though temporarily advancing Palestine's centralized controls, ultimately paralyzed the masses of dispersed Jewry when the great hour of decision struck for both groups.

Such exclusive concentration of leadership in Palestine and the natural proneness of these leaders to equate what seemed good for the homeland with the welfare of the whole people became doubly dangerous because of the vagaries of Rome's imperial policies toward Jews. Roman statesmen and legislators were often inconsistent, not so much because of individual whims and chance circumstances, but for reasons inherent in the genuine regional variations of Rome's imperial interests. Outside of Palestine and Italy, Jews could be treated as an imperially useful loyal minority helping to restrain any anti-Roman outbreaks. In Palestine, on the other hand, it was the rebellious Jewish majority itself whom Rome wished to restrain by favoring the pagan minorities. Italy, mistress of the Mediterranean, at times resented the presence of Jewish and other strong alien groups in Rome. That is why the same Tiberius who expelled the Jews from Rome or all of Italy, and sent thousands of their young men to Sardinian mines, nevertheless upheld the extensive privileges granted by his predecessors to the Jews of other provinces. That is also why Claudius who, in another outburst of intolerance, shut the Jewish places of worship in Rome, at the same time executed some of the "heathen martyrs" for their share in the anti-Jewish riots in Alexandria. Simultaneously, these and other emperors collected vexatious, often outright ruinous, taxes from Palestine's farming population and maintained there an extortionist and corrupt administrative machinery which, though not specifically anti-Jewish, embroiled Rome in endless controversies with that rebellious province. Despite the ultimate outbreak of the great Palestinian revolt, however, both Vespasian and Titus refused, as we shall see, to budge from the principles of a limited Jewish equality in either Antioch or Alexandria.

These and other constantly changing cross currents in Roman society and government, which perplexed even such keen political analysts as Polybius or Tacitus, would have taxed the mental capacities of the best-informed and most politically sagacious Jewish leadership. Only a group of very wise men, in part recruited from the various countries of the dispersion with their varying local interests and problems, might have successfully coped with the staggering complexities of Jewish status. The Palestinian leaders alone, even if they had had access to far better and more up-to-date information about these local difficulties than was possible under the existing slow media of communication, could hardly be expected to balance with complete impartiality their country's immediate exigencies against the long-range interests of the people as a whole. As it happened, they neither were sufficiently well informed nor sagacious enough to think in these broader terms. More, they were a house divided against itself. In fact, many of their political difficulties themselves stemmed from deep socio-economic and religious cleavages which set Jew against Jew in Palestine and elsewhere. Despite the vaunted solidarity of the Jewish people, so often denounced by Jew-baiting contemporaries, disunity and strife dominated all walks of life in the declining years of the Second Commonwealth.

VIII

SOCIAL TURMOIL

EXTENSION of the boundaries of the Jewish state under the
Maccabees to include almost all Palestine and Transjordan,
the rapid population increase, Jerusalem's rise to a position
of prominence in national and international affairs, the economic
and social effects of the *Pax Romana*—all had lasting influence on
the social conditions of the Second Commonwealth. With some justice a Graeco-Roman writer of the age declared that "the whole
inhabitable world is like one city." In fact, the empire's relations
extended far beyond its boundaries, into the Scandinavian countries, and what is now the Soviet Union, and China. The small
country watered by the Jordan could not help becoming a part of
the new economic system. Whether under the stringent economic
regime of the Ptolemies, the more nationally oriented Maccabean
rule, or the fiscal exploitation by Herodians and Romans, Palestine's methods of production, distribution, and even consumption
increasingly resembled those of the other parts of the *oikoumene*.

At the same time there persisted numerous local variations not
only on account of differences in natural equipment and historic
heritage, but also because of the frequent customs and other fiscal
barriers. "All along the route they keep on paying," Pliny graphically described the transportation of Arabian frankincense at the
height of the Roman peace, "at one place for water, at another for
fodder, or the charges for lodging at the halts, and the various oc-
trois; so that expenses mount to 688 denarii per camel before the
Mediterranean Coast is reached." Combined with the still primitive and costly methods of transportation, these constant surcharges
on the cost of production stimulated the forces of autarchy and regional diversity. These conflicting trends caused Palestine's economic differentiation to increase rapidly and to extend further
than at any previous period in its history, including that of King
Solomon.[1]

AGRICULTURE

The country's economy remained principally agricultural. Since
deforestation had not progressed very far, its natural fertility was

greatly enhanced by the accumulated capital investment of centuries and the new, more intensive methods of cultivation. Palestine produced wheat and particularly barley in such quantities that, despite the great population density, it could in good years sustain the heavy burden of taxation in kind by foreign rulers, and in addition sell cereals for export.

Even the Egyptian author of the Letter of Aristeas extolled Judaea's high agricultural productivity. Some rabbis boasted, with homiletical recklessness, that in blessed years the poorest region of Palestine gave a larger crop than the richest part of Egypt, which from time immemorial had been the granary of the Mediterranean world. Much more moderately, R. Jose enumerated five *se'ahs* (measures) of varying quality yielded by the sowing of one *se'ah* of grain. Although still higher than "the fourth corn"—the alleged average return of the Italian soil in the days of Columella (1st cent. c.e.)—this is much lower than Varro's previous estimate of a tenfold to fifteenfold harvest in Italy. It was also less than the yield of the more fertile Palestinian regions in the Old Testament period which, according to modern scholars, had produced more than fifteen times their seed, at least in barley. It appears that the increasing population necessitated more intensive exploitation of the soil and the use of much marginal land with proportionately larger investments of seed on smaller areas.[2]

Still richer was the fruit crop. As Plutarch, Pliny, and other classical writers tell us, Palestinian dates, figs, olives and grapes, wine and oil were of superior quality and prized even in other Mediterranean countries rich in these products. They were served on the imperial tables in Rome. With truly oriental abandon a rabbi contended that "there is not a vine in the land of Israel whose harvesting does not require the labor of a whole town." Another explained a three-day absence from his job by saying, "My father left me a vine branch from which I harvested on the first day three hundred clusters each yielding a barrel, on the second day I cut three hundred clusters yielding half a barrel each, on the third day the three hundred clusters produced one-third of a barrel each; and I still left behind more than half the crop." Still another claimed that one early morning he had walked the three miles from Lydda to Ono, wading through an ankle-high lake of fig juice (Ketubot 111b).

More than ever before, the country became a land flowing "with milk and honey," or rather with fruit juices, if we so translate *de-*

bash in the well-known biblical formula. Not that "honey" had lost its importance in Palestine's economy. As in the rest of the Mediterranean world the sugar cane was either unknown or unexploited, and honey remained the main sweetening substance. Such of its by-products as wax were also widely used. Sirach still reflected Palestine's realities of his day when he wrote, "The chief of all the necessaries of life for man are water and fire, and iron and salt, the fat of [choice] wheat, milk and honey, the blood of the grape, oil and clothing" (39:26). However, honey could not compare in either quantity or general utility with the various fruit juices, including wine, which was part of the daily menu of large segments of the population.

Perhaps for this reason, as well as on account of the still greater importance of wheat and particularly barley for the feeding of the people, Jewish liturgy relinquished the biblical idiom in favor of the Greek-flavored blessing of *ereṣ ḥemdah ṭobah u-reḥabah* (fertile, good and wide land). Nor were such rather outlandish plants as the papyrus altogether lacking. It grew in the Negev; the manufactured product supplemented Egyptian imports, although the price, kept high by the Egyptian foreign trade monopoly, seems to have greatly curtailed the use of papyrus as compared with the more abundant parchment and the still less expensive ostracon.[3]

Only in the region around Jericho did the balsam tree flourish. Hence balsam commanded an enormous price and is said to have been sold for its weight in gold. According to Strabo, price-conscious Jewish growers intentionally limited cultivation to the Jericho region which, owing to intensive irrigation, was one of the most fertile sections of the country. The rabbis spoke admiringly of the "fat lands of Jericho." Pliny records a dramatic incident of the Great War, when, in the Jordan Valley, Jews tried to cut down all balsam trees lest they fall into the hands of the enemy. The Romans sought to save the precious plants and "there have been pitched battles in defense of a shrub." This was an act of despair on the part of the Jews, in some way resembling the heroic self-extermination of the garrison of Masada.[4]

In general, "cutting down plantations," the lifeblood of Palestinian economy, was recognized as such an indefensible crime that the expression came to be used metaphorically for the equally rampant attacks on religious fundamentals. To be called *qoṣeṣ ben qoṣeṣ* (cutter, son of a cutter) was superlative insult. The Jews so thoroughly identified themselves with Palestine's most representative plants that, in literary metaphor and artistic adornment, the palm tree and the vine became the paramount symbols of Israel. To a lesser extent this is also true of the pomegranate and the olive tree. Olives and olive oil were not only major nutrients, but the latter served also for illumination and as an important ingredient of a variety of drugs and cosmetics.

All of these trees appear on most Palestinian coins, as well as on many tombs in the Roman catacombs. The relative absence, on the other hand, of the fig tree from Jewish iconography is the more remarkable, since the tree furnished important foodstuffs (raw and in baked form) practically throughout the year, and since relaxed sitting under it had long been glorified as the acme of peace and security. Perhaps its frequent identification in the popular mind with the tree of knowledge which, according to the biblical cosmogony, had brought death into the world (Ginzberg's *Legends*, V, 97 f.), served as a deterrent.

Law often had to be adjusted to life's urgent necessities. For example, the biblical prohibition of *kilayim* (the cultivation of heterogeneous plants in the same field), now an obstacle to rational farming, was so circumscribed as to become almost meaningless. As in Rome from the days of Cato to those of Columella, so also in Palestine of the postbiblical age, the intensification of agriculture forced the Jews to utilize every available parcel of ground to the utmost limits. The new law therefore defined *kilayim* as referring merely to the simultaneous sowing of wheat, barley, and seeds of grapes, or on a spot which could be covered by the sowing of one hand (Qiddushin 39a). Except for this limitation, wheat could easily be grown in a vineyard. Truly, a simple evasion of the spirit of the biblical taboo!

For similar reasons a rabbi of the second century listed "those who rear small cattle" alongside of those who "cut down good trees" as persons "who will never see a sign of blessing." These two activities were not quite unrelated. Apart from fearing the direct damage which grazing sheep might inflict on trees, particularly in their tender years, the sages of the first and second centuries favored the more intensive grain and fruit cultivation. Less dangerous appeared to them the larger cattle (oxen and cows) which could be raised economically only in the extensive grasslands of Transjordan and other peripheral regions, where flocks of sheep were likewise permitted. A similar transition occurred in Rome where the great patriot Cato (2d cent. B.C.E.) had placed a meadow for cattle raising ahead of grain land as a safe way of making profit, while a century later Varro sharply denounced those who converted fields into pasture. In any case, meat was not a staple product in Palestine. According to R. Eleazar ben Azariah (2d cent.),

A man who owns a hundred shekels shall buy for his stew a pound of vegetables; a thousand shekels, shall buy a pound of fish; 5,000 shekels, a pound of meat [it is later explained: once a week]. Only if he owns 10,000 shekels, he may put his pot on the stove every day.

With the burning of the Temple disappeared also the need of a daily supply of sacrificial animals and birds. Animals needed for work in fields or for such by-products as hides and wool could readily be purchased from the neighboring seminomadic Nabataeans. Not that cattle raising totally disappeared from the Jewish economy before 70, but it was topographically as well as figuratively relegated to the periphery.[5]

Correspondingly, the high appreciation of a shepherd's life found in Old Testament literature (God himself was likened to the "good shepherd" in an almost standardized poetic metaphor) now gave way to considerable deprecation. Not only did the rabbis' general preoccupation with raising the educational level of the masses make them frown upon the lighthearted ignorance of the average shepherd, but they also treated him as a generally untrustworthy character, whose testimony was not fully acceptable in court. We shall see that it was only a reflection of the renewed appreciation of cattle raising that the third-century Sepphoris rabbi Ḥama ben Ḥanina pointed out the discrepancy between the shepherd's lowly calling and the biblical designation of God as shepherd (homily on Ps. 23:1 cited in *Yalqut Shime'oni* on Psalms, No. 690). Neither he nor any of his like-minded colleagues, however, could remove the old stigma from the shepherd's dependability as a witness. Because of the prevalence of aleatory games in the Graeco-Roman world, a pigeon fancier, too, was regarded as a reckless gambler, rather than a trustworthy witness (M. Sanhedrin III, 2–3; b. 25 ab).

By way of contrast the numerous fishermen at Lake Tiberias (Genezareth) or along the Mediterranean shore enjoyed a reputable, if not high, social standing. Since they were supplying a staple article of daily consumption in the shape of both fresh and salted fish, their great piety sometimes proved embarrassing. When on one occasion the fishermen of Tiberias, apparently forming a professional association, decided to abstain from work on the semi-holidays of Passover and the Feast of Tabernacles, this act of supererogation caused widespread complaints. Fresh fish deteriorates rapidly in the hot Palestinian climate, and many consumers found themselves deprived of that integral part of their holiday meal during the latter days of these important festivals. They could only secure salted fish which were an even more regular ingredient in the diet of the whole Graeco-Roman world. That is why, for example, Strabo stressed the importance of the Galilean city of Tarichaea, so called because it served as a center of an elaborate fish-salting industry and commerce.[6]

TRADE AND INDUSTRY

At the same time, a large class of artisans and merchants grew up in the capital and other cities. To be sure, the largest provincial cities and especially those on the Mediterranean coast were predominantly Greek. Thus far Josephus' apologetical statement, "Ours is not a maritime country; neither commerce nor the intercourse which it promotes with the outside world has any attraction for us" (*Ag. Ap.* I, 12.60), is not without foundation. No inland city in the third century B.C.E. could compare, for instance, with Gaza or Akko as a center of trade, according to references in the Zenon papyri. None the less, not only among the numerous Jewish residents of these Greek cities, but also among the upper classes of the Jewish settlement in the interior there were some who had accumulated enough capital to start a profitable trade and even to enter the banking business. Against this drive the warning by an aristocratic sage like Sirach that "hardly shall the merchant keep himself from wrongdoing" (26:29) proved of even less avail than the advice of a later teacher, R. Meir, that one ought to devote little time to business and much time to study (M. Abot IV, 12).

The persistent Maccabean struggle for the possession of the coast revealed the tenacity of a more or less conscious drive for access to the sea. The author of First Maccabees, a contemporary of the Maccabean dynasty and evidently writing under its inspiration, extolled Simon because he had taken Jaffa "for a haven and made an entrance to the isles [the Syriac reads: ships] of the sea." Simon was prepared to pay a high price for this port city, while his successor, John Hyrcanus, successfully appealed to the Romans "that Joppa and its harbors" be restored to the Jews. Although the ensuing decree of the Roman Senate gave the whole affair a fiscal coloring, the primary intention of the Maccabean rulers doubtless was to promote Jewish commerce. For this purpose Jaffa also had to be forcibly Judaized. Herod, to be sure, seems to have favored pagan over Jewish merchants and, after building Caesarea's magnificent harbor, attracted to it chiefly Greek settlers. But even he could not prevent the entry of that city's numerous Jewish residents into its commercial life. More and more Jews were able now to put to sea in their own vessels, transport their own goods, and enter the flourishing East Mediterranean trade. Not even that frequent by-line of ancient sea commerce, piracy, was completely absent. During the war with the Romans Jewish pirates from Jaffa "made raids on the traffic along the coast of Syria and Phoenicia and the route to Egypt, rendering the navigation in those seas quite impossible." Ultimately a second-century rabbi could claim that Israel's sea trade caused many foreign merchants to adopt Judaism.[7]

Before the fall of Jerusalem, to be sure, these developments were still in their early stages. Apart from a minority precariously living in Greek cities, Palestinian Jewry must have embraced but a small fraction of petty merchants, selling goods in their local stores, at periodic markets, or peddling them among the farmers. Many pursued their trade as a mere by-line to their main occupation of farming or industry. The high priest was certainly entitled to pray on the Day of Atonement that God should grant the country a prosperous year, "a year of low prices, plentiful crops and [extensive] trade," but at the same time to ask God not to allow the requests of travelers (that is, businessmen) to interfere with rainfall. In case of conflict the farmers' interests came first.[8]

Industrial occupations seem to have gained ground more speedily. Here, too, the Jews engaged in petty crafts requiring few laborers, rather than in large-scale industry, even in the restricted meaning of this term in the ancient world. Nor can one attribute this deficiency entirely to lack of raw materials. Of course, Palestine had neither coal nor oil. But neither of these sparkplugs of modern industry was significantly exploited in any other part of the Western world. The country was also poor in metals. Particularly since the suspension of Egyptian copper mining on the Sinaitic peninsula, the local supply of copper, as well as iron, must have been very small. Like gold or silver these metals had to be imported from other lands at very high cost. Hence, perhaps, Herod's endeavors, temporarily successful, to exploit under a direct grant from Augustus the famous copper mines of Cyprus. Nor was Palestine, except in its northern Lebanese extension, blessed by any noteworthy supply of lumber, particularly of the varieties needed for home construction. If anything, conditions had worsened since the days of Solomon when cedar for the building of Temple and royal palace had to be brought down from Lebanon.[9]

On the other hand, there were ample stone quarries up and down the land, and stone houses, in any case more appropriate to the local climate, could be built very inexpensively even by inexperienced masons. Certain minerals were plentiful, particularly in the vicinity of the Dead Sea, which the Romans called the *Lacus Asphaltitis*. Transjordanian and southern steppes furnished sufficient wool, all of Palestine enough flax for the development of a flourishing textile industry. In describing the battle for Jerusalem, Josephus mentions the Romans storming "that district of the new town, where lay the wool-shops [*eriopolia*], the braziers' smithies and the clothes-market." Three centuries later Diocletian's edict regulating maximum prices set the very highest price on the fine linen produced at Beth-Shan (Scythopolis). There was also enough local raw material for the food processor, leather manufacturer, and potter, although much ceramic ware was steadily imported from abroad.[10]

Nevertheless we have little evidence of any major technological or organizational advances. From time immemorial there had been whole villages of artisans engaged exclusively in one trade. Excavators have discovered traces of such villages even in the pre-Israelitic period. On the other hand, special quarters in Jerusalem, devoted to a particular line of production, are referred to in Nehemiah (3:8). This sort of specialization progressed with the increase in the general division of labor. We have no Palestinian counterpart to the large Alexandrian Jewish guilds which occupied separate sections in the celebrated *diplostoön*, probably a double-colonnaded synagogue. This enormous structure so deeply impressed the Palestinian R. Judah that he exclaimed, "Whoever has not seen the *diplostoön* in Alexandria of Egypt has never in his life seen Israel's glory" (T. Sukkah IV, 6, 198). Here new arrivals in search of employment readily contacted master artisans in their respective trades. In the more sedentary population of Jewish Palestine, crafts were still largely hereditary.

Even among the Palestinians, however, there gradually developed, particularly in the transport industry, some professional associations which, during the later period of economic regimentation, were to play a great role in regulating conditions of work. Some of them went so far as to assign special working days to each member and to insure him against losses of ships or donkeys. Having ancient roots in Palestine's economy, such guilds were doubtless stimulated by the widespread professional *collegia* throughout the Graeco-Roman world. They must have played a far greater role in the country's economic and political life than appears from the few incidental references in extant sources.[11]

Jewish religious demands likewise served as a stimulus. The extremely favorable attitude of the rabbis to labor and to earning a living may have been the effect, rather than the cause, of economic developments, but there were inherent in the religion, as such, many impulses to Jewish economic endeavor. For example, the rigid prohibition of admitting Gentiles to the sanctuary forced even such a "liberal" as Herod to employ exclusively Jewish labor in the reconstruction of the Temple. Wherever the holiness of the place precluded laymen, the priests had to serve as masons and carpenters, a thousand of them having mastered these trades, according to Josephus. In addition, ten thousand lay laborers were needed. Aside from its construction, the Temple permanently supplied work to numerous artisans of all kinds. Here again extreme punctiliousness in matters relating to consecrated objects favored priestly artisans. If a lay worker ate some fruit belonging to sacred property (*heqdesh*) on which he had been working or demanded payment in kind, he was told that he had committed outright sacrilege. The annual pilgrimages to Jerusalem not only brought Palestinian Jewry into contact with the far-flung Diaspora in a commercial way, but also created a whole class of Palestinian bankers and money changers for pilgrims. When Jesus "overthrew the tables of the money-changers, and the seats of them that sold doves," he merely revolted against certain conveniences that had become attached to an institutionalized "house of prayer." Such examples could easily be multiplied. It is almost self-evident that the Jewish religion had, by that time, become a tremendous social force in itself.[12]

Despite the great differences in the impact of the respective religions on economics and the ethnic separation of the coast from the interior, it may nevertheless be asserted that economic conditions in Palestine in many ways resembled those of the neighboring countries, Egypt and Syria. Taken as a whole, this southeastern corner of the Mediterranean was economically the most advanced region of the Roman Empire.

DIASPORA ECONOMY

Economic differentiation in the mother country was far surpassed by that of the Jewish communities in the dispersion. If Palestine, politically autonomous and dependent on local natural and historic factors, was irresistibly drawn into the vortex of Graeco-Roman economic developments, the Jewish minorities in the Diaspora were almost entirely the objects of economic forces beyond their collective control. Particularly those large segments of Jewry forcibly brought to other lands as prisoners of war and slaves had no choice but to adjust themselves to the requirements of their masters. To be sure, most of them seem not to have remained in bondage for a long time. Because many tried to live up to ritual diet and Sabbath commandments, their owners may have found possession quite irksome and may have released them at an early date. This was especially the case in those Graeco-Roman areas where the existing laws made possible a more profitable employment of their services as freedmen.

Moreover, the families of Jewish prisoners, as well as the Jewish communities already established in the vicinity of their new places of settlement, left no stone unturned until they secured their freedom, since the commandment to "ransom captives" ranked among the highest in Jewish religious law (M. Gittin IV, 6, 9). While our direct records of such communal redemptions date from the third century C.E. and later, there is little doubt that even earlier large-scale Jewish slavery was but a sporadic accompaniment of Palestinian wars and was reduced to a minimum in periods of peace. Even the Maccabean revolt which, particularly during its early phase of guerrilla warfare, must have given the Syrian armies ample opportunity to dispose of Jewish fighters and civilians, proved rather disappointing to the slave traders in the wake of Lysias' expedition. As soon as the Maccabeans succeeded in securing favorable terms from Demetrius I (152 C.E.), they exacted from him the promise to set free without price "every soul of the Jews that hath been carried away captive from the land of Judah into any part of my kingdom" (I Macc. 3:41; 10:33).

It is small wonder, therefore, that the manumissions in the great commercial center of Delphi during a century and a half (201–50 B.C.E.) included, among 934 slaves of various nationalities, only four Jews and three Egyptians. Three of these four Jewish slaves, moreover, were feminine members of a single family released about

158 B.C.E. and evidently brought to Delphi by slave merchants at the time of the Maccabean revolt. While the paucity of Egyptian slaves may be explained by the infrequency of campaigns in Egypt, the state-capitalistic exploitation of "free" villeins, and the governmental control over foreign trade, that of Jews is understandable only as the result of concerted communal resistance.[13]

Even if liberated, however, these Jewish settlers had to earn a living under varying local conditions. Many were used by their masters to reinforce the garrisons of outlying fortresses, but even they could in peacetime pursue their traditional agricultural activities. Others, too, were employed by their masters on farms or voluntarily settled on land. In Egypt they, like the Greeks, seem to have been encouraged by the government to develop previously neglected viticulture.

On the other hand, a very large proportion of slaves must have found its way into the households and industrial or commercial establishments of urban masters. The free immigrants were doubtless attracted most to the ever-growing, manpower-hungry metropolitan areas. The larger and better organized the Jewish communities in the larger cities became, the more effective welcome could they extend to more recent arrivals. In such cities the Jews, too, largely lived on trade and commerce, in some branches of which they had been trained by their masters. We recall that in Alexandria they formed regular artisan guilds of their own. Some Alexandrian metal workers possessed skills unknown among their less specialized Palestinian confreres, and were called to the Temple in Jerusalem whenever difficult repairs required particular skills. In short, L. Fuchs's description of the economic diversification of Egyptian Jewry also fits, with minor modifications, other countries of the dispersion.

Under the Roman emperors [he writes] they were beggars, sorcerers, peddlers, artisans and traders of all kinds, dealers in antiques and usurers, bankers, farmers, tenants, workingmen and sailors, in short, they did everything from which they could hope to derive a livelihood.[14]

It is possible, none the less, that their alien quality and interterritorial solidarity brought about a gradual increase of artisans and, especially, of merchants among the Jews. However, even then the proportion of Jews in the commercial life of those countries was not much higher than their proportion in the population. At any rate, for centuries to come the Jewish merchant was to be outranked by his pagan and later Christian competitor, the Syrian, about whom a provincial "hundred per cent" Italian poet reproachfully sang, "The Syrian Orontes has long since poured [dregs] into the Tiber" (Juvenal's *Satires*, III, 62).

Curiously, banking, which in later ages was to become a characteristically Jewish occupation, still attracted but few Jews. Among the considerable number of bankers in Graeco-Roman Egypt listed by Calderini not one name could be safely identified as Jewish, although a number of Jews seem to have served as officials in state banks. It has even been suggested that the loan contracts without interest included in the Adler papyri reflected the influence of Jewish aversion to usury. Be this as it may, one Tebtunis papyrus of 182 B.C.E., recording a mortgage loan between two Jews, specifically provided that no interest was to be paid for a year. Only "if he does not repay it as stated, Sostatus shall forthwith forfeit to Apollonius the loan increased by one-half and for the overtime interest at the rate of two drachmas per mina per month." The same fairly customary rate of 24 per cent is recorded also in another loan contract between two Jews of Tebtunis (of 174 B.C.E.). However, here, too, we deal with the renewal of the loan, further complicated by the prospect of repayment in "the eighth year," which may have had some bearing on the legal cancellation of debts during the Jewish Sabbatical year. In any case, the original loan may have been granted without interest. It stands to reason, however, that once they became a professional group, the Jewish moneylenders in Egypt and elsewhere could not long indulge in such profitless transactions.[15]

Some Jews ultimately gained a footing at the top of capitalistic activities, particularly in Alexandria which, according to the Letter of Aristeas, surpassed "all cities in size and prosperity." Some of them became prominent bankers, shipowners, and contractors. Certainly, Philo's relatives, the "alabarchs" Alexander and Demetrius, did not derive their great wealth from the revenue of the district under their fiscal administration, if this be the meaning of their title. Alexander's far-flung banking relations are well illustrated by his loan of 200,000 drachmas (some $30,000) to the future King Agrippa I. Fearing Agrippa's widely known prodigality, Alexander gave him less than a third of the amount in cash and the rest in a draft on Dicaearchia (Puteoli) in Italy, where he had a correspondent or, possibly, a branch office of his own.[16]

The assumption of some modern scholars that the Egyptian Jews monopolized the papyrus and corn trades in their country is almost certainly erroneous. But there is no doubt that many of them played a significant role in these and other state monopolies. Neither is it a mere accident that Strabo, speaking of restrictions in the production of papyrus in Egypt, mentioned as a parallel Jewish speculators who limited their palm-tree plantations in order to maintain the price of dates. Many Jews derived a large income from farming the public revenue for a contractual lump sum. There must also have been some rich Jewish corn merchants in the adjacent provinces of Cyrenaica and Africa, where Italian excavations have revealed the existence of important commercial centers dating from the Roman period.[17]

RICH AND POOR

A few examples of great Jewish fortunes must not blind us to the appalling poverty prevailing among the masses. Contemporaries as well as modern scholars were often misled. Even Tacitus looked for some explanation of the reputed Jewish communal wealth. Compassion rather than resentment was evoked by ladies like Martha, daughter of Boethos, who allegedly acquired for her second husband, Simon son of Gamala, the high-priestly office for three *qabs* (approximately 1½ gallons) of gold denars. Martha could walk to the Temple only on carpets; she subsequently perished from eating unaccustomed coarse food during the siege of Jerusalem. She was remembered with great sympathy, for example, by R. Johanan ben Zakkai, who himself had been a trader for forty years. Wealthy benefactors were not only gratefully remembered in synagogue inscriptions, but a famous brass gate at the Temple, which allegedly required twenty men to push open, was named after its donor, Nicanor of Alexandria.[18]

Herod, in particular, seems to have been generally recognized as Rome's richest vassal. Tribute to his munificence, praised all over the Mediterranean world, was made by means of a statue erected in the Acropolis of Athens. But the oppressive burden of taxation which made possible all this splendor brought the people of Palestine to the brink of ruin. Certainly the approximate amount of 1,000 talents of Herod's annual revenue, which can be deduced from Josephus, constituted only a fraction of the royal budget. Even so, the per capita burden of approximately half a dollar annually was rather heavy. Moreover, it is difficult to overestimate the amount which tax collectors extorted from the population but which never reached the royal treasury; the amount which poured in every year under the guise of voluntary or involuntary donations; and, finally, the extent of confiscations which resulted in the extraordinary increase of the royal domains. Herod's fiscal reign of terror, with his expropriatory regular taxes and highly irregular direct expropriations, horrified even the oriental chroniclers, accustomed though they were to tyrannical government.[19]

In its complaints before Augustus against Herod's regime the Palestinian delegation stressed particularly his property confiscations under flimsy excuses (whether or not he combined them with the execution of owners), his ruthless collection of the regular revenue, including a large variety of customs, and the corruption of his officials who, at every step, exacted heavy bribes (*Antt.* XVII, 8, 4.204; 11, 2.306–7). The delegates may have exaggerated the general economic decline of the country, but their complaints about Herod's expropriation of the ruling classes made a greater impression in Rome, where the colonial policy had largely favored the local aristocracies as the mainstay of imperial rule. Herod's ruthless execution of members of his own family was well known in the capital. Augustus himself once quipped that he would "rather be Herod's pig than Herod's son." This may have been a weighty reason for the Crown Council in Rome to replace the vassal kingdom by more direct procuratorial control in 6 C.E.

Palestine Jewry thus merely exchanged one oppressive master for another. The first act of the new administration was to institute a general census of persons and property. Although Quirinius, the new legate of Syria, partly masked this undertaking under the guise of liquidating Archelaus' possessions, the people were filled with forebodings of evil. Extremists, led by Judas of Galilee, staged a short-lived revolt, but the majority acquiesced under the persuasive urging of their high priest. The first decade seems to have passed quietly enough, if we are to judge from the absence of specific complaints and from the fact that one of the Temple gates was named in honor of the first procurator, Coponius. But, as elsewhere, the Roman fiscal administration proved extremely ingenious in finding new objects of taxation, both regular and extraordinary. Ultimately a century after the fall of Jerusalem, Pescennius Niger informed some plaintive Palestinians, "Verily, if I had my way, I would tax your air." Methods of collection also became the more ruthless, bribery the more rampant and universal, as Roman colonial officials enjoyed only relatively brief tenure and tried to amass the greatest fortunes possible in a short time. According to Josephus, Tiberius extended the term of office of his provincial administrators (including the two procurators who served in Judaea for a decade each), in order that, having amassed fortunes in the early years, they would prove less extortionate for the remainder of their terms. But after Tiberius' death the old system reasserted itself and, especially after Agrippa I's brief royal interlude, the procurators changed for the most part after two or three years. The Romans themselves poked fun at such typical governors as Ventidius who had "entered rich Syria poor and left poor Syria rich." [20]

Despite Palestine's considerable natural wealth and economic self-sufficiency, the masses lived in dismal poverty. While the favorable climate reduced to a minimum expenditures for housing and even for food, clothing was comparatively expensive. The majority seems to have been forced to get along with one set of garments. This circumstance was exploited by Graeco-Roman vaudeville entertainers, who found the derision of Jews an enjoyable and profitable undertaking. One may get an inkling of the coarse cruelty of these vaudeville performances from the later homily of the Palestinian R. Abbahu (about 300 C.E.). Although, as we shall see, poverty had greatly increased in Palestine and elsewhere as a result of the third-century inflation and political disorganization, there is no reason for assuming that either the character of these performances or their underlying causes were totally different before the fall of Jerusalem.

"They that sit in the gate talk of me" [R. Abbahu quoted Ps. 69:13], these are the heathens who sit in their theaters and circuses, "and I am the song of the drunkards" [ibid.], after they had eaten and drunk and become intoxicated they sit and talk about me and mock me and say: "[Let us hope] that we shall not need carob [the poor man's food] as the Jews do." They say to one another: "How many years do you wish to be smitten?" And they answer: "As a Jewish Sabbath shirt [which needs thorough cleaning after many years of constant use]." They bring into their theaters a camel with covers on and they say to one another: "What is he mourning for?" And they say: "These Jews observe their Sabbatical year, and having no vegetables they have eaten this camel's thorns, over which he is mourning now." They also bring into their theaters a mime with his head shaved, and they say to one another: "Why is this man's head shaved?" And he answers: "These Jews are Sabbath observers and all that they earn during the week they consume on Sabbath, and thus they have no wood to cook with, so they break their beds and cook with them, then they sleep upon the bare ground and become soiled with mud and finally rub themselves with oil, wherefore oil is so expensive." [21]

A second-century rabbi's rueful exclamation, "The daughters of Israel are comely, but poverty makes them repulsive" (M. Nedarim IX, 10) is characteristic of the sufferings of women, which must have exceeded those of men. In conjunction with climatic and current social institutions, such as child marriages, poverty must also have caused widespread premature aging. Already in the relatively prosperous pre-Maccabean period the patrician Sirach envisaged little social intercourse between rich and poor. "What association," he inquired, "can jar and kettle have in common, where, if one smite, the other is smashed?" (13:2). Even the scholars, although very likely enjoying a certain preference in obtaining employment, often found it extremely difficult to eke out a minimum of subsistence. Hillel, for instance, was for a long time able to earn only the equivalent of fourteen American cents daily for the maintenance of his family. There is a bitter personal undertone in R. Joshua's censure of Rabban Gamaliel, the patriarch, for his ignorance of the ordinary scholar's difficulty in earning a living (Berakhot 28a).

Needless to say that the revolts against the Romans (66–135 C.E.) further increased this impoverishment of the masses. Theoretically, all land was once again taken over by Vespasian, the Jewish landowners and peasants remaining, so to speak, mere freeholders. In practice, too, certain sections were given to Roman veterans or Jewish partisans of Rome as a reward for their services. Those permitted to continue tilling their fields or orchards were crushed under the ever-increasing load of taxation. The devastation of whole regions through warfare, the depopulation of the country as a whole, and the ensuing shortage of farm hands must also have caused an abrupt decline in agricultural production. We shall see that a Palestinian teacher living in the period of Bar Kocheba (R. Eleazar ben Perata) believed that nature itself had changed its course. "Since the day of the destruction of the Temple," he said, "rains have become scanty" (ṣimmuqim: Ta'anit 19b).

In the ancient Diaspora, too, Jews were known for poverty rather than for wealth. Even in Alexandria bankers like Alexander and Demetrius were rare exceptions. From Philo we learn that there were moneylenders in Alexandria who charged as much as one hundred per cent for their loans, but these need not have been Jewish nor, for that matter, more than petty loan sharks. Similarly Philo's ringing denunciation of the conspicuous display by the *nouveaux riches* applied equally well to landowners, speculators and bureaucrats of all the ethnic and pseudo-ethnic groups which resided in the cosmopolitan city. At the same time, however, we also learn from him that in the richest Jewish community in the world the masses lived in dark, congested, and unhealthy quarters, and that their whole life was pervaded by economic insecurity, if not positive misery. With the rise of antisemitism, the Egyptian Jewish communities, in particular, must have felt their whole economic basis to be seriously impaired. Philo's description of the catastrophic results of the pogrom movement in the year 38 is revealing:

But cessation of business was a worse evil than plundering [he writes in his indictment of Flaccus]. The provision merchants had lost their stores, and no one was allowed, either farmer or shipper or trader or artisan, to engage in his normal occupation. Thus poverty was brought about from both quarters, both from plunder, for in one day they were dispossessed and stripped of their property, and from inability to earn a living from their normal occupations.

The permanent effects of both pogroms and revolts were no less disastrous.[22]

Egyptian Jewry outside the capital must have been even less prosperous. In this sense Strabo's generalization that "this nation has flourished in Egypt," though less extreme than his prior assertion concerning Jewish domination of "any place in the habitable world," is in its context more justified with respect to Jewish autonomy than to Jewish wealth. About 150 B.C.E., for example, the military colony of Samareia, Fayyum, seems to have owned a total of but 1,404 sheep and goats, the possessions of individual soldiers ranging from as little as five to a maximum of 140 heads. Under the Egyptian system they did not own their land, but merely leased it from the government or temple. In Tebtunis, another Fayyum community of the same period, the Jews were forced to build their very synagogue in a "sacred garden," that is, on the property of an Egyptian temple. Moreover, like the rest of the population they smarted under the heavy yoke of taxation, even before Vespasian enacted the special Jewish fiscal tax. For one example, a simple Jewish donkey driver of Edfu is recorded in two Greek ostraca to have paid, some twenty years apart, both a transport tax for donkey driving and a specific tax for his occupational permit. Indeed, all over the empire the Jews were prominent among the proletarians, Jewish peddling, magic, and beggary furnishing ample material for satirists in the imperial city.[23]

SLAVES AND FREE WORKERS

This growing differentiation in the economic life of Palestinian and world Jewry had, of course, a tremendous effect upon the social structure in the home country and abroad. On a higher plane, conditions in many ways resembled the age of the kings, with its relatively advanced economy, accompanied by numerous social evils. As in the days of the prophets, there was a relative lack of slaves. Not only were theocratic states in general less desirous and less in need of exorbitant slave labor than expansive military nations, but in Palestine specific circumstances effectively militated against slavery.

In the first place, the local "Hebrew" slave began to disappear altogether toward the end of the Second Commonwealth, owing to the antipathy of the nationalist and democratic Pharisees to the enslavement of a Jew even by a coreligionist. A whole system of laws was evolved to eliminate every conceivable abuse and, finally, to abolish the entire institution. The rabbis declared that the dedication of Hebrew male and female slaves to sacred use is, like that of children, null and void, "because nobody can renounce the use of what does not belong to him." They emphasized the fact that the biblical phrase, "because he fareth well with thee," indicates that a master must afford to his Hebrew slave a standard of life equal to his own and provide him with the same food, wine, and bed. In the light of this and other protective laws in similar vein it is easy to understand the popular proverb, "Whosoever buys a Hebrew slave acquires a master unto himself." At a time when rabbinic authority was constantly mounting, the oppressed class undoubtedly could invoke the protection of the court against the violation even of those talmudic legal enactments which were purely academic. Indeed, the Hebrew slave seems eventually to have gone out of existence, the rabbis devising for it a hyperbolical formula, "The Hebrew slave existed only in the period when the Jubilee year was in force." [24]

Many of these statements, to be sure, bear the earmarks of schoolmasterly idealism, rather than daily practice. Largely of tannaitic origin, they may also represent the growing feeling of national soli-

darity concomitant with the national catastrophes between 70 and
135. On the other hand, even before the fall of Jerusalem, default-
ing debtors seem no longer to have worked off their indebtedness
through that limited, temporary bondage which had, in the Old
Testament period, been the main source of supply of "Hebrew"
slaves. Exposure of children, another major source in Egypt and
elsewhere, was effectively outlawed by Jewish legal tradition. A
father was still permitted to sell his minor daughter, but this was
largely another form of arranging for her marriage. Only court
sales of thieves, unable to meet the fine, seem to have continued.
One or another individual in despair could still sell himself into
bondage, but if acquired by a Gentile master he immediately became the subject of obligatory ransom on the part of his relatives
and the community at large.[25]

We do not know how strictly these laws were adhered to, but the
existence of a large class of Hebrew slaves is, under these circumstances, highly improbable. If, at the inception of the Great War,
Simon son of Giyoras seems successfully to have appealed to numerous slaves to join his ranks under the promise of freedom, he
probably attracted Gentile rather than Hebrew slaves. Since the
former not only had to be circumcised, but also observed the seven
Noahide commandments and in general lived practically as Jews in
Jewish households, they could well take an interest in that great national as well as social upheaval. Later, too, a fugitive slave often
joined one or another gang of freebooters.[26]

At this time, however, when Jewry was no longer a conquering
nation, Gentile slaves had to be purchased at comparatively high
prices. Once more the densely populated country, with its economic inequalities, furnished a large number of hired laborers
with whom the slaves could not altogether compete. The wage of a
hired worker amounting, as certain records indicate, to twenty-
eight cents daily or less, to pay a minimum purchase price of fifty to
eighty dollars for a slave scarcely appeared profitable in a period of
severe capital shortage. Moreover, the rabbis extended protection
to Gentile slaves in a degree surpassing even the biblical legislation.
There was nothing in the Jewish attitude even remotely resembling the snobbery of that Roman lady whom Juvenal describes as
asking, "Is a slave a man?" (Satires, VI, 222) or the detachedness of
the Roman law, which for centuries classified the slave among
"things" (res). Gaius' injunction, "Whosoever kills his slave without reason [sine causa] should be held not less responsible than one

who kills anybody else's slave" (I, 53) was heralded as a great advance by Roman humanitarians and, indeed, reflected the changing economic and moral attitudes of the age that resulted from the decline in the number of available slaves and the propaganda of the Stoa. This was, however, a matter of course with the earliest Israelitic lawgiver in the Book of the Covenant. Rabbinic legislation went much farther. Although it did not make the lot of the Gentile slave enviable, it sufficiently reduced his attractiveness to the master to make him ever less competitive to the hired worker.

By sharply combating concubinage with slaves the rabbis also helped dry up another major source of demand. Hillel's remark, "He who multiplies female slaves, increases licentiousness, while he who multiplies male slaves, increases robbery," well epitomizes the general Pharisaic-rabbinic moral aversion at least toward the practical manifestations of slavery. To justify their opposition to the Sadducean insistence on a master's responsibility for damages inflicted by his slave—which view they had themselves held before, as also did the Romans—the Pharisees emphasized that the slave had a mind of his own and, hence, if "angered by me, he might set fire to my neighbor's crop and I should be obliged to pay." The rabbis believed that thievery and gambling were so characteristic of the general run of slaves that a purchaser discovering these faults was not entitled to annul the transaction. Another tannaitic source lists the following five injunctions which Canaan, the alleged progenitor of all "Canaanite" slaves, supposedly bequeathed to his descendants: "Love one another, love robbery, love licentiousness, hate your masters, and never tell the truth." [27]

In view of this low estimate of the slaves' morals it is not astonishing that the rabbis greatly discouraged their manumission. Once freed, they were treated legally, and even socially, on a par with proselytes and, hence, enjoyed nearly complete equality with born Jews. A mass influx of freedmen into the Jewish community was, therefore, considered undesirable on moral as well as ethnic grounds. Combined with the general paucity of slaves, this attitude explains the relatively small number of freedmen within the Jewish communities of Palestine and the dispersion.

One should not underestimate the importance of this fact for the entire sociopolitical structure of ancient Jewry. Almost all other areas of the Graeco-Roman world, and particularly Rome itself, possessed an influential class of freedmen who, in continued relationships with their former masters, strengthened the economic and political control of the upper classes. Jewish law, on the contrary, failed to link the freedman permanently with the interests of his previous master. Very likely the few freedmen speedily dissociated themselves from their Jewish overlords and joined the proletariat. Nor was freedom an unmitigated blessing to unskilled, aged, or diseased slaves, since the Deuteronomist's humanitarian provision for the endowment of a Hebrew slave at his release from bondage never applied to a Gentile freedman. It is small wonder that the rabbis seriously debated the problem of how much credence one ought to give a slave who denied the emancipation asserted by his master (Giṭṭin 40b).

The mere existence of slaves and freedmen, however, and particularly their ready availability in slave markets, necessarily depressed the price of free labor. From the scattered talmudic records we are able to judge that few skilled workingmen received a daily wage as high as one dollar, while the scale for the unskilled often sank to a few cents. In addition, there were many unemployed (po'alim beṭelim), as indicated by the Talmud. This eternally renewed "industrial reserve army" (and to an even greater extent the reserve army of slaves whose potential number seemed unlimited in the earlier periods of constant wars and piracy) made utterly hopeless the purely economic struggle of the hired laborer.

Hence, the paucity of strikes in the entire Graeco-Roman world and their almost total absence in Palestine. A strike, to be sure, of some temple officials who refused to instruct others in singing and writing or in the skillful preparation of showbread and incense is mentioned disparagingly in the Mishnah and in several Baraitot. Even the motive may have been purely economic. At any rate, when the "strike breakers," imported from Alexandria, failed to perform satisfactorily, the original craftsmen, belonging to the houses of Garmo and Euthinos which for generations had been entrusted with this service, resumed their positions with a 100 per cent increase in wages. But the peculiar character of this service obviously puts the abstention from work in a class by itself. Only thus can we understand the ire of those rabbis who, a long time after, wished to see these two names exposed to eternal shame, and the leniency of those who declared themselves satisfied with a purported declaration of the returning strikers. They had only refrained from teaching their art, they were reputed as saying, lest it be abused for idolatrous purposes after the destruction of the Temple, of whose doom they had been forewarned by a family tradition. In general, it seems that neither Roman nor Jewish legislators and officials would have seriously interfered with an organized strike movement, picketing, and the like, so long as public order was not disturbed. But in the prevailing economic situation class struggle could have meaning only if aimed at final seizure of power. Hence the perennial socio-political strife in the Hellenistic industrial centers of the East.[28]

SOCIAL STRATIFICATION

The "theocratic" form of government, or its skeleton retained by the Romans, could no longer maintain the social equilibrium. Not even the priestly class was safe behind its walls. Having abandoned its major function in society, this class became a grave liability to the Jewish people. The priest was no longer intellectual leader, judge, and educator, as well as the main bearer of the nation's tradition. All these functions were now gradually taken over by the lay "scribe." The purely sacerdotal duties of the Temple, still the exclusive domain of priests, may have retained some romantic appeal, but they had long lost their intrinsic value to the daily life of the millions living in the more distant regions of Palestine and the Diaspora.

By virtue of their class position, the priests increasingly identified themselves with the Sadducean group lying athwart the living flow of tradition. Together with the whole Sadducean movement the Jewish priesthood gradually atrophied, and was essentially dead long before the Temple's destruction. In its protracted *stupor mortis,* it forfeited whatever veneration might have persisted among the masses for the sacerdotism of bygone days by its unmitigated worldliness and the barter of the high priest's office, ever more openly practiced since the time of Herod.

Farsighted leaders, even among the lay scribes, did not wish to undermine the prestige of the priesthood, which they revered as a God-given and time-honored national institution. Within the precincts of the Temple at least they were sure that, by virtue of the priests' hereditary charisma, aliens like the Herodians or Romans would not be able to exercise direct control. Unlike Greece and Rome, where most sacrificial functions were performed by civil magistrates, only born priests without mental or physical blemish could sacrifice at the Temple of Jerusalem. The Second Commonwealth had long eliminated even the sacerdotal functions of kings, other than those of the priestly family of Hasmoneans.

Exact genealogical records were kept in the archives to discourage pretenders. Josephus, proud of his priestly lineage, was able to list his direct forebears over a century and a half and to note the year of each ancestor's birth. If Herod ever toyed with the idea of personally assuming the high-priestly office as heir of the Hasmoneans (this was possibly the purpose of Nicolaus of Damascus' fabrication of his family's genealogy from "the leading Jews who came to Judaea from Babylon"), he must have given it up as totally unworkable. Pharisees vied with the Sadducees in trying to increase the priestly revenues. The pro-Sadducean Sirach constantly harped on the duty of honoring Temple and priests and echoed the appeal of the early teachers of wisdom to the self-interest of the Jewish farmer, "Honor the Lord with thy substance and, with the first fruits of all thine increase; so shall thy barns be filled with plenty and thy vats shall overflow with new wine." The Pharisaic rabbis, on their part, elaborated in great detail the twenty-four different types of temple and priestly dues and, by injunction, homily, and personal example, exhorted their followers to pay them with utmost care. To enhance their popular appeal, some of these dues (for example, the first fruits) were delivered by provincials in picturesque processions from their district towns to Jerusalem. Here these mass delegations were greeted joyously by priestly and lay dignitaries as well as by the populace, represented by artisan guilds and others.[29]

The very frequency of the appeals, however, shows that these laws were often honored in the breach. Quite apart from its inherent weaknesses, the priestly aristocracy was numerically too insignificant to keep the masses in check. It has been estimated that there were some 18,000 adult priests and levites in the country. Accepting this as approximately correct, the whole class amounted only to about 3 per cent of Palestine's Jewish population and not more than one or two per cent of the Jews throughout the world. At least 10,000 of these Palestinians were levites, while the majority of the remainder were priests of a lower order, who, no less than the lay masses, resented the excesses of the few influential families at the top. The priests' appropriation of the tithe against the Bible's express injunction, although more and more sanctioned by custom, must have antagonized the levites, legally the major beneficiaries of that revenue.[30]

The *kohanim* were divided among themselves, as is indicated by the abuses of the servants of Ananias, the high priest (47–59), who "went to the threshing floors and took away tithes that belonged to the priests by violence, and did not refrain from beating such as would not give these tithes to them . . . so that priests that of old were wont to be supported with those tithes, died for want of food." Ananias, like some of his predecessors and successors, considered the high-priestly office as a pure business enterprise. These hierarchs tried to recoup not only their original, usually large investment, but also to get rich quickly during their brief and precarious tenure of office. They succeeded in introducing a number of permanent changes in the distribution of certain types of Temple revenue. Originally divided among the priestly groups serving on each particular day, this revenue, according to the Tosefta, now fell prey to the leading priests using strong-arm methods. These proceedings called forth a popular dirge naming the chief priestly families, whose heads "are high priests, while the sons are treasurers, the sons-in-law superintendents, and the slaves swing their sticks over our heads." A rabbi's sweeping generalization that "most priests are rich," understandable only because of the still greater penury of the masses and the more orderly system of distribution after 70, would have sounded bitterly ironical to the rank and file of the priestly class before the destruction of the Temple. It was slight comfort for the people or for the many self-respecting lower priests that these rascals on top were not "anointed" priests, since this ceremony seems to have gone into total disuse in the days of Herod or earlier. This deep cleavage within the priesthood itself, somewhat resembling that between the higher and lower clergy in France on the eve of the Revolution, must have further reduced its stabilizing power in the approaching crisis.[31]

Moreover, the main body of priests, concentrated around the capital, had little direct contact with the people in the provinces. Although they performed functions at the Temple only at stated periods and lived partly outside Jerusalem (such a flight from the capital was recorded in Neh. 13:10), all priests and levites were necessarily descendants of those who were established ecclesiastics before the Maccabean expansion. The majority remained within the confines of the former Judaean theocratic state, the newly annexed provinces receiving only a sprinkling of each group. The masses of provincials now looked, in any case, to the local synagogue, teacher, and scribe, rather than to the distant Temple and its officialdom, for the satisfaction of their religious and cultural wants. The handful of country priests and levites rendered few services to their respective communities. They seem to have busied themselves exclusively with collecting the heave-offering and tithe, which certainly did not enhance their popularity in the farming population.

Despite all this, the priesthood was believed to be endowed with a supernatural charisma, a claim to distinction such as lay aristocracy did not possess. Josephus rightly asserts, "Different races base their claim to nobility on various grounds; with us a connection with the priesthood is the hallmark of an illustrious line" (*Life* I, 1.1). Of course, there were in the country many noble families, some of which traced their descent back to personages and lines recorded in the Old Testament. However, the frequent and abrupt changes in social structure under the Hellenistic, Maccabean, Herodian, and Roman administrations, shifting political constellations and meteoric personal careers, make most such claims appear doubtful. And even when they were acknowledged, as in the case of the eight families called upon to furnish lumber for burnt offerings at the Temple (M. Ta'anit IV, 5), they did not, according to Jewish law, carry with them any special rights. Before the law every born Jew was an "Israelite," in some respect inferior in rank to a "Kohen" or "Levi," but absolutely equal to any other Jewish layman. Thus the lay aristocracy wielded only the power granted by wealth and political connections. But a descendant of a proselyte, such as Herod, easily possessed even more power!

Of course, the lay aristocracy of landowning gentry or successful merchants and officials had great influence upon the affairs of the country. From this class came most of the "elders" and "archontes," whether of the great governing and judicial bodies, the Sanhedrins, or the municipal councils. Curiously enough, however, this function of the aristocracy added fuel to the growing animosity. The municipal elder, as a rule, was forced by the government to assist in the odious task of tax collecting (Josephus' *War* II, 17, 1.405). Although refraining from the unscrupulous methods of the commercial tax collectors, the elders could not but incur a share of the opprobrium attached to the whole system. Naturally the more excessive the burden of taxation became, the more the elders shifted its incidence to the shoulders of the defenseless masses. There was no end to rumors and suspicion. If inefficient in delivering their quota, they had to face the uncontrollable wrath of a Herod and his underlings or that of a rapacious and ruthless procurator.

At the other end of the social ladder were many groups which, although recognized as Jewish, were inferior in rank even to the humblest Jewish proletarian. The following scale appears in a famous tannaitic discussion of prohibited degrees of marriage:

Ten genealogical classes returned from Babylon: priests, levites, Israelites, disqualified priests, proselytes, freedmen, bastards [offspring of adulterous or incestuous relations], *netinim* [alleged descendants of the Gibeonites], children of unknown fathers and foundlings [M. Qiddushin IV, 1; elaborated in j. IV, 11, 66c].

It seems, however, that except for the mass of Israelites all these groups were small. The largest, those of proselytes and freedmen, usually merged by intermarriage with the large body of Israelites after two or three generations. The last four groups, although excluded from marrying an Israelite, were likewise eventually absorbed in a roundabout way. None the less, there must have been some such virtual social outcasts in every generation.

Others, though suffering from but minor legal disabilities, lived under the shadow of popular suspicion. The publicans or tax-farmers long constituted, as elsewhere in the Roman Empire, a parasitic class, bitterly resented by the masses and condemned by the intellectual leaders. Some other occupations were likewise tinged with popular disapproval. Apart from distrusting, as we recall, shepherds and pigeon-fanciers, the rabbis seriously debated the professional morals of most transport workers, butchers, and doctors, and like the Greeks relegated tanners outside the confines of cities. Numerous orphans and widows, though legally privileged, were in fact members of the underprivileged majority. So were the numerous professional beggars, whose number increased rather than diminished as a result of the traditional Jewish emphasis on charity. It is difficult to imagine, today, how large a portion of the ancient populations was stricken by leprosy and forced to live for years in physical segregation. While in ancient times Jews seem to have been relatively more immune to that disease than their Egyptian and other neighbors, they must have had their share of lepers, as well as of cripples and mentally deranged persons. Many of these social misfits doubtless swelled the ranks of the discontented, without being a sufficiently homogeneous group to serve as an object of contempt to the Jewish proletarians, who, through a resultant feeling of superiority, might have been induced to accept their lot more passively.[32]

Jewish society thus was even more deeply divided than in the days of the Israelitic monarchy. All the old causes of dissension were now further exacerbated, many new ones were added. Only the blood feuds, that eternal source of social disequilibrium in more primitive Near Eastern societies, seem to have all but disappeared from the late Second Commonwealth. Even if we accept S. Klein's reconstruction from scattered, often incorrigibly doctrinaire, sources and assume the reëstablishment of cities of refuge during the reigns of John Hyrcanus and Alexander Jannaeus, we shall admit that there is no record of their persistence after the days of Pompey. The evident reason is not the restoration of these cities' independence by the Romans (some had undoubtedly been located in what remained the Jewish area, others could be newly assigned), but the absence of any urgent social need.[33]

POPULAR UNREST

Other social factors further magnified the results of economic conflicts. More than anywhere else, the inhabitants of the whole country, and not merely of a single municipality, felt themselves equal, by birth and destiny, to the members of the privileged classes. The conviction of choseness, rooted in every Jew even more deeply now than in the days of the prophets, was further enhanced by the new individualistic doctrines of personal merit and reward. After the Maccabean upheaval, the rank and file of Jewry must have felt cheated of the fruits of victory by those small groups of priests and landowners who became the dominant classes. For a while, the glory of conquest and expansion, with the concomitant general prosperity, obscured the widespread inequalities and the great suffering of the masses. But after the Roman occupation, the glamor of national independence was gone. With power slipping out of their hands, the privileged classes could offer no psychological compensation to the urban and rural working classes, whose privations had multiplied under the stress of relating Palestinian to imperial economy and under the increasingly burdensome tax yoke. Secret or open rebellion was inevitable.

At the same time the distinction between the urban and rural population, although less sharp than in the Western world today, became more pronounced in the first century than ever before. In the numerous hamlets and small towns, more inhabitants were still engaged in agriculture than in any other pursuit. But the ancient and newer large cities necessarily turned to a more intensive employment of capital and labor. The metropolitan economy of Jerusalem, in particular, with more than 100,000 inhabitants surrounded by arid country, was bound to have artificial foundations. Lacking even the most basic raw materials, and having practically no natural lines of communication, this political and religious superstructure of Palestinian and world Jewry revealed some of the typical vices of metropolitan life: absentee landlordism, corrupt officialdom, and *Lumpenproletariat*. Thus the contrast between capital and countryside was even more obvious than in the days of the prophets.

Unfortunately, we possess no information concerning the price movements in Palestine during that period, but it is likely that the same factors which operated to raise steadily the cost of living in neighboring Egypt also exerted inflationary pressures in overcrowded Palestine. Although it was the landowner, rather than his tenant or worker, who benefited most from the ensuing rise of farm income, the additional hardships for the urban working classes must have increased the antagonism between these major groups. Nor would it be surprising if the farmers placed the blame on the urban grain speculators, against whom later rabbis had to take stringent measures. Even such foreign cities as Tyre and Sidon depended on the Palestinian countryside's food supply, a fact which was highlighted when Agrippa I's economic blockade of these cities brought about their speedy submission.[34]

We also know very little about the relative ratio of the large and small landholdings in ancient Palestine. The country seems never to have witnessed such concentration of landownership in a few hands as characterized the Italian *latifundia*. Hence the small Jewish farmer, and not the slaveholding landlord, permanently remained the backbone of Palestinian agriculture, indeed of Jewish society at large. Nevertheless, large estates, both royal and private, were sufficiently numerous to set the pace for production and prices. They must have increased in number and size as a result of the Maccabean conquests and Herodian expropriations. Together with the growing population density and high birth rate, which must have resulted in constant subdivisions of the small farms, these large estates accounted for many of the characteristic evils of widespread land tenancy and absentee landlordism.[35]

While ethnic and religious factors were the basis of any real or apparent unity, they also increased the disparity of the various sections of the population. The ancient and deeply rooted Jewishness of the inhabitants of the former theocratic state of Judaea contrasted sharply with the relative neophytism of the majority in the other provinces. Galilee, the richest and most populous region, must have resented the discrepancy particularly. Its population, even before the mass conversions of the Maccabean era, had belonged to a closely related racial stock, and its acceptance of Judaism, its tenets and observances, was more complete and unrestricted than anyone could have expected. Nevertheless, the Galileans were bullied by the political "bosses" in Jerusalem, exploited by the absentee landlords, oppressed by the tax collectors, and made to feel that their Jewishness was permanently suspected.

It is no mere chance that Galilee was the main center of the so-called 'am ha-areş (people of the land), that group of the population whose Jewish education was slight and whose orthodoxy was looked upon with much suspicion by the more rigid Pharisees. To be sure, such talmudic statements as the following concerning this class of the population are to be taken with a grain of salt:

A Jew must not marry a daughter of an 'am ha-areş, because they are unclean animals [sheqeş] and their women forbidden reptiles [shereş] and with respect to their daughters the Scripture writes: "Cursed be he that lieth with any manner of beast [Deut. 27:21]!" . . . Said R. Eleazar: one may butcher an 'am ha-areş on a Day of Atonement that happens to fall on a Sabbath [when any kind of work constitutes a violation of a double prohibition]. His disciples said to him: Master, say "slaughter" [instead of the vile word, butcher]. But he replied: "slaughtering requires a benediction, butchering does not require a benediction" [Pesaḥim 49b].

Undoubtedly the authors themselves consciously were using gross exaggerations in a truly oriental fashion in order to impress their teachings upon their hearers. Nevertheless, it may be taken for granted that even before the rise of Christianity the conflict was deeply rooted.

The rabbis knew very well that their feelings were reciprocated. In their statement, "the hatred with which the 'ame ha-areş hate a scholar is greater than the hatred of the heathens against Israel, and their women hate still more ardently, while one that had applied himself to learning and afterwards abandoned it, hates most of all" (Pesaḥim 49b), lies a more tragic and sincere resignation than in all their violent arraignments. The Christian agitation must have inflamed the smouldering antagonisms, and the rabbis necessarily denounced more vigorously than ever that class from which had sprung the main founders of the new religion. Shortly after the destruction of the Temple R. Johanan ben Zakkai addressed the cradle of the new faith, "Galilee, Galilee, thou hatest the law. Before long thou wilt make common cause with the tax assessors [the Romans]." [36]

It was, indeed, much more difficult for a Galilean peasant than for most members of the artisan and petty merchant class to adhere strictly to the law. Jewish agricultural regulations, not to mention the laws of purity and impurity, must have appeared increasingly burdensome. Even according to Caesar's most friendly decree, the Romans levied a tax as high as one-fourth of the crop (it had been one-third under the Seleucids) every year or every other year. Caesar's successors and their local administrators exacted these payments harshly and probably disregarded the limitations of that decree with respect to additional services. Especially after the country's direct reincorporation in the empire in 6 c.e., the multiple payments in kind and personal services for the maintenance of Roman officials and soldiers, as well as such indirect taxes as the numerous tolls and customs duties, must have made the life of a Palestinian farmer extremely arduous. No wonder that the toll collector (mokhes), often a private entrepreneur who farmed out the state revenue, was the most widely hated fiscal agent. His whole family shared in the opprobrium. "There is no family," states a rabbinic dictum, "having a publican as a member, which does not all ultimately turn publican." [37]

From the standpoint of Jewish law, on the other hand, the farmer was supposed to put aside about 12 per cent of the remainder of his crop for the priestly tithe and heave-offering, plus a "second tithe" for the poor or for spending it in the distant city of Jerusalem. There may actually have been a third tithe for the poor every third year. [38] All these dues, coming after the farmer had already delivered the "first fruits" to the Temple and carried out during the harvest the biblical injunctions concerning "gleanings, sheaf and corner" which had to be left on the fields, were almost unbearable charges even in the most fertile regions of the country. Superimposed upon them all was the extremely rigid observance of the sabbatical year, involving the loss of at least a year and half of agricultural produce in every seven-year cycle—a crushing burden, indeed, upon a people which was unable in any year to save a substantial part of the crop.

The peasant thus simply faced the alternatives of complying with Jewish religious, or Roman civic, duties. In the face of the ruthless

Roman administrative methods, the decision was seldom in doubt. The division of land into ever-smaller parcels, moreover, made the choice almost a matter of life and death. Although outspoken opposition to priestly dues, such as seems to have existed in the days of Malachi (3:8–14), had long been silenced through the combined efforts of Sadduceeism and Pharisaism, many a farmer saw himself forced to refuse publicly or secretly to set aside the prescribed tithe for the levite. Even the threat of an ultimate famine as the result of noncompliance (M. Abot V, 8) deterred but few of those who faced the spectre of immediate starvation. Hence the many accusations hurled against the ʿam ha-areṣ, whose food might not be eaten by an observant Jew, since it presumably contained grain from which the tithe and other priestly portions had not been subtracted. Finally, one must also bear in mind that, as a rule, the yoke of the law appeared less burdensome to a Jew, who for generations had been inured to it, than to some comparative newcomers in Galilee and other newly conquered areas.

Most decisive for the social disequilibrium was the absence of a strong Jewish bourgeoisie, such as existed in the other countries of the Graeco-Roman world and formed the backbone of the successive imperial regimes. At no time did Palestine possess a strong conservative class of "substantial" citizens resembling the Athenian bourgeoisie of 322 B.C.E. A census taken in that year showed that the latter mustered 9,000 members owning 2,000 drachmas or more, as against only 12,000 citizens of the lower classes. Whatever third estate of this type existed in Palestine was largely concentrated in the "Greek" cities, which enjoyed complete political and social autonomy. In this respect, the declining Second Commonwealth resembled Poland on the eve of partitions, except that its "Greek" middle class (such as the residents of Samaria-Sebaste and Caesarea) was actively disloyal; indeed, on every occasion, it exhibited profound hatred of its Jewish neighbors.

The landowning gentry, on the other hand, did not feel altogether secure in their holdings, since theoretically all land belonged to the state. They were also much too frequently decimated or displaced by the arbitrary acts of Herod and the other rulers to maintain a stable social order. Ever since the Ptolemies had established the "large estate," handed it over to an individual master for direct or indirect exploitation, but also subjected it to arbitrary withdrawal, there occurred too many changes in these landowner-tenant relationships to guard the necessary continuity. Under this system, the petty tenant and agricultural laborer suffered most severely. But the landowning class, too, developed those characteristics of servility toward political superiors and of utmost ruthlessness toward underlings which often forced the latter to flee and join the roving bands of brigands. This was the usual, extreme way out for oppressed farmers, as well as slaves, in the ancient world. With the Herodian dynasty and the priesthood likewise in increasing disrepute, the country was speedily heading toward some ultimate catastrophic breakdown.[39]

Deep divisions, although of a somewhat different order, existed also within Diaspora Jewry. Class distinctions which prevailed there were not Jewish class distinctions. The integration of the Jewish settlements into the economic structures of the various lands and the generally prevailing legal equality of opportunity scattered the Jews among diverse social levels along with members of other creeds and nationalities. In most countries the overwhelming majority of Jews belonged to the urban proletariat, thus becoming cobearers of the main revolutionary movements. In the older and more prosperous communities, especially Egypt and Babylonia, there also existed a considerable Jewish middle class, and even a fair-sized patrician group. In the economic struggle, Jews usually behaved in accordance with their class position.

In one respect, however, Jewry as a whole somewhat resembled the dominant element in the empire, the Romans. Jewish slavery, we recall, was neither a permanent nor a numerically significant factor in Jewish life, except for the few periods of Jewish wars or rebellions, since Jewish captives were ransomed as soon as possible by relatives or by the community. From this mutual responsibility arose a certain solidarity among all Jews regardless of class, further strengthened by the spread of antisemitism and the ensuing rise of a specifically Jewish economic problem. Some Jews, weary of their specifically Jewish economic struggle or because they cherished their accumulated possessions whose loss they feared during one of the recurrent crises, gave up their Jewishness and joined the majority. The author of Third Maccabees, in particular, pointed an accusing finger at these materialistic renegades (7:10–11: "for their belly's sake"). Others, however, closed their ranks and, through greater communal solidarity and mutual self-help, tried to counteract the economic effects of Jew-baiting.

For this reason they, no less than the Jews of Palestine, stressed the idea of charity. Already the author of Tobit, apparently an

Egyptian Jew, made the hero enjoin his son, "As thy substance is, give alms of it according to thine abundance . . . if thou hast little bestow it, and be not afraid to give alms according to that little; for thou layest up a good treasure for thyself against the day of necessity." If, in the fourth century, Emperor Julian praised the Roman Jews for having stamped out mendicity in their midst, he probably meant to say that the community was now effectively taking care of its beggars, who had previously been a choice target of Roman satirists.[40] Nevertheless, the great contrasts in the outside world necessarily had strong reverberations even within the powerful frame of Jewish self-government.

Still more crucial were the divisions among the Jewries of various lands. The economic, ethnic, and religious structure of Babylonia, in particular, was altogether different from that of the rest of the Diaspora. Notwithstanding centuries of separation when Palestine was under Ptolemaic and Roman rule while the Parthians occupied the Euphrates Valley, Babylonia resembled Palestine more than any other land. The modicum of Hellenistic influence which had penetrated the core of Palestinian Jewish life was not a sufficiently differentiating factor, inasmuch as Babylonia, too, during the centuries of Syrian and Parthian rule, was exposed to deep inroads of Hellenistic ways of life and modes of thinking. In a sense, Babylonia, during and long after the Second Commonwealth, was the great hinterland, the mainstay of the Palestinian center. To such a degree had Jewry learned to disregard state boundaries!

Over against the Palestino-Babylonian complex was the vast world of Hellenistic Jewry. Jewish Hellenism is still commonly but fallaciously regarded as a homogeneous unit and discussed almost exclusively in terms of Egyptian-Jewish culture. For two or three centuries Egypt undoubtedly led the Graeco-Roman Diaspora in cultural and social achievements. The survival of a body of Egyptian-Jewish writings and papyri, vast in contrast with the rare sources pertaining to Jewish settlements in Syria, Asia Minor, the Balkans, and the East Mediterranean islands, have led most historians to overlook the profound differences which must have prevailed among the various Jewries of these regions. Even under Roman domination, Egypt, as a result of its millennia of unique historical evolution, its special climatic and geographic position, and its state socialism, was vastly different from the countries on the northeastern shores of the Mediterranean. The distinctions must also have held true with respect to the Jewish settlements. Disregarding all memories of the pre-Mosaic age, the history of Egyptian Jewry went back to the seventh or eighth century B.C.E. Jews came to Egypt in large groups after the destruction of Samaria and Jerusalem, and again under Alexander and Ptolemy I. At a very early period, as in the Elephantine colony, Alexandria or Edfu, they had a strong Jewish group life.

In contrast thereto, the Jewish settlers in Syria, Asia Minor, and southeastern Europe had a much briefer local history. Their settlements, with few exceptions, grew up through the immigration of individuals from many lands, whose capacity to develop an organized Jewish life was limited by lingering discrepancies in custom and outlook. Their cohesiveness must have been much slighter than that of the Egyptian communities.

The influence of Greek culture, too, must have been stronger in Asia Minor and Europe than on the Nile, except perhaps in Alexandria. Purely Greek settlements had existed on the coast of Asia Minor, in the Balkans, in southern Italy, and on the islands, before the conquest of Alexander. Jews, too, must have felt these Hellenic influences for a long time. Aristotle's Syrian-Jewish interlocutor could become "a Greek not only in language but also in spirit" in the pre-Hellenistic age only in these regions directly exposed to Hellenic infiltrations. Moreover, Jew-baiting never became as violent in Asia Minor, Greece, or even Syria, as it had been in Egypt. After the days of Augustus, the controversies seem to have quieted down, particularly in Asia Minor. The *rapprochement* between the two parts of the population could thus proceed unhindered. In short, using the figures cited above, we may assume that before the fall of Jerusalem about 3,000,000 Jews, living north of a line extending from Crete to Armenia and including Syria, felt most keenly the combined influences of Greece and Iran.

Another important consideration is the character of these Jewish settlements themselves. There is a basis for the assumption that the farther away from Palestine a country was situated, the less pure racially and ethnically its Jewish settlers were. But while Babylonia and Egypt contained large aboriginal Jewish groups, the community in near-by Syria grew through a slow process of evolution. A large section of Syrian Jewry, and probably a still larger section of the Jewries of Asia Minor, the East Mediterranean islands, and the Balkans, must have consisted of former proselytes and their descendants. The same is true of the Jews in Italy, Carthage, and Armenia. Only the large Jewish community in the city of Rome, composed at least partly of former Palestinian captives, must have contained more purely Jewish blood. The several hundred inscriptions, preserved in the Roman catacombs, not by sheer chance show less than a score of references to proselytes and *sebomenoi*, the majority, characteristically, being women. In addition to full Jews, in the religious sense, whether of Jewish or Gentile descent, there must have been in all these countries large numbers of semi-proselytes at different stages of conversion.[41]

WEAKNESS OF CONFUSION

When the hour of decision struck, this enormous and heterogeneous mass, called world Jewry, could not possibly be of one mind. Still less could it develop singleness of purpose or simultaneity of action. United for a moment by Caligula's attack on the very fundamentals of their Jewishness, the classes and groups making up the various Jewish communities fell apart on almost all other crucial political and economic issues. By the inner corrosion of the Temple hierarchy and the Pharisaic-Sadducean-Zealotic struggles in Palestine they were deprived even of a single spiritual leadership and allowed to shift for themselves or follow the lead of individuals who happened to appear on the scene in decisive moments.

Palestinian Jewry, too, long the tower of strength of the whole people, was rapidly disintegrating. So long as it had its native Maccabean regime it could somehow gloss over these inner weaknesses and lend a semblance of direction to the course it steered through the uncharted seas of destiny. Not only its older and newer members, but also the communities of the dispersion could look to Jerusalem, its Temple and its priestly monarchs, for spiritual guidance and political support. But sooner or later the growing inner corruption of the Hasmonean dynasty and the ruling classes behind it had to come to the fore. It was the same type of corruption which had undermined the strength of all Near Eastern nations and made them fall easy prey to Roman imperialists.

When afterwards the rapacity of Rome and the mismanagement of the Herodian dynasts had eaten away much of the country's substance, when the priesthood stood denuded of its ancient glory and the landowning gentry became the extortionist collaborator of alien oppressors, when the native middle class was prevented from playing its usual moderating role by the overwhelming competition of a hostile population in the leading centers of trade and industry, an inner and outward debacle became well-nigh unavoidable. At the same time the millions of Diaspora Jews, at first a source of great economic and political strength for the Palestinian center, now became involved in a prolonged, hopeless struggle with an increasingly ferocious antisemitic movement.

In this state of extraordinary tension, the people's creative forces searched for ever new intellectual and spiritual solutions. Responding to unprecedented challenges the leaders constantly expanded the frontiers of their religious experience. As in the declining First Commonwealth, the stresses and strains of these deep conflicts in society and religion produced deeply creative quests for new socioreligious answers which, now experimented with on an almost world-wide scale, ultimately changed the destinies of mankind.

NOTES

ABBREVIATIONS

AASOR	Annual of the American Schools of Oriental Research
Abhandlungen Chajes	Abhandlungen zur Erinnerung an Hirsch Perez Chajes. Vienna, 1933.
Abrahams Mem. Vol.	Jewish Studies in Memory of Israel Abrahams. New York, 1927.
Ag. Ap.	Josephus' Against Apion
AJA	American Journal of Archaeology
AJSL	American Journal of Semitic Languages and Literatures
Annuaire	Brussels, Université libre, Institut de philologie et d'histoire orientales et slaves, Annuaire
Antt.	Josephus' Antiquities
AOF	Archiv für Orientforschung
AR	Archiv für Religionswissenschaft
ARN	Aboth de-Rabbi Nathan. Ed. by S. Schechter
ASAE	Annales de Service des Antiquités de l'Egypte
ATR	Anglican Theological Review
'A.Z.	'Abodah Zarah
b.	Babylonian Talmud
BA	Biblical Archaeologist
BASOR	Bulletin of the American Schools of Oriental Research
B.B.	Baba Batra
BJPES	Bulletin (*Yediot*) of the Jewish Palestine Exploration Society
BJRL	Bulletin of the John Rylands Library, Manchester
B.M.	Baba Meṣiah
B.Q.	Baba Qamah
BSOS	Bulletin of the School of Oriental Studies (University of London)
CBQ	Catholic Biblical Quarterly
Cohen Mem. Vol.	Freedom and Reason: Studies in Philosophy and Jewish Culture in Memory of Morris Raphael Cohen. Glencoe, Ill., and New York, 1951.
C. TH.	Theodosian Code
CRAI	Comptes rendus de l'Academie des Inscriptions et des belles lettres
EJ	Encyclopaedia Judaica, Vols. I–X. Berlin, 1928–35.
Essays Hertz	Essays in honour of J. H. Hertz. London, [1942].
Festschrift Bertholet	Festschrift Alfred Bertholet. Tübingen, 1950.
Festschrift Breslau	Festschrift zum 75 jährigen Bestehen des Jüdisch-Theologischen Seminars. 2 vols. Breslau, 1929.
Festschrift Freimann	Festschrift Jakob Freimann . . . gewidmet. Berlin, 1937.
Festschrift Kaminka	Festschrift für Armand Kaminka. Vienna, 1937.

Festschrift Schwarz	Festschrift Adolf Schwarz. Berlin, 1917.
FJF	Forschungen zur Judenfrage
Gaster Anniv. Vol.	Occident and Orient . . . Gaster Anniversary Volume. London, 1936.
Ginzberg Jub. Vol.	Louis Ginzberg Jubilee Volume. 2 vols. New York, 1945. A volume each of English and Hebrew essays.
G.S.	Gesammelte Schriften
GSAI	Giornale della Società asiatica italiana
Gulak-Klein Mem. Vol.	Sefer Zikkaron (Studies in Memory of Asher Gulak and Samuel Klein). Jerusalem, 1942.
HJ	Historia Judaica
HTR	Harvard Theological Review
HUCA	Hebrew Union College Annual
HVLA	Kungl. Humanistika Vetenskapssamfundet i Lund Årsberättelse (Bulletin de la Société Royale des Lettres de Lund)
HZ	Historische Zeitschrift
j.	Palestinian Talmud (Jerushalmi)
JA	Journal asiatique
JAOS	Journal of the American Oriental Society
JBL	Journal of Biblical Literature
JE	The Jewish Encyclopedia. 12 vols. New York, 1901–6.
JEA	Journal of Egyptian Archaeology
JEOL	Jaarboek "Ex Oriente Lux"
JJGL	Jahrbuch für jüdische Geschichte und Literatur
JJLG	Jahrbuch der jüdisch-literarischen Gesellschaft, Frankfurt a.M.
JNES	Journal of Near Eastern Studies (continuation of *AJSL*)
JPOS	Journal of the Palestine Oriental Society
JQR	Jewish Quarterly Review (new series, unless otherwise stated)
JR	Journal of Religion
JRAS	Journal of the Royal Asiatic Society
JRS	Journal of Roman Studies
JSS	Jewish Social Studies
JTS	Journal of Theological Studies
Kohut Mem. Vol.	Jewish Studies in Memory of George A. Kohut. New York, 1935.
Krauss Jub. Vol.	Sefer ha-Yobel la-Professor Shemuel [Samuel]Krauss. Jerusalem, 1937.
KS	Kirjath Sepher, Quarterly Bibliographical Review
Lewy Mem. Vol.	Sefer Johanan Lewy (Commentationes Judaico-Hellenisticae in memoriam Johannis Lewy). Jerusalem, 1949.
Löw Mem. Vol.	Semitic Studies in Memory of Immanuel Löw. Budapest, 1947.
M.	Mishnah
Mahler Jub. Vol.	Emlékkönyv (Dissertationes) in honorem Dr. Eduardi Mahler. Budapest, 1937.

Marx Jub. Vol.	Alexander Marx Jubilee Volume. 2 vols. New York, 1950. A volume each of English and Hebrew essays.
Mélanges Dussaud	Mélanges syriens offerts à M. René Dussaud. Paris, 1939.
MGH	Monumenta Germaniae Historica
MGWJ	Monatsschrift für Geschichte und Wissenschaft des Judentums.
Miller Mem. Vol.	Essays and Studies in Memory of Linda R. Miller. New York, 1938.
Miscellanea Mercati	Miscellanea Giovanni Mercati. 6 vols. Vatican City, 1946. Studi e testi, CXXI–XXVI.
M.Q.	Mo'ed Qaṭan
M.T.	Moses ben Maimon's Mishneh torah (Code)
OLZ	Orientalistische Literaturzeitung
OS	Oudtestamentische Studien
PAAJR	Proceedings of the American Academy for Jewish Research
PEQ	Palestine Exploration Quarterly *or* Palestine Exploration Fund Quarterly Statement
PG	J. P. Migne's Patrologiae cursus completus, series Graeca
PJB	Palästina-Jahrbuch
PL	J. P. Migne's Patrologiae cursus completus, series Latina
PWRE	Pauly-Wissowa-Kroll, Realencyclopädie der classischen Altertumswissenschaft
Quantulacumque	Studies presented to Kirsopp Lake. London, 1937.
R	Rabbi or Rab
r.	Midrash Rabbah (Gen. r. = Bereshit rabbah; Lam. r. = Ekhah rabbati, etc.)
RB	Revue biblique (includes wartime *Vivre et Penser*)
REJ	Revue des études juives
RES	Revue des études sémitiques
R.H.	Rosh Hashanah
RHPR	Revue d'histoire et de philosophie religieuses
RHR	Revue d'histoire des religions
RIDA	Revue internationale des droits de l'Antiquité (II–V = Mélanges Fernand de Visscher, I–IV)
RR	Review of Religion
SB	Sitzungsberichte der Akademie der Wissenschaften (identified by city: e.g., *SB* Berlin, Heidelberg, Vienna)
Schorr Mem. Vol.	Qobeṣ madda'i (Studies in Memory of Moses Schorr). New York, 1944.
SH	Sefer ha-Shanah li-Yehude Amerika
Studies Robinson	Studies in Old Testament Prophecy Presented to Theodor H. Robinson. Edinburgh, 1950.
T.	Tosefta. Ed. by M. S. Zuckermandel
TZ	Theologische Zeitschrift (Basel, 1945–)
WZKM	Wiener Zeitschrift für die Kunde des Morgenlandes

ZAW	Zeitschrift für die alttestamentliche Wissenschaft und die Kunde des nachbiblischen Judentums
ZDMG	Zeitschrift der deutschen morgenländischen Gesellschaft
ZDPV	Zeitschrift des Deutschen Palästina Vereins. Vols. LXVIII (1948) ff. are entitled Beiträge zur biblischen Landes- und Altertumskunde.
ZNW	Zeitschrift für die neutestamentliche Wissenschaft und die Kunde der älteren Kirche

NOTES

CHAPTER I: JEWISH SOCIETY AND RELIGION

1. The best guides for the entire field of Jewish social and religious history are still such general works as H. Graetz's *Geschichte der Juden* which, although begun nearly a century ago, has not yet been superseded. Most of the volumes have appeared in revised editions; the English translation under the title *History of the Jews* includes a full index, but omits the scholarly apparatus. S. M. Dubnow's *Weltgeschichte des jüdischen Volkes; Z.* Jawitz's *Toledot Yisrael* (Jewish History: Revised on the Basis of Primary Sources); M. L. Margolis and A. Marx's *History of the Jewish People;* and *The Jews: Their History, Culture and Religion,* ed. by L. Finkelstein, are the most important more recent publications. For a systematic survey of the main doctrines of the Jewish religion, with some reference to their historical development, cf. K. Kohler's *Jewish Theology* and L. Baeck's *Essence of Judaism.* No searching philosophy of Jewish history has been presented since the days of Naḥman Krochmal's *Moreh nebukhe ha-zeman* (The Guide of the Perplexed of Our Time), first published in 1851. Among later attempts at such a philosophy, Malkizedek's *Probleme der jüdischen Geschichte und Geschichtsphilosophie* merely scratches the surface; while Y. Kaufmann's *Golah ve-nekhar* (Exile and Alienage) presents a vivid interpretation of the Jewish past from an extreme "territorialist" point of view. Cf. also the brief analyses of "Emphases in Jewish History," by S. W. Baron, and of "Philosophies of Jewish History" by M. R. Cohen in *JSS,* I, 15–38, 39–72.

It is a deplorable sign of the waning interest of Jewish and general scholarship in the totality of Jewish historic experience and of the inability of our generation creatively to synthesize the vast monographic literature accumulating from year to year that the present note, which appeared in our 1937 edition, could not be amplified by any comprehensive newer publications on the philosophy of Jewish history. Nor were the aforementioned general historical works of Graetz, Dubnow, Margolis and Marx, all of them more than two decades old or older, brought up to date. The articles published in the *Universal Jewish Encyclopedia;* the general essays included in Finkelstein's comprehensive review; and *The Jewish People Past and Present,* ed. by R. Abramovich, *et al.* (of which thus far only Vols. I–II have appeared) are, of course, not sufficient substitutes. Various projects for the publication of a large collective work on Jewish history, in which the usual deficiencies of diverse approaches and styles would be compensated by each contributor's expert familiarity with his specialized field of research, have likewise failed to materialize so far. Perhaps it is still too early for the Jewish people to digest mentally the historic meaning of its recent tragedies and achievements, and to review afresh its entire historical record from some such novel approaches.

At the same time detailed investigations have proceeded apace even during the Second World War. Many of them will be quoted briefly in the following notes and, more fully, in the alphabetically arranged "Bibliography" in the concluding volume. Shortly before the War historical, sociological, linguistic, and theological investigations of various phases of Jewish life in the past and present, made by both Jews and non-Jews, reached unprecedented dimensions. Cf., in particular, my *Bibliography of Jewish Social Studies, 1938–39* which, unwittingly, has become a monument to an epoch of rich exploration and discussion abruptly ended by the Nazi onslaught. A useful work for the whole field is S. Shunami's *Bibliography of Jewish Bibliographies.*

2. Gen. 1:16–18; Sirach 43:6–7 (cf. 33:7–9). The Pharisaic quest for historical motivations is well illustrated by a statement of R. Eliezer the Great, usually the mouthpiece of older traditions: "In Tishre [the first month of the Jewish calendar] the world was created, in Tishre the patriarchs were born, in Tishre the patriarchs died . . . on New Year's day Sarah, Rachel and Hannah were remembered [to become mothers], on New Year's day Joseph was discharged from prison, on New Year's day ceased the hard labor of our forefathers in Egypt, in Nisan [the seventh month] they were redeemed, in Tishre the Jews will be redeemed in the future" (R. H. 10b–11a). Even R. Joshua, Eliezer's great opponent, who clung to the older chronology according to which the world was created in Nisan, did not suggest transferring the celebration of the New Year to that month. If he was at all aware of the Babylonian mythology concerning the conquest of the dragon by an annually reborn god, he revealed the even more "pious and heroic" conviction that during the autumn, i.e., the period of the God's progressive eclipse, the Jew is to celebrate the victory of the deity over all opposing forces. Cf. A. Jeremias's data in *Das Alte Testament im Lichte des alten Orients*, 4th ed., pp. 409 f. At any rate, R. Joshua, too, accepted several of the above chronological identifications for Tishre and the New Year. Cf. also T. H. Gaster's semipopular analysis of *Passover: Its History and Tradition*. As to Ḥanukkah, cf., especially O. S. Rankin's *Origins of the Festival of Hanukkah;* and L. Finkelstein's review of this work in *JQR*, XXII, 169 f. Cf. also J. Morgenstern's comprehensive study of "The Chanukkah Festival and the Calendar of Ancient Israel," *HUCA*, XX, 1–136; XXI, 365–496. This historicism became so deeply ingrained in the minds of the rabbis, that several later Amoraim tried in every possible manner to obtain a Jewish historical basis for the ancient Ishtar-Sirius festival of mating on the fifteenth of Ab. Cf. M. Ta'anit IV, 8; and the comments thereon in both j. and b. Ta'anit, end. The impact of history eventually led to the creation of new, purely historical commemorative days. The great Jewish fasts, particularly, from the Fast of Gedaliah to the Ninth of Ab, are all days of mourning commemorating fateful events in the history of the people for which no natural background need be sought.

3. The purport of this discussion is not, of course, to minimize the influence of ethics upon Jewish religion in any way. Jewish apologists of all shades, and sympathetic outsiders as well, have often rightly glorified Jewish ethics as the major contribution of Judaism in the past as well as for the future. There is doubtless a grain of truth even in the bizarre exclamation of Frank Wedekind, the non-Jewish poet, "The Jew, unproductive in the political field, only once possessed a state of his own which, if one is to accept the biblical tradition, covered only a small area and endured only for a short time. The non-Jew, on the other hand, unproductive in the moral field, has depended for two millennia upon Jewish morality which he adopted with great zeal but which, intrinsically, is still foreign to him. Under these circumstances, every Jew appears as his own moralist and father confessor and constantly arouses by this capacity the ire of the non-Jew to its highest pitch" (Sombart *et al., Judentaufen*, p. 134). In our discussion an attempt has been made merely to penetrate beneath the surface of ethics to its more hidden source, the historical trend. It is quite natural that in Judaism, an intrinsically actional rather than speculative creed, the ethical and legal side of human behavior should be treated in the sources with much greater emphasis than its philosophical or theological motivation through the imprint of history.

4. "From the point of view of Judaism," rightly comments M. S. Enslin, "there was only one real remedy to sin, viz., repentance. . . . Christianity has often failed to recognize the centrality of that note in Judaism. The failure of Paul to stress it in his treatment of Israel's attitude to the law has done no little to raise barriers between the synagogue and the church. Before the world was created, before the law had been promulgated, while it was still only in the mind of God, coëval with it was

the idea of repentance in the mind of God" ("Atoning Work of Christ in the New Testament," *HTR*, XXXVIII, 43 f.). On the ramified Jewish doctrine of repentance, cf. E. K. Dietrich's detailed analysis of *Die Umkehr (Bekehrung und Busse) im Alten Testament und im Judentum;* and S. Herner's "Sühne und Vergebung in Israel," *HVLA*, 1941–42, pp. 47–122.

5. Although still adhering to his older view that Exod. 3:13–15 is a later theological interpolation, J. Morgenstern stresses its appropriateness for the days of Moses. "And in just this particular setting, as the Deity who purposes to shape the course of history and destiny not only of Israel but also, in relation thereto, of Egypt as well, He is not only 'the eternally existent One,' but is also the God of history" ("Deutero-Isaiah's Terminology for 'Universal God,'" *JBL*, LXII, 277). This interpretation is essentially correct, whether or not we accept the translation of the divine name itself as "He causes to be" (W. F. Albright, *From the Stone Age to Christianity*, pp. 197 f.); identify it with the personal pronoun, *hu* (He; cf. Morgenstern, *loc. cit.;* and J. A. Montgomery in his "Hebrew Divine Name and the Personal Pronoun *HU*," *JBL*, LXIII, 163: "The Name then means, 'He is He,' an early theologumenon, but at the basis of all theology"); translate it by a term like "Sustainer" (J. Obermann in "The Divine Name YHWH in the Light of Recent Discoveries," *JBL*, LXVIII, 301–23); or adopt any of the numerous other explanations offered in recent years. Cf. O. Grether's *Name und Wort Gottes im Alten Testament;* O. Eissfeldt's "Neue Zeugnisse für die Aussprache des Tetragramms," *ZAW*, LIII, 59–76; R. Dussaud's "Yahwé," *CRAI*, 1940, pp. 364–70; Y. Kaufmann's *Toledot ha-emunah ha-yisre'elit* (History of Israelitic Religion), II, 51, n. 3; S. I. Feigin's *Missitre heavar* (Biblical and Historical Studies), pp. 355, 429 ff.; R. A. Bowman's "Yahweh the Speaker," *JNES*, III, 1–8; and the pertinent essays by B. D. Eerdmans and G. J. Thierry in *OS*, V, 1–42. Cf. also A. Alt's "Aegyptisches Seitenstück zu Ex. 3:14," *ZAW*, LVIII, 159–60 (in the teaching for King Merikare); T. C. Vriezen's "'Ehje 'ašer 'ehje," *Festschrift Bertholet*, pp. 498–512 (pointing out the uniqueness of this designation among ancient deities and its early intimation of the combination of God's simultaneous nearness and remoteness); J. Schmidt's careful analysis of *Der Ewigkeitsbegriff im Alten Testament* which shows how close this concept is to the modern views of eternity; A. M. Dubarle's "Signification du nom de Jahwe," *Revue des sciences philos. et théol.*, XXXV, 3–21; and *infra*, Chap. II, n. 15.

6. The historical basis of Judaism has long been recognized by Jewish and Christian theologians. Next to Yehudah Halevi it was especially Samuel Hirsch who, in 1842, based upon this recognition a penetrating analysis of the Jewish religion. Cf. his *Religionsphilosophie der Juden*, the first and only volume of a larger *System of the Religious Tenets of the Jews* which he never completed. Hermann Cohen, in contrasting the social ideal of Plato with that of the prophets, clearly perceived the difference between the spatial orientation of the Greek thinker and the dominance of time in the Israelitic conception. "For the prophets," he declared, "the earth and the universe are almost wholly concentrated upon time. . . . It is the 'end of days,' the infinity of time, with which they overcome the antinomies in space, in the geographic distribution of mankind" (*Jüdische Schriften*, I, 325). Cf. also *infra*, Chaps. VI, n. 22; IX, notes 1–4. If Buber, in recent years, sometimes spoke of the Jewish belief in God as overcoming both "nature" and "history," he immediately qualified the meaning of "history" in this sense as equivalent to the popular conception, namely, the history of earthly success and victory. Cf., for example, his fascinating essay on biblical leadership written in 1928 and reprinted in his *Kampf um Israel*, pp. 84–106; and in English transl. in his *Mamre*, pp. 44 ff. From Protestant theologians one might quote R. Kittel's enthusiastic comment on the enduring work of Moses: "History has here become Revelation. And as long as Israel lived, its religion remained linked up with its history and its history with its religion. History is, indeed, the work of God and the supreme religious experience" (*Geschichte des Volkes*

Israel, I, 387). Cf. also E. Sellin's early study, *Die alttestamentliche Religion im Rahmen der andern altorientalischen*.

Of a somewhat different, though related, order is the question of the interrelations between "faith and history." Long agitating the minds of Christian theologians, it was brought into clearer focus in the last two decades by the Barthian school's sharp attacks on theological historicism and relativism. Out of this concern grew such studies as J. Hempel's *Altes Testament und Geschichte* and A. Weiser's *Glaube und Geschichte im Alten Testament*. Cf. also, more generally, the different approaches exemplified by H. G. Wood's *Christianity and the Nature of History;* the collection of essays prepared for the Oxford Conference of 1938 under the title, *The Kingdom of God and History;* R. Niebuhr's *Faith and History;* and S. J. Case's *Christian Philosophy of History*. C. C. McCown was, indeed, right when, surveying the various schools of thought, he noted that "numerous current publications testify that the relationship of Christianity and its doctrine of revelation to history is one of the most serious problems that the present generation of theologians has to face. Paul Tillich has characterized history as *the* problem of our age" ("In History or beyond History," *HTR*, XXXVIII, 151). For Jewish theology this entire problem is far less important, for reasons which may become clearer in the light of our discussion of Christian origins, *infra*, Chap. X. However, a thoroughgoing investigation of the successive stages in Jewish historical thinking throughout the ages remains an urgent scholarly desideratum. For the time being, cf. such monographs as N. N. Glatzer's *Untersuchungen zur Geschichtslehre der Tannaiten* and S. W. Baron's "Historical Outlook of Maimonides," *PAAJR*, VI, 5–113. Cf. also *infra*, Chaps. III, n. 51; X, notes 10, 35; XII, n. 17.

Our views expressed in the 1937 edition were criticized by W. F. Albright in his *Stone Age*, p. 318, n. 21. Although as far as possible steering clear of polemics, we must briefly take up his arguments, since they relate to a focal point in our treatment. To begin with, it is questionable whether the dichotomy between "history" and "nature" which plays such a role in the philosophic outlook of Windelband, Rickert and Max Weber, can really be traced back first to Johann Gustav Droysen, as suggested by E. Rothacker in his "J. G. Droysens Historik," *HZ*, CLXI, 89 f. After all, Droysen's views themselves were fully developed only in his lectures which, though of great influence on his students, became generally known only after their publication from the historian's notebooks in 1937. Be this as it may, Droysen has thus merely replaced the older antinomy between "spirit" and "nature," which had played a very great role in the German idealistic philosophy. Terminologically "history" seems preferable inasmuch as it contrasts more sharply the historic dynamism with the more static forces of nature. Under whatever guise, this dichotomy has long been felt by keen observers of the historic process. Rudolf Anthes's criticism of this view in connection with his critique of W. Wolf's *Wesen und Wert der Aegyptologie*, to which Albright refers, is in fact focused on Wolf's identification of his theory of evolution with nature and of his theory of circular movements (*Kreislauftheorie*) with history. See Anthes's "Zu Walther Wolf's 'Wesen und Wert der Aegyptologie,' " *ZDMG*, XCII, 430. Moreover, both author and reviewer clearly caught something of the intellectual atmosphere bred by Nazism's truly antihistorical attempt at remaking history on the basis of "natural" racial factors. Cf., on the other hand, Johannes Lindblom's analysis, "Zur Frage der Eigenart der alttestamentlichen Religion" in *Werden und Wesen des Alten Testaments*, ed. by P. Voltz, *et al.*, pp. 128–38; and P. Tillich's unpublished address on "The Struggle between Time and Space and the Prophetic Message," to which the present writer listened in 1938 and which, owing to Professor Tillich's kindness, he recently reread. The fact that Lindblom's and Tillich's penetrating minds *independently* reached conclusions so strikingly similar to those presented here in 1937 points to the encouraging possibility of a more general agreement in this admittedly speculative area. Needless to say that Judaism's historical emphases have nothing to do with depreciation of the beauties of man's natural environment, on which cf., e.g., S. Herner's interesting study of "Die Natur im Alten Testament," *HVLA*, 1940–41, pp. 27–148.

7. The phrase, though not the concept, of the pariah status of Jews was first given wide circulation by the authority of Max Weber. "Sociologically speaking, what were the Jews? A pariah people," he declared in the introductory definition to his otherwise admirable volume on the social ethics of ancient Judaism (*Gesammelte Aufsätze zur Religionssoziologie*, III, 2 f.). "This means," he continued, "as we know it from India, a guest-people which is ritualistically segregated from its social environment, either formally or actually." It could not escape Weber's sharp eyes, of course, that there have always existed fundamental differences between the position of Diaspora Jewry and that of the pariah caste of India. He himself enumerated three such basic distinctions. More important than these qualifications is, evidently, the religious disparity between the Jews and their Gentile rulers. In India it was within the same religion that the position of an inferior, unchangeable caste was determined by the dominant religious doctrine and, on the whole, accepted by the pariahs themselves. Judaism has remained an extraneous religion with its own values and countervalues. It has always regarded the passing of a member to another camp as a forfeiture of rights by the person concerned, rather than as a reward. His family mourned for him by following the same ritual as if he had died.

It must be admitted that contemptuous treatment by outsiders necessarily had many a harmful effect upon Jewish mentality. No one was more eloquent in describing the sufferings of the Exile and the disgrace of living in subjection to foreign rulers than were the Jews themselves, beginning with the ancient rabbis. Cf. *infra*, Chap. VII, notes 27–29. But at no time in antiquity or in the Middle Ages did they admit that their sufferings were due to their personal or group inferiority. It was their own God, they believed, who castigated them for their sins and the sins of their forefathers. At the same time, He regarded Israel as his first-born, towering high above all the other nations even at its lowest. Not until the Emancipation era did Jewish theologians and historians assimilate, along with the other non-Jewish concepts, the distorted view of the Jews' past, or what I have called the "lachrymous conception of Jewish history." The depressing spectacle, already anachronistic, of a more or less distinct Jewish group persisting in increasingly homogeneous democratic societies encouraged this view, as did the desire to use it as a weapon in the prolonged struggle for equality in which medieval oppression was contrasted to modern freedom as black to white. Even the Zionist opponents of liberal writers preferred to display the shining glory of the forthcoming rebirth of the people in Zion against a dark background. A more unbiased historical estimate, however, shows that, if measured objectively, neither the ancient nor the medieval Jew was ever a "pariah" in any real sense.

8. These biological factors, underlying all historical developments in Jewish society and religion, have thus far received scant attention. Population problems have been carefully investigated only with respect to the last century or two, and even here stupendous tasks still await the scholar. For earlier periods this study is in its infancy, as will be seen by the scarcity of bibliographical references in subsequent chapters. The source material is, of course, very inadequate, but dispassionate inquiries into these truly basic aspects of the Jewish past are nevertheless possible, and wellnigh imperative.

CHAPTER II: ISRAEL'S ORIGIN

1. Innumerable books and articles have been written on Israel's history and religion in the Old Testament period. Among the outstanding and most comprehensive works are R. Kittel's *Geschichte des Volkes Israel;* E. Sellin's *Geschichte des israelitisch-jüdischen Volkes;* A. T. Olmstead's *History of Palestine and Syria to the Macedonian Conquest;* T. H. Robinson and W. O. E. Oesterley's *History of Israel* (down to the Bar Kocheba revolt); G. Ricciotti's *Histoire d'Israël* (covering the same period); M. Noth's *Welt des Alten Testaments* (a good general introduction to the problems of geography, archaeology, Near Eastern background and Old Testament text); his *Geschichte Israels;* and W. F. Albright's *From the Stone Age to Christianity* (most comprehensive treatment from the standpoint of archaeology and Albright's philosophy of history). Cf. also the more popular surveys by H. H. Rowley, *The Re-discovery of the Old Testament;* I. G. Matthews, *The Religious Pilgrimage of Israel;* G. E. Wright, *The Old Testament against Its Environment;* as well as various chapters in *Cambridge Ancient History.* Major recent works in the field of biblical religion and thought include W. Eichrodt's *Theologie des Alten Testaments;* D. B. Macdonald's *Hebrew Philosophical Genius;* Y. Kaufmann's *Toledot ha-emunah ha-yisre'elit* (an English transl. of this comprehensive and original work seems long overdue; cf. also Kaufmann's reply to his early critics in "The Secret of National Creativity" [Hebrew], *Moznayim,* XIII, 237–51); W. F. Albright's *Archaeology and the Religion of Israel;* N. H. Snaith's *Distinctive Ideas of the Old Testament;* M. Burrows's *Outline of Biblical Theology;* B. D. Eerdmans's *Religion of Israel;* and P. Heinisch's *Theology of the Old Testament.* For the early period, cf. also A. Lods's *Israel from Its Beginnings to the Middle of the Eighth Century;* and B. Maisler's *Toledot Ereṣ Yisrael* (History of Palestine), I. The collective works, *The People and the Book,* ed. by A. S. Peake; *The Haverford Symposium on Archaeology and the Bible,* ed. by E. Grant; *Record and Revelation,* ed. by H. W. Robinson; and *The Study of the Bible Today and Tomorrow,* ed. by H. R. Willoughby consist of many informative and stimulating essays. Good general reference works are K. Galling's *Biblisches Reallexikon;* J. D. Davis's *Westminster Dictionary of the Bible* (revised by H. S. Gehman); and the more ambitious *Enṣiqlopediah miqra'it* (Encyclopaedia Biblica), ed. by M.D. (U.) Cassuto, *et al.* (one volume of which appeared in 1950). Fairly full bibliographical surveys appear regularly in various journals, especially *Biblica.*

Extrabiblical sources, in so far as they were known a quarter of a century ago, were well collected and translated into German by several specialists in *Altorientalische Texte und Bilder zum Alten Testament,* ed. by H. Gressmann, 2d ed. A more up-to-date translation into English which, despite the omission of certain Phoenician and Aramaic texts, includes almost twice as many documents, has recently been edited by J. B. Pritchard under the title, *Ancient Near Eastern Texts.* A companion volume of plates is likewise planned. For the important new archaeological discoveries, cf. G. A. Barton's *Archaeology and the Bible,* 6th ed. (includes transl. of many extrabiblical texts); W. F. Albright's *Archaeology of Palestine and the Bible,* 3d ed.; his popular *Archaeology of Palestine;* S. A. Cook's *Religion of Ancient Palestine in the Light of Archaeology;* C. Watzinger's *Denkmäler Palästinas;* A. G. Barrois's *Manuel d'archéologie biblique;* F. Kenyon's *Bible and Archaeology;* M. Burrows's *What Mean These Stones? The Significance of Archaeology for Biblical Studies;* J. Finegan's *Light from the Ancient Past: the Archaeological Background of the Hebrew-Christian Religion;* and N. Glueck's *River Jordan.* In view of the rapid progress in the discovery of ever new data and the reinterpretation of old ones, the date of publication of a particular work is of utmost significance. Even articles in scholarly journals sometimes become obsolete in the short span between writing and publication. W. F. Albright, in particular, keeps the scholarly public abreast of new developments in his regular surveys and reviews appearing in *BASOR*. He is ably seconded, on a more popular level, by the various contributors to *BA*. Cf. also A. Parrot's related reference work, *Archéologie mésopotamienne;* and such specialized handbooks as G. E. Wright's *Pottery of Palestine from the Earliest Times to the End of the Early Bronze Age;* and M. Walker's *Painted Pottery of the Near East in the Second Millennium B.C.* A word of caution, however, voiced a decade ago by M. Noth in his "Grundsätzliches zur geschichtlichen Deutung archäologischer Befunde auf dem Boden Palästinas," *PJB*, XXXIV, 7–22, still merits attention, as do the warnings sounded by J. A. Wilson in his "Archaeology as a Tool in Humanistic and Social Studies," *JNES*, I, 3–9; and T. J. Meek in his address on "The Challenge of Oriental Studies to American Scholarship," *JAOS*, LXIII, 83–93. For one example the much-debated problem of the destruction of Ai by the Israelitic conquerors largely depends on the identification of that city with Al-Tell, denied by J. Simons in his Dutch essay, "An Observation on the Problem of Ai," *JEOL*, IV, 157–62. Cf. also B-Z. Luria's *Gelilot ba-moledet* (essays and studies in the history and topography of Palestine), pp. 211 ff. (suggesting Ai's location in the district of Jericho); and, more generally, the discussion between W. F. Albright ("Archaeology Confronts Biblical Criticism") and W. C. Graham ("Higher Criticism Survives Archaeology") in the *American Scholar*, VII, 176–88, 409–27.

The epigraphic material is well assembled in D. Diringer's *Iscrizioni antico-ebraiche palestinesi.* It is to be supplemented by the same author's methodological remarks on "The Dating of Early Hebrew Inscriptions," *PEQ*, 1943, pp. 50–54 (with reference to S. Birnbaum's ingenious new approach to the dating of the Gezer tablet and the Samarian ostraca, *ibid.*, 1942, pp. 104–8); and W. F. Albright's comments and paleographic table in his "Gezer Calendar," *BASOR*, 92, pp. 16–26. Our knowledge of ancient Hebrew paleography has also been enriched by such newer material as H. Torczyner's edition of *The Lachish Letters.* Cf. also *infra*, notes 7, 13. The geography of Palestine as related to history is best treated in the well-known works of G. A. Smith, *Historical Geography of the Holy Land*, 25th ed.; and F. M. Abel, *Géographie de la Palestine;* as well as in *Ereş Yisrael* (A Topographical-Historical Encyclopaedia of Palestine), ed. by I. Press, Vols. I–II. Cf. also L. Picard's geological survey of the *Structure and Evolution of Palestine;* M. Blanckenhorn's bibliographical "Bericht über die Fortschritte der geologischen Erforschung Palästinas von 1931–1938," *ZDPV*, LXII, 22–52; and the *Westminster Historical Atlas to the Bible*, ed. by G. E. Wright and F. V. Filson. Many relevant historical data are also included in Z. Braslavski's comprehensive geography, *Ha-yadata et ha-areş?* (Do You Know the Country?) the three volumes hitherto published cover Galilee and the northern valleys, the Negev and the Dead Sea region); and, from the bio- and zoölogical points of view, in S. Bodenheimer's *Ha-Ḥay be-areşot ha-miqra* (Living Beings in the Lands of the Bible . . . from the Stone Age to the End of the Biblical Period).

Extremely complex literary and textual problems are discussed most fully in the various commentaries on the Old Testament. Cf. especially the *International Critical Commentary* ed. by S. R. Driver, *et al.;* the *Handkommentar zum Alten Testament* ed. by W. Nowack; the *Kommentar zum Alten Testament*, ed. by E. Sellin; and the *Handbuch zum Alten Testament* ed. by O. Eissfeldt (many of the older volumes in the former three series were already partially obsolete before the latest volumes appeared). They are also reviewed, from different approaches, in J. A. Bewer's *Literature of the Old Testament;* S. Bernfeld's *Mabo sifruti-histori le-kitbe ha-qodesh* (Literary and Historical Introduction to the Holy Scriptures); J. Hempel's *Althebräische Literatur und ihr hellenistisch-jüdisches Nachleben;* A. Lods's *Histoire de la littérature hébraïque et juive depuis les origines jusqu'à la ruine de l'état juif;* O. Eissfeldt's *Einleitung in das Alte Testament;* R. H. Pfeiffer's comprehensive *Introduction to the Old Testament;* A. Bentzen's work under the same title; M. Z. [H.] Segal's *Mebo ha-miqra* (Introduction to Scripture); J. E. Steinmueller's voluminous *Companion to Scripture Studies* (includes Vol. II, Pt. 1: Special Introduction to the Old Testament); and S. Goldman's even more comprehensive *Book of Human Destiny*, Vols. I–II. Cf. also W. F. Albright's and H. L. Ginsberg's detailed reviews of Pfeiffer's volume in *JBL*, LXI, 111–26; and *JQR*, XXXIII, 481–85; D. B. Macdonald's *Hebrew Literary Genius*; H. H. Rowley's plea for the "Unity of the Old Testament," *BJRL*, XXIX, 326–58; his *Growth of the Old Testament*; E. Robertson's collected essays on *The Old Testament Problem*; and A. Sperber's "Biblical Exegesis; Prolegomena to a Commentary and Dictionary to the Bible," *JBL*, LXIV, 39–140 (preparatory to his projected new edition of the Hebrew Bible on the basis of "objective" data). Brief historical surveys of biblical research are given in S. Klein's *Toledot ḥaqirat Ereṣ-Yisrael* (History of Palestine Exploration in Hebrew and Universal Literature); C. C. McCown's *Ladder of Progress in Palestine: a Story of Archaeological Adventure*; G. Contenau's *Manuel d'archéologie orientale*, Vol. IV (reviewing the decade of 1930–39 of Near Eastern archaeological discoveries); J. Coppens's *Old Testament and the Critics*; A. Causse's "Notes sur le développement des études d'Ancien Testament en France," *RHPR*, XX, 47–76; and, from another angle, J. H. Scammon's brief survey of "Trends in Old Testament Introductions from 1930 to the Present," *ATR*, XXX, 150–55. Of interest are also B. Hessler's "De theologiae biblicae Veteris Testamenti problemate," *Antonianum*, XXV, 407–24 (a discussion of recent trends in the study of the Old Testament theology); and O. S. Rankin's brief sketch of "Old Testament Interpretation, Its History and Development," *Hibbert Journal* XLIX, 146–53. A fine comprehensive dissertation on the major trends in biblical criticism since Wellhausen by my pupil, Herbert F. Hahn, is now awaiting publication.

The social history of ancient Israel has been treated from different angles in M. Weber's *Gesammelte Aufsätze zur Religionssoziologie*, Vol. III; I. Benzinger's *Hebräische Archäologie*, 3d ed.; A. Bertholet's *History of Hebrew Civilization*; C. R. Smith's *Bible Doctrine of Society in Its Historical Evolution*; M. Lurie's *Studien zur Geschichte der wirtschaftlichen und sozialen Verhältnisse im israelitisch-jüdischen Reiche*; R. H. Kennett's *Ancient Hebrew Social Life and Custom as Indicated in Law, Narrative and Metaphor*; T. H. Robinson's "Some Economic and Social Factors in the History of Israel," *Expository Times*, XLV, 264–69 and 294–300; L. Wallis's *God and the Social Process*; D. Jacobson's *Social Background of the Old Testament*; J. Pedersen's *Israel, Its Life and Culture*, Vols. I–IV (comprehensive and original); and (for the early period) J. Garstang's *Heritage of Solomon*. Much significant material, on the basis of contemporary observations, has also been assembled by G. Dalman in his voluminous *Arbeit und Sitte in Palästina*. Cf. also N. M. Nikolskii's Russian review of "Problems of Biblical Criticism in Soviet Science" in *Vestnik drevnei istorii*, 1938, pp. 30 ff. More recent discussions of general problems include also A. T. Olmstead's "Hebrew History and Historical Method," in *Persecution and Liberty*, pp. 21–54; and "History, Ancient World and the Bible: Problems of Attitudes and of Method," *JNES*, II, 1–34; S. A. Cook's "Salient Problems in Old Testament History," *JBL*, LI, 273–99; F. Dornseiff's "Antikes zum Alten Testament, I–IV," *ZAW*, Vols. LII–LIII, LV–LVI; and W. F. Albright's "Ancient Near East and the Religion of Israel," *JBL*, LIX, 85–112.

2. "The Canaanite royal cities," observes G. E. Wright on the basis of ever-growing archaeological evidence, "of Bethel, Beth-shemesh and Kiriath-sepher, for example, possessed a comparatively high degree of material civilization. A native art had developed and was flourishing. Houses were well built. Floors were paved and plastered. City drainage was in operation. Metal workers, artisans in copper, bronze, lead and gold were active. Extensive world trade was carried on with Syria, the Aegean and Egypt. Wares were even purchased from Egyptian tomb robbers." Cf. his "Archaeological Observations on the Period of the Judges and the Early Monarchy," *JBL*, LX, 31. The recently excavated royal palace of Mari in Northern Syria which covered

an area of some six acres and possessed more than two hundred and fifty rooms, including many bathrooms, has served to illustrate the high degree of well-being attained by the upper classes in Canaan and its vicinity in the eighteenth century B.C.E. Cf. G. Dossin, et al.'s ed. of Archives royales de Mari; the extensive bibliography by A. Spycket in A. Parrot's Studia Mariana, pp. 127 ff.; Parrot's "Tablettes de Mari et l'Ancien Testament," RHPR, XXX, 1–11; and the brief summary in G. E. Mendenhall's "Mari," BA, XI, 1–19. We shall see that general intellectual and cultural progress, too, had kept pace with this advance in physical amenities. Only in the area of religious doctrine and ritual may one legitimately speak of "the extremely low level of Canaanite religion, which inherited a relatively primitive mythology and had adopted some of the most demoralizing cultic practices then existing in the Near East," as observed by W. F. Albright in his "Role of the Canaanites in the History of Civilization," Studies in the History of Culture, pp. 28 f. However, even some of these religious extremes were symptoms of cultural decadence, rather than of sheer primitivism. Cf. also R. T. O'Callaghan's comprehensive analysis of the history of Aram Naharaim in the second millennium B.C.E.; and, on the perennial "Struggle between Cultivation and Wilderness" in Palestine, A. A. Reifenberg's Hebrew work under this title (Milḥemet ha-mizra' ve-ha-yeshimon).

3. Contemporary scholarship has slowly, but perceptibly, moved away from the long-prevailing identification of the life of early, "patriarchal" Hebrews with that of present-day Bedouins. W. F. Albright pointed out that, before the camel was introduced into common use in Palestine about the twelfth century, the Hebrews could only be ass nomads whose mobility was far more restricted. This condition stimulated more or less sedentary occupations, including agriculture. See his Stone Age, pp. 120 f., 196. Albright's observation remains essentially valid notwithstanding the fairly conclusive evidence assembled by J. P. Free for the more or less sporadic use of camels in Egypt ever since the First Dynasty or earlier ("Abraham's Camels," JNES, III, 187–93). Cf. also B. S. J. Isserlin's "On Some Possible Early Occurrences of the Camel in Palestine," PEQ, 1950, pp. 50–53. According to A. Alt, the mere transition from raising sheep to that of larger cattle served likewise as an incentive for the Israelites to strike early roots in the sparsely inhabited hill areas of Palestine ("Erwägungen über die Landnahme der Israeliten in Palästina," PJB, XXXV, 34 ff.). More recently F. Helling has plausibly argued that more credence ought to be given to the biblical narratives depicting the patriarchs as owners of money, as well as of agricultural land, and that, hence, the latter were anything but typical nomads. Helling's Frühgeschichte des jüdischen Volkes, though at times leaning too heavily on H. Grimme's fantastic conclusions from the Sinaitic inscriptions and A. S. Yahuda's strained Egyptian parallels, offers many interesting sociological observations. Cf. infra, n. 7, and Chap. IV, n. 20. Cf. also infra, Chap. III, n. 36.

4. A. Jeremias in Das Alte Testament, p. 289. The fact that at a much later date the Septuagint evidently misread ereṣ for ur in both crucial passages (Gen. 11:28, 31) need not controvert the patriarchs' original association with that ancient emporium of trade and culture. The date of Abraham's activity in and outside of Palestine is placed by F. M. T. Böhl at about 1600 B.C.E. Cf. Das Zeitalter Abrahams. Cf. also L. Woolley's Abraham, and S. I. Feigin's remarks thereon in his Missitrei heavar, pp. 343 ff. In view of the constant lowering of dates in ancient Near Eastern chronology it may be possible again to identify Amraphel, King of Shinear, mentioned among Abraham's foes (Gen. 14) with Hammurabi, although philologically this equation remains dubious. Hammurabi's reign is now dated by Albright as of 1728–1686 B.C.E. (Albright, "Third Revision of the Early Chronology of Western Asia," BASOR, 88, pp. 28–36; cf. G. Goossens's "Révision de la chronologie mésopotamienne et ses conséquences pour l'histoire orientale," Muséon, LXI, 1–30).

When Charles Virolleaud, in 1934, first identified a passage in the Keret legend, which he was then preparing for publication, with Terah, he immediately secured a wide and enthusiastic following. Cf. his "Epopée de Kéret, roi des Sidoniens," *RES*, I, Pt. 1, vi–xiv. He was supported by scholars of the rank of R. Dussaud who even in the 1941 edition of *Les Découvertes de Ras Shamra (Ugarit) et l'Ancien Testament* still adhered to this interpretation. On the other hand, Cyrus H. Gordon, after close examination of the respective passages (*The Birth of the Beautiful and Gracious Gods*, 64) came to the sweeping conclusion that "there is no valid evidence pointing to the mention of Terah in any Ras Shamra text published so far" ("TRḤ, ṮN and NKR in the Ras Shamra Tablets," *JBL*, LVII, 410). Gordon's views are shared by such other specialists as Albright and H. L. Ginsberg (cf. the latter's edition and transl. of *The Legend of King Keret*, verses 100 ff., pp. 16, 38), who, by the way, also deny any mention of Asher and Zebulun in these Ugaritic tablets. Incidentally, the word *Terah* found on eight or nine Safaitic inscriptions of some twelve centuries later has likewise been explained as a common noun by G. Ryckmans in his "Nom propre Teraḥ est-il attesté en safaïtique?" *RB*, LVI, 579–82. Cf. also R. de Langhe's independent interpretation of the pertinent passages in his comprehensive *Textes de Râs Shamra-Ugarit et leurs rapports avec le milieu biblique de l'Ancien Testament;* R. de Vaux's brief survey, "Les Patriarches hébreux et les découvertes modernes," *RB*, LIII, 321–48; LV, 321–47; and *infra*, n. 21.

5. The identity of the *Ḥabiru* with the biblical *'Ibrim* (Hebrews), for a while almost universally accepted, was again vigorously debated several years ago. The older data and views are well summarized in the discussions of E. Chiera, H. Parzen, and J. A. Wilson in *AJSL*, XLIX, 115–24, 254–61, 275–80; and M. Noth's "Erwägungen zur Hebräerfrage" in *Festschrift Otto Procksch*, pp. 99–112. However, the cumulative evidence of Nuzi and other tablets, reflecting the Ḥabiru status as that of an under-privileged class, rather than an ethnic group, has raised new questions. While M. Burrows could write in 1941 "that the words Ḥabiru and Hebrew are identical in origin is now generally agreed" (*What Mean These Stones?*, p. 92), A. Alt had already advised in 1939 the complete divorce of the problem of the Israelite conquest of Palestine from that of the Ḥabiru. See Alt's remarks in *PJB*, XXXV, 60. Some scholars, stressing the original meaning of Ḥabiru as the equivalent of raiders, treated them as a social class rather than an ethnic group, forgetting that ethnic names had often originated from characteristics prominently associated in the mind of neighbors with particular occupations. For example, E. Speiser and B. Maisler have shown that the name "Canaan" owes its origin to early Nuzi and Egyptian identification of the inhabitants of Palestine and southern Syria with a prominent class of traders. In fact, *kina*, originally meaning merchandise, became later identified particularly with "red purple" which, subsequently known under the name *phoinos*, became also the source of the ethnic designation, Phoenicians. Cf. Maisler's "Canaan and the Canaanites," *BASOR*, 102, pp. 7–12; and T. J. Meek's *Hebrew Origins*, rev. ed., pp. 1–45.

The debate received a new impetus when Virolleaud discovered a reference to *Ḥapiri*, rather than *Ḥabiri*, in a Ugaritic document. Because of this spelling he and E. G. Kraeling denounced altogether the possibility of any philological equation with *'ibri*. See Kraeling's "Origin of the Name 'Hebrews,'" *AJSL*, LVIII, 237–53. This philological argument is vitiated, however, by the fact that the Ugaritic texts them-selves seem to use both forms interchangeably. Cf. Julius Lewy's "New Parallel be-tween Ḥabirū and Hebrews," *HUCA*, XV, 48 n. 7; and H. H. Rowley's "Ḥabiru and Hebrews," *PEQ*, 1942, pp. 41–53. We may add that in medieval Hebrew such inter-changeable use in names became very frequent. For one example, when a controversy broke out between two Polish families descended from Meir Katzenellenbogen, a famous fifteenth-century rabbi of Padua, the Council of the Four Lands allegedly decided that only Meir's descendants by male line be entitled to use the customary spelling, whereas the others should spell their name Katzenellenpogen. See the text published by A. A. Harkavy in *Ḥadashim gam yeshanim* (New and Old, II, 3; Supplement to the Hebrew transl. of Graetz's *Geschichte*, VII, 44). Certainly if one finds in many medieval Hebrew sources the city of Heilbronn spelled *Heilpronn* (with many such family derivatives as Halpern still in common use today), one need not look for some other locality. Even Rowley, however, later came to the conclusion that "the Habiru of the Amarna letters were Hebrews, but not those led by Joshua." See his *Re-discovery*, pp. 62 f. Cf. also E. Dhorme's "Question de Ḥabiri," *RHR*, CXVIII, 170–87; Julius Lewy's "Habiru and Hebrews," *HUCA*, XIV, 587–623 (Lewy's thesis that Ḥabiru as unfree workers in Nuzi are a close parallel to the "Hebrew slave" of Exod. 21:2–6 is reinforced by an old Babylonian document in J. B. Alexander's *Early Babylonian Letters and Economic Texts*, No. 93); M. Noth's "Syrisch-palästinische Bevölkerung des zweiten Jahrtausends v. Chr.," *ZDPV*, LXV, 12–15, 20–34; his "Herrenschicht von Ugarit im 15–14. Jahrhundert v. Chr.," *ibid.*, pp. 144–64; De Langhe's *Textes*, II, 254 ff.; S. I. Feigin's "Hebrews in Cuneiform Inscriptions" (Hebrew), *SH*, VIII–IX, 221–39; Kaufmann's *Toledot*, III, 8 ff., 328 ff.; and A. Guillaume's somewhat far-fetched study of "Habiru, the Hebrews and the Arabs," *PEQ*, 1946, pp. 64–85.

6. The perennial story of the action and counteraction between Egypt and Asia is summarized by J. Wilson in his "Egyptian Middle Kingdom at Megiddo," *AJSL*, LVIII, 225: "The late predynastic age showed strong Asiatic influences coming into the land of the Nile. Then the old Kingdom exploited Sinai, Phoenicia and perhaps Palestine economically. In the First Intermediate Period Asiatics invaded the Egyptian Delta. The Middle Kingdom moved again into Asia in some measure and with some authority. The Second Intermediate Period saw the Hyksos invasion of Egypt. The New Kingdom set up an Egyptian Empire in Asia. The balance swung again with attempted invasions of Egypt in the thirteenth and twelfth centuries B.C." Among more recent discussions of the Hyksos problem as related to ancient Israelitic history are R. Dussaud's "Quelques précisions touchant les Hyksos," *RHR*, CIX, 113–28; and particularly R. M. Engberg's *Hyksos Reconsidered*. The duration of their reign in Egypt has been reduced to but 108 years, as a result of G. Farina's careful investigation of the Turin papyrus in *Il Papiro dei re*, and is now dated in the years 1675–1567 by H. E. Winlock in *The Rise and Fall of the Middle Kingdom in Thebes*, pp. 104 ff. Cf. also H. Stock's *Studien zur Geschichte und Archäologie der 13. bis 17. Dynastie Aegyptens;* J. Vandier's review thereof in *Journal des savants*, 1944, pp. 154–68; and B. Maisler's "Palestine at the Time of the Middle Kingdom in Egypt," *Revue de l'histoire juive en Egypte*, I, 33–68.

7. Cf. H. Grimme's *Altsinaitische Forschungen*, particularly; pp. 23, 88 f., Nos. 358, 369; and the sociological interpretation of these inscriptions in Helling's *Frühgeschichte*, pp. 120 ff. For entirely different readings, however, cf., e.g., J. Leibovitch's *Inscriptions protosinaïtiques* (denying altogether their Semitic character); W. F. Albright's "Some Suggestions for the Decipherment of the Proto-Sinaitic Inscriptions," *JPOS*, XV, 334–40 (defending their connection with Semitic languages but admitting that they are still largely illegible); and his wholly negative review of Grimme's volume in *JQR*, XXVIII, 333–35. Albright's own new decipherment arrived at during a recent visit on Sinai is now eagerly awaited. Cf. his "Early Alphabetic Inscriptions from Sinai and Their Decipherment," *BASOR*, 110, pp. 6–22 (he considers them written in the ordinary Canaanite language and script of the early 15th cent. B.C.E.). In the meantime, cf. also J. Černý's "Semites in Egyptian Mining Expeditions to Sinai," *Archiv orientalni*, VII, 384–89; S. Yeivin's "Palestino-Sinaitic Inscriptions" (Hebrew), *BJPES*, V, 1–10; H. Grimme's "Südpalestinensische Inschriften in altsinaitischer Schriftform," *Muséon*, LV, 45–60; his "Aussehen und Aufschrift der mosaischen Gesetzestafeln," *Nieuwe theologische Studiën*, XXV, 81–90; H. G. May's

"Moses and the Sinai Inscriptions," *BA*, VIII, 93–99; and J. Boüüaert's survey of "Nouvelles hypothèses concernant la constitution de l'alphabet proto-sinaïtique et des alphabets grecs," *Antiquité classique*, XIV, 331–51.

8. Text translated by B. Gunn and A. H. Gardiner in their "Expulsion of the Hyksos," *JEA*, V, 55. Despite the translators' warning against the use of this much-damaged inscription as basic evidence, it clearly indicates that religious restoration went hand in hand with that in the political sphere. It is also borne out by the more recently published inscription praising Ḥatshepsut as one "who builds our temples, who restores our fanes, who renews our altars, she who is beloved by us." Cf. H. W. Fairman and B. Grdseloff's "Texts of Ḥatshepsut and Sethos I inside Speos Artemidos," *JEA*, XXXIII, 17. The propagation, by the Hyksos, of the worship of Seth, the Egyptian counterpart to the Canaanite Baal, has long been recognized as an attempt to harmonize Egyptian worship with their own. Because of this religious antagonism A. S. Yahuda combated the old hypothesis of Joseph's spectacular Egyptian career having been made possible by the Hyksos regime. See his *Accuracy of the Bible*, pp. 52 ff. However, his main argument that the biblical narratives reflect a truly Egyptian, rather than Hyksos, setting is weakened by the general historical observation that conquerors, if culturally inferior, are apt speedily to forego their racial and religious separation and to become absorbed by the superior culture of the native majority. Despite the persistence of western Semitic names among the Hyksos rulers, therefore, it is not surprising to find this process of speedy amalgamation well attested by the sources. Cf. Albright, *Stone Age*, p. 323, n. 4.

9. The identity of several Semitic localities in the Delta region and the existence of a locality "Goshen" in southern Palestine as well is discussed by W. F. Albright in "The Town of Selle (Zaru) in the Amarnah Tablets," *JEA*, X, 7 f. Cf. also his review of Abel's *Géographie*, II, in *JBL*, LVIII, 186 f.; such works by P. Montet, the chief excavator, as *Le Drame d'Avaris, essai sur la pénétration des Sémites en Egypte*, and *Tanis, douze années des fouilles dans une capitale oubliée du Delta égyptien;* and H. Kees's "Tanis. Ein kritischer Ueberblick," *Nachrichten von der Akad. der Wiss. Göttingen*, 1944, pp. 145–82.

10. Albright's *Stone Age*, pp. 183 f., 193 ff. Cf. also B. Couroyer's "Résidence ramesside du Delta et le Ramsès biblique," *RB*, LIII, 75–98. Perhaps more attention than hitherto should be paid in this connection to the account of the Hellenistic Jewish historian Artapanus. Living in pre-Christian Alexandria, Artapanus, like Manethon, may well have had at his disposal sources of information which were not available even to the ancient Palestinian writers, Jewish or Christian. Though disfigured by many fanciful accretions and etymologies (particularly with reference to Moses) and frequently colored by the author's obvious syncretistic and apologetic biases, his story measures up to historical facts and probabilities no less well than similar accounts by other Hellenistic writers. When he tells us, for instance, that Abraham spent twenty years in Egypt and that, after his return to Syria, many of his followers remained behind in Egypt because of the country's fertility, he seems to reflect some authentic tradition. So does his statement that the Hebrews—whom he twice calls *Ermiuth* or *Hermiuth*, possibly a bad corruption from *Apiru*—settled in the "city" of Kessan (Goshen; Manethon, too, speaks of a "city" only) and built temples in Athos and Heliopolis. One wonders whether Athos, which has baffled commentators, is not really some historic reminiscence of both Avaris and Tanis. Cf. the text in J. Freudenthal's *Alexander Polyhistor*, pp. 231 ff. It is also noteworthy that later rabbinic tradition seems to have retained a dim recollection of certain relationships between the free Hebrew settlers in Palestine and their oppressed brethren in Egypt. Cf. S. Krauss's "Exodus vor dem biblischen Exodus," *WZKM*, XXXVIII, 76–90.

The reference here and in several other connections to legends which first appear in the literature of the late pre-Christian or Christian era need not be as pointless as it might appear from the time lag between event and record. Biblical narratives and laws, too, are often based on traditions carried orally for several centuries. They have nevertheless stood up remarkably well against whatever external evidence had become available in recent decades. The "form critics," in particular, have made the fully justified effort to detect such oral traditions behind both the Old and the New Testament texts. Cf. also, e.g., S. Mowinckel's recent studies, *Zur Frage nach dokumentarischen Quellen in Josua 13–19,* and *Prophecy and Tradition.* The mere length of the period of oral transmission down the Hellenistic or rabbinic age need not completely vitiate its value for historical research in view of the great tenacity of oral traditions in all ancient civilizations and their frequently surprising historical accuracy. Cf. in particular, H. W. Hertzberg's "Tradition in Palästina," *PJB,* XXII, 84–104; S. Gandz's "Dawn of Literature, Prolegomena to a History of Unwritten Literature," *Osiris,* VII, 261–522; and H. Birkeland's *Zum hebräischen Traditionswesen.* To be sure, like his teacher, H. S. Nyberg, Birkeland goes to the extreme of postulating that most preëxilic "writings" owed their origin to oral transmission. Cf. J. van der Ploeg's legitimate reservations in "Le Rôle de la tradition orale dans la transmission du texte de l'Ancien Testament," *RB,* LIV, 5–41. Cf. also H. Ringgren's "Oral and Written Transmission in the Old Testament," *Studia theologica,* III, 34–59. But this is no reflection on either the vast range or the general dependability of the ancient oral traditions. There certainly are kernels of good historic recollection even in the "Rabbinische Nachrichten über das alte Aegypten," analyzed by S. Krauss in the *Mahler Jub. Vol.,* pp. 446–63, although, of course, such late records must be used with the utmost caution. Cf. also *infra,* Chap. XV, n. 3.

11. Cf. especially G. Posener's *Princes et pays d'Asie et de Nubie, Textes hiératiques* (showing close Egyptian relationships with Palestine and Syria before 1800); G. Steindorff and K. C. Seele's *When Egypt Ruled the East;* and Albright's notes on Posener's work in *BASOR,* 81, pp. 16–21. Cf. also the complementary studies by J. Simons, *Handbook for the Study of Egyptian Topographical Lists Relating to Western Asia;* A. Jirku, *Die ägyptischen Listen palästinensischer und syrischer Ortsnamen;* M. Noth, "Die Wege der Pharaonenheere in Palästina und Syrien," *ZDPV,* Vols. LX, LXI, LXIV; and E. de Martonne, "Reconnaissance géographique au Sinaï," *Bulletin de la Société r. de géographie d'Égypte,* XXII, 105–36. The Egyptian names in Moses' family are discussed by T. J. Meek in his "Moses and the Levites," *AJSL,* LVI, 113–20.

Our reconstruction of Israel's sojourn in Egypt, though suggested here with considerable diffidence because of the nearly total absence of reliable sources, seems to resolve a great many difficulties and to reconcile most contradictions, apparent as well as real, in the few extant data. There is a real dearth of monographic treatment of this vitally significant phase of Israelitic history since A. Mallon's *Les Hébreux en Égypte;* and T. E. Peet's *Egypt and the Old Testament,* large sections of which are now obsolete. Most recent studies (e.g., H. H. Rowley's "Israel's Sojourn in Egypt," *BJRL,* XXII, 243–90) limit themselves to an examination of the chronological framework. For Helling's more searching inquiry, cf. *supra,* n. 3.

12. Gen. 24:3, 25:1–6, 38:2–6, 41:45 and 50, 46:10; Exod. 2:21–22, 6:15, 18:2–5. Cf. E. A. Speiser's *Ethnic Movements in the Near East in the Second Millennium B.C.;* and F. Stähelin's brief sketch of "Völker und Völkerwanderungen im alten Orient," *Schweizer Beiträge zur allgemeinen Geschichte,* I, 8–33. Recent craniological investigations have also disproved Von Luschan's long widely accepted view that the populations of the ancient Near East had been predominantly brachycephalic. An examination of 92 skulls from that region dating from the tenth to the eighth centuries

B.C.E. showed 44 long as against 26 medium and but 22 short heads. Cf. M. R. Sauter's "Races brachycéphales du Proche Orient des origines à nos jours," *Archives suisses d'anthropologie générale*, XI, 68–131.

13. The early relations between Palestine and Phoenicia are now emerging from age-old obscurity. Cf. in particular Albright's aforementioned essay in *Studies in the History of Culture*, and his "New Light on the Early History of Phoenician Civilization," *BASOR*, 83, pp. 14–22. Cf. also R. Weill's *Phoenicia and Western Asia;* O. Eissfeldt's *Ras Shamra und Sanchunjaton;* and "Phoiniker und Phoinikia" in *PWRE*, XX, Pt. 1, pp. 350–80; G. Bonfante's "Name of the Phoenicians," *Classical Philology*, XXXVI, 1–20; A. Garcia y Bellido's *Fenicios y Carthagineses en Occidente;* and R. Dussaud's *Religions des Hittites, et des Hourrites, des Phéniciens et des Syriens.*

Amazing progress has been made in the last two decades as a result of the great discoveries of Schaeffer and Chenet at Ras Shamra (Ugarit) and Minet el-Beida in northern Syria. The twelfth-century Canaanite library unearthed there has furnished much unexpected vital information. The publication of large Ugaritic epics and many administrative documents dating from 1400–1200 by C. Virolleaud has already revolutionized our views on many phases of biblical mythology and custom. Cf. especially his important publications and announcements in *Syria*. The earlier publications, which included the comprehensive works by J. A. Montgomery and Z. S. Harris, *The Ras Shamra Mythological Texts;* H. L. Ginsberg, *Kitbe Ugarit* (The Ugarit Texts); and Virolleaud, *La Légende phénicienne de Danel; La Légende de Kéret;* and *La Déesse 'Anat* are fully listed by the chief excavator, C. F. A. Schaeffer, in his *Ugaritica: Etudes relatives aux découvertes de Ras Shamra*, I, 147 ff. Cf. also Schaeffer's more recent report in his *Ugaritica*, II.

The texts as well as the underlying philological and historical problems were immediately subjected to an ever closer scrutiny by other scholars. More recent monographs include Virolleaud's summary of the historical significance of his earlier publications in "Les Poèmes de Ras-Shamra," *Revue historique*, CLXXXV, 1–22; Z. S. Harris's *Development of the Canaanite Dialects;* O. Eissfeldt's "Zum geographischen Horizont der Ras-Schamra-Texte," *ZDMG*, XCIV, 59–85, and his "Bestand und Benennung der Ras Schamra Texte," *ibid.*, XCVI, 507–39; H. L. Ginsberg's *Keret;* and, particularly, De Langhe's *Textes;* J. Obermann's *Ugaritic Mythology;* C. H. Gordon's *Ugaritic Handbook;* and his *Ugaritic Literature* (offering the fullest translation of texts hitherto published). The latter four also list the numerous detailed reconstructions of various texts suggested by Albright, Gaster, Ginsberg, Goetze, Pedersen, and others. Cf. also T. H. Gaster's comparative study, *Thespis;* H. E. Del Medico's French transl. of *La Bible cananéenne découverte dans les textes de Ras Shamra;* A. Herdner's "Légende cananéenne d'Aqhat d'après les travaux récents," *Syria*, XXVI, 1–16; C. Virolleaud's semipopular survey of *Légendes de Babylone et de Canaan;* and O. Eissfeldt's analysis of the "Bedeutung der Funde von Ras Schamra für die Geschichte des Altertums," *HZ*, CLXVIII, 457–86. The ever-growing epigraphic material was collected in 1942 by N. Slouschz in his *Oṣar ha-ketobot ha-feniqiot* (Thesaurus of Phoenician Inscriptions); and commented on, among others, by A. Mentz in his *Beiträge zur Deutung der phönizischen Inschriften;* and by W. F. Albright in his "Phoenician Inscriptions of the Tenth Century B.C. from Byblus," *JAOS*, LXVII, 153–60.

Of greatest interest to scholars and general public alike were, of course, the relationships between these newly discovered religious and cultural data and Old Testament literature and religion. Apart from De Langhe's voluminous and painstaking *Textes*, cf. especially the revised ed. of Dussaud's *Découvertes de Ras Shamra;* H. L. Ginsberg's "Ugaritic Texts and Textual Criticism," *JBL*, LXII, 109–15, and "Ugaritic Studies and the Bible," *BA*, VIII, 41–58; U. Cassuto's "Biblical Literature and Canaanite Literature" (Hebrew), *Tarbiz*, XIII, 197–212, XIV, 1–10; J. H. Patton's *Canaanite Parallels to the Book of Psalms;* and such detailed comparative studies as

O. Eissfeldt's "Ba'alšamēm und Jahwe," *ZAW*, LVII, 1–31; W. F. Albright's "Are the Ephod and Teraphim Mentioned in Ugaritic Literature?" *BASOR*, 83, pp. 39–42; and S. Spiegel's "Noah, Danel and Job Touching on Canaanite Relics in the Legends of the Jews," *Ginzberg Jub. Vol.*, pp. 305–55. Kaufmann has rightly pointed out that this triad of ancient sages, mentioned by Ezekiel (14:14, 20), well mirrors the three main traditions which together built the Israelitic culture: Noah represents the Babylonian heritage; Job is the spokesman of the ancient Hebrew (Edomite, Aramaean) tradition; while Danel personifies the influx of Canaanite ideas. See Kaufmann's *Toledot*, II, 21.

The fascinating story of the gradual and independent deciphering of the approximately thirty letter signs of the Ugaritic alphabet by H. Bauer and E. Dhorme is told by the latter in *JPOS*, XI, 1–6; and by Bauer in *Das Alphabet von Ras-Schamra*. The importance of these and other recent finds for the history of writing is fully discussed in D. Diringer's *Alphabet*. More recently, H. Tur-Sinai (Torczyner) tried in several essays to prove the Israelitic origin of the Hebrew-Phoenician alphabet, at least with respect to the names and order of the letters. See especially his "Origin of the Alphabet," *JQR*, XLI, 83–109, 159–79, 277–301. This view was sharply repudiated, however, by W. F. Albright in his review of "Some Important Recent Discoveries," *BASOR*, 118, pp. 11 ff. Both Tur-Sinai (in a postscript) and Albright took note of the significant discovery, by Schaeffer in 1949, of a Ugaritic alphabet of the fourteenth century or earlier. Cf. E. A. Speiser's brief "Note on Alphabetic Origins," *BASOR*, 121, pp. 17–21. Cf. also K. Sethe's *Vom Bilde zum Buchstaben*, with O. Krückmann's detailed comments thereon in *Orientalia*, X, 254–71; S. Yeivin's *Toledot ha-ketab ha-'ibri* (History of the Jewish Script); M. Dunand's *Byblia grammata*; B. Maisler's "Phoenician Inscriptions from Byblos and the Evolution of the Alphabetical Phoenician-Hebrew Script" (Hebrew), *Leshonenu*, XIV, 166–81; and G. R. Driver's *Semitic Writing from Pictograph to Alphabet*, and, on the persistence of the "Early Hebrew Writing" beyond the rise of Christianity, Diringer's data in *BA*, XIII, 74–95.

14. The date of the Exodus is still highly controversial. While many scholars cling to the dating during the reign of Merneptah (about 1230), an increasing number of archaeologists are inclined to put it in the fifteenth century. J. Garstang, for instance, suggested 1407 as the date of the conquest of Jericho by Joshua. See his *Joshua-Judges*. Notwithstanding their serious methodological shortcomings, pointed out by A. Alt in his review in *JPOS*, XII, 172–80, Garstang's investigations have made a strong impression. On these and other grounds T. H. Robinson (*History of Israel*, I, 80) decided that "the date of the Exodus can hardly have been later than the early part of the fifteenth century." A. Lucas, adding the forty years of the desert migration to Garstang's date of the fall of Jericho, concluded that 1446 was the precise "Date of the Exodus" (*PEQ*, 1941, pp. 110–21; cf. also H. H. Rowley's reply, *ibid.*, pp. 152–57). A. S. Yahuda accepted 1445 in his Hebrew essay in *SH*, VII, 126–35.

On the other hand, the eminent Palestinian archaeologist Père L. H. Vincent, after careful reëxamination of the available evidence, particularly the unearthed pottery, has consistently advocated 1250 as the most likely date of Jericho's fall. See especially his "Jericho et sa chronologie," *RB*, XLIV, 583–605. Moreover, beginning in 1934 several expeditions of the American Schools of Oriental Research in Jerusalem, headed by N. Glueck, have shown that Transjordan, which had had a flourishing civilization before 1900, had almost become a wasteland in the subsequent centuries and that the Edomite and Moabite settlement in southeastern Palestine did not precede the thirteenth century. Consequently, Numbers 20:14–21, etc., could record events of that century only. Cf. N. Glueck's "Explorations in Eastern Palestine," *AASOR*, XIV, 1–113, XV, XVIII–XIX; his *Other Side of the Jordan* and *River Jordan*. On these and other grounds, Albright suggested the separation of the conquest of Jericho, which he placed at some time between 1375 and 1300, from the story of the Exodus. Counting back from the Merneptah stele's mention of "Israel" in 1229, he added the forty years of desert migration and further time for the slow conquest of Transjordan. He computed, therefore, the Israelite departure from Egypt at about 1290. Cf. his "Israelite Conquest of Canaan in the Light of Archaeology," *BASOR*, 74, pp. 11–23, and *Stone Age*, pp. 194 f. Cf. also G. E. Wright's "Epic of Conquest," *BA*, III, 25–40, and "Two Misunderstood Items in the Exodus-Conquest Cycle," *BASOR*, 86, pp. 32–35; J. and J. B. E. Garstang's *Story of Jericho*, rev. ed. (prepared to lower the date to "any year between 1400 and 1385" [p. 135], though not yet accepting Albright's chronology of 1375–1300 for Jericho's fall); A. Servin's careful review of "La Tradition judéo-chrétienne de l'Exode," *Bulletin de l'Institut d'Egypte*, XXXI, 315–55 (the texts have decided historical value); and A. Shafei's "Historical Notes on the Pelusian Branch, the Red Sea Canal and the Route of the Exodus," *Bulletin de la Société royale de géographie d'Egypte*, XXI, 231–87 (proves the location of Yam Suf east of Zoan-Tanis). Cf. also B. Weitzel's "Era of the Exodus in the Talmud," *Mizraim*, VIII, 15–19; and, for the geographic aspects, A. Lucas's *Route of the Exodus of the Israelites from Egypt*, and M. Noth's "Wahlfahrtsweg zum Sinai," *PJB*, XXXVI, 5–28 (concluding that Num. 33:3–49 is based on independent older sources). For the purposes of our discussion the decision between the conflicting chronologies may be left in abeyance until new and more decisive evidence is forthcoming.

On Israel's settlement in Canaan, see in particular A. Alt's *Landnahme der Israeliten in Palästina*, showing the gradual process of Israelite penetration. Alt has also pointed out that, by its very nature, an archaeological excavation could reveal only traces of permanent destruction, i.e., some catastrophic interruption in historic continuity. The latter need not, in all cases, reflect Israelitic conquest, for considerable destruction was also wrought by the recurrent Egyptian expeditions, Philistine invasions and the constant internecine struggles among the Canaanite rulers themselves. Moreover, the Israelites may have been peacefully established in a city's vicinity for several generations before they felt strong enough, or were provoked by some hostile act, to attack it. Cf. Alt's remarks in *PJB*, XXXV, 40 ff.; R. M. Engberg's "Historical Analysis of Archaeological Evidence: Megiddo and the Song of Deborah," *BASOR*, 78, pp. 4–7; and Albright's remarks thereon, *ibid.*, pp. 7–9. The opposite is represented by Y. Kaufmann who, accepting the late days of Merneptah and his weak successors as the best date for a speedy conquest, pointed out that only a sudden overpowering of the Canaanite natives by the Israelitic tribes would account for the negligible military role played by the former in the subsequent Israelitic campaigns, as well as for the absence of both internecine struggles and covenants among the conquerors concerning the possession of disputed areas (*Toledot*, II, 308 ff.). These arguments, however, do not suffice to invalidate the widely held view that Palestine's conquest was accomplished in successive stages extending over several centuries. Cf. the extensive literature listed in H. H. Rowley's *From Joseph to Joshua*.

15. "Canaanite, Amorite and Accadian deities," says W. F. Albright, "were exchanged and identified to a disconcerting degree. Gods like Hadad and Dagan, Asherat (Asherah) and Astarte (Ishtar) were worshipped in the second millennium from the Delta of Egypt to the mountains of Iran" (*JBL*, LIX, 108). Cf. A. Bertholet's *Götterspaltung und Göttervereinigung* and O. Eissfeldt's "Wanderung palästinisch-syrischer Götter nach Ost und West im zweiten vorchristlichen Jahrtausend," *JPOS*, XIV, 294–300. The final act of unification may, indeed, have come about in the covenant concluded at Shechem. Here Joshua is said to have bluntly placed before the Israelites the alternative, "And if it seem evil unto you to serve the Lord, choose you this day whom ye will serve; whether the gods which your fathers served that were beyond the River, or the gods of the Amorites, in whose land ye dwell; but as for me and my house, we will serve the Lord" (Josh. 24:15). Cf. Sellin's *Geschichte*, I, 97 ff.; M. Noth's *Buch Josua*, pp. 105 ff.; and *infra*, Chap. III, n. 15.

Exod. 6:3 has, of course, been subjected to a variety of interpretations. Some scholars explained it altogether as a later reconstruction by the "Elohistic" author. However, no conclusive argument has yet been advanced against the traditional interpretation that only the patriarchs were unfamiliar with this divine name adopted by Moses. The prevalent critical view, moreover, concerning the theology of the Elohist appears considerably weakened as a result of U. Cassuto's analysis in his *Questione della Genesi* and *Torat ha-te'udot* (The Documentary Hypothesis and the Arrangement of the Pentateuch). Cassuto's criticism of the accepted views is frequently valid, even where his own constructive suggestions may appear equally untenable. Cf. also P. Volz and W. Rudolph's analysis of *Der Elohist als Erzähler, ein Irrweg der Pentateuch-kritik?*; supplemented by Rudolph in *"Der Elohist" von Exodus bis Josua*. In fact, the ready acceptance of the divine name YHWH by all the tribes would be even more astonishing if, as some scholars assume, that name had been known and worshiped by many non-Israelitic peoples for centuries before Moses. Cf. the various theories mentioned by K. G. Kuhn in his "Ueber die Entstehung des Namens Jahwe," *Fest-schrift für Enno Littman*, pp. 25–42. The discovery of a deity YW, son of El, in the pantheon of Ras Shamra, if indeed this be the meaning of the questionable passage, has made it still less likely that the YA-compounds found outside of Israel were abbreviations of YHWH, and has strengthened the hypothesis that we are here confronted by a strange historical coincidence. Cf. H. Bauer, "Die Gottheiten von Ras Shamra," *ZAW*, LI, 92. On different readings, cf. A. Bea's "Archäologisches und Religions-geschichtliches aus Ugarit-Ras-Šamra," *Biblica*, XX, 440 f.; Albright's *Stone Age*, p. 197. Cf. also *supra*, Chap. I, n. 5.

16. The El-Amarna letters which, ever since their discovery in 1887, have thrown so much light on the period of Egypt's prolonged regime in Palestine, have been subjected to renewed scrutiny in recent years. S. A. B. Mercer published the first full English transl. of all *The Tell el-Amarna Tablets* which, though subjected to severe criticisms by such reviewers as W. F. Albright (in *JBL*, LIX, 313–15) and C. J. Gadd (*PEQ*, 1940, pp. 116–23), has at least the advantage of ready accessibility. Eight additional tablets, recovered from that Egyptian archive by J. D. S. Pendle-bury in 1933 have recently been analyzed by C. H. Gordon in his "New Amarna Tablets," *Orientalia*, XVI, 1–21 (also listing all letters previously published). There is no complete agreement, however, on the date of most of these important documents. While Albright is inclined to place a great many at a relatively late date (cf. especially "The Egyptian Correspondence of Abimilki, Prince of Tyre," *JEA*, XXIII, 190–203), W. Riedel has vigorously defended at least the earlier dating of the letters from Babel ("Archiv Amenophis IV," *OLZ*, XLII, 145–48). Cf. also J. Sturm's "Zur Datierung der El-Amarna Briefe," *Klio*, XXVI, 1–28; Albright's general remarks in his "Two Little Understood Amarna Letters from the Middle Jordan Valley," *BASOR*, 89, pp. 7–17 (referring to Knudtzon, Nos. 256, 274); and, especially, the detailed *Studien over de El-Amarna brieven en het Oude-Testament* by J. de Koning. The general historical situation is analyzed in J. Baikie's *Amarna Age: a Study of the Crisis of the Ancient World*; J. D. S. Pendlebury's *Tell el Amarna*; and S. Furlani's "Cor-rispondenza diplomatica del II millennio a.C.," *Nuova Rivista storica*, XXX, 1–26.

17. Gen. 43:32. The explanation, given by the Targum (*ad loc.*), that the Egyptians resented the Israelites' consumption of their sacred animals may be a later Hellenistic rationalization, but it reflects some of the difficulties which must have arisen because of that ritualistic disparity.

18. Origin and meaning of this name, long debated by scholars, have been sub-jected to renewed careful scrutiny by G. A. Danell in his *Studies in the Name Israel in the Old Testament*. The widespread assumption that the name is of Canaanite origin is flatly contradicted by R. Marcus who considers its integral "s" sound char-acteristically Amorite or Proto-Aramaic and, hence, evidently brought by the Israelites

into their country of adoption. See his "Hebrew Sibilant Śin and the Name Yiśrael,"
JBL, LX, 141–50. Cf. also L. Rost's Israel bei den Propheten; and, for the etymology
(Yisrael = God Heals), W. F. Albright's "Names 'Israel' and 'Judah' with an Excursus
on the Etymology of todah and torah," JBL, XLVI, 151–85. The pairing of the names
Jacob-Israel, although going far beyond the similar equations of Abram-Abraham and
Sarah-Sarai, may well reflect the writer's propensity for double names encountered in
many literatures. Cf. the parallels assembled by Dornseiff in ZAW, LII, 60.

19. Cf. S. A. Cook's remarks, from another angle, in "The 'Evolution' of Biblical Religion," Modern Churchman, XXIV, 471–84; F. Boschwitz's keen analysis of Julius
Wellhausen. Motive und Masstäbe seiner Geschichtsschreibung; and F. Helling's
Frühgeschichte, pp. 27 ff. In his Beduinentum und Jahwismus, however, S. Nyström
still follows largely the earlier view, while E. König goes to the other extreme in
his attack, Ist die moderne Pentateuchkritik auf Tatsachen begründet?.

20. Cf. D. Nielsen's suggestive essay, "Die altsemitische Muttergöttin," ZDMG,
XCII, 504–51; and L. Franz's brief survey of Die Muttergöttin im Vorderen Orient
und in Europa. Recent Palestinian excavations have shown that even among the
Canaanites these female figurines may have been semimagical implements (intended to
help, for example, a childbearing woman during her hour of trial) rather than ob-
jects of worship. Cf. W. F. Albright's "Astarte Plaques and Figurines from Tell Beit
Mirsim," Mélanges Dussaud, I, 107–20; his Archaeology and Religion, pp. 114 f.; J. B.
Pritchard's Palestinian Figurines in Relation to Certain Goddesses Known through
Literature; and G. E. Wright's review of this book in JBL, LXIII, 426–30.

The independence of the belief in God's fatherhood from ancestor worship has been
convincingly demonstrated by Count W. W. Baudissin in his Kyrios als Gottesname im
Judentum und seine Stelle in der Religionsgeschichte, III, 336 f. Even scholars who
try to prove the persistence of matriarchal forms of marriage down to the period of
the kings (see J. Morgenstern's "Beena Marriage (Matriarchat) in Ancient Israel,"
ZAW, XLVII, 91–110; XLIX, 46–58) admit that "more and more, even within the
desert, ba'al marriage supplanted beena marriage" (ibid., XLVII, 103). Certainly, the
matriarchal reminiscences preserved in the Old Testament, if any, are purely peripheral. The supremacy of the father within the family, even in the earliest stages of
Israel's history, can hardly be contested. See Jacobson's Social Background, pp. 3 ff.,
28. On the other hand, the survival of certain matriarchal elements in Jewish life
during the postbiblical age and, to a certain extent, even today (e.g., the prohibition
of marriage between an aunt and a nephew and not between an uncle and a niece)
would not seem astonishing if one considers the tenacity of basic social institutions.
Cf. V. Aptowitzer's "Spuren des Matriarchats im jüdischen Schrifttum," HUCA, IV,
207–40, V, 261–97; S. Zuri's "Family Organization" (Hebrew), Ha-Mishpaṭ ha-'Ibri,
IV, 1–25; A. S. Hershberg's "Research in the Ancient Hebrew Family" (Hebrew),
Hatekufah, XXVIII, 348–62; and, on the other hand, W. Koshland's critical remarks
in his Mother-Right and Biblical Judaism, pp. 78 ff. Cf. also P. Koschaker's "Fra-
triarchat, Hausgemeinschaft und Mutterrecht in Keilschriftrechten," Zeitschrift für
Assyriologie, XLI, 1–89; and C. H. Gordon's "Fratriarchy in the Old Testament,"
JBL, LIV, 223–31. We should bear in mind, however, that many of these discussions
have become meaningless in the light of more recent anthropological evaluation of the
primitive institution of matriarchate. Cf. F. Kern's pertinent remarks in his "Mutterrecht—einst und jetzt," TZ, VI, 292–305.

21. A. Alt in his Gott der Väter, p. 67. Still more conservative views are expressed
by I. Rabin in his "Studien zur vormosäischen Gottesvorstellung," Festschrift Breslau,
I, 253–356. Alt's findings were reinforced by significant northern sources discussed in
Julius Lewy's "Textes paléo-assyriens et l'Ancien Testament," RHR, CX, 29–65; and

W. F. Albright pointedly asserted that "in any event, the material presented by Alt and Lewy makes it all but impossible hereafter to regard the tradition about the 'Gods of the Fathers' as late or secondary" ("Names Shaddai and Abram," *JBL*, LIV, 173–204). Alt, Lewy, and Albright have substantially adhered to that position in their subsequent writings. Cf. also F. X. Kortleitner's *Religio a patriarchis Israelitarum exercitata*; H. S. Nyberg's "Studien zum Religionskampf im Alten Testament, I: Der Gott 'Al: Belege und Bedeutung des Namens," *AR*, XXXV, 328–87; R. Weill's "Légende des patriarches et l'histoire," *RES*, 1937, pp. 145–206; H. G. May's "Patriarchal Idea of God," *JBL*, LX, 113–28; and H. H. Rowley's "Recent Discovery and, the Patriarchal Age," *BJRL*, XXXII, 44–79. On the other hand, B. Balscheit's *Alter und Aufkommen des Monotheismus in der israelitischen Religion*, although strongly influenced by Alt, still harps on the somewhat outworn idea of patriarchal and Mosaic "henotheism," as contrasted with the pure monotheism of the later prophets. See also *infra*, n. 33.

22. Cf. the much-debated books by Father W. Schmidt, *Der Ursprung der Gottesidee* and *The Origin and Growth of Religion*; S. A. Cook's defense of the "evolutionary" method against Schmidt's exclusively "ethnological" approach, *JTS*, XXXIII, 1–17; T. J. Meek's "Primitive Monotheism and the Religion of Moses," *RR*, IV, 286–303 (likewise attacking Father Schmidt); and G. van der Leeuw's "Struktur der Vorstellung des sogenannten höchsten Wesens," *AR*, XXIX, 79–107 (showing the structural identity of this primitive god idea with that of the modern deists). Cf. also C. Clemen's interesting survey of three decades of discussion in "Der sog. Monotheismus der Primitiven," *AR*, XXVII, 290–333. Renan's older theory of a specific Semitic primitive monotheism has, however, been rejected by the majority of scholars. Cf. the bibliographical material in D. Nielsen, *et al., Handbuch der altarabischen Altertumskunde*, I, 221 f.

23. It is often suggested that there is a connection between: Laban and *lebanah* (moon); Sarah and Sarrati (an epitheton of the Moon goddess of Haran); Milcah and the royal attributes ascribed to Ishtar all over Babylonia; Terah and *Yareaḥ* (Yerah, moon); and between Abram, which apparently means the "father is exalted" (A. Reubeni, *Shem, Ḥam ve-Yafet*, pp. 49 ff.), or the "father's beloved" (E. Dhorme's "Abraham dans le cadre de l'histoire," *RB*, XL, 368 n. 2), or "he is exalted with respect to father—he is of distinguished lineage" (W. F. Albright, *JBL*, LIV, 202), and the frequently found father epithet of the Moon god. Cf. A. Jeremias, *Das Alte Testament*, pp. 296 f., and E. Dhorme's *Evolution religieuse d'Israël*, I, 69 ff. This connection remains unimpaired by the controversy over the alleged appearance of Terahites in the Ugaritic poems mentioned *supra*, n. 4. Cf. also M. D. Cassuto's *Mi-Noaḥ 'ad Abraham* (From Noah to Abraham). D. Nielsen goes too far, however, in elevating the Moon god among the early Hebrews to a position of supreme deity of a triad which included also the Sun goddess and their son, Venus. See his suggestive study of *Der dreieinige Gott in religionshistorischer Beleuchtung*. The worship of the "Queen of Heaven," on the other hand, appearing at the end of the First Commonwealth, if it be a moon cult at all, reflected the new influx of Babylonian cults accompanying the military expansion of Assyria and Chaldaea, although some slumbering age-old traditions may thus have suddenly been brought back to life.

24. Cf. H. G. May's "Some Aspects of Solar Worship at Jerusalem," *ZAW*, LV, 269–81; Albright's *Archaeology and Religion*, p. 83. The antecedents of the Egyptian worship of the sun ray, *Aton* have been reëxamined by M. and J. Doresse in "Le Culte d'Aton sous la XVIIIe dynastie avant le schisme amarnien," *Journal asiatique*, CCXXXIII, 181–99. Cf. also L. G. Leeuwenberg's Dutch booklet, *Ekhnaton*; E. Drioton's "Monothéisme de l'ancienne Égypte," *Cahiers d'histoire égyptienne*, I, 149–68.

25. This identification is probably very old, notwithstanding the arguments to the contrary advanced by A. Marmorstein in his *Old Rabbinic Doctrine of God*, I, 45 ff., and "Philo and the Names of God," *JQR*, XXII, 295–306. Cf. also C. H. Gordon's examination, on the basis of Nuzi parallels, of *"Elohim* in its Reputed Meaning of *Rulers, Judges,*" *JBL*, LIV, 139–44; M. H. Segal's analysis of "The Names *YHWH* and *Elohim* in the Books of the Bible" (Hebrew), *Tarbiz*, IX, 123–62 (discussing the frequency of their occurrence and its relevance to biblical history); Segal's "Revelation of the Name YHWH" (Hebrew), *ibid.,* XII, 97–108 (arguing for its pre-Mosaic date); and on the combination of the two divine attributes in rabbinic Judaism, *infra,* Chap. XV, n. 23.

The divine name *Elyon* has received new meaning since the discovery of the Aleyan Epic in Ras Shamra, although the etymology of the latter name still is somewhat dubious. The usual translation of Elyon, however, by "Most High" and its relation to the Greek attribute *hypsistos* in later Hellenistic inscriptions seems clearly indicated. On the assumption that monarchical polytheism centered around the divine name "El" prevailed in Melchizedek's Jerusalem, G. A. Barton suggested that the Ugaritic poem, *The Birth of the Gracious and Beautiful Gods* (first published by Virolleaud in *Syria,* XIV, 128–51) was intended for use there as "A Liturgy for the Celebration of the Spring Festival" (*JBL*, LIII, 61–78). This hypothesis, in itself farfetched, has been further weakened, however, by G. Levi della Vida's discovery in Punic inscriptions of a clear dichotomy between *El,* the god of the earth, and *Elyon,* the god of heaven. He concluded, therefore, that the combination *El Elyon* as a single deity of both heaven and earth originated with the monotheistic author of Gen. 14, whether or not the latter intended to buttress therewith David's claim to the possession of Jerusalem, as proposed by Nyberg. Cf. Della Vida's "El Elyon in Genesis 14¹⁸⁻²⁰," *JBL*, LXIII, 1–9. J. Morgenstern went further and considered Elyon (or Eloah) as but a member of "The Divine Triad in Biblical Mythology," *JBL*, LXIV, 15–37. At the same time, Julius Lewy has consistently espoused the view that the proper name of Melchizedek's god was not *Elyon* at all, but *Shalim* which became an integral part of the name of the city. Cf. his essay in *RHR*, CX, 60 ff., and "The Šulman Temple in Jerusalem," *JBL*, LIX, 519–22. But there is nothing in the evidence invalidating either the ancient origin of Gen. 14 or the probability that Melchizedek worshiped one supreme deity. Nor would the validity of either be impaired by the acceptance of H. H. Rowley's rather implausible combination of "Melchizedek and Zadok" and his dating of both Gen. 14 and Ps. 110 in the period of David's conquest of Jerusalem (*Festschrift Bertholet,* pp. 461–72).

The mysterious personality of the priest of Salem naturally struck the imagination of the later teachers of the synagogue, church, and mosque. The rabbis, homiletically amplifying these biblical statements, even engaged in a controversy as to whether Melchizedek instructed Abraham in the entire Torah or only in the laws concerning the high priesthood. Cf. Gen. r. XLIII, 6–7, pp. 420 f. For further details, cf. L. Ginzberg's *Legends of the Jews*, I, 233, and V, 225, notes 102–3; V. Aptowitzer's "Malkizedek," *MGWJ*, LXX, 93–113; G. Bardy's "Melchisédech dans la tradition patristique," *RB*, XXXV, 496–509, XXXVI, 25–45; G. Wuttke's *Melchisedech;* M. Simon's "Melchisédech dans la polémique entre juifs et chrétiens et dans la légende," *RHPR*, XVII, 58–93; and G. Vajda's "Melchisédec dans la mythologie ismaélinienne," *JA*, CCXXXIV, 173–83.

26. Num. 24:16. This admission becomes even more significant when the present formulation of the legend is ascribed to the highly nationalistic age of Josiah. See S. Mowinckel's "Ursprung der Bil'amsage," *ZAW*, XLVIII, 233–71. W. F. Albright, however, after careful reëxamination of Num. 23–24 and an ingenious reconstruction of the consonantal text, came to the conclusion "that Balaam was really a North-Syrian diviner from the Euphrates Valley, that he spent some time at the Moabite court, that he became a convert to Yahwism, and that he later abandoned Israel and

joined the Midianites in fighting against the Yahwists (Num. 31⁸, ¹⁶). We may also infer that the Oracles preserved in Num. 23–24 were attributed to him from a date as early as the twelfth century, and that there is no reason why they may not be authentic, or may not at least reflect the atmosphere of his age" ("The Oracles of Balaam," *JBL*, LXIII, 207–33). Cf. also A. S. Yahuda's "Name of Balaam's Homeland," *JBL*, LXIV, 547–51.

The impact of the southern tribes on Moses' monotheism (a theory advanced as early as 1862 by Ghillany) was much debated in the first three decades of this century. For a circumspect and, on the whole, approving survey of this vast literature, see L. E. Binns's "Midianite Elements in Hebrew Religion," *JTS*, XXXI, 337–54. A few additional arguments were advanced by H. Schmökel in his "Jahwe und die Keniter," *JBL*, LII, 212–29. It remains true, nevertheless, that "one may learn from the Old Testament the position which it ascribes to the Kenites, but not what they really were or stood for" (W. Vischer in *Jahwe der Gott Kains*, p. 2). Neither has archaeology been able to shed any significant new light; cf. N. Glueck's "Ḳenites and Ḳenizzites," *PEQ*, 1940, pp. 22–24. J. Lewy's suggestion (in his "Influences ḥurrites sur Israël," *RES*, 1938, pp. 49–75) that both the Kenites and Midianites were Hurrians, if true, would merely compound our ignorance of these lesser tribes with that of a large, but no less obscure, ethnic and cultural movement. Cf. also J. Paterson's "Hurrians" in *Studia Semitica et Orientalia*, II (Presentation Volume to W. B. Stevenson), ed. by C. J. M. Weir, pp. 95–115. Nor is the letter unearthed in Taanach, in which the addressee is blessed, "May the Lord of the Gods preserve thy life" (E. Sellin's *Tell-Ta'annek*, p. 115) conclusive in regard to the Canaanite faith, since it may have been written by an early Hebrew settler. However that may be, "it is precisely between 1500 and 1200 B.C., i.e., in the Mosaic age, that we find the closest approach to monotheism in the ancient Gentile world before the Persian period" (Albright, *Archaeology and the Bible*, p. 163).

27. Cf. H. Fredriksson's *Jahwe als Krieger*. Emphasis upon military exploits also displaced the previous pacific penetration in the memory of the people and became the keynote of its historical literature and liturgy, as stressed by G. von Rad in *Das formgeschichtliche Problem des Hexateuchs*, pp. 3 ff., 37 ff., 46 ff., 62 ff., 69 ff.

28. Cf. A. Heidel's careful analyses of *The Babylonian Genesis*, 2d ed.; and *The Gilgamesh Epic and Old Testament Parallels;* U. Cassuto's *Me-Adam ve-'ad Noaḥ* (From Adam to Noah; commentary on Gen. 1:1–6:8); J. Coppens's *Connaissance du bien et du mal et le péché du Paradis* (interpretation of Gen. 2–3); and the debate between S. Mowinckel and Albright on the former's theses concerning "The Two Sources of the Predeuteronomic Primeval History (JE) in Gen. 1–11" in *JBL*, LVII, 230–31, LVIII, 87–103. Cf. also P. Humbert's *Etudes sur le récit du paradis et de la chute dans la Genèse;* and A. Bea's critical review of some "Neuere Probleme und Arbeiten zur biblischen Urgeschichte," *Biblica*, XXV, 70–87.

29. "It is a covenanted society," rightly comments G. E. Wright, "and for it there is no direct Near Eastern parallel" ("How did Early Israel Differ from her Neighbors?" *BA*, VI, 18). The theological and ethical implications of the Old Testament idea of Covenant have been frequently analyzed. Cf., e.g., J. Begrich's "Berit. Ein Beitrag zur Erfassung einer alttestamentlichen Denkform," *ZAW*, LX, 1–10; A. Causse's analysis of "la transformation de la notion d'alliance et la rationalisation de l'ancienne coutume dans le réforme deutéronomique" in his *Du groupe ethnique à la communauté religieuse*, pp. 114 ff.; and B. D. Eerdmans's brief comparative study of the *Covenant at Mount Sinai Viewed in the Light of Antique Thought*. That idea's sociopolitical impact, however, on the ultimate exaltation of the Law and the ever self-rejuvenating egalitarian trends in Jewish society deserves fresh monographic treatment.

30. Unfortunately archaeology has thus far been unable to contribute substantially to the solution of the much-debated problems of Israel's imageless worship and its specific application to the Tabernacle, the Ark, and the oracular lots. No such objects having been identified, we must be satisfied with the always dubious negative evidence. It is, nevertheless, remarkable that, while many male figurines were found in the ruins of the Canaanite cities, not one has so far been dug up in any Israelitic mound. See Wright in *BA*, VI, 16. The meaning of female figurines is discussed *supra*, n. 20. On the basis of much comparative material (including such as had been assembled by Père H. Lammens) J. Morgenstern has reëxamined in detail the biblical records concerning *The Ark, the Ephod and the "Tent of Meeting."* Cf. also H. Thiersch's *Ependytes und Ephod;* N. H. Torczyner's "Urim and Tummim" (Hebrew), *Sefer Zikkaron* (Memorial Volume for the Jewish Theological Seminary in Vienna), ed. by J. Bergmann, *et al.*, pp. 144–54; A. Bentzen's "Cultic Use of the Story of the Ark in Samuel," *JBL*, LXVII, 37–53; F. M. Cross, Jr., "Tabernacle: a Study from an Archaeological and Historical Approach," *BA*, X, 45–68; and, more generally, R. Brinker's *Influence of Sanctuaries in Early Israel;* and W. A. Irwin's "Images of Yahweh," *Crozer Quarterly*, XIX, 292–301. The central position of the prohibition of imagery in the Decalogue is obvious. Catholics, since Augustine, and Lutherans have included it in the first commandment, although Jewish tradition, at least since the days of Philo, also followed by the Greek Orthodox and most Protestant churches as well as by the majority of modern critics, has considered it as the Second Commandment. On its manifold interpretations, cf. W. Zimmerli's "Zweite Gebot," *Festschrift Bertholet*, pp. 550–63.

31. Cf. J. Hempel's succinct analysis of "Die Grenzen des Anthropomorphismus Jahwes im Alten Testament," *ZAW*, LVII, 75–85; and P. Volz's comments on "Die Würde des Menschen im Alten Testament" in *Glaube und Ethos* (Festschrift . . . G. Wehrung), pp. 1–8.

32. Among the representatives of the older school G. A. Barton, for example, contended that the ethical Decalogue was intended to perpetuate the teachings of Elijah, "the second founder of Hebrew religion" (cf. his *Semitic and Hamitic Origins*, pp. 350 ff.), while others dated them as late as the seventh century or even later. Cf. S. Mowinckel's *Décalogue* and "Zur Geschichte der Dekaloge," *ZAW*, LV, 218–35. Various compromise solutions have also been advanced. H. H. Rowley, for example, suggested that the ritual commandments were formulated in more backward Judah during its contacts with its Kenite neighbors, while the ethical decalogue stemmed from the Joseph groups which had participated in the Exodus (*Re-discovery*, pp. 120 f.).

A comprehensive defense, on the other hand, of the Decalogue's Mosaic authorship is offered especially by P. Volz in his *Mose und sein Werk*, 2d ed. Cf. also S. Spiegel's "Prophetic Attestation of the Decalogue: Hosea 6:5," *HTR*, XXVII, 105–44; M. Valentini's "Condizioni sociali del Decalogo e la sua autenticità mosaica," *Salesianum*, I, 407–20; T. C. Vriezen, "Literary and Historical Questions Concerning the Decalogue" (Dutch), *Nieuwe theologische Studiën*, XXII, 2–24, 34–51; and, more generally, M. Buber's *Moses;* and Albright's *Archaeology and the Bible*, pp. 167 f. The distinctiveness of Mosaic monotheism as opposed, for instance, to incipient Babylonian pantheism, is well pointed out in F. M. T. Böhl's "Some Notes on Israel in the Light of Babylonian Discoveries," *JBL*, LII, 140–46. Cf. also A. Lods's "Le Monothéisme israélite a-t-il eu des précurseurs parmi les 'sages' de l'ancien Orient?" *RHPR*, XIV, 197–205, which, referring primarily to the monotheism of the later prophets, answers the question in the negative. While Grimme's attempt to identify the two "tables of the testimony" among the Sinaitic inscriptions has been thoroughly discredited, our increased knowledge of the art of writing about the middle of the second millennium (there was a special school for scribes at Ras Shamra), makes it seem likely that Moses himself wrote down a few fundamental commandments.

The absence of more definite sources in regard to the life and work of Moses may be explained by the peculiar nonliterary way in which all the great ancient religious reformers addressed their followers. Gotama Buddha preached to a nation with a long history of religious and philosophic thought, yet the historical records concerning him are very obscure. One can, then, expect little in the case of Moses or Zoroaster, both of whom appeared at the threshold of the history of their peoples. Cf. N. Schmidt's stimulating remarks in "Problems Concerning the Origin of Some of the Great Oriental Religions," *JAOS*, LIII, 191–214.

On the name "Moses," whose Egyptian origin is suggested by the Bible, cf. the identification with *Mi-Shu* or *Ma-Shu* (like the Sun) by J. R. Towers in "The Name Moses," *JTS*, XXXVI, 407–9; and with *Mu-sheh* (child of the Nile) by Yahuda in his *Accuracy*, p. 66. The weight of scholarly opinion, however, still leans toward the old derivation from *Mase* or *Mose* (is born) which is also a component part of such well-known names as Ahmose, Thutmose, etc. If there is any validity in the persistent tradition that Moses was brought up in an Egyptian palace (the biblical narrative is greatly embroidered by later traditions mentioned by B. Beer in his *Leben Moses nach Auffassung der jüdischen Sage* and by Ginzberg in his *Legends*, V, 398, 402), his Egyptian foster mother naturally gave him an Egyptian name, whose theophoric element he later dropped as a sign of his repudiation of Egyptian paganism. Cf. also B. Jacob's "Childhood and Youth of Moses, the Messenger of God," *Essays Hertz*, pp. 245–59 (based on a forthcoming commentary on Exod.); J. B. Chabot's "Comment s'appelait la mère adoptive de Moïse?" *CRAI*, 1942, pp. 396–401 (reviewing the various names suggested since Josephus); and the semi-imaginative and semihistorical reconstructions in L. Golding's journey *In the Steps of Moses*. On the other hand, Sigmund Freud's attempt at a psychoanalytical interpretation of *Moses and Monotheism* is built upon such weak philological and historical foundations that even the author's great reputation could not salvage it from deserved oblivion. Cf., e.g., my relatively moderate criticisms in the *American Journal of Sociology*, XLV, 471–77, and, on the other hand, A. A. Feldman's "Freud's 'Moses and Monotheism' and Three Stages of Israelitish Religion," *Psychoanalytic Review*, XXXI, 361–418.

33. The picturesque descriptions of Abraham's missionary activities in later Jewish legends (cf. the references in Ginzberg's *Legends*, V, 215, notes 42–43, and 220, n. 61; W. L. Knox's "Abraham and the Quest for God," *HTR*, XXVIII, 55–60; and S. I. Feigin's "Hebrews in Cuneiform Inscriptions" [Hebrew], *SH*, VIII–IX, 239) reflect Judeo-Hellenistic and talmudic ideology rather than happenings of the patriarchal age. It was particularly in the seminomadic age that the two fundamental ideas underlying the Israelitic sacrificial system came clearly to the fore. Whether as a gift to the deity of a precious object, as stressed by G. B. Gray in his *Sacrifice in the Old Testament*, or as a symbol of communion between the worshiper and his God, as pointed out by W. R. Smith in his *Lectures on the Religion of the Semites* (3d ed., p. 240; and Cook's notes, pp. 630 f.), there could hardly have been a better object for a seminomadic tribe than communally owned cattle. Both these ideas retained their vitality in the later more advanced civilization, whereas A. Bertholet's "dynamistic conception of sacrifice" ("Zum Verständnis des alttestamentlichen Opfergedankens," *JBL*, XLIX, 218–33)—according to which the main function of the sacrifice was to furnish nourishment and power to the deity—had its place only in the pre-Mosaic and the "popular" Israelitic sacrificial order. Doubtless too crude for Moses and his more thoughtful successors, it was, at most, a vestige of more primitive thinking, coloring one or another ceremony but certainly unable to give meaning to the whole institution.

Such reinterpretation of ancient rituals without any change in form has been an almost universal human method of reconciling deep-rooted ritualistic conservatism with changing outlooks on life. Cf. the interesting examples assembled by Bertholet himself in his "Ueber kultische Motivverschiebungen," *SB* Berlin, 1938, pp. 164–84. Of course, after their settlement in Palestine the Israelites became also greatly indebted to Canaanite prototypes. Such indebtedness, long ago suggested by R. Dussaud, has been strikingly confirmed by the bread and wine offerings of the epics of Ras Shamra which corresponded to the biblical *Tamid* and the *Shelamim* (Dussaud, "Sanctuaire et les dieux phéniciens de Ras Shamra," *RHR*, CV, 285 ff.). But there also were basic differences between the worship of Israel's "historic" god who did not require ceremonial "rebirth" and that of the Canaanite Baal. Cf. J. Pedersen's older "Canaanite and Israelite Cultus," *Acta Orientalia*, XVIII, 1–14. Cf. also A. Rowe's archaeological study of *The Four Canaanite Temples of Beth-Shan*; and, more generally, A. Lods's older surveys, "Examen de quelques hypothèses modernes sur les origines du sacrifice," *RHPR*, I, 483–506; and W. O. E. Oesterley's *Sacrifices in Ancient Israel* (reviewing the different periods in terms of the three fundamental purposes "as gifts to the Deity, as a means of union with Him, and as a means of liberating life"); and, from other angles, L. B. Cross's "Blood Ritual in the Old Testament," *Modern Churchman*, XXXI, 295–312; A. Metzinger's comprehensive analysis of "Die Substitutionstheorie und das alttestamentliche Opfer," *Biblica*, XXI, 159–87, 247–72, 353–77 (with reference to Lev. 17:11); and H. H. Rowley's "Meaning of Sacrifice in the Old Testament," *BJRL*, XXXIII, 74–110.

34. If, on the basis of such passages T. J. Meek criticizes Albright's effective defense of Mosaic monotheism, for "there can be grades of approximation to monotheism, but not of monotheism itself" (*JBL*, LXI, 22), he seems to overstress the importance of verbal precision in the case of these ancient poets and preachers. The rabbis were undoubtedly right in saying that "the Torah speaks in the language of the people" and thus explaining the frequent discrepancies between highly refined thoughts and their less precise formulation. In fact, even Albright seems to give too little credit to the speculative propensities of the great thinkers of the "pre-logical" age antedating the great achievements of Greek philosophy. The distinction in the quality of thinking is at times more formal than substantive. Cf. the stimulating collection of essays on *The Intellectual Adventure of Ancient Man*, ed. by H. Frankfort, which includes a study of ancient Hebrew thought by W. A. Irwin. Cf. also J. Leclant's "Spéculations égyptiennes sur la vie, la mort, l'être et le devenir," *Revue philosophique*, 1946, pp. 337–42, with reference to G. Thausing's *Auferstehungsgedanke in ägyptischen religiösen Texten;* F. James's affirmative answer to his query, "Was There Monotheism in Israel before Amos?" *ATR*, XIV, 130–42; and T. Weindl's somewhat venturesome psychological thesis concerning the *Monotheismus und Dualismus in Indien, Iran und Palästina als Religion junger, kriegerischer nomadistischer Völker im Gravitationsbereich von Völkern alter Kultur*.

35. Burrows's *What Mean These Stones?* pp. 99, 140 f. Palestine's great wealth, as exemplified in the objects carried away from the country by the Pharaohs of the Twelfth and Eighteenth Dynasties, is graphically described by M. E. Kirk in her "Outline of the Cultural History of Palestine down to Roman Times," *PEQ*, 1943, pp. 31, 37. Here, too, however, one must bear in mind Noth's warning that not all the decline in the standards of material goods during the Early Iron Age should be ascribed to the Israelite conquest (*PJB*, XXXIV, 18 f.). On the general evolution of Palestinian agriculture during the Old Testament period, cf. A. A. Reifenberg's *Milḥemet ha-mizra' ve-ha-yeshimon*, pp. 90 ff.; and the detailed analysis of '*Abodat abotenu* (The Work of Our Ancestors or Hebrew Agriculture According to the Bible) by M. Zagorodsky.

There also is a frequent dichotomy between whatever ethnic changes seem indicated by the sudden destruction of a city and the far slower cultural transformations.

Combined with the general obscurity of the literary tradition this dichotomy, for example apparent in the various archaeological layers (VII to V) at Megiddo, has induced R. M. Engberg to date the Israelitic victory in the Plain of Esdraelon and, with it, the Song of Deborah at about 1050 B.C.E. This date would telescope the story of Deborah, Gideon, and Jephtah into the brief span of fifty years (1100–1050 B.C.E.). Cf. *BASOR*, 78, pp. 6 ff. What is worse, since the destruction of Shiloh, presumably by the Philistines, likewise occurred around 1050 according to the ceramic chronology (cf. H. Kjaer's "Excavation of Shiloh 1929," *JPOS*, X, 87–174; and Albright's *Archaeology and Religion*, pp. 103 f.), Deborah and Samuel would appear to have been contemporaries. Cf. however, A. Alt's more reasonable explanation in his "Megiddo im Uebergang vom kanaanäischen zum israelitischen Zeitalter," *ZAW*, LX, 67–85. No wonder, then, that E. Robertson refers to "The Period of the Judges: a Mystery Period in the History of Israel" in his *Old Testament Problem*, pp. 159 ff. Cf. also, from other angles, P. A. Munch's "Wirtschaftliche Grundlage des israelitischen Volksbewusstseins vor Saul," *ZDMG*, XCIII, 217–53; and O. Grether's analysis of the "Bezeichnung 'Richter' für die charismatischen Helden der vorstaatlichen Zeit," *ZAW*, LVII, 110–21.

36. In analyzing the pertinent, often perplexing, biblical passages, one must allow for this necessary time lag in the transition from one social organization to another and the still greater lag in the corresponding terminological adjustments. One must bear in mind, for example, that, to quote J. Pedersen (*Israel*, I, 49), a "tribe, when still a living term, was not essentially different from the family, the family, not being an extensive, clearly limited quantity, but the appellation of those who are of common blood." It is small wonder, therefore, that the clans of the extinct tribe of Simon retained their genealogical identity as late as the reign of Hezekiah. Cf. I Chron. 4:24–43. Cf. also J. van der Ploeg's "Social Groupings in Ancient Israel" (Dutch), *JEOL*, VIII, 642–50; C. U. Wolf's "Some Remarks on the Tribes and Clans in Israel," *JQR*, XXXVI, 287–95; and his "Terminology of Israel's Tribal Organization," *JBL*, LXV, 45–49; and, on the geographic differences, D. H. Kallner's "Outlines of the Geomorphology of Judea," *Bulletin de la Société r. de géographie d' Égypte*, XXI, 35–49.

37. It was perhaps such pressure from the Amalekites which, ever since the obscure battle at Rephidim (Exod. 17:8–16), caused that bitter enmity which finally led to the war of extermination in the days of Samuel and Saul. See Alt in *PJB*, XXXV, 33. E. Robertson goes too far, however, in using this vindictive passage, reiterated in Deut. 25:17–19, as an argument for his theory that a council presided over by Samuel assembled much of the canonical material which later became part and parcel of our Pentateuch. Cf. his *Old Testament Problem*, pp. 33 ff., 137 ff. At the other extreme W. A. Irwin doubts the historicity of most of the biblical traditions about Samuel and contends that, like Moses, he is sketched "not in the precise delineation of history, or even the realism of contemporary hero-tales, but rather in the romantic embellishments with which the loyalties and admiration of a later time adorned" his achievements ("Samuel and the Rise of the Monarchy," *AJSL*, LVIII, 133). Cf. also R. Press's "Prophet Samuel: eine traditionsgeschichtliche Untersuchung," *ZAW*, LVI, 177–225; M. Buber's "Samuel and the Evolution of Authority in Israel" (Hebrew), *Zion*, IV, 1–29; his "How Saul Was Made King" (Hebrew), *Tarbiz*, XXII, 1–20, 65–84; K. Möhlenbrink's "Sauls Amoniterfeldzug und Samuels Beitrag zum Königtum des Saul," *ZAW*, LVIII, 57–70; and on the much-debated phrase, "Is Saul also among the Prophets" (I Sam. 10:12), N. H. Tur-Sinai's (Torczyner's) ingenious, perhaps overingenious, interpretation in his *Ha-Lashon ve-ha-sefer* (The Language and the Book: Basic Problems in the Study of the Hebrew Language and Its Literary Sources), II, 233–37. In any case it was not until the time of the monarchy that these diverse elements ultimately emerged as two distinct groups of tribes, the northern and the southern. Cf. Alt's *Staatenbildung der Israeliten in Palästina*.

38. The name "mother-earth," may be primarily Greek (Pindar), but the idea was by no means strange to the Semites. It may perhaps be traced even in some of the later Hebrew writings. Cf. W. R. Smith's *Religion of the Semites*, p. 537 (Cook); Heinrich Lewy's "Beiträge zur Religionsgeschichte und Volkskunde," *AR*, XXIX, 187 ff.; M. (E.) Stein's "Mother Earth in Old Hebrew Literature" (Hebrew), *Tarbiz*, IX, 257–77; and E. Roellenbleck's psychoanalytical study of the *Magna Mater im Alten Testament*. The idea of a mother-goddess of the clan, which we encounter as far back as the early Sumerian and Akkadian records is, of course, different, but it, too, may have been imported from Asia Minor. See Baudissin's *Kyrios*, III, 364. It is small wonder that the conglomerate commercial population of Ras Shamra should have worshiped both the male Athtar and the female Astarte. Cf. Bauer's remarks in *ZAW*, LI, 91; Nielsen's *Handbuch*, I, 232; W. L. Reed's *Asherah in the Old Testament;* R. Dussaud's "Astarté, Pontos et Baal," *CRAI*, 1947, p. 203, n. 3; and, particularly, J. Gray's "Desert God 'Attr in the Literature and Religion of Canaan," *JNES*, VIII, 72–83.

In recent years, however, a reaction has set in against the exaggerated importance attributed to fertility cults in the early phases of Israelitic religion, a theory, expounded, among others, by W. C. Graham and H. G. May in their *Culture and Conscience*, pp. 24–56; and by B. A. Brooks in her "Fertility Cult Functionaries in the Old Testament," *JBL*, LX, 227–53. The nearly total absence of large statues of Astarte in the excavations of Canaanite cities and the likely use of the small figurines for magical rather than ritual purposes (cf. *supra*, n. 20) have served to tone down some of these assertions.

39. L. Waterman, among others, takes the extreme position of denying that either Moses or Aaron ever belonged to the "tribe" of Levi. Cf. his "Moses the Pseudo Levite," *JBL*, LIX, 397–404, and "Some Repercussions from Late Levitical Genealogical Accretions in P and the Chronicler," *AJSL*, LVIII, 49–56. On the other hand, T. J. Meek effectively defends Moses' levitical ancestry in his *Hebrew Origins*, rev. ed., pp. 121 ff., and in *AJSL*, LVI, 113 ff. The rabbinic traditions concerning the special treatment of the levites during the Egyptian oppression are summarized in Ginzberg's *Legends*, II, 248; V, 391, n. 6. Cf. also *infra*, Chaps. III, n. 26, and V, n. 24.

40. Judg. 6:11, 32, and 9:26–31 (LXX); I Chron. 12:5. On the meaning of some of these names, see Albright's *Archaeology and Religion*, pp. 112 ff. J. W. Jack's query *(Samaria in Ahab's Time*, p. 157), whether we can deduce from the ostraca any conclusions for children born under the reign of Ahab, is easily answered in view of the Yahwistic names of Ahab's own offspring.

41. The existence of money is well exemplified in the ancient Song of Deborah, which triumphantly exclaims: "They [the enemies] took no gain of money" (Judg. 5:19). The very old narrative in Judg. 17 likewise speaks of *keseph* (silver and money). The fact stressed by A. Menes *(Die vorexilischen Gesetze Israels*, p. 25) that even Solomon collected taxes and made payments in kind proves only that the amount of currency was insufficient for the rapidly expanding needs of the state. Even much later, when coins enjoyed wide circulation, taxes were usually paid in kind. Certainly, I Kings 10 conclusively demonstrates how highly developed Israelitic trade was in the reign of Solomon, with gold and silver serving as the principal standards of value and, consequently, as the means of exchange. Cf. also W. H. Dubberstein's "Comparative Prices in Later Babylonia (625–400 B.C.)," *AJSL*, LVI, 21 f., showing that regular coins existed in the Near East in the days of Sennacherib and possibly earlier; and the general, well documented, survey of "Silver and Lead in Antiquity" by R. J. Forbes in *JEOL*, VII, 489–524. It should also be noted that, according to C. F. A. Schaeffer, Syria, and particularly the region of Byblos, had significantly contributed to the invention of bronze as early as the third millennium. See his brief

French essay in *JEA*, XXXI, 92–95. Cf. also, more generally, H. Maroyou's "Metal Working in the Ancient World," *AJA*, LIII, 93–125.

42. The authenticity of the historical division into twelve tribes and of their festive gatherings, reminiscent of the Greek amphictyonies, has been made plausible by M. Noth in *Das System der zwölf Stämme Israels*. Noth has also pointed out that "the judge of Israel," still mentioned by Micah (4:14), was very likely a reminiscence of the premonarchical leader who was entrusted by the amphictyony with the adjudication of particularly difficult cases. This type of leadership underscored the peculiarity of Israelitic society, which from earliest times lived under the rule of the divine law and its exponents. See Noth's "Das Amt des 'Richters Israels,'" *Festschrift Bertholet*, pp. 404–17. Of course, such judicial function could, and often did, go hand in hand with leadership in war and it is not at all surprising that the book of "Judges" tells us more about these chieftains' warlike exploits, than about their less dramatic judicial functions. See O. Grether's remarks in *ZAW*, LVII, 110 ff. We are unfortunately very much in the dark about the public activities, other than cultic, at these amphictyonic gatherings. But K. Galling has made a case not only for the pre-Deuteronomic origin of Deut. 23, but also for its serving as an illustration of decisions taken at such an amphictyonic "assembly of the Lord." Here the leadership of all the tribes, convened for general communal as well as ritualistic purposes, passed judgment on the admission of new members and set up those basic rules barring certain groups of aliens which were to play such a great role in the subsequent Judeo-Gentile relations. See Galling's "Gemeindegesetz in Deuteronomium 23," *Festschrift Bertholet*, pp. 176–91.

CHAPTER III: KINGS AND PROPHETS

1. Although about the same time iron appears also in Transjordan, the Philistines made far more extensive use of it in their armaments, thereby undoubtedly facilitating their rapid conquests. They also brought with them a distinct type of pottery, found in the ruins of Beth-shan, Gezer, and Beth-shemesh. Its presence in Beth-shemesh seems to indicate their control over the city even after the Israelite conquest. Cf. Wright's comments in *JBL*, LX, 33 ff., his "Iron," *AJA*, XLIII, 458–63; and *supra*, Chap. II, n. 41. On the other hand, R. M. Engberg has pointed out that the Philistine pottery found in the strata VII–VI in pre-Israelitic Megiddo may well have been imported from a neighboring Philistine city and need not presuppose actual occupation ("Megiddo—Guardian of the Carmel Pass," *BA*, III, 41–51; IV, 11–16). With respect to the title *tyrannos* it should be borne in mind that it first appears in Greek documents of the late seventh century "on Ionian territory or such areas as were under Ionian influence." Cf. T. Lenschau's "Tyrannis," *PWRE*, 2d ser., VII (XIV), 1821–42.

In his Hebrew essays "The Philistines of Gerar and the Philistines of the Seacoast" in *Schorr Mem. Vol.*, pp. 96–112, and "The Immigration of the First Philistines in the Inscriptions" in *Tarbiz*, XVII, 32–42, J. M. Grintz suggested that there were three distinct Aegean waves which hit Palestine during the 21st, the 16th, and the 12th centuries. But this theory was rejected by Albright who, on the other hand, called attention to the similarity of a passage in the oracles of Balaam (Num. 24:23–24) to several Egyptian accounts of the invasion of the "sea peoples." Cf. his review of the *Schorr Mem. Vol.* in *JBL*, LXV, 418 f., and his remarks *ibid.*, LXIII, 230. Cf. also R. A. S. Macalister's *Philistines: Their History and Civilization* which, though obsolete in many sections, still offers the most comprehensive survey. More up to date are O. Eissfeldt's "Philister," *PWRE*, XIX, 2390–2401, and *Philister und Phönizier;* A. Jirku's "Herkunft und Bedeutung der Philister," *Rasse*, IX, 284–90; A. Alt's "Aegyptische Tempel in Palästina und die Landnahme der Philister," *ZDPV*, LXVII, 1–20 (trying to show that, like the Israelites, the Philistines slowly infiltrated into the Palestinian sea coast before they engaged in open warfare and that they were abetted by the Egyptians who thus attempted to divert them from their own shores); and G. Bonfante's "Who Were the Philistines?" *AJA*, L, 251–62 (defending the hypothesis of their "Illyrian" origins). Cf. also, for the later period, O. Eissfeldt's "Israelitisch-philistäische Grenzverschiebungen von David bis auf die Assyrerzeit," *ZDPV*, LXVI, 115–28; and M. Noth's "Zur Geschichte des Namens Palästina," *ibid.*, LXII, 125–44.

2. The figures for which, of course, no finality can be claimed, have been computed after careful investigation of available archaeological and literary records. On a detailed analysis of this complex subject, as well as on many other points in this chapter, cf. S. Baron's "Israelitic Population under the Kings" (Hebrew), *Abhandlungen Chajes*, pp. 76–136. These computations greatly differ from those of other writers, most of whom assume a steady growth of the Israelitic population under the later kings and, hence, postulate a far lesser population density under the reigns of David and Solomon. W. F. Albright, for instance, still adheres to his assumption that the biblical figure of 600,000 Israelite adult males in the days of the Exodus really represents the total population under David, including women and children. Apart from that rather arbitrary inclusion, this assumption is vitiated by its dependence on another debatable hypothesis that the two lists in Num. 1 and 26 are but variants of the results of the census taken under David. Cf. Albright's "Administrative Divisions of Israel and Judah," *JPOS*, V, 20 ff., and *Stone Age*, pp. 222 f. None of the data,

hitherto assembled, however, not even Albright's own estimate of some 2,000–3,000 inhabitants of Debir (Beit Mirsim; cf. his report on "The Excavations of Tell Beit Mirsim, III," *AASOR*, XXI–II, 39) seem to offer conclusive evidence for the lower estimates. A. Lucas's denial, on the other hand, of the traditional "Number of Israelites at the Exodus" in *PEQ*, 1944, pp. 164–68, merely confirms a widely held conviction.

3. In his "Gottesurteil auf dem Karmel," *Festschrift Georg Beer*, pp. 1–18, A. Alt has shown that, as a price for Tyre's collaboration, Solomon gave up all the Phoenician areas beyond Sidon formerly controlled by his father and that he, or one of his successors, also lost to the Phoenicians some ethnically Israelitic areas down to Mount Carmel. There still is no general agreement as to the location of Ophir, the destination of that combined Tyro-Israelitic expedition. J. Hornell has made a strong case, however, for considering it "a great mart on the west coast of India, where the produce of the gold mines of Hyderabad, of the spice lands of Malabar and of the gem-workings and pearl-fisheries of Ceylon, were collected by merchants to meet the foreign merchant-king's requirements" ("Naval Activity in the Days of Solomon and Rameses III," *Antiquity*, XXI, 72). W. F. Albright has suggested that the ships of Tarshish, recorded in these journeys, be translated by "refinery ships" and that its locale be looked for in Sardinia rather than in Spain. Cf. his *Archaeology and Religion*, pp. 131 f., 135 ff., and *BASOR*, 83, pp. 21 f., and 95, p. 38. One need not completely give up, however, the traditional assumption that some Israelites participated also in expeditions to the Phoenician colony of Tartessus in Spain, which also doubtless originated from the Phoenician quest for copper. See Garcia y Bellido's *Fenicios*. On the excavations at Ezion Geber, cf. N. Glueck's detailed report in *AASOR*, Vols. XIV, XV, and XVIII–XIX; and his summary in *The Other Side of the Jordan*, pp. 50 ff.

4. II Sam. 7:6. "The Story of the Capture of Jerusalem in the Time of David" has been analyzed with fresh insight by B. Z. Dinaburg in his Hebrew essay in *Zion*, XI, 153–67. The name "Jerusalem" (probably meaning "May the Perfect One found") has been traced back to the twentieth century B.C.E. Cf. Abel's *Géographie*, II, 360 f., and Albright's review thereof in *JBL*, LVIII, 183 f. Cf. also A. Jirku's "Name der Stadt Jerusalem," *WZKM*, XLVI, 205–8, and S. Krauss's extensive analysis of the names "Zion and Jerusalem," *PEQ*, 1945, pp. 15–33. An early mention of the tribe of Benjamin in whose area the new capital was located was first pointed out by G. Dossin in his "Benjaminites dans les textes de Mari," *Mélanges Dussaud*, II, 981–96. Cf. also the second volume of R. Weill's *Cité de David* (reporting on the excavations of 1923–24); S. Yeivin's "Beginnings of the House of David" (Hebrew), *Zion*, IX, 49–69 (stressing the impact of the monarchical traditions of the non-Jewish wives of the Davidic family, including Bath-Sheba); M. Noth's "Jerusalem und die israelitische Tradition," *OS*, VIII, 28–46; and, *supra*, Chap. II, n. 25.

5. This has been made clear by K. Möhlenbrink's comprehensive reconstruction of *Der Tempel Salomos*, supplemented from archaeological data by Watzinger in his *Denkmäler*, I, 88 ff.; G. E. Wright in his "Solomon's Temple Resurrected," *BA*, IV, 17–31; R. de Vaux in his "Notes on the Temple of Solomon" (Hebrew), *Kedem*, II, 48–58; and J. L. Myres's "King Solomon's Temples and Other Buildings and Works of Art," *PEQ*, 1948, pp. 14–41. R. B. Y. Scott ingeniously explained also, with the aid of comparative foreign material, "The Pillars Jachin and Boaz" described in I Kings 7:15–22. See *JBL*, LVIII, 143–49. Despite their foreign antecedents, however, they may have been intended to commemorate historically the pillars of fire and cloud of the days of the Exodus, a truly Hebraic motif. See H. G. May's "Two Pillars before the Temple of Solomon," *BASOR*, 88, pp. 19–27. "The Date of the Founding of Solomon's Temple" is analyzed by M. B. Rowton *BASOR*, 119, pp. 20–22 (confirming,

on the basis of Phoenician chronology, the date of 959 B.C.E. suggested by Albright), while P. L. Garber (in collaboration with E. S. Howland) has made a fresh attempt at "Reconstructing Solomon's Temple." Cf. *BA*, XIV, 2–24. Unfortunately, "no authentic Jewish temples have been excavated" (not even that unearthed in Megiddo IV by Schumacher), while the pre-Israelitic sanctuaries can furnish only some more or less remote parallels. Cf. M. V. Seton Williams's "Palestinian Temples," *Iraq*, XI, 88.

6. I Kings 12:30, 15:13; II Kings 18:4. Cf. H. T. Obbink's "Jahwebilder," *ZAW*, XLVII, 264–74; and H. H. Rowley's "Zadok and Nehushtan," *JBL*, LVIII, 113–41. If true, Rowley's theory concerning the Jebusite snake symbol would dovetail with the aforementioned hypothesis that David tried to appease the Jebusites also by claiming to be the successor of their own king-priest, Melchizedek. On this basis E. R. Hardy, Jr., ascribes to David Psalm 110 which extols such a priestly warrior, the only other alternative being, in his opinion, that the psalmist tried to glorify some Maccabean ruler. Cf. his "Date of Psalm 110," *JBL*, LXIV, 385–90; and Rowley's essay cited *supra*, Chap. II, n. 25. The problem of images in Jerusalem is reviewed also by J. Morgenstern in his *Amos Studies*, I, 227 ff. Morgenstern asserts that even in the days of Solomon there was in the *debir* "an image of Yahweh, in all likelihood either made of, or else richly overlaid with, precious metal. It probably represented Yahweh sitting as the divine king, the lord of all the gods, upon a lofty throne, with His feet resting upon a cushion or footstool" (p. 229). Cf. also the general "Vindication of Jerobeam I" in the excursus in *HUCA*, XXI, 481 ff. S. Mowinckel has likewise argued that not until Amos and Hosea did the partisans of imageless worship win the upper hand over its opponents ("À quel moment le culte de Yahvé à Jérusalem est-il officiellement devenu un culte sans image?" *RHPR*, IX, 197–216). On the other extreme, R. H. Pfeiffer denies outright (in *JBL*, XLV, 211–22) the existence in Jerusalem of any real "Images of Yahweh." Cf. also R. de Vaux's analysis of "Le Schisme religieux de Jéroboam I," *Angelicum*, XX, 77–91. The weight of evidence seems to favor the former point of view.

7. Even Asa's decisive victory of 895 over "the Ethiopian" Zerah (Osorkon I of Egypt?), is recorded only by the Chronicler (II Chron. 14:8 ff.). The undoubtedly authentic previous invasion of Palestine by King Shoshenk ("Shishak" in the biblical records) in 926, on the other hand, seems to have occurred as part of widespread restlessness in western Asia, Shoshenk himself being apparently of Elamite or Persian origin. Even Turkestan, the cradle of so many migrations, is said to have furnished soldiers for the bodyguard of King David. See F. Petrie's "Shishak Migration," *Ancient Egypt*, 1928, pp. 101–4. Only Egypt's subsequent withdrawal from the Asiatic scene made possible the speedy rise of Damascus. During his first invasion of Israel (about 874), Hadad I was actually aided by Asa of Judah, whose shortsighted policy was rightly castigated by the seer, Hanani (II Chron. 16:1–10; as usually the Chronicler gives the prophetic reprimand a purely theological slant). Perhaps in anticipation of this Aramaean danger, Omri, soon after his rise to power, married off his son Ahab to the Tyrian princess Jezebel, hoping to secure Tyre's assistance in the forthcoming conflict. Cf. J. Morgenstern's computation of the "Chronological Data of the Dynasty of Omri," *JBL*, LIX, 385–96. Hadad, however, seems to have neutralized Tyre by marrying another daughter of its king, Ittobaal, and by outdoing Ahab in worshiping outright the Tyrian god, Melcart. Cf. G. Levi della Vida's "Some Notes on the Stele of Ben Hadad," *BASOR*, 90, pp. 30–32. Cf. also H. Parzen's "Prophets and the Omri Dynasty," *HTR*, XXXIII, 69–96; A. Jepsen's ingenious reconstruction, largely from Assyrian records, of the background of relations between "Israel und Damaskus," *AOF*, XIV, 153–72; M. F. Unger's "Archaeology and the Israelite-Aramean Wars," *Bibliotheca Sacra*, CVI, 178–86, 303–11; A. Dupont-Sommer's brief historical survey of *Les Araméens*; and, on the relations with Israel's immediate neighbors, A. Alt's

"Beiträge zur Geschichte des Ostjordanlandes, I–III," *PJB*, XXXVII, 50–101; *ZAW*, LX, 11–57; *ZDPV* (Beiträge), LXVIII, 1–50. For the dates given here and elsewhere in this chapter, cf. E. R. Thiele's "Chronology of the Kings of Judah and Israel," *JNES*, III, 137–86. Cf. also his *Mysterious Numbers of the Hebrew Kings: a Reconstruction of the Chronology of the Kingdoms of Israel and Judah.*

8. The story that an ordinary boy caught by Gideon could write "down for him the princes of Succoth, and the elders thereof, seventy and seven men" (Judg. 8:14) has long been doubted. But the Gezer calendar discovered by Macalister in 1908 has shown that an average farmer in the Shephelah, perhaps even a schoolboy, had a fair command of what had already become a sort of cursive Hebrew script. Cf. the extensive bibliography in Diringer's *Iscrizioni*, pp. 18 f.; W. F. Albright's "Gezer Calendar," *BASOR*, 92, pp. 16–26; S. A. Birnbaum's "On the Possibility of Dating Hebrew Inscriptions," *PEQ*, 1944, pp. 213–17; H. Torczyner's "Toward an Understanding of the Gezer Calendar" (Hebrew), in his *Ha-Lashon ve-ha-sefer*, I, 40–47; and J. G. Février's "Remarques sur le calendrier de Gezer," *Semitica*, I, 33–41.

The biblical sources give us regrettably few glimpses of the general state of education in preëxilic Palestine. Cf. L. Dürr's brief comparative study of *Das Erziehungswesen im Alten Testament und im antiken Orient;* and N. Morris's general survey of *The Jewish School from the Earliest Times to the Year 500 of the Present Era.* Both of these monographs may now be supplemented by more recent information concerning the pre-Israelitic schools at Mari (ab. 1800) and Ugarit (1400).

9. Unfortunately no loan contracts of the period of the Israelitic monarchy have as yet come to light, but the rate of interest negotiated, for instance, by the Aramaic-speaking inhabitants of the provincial capital of Guzana (the biblical Gozan) in the seventh century ranged from 50 per cent for loans in silver up to 100 per cent in grain. Cf. J. Friedrich, *et al., Inschriften vom Tell Halaf*, pp. 48 ff., Nos. 101–2, 108; and E. F. Weidner's comments, *ibid.*, p. 7. Elephantine Jews in the fifth century paid about 60 per cent per annum. Cf. E. Meyer's *Papyrusfund von Elephantine*, pp. 30 f.; and A. Cowley's *Aramaic Papyri of the Fifth Century B.C.*, Nos. 10–11. Credit as a whole certainly was cheaper in Egypt in 461 or even in the troubled year 455 than in Palestine in the days of the kings. Cf. also the data collected by I. Mendelsohn in his *Slavery in the Ancient Near East*, pp. 23 ff.; and W. F. Leemans's "Rate of Interest in Old-Babylonian Times," *RIDA*, V, 7–34.

10. Cf. I. Mendelsohn's "Guilds in Ancient Palestine," *BASOR*, 80, pp. 17–21 ("perhaps as early as the Hyksos period"), and "Gilds in Babylonia and Assyria," *JAOS*, LX, 68–72. That some such political and economic factors, rather than absence of native ability, were mainly responsible for the relative paucity of high-grade Palestinian products in the excavated cities is evidenced both by some extant specimens of pre-Israelitic craftsmanship and the wide use of beautiful seal cylinders made by Israelitic artisans during the Middle Iron Age. Cf., e.g., Y. Sukenik's [Yadin's] "On the Technique of Khirbet Kerak Ware," *BASOR*, 106, pp. 9–17 (this ware is particularly interesting because of its lustrous black or red polish); G. E. Wright's "Palestine's First Great Artist," *BA*, II, 16–20 (referring to a possibly itinerant painter of the mid-sixteenth century B.C.E.); Burrows's *What Mean These Stones?* p. 194. Cf. also the comparative modern materials assembled by G. M. Crowfoot in her "Handicrafts in Palestine," *PEQ*, 1943, pp. 75–88; 1944, pp. 121–30; and "The Tent Beautiful," *ibid.*, 1945, pp. 34–46. On the other hand, there is no up-to-date detailed study of ancient Israel's international and domestic commerce. I. Ben-Dor's survey of "Trade Relations between Palestine and Egypt in the Canaanite Period," in S. Yeivin's *Ha-Mishar* (Trade, Industry and Crafts in Ancient Palestine), pp. 31–50, has not been extended into the Israelitic period. Cf., however, the literature listed *supra*, n. 3; and *infra*, Chap. VIII, n. 8.

11. As in other areas of government, Solomon merely followed Egyptian models. In the Egyptian Empire (1580–1085) free laborers were often conscripted for government work in distant parts of the country. Cf. W. F. Edgerton's "Government and the Governed in the Egyptian Empire," *JNES*, VI, 160; W. Spiegelberg's *Arbeiter und Arbeiterbewegung im Pharaonenreich unter den Ramessiden;* and *infra*, n. 16. In addition to the irregular *corvée* of free Israelites, I. Mendelsohn distinguishes more or less permanent "state slaves" (those subject to *mas 'obed*), temple slaves (the *netinim*) and "free proletarians" or coloni (the so-called *hofshim*). Cf. his essays in *BASOR*, 83, pp. 36–39; 85, pp. 14–17; and *Slavery*, pp. 92 ff., 148 ff. The latter identification is somewhat dubious because, apart from the likely better rendering of *hofshi* by "half-free" (cf. E. R. Lacheman's "Note on the Word Ḫupšu at Nuzi," *BASOR*, 86, pp. 36–37), the very essence of the later Roman colonate, in so far as it is at all comparable with ancient Israelitic conditions, consisted in the early attachment of the colonus to the soil and his inability freely to choose his employment or residence. See also W. Caspari's "Alter des palästinischen Kolonats," *Archiv für Sozialwissenschaft*, XLIX, 54–107, and on the self-sale of slaves the comparative data assembled in J. Pirenne's "Contrats de vente de soi-même en Égypte à l'époque saïte," *Bulletin de l'Académie r. de Belgique*, 5th ser. XXXIV, 581–93.

12. That extensive legal protection was granted to Gentile slaves as early as the Book of the Covenant has frequently been doubted. Precisely its profoundly humanitarian spirit seemed to offer justifiable grounds for suspicion. However, all attempts to read Exod. 21:20–21, 26–27, as referring to a Hebrew slave like 21:2–6 (cf. Morgenstern's "Book of the Covenant," *HUCA*, VII, 38 n. 24, 94) appear to meet an insurmountable barrier in Exod. 21:32, which admittedly refers to a non-Israelitic slave. The traditional explanation, distinguishing between the first eleven verses as referring to a "Hebrew" slave, male or female, and the other passages which treat of a slave without the adjective *'ibri*, appears much more convincing.

On the other hand, the extreme Deuteronomic prohibition of returning fugitive slaves may indeed have come late and perhaps merely reflected the unrealistic bent of much of the Deuteronomic reform. It certainly was at complete variance with the general oriental practice as expressed in the *Code of Hammurabi*, articles 15–16, 18–19; or in J. B. Alexander's *Early Babylonian Letters*, No. 93, where the possessor of two fugitive slaves was fined. Cf. also Mendelsohn's *Slavery*, pp. 58 ff. In the only case recorded in Scripture (I Kings 2:39–40) Shimei seems to have encountered no serious difficulty in bringing back his two runaway slaves from Gath. But since this was extradition from a non-Israelitic territory, it may well have been secured by some extralegal means. Certainly the similar forcible return of the fugitive prophet Uriah from Egypt (Jer. 26:21–23) smacks of the kind of kidnapping made familiar by the Nazis. Nor does the meager evidence available sufficiently sustain I. Mendelsohn's suggestion that the *amah* of the Book of the Covenant was an exceptionally privileged "conditional" slave, while other Hebrew slaves could be freely disposed of. See his "Conditional Sale into Slavery of Free-born Daughters in Nuzi and the Law of Ex. 21:7–11," *JAOS*, LV, 190–95. Even the two seals (apparently both preëxilic) bearing the inscription *amah* found in Palestine in recent years may be explained either by these ladies' widowhood or foreign influence or both. See N. Avigad's "Seal of a Slave-Wife (Amah)," *PEQ*, 1946, pp. 125–32. Cf. also P. A. H. de Boer's "Some Remarks on Exodus XXI, 7–11" in *Orientalia neerlandica*, pp. 162–66.

With respect to the price of slaves, we have the record of an early transaction concerning the purchase of forty beautiful girls at the rate of 40 silver shekels each (G. Dossin's "Une Nouvelle lettre d'el-Amarna," *Revue d'Assyriologie*, XXXI, 125–36). It must be borne in mind, however, that female slaves, purchased for a harem, commanded an extraordinary price. Later on, in the days of Nebukadrezzar, even ordinary slaves seem to have been worth 40 shekels in Babylonia. The price rose further to 60 shekels under the reign of Cyrus. At the same time an unskilled free workman could be hired for one shekel a month; a young boy for as little as 4 shekels a year (Dubberstein in *AJSL*, LVI, 34 ff., 39 f.). This uneconomical ratio between free and slave labor doubtless was aggravated in Israel with its limited supply of prisoners of war.

13. It is small wonder, therefore, that Benzinger (in his *Archäologie*) and Lurie (in his *Studien*) deem the hired laborers unworthy of special consideration, while M. Sulzberger (in his *Status of Labor in Ancient Israel*) identifies them with the *gerim*, the resident aliens of preëxilic times. Cf., on the other hand, the comparative study by K. Fuchs, *Die alttestamentliche Arbeitergesetzgebung;* and, more generally, A. Kuschke's "Arm und reich im Alten Testament," *ZAW*, LVII, 31–57; N. Peters's *Soziale Fürsorge im Alten Testament;* E. T. Root's *Bible Economy of Plenty;* and O. Weinberger's *Wirtschaftsphilosophie des Alten Testamentes.*

14. A Ras Shamra text (first published by C. Virolleaud in *Syria*, XIII, 151 f.: B VI 47–54) now offers striking documentary proof of the early existence of such an eight-day Canaanite festival. Cf. J. A. Montgomery's interpretation in his "Ras-Shamra Notes," *JAOS*, LIII, 120 f. The agricultural character of the small towns in Palestine has already been pointed out by W. Caspari in his *Gottesgemeinde von Sinaj und das nachmalige Volk Israel,* p. 42, against Weber's too far-reaching division between the rural and the urban interests. In other connections, however, Weber himself was most outspoken in drawing a distinction between the ancient and medieval worlds, precisely on the ground of the greater prevalence of towns in antiquity. For a detailed discussion of this ramified problem, and an attempt to establish the approximate number of towns in ancient Israel, see my computations in *Abhandlungen Chajes*, pp. 114 ff. R. Gordis's efforts to explain many conflicts in ancient Israel on the basis of the contrast between town and village ("Sectional Rivalry in the Kingdom of Judah," *JQR*, XXV, 237–59) are greatly vitiated by his failure to take cognizance of these peculiarities of the Israelitic town. Many of his remarks may be applied, however, to the diverse attitudes of capital and provinces.

15. Exod. 12:21, 27–28; 19:6–8. In the convocation of "all the people" by Jehu (II Kings 10:18 ff.) some see the historical basis for the great Shechem covenant, allegedly concluded by Joshua with the people (Josh. 24). The content of Jehu's covenant could thus be easily reconstructed from this record, composed about 800. Cf. K. Galling's *Israelitische Staatsverfassung in ihrer vorderorientalischen Umwelt*, p. 55. The identification remains very doubtful, however. Cf. also *supra*, n. 15.

The problems of ancient Hebrew "democracy" attracted considerable attention in recent years, when the modern democratic countries faced the onslaught of totalitarian powers. Its origin undoubtedly goes back to the earliest stages of Near Eastern democracy which, in Mesopotamia and elsewhere, was subsequently submerged by a strong monarchical and priestly autocracy. Vestiges of such a "Primitive Democracy in Ancient Mesopotamia" are plausibly analyzed by T. Jacobsen in *JNES*, II, 159–72. It was perhaps fortunate for the Israelites that their political weakness, both domestic and international, combined with the strength of their religious and legal traditions, prevented the suppression of their own "primitive democracy." Cf. the fuller treatment of this subject in my *Jewish Community*, I, 31 ff.; III, 6 ff.; A. H. Silver's "Prophetic Conception of the Ministry," *Harvard Divinity School Bulletin*, 1940–41, pp. 19–33; C. U. Wolf's "Traces of Primitive Democracy in Ancient Israel," *JNES*, VI, 98–108; P. Ramsay's "Elements of a Biblical Political Theory," *JR*, XXIX, 258–83; and the literature listed *infra*, n. 40–41. In general, the rebel kings of Northern Israel, who owed their sovereignty to a popular upheaval against Solomon's autocratic regime, emulated his governmental methods much more ruthlessly than did his legitimate Judean successors. Cf. R. Dussaud's "Samarie au temps d'Achab," *Syria*, VI, 314–38; VII, 9–29; and E. Robertson's "Disruption of Israel's Monarchy—

Before and After" in his *Old Testament Problem*, pp. 10–32. Cf. also, more generally, A. Alt's recent study of "Das Königtum in den Reichen Israel und Juda," *Vetus Testamentum*, I, 2–22.

16. The actual boundaries of these new provinces described in I Kings 4 are subject to debate. Cf., in particular, the divergent interpretations by A. Alt in his "Israel's Gaue unter Salomo," *Alttestamentliche Studien Rudolf Kittel . . . dargebracht*, pp. 1–19; and W. F. Albright in *JPOS*, V, 25 ff. But there is general agreement that they greatly differed from the old tribal boundaries. The unnamed thirteenth officer who was "in the land" (I Kings 4:19) evidently was not "over all the officers," but a sort of vice-regent in charge of Judah. He may or may not have served also as "governor of the city" of Jerusalem recorded later in the days of Josiah (II Kings 23:8). A similar exemption of the home province of Ashur is recorded also in the later Assyrian Empire. See J. A. Montgomery's "Hebraica," *JAOS*, LVIII, 133. Apart from thus leaning heavily on the loyalty of their own tribe, David and Solomon also employed foreign mercenaries and such foreign officials as Uriah, the Hittite. King Ahaz, too, may have later employed an Assyrian as a high government official, as suggested by C. C. Torrey, whatever may otherwise be the merits of his interpretation of the inscription found on "A Hebrew Seal from the Reign of Ahaz" in *BASOR*, 79, pp. 27–28. Cf. his debate with Albright and Sukenik, *ibid.*, 82, pp. 16–17; 84, pp. 17–19. These practices help explain the vehemence of the Deuteronomic injunction, "One from among thy brethren shalt thou set king over thee; thou mayest not put a foreigner over thee, who is not thy brother" (17:15). The Egyptian influences on the administrative setup under the first kings are discussed, affirmatively, in R. de Vaux's "Titres et fonctionnaires égyptiens à la cour de David et de Salomon," *RB*, XLVIII, 394–405;. and J. Begrich's "Sōfēr und Mazkīr," *ZAW*, LVIII, 1–29; and, negatively, in B. Maisler's "Scribe of King David and the Problem of the High Officials in the Ancient Kingdom of Israel" (Hebrew), *BJPES*, XIII, 105–14.

17. Cf. J. W. Crowfoot *et al.*, *Buildings of Samaria*. Our knowledge of ancient Israelitic taxation and fiscal structure is still very inadequate. Neither the few tangential statements in the Bible (including I Sam. 8:14–17) nor the incidental archaeological finds allow for any safe generalization. Even the problem of the Samarian "tax receipts" is still unsolved. A quarter of a century ago M. Noth made a strong case for considering them simple receipts in business transactions of the royal domain. Cf. his "Krongut der israelitischen Könige," *ZDPV*, L, 211–44. Similarly the question of the royal monopoly in pottery, long considered settled by the numerous jar handles bearing the inscriptions *Le-melekh* (to the king) found in various archaeological sites, has been reopened in recent years. E. L. Sukenik (in his "Meaning of the 'Le-Melekh' Inscriptions" [Hebrew], *Kedem*, I, 32–36) interpreted these stamps as mere official confirmations of certain standard sizes, while E. Sellin suggested that the jars were so stamped because they were used for wine and oil produced in the royal domain. See "Die palästinischen Krughenkel mit den Königsstempeln," *ZDPV*, LXVI, 216–32; and, on some palaeographic aspects, D. Diringer's "Royal Jar-Handle Stamps of Ancient Judah," *BA*, XII, 70–86. Curiously, these inscriptions have frequently appeared in Judean sites, including Tell en-Nasbeh (ancient Mizpah?), but none have turned up thus far in neighboring Bethel which belonged to the Northern Kingdom. Cf. the comprehensive recent report by C. C. McCown, *et al.* on *Tell en Nasbeh;* and G. E. Wright's comments thereon in *BA*, X, 71. Royal manufacture of pottery seems sufficiently borne out, however, by the biblical reference to potters "occupied in the king's work" (I Chron. 4:23).

Nor is there any reason for assuming that Solomon's extensive industrial and commercial undertakings, confirmed by the archaeological evidence from Ezion Geber, were completely abandoned by his successors. For example, the large stables accommodating some 450 horses and 150 chariots which were unearthed at Megiddo were apparently built by Solomon, but they evidently survived the city's destruction by Shishak and were still used by Jeroboam I and later. In fact, J. W. Crowfoot claims that they were first built by Ahab ("Megiddo—a Review," *PEQ*, 1940, pp. 146 f.). While these stables primarily served as arsenals, Solomon certainly used them also as commercial warehouses for his horses and chariots, which were imported and exported in large numbers by his "king's merchants" (I Kings 10:26–29). The subsequent disruption of trade routes occasioned by the division into two kingdoms and the loss of control over Edom and Philistia greatly reduced Palestine's role in international trade, but the kings must have tried the more fully to exploit the few remaining avenues.

18. Cf. M. Noth's data in *Die israelitischen Personennamen im Rahmen der gemeinsemitischen Namengebung,* p. 120. A list of names found at Lachish written shortly before the fall of Jerusalem showed that seven out of nine were compounded with Yahu "and in the eighth, Ṭobshillem, it may be implied '(Yhwh) has repaid good.'" Cf. H. Torczyner's *Lachish Letters,* pp. 28 f., 72, 198. Torczyner goes too far, however, in deducing from these onomatological statistics that the Lachish garrison felt more strongly than most Jerusalemites the impact of the Deuteronomic reformation and that it belonged to a particular religious party led by the prophet Uriah. Similarly, the change of the king's name from Eliakim to Jehoiakim, ascribed to Pharaoh Necho (II Kings 23:34), need not have been the effect of that reformation, but rather the acceptance of a custom fairly well established among the Davidic rulers since Jehoshaphat. Cf. also *supra,* Chap. II, n. 40; and *infra,* n. 33.

19. Legal principles and observances, springing from analogous social conditions, are often strikingly similar. Perhaps even more than in other fields scholars must refrain here from drawing hasty parallels and, particularly, from postulating historic influences. The early enthusiasm which followed the successive discoveries of the Code of Hammurabi, the Hittite and Assyrian codes, and the vast contractual records of Nuzi has given way to more sober second thoughts. Cf., e.g., the negative results of M. David's investigation of "The Code of Hammurabi and Its Relation to the Legal Provisions in Exodus" (Dutch), *Tijdschrift voor Rechtsgeschiedenis,* XVII, 73–98. However, using the necessary caution and always remembering that parallels need not reflect influence and that differences are at least as important as similarities, the student of biblical law may learn a great deal from such comparative material. For example, the town's responsibility for unsolved crimes has been elucidated by a Nuzi tablet examined by C. H. Gordon in his "Akkadian Parallel to Deuteronomy 21:1 ff.," *Revue d'Assyriologie,* XXXIII, 1–6. Cf. also R. Patai's "'Egla 'Arufa or the Expiation of the Polluted Land," *JQR,* XXX, 59–69. Many other insights have been secured by such general comparative studies as E. Ring's *Israels Rechtsleben im Lichte der neuentdeckten assyrischen und hethitischen Gesetzesurkunden;* E. Cuq's *Etudes sur le droit babylonien, les lois assyriennes et les lois hittites;* J. M. P. Smith's *Origin and History of Hebrew Law;* and P. Korngreen's *Ḥuqqe ha-mizraḥ ha-qadmon* (The Laws of the Ancient Near East).

These comparative studies have received new impetus by the recent discovery of two Sumerian law codes (Eshnunna and Lipit-Ishtar), both of which antedated that of Hammurabi by more than a century. Cf. especially F. R. Steele's "Lipit-Ishtar Law Code," *AJA,* LI, 158–64; his "Code of Lipit-Ishtar," *ibid.,* LII, 425–50; A. Goetze's "Laws of Eshnunna Discovered at Tell Harmal," *Sumer,* IV, 63–102; and, as a sample of preliminary comparative investigations, M. San Nicolò's "Religionsgeschichtliches zum Gesetz des Bilalama von Ešnunna," *Orientalia,* XVIII, 258–62.

Ring has pointed out that, much as the other ancient legal compilations likewise depended on ultimate religious sanctions (the well-known Louvre stele represents Hammurabi as receiving his code from his god, Marduk), they were essentially secular codes of law, whereas biblical law was an integral part of Israel's religion.

This distinction is evident in the differentiation between "Error and Accident in the Bible" as analyzed by D. Daube in *RIDA*, III, 189–213. It comes to the fore with particular clarity in the domain of family relations, which have almost always hovered on the borderline between civil and religious law. One need but compare, for instance, A. van Praag's survey of the *Droit matrimonial assyro-babylonien* with L. M. Epstein's *Marriage Laws in the Bible and the Talmud;* M. Burrows's *Basis of Israelite Marriage;* and G. E. van Randenborgh's *Von der Ordnung der Ehe,* or to peruse E. Neufeld's *Ancient Hebrew Marriage Laws, with Special Reference to General Semitic Laws and Customs,* to notice the difference in their basic approach. Cf. also J. M. Mittelmann's *Altisraelitische Levirat;* Burrows's "Levirate Marriage" in Israel," *JBL,* LIX, 23–33; and "The Marriage of Boaz and Ruth," *ibid.,* pp. 445–54 (concluding that the latter corresponded "to a stage of folk-custom in Israel earlier than those represented by the Pentateuchal laws regarding inheritance, redemption and levirate marriage"); and more generally, the older literature listed by H. Duesberg in his "Introduction bibliographique du droit du peuple hébreu," *Archives d'histoire du droit oriental,* II, 143–69; E. J. White's *Law in the Scriptures;* C. Tchernowitz's *Toledoth ha-halakah* (History of the Halakah); M. Noth's *Gesetze im Pentateuch, ihre Voraussetzungen und ihr Sinn;* J. van der Ploeg's "Studies in Hebrew Law," *CBQ,* XII–XIII; and D. Daube's *Studies in Biblical Law* (supplemented by a defense of his method in *Archiv Orientalni,* XVII, 88–99).

20. See Alt's "Ursprünge des israelitischen Rechts," *Berichte über die Verhandlungen der Sächsischen Akademie der Wissenschaften,* LXXXVI, 1–72. Despite the enthusiastic acceptance of Alt's theory by many scholars, the Canaanite background of the "casuistic" laws in the Book of the Covenant is still rather dubious. Cf. the generally divergent views reached after a detailed examination of that earliest Hebrew collection of laws by Morgenstern in *HUCA,* V, VII–IX; and by H. Cazelles in his *Études sur le Code de l'Alliance.* Cf. also W. Caspari's "Heimat und soziale Wirkung des alttestamentlichen Bundesbuchs," *ZDMG,* LXXXIII, 97–120; Tchernowitz's *Toledoth ha-halakah,* I, Pt. 2, pp. 210 ff. (citing the views of R. Ishmael, Ibn Ezra and Naḥmanides); S. I. Feigin's "Jethro's Book of Laws" (Hebrew), *SH,* VII, 89–125; and *supra,* Chap. II, n. 31.

21. Cf. L. Köhler's stimulating address on *Die hebräische Rechtsgemeinde* (comparing it with the Swiss "street courts"); and my *Jewish Community,* I, 39 f., 48 f.; III, 7 n. 3. In his "Judicial Reform of Jehoshaphat," *Marx Jub. Vol.,* pp. 61–82, W. F. Albright argued not only for the essential historicity of the Chronicler's account (II Chron. 19:4–11) concerning that reform, but also asserted, "That the administration of civil justice was transferred long before the Exile from the 'elders' to royally appointed judges may be taken as certain" (p. 75). Much as we may agree with Albright's greater appreciation of the Chronicler's veracity (see *infra,* Chap. IV, n. 4) there is no evidence of any permanent success of Jehoshaphat's reform. On the contrary, the constant decline in the royal power in both kingdoms would have nullified any permanent monarchical control over the local judiciary, even if Jehoshaphat's attempt had proved initially more successful than we have any reason for assuming. Cf. also P. L. Ross's "Lawyers and Judges in Hebrew Jurisprudence," *United States Law Review,* LXVII, 19–26; and J. A. Montgomery's "Law and Religion in the Ancient World as Illustrated in the Bible," *ATR,* XXIII, 293–306.

22. The connection between the biblical prohibition of seething a kid in its mother's milk and the somewhat uncertain reading of *tb [ẖ g] d bḥlb* (prepare the kid in milk) in the Ugaritic Poem of *The Birth of Gracious and Beautiful Gods,* 13, was first suggested, soon after that poem's publication, by R. Dussaud in "Les Phéniciens au Négeb et en Arabie," *RHR,* CVIII, 7 f. Unwittingly Dussaud thus confirmed an explanation offered in the twelfth century, on the basis of reasoning rather than direct

evidence, by Maimonides in his *Guide for the Perplexed*, III, 48 (in Friedlaender's transl. p. 371).

23. Num. 5. Considering the widespread use of river and other ordeals in the legal procedures of Assyria, Nuzi, etc., it must have been owing to an equally conscious suppression of this practice by Israelitic legislators that we have so few vestiges of it in the Bible. Cf. J. Morgenstern's "Trial by Ordeal among the Semites and in Ancient Israel," *HUCA*, Jubilee Vol., pp. 113–43; and R. Press's "Ordal im Alten Israel, I," *ZAW*, LI, 121–40. The ascertainment of the divine will through throwing lots played a great role in public affairs (e.g., the detection of Achan and the election of Saul). Cf. A. Lods's "Rôle des oracles dans la nomination des rois, des prêtres et des magistrats chez les Israélites, les Egyptiens et les Grecs," *Mémoires de l'Institut Français du Caire*, LXVI, Pt. 1, pp. 91–100. But it seems not to have been given much leeway in civil proceedings. Apart from the dubious passage, "The lot causeth strife to cease, and parteth asunder the contentions" (Prov. 18:18), which may refer to extra-legal settlement of disputes and, like much else in the book of Proverbs, may reflect general oriental, rather than specifically Israelitic practice, we find no record of outright judicial reliance on this type of evidence. Even if we were to accept the somewhat tenuous interpretation by W. F. Albright of "The Copper Spatula of Byblus and Proverbs 18:18," *BASOR*, 90, pp. 35–37, we would have here but a physical specimen of lots used in non-Israelitic Byblus.

24. Cf. J. Morgenstern's "Chapter in the History of the High-Priesthood," *AJSL*, LV, 11 f.; A. Maecklenburg's analysis of "Die Anschauung der Bibel über die hebräische Musik," *Biblische Zeitschrift*, XXII, 101–17, 332–49; H. F. Vos's "Music of Israel," *Bibliotheca Sacra*, CVI, 446–57; CVII, 64–70; M. Wegner's *Musikinstrumente des Alten Orients*; and other literature listed in A. Sendrey's comprehensive *Bibliography of Jewish Music*, pp. 23 ff. The early conflict between the spiritual and temporal powers in the days of Samuel and Saul is interestingly analyzed by E. Robertson in his Hebrew essay on "Priesthood and Monarchy" in *Melilah*, II, 279–99. Cf. also *infra*, Chap. V, n. 21.

25. There is little new evidence for the extent to which the ancient Hebrews indulged in magical practices frowned upon by their leaders. The older views are well summarized in A. Lods's comparative study of "Magie hébraïque et magie cananéenne," *RHPR*, VII, 1–16; and E. Dhorme's "Prêtres, devins et mages dans l'ancienne religion des Hébreux," *RHR*, CVIII, 113–43. However, even the meaning of the so-called "Magical Terms in the Old Testament" is highly controversial. Cf. the debate between A. Guillaume and G. R. Driver in *JRAS*, 1942, pp. 111 ff.; 1943, pp. 6 ff., 251 ff.; 1944, pp. 165 ff.; 1946, pp. 79 f. Although it is likely that ancient Israelitic women employed Astarte figurines as talismans of a sort during childbirth (*supra*, Chap. II, n. 20) and had even less compunctions about using for that purpose objects inscribed with pertinent incantations (as did their medieval descendants), the only text of this kind written in preëxilic Hebrew was recently found in Arslan Tash, Upper Syria, and was doubtless written by a Phoenician. Cf. Comte du Mesnil du Buisson's "Tablette magique de la region du moyen Euphrate," *Mélanges Dussaud*, I, 421–34; T. H. Gaster's "Canaanite Magical Text," *Orientalia*, XI, 41–79; and his debate with H. Torczyner (in *JNES*, VI, 18–29, 186–88) as to whether the incantation was aimed at night demons generally or, in particular, at a child-stealing night hag. Cf. also *infra*, Chap. V, n. 9.

26. The biblical references to the genealogies of the tribe of Levi (e.g., Exod. 6:16–19 and Num. 26:58), the descendants of either Moses or Aaron and relations between the "priests" and the "levites" (Deuteronomy calls them as a rule in one breath "the priests the levites"), are full of obscurities and have been the subject of

almost endless controversies. See K. Möhlenbrink's survey of "Die levitischen Ueber-
lieferungen des Alten Testaments," ZAW, LII, 184–231; and C. Lattey's "Tribe of
Levi," CBQ, XII, 277–91. Zadok, in particular, who started as a provincial priest in
Gibeon (I Chron. 16:39), then served with Abiathar at David's court, and, finally,
after helping secure Solomon's accession to the throne, became the founder of the
chief priestly dynasty in Jerusalem, became a highly controversial figure in both
ancient and modern discussions. While A. Bentzen tried to defend his descent from
Aaron, as construed by the Chronicler (I Chron. 5:27–34; 6:35–38), H. H. Rowley
suggested that he had been a Jebusite priest in Jerusalem taken over by David after
the city's conquest. Cf. Bentzen's Studier over det zadokidiske praesterskabs Historie
(Studies in the History of the Zadokite Priesthood; "Zur Geschichte der Ṣadoḳiden,"
ZAW, LI, 173–76; and Rowley's essays in JBL, LVIII, 130 ff., and in Festschrift
Bertholet, pp. 461 ff. Cf. also K. Budde's critique in "Die Herkunft Ṣadoḳ's," ZAW,
LII, 42–50; and supra, Chap. II, n. 39. Nevertheless, in trying to defend its own
sacerdotal legitimacy through its claim to descent from the family of Moses, the
priestly class as a whole was bound more or less staunchly to uphold the Mosaic
tradition. On the priest cities, cf. infra, Chap. V, n. 16.

27. Deut. 6:20–25. The Deuteronomic overemphasis on such protestations was evidently intended even more to appease the author's own conscience than to forestall
the objections of opponents. So is his assurance that "this commandment which I
command thee this day, it is not too hard for thee, neither is it far off. It is not in
heaven. . . . Neither is it beyond the sea. . . . But the word is very nigh unto thee,
in thy mouth and in thy heart, that thou mayest do it" (Deut. 30:11–14). Cf. also
A. Causse's Du groupe ethnique, pp. 144 ff., emphasizing the idea of Israel's brotherhood as the outstanding element in the political and social ideal of the book of
Deuteronomy.
The position here taken that this book, in its essential parts, is the product of the
religious and social reformation under Josiah, is still shared by the regnant scholarly
opinion. The significant researches of T. Oestreicher, A. C. Welch, and E. Robertson,
which have demonstrated the necessity of dating earlier substantial sections, and, on
the other hand, G. Hölscher's equally penetrating arguments in favor of the exilic
provenance of many passages, have not succeeded in wholly eliminating the older
theory. They have undoubtedly proved the shakiness of this corner stone of Graf
and Wellhausen's classical structure, but they have thus far failed to evolve a complete positive hypothesis which would as fully explain the major difficulties as did
the older theory in the heyday of higher criticism. Cf. "The Problem of Deuteronomy:
a Symposium," by J. A. Bewer, L. B. Paton and G. Dahl in JBL, XLVII, 305–79; W.
A. Irwin's "Objective Criterion for the Dating of Deuteronomy," AJSL, LVI, 337–49
(Deut. 28 proves the preëxilic existence of the code); G. R. Berry's "Date of Deuteronomy," JBL, LIX, 133–39 ("about 520 or, more probably, a few years later"); R. H.
Pfeiffer's Introduction, pp. 178 ff. (the bulk of the code was compiled in 621, but it
underwent three revisions down to 400 B.C.E.); and E. Robertson's essays cited supra,
Chap. II, n. 37. Nor have the fundamentalists been completely silenced. An able
defense of the Mosaic authorship of the whole Pentateuch is presented, for instance,
by O. T. Allis in his Five Books of Moses. Cf. also G. von Rad's more recent
Deuteronomium-Studien (chiefly concerned with the problem of its sources; uses the
techniques of form criticism); S. Yeivin's complementary Hebrew essays on "The
Date of Deuteronomy," Dinaburg Jub. Vol., pp. 31–48, and "Torah as Legislation in
Judah and Israel," Tarbiz, XX, 58–60 (ably, but not altogether convincingly, arguing
that in its essentials Deut. dates back to the days of Solomon or soon after); C. A.
Simpson's Early Traditions of Israel (an attempt to reconstruct the pre-Deuteronomic
layers in the narratives of the Hexateuch); M. Noth's Ueberlieferungsgeschichte des
Pentateuchs; O. Eissfeldt's detailed review of Simpson's work in Die ältesten Tradi-
tionen Israels; his more general survey, "Die neueste Phase in der Entwicklung der

Pentateuchkritik," *Theologische Rundschau*, XVIII, 91–122, 179–215, 267–87, with special reference to F. V. Winnett's *Mosaic Tradition;* and, on the long earlier history of these debates, H. H. Krause's survey, *Das Deuteronomium in der wissenschaftlichen Bearbeitung des 19. und 20. Jahrhunderts.*

Perhaps this entire problem, as that of the other sections of the Pentateuch, will appear in a new light when the numerous small fragments discovered in the 'Ain Fashkha cave, will have been published and carefully scrutinized. Because of the great time lag, however, between the original composition and the date of the present copies, which hardly antedate the Maccabean or Herodian period, these finds may be more enlightening for the story of the Second than for that of the First Commonwealth. Moreover, these hundreds of lesser fragments still await publication. Only some of the larger scrolls, including that of the book of Isaiah, have so far seen the light of day. See *infra*, Chap. IV, n. 3. The Pentateuchal fragments, perhaps of even more direct interest to research in preëxilic literature, including fragments of Lev. 19–22, parts of Gen. and Deut., etc., were first briefly discussed by G. L. Harding in his "Dead Sea Scrolls," *PEQ*, 1949, pp. 112–16; and R. de Vaux, in "La Grotte des manuscrits hébreux," *RB*, LVI, 586–609.

There has, in fact, already grown up a fantastic secondary literature around those scrolls. Apart from offering a host of exegetical comments, most writers evinced great concern for the problem of dating. Many recent issues of *JQR*, *BASOR* and other journals have devoted most generous space to this question. Cf., e.g., the debate between E. R. Lacheman, W. F. Albright, M. Burrows and S. Zeitlin in *JQR*, XL, 15–78; XLI, 1–58; G. R. Driver's "New Hebrew Manuscripts," *ibid.*, pp. 359–72; and W. F. Albright's and S. A. Birnbaum's comments in *BASOR*, 115, pp. 10–22. The divergence of views even among such experts on ancient writing as S. A. Birnbaum and S. Yeivin is illustrated by their recent discussion of the Leviticus fragment. In their independently written essays in *BASOR*, 118, pp. 20–30, Birnbaum came to the conclusion that the most likely date is the second half of the fifth century B.C.E., whereas Yeivin asserted that we have here remains of a Samaritan manuscript of Leviticus of about 100 B.C.E. Cf. also Birnbaum's "Date of the Covenant Scroll," *PEQ*, 1949, pp. 140–47 (dating it at 200–50 B.C.E.); and, more generally, R. de Vaux's "À propos des manuscrits de la Mer Morte," *RB*, LVII, 417–29. Although the main, paleographic argument in favor of dating these scrolls in the pre-Christian era is far from conclusive—there is too little comparative material available—the weight of evidence favors the Maccabean or Herodian age as the most likely period of the composition of most of these fragments. This date is confirmed by the evidently Hellenistic jars in which the manuscripts were found and the cloth used for their wrapping which, when measured by the new nuclear Carbon 14 process, yielded a date between 167 B.C.E. and 233 C.E. Cf. O. R. Sellers's brief communication in *BA*, XIV, 29.

28. After carefully analyzing the use of the term "Torah" in the Book of Jeremiah *(JBL*, LX, 381–96), J. P. Hyatt comes to the conclusion that, although not attaching great importance to this concept and generally denying that the true Torah was incorporated in any book, Jeremiah nevertheless identified it with the "ancient paths" and preached a new covenant rather than a new Torah. These conclusions will be accepted by many who share neither the author's overcritical appraisal of the text which reduces to only five the genuine occurrences of the word *torah*, nor the chronology elaborated elsewhere (in Hyatt's "Jeremiah and Deuteronomy," *JNES*, I, 156–73), according to which Jeremiah began his public career about a decade after Josiah's reform of 621. Cf. also H. G. May's "Chronology of Jeremiah's Oracles," *ibid.*, IV, 217–27; and *infra*, Chap. V, n. 11.

Neither is there any evidence that Jeremiah ever opposed the centralization of worship. Whether or not he was, like Josiah, interested in the destruction of local sanctuaries because they had focalized the political aspirations of provincial nobles and priests, he certainly objected to their harboring the surviving vestiges of ancient polytheistic cults. Cf. also A. Robert's "Jérémie et la réforme deutéronomique," *Science religieuse*, 1943, pp. 5–16; and H. H. Rowley's "Prophet Jeremiah and the Book of Deuteronomy," *Studies Robinson*, pp. 157–74, culminating in the assertion "that Jeremiah had some knowledge of its contents and style, though not the sort of access that possession of a copy might have given, and that he at first advocated the Deuteronomic reform, but later perceived its spiritual failure and therefore condemned its insufficiency." H. Cazelles, on the other hand, looks chiefly to the editors of both books for the explanation of the obvious mutual influences which, he points out, have been heatedly debated ever since 1839. Cf. his "Jérémie et le Deutéronome," *Recherches de science religieuse*, XXXVIII, 5–36.

In his "Reichstempel und Ortsheiligtümer in Israel," *Beiträge zur Förderung christlicher Theologie*, XXXIII, 139–94, T. Oestreicher tried to prove the coëxistence throughout the preëxilic period of purely religious local sanctuaries, the *bamot*, and the *hekhal* (the royal temple), in which the political played as strong a part as the religious element. However, this hypothesis, expounded in consonance with Oestreicher's older theories concerning the early composition of Deuteronomy, cannot be said to have stood the test of either a careful analysis of the sources, or of broader historical considerations. It is, in particular, vitiated by the unwarranted assumption that Josiah, undertaking the war of liberation of Samaria from Assyrian domination, would not have dared to antagonize the vested interests of the *bamot*. One certainly ought not to underestimate the propelling religious force which determined the enthusiastic reformer to purify his own camp before removing all vestiges of the Assyrian cults in the northern province.

29. Cf. E. Junge's *Wiederaufbau des Heerwesens des Reiches Juda unter Josia*, and Y. Yadin's comments on the same subject in *BJPES*, XV, 86–98. The Deuteronomic laws of military organization (20:1–9) are, however, ideals rather than practical norms. It was an utopian attempt to restore the army of free peasants as it had existed in the days of Deborah (Judg. 5:11) and to eliminate costly cavalry and heavy equipment. This tendency found telling expression in the prophetic denunciation of the importation of horses and chariots from Egypt, and possibly also in the elaboration of the popular legend depicting the victory of the unarmed shepherd David over the well-accoutered "knight" Goliath. Cf. Menes, *Gesetze*, pp. 109 ff. The memory of the two thousand chariots of Ahab at Karkara, instead of evoking a sense of pride, merely added to the opprobrium attached in prophetic circles to all undertakings of that much-hated king. Nevertheless, a certain amount of mass participation in the perpetual warfare may be taken for granted, if the figures of combatants, recorded in the most reliable historical sections of the Old Testament, are to be given any credence at all. Cf. also H. E. Del Medico's brief survey of *Armées et finances dans l'Ancien Testament*.

30. Lev. 25:29–31. The conviction, long widely held by critical scholars (cf. A. Jirku's analysis of "Das israelitische Jobeljahr" in the *Reinhold Seeberg Festschrift*, II, 169–79; and N. M. Nicolsky's note in *ZAW*, L, 216) that the biblical Jubilee year had never been observed, has been somewhat shaken in recent years. Although nothing so far-reaching and so deeply permeated with passion for social justice has been found anywhere else, some minor parallels have been detected in Nuzi. Cf. Gordon's remarks in *RB*, XLIV, 34 ff. The Nies Babylonian collection at Yale has likewise yielded evidence that at times, though not at fixed periods, the Babylonian kings also enacted a general cancellation of contracts. Cf. J. B. Alexander's "Babylonian Year of Jubilee?" *JBL*, LVII, 75–79. The Hebrew Jubilee year itself may have been but an attenuation of a regular system of restitution every seventh year (the biblical lawgiver refers to this background of "seven times seven years," Lev. 25:8) which seems to have prevailed among the Hebrews of the patriarchal age. Both A. Musil

(in his *Arabia Petraea*, III, 293 f.) and G. Dalman (in his *Arbeit und Sitte*, II, 36, 38 f., 131 ff.) have pointed out that many seminomadic tribes in and around Palestine have often practiced redistribution of land at intervals of seven years or less. The priestly redactor may have tried to revive here, as elsewhere, a very old practice, abandoned or modified during the subsequent more "advanced" social evolution. Certainly the preëxilic observance of a year of fallowness appears the more likely, as that institution, though devoid of the regularity of a seven-year cycle and the sanctification by the Sabbath idea, has also been found among contemporary Bedouins. Cf. Alt's remarks in *PJB*, XXXV, 36; and *infra*, Chap. V, notes 13–15.

31. Judg. 9:4. Nor is there any evidence for the Hebrew sanctuaries serving as fiscal agencies, a practice extensively employed in medieval Islam but traced back to ancient Babylonia by A. L. Oppenheim in his "Fiscal Practice in the Near East," *JNES*, VI, 116–20. They may have been used, however, as depositaries, offering because of the awe of sacrilege greater protection than individuals entrusted with the safekeeping of movables. This widespread ancient and medieval practice, though recorded only at the Second Temple (cf. *infra*, Chap. VIII, n. 29) was possibly reflected in one of the various shades of meaning given by prophets and psalmists (Isa. 56:5; Zech. 6:14–15, etc.) to the "Sojourn in the Tent of Jahu," according to B. Eerdmans's interpretation in *OS*, I, 1–16.

32. Amos 7:12, 14; Micah 3:5; Jer. 23:13 ff. T. J. Meek is right in saying that, even if *nabi* originally meant "one who is called" (akin to the Akkadian *nabu*), as suggested by Albright, the Hebrews used it as the equivalent of "spokesman." Cf. Exod. 7:1; 4:16; and *JBL*, LXI, 40 f. The frequently involuntary nature of Israelitic prophecy is well rendered by the frequent use of the term *massa* (burden) for a prophetic vision. The rabbis underscored this double meaning by comparing it with the "heavy burden" of sins in Ps. 38:5 (Gen. r. XLIV, 6, p. 429). Cf. also H. S. Gehman's analysis of that term in *JQR*, XXXI, 107–21.

Numerous attempts have been made to find objective criteria to differentiate "true" from "false" prophets, but J. Skinner is still perfectly right in asserting that "in externals there was nothing to distinguish the one kind of prophet from the other." Cf. his *Prophecy and Religion*, p. 188. Of course, the picture of the "false prophets" often appears polemically distorted. There were among them sincere devotees of the Israelitic religion, as they conceived it. Only few of them consciously tried to perpetuate Canaanite ideals, as Mowinckel thought, even where they appear to have borrowed heavily from Canaanite prototypes. They frequently represented merely an older stage in religion, and preached theological principles which had been regarded as sound in the preceding period, but which had been discarded during the subsequent historical evolution. The "true" prophets, on the other hand, were primarily those whose minds were open to the meaning of the new historic experience from which they deduced the wish of God. Cf. G. von Rad's "Die falschen Propheten," *ZAW*, LI, 109–20, and especially his statement: "History always was for Israel the place in which God's reign became manifest. The true prophet viewed the concrete historic evolution with complete lack of predetermination [*Ungesicherheit*]" (p. 119). Cf. also E. F. Siegman's *False Prophets of the Old Testament*; and M. Buber's "Falsche Propheten," *Wandlung*, II, 277–83 (the true prophets were "Realpolitiker," the false prophets "Illusionspolitiker"). It is not surprising, on the other hand, that the exalted teachings derived by the prophets from the changing course of events, often appeared starkly utopian to more "realistic" statesmen.

The limitations of the present treatment prevent us from surveying the impact of social developments upon the successive stages of preëxilic prophecy, from Elijah to Amos and down to Jeremiah. For such a chronological discussion, cf., for instance, A. Causse's *Du groupe ethnique*, pp. 61 ff.; A. Lods's *Prophets and the Rise of Judaism*; F. James's *Personalities of the Old Testament*; B. D. Cohon's *Prophets*; and J. M. P.

Smith's *Prophets and Their Times*, 2d ed. Neither can the much-debated psychological background of prophetic ecstasy (as recorded in Northern Syria as early as 1100 by the Egyptian traveler Wenamon) and its impact upon both true and false prophecy be discussed here. Cf. the general surveys by W. Baumgartner, "Die Auffassungen des 19. Jahrhunderts vom israelitischen Prophetismus," *Archiv für Kulturgeschichte*, XV, 21–35; A. Lods, "Recherches récentes sur le prophétisme israélite," *RHR*, CIV, 279–316; and H. H. Rowley, "Nature of Prophecy in the Light of Recent Study," *HTR*, XXXVIII, 1–38. Cf. also S. Mowinckel's "Ecstatic Experience and Rational Elaboration in Old Testament Prophecy," *Acta Orientalia*, XIII, 264–91; M. Sister's "Typen der prophetischen Visionen in der Bibel," *MGWJ*, LXXVIII, 399–430; A. Heschel's *Prophetie*; P. Volz's *Prophetengestalten des Alten Testaments*; J. Lindblom's "Religion der Propheten und die Mystik," *ZAW*, LVII, 65–74; J. P. Hyatt's *Prophetic Religion*; G. Widengren's *Literary and Psychological Aspects of the Hebrew Prophets*; various essays in *Studies Robinson*; and the works listed *infra*, n. 38.

33. These "pamphlets" were undoubtedly written on ostraca, which were far less expensive than papyri. One need not give up hope, therefore, that some day potsherds will turn up containing original fragments of some prophetic oration. They may even prove to be autographs. The fact that Jeremiah, for example, is known to have employed Baruch to write down his prophecies is no more proof of his ignorance of writing than is the use of secretarial services by modern writers. J. P. Hyatt's suggestion that this may have been the case, because "the great majority of people could neither read nor write" (cf. his "Writing of an Old Testament Book," *BA*, VI, 72) seems clearly controverted by the Lachish ostraca. Written by different scribes these letters indicate, according to Torczyner, "that the ancient Jews could write quickly and boldly, in an artistic flowing hand, with the loving penmanship of those who enjoy writing" (*The Lachish Letters*, p. 15). We certainly must not assume, without further proof except a general disposition to exaggerate ancient illiteracy, that the small Lachish garrison included several professional scribes, lay or priestly.

The publication of these letters by Torczyner in 1938 (also in a revised Hebrew edition, entitled *Te'udot Lakhish*, which includes three additional letters) caused a great stir in biblical scholarship. Here were original letters written in the days of Jeremiah in pure biblical Hebrew, which shed unexpected new light on many aspects of life in the vicinity of Jerusalem shortly before its destruction. More than a score of significant articles by scholars of various lands appeared in quick succession. Cf. the list in S. W. Baron's *Bibliography of Jewish Social Studies, 1938–39*, No. 1217. Among more recent comments, cf., e.g., H. L. Ginsberg's "Lachish Ostraca New and Old," *BASOR*, 80, pp. 10–13; W. F. Albright's "Lachish Letters after Five Years," *ibid.*, 82, pp. 18–24; H. Michaud's "Témoignage des ostraca de Tell Douweir concernant le prophète Jérémie," *RES*, 1941, pp. 42–60; B. Chapira's "Lettres de Lakiš," *ibid.*, 1942–45, pp. 105–73; and M. A. van den Oudenrijn's address on *Fouilles de Lakis et l'étude de l'Ancien Testament*.

An interesting sidelight on the situation in Palestine at that time has been shed by a newly discovered Aramaic letter addressed by Adon, king of Ascalon (?) to the King of Egypt and asking for aid against the onrushing hosts of Chaldaea (probably dated in 603–602 or 599–98). Published by A. Dupont-Sommer, in *Semitica*, I, 43–68, this letter has been reinterpreted by H. L. Ginsberg in his "Aramaic Contemporary of the Lachish Letters," *BASOR*, 111, pp. 24–27. Cf. also J. Bright's "New Letter in Aramaic," *BA*, XII, 46–52; A. Malamat's "New Aramaic Saqqârah Papyrus from the Time of Jeremiah" (Hebrew), *BJPES*, XV, 33–39 (dating it in 599–98); and, more generally, his "Last Wars of the Kingdom of Judah," *JNES*, IX, 218–27.

34. The new light thrown by the Ugaritic poems on the Baal cult at Carmel which underlay the decisive struggle between Jezebel and the prophetic party has put into bolder relief Elijah's uncompromising purism. Cf., in particular, A. Alt's remarks in

Festschrift Georg Beer, pp. 1 ff.; R. Dussaud's "Vrai nom de Baal," *RHR*, CXIII, 5–20; M. Astour's "Original Concept of Yahweh" (Yiddish), *Yivo Bleter*, XIII, 477–504; and R. de Vaux's "Prophètes de Baal sur le Mont Carmel," *Bulletin du Musée de Beyrouth*, V, 7–20. In view of the sharp attacks in Hosea 1–3 on Baal worship, which allegedly had been extirpated by Jehu (II Kings 10:28), Y. Kaufmann argues for their great antiquity. See his "Three Chapters of the Earlier Hosea" (Hebrew), *Keneset*, X, 121–29. Whether or not the "idols" (*gillulim*) at the Temple of Jerusalem which provoked Ezekiel's wrath (8:10) were connected with the worship of Osiris, certainly the existence there of "every detestable form of creeping things and beasts" sufficed to justify the prophet's anger. In fact, he could have been equally aroused by a mere stele of stone or wood, if unsophisticated worshipers regarded it as an agent of redemption. Cf. Torczyner's ingenious interpretation of Ez. 8:3, 5, in his "Image of Jealousy which Provoketh to Jealousy" (Hebrew) in *Ha-Lashon ve-ha-sefer*, II, 275–96 (summarized from an earlier essay in *JBL*, LXV, 293–302); A. S. Yahuda's "Osiris Cult and the Designation of Osiris Idols in the Bible," *JNES*, III, 194–97; and C. Virolleaud's "Sur l'idole de la jalousie," *RES*, 1945, pp. 59–63.

One must not imagine, however, that in their opposition to imagery the prophets had any of the compunctions of the later anti-anthropomorphic thinkers. They did not hesitate to describe their own visions with much picturesque detail. B. L. Goff rightly remarks that in "Isaiah's attitude to the seraphim and Ezekiel's vision of the living creatures with the chariot . . . the symbols did not serve even remotely as objects of worship, but added emotional richness and majesty to the awareness of divinity" ("Syncretism in the Religion of Israel," *JBL*, LVIII, 161). Cf. also F. Weinrich's *Religiös-utopische Charakter der "prophetischen Politik"*; S. Mowinckel's "Connaissance de Dieu chez les prophètes de l'Ancien Testament," *RHPR*, XXII, 69–105; and *supra*, Chap. II, n. 32.

35. Josh. 24:13. No less expressive is the injunction in Deut. 6:10–12. As against this frank admission, the self-assertion of the Judaism of the Second Commonwealth and after, and the growing conviction that the Jews have a primordial and exclusive claim to Palestine, are best illustrated by the words put into the mouth of Noah's son Ham and his children, Cush and Mizraim, who addressed Canaan (their son and brother respectively), "Thou hast settled in a land that is not thine, and which did not fall unto us by lot" (Book of Jubilees 10:29–34). For further references, see Ginzberg's *Legends*, V, 220, n. 62; and especially Hans Lewy's "Rechtsstreit um den Boden Palästinas," *MGWJ*, LXXVII, 84–99, 172–80. See also G. von Rad's "Verheissenes Land und Jahwe's Land im Hexateuch," *ZDPV*, LVI, 191–204, where the emphasis of the biblical narratives on the divine pledge to the patriarchs to *give* the land to their descendants is contrasted with the legal sections' stress on God's continued *ownership*. These two ideas, however, rather than contrasting, are genuinely complementary.

36. Isa. 9:6; Jer. 35:16; Deut. 28:16. Cf. also Isa. 11:1–10; Amos 5:11, etc. Ever since Karl Budde published, more than half a century ago, his essay on "The Nomadic Ideal in the Old Testament," *New World*, IV, 726–45, this ideal of the ancient prophets harking back to the age of the "nomadic patriarchs" became one of the shibboleths of biblical historians and critics. Cf., e.g., J. W. Flight's "Nomadic Idea and Ideal in the Old Testament," *JBL*, XLII, 158–226. On closer examination, however, it turned out that not only was the patriarchal age itself neither so primitive nor so pastoral as it is somewhat inconsistently depicted in the book of Genesis, but also that the prophets themselves were not wholly of one mind on this subject. Most of the older theories concerning the Bedouin-like patriarchal society were based on the superficial similarity between the stereotyped praise of Bedouins in medieval and modern Arab poetry and the attitude of some biblical authors toward the idyllic life of the Israelitic patriarchs. Only in recent years have several important on-the-spot in-

vestigations produced enough reliable evidence about the life of present-day Bedouins to show that the differences far exceed the similarities. Cf. in particular the detailed studies of Bedouin life in Northern Palestine, Transjordan, and the Negeb (including Beersheba) listed in my *Bibliography*, Nos. 2834–35, 2839–42, 2844, 2848; E. Bräunlich's "Beiträge zur Gesellschaftsordnung der arabischen Beduinenstämme," *Islamica*, VI, 68–111, 182–229; Josef Henninger's "Familie bei den heutigen Beduinen Arabiens und seiner Randgebiete," *Internationales Archiv zur Ethnographie*, XLII, 1–188; and Baron von Oppenheim's *Beduinen*. Cf. also J. L. Myres's basic observations on "Nomadism" in the *Journal of the Royal Anthropological Institute*, LXXI, 19–42. The early Hebrews, moreover, being strangers to the land, did not even enjoy the advantages of the autochtonous nomadic tribes, but possibly belonged for a while to some such inferior groups as are described in J. Henninger's *Pariastämme in Arabien*. Cf. also Causse's pertinent remarks in his *Du groupe ethnique*, pp. 73 ff.; J. Pedersen's "Role Played by Inspired Persons among the Israelites and the Arabs," *Studies Robinson*, pp. 127–42; and *supra*, Chap. II, n. 3. In other words, whatever relatively minor role the "nomadic ideals" played in the socioreligious outlook of the prophets was based not on any recollection, or even mistaken assumption, of a nonexistent bliss during the patriarhal era, but on the general penchant of these "historical monotheists" to contrast the golden ages of Adam or Abraham, as well as of the messianic future, with the corruption of their contemporary civilization. Cf. also J. Rieger's *Bedeutung der Geschichte für die Verkündigung des Amos und Hosea*.

37. The genuineness of the Mesha inscription, long considered definitely established, has been timidly impugned by A. S. Yahuda, but effectively defended by W. F. Albright in *JQR*, XXXV, 139–64, 247–50. Cf. also, from other angles, R. H. Pfeiffer's "Patriotism of Israel's Prophets," *Harvard Divinity School Bulletin*, 1941–42, pp. 45–54; and M. E. Andrews's comparison between "Hesiod and Amos," *JR*, XXIII, 194–205.

38. The record of Hosea's married life and his preachment of God's love for Israel have been subjected to critical scrutiny by many modern scholars. Those who deny the authenticity of both (e.g., L. W. Batten in his "Hosea's Message and Marriage," *JBL*, XLVIII, 257–73) are forced to resort to an extremely radical suppression and emendation of the Masoretic text—always a very dubious proceeding. An interesting psychoanalytic treatment of internal conflict between physical love for a prostitute and deep religious feeling, and of the sublimation of this conflict into the conception of God's love for an unworthy people, is given by A. Allwohn in *Die Ehe des Propheten Hosea in psychoanalytischer Beleuchtung*. In "The Prophet Hosea and His Life as a Symbol for the Relations between Israel and Its God" (Hebrew), *Dinaburg Jub. Vol.*, pp. 49–64, N. H. Torczyner has made it plausible that Hosea did not envisage the mere return of his people to the more primitive conditions of the desert, but rather, like in marriage, a completely fresh start. He daringly intimated that God might again exile the people, as he had sent its ancestors into Egypt, and only subsequently redeem and make a new covenant with it. Cf. also J. W. Povah's *New Psychology and the Hebrew Prophets*; J. Lindblom's "Gesichte der Propheten," *Studia theologica*, I, 7–28; A. Guillaume's *Prophecy and Divination*; C. Toussaint's "Psychologie des prophètes," *Revue des Cours et Conférences*, XXXIX, 673–96; I. P. Seierstad's *Offenbarungserlebnisse der Propheten Amos, Jesaia und Jeremia*; and J. J. Stamm's terminological analysis of *Erlösen und Vergeben im Alten Testament*.

39. II Sam. 14:17; W. F. Albright's "Oldest Hebrew Letters," *BASOR*, 70, p. 15; 82, p. 21 (interpreting the Lachish letter V); and his "Case of Lèse-Majesté in Pre-Israelite Lachish," *ibid.*, 87, pp. 32–38. Nor does the Song of Songs claim any divine qualities for the king. This restraint would appear doubly significant were we to assume with R. Gordis (in his "Wedding Song for Solomon," *JBL*, LXIII, 263–70)

that, apart from later accretions, the Song was composed on the occasion of one of Solomon's marriages to a foreign princess. Cf., on the other hand, D. Buzy's spirited defense of the traditional allegorical interpretation by both Synagogue and Church, in his "Alliance matrimoniale de Jahvé et d'Israël et le Cantique des Cantiques," *RB*, LII, 77–90; H. Torczyner's "historistic" explanation mentioned *infra*, n. 51; and Chap. XII, n. 23.

40. This is not to deny that the king had a variety of important ritualistic functions (cf. II Sam. 6:13; 24:25; II Kings 16:12–13, etc.), although A. R. Johnson far overshoots the mark in his ingenious reconstruction of "The Role of the King in the Jerusalem Cultus" in *The Labyrinth*, ed. by S. H. Hooke, pp. 71–111. R. Patai's study of "Hebrew Installation Rites," *HUCA*, XX, 143–225, though more restrained, is somewhat weakened by the author's excessive attempt to fit the ancient Hebrew ceremonies into the pattern of the better observed installation rites in Africa (the author finds fully twenty-one of a possible maximum of twenty-seven parallels) and his rather indiscriminate use of biblical and rabbinic materials. The latter are not only slanted for exegetical and homiletical purposes—such theorizing is particularly pronounced in all domains of public law—but, in so far as they are based upon genuine historic reminiscences, reflect the realities of the Maccabean and Herodian dynasties rather than those of the ancient Israelitic kingdoms. The difference between the ideological underpinnings of the latter and those of the other Near Eastern monarchies is intimated by I. Engnell in his *Studies in Divine Kingship in the Ancient Near East*, although he has reserved the treatment of the Old Testament doctrines to a separate monograph. Cf. also H. Frankfort's *Kingship and the Gods* and H. Jacobsohn's study of *Die dogmatische Stellung des Königs in der Theologie der alten Aegypter*.

41. Ps. 45:8; 72; I Sam. 12; 30:25; I Kings 12; E. R. Goodenough's "Kingship in Early Israel," *JBL*, XLVIII, 203. In the absence of clear legal definitions one may assert that the royal power in Israel was generally more limited than any so-called "limited monarchy" of more modern times. Cf. M. Burrows, "Democracy in the Hebrew-Christian Tradition: Old and New Testaments," *Second Symposium of the Conference on Science, Philosophy and Religion*, pp. 403, 412; H. Silving's "State Contract in the Old Testament," *JR*, XXIV, 17–32; K. C. Evans's "Image of the King," *Christendom*, VIII, 362–73; and *supra*, n. 15.

42. Cf. O. Eissfeldt's "Jahwe als König," *ZAW*, XLVI, 81–105. The fact, stressed by him, that Isa. 6:5 ("For mine eyes have seen the King, the Lord of hosts") is the first biblical statement of more or less certain date concerning the "kingdom" of Yahweh, thus finds its best explanation. The emphasis upon God's exclusive royal prerogative undoubtedly fits best into the antimonarchical eighth century. Even at that time, however, the kingdom of God no longer meant the territorial kingdom analogous to that of Baal, the lord of a certain locality, as assumed by E. Dhorme in "Le Dieu parent et le dieu maître dans la religion des Hébreux," *RHR*, CV, 229–44. It was rather that type of divine monarchy which was synonymous with God's fatherhood of all Israel, divided though it be into two kingdoms. This combination of divine kingship and fatherhood became increasingly emphasized in the subsequent glorification of the kingdom of heaven, for which consult the references in A. E. Silverstone's "God as King," *Journal of the Manchester Egyptian and Oriental Society*, XVII, 47–51. Cf. in general also the stimulating papers by C. R. North, "The Old Testament Estimate of the Monarchy," *AJSL*, XLVIII, 1–19 and "The Religious Aspects of Hebrew Kingship," *ZAW*, L, 8–38; as well as C. J. Gadd's *Ideas of Divine Rule in the Ancient East*; M. Buber's *Königtum Gottes*, 2d ed.; K. F. Euler's "Königtum und Götterwelt in den altaramäischen Inschriften Nordsyriens," *ZAW*, LVI, 272–313; and W. F. Albright's "Historical Adjustments in the Concept of Sovereignty in

the Near East," *Approaches to World Peace* (IV Conference on Science, Philosophy and Religion), pp. 1–16.

43. By W. Zimmerli in his *Geschichte und Tradition von Beersaba im Alten Testament*. If true, such encouragement would be an even stronger proof for the ethnoreligious unity of the people, which the northern kingdom could not help but acknowledge in one form or another. Similarly, M. Noth interprets the various stations recorded in Num. 33 as referring not to early Israelitic migrations but rather to a regular "Wahlfahrtsweg zum Sinai" taken by Israelitic as well as Judean pilgrims in later ages. Cf. *PJB*, XXXVI, 5–28. However, the evidence in support of either of these two hypotheses is far from conclusive.

44. Cf. Barton's *Archaeology and the Bible*, p. 471; L. Honor's *Sennacherib's Invasion of Palestine;* and A. Ungnad's "Zahl der von Sanherib deportierten Judäer," *ZAW*, LIX, 199–202. The latter's attempt to reduce the number of Sennacherib's deportees to 2,150 is not only based on daring arithmetic, but would render the royal boast perfectly senseless. The complicated political situation in Syria and Palestine in the period preceding these deportations is described by A. Alt in "Die syrische Staatenwelt vor dem Einbruch der Assyrer," *ZDMG*, LXXXVIII, 233–58. Cf. also his "Neue assyrische Nachrichten über Palästina und Syrien," *ZDPV*, LXVII, 128–59. The existence of a large Diaspora, long before 586, is clearly reflected in many biblical passages discussed by C. C. Torrey in his *Ezra Studies*, pp. 294 ff.; and A. Causse in his *Dispersés d'Israël*, pp. 17 ff. Cf. *infra*, Chap. IV, n. 2, 4.

45. The impact of these Scythian invasions on the prophecies of Jeremiah (4:6: "For I will bring evil from the north, and a great destruction," etc.) has been doubted ever since F. Wilke's analysis, some four decades ago, of "Das Skythenproblem im Jeremiabuch," *Alttestamentliche Studien Rudolf Kittel . . . dargebracht*, pp. 222–54. With his usual extremism C. C. Torrey rejected altogether the authenticity of the first ten chapters which, in his opinion, are a late pseudepigraphon projecting Alexander's conquest of western Asia back to preëxilic days. Cf. his "Background of Jeremiah 1–10," *JBL*, LVI, 193–216. More moderately J. P. Hyatt identified the Chaldaeans as the source of "The Peril from the North in Jeremiah," *ibid.*, LIX, 507 ff. Cf. also F. Horst's related comments on Zephaniah's prophecies in his *Zwölf Kleine Propheten*, Pt. II, pp. 184, 191; and, more generally, D. W. Thomas's "Age of Jeremiah in the Light of Recent Archaeological Discoveries," *PEQ*, 1950, pp. 1–15; and N. Hareubeni's *Or ḥadash 'al Sefer Yirmiyahu* (New Light on the Book of Jeremiah). But whether we accept any of these or other suggestions, there is no doubt that the tremendous events in the North made the greater an impression on Israelitic minds, as immemorial mythological associations had long prepared them for a great cosmic menace perennially looming from that region. Cf. A. Lauha's *Zaphon, der Norden und die Nordvölker im Alten Testament;* J. Morgenstern's "Psalm 48," *HUCA*, XVI, 47 ff.; his "Psalm 23," *JBL*, LXV, 19 f.; and W. F. Albright's "Baal-Zaphon," *Festschrift Bertholet*, pp. 1–14.

Understandably Israel, too, reacted sharply to the fall of Nineveh. Its elation is best illustrated by the vindictive prophecies against "the bloody city" in Nahum, "the only book in the Bible entirely filled with invective directed against a single nation" (Hunkin in T. H. Robinson, *et al.*, *Palestine in General History*, p. 47). Cf. also J. Reider's suggestion that Nah. 1:12 contains an acrostic, underscoring the prophet's gloating over the downfall of that "strong nation." Cf. his "Name Ashur in the Initials of a Difficult Phrase in the Bible," *JAOS*, LVIII, 153–55. That Nahum preached after the destruction of Nineveh seems conclusively proved by P. Humbert in his "Essai d'analyse de Nahoum, 1:2–2:3," *ZAW*, XLIV, 266–80, and his *Problème du livre de Nahoum*, despite arguments to the contrary advanced by H. Junker and F. Horst in their respective commentaries on the Minor Prophets. Cf. also A. Haldar's

Studies in the Book of Nahum. The tragic end of Josiah, as described in II Chron. 35:20–27, and its diplomatic military background are analyzed by B. Couroyer in "Le Litige entre Josias et Néchao," RB, LV, 388–96.

46. Without having any of the modern racial undertones, the declaration of "all the tribes of Israel" to David at Hebron, "Behold, we are thy bone and thy flesh" (II Sam. 5:1) well illustrates this consciousness of ethnic unity transcending all tribal divisions. Political consolidation under the monarchy merely enhanced this feeling of belonging to one large family, notwithstanding the general loosening of clan ties and the growing territorial divisions. Cf. the fine analysis of the pertinent data in Pedersen's Israel, I, 266 ff. Cf. also J. N. Schofield's " 'All Israel' in the Deuteronomic Writers," Essays and Studies Presented to Stanley Arthur Cook, pp. 25–34.

47. It is small wonder that these ramified teachings have been and doubtless will long remain the subject of unceasing debate. Cf. the extensive summaries in the handbooks on the Hebrew religion listed supra, Chap. II, n. 1; as well as more recent monographs such as K. Galling's Erwählungstraditionen Israels; W. Staerk's "Zum alttestamentlichen Erwählungsglauben," ZAW, LV, 1–36; M. Buber's "Erwählung Israels. Eine Befragung der Bibel," Almanach des Schocken Verlags . . . 5699, pp. 12–31; and H. H. Rowley's lectures on The Biblical Doctrine of Election. Cf. also H. Bückers's "Des Propheten Isaias messianische Erwartungen für die Heidenvölker," Theologisch-praktische Quartalschrift, XCI, 16–23, 222–34; W. E. Müller's dissertation, Die Vorstellung vom Rest im Alten Testament; and F. M. T. Böhl's "Missions- und Erwählungsgedanke im Alt-Israel," Festschrift Bertholet, pp. 77–96 (pointing out that these apparently contradictory ideas were fully reconciled in Israel's outlook on the world).

48. Hugo Gressmann, chief exponent of the oriental origins of Israel's messianic ideas, readily admits with respect to Israelitic prophecy in general that "if Babylonian influences are really present, they are peripheral and not central" (The Tower of Babel, p. 39). Cf. also his Messias; M. Buber's Königtum Gottes; and W. Staerk's Erlösererwartung in den östlichen Religionen.

49. II Kings 2:11. That we have no reference to a messianic expectation in connection with Elijah before Mal. 3:23 may be due to a mere accident. There is no reason why this expectation should have arisen in the exilic or postexilic age, while the spread of a legend about any prophet's supernatural death seems to presuppose popular belief in his ultimate return.

50. Isa. 1:21, 26–27. Even Isaiah, however, dreamed of the reëstablishment of a just government as it had existed in the days of Moses. This is clearly the meaning of verse 1:26a, as emphasized by B. Duhm in his commentary ad locum, and by H. Gressmann in his Messias, p. 183. The Deuteronomic lawgiver and historian, likewise a Jerusalemite, while glorifying more than any other biblical author the Holy Land and the Holy City (which for obvious reasons he did not mention by name), expected a change for the better from his own laws, written wholly in the spirit of Moses. The psalms, on the other hand, naturally extolled the royal house. Being poetically even more vague than the prophetic oracles, generally of uncertain date and often revealing strong Canaanite and other oriental influences, these messianic psalms have been a major battle ground of biblical scholarship. Even their number is controversial. W. Stade listed as many as thirty-six psalms filled with messianic content and fifty-two others with less specific messianic references. Cf. "Messianische Hoffnung im Psalter," Ausgew. Akademische Reden und Abhandlungen, p. 63. Others, including H. Gunkel, S. Mowinckel, and G. Dahl have presented different computations. See the latter's "Messianic Expectation in the Psalter." JBL, LVII, 1–12. Al-

though the recent trend toward dating most psalms in the preëxilic age (cf. *infra*, Chap. V, n. 22) has enhanced the possibility of connecting particular psalms with certain rulers, such specific identifications have thus far been crowned with little success. Equally futile is the other extreme of denying all personal aspects, because the prophets, especially Amos and Isaiah, allegedly looked forward only to an eschatological end of days wholly outside the affairs of this world. Cf., e.g., W. Vollborn's thesis, *Innerzeitliche oder endzeitliche Gerichtserwartung?* It is a wholesome corrective, therefore, to find, e.g., J. J. Stamm's analysis of "La Prophétie d'Emmanuel" (*Revue de théologie et de philosophie*, n.s. XXXII, 97–123), despite its strong Barthian and christological overtones, reach the simple conclusion that this Emmanuel was but one of Isaiah's children.

51. E. Meyer in *Die kulturelle, literarische und religiöse Entwicklung des israelitischen Volkes in der älteren Königszeit*, p. 4. Referring to the widely held view that Abiathar, King David's chief priest and hence in many respects an eyewitness, was the author of the original sections of the book of Samuel, A. T. Olmstead commented that "whether or not Abiathar was our historian, his work is almost a miracle to his modern successors. History such as this had never before been written" (*History of Palestine and Syria*, p. 337). If we are to accept E. Auerbach's theory that the first chapter of Judges was composed and written at the beginning of the twelfth century (even before the Song of Deborah), this historical literature would have to be dated further back to the earliest post-Mosaic age—an astounding phenomenon indeed. There is, however, a fairly general consensus of opinion that even before Abiathar there must have been prominent historical writers to pave the way for his remarkable achievement. The superiority of Israel's historians over the "father" of Greek historiography is stressed with convincing argument by H. T. Fowler in his "Herodotus and the Early Hebrew Historians," *JBL*, XLIX, 207–17. An interesting attempt to establish "Archival Data in the Book of Kings" is made by J. A. Montgomery in *JBL*, LIII, 46–52. What is more, H. Torczyner has advanced the intriguing theory that most biblical poems, including the Psalms and the Song of Songs, as well as many prophetic speeches, were recorded only because of their integration into various narratives. Cf. "Das literarische Problem der Bibel," *ZDMG*, LXXXV, 287–324; *Shir ha-Shirim* (Song of Songs); and "What Is Biblical Literature?" (Hebrew) in his *Ha-Lashon ve-ha-sefer*, II, 3–57.

A fuller analysis of the historical writings is given in the various introductions to the Old Testament and commentaries on individual books listed *supra*, Chap. II, n. 1; as well as in H. Schmidt's *Geschichtsschreibung im Alten Testament;* M. Noth's *Ueberlieferungsgeschichtliche Studien*, I. Cf. also S. A. Cook's "Arrière-plan historique de l'Ancien Testament," *RHPR*, IX, 295–318; Kaufmann's *Toledot*, III, 153 ff., 308 ff., 355 ff.; G. Hölscher's "Anfänge der hebräischen Geschichtsschreibung," *SB* Heidelberg, 1941–42; J. Obersteiner's *Biblische Sinndeutung der Geschichte;* C. North's *Old Testament Interpretation of History;* O. Eissfeldt's critical review of recent publications by Hölscher and Noth in his *Geschichtsschreibung im Alten Testament;* his own positive analysis of "Geschichtliches und Uebergeschichtliches im Alten Testament," *Theologische Studien und Kritiken*, CIX, 9–53 (includes an analysis of the God idea in the Old and New Testaments); H. G. Güterbock's "Historische Tradition und ihre literarische Gestaltung bei Babyloniern und Hethitern bis 1200," *Zeitschrift für Assyriologie*, XLII, 1–91; XLIV, 45–149; and L. Landau's *Geschichtsauffassung der Propheten im Verhältnis zur Geschichtsphilosophie des Idealismus der Gegenwart*.

CHAPTER IV: CRUCIAL TEST

1. S. Smith's *Isaiah Chapters XL–LV*, p. 26. Cf. also S. A. Cook's "VIe siècle, moment décisif dans l'histoire du judaïsme et dans l'évolution religieuse de l'Orient," *RHPR*, XVIII, 321–31. Neither ancient sources nor modern scholars agree in the matter of Zoroaster's chronology. Following Xantus of Lydia, E. Meyer, Christensen, and others, G. Messina in his *Ursprung der Magier und die zarathuštrische Religion*, tried to prove that Zoroaster lived some six hundred years before Xerxes. This chronology would put the prophet back into the first half of the eleventh century. If such lofty religious ideas could have originated so early in a comparatively backward corner of the Iranian plateau, there would be even more reason to believe in the historicity of Moses and his great religious reform. On the other hand, C. F. Lehmann-Haupt and E. Herzfeld, following A. V. W. Jackson and others, accept the essential authenticity of the Pehlevi records, and think that the founder of Mazdaism lived between 570 and 520. Cf., respectively, their independently written articles, "Wann lebte Zarathuštra?" and "The Traditional Date of Zoroaster" in *Oriental Studies . . . Pavry*, pp. 251–80, 132–36; as well as Herzfeld's comprehensive recent work on *Zoroaster and His World*. Here Herzfeld marshals strong arguments for the tradition that the founder of Parsiism lived "258 [years] before Alexander" (p. 22). H. S. Nyberg, finally, after reëxamining the entire evidence comes to the conclusion that Zoroaster "lived before 485 B.C.—that is all that can be said from the historic standpoint." Cf. his comprehensive work on *Religionen des Alten Iran*, p. 45. Cf. also A. D. Nock's rather negative review of Herzfeld's work in "The Problem of Zoroaster," *AJA*, LIII, 272–85.

Of course, it was to the best advantage of Jews, and later also of Christians, living under a Zoroastrian regime to profess the belief that Zoroaster, too, had been indebted to Judaism. Such Muslim historians as Ṭabari mention that, in their day, many "people of the book" believed that the founder of Parsiism had been a native of Palestine; a disciple of Jeremiah's pupil, Baruch; perhaps even a direct descendant of Isaac, the patriarch. Cf. Ṭabari's *Annales*, ed. by M. J. de Goeje, I, Pt. 2, pp. 648, 681; A. V. W. Jackson's *Zoroaster*, pp. 165 ff.; and J. Horovitz's "Hebrew-Iranian Synchronisms," *Oriental Studies . . . Pavry*, pp. 151–55. However, such identifications seem to reflect the spirit of the syncretistic age of the neo-Persian Empire after 226 C.E. much more than that of the overtly "separatist" Jews under the Achaemenid dynasty. The latter were at best ready to tone down differences when they addressed their Zoroastrian overlords. Cf. *infra*, n. 37; and Chap. V, n. 32. On the other hand, it is not impossible that Israelitic monotheism had had some influence on the great Persian religious reformer. Cf. in particular, R. Pettazzoni's *Religione di Zarathustra*, *passim*.

2. "It is taking the historians of Israel a long time to find out the truth . . . that that author of Chronicles—Ezra—Nehemiah wrote fiction, not history; that the politically and economically impossible Golah and Return which he described (unknown to any other Hebrew writer, virtually denied many times over and expressly denied once, Isa. 11:11), existed only on paper; and that his theory, at first discredited, was ultimately accepted and accordingly supported, as the true theory, by the authorities in Palestine." In these words C. C. Torrey (in his "Notes on Ezekiel," *JBL*, LVIII, 82) summarized three decades of research which had culminated in the publication over the years of his trilogy, *Ezra Studies; The Second Isaiah;* and *Pseudo-Ezekiel*. The latter volume attempted to prove that the whole book of Ezekiel was but a pseudepigraphon fabricated by the school of the Chronicler about 230 B.C.E. and

attributed to a prophet Ezekiel, said to have preached in Babylonia before and after the national disaster of 586. These radical views have not been accepted by "regnant opinion," however. For example, most arguments in Torrey's *Pseudo-Ezekiel* have been convincingly refuted by S. Spiegel in his "Ezekiel or Pseudo-Ezekiel?" *HTR*, XXIV, 245–321. Cf. also the additional remarks of both author and reviewer in *JBL*, LIII, 291–320; LIV, 145–71; and Spiegel's "When Was Ezekiel Exiled?" (Hebrew), *Sefer Touroff* (N. Touroff Anniversary Volume), pp. 206–12 (suggesting the date of 592, rather than the more widely accepted year, 597). Torrey's views have also been rejected by more recent commentators as A. Bertholet and G. A. Cooke. In his *Ezechielfragen*, Nils Messel took the intermediary position that the book was written about 400 B.C.E. and rewritten by the redactor so as to appear an older collection.

It is small wonder that, after briefly reviewing the whole history of Ezekiel research, W. A. Irwin came to the discouraging conclusion that "at this moment [1943] the work of the prophet Ezekiel is cloaked in the darkest obscurity. No one at all has given us reason to believe that he knows what the prophet taught." Cf. his *Problem of Ezekiel: an Inductive Study*, p. 29. Irwin's own literary reconstruction, however, though based on the assumption that the prophet had begun to prophesy about 600 and was exiled to Babylonia in 586, eliminated as spurious not only the really dubious chapters 40–48 but about three-quarters of the remaining text, including some of the most vigorous and historically influential passages. Cf. R. H. Pfeiffer's review in *RR*, VIII, 386–89. In short, we may still speak today, as G. Dahl did a decade and a half ago, of a "Crisis in Ezekiel Research," *Quantulacumque*, pp. 265–84. On the other hand, in his dissertation on *The Date and Composition of Ezekiel*, C. G. Howie has plausibly argued for the return to the traditional date of 593–70 and Babylonian locality of Ezekiel's prophetic work. Cf. also M. H. J. Gruenthaner's review of "Recent Theories about Ezekiel," *CBQ*, VII, 438–46. Under these circumstances we must be doubly grateful for the discovery, among the John H. Scheide papyri, of twenty-one leaves giving us the Greek transl. of Ez. 19:12–39:29. These papyri, dating from about 200 C.E. at least help confirm the authenticity of the Masoretic text. Cf. *The John H. Scheide Biblical Papyri: Ezekiel*, ed. by A. C. Johnson, *et al.;* and H. S. Gehman's study of "The Relations between the Hebrew Text of Ezekiel and that of the John H. Scheide Papyri," *JAOS*, LVIII, 92–102.

3. Cf. Burrows's remarks in J. C. Trever and his "Newly Discovered Jerusalem Scrolls," *BA*, XI, 61. This is borne out by Burrows's detailed analysis of many "Variant Readings in the Isaiah Manuscript," *BASOR*, 111, pp. 16–24; 113, pp. 24–32. Cf. also E. L. Sukenik's *Megillot genuzot* (Hidden Scrolls from an Ancient Genizah Found in the Wilderness of Judah), I, 34 ff.; and the *Dead Sea Scrolls*, ed. by M. Burrows, *et al.*, Vol. I. Cf. also *supra*, Chap. III, n. 27. Little assistance, however, may be expected from these scrolls in the resolution of such old problems, raised by higher criticism, as the authorship of Isa. 56–66. The extensive literature on the question whether these chapters were written by several authors, one single disciple of Deutero-Isaiah or by the latter himself, is therefore, far from obsolete. Cf., e.g., L. Glahn's "Quelques remarques sur la question du Trito-Esaïe et son état actuel," *RHPR*, XII, 34–46; and S. Smith's *Isaiah*, pp. 4 f. The weight of evidence now favors the basic unity of Isa. 40–66 (despite some later interpolations) on both historical and linguistic grounds. On the latter, cf. also J. W. Behr's *Writings of Deutero-Isaiah and the Neo-Babylonian Royal Inscriptions;* and S. H. Blank's "Studies in Deutero-Isaiah," *HUCA*, XV, 1–46. Nor have the voices arguing for the unity of the whole book of Isaiah been completely silenced. One of its more recent staunch champions, on scholarly rather than fundamentalist grounds, has been A. Kaminka. Cf., e.g., his stimulating remarks on "Le Développement des idées du prophète Isaïe et l'unité de son livre," *REJ*, LXXX, 42–59, 131–69; LXXXI, 27–47; and his *Meḥqarim be-*

miqra ve-talmud (Studies in Bible, Talmud and Rabbinic Literature), I, 1–89. These studies have at least pointed up the profound similarity between the teachings of the First and Second Isaiahs, the latter prophet evidently following closely in the footsteps of his great predecessor. Cf. also W. S. McCullough's "Re-Examination of Isaiah 56–66," *JBL*, LXVII, 27–36.

4. The authenticity of the books of Ezra and Nehemiah and the documents included therein, long impugned by such critics as Wellhausen, Hölscher, and Mowinckel, has found able defenders in recent years. H. H. Schaeder has shown (especially in his *Esra der Schreiber*) how well the historical records concerning Ezra the Scribe (i.e., the Persian chancery official) fit into the whole framework of the Persian administration. His findings, supplementing earlier researches by E. Meyer and others, have been borne out also by E. J. Bickerman's brilliant analysis of "The Edict of Cyrus in Ezra I," *JBL*, LXV, 249–75. They stand unrefuted by A. S. Kapelrud's "lexical investigation" of *The Question of Authorship in the Ezra-Narrative*. In fact, the entire work of the Chronicler has received a much higher appreciation and been dated much further back than before (about 400 B.C.E.) in J. W. Rothstein's comprehensive commentary in the Sellin series. Cf. also G. von Rad's *Geschichtsbild des chronistischen Werkes;* and A. C. Welch's *Work of the Chronicler.* While postulating a double strand running through the whole narrative (an original chronicler from among those who had remained in Palestine and closely followed the Deuteronomic law, and a reviser from the midst of the returning exiles who appealed to the Priestly law and ignored Deuteronomy), Welch believes in the essential authenticity of I Chron. 10:1–II Chron. 36:21 and its being in substance a reasoned program for the Restoration. Cf. *ibid.,* pp. 149 f., 155 ff. The earlier dating of Chronicles may thus be considered the accepted opinion, despite M. Noth's attempt at returning to the older date of about 300–200 B.C.E. Cf. his *Ueberlieferungsgeschichtliche Studien,* I, 192 ff. Cf. also A. Noordtzij's comprehensive *Boeken der Kronieken;* supplemented by his suggestive observations on "Les Intentions du Chroniste," *RB*, XLIX, 161–68; F. Ahlemann's careful analysis "Zur Esra Quelle," *ZAW*, LIX, 77–98; M. H. Segal's "Books of Ezra and Nehemiah" (Hebrew), *Tarbiz*, XIV, 81–103, 141; W. Rudolph's detailed commentary on *Esra und Nehemia* (rejecting Noth's attempt); and A. Bea's older survey of "Neuere Arbeiten zum Problem der Chronikbücher," *Biblica*, XXII, 46–58. Nor are the subsequent traditions concerning Ezra and his work devoid of historical interest. Cf. M. Munk's detailed analysis of "Esra Hasofer nach Talmud und Midrasch," *Jahrbuch der jüdisch-liter. Gesellschaft, Frankfurt,* XXI, 129–98; XXII, 223–44.

With respect to the book of Lamentations, too, H. Wiesmann's study, "Der geschichtliche Hintergrund des Büchleins der Klagelieder," *Biblische Zeitschrift,* XXIII, 20–43, makes it seem very plausible that these "Jeremiads" reflect, indeed, the historical situation of the sixth century. M. H. Segal has even attempted to prove that Chap. 3 was written by the youthful King Jehoiachin himself. Cf. his Hebrew essay on "Lamentations III" in *Tarbiz*, XI, 1–16. Cf. also R. G. Castellino's comparative study of *Le Lamentazioni individuali e gli inni in Babilonia e in Israele.*

A more comprehensive treatment of the entire period is given by E. Klamroth in *Die jüdischen Exulanten in Babylonien;* and A. C. Welch in *Post-Exilic Judaism.* Although the former is partly obsolete, and the latter is subject to considerable reservations with respect to both general outlook and details, these works still are very useful. A new valiant effort to scrutinize the present state of our knowledge concerning this vital, though obscure period, has been made by J. Klausner in his *Historiah shel ha-bayit ha-sheni* (A History of the Second Commonwealth). The first two (of the total of five) volumes dealing with the period before the Maccabean Revolt are new, while Vols. III–V present a somewhat revised edition of Klausner's earlier *Historiah Yisre'elit* (Jewish History). Cf. also E. B. Cross's "Rhapsody of 'Exile,'"

Colgate-Rochester Divinity School Bulletin, XIV, 119–61; and W. F. Albright's "Brief History of Judah from the Days of Josiah to Alexander the Great," *BA*, IX, 1–16 (the attempt here, p. 13, to date Ezra at 428 B.C.E. about a dozen years after Nehemiah's arrival is based upon an emendation of Ezra 7:7 to read "thirty-seven," instead of "seven"—always a desperate expedient). On the Palestinian situation in the early period of the Restoration, cf. also S. A. Cook's "Age of Zerubbabel," *Studies Robinson*, pp. 19–36; J. Morgenstern's "Two Prophecies from 520–516 B.C.," *HUCA*, XXII, 365–431 (on Isa. 55:1–5; 60:1–3, 5–7); A. Alt's "Judas Nachbaren zur Zeit Nehemias," *PJB*, XXVII, 66–74; K. Galling's "Denkmäler zur Geschichte Syriens und Palästinas unter der Herrschaft der Perser," *ibid.*, XXXIV, 59–79; and from the geographical angle, M. Avi-Yonah's *Geografiah historit shel Ereṣ Yisrael* (Historical Geography of Palestine from the Return to Zion to the Beginning of the Arab Conquest); and *infra*, n. 37–38.

5. Our assumption of the deportation of but one-third of the population is rather conservative. Cf. the aforementioned Hebrew essay on the "Israelitic Population," where an attempt is also made to explain the apparently contradictory statements in II Kings 24 and Jeremiah 52. R. Kittel in his *Geschichte*, III, 62; and E. Sellin in his *Geschichte*, II, 1 ff., reach similar absolute figures, but the proportion of the deported to the rest of the population appears to them much higher. Cf. also R. de Vaux's "Décrets de Cyrus et de Darius sur la reconstruction du Temple," *RB*, XLVI, 29–57; and Albright's *Stone Age*, pp. 246 f.

The date of 602–582, given parenthetically in our text, refers, on the one hand, to the rebellion against the Babylonians and the assassination of Gedaliah, according to Klamroth's *Exulanten*, p. 22, and, on the other hand, to Nebukadrezzar's earliest invasion of Palestine (601), suggested by Julius Lewy in his *Forschungen zur alten Geschichte Vorderasiens*, pp. 37 ff. Cf., however, the arguments against the latter date in W. Caspari's "Vorfahren und Vorgeschichte des letzten Judäischen Königs," *Klio*, XXVI, 192 ff. The generally complex chronological problems of the period have been treated, among others, in J. Begrich's *Chronologie der Könige von Israel und Juda*; R. Fruin's "Studies in the Old Testament, I–VI" (Dutch), *Nieuw theologisch Tijdschrift*, XX–XXIII; R. A. Parker and W. H. Dubberstein's *Babylonian Chronology 626 B.C.–A.D. 45*; and J. Morgenstern's review thereof in *JNES*, II, 125–30.

6. Cf. C. C. Edgar's *Zenon Papyri*, I, 36 ff., No. 59015 verso l. 42; A. Tcherikover's "Palestine in the Light of the Zenon Papyri" (Hebrew), *Tarbiz*, IV, 238 ff. If Albright's dating of Ostracon 6043 from Elath is correct, this sherd containing four Edomite but no Arabic names would indicate that at least in the early sixth century the city was still safely in Edomite hands. Cf. his and Glueck's readings of these inscriptions in *BASOR*, 80, pp. 3–10, and 82, pp. 3–15; Glueck's previous study of "The Boundaries of Edom," *HUCA*, XI, 141–57; and, for the earlier period, B. Grdseloff's "Edom, d'après des sources égyptiennes," *Revue de l'histoire juive en Egypte*, I, 69–99. This gradual displacement of ancient Jewish settlers from Beersheba to Hebron helped nurture among the Jews the conviction that the Edomites had always been their "hereditary enemies" (Mal. 1:3, etc.). They hoped that some day they would not only regain their former possessions, but also occupy the "Mount of Esau" itself. Cf. Ob. 18–19, and S. Klein's comments thereon in his *Ereṣ Yehudah* (Judaea from the Return from Babylonia to the Conclusion of the Talmud), p. 3. This hope remained unfulfilled, however, until the Maccabean age. Even Darius' alleged decree ordering the Edomites to "give over the villages of the Jews which then they held" (reported in the apocryphal III Esdras 4:51) represented but wishful thinking. Cf. also Alt's remarks on "Die Rolle Samarias bei der Entstehung des Judentums," *Festschrift Otto Procksch*, pp. 5 ff.; S. H. Blank's "Studies in Post-Exilic Universalism," *HUCA*, XI, 174 ff.; and particularly H. L. Ginsberg's "Judah and the Transjordan States from 734 to 582 B.C.E.," *Marx Jub. Vol.*, pp. 347–68.

7. The usual explanation that Judah had extended its boundaries much farther north under the reign of Josiah (cf. the felicitous reconstruction of "Judas Gaue unter Josia" by A. Alt in *PJB*, XXI, 100–17) leaves too many difficulties unsolved. Cf. also the judicious discussion of these problems in W. Rosenau's "Ezekiel 37:15–28. What Happened to the Ten Tribes?" *HUCA Jub. Vol.*, pp. 79–88; and, more generally, the vast material accumulated in A. H. Godbey's *Lost Tribes, a Myth*.

8. Isa. 43:5–6; Esther 3:8. That the book of Esther was written in Persia before the time of Alexander has been conclusively proved by H. Gunkel in *Esther* and by J. Hoschander in *The Book of Esther in the Light of History*. The school of Wellhausen, of course, had to postdate this work (notwithstanding its vivid local colors of obvious authenticity) to a late Hellenistic age—if for no other reason than for a passage like the one quoted here. Wellhausen himself was so spellbound by his conviction that the Pentateuch became known to the Jews only through Ezra and his disciples that he could not explain its universal acceptance by Diaspora Jewry in the Hellenistic age except by assuming the total disappearance of the exiles of Samaria and Jerusalem before that time. It was, he thought, only the subsequent emigration from Palestine and the ensuing religious propaganda which suddenly filled all the neighboring countries with Jewish masses. Cf. his *Sketch of the History of Israel and Judah*, pp. 137 ff. Seeing that many statements in the Prophets and Hagiographa contradicted this theory, the master and his school immediately proceeded to revise downward the accepted dating of these passages and even of whole chapters and books. Thus not only Isaiah, but also the exilic prophets were radically purified of all such "interpolations." Subsequent discoveries, however, e.g., of the Elephantine papyri, and the accumulated results of many independent lines of research (by Meyer, Torrey, Gunkel, Causse, and others) overthrew the theory, along with much that depended on it. Scholars are only now beginning to realize the full consequences of this unbroken continuity in the evolution of the Jewish dispersion. Cf. also Julius Lewy's "Feast of the 14th Day of Adar," *HUCA*, XIV, 127–51; W. F. Albright's comments thereon in *JBL*, LIX, 301; C. C. Torrey's "Older Book of Esther," *HTR*, XXXVII, 1–40; and A. S. Yahuda's "Meaning of the Name Esther," *JRAS*, 1946, pp. 174–78 (suggesting that it was the translation of Hadassah or myrtle in old Persian or rather in its Medic dialect spoken by Jews).

9. These words are quoted by Josephus, *Antt.* X, 11, 1.223 from the Babylonian Berossos, whose *Babyloniaca* were completed before 275–274 B.C.E., according to C. F. Lehmann-Haupt's "Neue Studien zu Berossos," *Klio*, XXII, 125–60.

10. It is still a moot question whether or not Israelitic exiles are mentioned in certain Assyrian records soon after the fall of Samaria. Although S. Schiffer's attempt to find *Keilschriftliche Spuren der in der zweiten Hälfte des 8. Jahrhunderts von den Assyrern nach Mesopotamien deportierten Samarier* has been rejected by many scholars, the occurrence of several such names as Pakaḫa (Pekaḫ) "the chief of cities" in deeds of the days of Sennacherib (cf. C. H. W. Johns's *Assyrian Deeds and Documents*, No. 234, Rev. ll. 8 f., in Vol. I, 60; cf. III, 456) has raised the intriguing question as to whether deportees from Northern Israel may not have achieved positions of trust in the imperial administration within a few years after their arrival. Cf. B. Meissner's informative, though biased, study of "Die Achämenidenkönige und das Judentum," *SB* Berlin, 1938, p. 6, n. 2. It may not be too venturesome to suggest that these individuals belonged to the pro-Assyrian party at home and, after their deportation, were rewarded with good administrative positions. That the Assyrians entrusted such Israelites with "dominion" in neighboring Moab is asserted, without much ado, by the Chronicler (I, 4:22) and seems confirmed by the name Pahath-moab in the postexilic community (Ezra 2:6; 8:4; Neh. 3:11). Unfortunately the cuneiform and Aramaic documents discovered at Tell Halaf (the biblical Gozan), though largely

written in the eighth or seventh pre-Christian centuries, have failed to shed any light on the Israelitic exiles there. None of the names listed by G. R. Meyer in J. Friedrich, *et al.*, *Inschriften vom Tell Halaf*, pp. 79 ff., seem of Hebraic origin. Even the name Elimelech, occurring in one of the few seals written in a Western Semitic alphabet (*ibid.*, pp. 75 f.), was a fairly widespread Semitic name. The absence of any *yahu* ending is underscored by the presence of nearly a dozen other divine prefixes or suffixes, including Adad, Ashshur, and Bel. Transplanted into an Aramaic-speaking environment, the deported Israelites may either have speedily adopted Aramaic names (not necessarily theophorous) or been given such names by the official scribes recording the various transactions.

11. Jer. 29:5; Josephus' *Antt.* XI, 3, 10.68. The latter passage does not justify, however, E. Bickermann's attack (in *JBL*, LXV, 262) on the "professorial mythology" concerning the entry of some exilic Jews into trade and moneylending. The considerable role played by Jewish merchants in fifth-century Nippur undoubtedly reflected only the acceleration of this process during the first postexilic century. But there is no reason for assuming that it had not begun immediately after the arrival of the first deportees from Samaria. At the other extreme, F. F. Zimmermann's exaggerations of the nexus between "Die babylonische Kapitalistenherrschaft und die Begründung des Judentums" (*Odal*, V, 166–81) may safely be discounted as a typical Nazi perversion. On the frequency of renting rather than owning houses in Babylonia, cf. Dubberstein's remarks in *AJSL*, LVI, 41.

Unfortunately almost all of our information still is based on the tablets published half a century ago by Albert T. Clay and in part analyzed at that time, with special reference to the Babylonian exiles, by S. Daiches in his *Jews in Babylonia in the Time of Ezra and Nehemiah*; and E. Ebeling in his *Aus dem Leben der jüdischen Exulanten in Babylonien*. Perhaps the new excavations at Nippur now being conducted jointly by the Oriental Institute and the University of Pennsylvania Museum will yield answers to some of these tantalizing problems. Cf. also A. T. Olmstead's *History of the Persian Empire*, pp. 83 ff., 192, 299, 356 ff. Olmstead's assumption, however, that, because the later chiefs of the house of Egibi bore pagan names, they must have been apostate Jews is far from conclusive. Cf. *infra*, n. 25.

12. Origin and date of establishment of the Elephantine colony are still as controversial as ever. On the one hand, W. Struve argued that this self-styled "Jewish" army (not "Israelitic" army) was recruited by Apries from the Judean exiles about 586 B.C.E. Cf. his "Zur Geschichte der jüdischen Kolonie von Elephantine," *Bulletin of the Academy of Science of the U.S.S.R.*, 6th ser., XX, 445–54. On the other hand, A. Vincent in his *Religion des Judéo-Araméens d'Eléphantine*, pp. 8 ff., has restated the case for considering Psammetichus I (663–609) as the founder and connected this event with Josiah's destruction of Bethel (II Kings 23:4–5). Struve's main contention that the Jewish soldiers probably replaced the mutineers, recorded in an Egyptian inscription (J. H. Breasted's *Ancient Records*, IV, 506 ff., No. 989), is so full of uncertainties as to the latter's location, date, and connection with the Jewish soldiers that it can hardly overcome the objections raised by J. Volkow and cited by Struve himself that the Jews were not likely to hasten with the building of another sanctuary *after* the destruction of that in Jerusalem. Together with other scholars, W. O. E. Oesterley pointed out that Israelitic mercenaries had previously been employed by the Assyrians during their occupation of Egypt and that, hence, after his successful revolt, Psammetichus I could utilize the former to guard Egypt's southern frontier. Cf. his and Robinson's *History of Israel*, II, 148, 161 ff., with special reference to Hebrew administrators mentioned in Assyrian texts. Cf. also *supra*, n. 10; *infra*, n. 15; C. G. Wagenaar's *Joodsche Kolonie van Jeb-Syene in de 5de Eeuw voor Christus*; P. Korngreen's *Moshabot ṣebaiyot shel ha-Yehudim* (Jewish Military Colonies in Antiquity); A. Dupont-Sommer's "Ostracon araméen inédit d'Éléphantine adressée

à Aḥuṭab," *RES*, 1942–45, pp. 65–75; his "Ostraca araméens d'Éléphantine," *ASAE*, XLVIII, 109–30; O. Neugebauer's discussion of a newly proposed "Chronology of the Aramaic Papyri from Elephantine," *Isis*, XXXIII, 575–78 (defending the accepted dates); L. H. Vincent's "Épigraphes judéo-araméennes postexiliques," *RB*, LVI, 274–94; and particularly, E. G. Kraeling's valuable edition of *The Brooklyn Museum Aramaic Papyri*. On the history of the discovery of these important papyri, cf. also the two letters written by C. Clermont-Ganneau on March 5 and 19, 1908, and published by J. B. Chabot in *Journal des Savants*, 1944, pp. 87–92, 136–42.

13. Cf. H. Bauer and B. Meissner's "Armäischer Pachtvertrag aus dem 7. Jahre Darius' I," *SB* Berlin, 1936, pp. 414–24; the comments thereon by C. C. Torrey and H. L. Ginsberg in *JAOS*, LVIII, 394–98; LIX, 105; and N. Aimé-Giron's *Textes araméens d'Egypte*, pp. 44 f., No. 33. Cf. also the patronymic Yehohanan found on an ostracon, *ibid.*, pp. 1 f., No. 1, and other data and discussions, *ibid.*, pp. 7 f., 10 f., 49, 58 ff. Many other Aramaic documents stemming from Egypt during the Persian occupation, which have become known in recent years, are also likely to shed significant light on the Jewish community of that period. Most of them still await publication and closer scrutiny by specialists. Cf., in particular, E. Mittwoch's brief description of "Neue aramäische Urkunden aus der Zeit der Achämenidenherrschaft in Aegypten," *MGWJ*, LXXXIII, 93–100 (14 letters written on leather and stemming from the chancery of the Persian governor of Egypt Arsham; they were probably written about 411–408 B.C.E. in Susa or Babylon and dispatched to Egypt); G. R. Driver's even more concise report on "New Aramaic Documents," *Bodleian Library Record*, II, 123–24 (giving the variegated content of 12 leather documents from Arsham's chancery recently acquired by the Bodleian Library; although writing in 1945, Driver, evidently because of the Nazi suppression of that volume of *MGWJ*, was not familiar with Mittwoch's essay largely covering the same ground); his equally brief communication to the Twenty-First International Congress of Orientalists in Paris, 1949, published in its *Actes*, pp. 108–9. Cf. also Murad Kamil's "Papyri araméens découverts à Hermoupolis-ouest." *Bulletin de l'Institut d'Égypte*, XXVIII, 253–57; his "Notice on the Aramaic Papyri Discovered at Hermopolis West," *Revue de l'histoire juive en Égypte*, I, 1–3 (briefly noting the discovery of 8 new Aramaic papyri of the fifth-century—the full texts were to appear in the Publications of Fuad University); and *infra*, n. 33; and Chap. V, n. 19.

14. Prophetic passages like Hos. 2:18 ff., Isa. 8:3, and Ez. 24:18 clearly reflect an overwhelmingly monogamous population in practice, if not in theory. Lest one be tempted to attribute these prophetic utterances to some semiconscious profeminist bias, one must bear in mind that, on religious grounds, the prophets often denounced Israelitic women for their proneness to fall back on magic and "popular" rituals. Cf. I Kings 15:13; Isa. 3:16–24; 32:9–12, etc. Cf. also M. Radin's *Life of the People in Biblical Times*, pp. 40 ff.; L. M. Epstein's *Marriage Laws*, pp. 3 ff., 34 ff.; and *infra*, Chap. XIV, n. 12.

15. Jer. 44:24. It should be noted that one of the recently discovered Hermopolis papyri likewise refers to the *malkat shamin* (Queen of Heaven). Egyptian Jews of the period were generally exposed to the influence of local Semitic as well as Egyptian cults. This is evidenced also by the penetration of the Baal Zaphon worship to such frontier cities as Daphne-Taḥpanḥes. Cf. N. Aimé-Giron's "Baal Saphon et les dieux de Taḥpanḥes dans un nouveau papyrus phénicien," *ASAE*, XL, 433–60, and *supra*, Chap. III, n. 45.

16. Cowley's *Aramaic Papyri*, No. 22. E. Meyer's figures in his *Papyrusfund*, p. 37, have to be corrected accordingly. Polygamy, too, must have been all but eliminated from the colony, not by law, but by the operation of social factors. That is why there

is nothing intrinsically improbable in A. Dupont-Sommer's reconstruction of Ostracon No. 175, whereby a husband declared his intention not to marry a particular slave girl or any other woman, despite his wife's sterility. Unfortunately, however, both reading and translation of several crucial words are very dubious. Cf. his " 'Yahô' et 'Yahô-Sebaôt' sur des ostraca araméens inédits de l'Elephantine," *CRAI*, 1947, pp. 181 f. (in this essay Dupont-Sommer announces the preparation of a complete ed. of these ostraca from Clermont-Ganneau's collection; cf. his brief communication to the Twenty-First International Congress of Orientalists in Paris, 1949, published in the latter's *Actes*, pp. 109–11). Cf. also U. Türck's "Stellung der Frau in Elephantine als Ergebnis persisch-babylonischen Rechtseinflusses," *ZAW*, XLVI, 166–69, who, however, because of her failure to consider the abnormal population structure in a military colony, was unable to account for the full extent of the new rights of Jewish women. In fact, these rights sharply contrasted with both the Old Testament and other oriental laws. Cf. E. M. Macdonald's *Position of Women;* and W. Erichsen's *Demotischer Ehevertrag aus Elephantine.*

17. Cf. W. F. Albright's "Seal of Eliakim and the Latest Preëxilic History of Judah," *JBL*, LI, 77–106; H. G. May's "Three Hebrew Seals and the Status of Exiled Jehoiakin," *AJSL*, LVI, 146–48; and, more generally, A. Reifenberg's *Ancient Hebrew Seals.* The tablets relating to Yaukin were published in 1939 by E. F. Weidner in his "Jojachin, König von Juda, in babylonischen Keilschrifttexten," *Mélanges Dussaud*, II, 923–35. Cf. also W. F. Albright's "King Joiachin in Exile." *BA*, V, 49–55; and G. R. Driver's "Jehoiakin in Captivity," *Expository Times*, LVI, 317–18. Evidently the biblical historian's statement that Jehoiachin had been in "prison" (*bet kele*) and wore "prison garments" (*bigde kileo*) did not refer to any kind of dungeon, but rather to some formal "prisoner of war" status (incidentally, this may also have been the extent of King Hosea's "imprisonment," II Kings 17:4). Only the other exiles' greater sufferings during the early years of their sojourn in Babylonia made them exaggerate the misery of the royal prisoner as well. Except for this mental attitude there is little support for the aforementioned attempt to ascribe to Jehoiachin the authorship of the moving *qinah* in Lam. 3. Cf. *supra*, n. 4.

18. Such Jewish sounding names as Niriiau, Palṭiiau, and, possibly, Iaabi'lu (reminiscent of the syncretistic biblical name Yobel) appear also among the higher Babylonian bureaucracy in L. Waterman's *Royal Correspondence of the Assyrian Empire*, I, No. 633; II, No. 1331. According to Schaeder's ingenious reconstruction of Ezra 4–5, Tabeel, too, was but another Jewish court official who, rather than denouncing the Jerusalem community for its alleged disloyalty, defended it successfully before Darius. Cf. his *Esra der Schreiber*, pp. 34 ff.; and his *Iranische Beiträge*, I, 215 ff.

19. G. Barton's *Archaeology and the Bible*, p. 483; Ezra 1:2; S. Smith's *Isaiah*, pp. 48 f. Wherever imperial policy demanded it, however, Persian kings could be extremely intolerant. The Zoroastrian, Xerxes, boasted in his Persepolis inscription that, in reprisal for an unspecified rebellion, he had destroyed a Daiva temple and "where formerly idols were worshiped, I worshiped Ahuramazda." Cf. R. G. Kent's "Daiva-Inscription of Xerxes," *Language*, XIII, 292–305; H. Hartmann, "Zur neuen Inschrift des Xerxes von Persepolis," *OLZ*, XL, 145–60; and E. Herzfeld's *Altpersische Inschriften*, No. 14. All these scholars relate the inscription to Babylon. On the other hand, with reference to Herodotus' report (VIII, 53) that Xerxes had "plundered the temple and burnt the whole of the Acropolis" in Athens, I. Lévy connected this "Inscription triomphale de Xerxès" with that religious persecution (*Revue historique*, CLXXXV, 105–22). A. Christensen and H. H. Schaeder, finally, insisted that the destruction of the Daiva temple must have occurred among the Parsees themselves. Cf. also P. de Manasce's summary in his "Observations sur l'inscription de Xerxès à Persépolis," *RB*, LII, 124–32. Be this as it may, Herodotus' reports of Xerxes'

religious intolerance (*loc. cit.* and I, 183), if not confirmed, have by no means been controverted. Nor has there been any fresh evidence to contradict the long-accepted fact that even the apparently non-Zoroastrian Cambyses had behaved with equal ruthlessness in recalcitrant Egypt. Cf. G. Posener's collection of hieroglyphic inscriptions pertaining to *La Première domination perse en Egypte*. Neither was the Jewish position absolutely secure. While, on the whole, wise rulers like Darius I and II and Artaxerxes I and II found it profitable to protect Jewish rights, farsighted as well as hotheaded Jews often resented this precarious dependence on the shifting requirements of power politics. Hence those occasional revolutionary, messianic outbursts of the Palestinian community to which reference is made *infra*, notes 38–39. Cf. also in general, K. Galling's *Syrien in der Politik der Achaemeniden* and Schaeder's comments thereon in *OLZ*, XLI, 101–6.

20. If we accept Rothstein's emendation of *hu Shenazzar*, instead of *ve-Shenazzar* in I Chron. 3:18 (cf. his commentary *ad loc.*), Shenazzar also had the Hebrew name of Pedaiah. But if so, we shall either have to abandon the latter's identification with Sheshbazzar, or else seek some explanation for the failure of the ancient chroniclers to mention Pedaiah in other connections. Neither does the compound Bali Yama (i.e., Baal in YHWH), found in the Murashshu records, necessarily indicate the revival of the ancient Israelitic syncretism which had once found expression in Bali Yama's Palestinian equivalents: Bealiah and Yobel. Curiously Nabonidus' prolonged sojourn in the North Arabian oasis of Teima (where Miss Caton-Thompson has unearthed a sixth-century temple of Sin) so deeply impressed all neighboring populations that, a century later, Nehemiah's archenemy, Sanballat the Horonite, still bore a Babylonian name meaning "Sin has given life." But he gave his sons purely Hebraic names. Cf., in general, R. P. Dougherty's *Nabonidus and Belshazzar*, pp. 153 ff.; and Julius Lewy's "Late Assyro-Babylonian Cult of the Moon," *HUCA*, XIX, 405–89.

21. Mardukedri (Marduk is my succor), however, who worked in the Memphis arsenal was very likely a non-Jewish Asiatic, as was the other worker, mentioned in the same list, whose father had the characteristic name Ashtarya[ton]. Cf. Aimé-Giron's *Textes*, pp. 37 f., No. 25. We must beware, however, of judging such onomatological adjustments by present-day standards. In the ancient Near East, it appears, even politically dominant groups often preferred to adopt native names prevalent in their places of residence. This seems, in fact, the most reasonable explanation of the curious phenomenon that the sixth-century Babylonian colonists in Nerab, near Aleppo, used cuneiform tablets but adopted Aramaic names. Cf. E. Dhorme's "Tablettes babyloniennes de Neirab," *Revue d'Assyriologie*, XXV, 53–82.

22. M. Noth is certainly right in emphasizing, against Daiches, the purely Hebrew character of Shabbetai and Haggai. Cf. his *Personennamen*, p. 222, n. 3. Cf. also D. Sidersky's "Onomastique hébraïque des tablettes de Nippur," *REJ*, LXXXVII, 177–99; and G. B. Gray's "Children Named after Ancestors in the Aramaic Papyri from Elephantine and Assuan," *Studien zur semitischen Philologie . . . Julius Wellhausen . . . gewidmet*, pp. 163–76.

23. By a curious misunderstanding, Cowley (No. 81, lines 9, 24–25, 127, translation and index) treats of three different Shabbetais as feminine names by conjecturing a missing *berat* (daughter). He was obviously induced to do so by the single word *titten* (No. 81, l. 24) with its feminine prefix. But this is too weak a support against the clear evidence of No. 58, l. 3, where Shabbetai appears as a father; and of 81, l. 3 itself, where a woman is distinctly called Shabbetit, daughter of Obadiah.

24. The attempt to bridge the gap between the two ancient cultures by means of philology, made by A. S. Yahuda in his *Language of the Pentateuch in Its Relation*

to Egyptian, was bitterly, much too bitterly, repudiated by both Semitists and Egyptologists. While some of his detailed suggestions merit consideration, his general thesis must be rejected. In any case, Egypt's cultural influences cannot be said to approximate those emanating from the Fertile Crescent, even if one rightly disregards the imaginative exaggerations of the old Babel-Bible extremists. Cf. also Yahuda's Accuracy of the Bible; his detailed examination of some "Hebrew Words of Egyptian Origin," JBL, LXVI, 83–90; and his "Medical and Anatomical Terms in the Pentateuch in the Light of Egyptian Medical Papyri," Journal of the History of Medicine and Allied Sciences, II, 549–74.

25. There is universal agreement as to the importance of names as a major criterion of the Jewish character of records, particularly from areas and periods of closer social relations between Jews and Gentiles (Graeco-Roman empires, the Caliphate, modern Europe and America). It is doubly astonishing, therefore, that careful onomatological studies are so few and far between. L. Zunz's Namen der Juden, though classical in its concise, pioneering treatment, is brief and cursory and far behind the present state of our knowledge. More, its fundamental approach is apologetic. Undertaken in 1837 to counteract projected Prussian legislation, it aimed to prove that Jews always adopted the names current among their neighbors, rather than to establish criteria of how to distinguish Jewish from non-Jewish bearers of such names. Much confusion and controversy in Jewish historical literature could be avoided, if disciplined research into the extant sources from various periods could develop rigorous standards for this much-needed differentiation. Cf. B. Klar's brief posthumous survey of Shemot Bene Yisrael (Names of the Children of Israel) from the biblical to the medieval period.

26. Isa. 19:19. This passage has been the subject of lengthy discussions. Some such critics as Duhm and Marti were inclined to regard it as an interpolation by a writer favorably disposed to the temple of Leontopolis in the second century B.C.E. The arguments of Meyer (Papyrusfund, pp. 35 f.) and others, in favor of a preëxilic date, seem irrefutable, however. On Ezekiel's recollection of the Temple architecture, cf. C. G. Howie's "East Gate of Ezekiel's Temple and the Solomonic Gateway at Megiddo," BASOR, 117, pp. 13–19 (pointing out that "this type of gate was no longer built in the ancient Near East after the early eighth century" and that the prophet must, therefore, have vividly remembered the actual gate built by Solomon).

27. Cf. Barton's Archaeology, p. 471. The use of psalms in the Canaanite ritual, frequently suggested before, was illustrated through twenty-four excerpts from El-Amarna records by A. Jirku (in his "Kana'anäische Psalmenfragmente in der vorisraelitischen Zeit Palästinas und Syriens," JBL, LII, 108–20); and still more by the Ugaritic poems. Cf. Patton's Canaanite Parallels; and J. Coppens's "Parallèles du psautier avec les textes de Ras-Shamra-Ougarit," Muséon, LIX, 113–42. Cf. also M. Liber's "Sur les origines de la prière publique dans le judaïsme," Annuaire de l'École pratique des hautes études. Section des sciences religieuses, 1933–34; A. Weiser's "Zur Frage nach den Beziehungen der Psalmen zum Kult," Festschrift Bertholet, pp. 513–31; S. H. Blank's "Confessions of Jeremiah and the Meaning of Prayer," HUCA, XXI, 331–54; and some of the literature listed infra, Chap. XI, n. 34.

28. Hos. 14:3; Ezra 2:65. As a link in this development there probably was a sacrifice connected with a prayer for God's favor. For this reason, for instance, O. Procksch is right when he explains "And Isaac entreated [vaye'etar] the Lord for his wife" (Gen. 25:21) as meaning that Isaac offered a "sacrifice of bidding" (Bittopfer). Cf. his Genesis übersetzt und erklärt, p. 164. The Elephantine soldiers, on the other hand, perhaps because they wished to differentiate between prayer and the sacrifices which they continued to offer, had to coin for it a new Aramaic word,

ṣalaʿ. Connoting prostration before the Lord, however, this term did not adequately describe the traditional posture of the Hebrew worshiper which, barring a few exceptions (I Kings 18:42; Num. 16:4; note, however, the evidently postexilic reference to incense in v. 7), was upright. Hannah certainly prayed standing up so that Eli could watch her lips move (I Sam. 1:13). As soon as Hebrew liturgy began to be standardized, one of the oldest and most significant prayers was called ʿAmidah (the standing-up prayer). Cf. A. Vincent's Religion des Judéo-Araméens, pp. 495 f.; and L. Finkelstein's "Development of the Amidah," JQR, XVI, 1–43, 127–70. Cf. also infra, Chaps. V, n. 22, and VI, n. 17.

29. This significant evolution is described in greater detail and with fuller documentation in my Jewish Community, I, 59 ff.; III, 10 ff.; and H. Zucker's Studien zur jüdischen Selbstverwaltung im Altertum, pp. 12 ff.

30. Cf. the respective lists in Ezra 2 and 8. Such disappearance of local units can hardly be reconciled with E. Meyer's widely accepted hypothesis that they had originally included only the landless exiles in contrast to the landowing groups which had steadily cultivated their clan loyalties. Cf. Meyer's Entstehung des Judentums, pp. 152 ff. This hypothesis seems untenable for other reasons as well, cf. my Jewish Community, III, 11, n. 11. More likely, these local units owed their origin to variations in rituals which must have developed in the various prayerful assemblies in preëxilic Palestine. Such ritualistic variations in different localities are recorded only during the Second Commonwealth (cf. L. Finkelstein's Pharisees, I, 43 ff., 61 ff.), but there is no reason for assuming any greater uniformity in the more spontaneous preëxilic assemblies. This ritualistic disparity may account, in part, also for the existence during the exilic and early postexilic periods of several synagogues, of which the Babylonian Talmud had some dim, but not necessarily unhistorical recollections (b. Megillah 29a; B. B. 15a). Cf. also infra, Chap. XIII, n. 38.

31. On the origins of that institution as well as of its Greek name synagogé (corresponding to the Aramaic kenishta and the Hebrew keneset), cf. my Jewish Community, I, 61 f.; III, 10 f. It is barely possible that the Elephantine papyri have preserved the intervening link between that designation and the older name bet ʿam (house of the people), first recorded in Jerusalem in the days of Jeremiah (39:8). Although the latter institution had very likely served as a political and social rather than religious center, Palestinian Jews as well as the Mandaean sectarians for many centuries continued using this designation for their respective places of worship. Cf. b. Shabbat 32a; and M. Lidzbarski's edition of Sidra d'Yahya. Das Johannesbuch der Mandäer, 18:67 (II, 75 f.). On the other hand, in two descriptions of the Elephantine Temple dated 447 and 416 B.C.E. (Cowley, Nos. 13 l. 14, and 25 l. 6), the structure is called egura or agora. While A. van Hoonacker is probably right in considering it a loan word from the Sumero-Accadian ekurru (house on the mountain top; cf. his Communauté judéo-araméenne à Eléphantine, pp. 52 f.), the Elephantine community may well have forgotten that etymology and rather associated that term with the root agar (assemble). Thus may have arisen the proper name for a "place of assembly," as suggested by Sachau. From here to the nonsacrificial synagogé was but a minor step. It should also be mentioned that C. C. Torrey believes to have detected the words bet kenisha and Yerushalem in an Elath ostracon (No. 2070) of the sixth century B.C.E., which would seem to indicate the presence of a "Jerusalem synagogue" on the Red Sea in that early period. Cf. his query, "A Synagogue at Elath?" BASOR, 84, pp. 4–5. However, both reading and chronology are too uncertain to justify definite conclusions.

32. Isa. 66:1, 3, 20; Mal. 1:11, 2:3, 13; Ps. 51:17–21. Cf. B. D. Eerdmans's "Reflections on a Synagogue Inscription (Isaiah 66)," Quantulacumque, pp. 35–40; A. Menes's

"Contributions to the Problem of Beginnings of Jewish Autonomy in the Biblical Period" (Yiddish), *Yivo Bleter*, I, 130–37, and "Tempel und Synagoge," *ZAW*, L, 268–76. The contrast between the First and Second Temples in the use of incense is so evident that Wellhausen was able to insist that no incense had ever been offered in preëxilic Jerusalem. This theory has been effectively controverted by Van Hoonaker, Wiener, Löhr, and others. But by reinterpreting a Palmyrene inscription known since 1751, H. Ingholt has identified the *ḥammanim* mentioned by the prophets with little incense altars used by the Canaanites and, following them, by some Israelites in private worship. Cf. his "Sens du mot ḥamman," *Mélanges Dussaud*, II, 795–802. We thus understand the virulent attacks on them by the preëxilic prophets. Apparently after the Exile the Temple's monopoly on all offerings was so firmly established that the leaders in Jerusalem saw no further need for combating such private worship. As we shall see, they even viewed with comparative complacency the offering of incense in far-off Elephantine.

33. Writing to a fellow Jew Micah, one Gadol did not hesitate to bless him in the name of "Yaho and Ḥnub" (a well-known Egyptian deity), if Dupont-Sommer's reading of Ostracon 70 from Clermont-Ganneau's collection is correct. Cf. his "Syncretisme religieux des Juifs d'Elephantine d'après un ostracon araméen inédit," *RHR*, CXXX, 17–28, and his remarks in *CRAI*, 1947, pp. 177 f. Dupont-Sommer also found on a dozen ostraca the form יהה, rather than the more usual יהו.

34. The problem of the various divine names mentioned in several Elephantine papyri (as Nos. 7, 22) and included also in some theophorous personal names recorded in Aimé-Giron's *Textes* has been the subject of lengthy debates for many years. The sudden appearance and ubiquity of theophorous names connected with Bethel after 650 has been emphasized by O. Eissfeldt in "Der Gott Bethel," *AR*, XXVIII, 1–30; and J. P. Hyatt in "The Deity Bethel and the Old Testament," *JAOS*, LIX, 81–98. The papyri of Hermopolis West likewise contain names like Bethelnathan and Bethelshazab; cf. Murad Kamil's observations in *Revue de l'histoire juive en Égypte*, I, 2. With reference to Amos (5:5–6), cf. also, in particular, K. Galling's "Bethel und Gilgal," *ZDPV*, LXVI, 140–55; LXVII, 21–43; M. Bič's suggestive "Bet'el—le sanctuaire du roi," *Archiv orientalni*, XVII, 46–63; and G. Zuntz's "Baitylos and Bethel," *Classica et medievalia*, VIII, 169–219 (arguing that the Greek magic stones and the Semitic temple had a common origin in the early pre-Semitic Mediterranean civilization).

Fewer and fewer scholars, however, are still prepared to condemn the entire Jewish colony in Upper Egypt as outright polytheists. These unsophisticated soldiers, including their priests and scribes, may well have thought that they increased the glory of their God by identifying him with the most powerful deities of the Asiatic world. Cf. A. Vincent's *Religion des Judéo-Araméens*, pp. 25–143, 562–680; Albright's *Archaeology and Religion*, pp. 165, 170 ff.; and *infra*, Chap. VI, n. 13. U. Cassuto has even tried to exonerate completely the Elephantine Jews by ascribing the various entries concerning donations for these deities (in Cowley, No. 22) to Aramaic-speaking pagans living in the Jewish colony. See his "Gods of the Jews of Elephantine" (Hebrew), *Kedem*, I, 47–52. His ingenious explanation is partially vitiated, however, by his failure to explain fully, for one example, why an indubitable Jew, called Malchiah, should challenge his opponent by "Herembethel the God" (No. 7). The assumption that Malchiah's opponent was a Gentile (p. 48, n. 13) would have to be proved by some supporting evidence, as would the very existence of a sizable Aramaic-speaking non-Jewish community in the midst of the "Jewish army camp." Cassuto's arguments from the inconsistency in the amounts recorded in the papyrus also leave much to be desired. Perhaps some further light on Egyptian Jewry's worship will be thrown by the publication of the new Aramaic papyri and ostraca by Kraeling, Dupont-Sommer, and others. Cf. *supra*, n. 12 and 16.

35. Cowley's *Aramaic Papyri*, No. 32. This explanation given by Van Hoonacker in his *Communauté* (p. 61) seems far more satisfactory than Causse's suggestion (in his *Dispersés*, pp. 93 f.) that it was merely a chance omission. The subsequent letter of the Elephantine Jews themselves (Cowley, No. 33) shows that they accepted this decision as excluding animal sacrifice. E. Meyer's hypothesis that the Persian governor acted under the impulse of his Zoroastrian belief that the sacred element of fire becomes defiled through the burning of an animal is, as Meyer himself admits, neither supported by the sources nor by what we know about the then extremely tolerant religious policy of the Achaemenid administration (*Papyrusfund*, pp. 88 f.). Cf. also F. Dijkema's "Temple in Elephantine and the So-Called Centralization of Worship in Jerusalem" (Dutch), *Nieuw theologisch Tijdschrift*, XX, 321–33; and A. Vincent's *Religion des Judéo-Araméens*, pp. 144 ff. Bagohi's arbitrary refusal to grant the Elephantine Jews the right to animal sacrifices, while allowing such offerings in Jerusalem, would seem even less likely if, as Meyer suggested, he had been the recipient of a substantial consideration. This bribery, supposedly intimated in Cowley, Nos. 30 and 33, is unduly played up by Meissner in *SB* Berlin, 1938, p. 15, and with equal zeal denied by M. Vogelstein in his "Bakshish for Bagoas?" *JQR*, XXXIII, 89–92. The latter resorts to the rather dubious expedient of eliminating two crucial words. Cf. also *infra*, n. 39.

As a matter of fact, however, we cannot even speak confidently about the Persian authorities' attitude toward the sacrificial worship of their own coreligionists. While Herodotus, for example, reports that the Persians did not "set up statues and temples and altars, but those who make such they deem foolish" (I, 131), Darius I, in his Behistun inscription, prided himself on having reconstructed the Parsee temples. To reconcile these contradictions K. Erdmann has suggested that high Parsee officials possessed private chapels, whereas the populace worshiped in the open air. Cf. *Das iranische Feuerheiligtum*. Cf. also, from another angle, W. B. Stevenson's "Hebrew 'Olah and Zebach Sacrifices," *Festschrift Bertholet*, pp. 488–97, pointing out that the flowering of the *zebaḥ* as family sacrifice depended on the existence of local *bamot* accessible to the whole population. As soon, however, as all sacrifices were monopolized by the Second Temple the *'olah* far overshadowed the *zebaḥ* in importance.

36. Ezra 6:1 ff.; 7:20 ff., etc. Cf. K. Galling's detailed analysis of "Der Tempelschatz nach Berichten und Urkunden im Buche Esra," *ZDPV*, LX, 177–83. On the coins struck by high priests, cf. E. L. Sukenik's ingenious interpretation of one Hebrew and two Aramaic inscriptions on coins of the fourth century in his "Paralipomena Palaestinensia," *JPOS*, XIV, 178–84; his "More about the Oldest Coins of Judaea," *ibid.*, XV, 341–43 (on one additional coin); and A. Reifenberg's "Hebrew Shekel of the Fifth Century B.C.," *PEQ*, 1943, pp. 100–104. The latter has plausibly argued that this shekel had been struck by a Jewish authority after Nehemiah's reduction of the temple tax from one-half to one-third of a shekel (10:33), but he has not proved Nehemiah's own role in its minting. It is more likely that this prerogative was exercised by the chief priest, whether or not he was called "high priest" before 411. Cf. Morgenstern's remarks in *AJSL*, LV, 193. In fact, it would not be surprising if the same postexilic priest who assumed the high-sounding title of *ha-kohen hagadol* were also the first Jew to order the minting of a coin, a right exercised by the high priests to the end of the Persian and deep into the Hellenistic period. Cf. also, in general, M. Narkiss's *Maṭbe'ot Ereṣ-Yisrael* (Coins of Palestine), Vol. I; A. Reifenberg's *Ancient Jewish Coins;* and *infra*, Chaps. VI, n. 1, and VII, n. 31.

37. Cowley's *Aramaic Papyri*, Nos. 30, 32, 38; Ezra 5:11, 6:10; Isa. 44:28, 45:1. The fact that the phrase referring to the holding of a right hand seems to be a direct borrowing from the official parlance at the Persian court (cf. R. Kittel's "Cyrus und Deuterojesaja," *ZAW*, XVIII, 149–62; and the subsequent debates summarized in S. Smith's *Isaiah*, pp. 73, and 180, n. 76) is not only a testimony to the prophet's

familiarity with Persian-Babylonian idioms, but also seems to bear out Bickermann's contention that, by issuing his edict, Cyrus did not confer any special favor on the Jews, but merely wished to appear as God's vicar in Palestine. Such was, indeed, the position of the Achaemenid rulers in Egypt and other provinces. Cf. *JBL*, LXV, 262 f. Cf. also C. E. Simcox's *"Rôle* of Cyrus in Deutero-Isaiah," *JAOS*, LVII, 158-71; and K. Galling's "Kyrusedikt und Tempelbau," *OLZ*, XL, 473-78 (suggesting with reference to Ezra 5:3, 9; 6:3, among other matters, that the reason why the Jews could not produce a copy of the original decree was that it had been deposited in a box and immured in the wall of the Temple).

38. These chronological aspects are analyzed by J. Morgenstern in his "Three Calendars of Ancient Israel," *HUCA*, I, 13-78, "New Year for Kings," *Gaster Anniv. Vol.*, pp. 439-56; and his "Two Prophecies from 520-516 B.C.," *HUCA*, XXII, 365-431. Cf. also his "Nashku bar," *JQR*, XXXII, 371-85 (which phrase in Ps. 2:12 he believes to be a corruption of *tenu li-shemo kabod =* pay homage to his [the Lord's] name); his remarks on Ps. 48:5-8 in *HUCA*, XVI, 5 ff. (in these and other biblical passages Morgenstern detects signs of Jewish unrest in the days of Xerxes); his review cited *supra*, n. 5; and A. Bentzen's "Quelques remarques sur le mouvement messianique parmi les Juifs aux environs de l'an 520," *RHPR*, X, 493-503. The evidence in all these cases is highly debatable, but there is considerable likelihood that at least Zechariah in his early prophecies (particularly 6:9-15) was "intent upon the establishment of an independent kingdom under Zerubbabel and Joshua." Cf. H. G. May's "Key to the Interpretation of Zechariah's Visions," *JBL*, LVII, 173-84.

39. This deportation, perhaps in some way connected with both a Phoenician uprising and the destruction of Jericho, is recorded by Eusebius and other church fathers. Cf. the respective excerpts in E. Schürer's *Geschichte des jüdischen Volkes im Zeitalter Jesu Christi*, III, 7 n. 11. Although in the 1st ed. of his *Geschichte des Altertums*, III, 211, E. Meyer raised some doubts as to the historicity of these events, they seem to be supported by the excavations at Jericho and other recent evidence. Meyer himself failed to repeat his doubts in the new ed. of his *Geschichte*, IV, Pt. 1, p. 199, n. 1. Unfortunately, we know very little about the inner developments in Judaea during the last century of Persian rule. But A. Shalit has made a case for considering the obscure, evidently much distorted, passage in Josephus' *Antt.* XI, 7, 1.297-301 as the reflection of "A Chapter in the History of Party Struggles in Jerusalem at the End of the Fifth and the Beginning of the Fourth Centuries B.C.E." Here Bagoas appears to have played a decidedly hostile role toward the faction in power. His measures, reported by Josephus, could not fail to affect adversely the whole of the Jewish Commonwealth and hence to add fuel to the existing disaffection of the population. Cf. Shalit's Hebrew essay in *Lewy Mem. Vol.*, pp. 252-72. Cf. also *supra*, n. 35.

In any case, the unfriendliness on the part of the later Persian administrators seems to have impressed itself sufficiently on the minds of the subsequent generations of Jews to make them almost forget the earlier benefactions from Cyrus to Darius II. On the latter's Passover circular of 419 and its textual reconstruction, cf. *infra*, Chap. V, n. 19. Even in the biblical writings the pusillanimity of Ahasuerus-Xerxes and the persecution of Daniel by Darius the Mede (Chap. 6-7) appeared to outweigh the favorable impressions offered by the books of Ezra-Nehemiah. Cf., e.g., H. H. Rowley's *Darius the Mede and the Four World Empires in the Book of Daniel*. In general, the Jews of Palestine retained but confused recollections about their experiences during the entire Persian period and its basic chronology. Cf. *infra*, Chap. VI, n. 44.

40. This concluding statement in E. Meyer's *Entstehung des Judentums* sounded the keynote for many such assertions repeated by himself and other scholars. B. Meissner went further and suggested that Babylonians and Jews were the only con-

quered populations so well treated by the Achaemenid rulers because both had conspired to open the gates of the unconquerable fortress of Babel to Cyrus (*SB* Berlin, 1938, p. 14). No effort was made to substantiate the queer idea that Jews, whose presence at that time in the Babylonian capital in any significant number is by itself rather dubious, collaborated with their chief enemies, the Bel priests, in subverting the regime of their friend Nabonidus. Deutero-Isaiah doubtless voiced more accurately their sentiments when he looked forward to Bel's downfall (46:1), which failed to materialize precisely because of the Bel priests' aid to Cyrus. Cf. also Morris Jastrow's *Civilization of Babylonia and Assyria,* pp. 184 f.; and R. de Vaux's remarks on "Les Décrets de Cyrus et de Darius sur la reconstruction du Temple" in *RB,* XLVI, 41. Of course, ultimately Jews must have rejoiced over Babel's fall and, if Xerxes' Persepolis inscription of 485 is to be interpreted to refer to a more thorough destruction of the city, J. Lindblom may indeed be right in connecting Isa. 24–27 with this event. Cf. his *Jesaja-Apokalypse: Jes. 24–27.*

CHAPTER V: RETHINKING FUNDAMENTALS

1. Ez. 37:11–12. The obvious irrationality and apocalyptic fervor of many Ezekelian visions have given rise to frequent doubts of the prophet's sanity. Summarizing many psychiatric studies, E. C. Broome, Jr., came to the conclusion that Ezekiel "exhibits behavioristic abnormalities consistent with paranoid schizophrenia," in particular, "(1) periods of catatonia; (2) 'the influencing machine'; (3) a narcissistic-masochistic conflict with attendant phantasies of castration and unconscious sexual repression; (4) schizophrenic withdrawal; (5) delusions of persecution and grandeur." Cf. "Ezekiel's Abnormal Personality," *JBL*, LXV, 291 f. Cf. also the literature listed *supra*, Chap. III, n. 38. But it required perhaps the presence of an almost insane religious genius like Ezekiel for the exilic community to recover so speedily from the shock and to follow some of his irrational solutions for the apparently insoluble perplexities of its new minority existence. At the same time neither the community nor its prophetic leader had any use for the mysterious rituals practiced by their neighbors. Ezekiel's famous vision, in the presence of the elders of Judah, of the "abominations" at the sanctuary, is aptly interpreted as a vivid satire on the oriental mystery cults by T. H. Gaster in his "Ezekiel and the Mysteries," *JBL*, LX, 289–310. Cf. also H. Knight's "Personality of Ezekiel—Priest or Prophet?" *Expository Times*, LIX, 115–20 (overstressing the irreconcilable nature of the two vocations); and *supra*, Chap. III, n. 34.

2. Isa. 48:3–6; 65:17, etc. The great significance of "The 'Former' and the 'Latter Things' in the Prophecies of Deutero-Isaiah" is rightly stressed by N. Rabban in his Hebrew essay in *Tarbiz*, XIV, 19–25, where the respective passages are assembled and brought into focus. We need not accept, however, the author's inconclusive argument that, for this reason, the prophet must have been familiar with both the prophecies of Isaiah (1–35) and the historical chapters (36–39), to which he himself appended the transcript of his prophecies. Neither is C. R. North's suggestion altogether plausible that by "former things" (*rishonot* without an article) the prophet had in mind such remote events as the Exodus, whereas he used *ha-rishonot* (with an article) for more recent developments, e.g., the victories of Cyrus. Cf. "The 'Former Things' and the 'New Things' in Deutero-Isaiah," *Studies Robinson*, pp. 111–26. In any case, Deutero-Isaiah's reiterated insistence upon the "good tidings," the "new song," etc., clearly shows that, in these passages, too, he did not have in mind the mere confirmation of former prophecies by subsequent events, but rather a total reshaping of Jewish and human destinies. Cf. also A. Bentzen's "On the Idea of 'The Old' and 'The New' in Deutero-Isaiah." *Studia theologica*, I, 183–87.

3. Cf. F. von Spiegel's *Eranische Altertumskunde*, III, 649 ff. On the meaning of the formula affirming the Jews' mutual responsibility (in Sifra to Lev. 26:37; b. Sanhedrin 27b) and its association with the responsibility of all Jewish copartners in the covenant with God, cf. A. Abeles's analysis of "Alle Israeliten sind Bürgen, Einer für den Anderen," *Festschrift Schwarz*, pp. 231–46. Cf. also H. W. Robinson's "Hebrew Conception of Corporate Personality" in *Werden und Wesen des Alten Testaments*, ed. by P. Volz, pp. 49–62.

4. Cf. K. Fullerton's "Job, Chapters 9 and 10," *AJSL*, LV, 267; R. Gordis's "Corporate Personality in Job," *JNES*, IV, 54 f.; other literature on the book of Job listed *infra*, n. 23; and, more generally, H. H. Rowley's *Submission in Suffering: a Comparative Study of Eastern Thought*. Interesting comparative data on Israel's and other

ancient peoples' concern with the problem of theodicy and the variety of solutions suggested by their religious thinkers are presented in the complementary studies by J. J. Stamm, *Das Leiden des Unschuldigen in Babylon und Israel;* and J. Paulus, "Le Thème du juste souffrant dans la pensée grecque et hébraïque," *RHR*, CXXI, 18–66. Referring in particular to Ps. 49 and 73 and the doctrine of the suffering Servant of the Lord, Stamm rightly emphasizes that, in contrast to Babylonians, Israel early accepted suffering as a meaningful manifestation of the divine guidance of history. It should be noted, however, that the Psalms, with their frequent emphasis on "I," as well as the Proverbs, both pre- and postexilic, have a strongly individualistic tinge. So have the ethical sanctions included even in the oldest laws of the Pentateuch. Cf. W. Eichrodt's pertinent remarks in *Das Menschenverständnis des Alten Testaments;* R. Tournay's "Eschatologie individuelle dans les Psaumes," *RB*, LVI, 481–508; P. J. Verdam's " 'On ne fera point mourir les enfants pour les pères' [Deut. 24:16] en droit biblique," *RIDA*, IV, 393–416; and A. R. Johnson's *Vitality of the Individual in the Thought of Ancient Israel.* Of some interest in this connection is also F. H. von Meyenfeldt's comprehensive Dutch study of the Hebrew terms for heart (*leb, lebab*). Cf. his *Het Hart . . . in het Oude Testament.*

5. Entire libraries could be filled with writings on the Old Testament doctrine of the Hereafter, even more than ordinarily contrasting with the paucity of the biblical statements themselves. This is not altogether surprising when one considers the enormous role this doctrine was to play in the subsequent world outlook of Judaism and its daughter religions. Among recent monographs, cf. in particular, such comparative studies as A. T. Nikolainen's *Auferstehungsglauben in der Bibel und ihrer Umwelt*, I; C. M. Edsman's *Body and Eternal Life* (with special reference to a ninth-century Christian writer's remarkable interpretation); O. R. Sellers's "Israelite Belief in Immortality," *BA*, VIII, 1–20; and H. Birkeland's "Belief in the Resurrection of the Dead in the Old Testament," *Studia theologica*, III, 60–78. Cf. also T. Zielinski's stimulating though undisciplined essay on "La Guerre de l'outre tombe chez les Hébreux, les Grecs et les Romains," *Annuaire*, II, 1021–42; A. Lods's "Notes sur deux croyances hébraïques rélatives à la mort et ce qui la suit," *CRAI*, 1943, pp. 271–97 (on the fate of the uncircumcized in the Hereafter with reference to Ez. 28:10, 31: 18, and elsewhere, and the Ugaritic background of the Leviathan); J. Taubes's *Abendländische Eschatologie;* and, on the possible connection with the Canaanite fertility rites, H. G. May's "Fertility Cult in Hosea," *AJSL*, XLVIII, 73–98. Of course, later generations read into the Bible their own cherished doctrines and even detected "Biblical Quasi-Evidence for the Transmigration of Souls," which is discussed, on the basis of Al-Qirqisani's tenth-century work by its editor L. Nemoy in *JBL*, LIX, 159–68. On the emergence of these teachings as major public issues during the Second Commonwealth and after cf. Chaps. VI, n. 53–54; IX, n. 47–48.

6. Isa. 55:8; I Sam. 4:4; Ez. 1:15 ff., 10:1 ff. "In the teaching of the Old Testament," rightly says H. H. Rowley, "no less than in that of the New, truth is found to lie in the tension between man's kinship with God, and God's otherness than man." Cf. his *Re-discovery*, p. 189. Cf. also the complementary studies of the related problems of "Fear and Love of God in the Old Testament" by B. J. Bamberger in *HUCA*, VI, 39–53, and by G. Nagel in the *Revue de théologie et de philosophie*, XXXIII, 175–86; and, from another angle, L. H. Brockington's "Hebrew Conception of Personality in Relation to the Knowledge of God," *JTS*, XLVII, 1–11. The ancient oriental background of the "chariot" has frequently been discussed. Cf., e.g., A. Salonen's brief essay on *Prozessionswagen der babylonischen Götter.* The Phoenician pantheon actually included a chariot-god, Rekhub-el. Cf. A. Dupont-Sommer's transliteration and translation of a ninth-century inscription (first published by F. von Luschan in 1943) in his "Inscription nouvelle du roi Kilamon et le dieu Rekoub-el," *RHR*, CXXXIII, 19–33.

7. "The notion 'holy,'" writes B. D. Eerdmans, "has in the O.T. a meaning very different from western conceptions. With us it refers to a spiritual attitude, to serenity, mercy, virtue. With the Hebrews it was a divine emanation, a fluid, covering the surroundings of a deity as an unseen atmosphere. Though invisible it was a concrete item" (*Religion of Israel*, p. 70). This sharp contrast, generally overstressing the picturesque concreteness of biblical Hebrew as opposed to modern abstractions even in the case of ordinary Israelites, is demonstrably untrue in that of the great prophets from Isaiah to Zechariah. In any case, the tremendous significance of the doctrine of holiness for Old Testament theology is evident from the presence in it of more than seven hundred passages containing the term *qadosh* or its derivatives. It is not accidental that these are found in greatest profusion in the Priestly Code, Ezekiel and Deutero-Isaiah. Cf. J. Haenel's comprehensive analysis of *Die Religion der Heiligkeit;* and J. W. Lambert's briefer review of "The Idea of Holiness in the Old Testament," *Shane Quarterly*, VII, 86–96.

8. Gen. 1:31; Deut. 30:15, 19. Though essentially preëxilic, indeed, probably quite old (cf. *supra*, Chap. II, n. 28), the biblical story of creation (Gen. 1–11) was undoubtedly rephrased by the writers of the Priestly school to suit the temper of the new age. Such rephrasing may be admitted even by those who reject J. Morgenstern's radical view that the Yahwistic strata in the whole story originated between 525 and 485 B.C.E. Cf. his "Mythological Background of Psalm 82," *HUCA*, XIV, 93, n. 114. Cf. also P. Humbert's detailed *Etudes sur le récit du paradis et de la chute;* and, on the Old Testament as well as Babylonian teachings concerning the meaning of death, E. Sellin's *Alttestamentliche Theologie auf religionsgeschichtlicher Grundlage*, II, 76 ff. Incidentally, the old rabbinic interpretation of the term *bara* as relating to creation *ex nihilo*, although representing a rather advanced type of philosophical speculation, has been confirmed by J. van der Ploeg's semantic analysis in *Muséon*, LIX, 143–57.

9. Cf., in particular, N. H. Ridderbos's detailed refutation of Mowinckel's theory in *De "Werkers der Ongerechtigheid" in de individuelle Psalmen* (The "Workers of Iniquity" in Individual Psalms), which remains essentially valid despite the modifications suggested by A. Lods in his review of that work in *RHR*, CXXI, 181–85. Ugaritic and other recent evidence has made it doubly clear that postexilic Jewry's increasing belief in demons was not a novel foreign importation, as was often assumed. Foreign material could never have shown such remarkable vitality as to last undiminished through Jewish, Christian, and Muslim influences to the present day. How widespread demonology is among the Muslims and Christians of Palestine today has been demonstrated by the Palestinian folklorist, T. Canaan, in his *Dämonenglaube im Lande der Bibel*. Generally human and native Palestinian influences, coupled with the "popular religion" of Israel, had sufficiently prepared the ground for a speedy and thorough assimilation of a few novel elements. Cf. the comprehensive analyses by H. Kaupel, *Die Dämonen im Alten Testament* (drawing a distinction between demons whose very existence was denied, and Satan, belief in whom was accepted as a legitimate religious doctrine); N. Johansson, *Parakletoi, Vorstellungen von Fürsprechern für die Menschen vor Gott in der alttestamentlichen Religion, im Spätjudentum und Urchristentum;* and E. Langton, *Good and Evil Spirits: a Study of the Jewish and Christian Doctrine*. Johansson and Langton rightly stress the autochtonous nature of certain phases of the ancient Israelitic belief in spirits, Langton also linking it with the Jewish doctrine of the future life which resulted "naturally, and we may say almost inevitably, from the special genius of the Yahwistic religion" (p. 198). Cf. also, from different angles, S. Langdon's "Babylonian and Hebrew Demonology," *JRAS*, 1934, 45–56; H. Torczyner's "Necromancy in the Biblical Period" (Hebrew), *Yellin Jub. Vol.*, pp. 69–77; A. Brock-Utne's " 'Der Feind.' Die alttestamentliche Satansgestalt im Lichte der sozialen Verhältnisse des nahen

Orients," *Klio*, XXVIII, 219–27; A. Lods's "Origines de la figure de Satan, ses fonctions à la cour céleste," *Mélanges Dussaud*, II, 649–60; M. J. Gruenthaner's "Demonology of the Old Testament," *CBQ*, VI, 6–27; A. Marmorstein's "Egyptian Mythology and Babylonian Magic in Bible and Talmud," *Mahler Jub. Vol.*, pp. 469–87; and W. G. Heidt's *Angelology of the Old Testament*.

Examples of early magical texts in Hebrew and Aramaic are the aforementioned text of the seventh century (cf. *supra*, Chap. III, n. 25); and "The Aramaic Incantation in Cuneiform" reinterpreted by C. Gordon in *AOF*, XII, 105–17. Really consisting of two incantations, the latter reflected formulas antedating the Seleucid era. Though basically rejecting Gordon's approach, B. Landsberger nevertheless seems to accept that dating. Cf. his "Zu den aramäischen Beschwörungen in Keilschrift," *AOF*, pp. 247–57. Cf. also *infra*, Chaps. IX, n. 22–23; XV, n. 27–28.

10. Isa. 42:9–10; 45:7; 63:10 ff. Although the "spirit of the Lord" had been an ancient concept (cf., e.g., I Sam. 16:14), it was imbued with a new and deeper significance by the anonymous immortal going under the name of the Second Isaiah. Cf. also M. Schmidt's searching investigation of the problem of God's nearness to man in his *Prophet und Tempel;* and H. Schrade's comparative study of *Der verborgene Gott*.

11. Judg. 5:11; Prov. 1:21; II Chron. 17:9. Overbearing lay, as well as priestly, teachers of both Torah and worldly wisdom had already become the target of Jeremiah's attack when he denounced "the vain pen of the scribes" overconfident of their possession of the Torah (8:8–9). The manifold shadings of the term *torah* in the Bible have long intrigued scholars. Among more recent monographs, cf. especially G. Ostborn's "semantic study" of the *Tora in the Old Testament;* and E. Robertson's "Riddle of the Torah: Suggesting a Solution" in his *Old Testament Problem*, pp. 80–104.

12. Ezra 7:6, 10. Precisely because so much of the preëxilic ceremonial law had been in the exclusive possession of the priestly class, its growth throughout the period of its oral transmission remains hidden from the eyes of modern investigators. That is why so many of the unceasing debates on the nature of the Priestly legislation and its older or newer sources are necessarily arid and unrealistic. Among more recent studies, cf. A. Bea's summary of "Der heutige Stand der Pentateuchfrage," *Biblica*, XVI, 175–200; and E. Robertson's "Priestly Code," in his *Old Testament Problem*, pp. 56–79. Cf. also the various introductions to the Old Testament and the vast pertinent literature on the oral transmission of biblical sources, listed *supra*, Chaps. II, n. 10; and III, n. 51.

13. Cf. Exod. 20:8–11 and 34:21; and Rowley's comments thereon in his *Rediscovery*, pp. 242 f. On the other hand, following Erdmann's argument, K. Budde, the famous protagonist of the Midianite-Kenite origins of Yahwism in general, declared the Sabbath to have been originally a *dies nefastus* and consequently also a rest-day for the Kenite smiths. Cf. his "Sabbath and the Week," *JTS*, XXX, 1–15. J. Meinhold's criticisms of this conception (in his "Zur Sabbathfrage," *ZAW*, XLVIII, 121–38) were much stronger on their negative side than in their positive defense of the old and widely discussed theory that the Sabbath was originally the festival of the full moon. More recently, N. H. Snaith suggested that it originated from a new-moon, rather than a full-moon holiday (*Jewish New Year Festival*, pp. 103 ff.). On the other hand, in his "Calendar and Sabbath" (Dutch), *Nieuwe theologische Studiën*, XXIII, 172–95, T. C. Vriezen has convincingly argued against its association with either phase of the moon as well as with the Babylonian unlucky day. He went too far, however, in minimizing the social vs. the ritualistic aspects of the Sabbath. Cf. also the denial of Babylonian borrowings in R. Ginns's "Rosh hash-Shanah: Its Date

and Significance," *Dominican Studies*, II, 385–94; and, on the opposing view, H. and J. Lewy's "Origin of the Week and the Oldest West Asiatic Calendar," *HUCA*, XVII, 1–152c (particularly pp. 78 ff., 136 ff.); Julius Lewy's brief discussion of the "Neo-Babylonian Names of the Days of the Week?" *BASOR*, 95, pp. 34–36; Albright's remarks on the *HUCA* essay in *JBL*, LXIV, 290, and his *Stone Age*, p. 329, n. 95. On the ramified older sociological and other theories, cf. E. G. Kraeling's survey of the "Present Status of the Sabbath Question," *AJSL*, XLIX, 218–28.

14. II Kings 4:23; Neh. 13:15 ff.; Isa. 58:13–14. Ordinary business transactions of professional traders were, of course, prohibited at an early date, as interfering with their obligatory rest. Even Amos denounced the impatience of those merchants who could not wait until the Sabbath was over once more to begin their cheating of the poor (8:5), although he did not accuse them of actual transgression of the Sabbath laws. Sabbath observance in trade seems also demonstrated by the apparent absence of contracts concluded by Elephantine Jews on that day. Cf. J. K. Fotheringham's "Dates in the Elephantine Papyri," *JTS*, XIV, 574 f. This contrasted with the uninterrupted succession of business days in Babylonia, where C. H. W. Johns could not establish, in his analysis of many extant contracts of different ages, any falling off of business on the seventh, fourteenth, etc., of the month, the alleged days of rest in the country. See his "Babylonian and Assyrian Sabbath," *Encyclopaedia Britannica*, 11th ed., XXIII, 961–62. Only one ostracon, however, may have direct reference to the Sabbath, if we accept A. Dupont-Sommer's rather dubious reading and interpretation in "L'Ostracon araméen du sabbat," *Semitica*, II, 29–39.

Otherwise, such paucity of specific injunctions on the sacredness of the Sabbath in the Elephantine papyri is fully understandable in view of the separation of this Egyptian group from Judah before the Deuteronomic reformation. Even the great prophets before Jeremiah did not attach to the Sabbath that overwhelming importance encountered everywhere in the postexilic literature. For this reason, Jeremiah's eloquent plea for the strict observance of the day (17:19–27) has been suspected as a later interpolation, although the emphasis upon the social prohibitions of work and carrying burdens is a strong indication of its authenticity. Cf. W. E. Barnes's "Prophecy and the Sabbath," *JTS*, XXIX, 386–90. It cannot be denied, however, that no preëxilic prophet would have made a statement exactly like that quoted here from Deutero-Isaiah, the authenticity of which need not be doubted.

15. Exod. 20:11 (P), 23:12, 34:21; Deut. 5:15; Ez. 20:12 ff. The importance of the Sabbath for the entire evolution of Judaism and its literature is well illustrated by the various excerpts assembled in the attractive Hebrew and English anthologies by I. L. Baruch in *Sefer ha-Shabbat* (Book of the Sabbath); and A. E. Millgram in *Sabbath: the Day of Delight*.

16. Deut. 21:18 ff.; I Chron. 6:39 ff.; Num. 36:6–7. The cities of refuge were undoubtedly established under the early monarchy which could not possibly tolerate endless blood feuds, often extending from generation to generation. Cf. in detail N. M. Nicolsky's "Asylrecht in Israel," *ZAW*, XLVIII, 146–75; M. Löhr's *Asylwesen im Alten Testament;* and C. L. Feinberg's "Cities of Refuge," *Bibliotheca Sacra*, CIII, 411–17, CIV, 35–48. Unlike the preëxilic localities, however, which had shrines of their own enhancing that right of asylum, those postulated by the Priestly legislation evidently did not require such added protection. The partial reëstablishment, on the other hand, of the "priest cities" was in line with the general revival of inbreeding in the local Palestinian communities, encouraged as a matter of principle by the later authors of the aprocryphal books Tobit (4:12–13; 6:10–13) and Jubilees (4:15, 25:3 ff.). It is still widespread among the Palestinian *felaheen* today, on social as well as economic grounds. Cf. H. Granqvist, *Marriage Conditions in a Palestinian Village*, I, 66 ff. On these "Cities of Priests and Levites and Cities of Refuge," cf. also

S. Klein's pertinent Hebrew study in *Qobeṣ* (Journal) *of the Jewish Palestine Exploration Society*, 1934-35, pp. 81-107, 367; and W. F. Albright's "List of Levitic Cities," *Ginzberg Jub. Vol.*, pp. 49-73 (placing, however, Josh. 21 and I. Chron. 6 in the tenth century B.C.E. and hence denying any connection with the postexilic institutions).

The new importance of the family in the exilic community also led to the sharpening of protective laws against such disruptive forces as adultery and conflicts between parents and children. Adultery had been outlawed by all ancient legal systems. But it was long treated as merely an offense against the individual concerned. Later on the state arrogated to itself the power to intervene in stemming a practice which might lead to serious antisocial complications. Only in Judaism, however, and particularly in the postexilic period, were all such family relations placed under the direct surveillance of God. Every offense now became not only a crime against the individual and society but a sin before the Lord. Cf. the interesting comparative studies by W. Kornfeld, "L'Adultère dans l'Orient antique," *RB*, LVII, 92-109; and S. J. Feigin, "Disrespect toward Parents in the Torah and the Near-Eastern Laws" (Hebrew), *SH*, X-XI, 301-15. Cf. also M. David's "Adultery According to Deut. 22:22 ff." (Dutch), *JEOL*, VIII, 650-54.

17. In her "Fertility Cult Functionaries in the Old Testament," *JBL*, LX, 227-53, B. A. Brooks exaggerates somewhat the importance of these officials even in preëxilic times. Apart from including in this category such questionable types as women sitting (*yoshebot*) at the Temple gate and "weeping for Tammuz" (Ez. 8:14) or the *'almah*, her list of recorded children of sacred prostitutes refers to persons who, if not altogether legendary, belong to the period before the divided monarchy. The main exceptions are Hosea's Gomer, Isaiah's "prophetess," and Ruth, but their connection with fertility cults has been postulated only by some extremists of the "cultic school." In any case, prophets, legislators, and historians unanimously condemned this institution as a foreign importation and tolerated none of it in the Second Temple.

18. Mal. 2:11. "Four definite attacks upon intermarriage," writes L. M. Epstein, "are to be found in Jewish history, and all of them came in the wake of a reformation movement consequent upon a national crisis. The first was the deuteronomic reformation, the second came with the Restoration under Ezra, the third with the Maccabean victory in the War of Independence, the fourth with the final fall of the Jewish State" (*Marriage Laws*, pp. 155 ff.). Nehemiah's specific concern about the people and language of Ashdod (4:1, 13:24) is understandable in the light of that city's prominence as a provincial capital. It had served as a focus of attraction to various neighbors ever since the Assyrians had deported its Philistine inhabitants. Cf. the fresh light thrown on that Assyrian province by two new fragments of Sargon II's prisms published by E. F. Weidner in *AOF*, XIV, 40 ff.; and reinterpreted by A. Alt in his "Neue assyrische Nachrichten über Palästina und Syrien," *ZDPV*, LXVII, 138 ff. Cf. also, in general, L. Löw's "Eherechtliche Studien" in his *G.S.*, III, 13-334; L. Freund's "Ueber Genealogien und Familienreinheit in biblischer und talmudischer Zeit," *Festschrift Schwarz*, pp. 163-92; and, in the sphere of laws of purity, H. M. Kamsler's "Hebrew Menstrual Taboos," *Journal of American Folk-Lore*, LI, 76-82.

19. Unfortunately the text of this Aramaic papyrus (in Cowley, No. 21) is badly preserved. It is cited here from Cowley's restoration (and translation) which seems far more plausible than that offered by A. Vincent in his *Religion des Judéo-Araméens*, pp. 237 ff. The latter's reading of *dibḥu pesaḥ* (sacrifice the Paschal lamb) in the decisive lacuna in line 9, is the less plausible as, according to his own view, the Palestinian authorities had favored the issuance of this decree. Cf. however, *ibid.*, pp. 279 ff. It is immaterial in this connection whether the Darius decree contained only a few lines, as assumed by M. Lidzbarski and Cowley (cf. the latter's remarks

loc. cit.), or, what is more probable, that the whole document emanated from the king himself (cf. Meyer's *Papyrusfund,* p. 92, n. 1). Nor is the reading of a crucial passage in an early Elephantine ostracon conclusive. Even if that text, dated by its editors on palaeographic grounds between 515 and 495, were to read in the equally important line 9, "When are you sacrificing the Pascha?" it would merely bear out the accepted fact that animal sacrifices had been regularly offered at the Elephantine temple until its destruction in 411. The main interest in this ostracon, therefore, consists in its apparent content showing that an outlying Egyptian community, though uncertain as to its calendar, likewise observed the Passover holiday. Cf. E. L. Sukenik and J. Kutsher's "Passover Ostracon from Elephantine" (Hebrew), *Kedem,* I, 53–56.

On governor Arsham or Arsames, who seems to have held sway over Egypt in the years 428–408 or longer, cf. the data assembled by Meissner in *SB* Berlin, 1938, pp. 10, 24 ff.; one of his letters, ed. (with a summary of several others) by J. Kutsher in collaboration with J. Polotsky in "An Aramaic Leather Scroll of the Fifth Century B.C." (Hebrew), *Kedem,* II, 66–74; and Mittwoch's essay cited *supra,* Chap. IV, n. 13.

20. Ez. 46:20; 44:19, etc. Even if one denies the exilic authorship of the constitutional proposals espoused in Ez. 40–48 and places them, as do some modern commentators, in the fifth century, their exilic antecedents can hardly be doubted. Cf. the literature listed *supra,* Chap. IV, n. 2.

21. Contrast especially Lev. 17:1–9 with Deut. 12:15. The evolution, here described, seems better to fit the wording of these and other scriptural passages than that suggested by S. H. Blank in his "Dissident Laity in Early Judaism," *HUCA,* XIX, 8 f. On the much-debated problem of relationships between the "priests" and "levites" we need but quote R. Meyer's correct, though rather disheartening, conclusion that "a connected story of the levitical group cannot be written." Cf. his "Levitische Emanzipationsbestrebungen im nachexilischen Zeitalter," *OLZ,* XLI, 728; Z. Karl's ingenious reconstruction of the story of "Priests and Levites in the Biblical Period" (Hebrew), *Keneset,* VII, 348–66 (his equation of levites with the preëxilic *netinim* is extremely dubious, however); A. Dupont-Sommer's rather questionable interpretation of a newly found Aramaic ostracon in his " 'Maison de Yahvé' et vêtemens sacrés à Eléphantine," *JA,* CCCXXXV, 79–87; and *supra,* Chap. III, n. 25–26.

22. Cf. I Chron. 25; Neh. 7:44. In the vivid discussions on the Psalms during the last decades, the belief in the preëxilic composition of many, if not most of them, has been steadily gaining ground. Cf., in particular, the arguments advanced by H. Gunkel in his *Einleitung in die Psalmen.* Although few will agree with I. Engnell (in his *Studies in Divine Kingship,* p. 176, n. 2) that "there is merely one psalm in the whole Psalter of which I am quite convinced that it is postexilic: Psalm 137," the fact that so many of them reveal decided Ugaritic affinities, which are otherwise attested only either before 900 or after 600, has induced many scholars to date some psalms in the tenth century. Albright, for instance, attributes Ps. 18, 29, 45, and 68 to that early period. Cf. also Patton's *Canaanite Parallels;* M. Buttenwieser's *Psalms;* W. O. E. Oesterley's *Psalms;* Kaufmann's *Toledot,* II, 201 ff.; B. D. Eerdmans's *Hebrew Book of Psalms;* and the brief review of recent approaches in C. L. Feinberg's "Date of the Psalms," *Bibliotheca Sacra,* CIV, 426–40. On the other hand, not only was the cultic origin of this species of poetry in general (which had been proved before through independent lines of research by Gunkel, Wundt, Heiler, and others) further confirmed, but S. Mowinckel's series of illuminating studies (especially his *Psalmenstudien,* I–VI) has demonstrated both the cultic objective and priestly authorship of almost all the extant poems. The subsequent criticisms by Gunkel, G. Kittel, G. Quell (in *Das kultische Problem der Psalmen*), and others, corrected Mowinckel's theory in details and modified its evident exaggerations, but also served to put into bolder relief its essential accuracy. Cf. J. Morgenstern's very detailed examination of

several psalms (e.g., 23 in *JBL*, LXV, 13–24; 48 in *HUCA*, XVI, 1–95; 82, *ibid.*, XIV, 29–126); his serious objections to Mowinckel's theories in his excursus, "The So-Called 'Thronbesteigungspsalmen'" in *HUCA*, XXI, 490 ff.; N. H. Tur-Sinai's "Literary Character of the Book of Psalms," *OS*, VIII, 263–81; H. Ubbelohde's *Fluchtpsalmen und alttestamentliche Sittlichkeit;* A. Lauha's *Geschichtsmotive in den alttestamentlichen Psalmen;* A. Barucq's "Péché et innocence dans les psaumes bibliques et les textes religieux de l'Égypte du Nouvel Empire," *Études de critique* of the Theological Faculty of Lyons, 1948, pp. 111–37 (emphasizing the great differences between these concepts, particularly with respect to repentance); and, from the musicological and liturgical angles, C. Sachs's *Rise of Music in the Ancient World*, pp. 79 ff.; and L. I. Rabinowitz's "Psalms in Jewish Liturgy," *HJ*, VI, 109–22, pointing out the remarkable fact that, with the exception of the so-called *Hallel* (Ps. 113–18), there is no record for the liturgical use of Psalms until the post-talmudic period. However, even then they were used extensively for private devotion. Cf. also *supra*, Chap. III, n. 24.

23. Prov. 3:9, 7:19–20; Job 42:7–8; Eccles. 5:3; Mal. 3:7–10; Neh. 10:33–40. Cf. Blank's remarks in *HUCA*, XIX, 20. Otherwise the biblical Proverbs are of such a worldly character, that it has been argued that they were written in the Diaspora (Causse) or at least for Palestinian travelers abroad (Sellin). Cf. also A. Wendel's *Säkularisierung in Israel's Kultur;* and A. Drubbel's "Conflit entre la sagesse profane et la sagesse religieuse," *Biblica*, XVII, 45–70, 407–28. R. Gordis has also made it plausible that most of these books of Wisdom reflect an upper class mentality. Cf. his "Social Background of Wisdom Literature," *HUCA*, XVIII, 77–118, and *Wisdom of Ecclesiastes*. Cf. also J. W. Gaspar's *Social Ideas in the Wisdom of the Old Testament*. Much as the content of these books, however, differs from that of the rest of the Old Testament, we can no more deny, for this reason, their partial priestly authorship than we can assert their non-Jewish origin merely because of their paucity of peculiar Jewish religious doctrines or of references to specific national and historical events. On the whole, Judaism's imprint on this Wisdom literature is so marked that, in his *Altorientalische Weisheit in ihrer israelitisch-jüdischen Ausprägung*, J. Fichtner could appropriately discuss the "nationalization of Wisdom in Israel." More recently, J. C. Rylaarsdam assembled interesting data on *Revelation in Jewish Wisdom Literature*. All attempts, on the other hand, to find in the "strange woman" of the Proverbs a reflection of the Canaanite goddess of love and in "Wisdom" its hypostatized counterpart have proved futile. Cf. G. Boström's *Proverbiastudien: die Weisheit und das fremde Weib in Spr. 1–9;* effectively controverted by P. Humbert in "La 'Femme étrangère' du livre des Proverbes," *RES*, 1937, 49–64. On the example of "The Tree of Life in Proverbs" (*JBL*, LXII, 117–20), R. Marcus has also shown how completely this-worldly and devoid of all mythological meaning this ancient symbol had become in the hands of the anonymous authors of the Hebrew proverbs.

This is not to deny all foreign influences. On the contrary, in a literature of so universal an interest and so reflective of the meditation of wise men among many nations (Job himself and his friends are depicted as Gentile sages), mutual borrowings must have gone on all the time. But particular foreign elements are more easily postulated than proved. Opinions are divided even in such an apparently obvious case as the relationships between the Egyptian Teaching of Amen-em-ope (variously dated between 1000 and 600) and Prov. 22:17–23:10 (24:22). While the majority of scholars agree on Egyptian priority, it has been denied as recently as 1939 by J. M. McGlinchey in his detailed comparison of *The Teaching of Amen-em-ope and The Book of Proverbs*. On the other hand, cf. especially the broader surveys by P. Humbert in his *Recherches sur les sources égyptiennes de la littérature sapientiale d'Israël;* B. Couroyer's "Chemin de vie en Égypte et en Israël," *RB*, LVI, 412–32; W. Baumgartner in his *Israelitische und altorientalische Weisheit;* H. Torczyner's notes on *Mishle Shelomo* (Proverbs of Solomon); J. H. Greenstone's and I. Bettan's more popular commentaries on *Proverbs* and the *Five Scrolls;* and the brief historic sketch by C. I. K. Story in the introductory remarks to his "Book of Proverbs and Northwest Semitic Literature," *JBL*, LXIV, 319 ff. The latter comes to the conclusion that "we may safely assign those parts of Proverbs ascribed to the Hebrew sages with their clear monotheistic point of view to a relatively early time in the history of Israel" (p. 336). The profound debates in the book of Job have, understandably, intrigued ever new commentators. Among recent writers, cf. especially G. Hölscher's *Buch Hiob*; A. Alt's "Zur Vorgeschichte des Buches Hiob," *ZAW*, LV, 265–68; H. Torczyner's *Sefer Iyob* (The Book of Job); J. Lindblom's "Composition du livre de Job," *HVLA*, 1944–45, pp. 101–205; and W. B. Stevenson's *Poem of Job*. Some of the older studies are reviewed by A. Lods in his "Recherches récentes sur le livre de Job," *RHPR*, XIV, 501–33. Cf. also the reviews of Torczyner's work by M. H. Segal in *Tarbiz*, XIII, 73–91; H. M. Orlinsky in *JBL*, LXII, 347–57; D. G. Maeso's "Sentido nacional en el libro de Job," *Estudios biblicos*, IX, 67–81; and R. Marcus's "Job and God," *RR*, XIV, 5–29, culminating in the assertion that "the author of Job was the first Existentialist."

On Ecclesiastes, cf. H. J. Blieffert's *Weltanschauung und Gottesglaube im Buche Kohelet*; W. E. Staples's " 'Profit' in Ecclesiastes," *JNES*, IV, 87–96; and, particularly, H. L. Ginsberg's *Studies in Koheleth*. H. Torczyner has suggested, however, that Kohelet, originally derived from *kehillat* (assembly of royal dignitaries) essentially goes back to King Solomon and even, in its present form, dates from the fifth century. Cf. his "Words of Koheleth" (Hebrew) in *Ha-Lashon ve-ha-sefer*, pp. 389–409. Cf. also, in general, O. S. Rankin's *Israel's Wisdom Literature*; H. Duesberg's *Scribes inspirés*; and S. Pollock's *Stubborn Soil*.

24. The fourfold repetition of the term "anointed priest" in Lev. 4:3, 5, 16; 6:15 (and there only) was probably intended to emphasize this substitution of king by priest in various cultic as well as political functions. Cf. J. Morgenstern's remarks in *AJSL*, LV, 187 f., 196 f. Josephus' reference to a Jewish theocracy is quoted from *Ag. Ap.* II, 16.164–65, *supra*, p. 223. Cf. also J. Kroeker's *Das Königtum und die Theokratie in Israel*; O. Procksch's "Fürst und Priester bei Hesekiel," *ZAW*, LVIII, 99–133; and E. Margalioth's "Laws of the Priests and of the Sacrifices in Ezekiel" (Hebrew), *Tarbiz*, XXII, 21–27 (showing that, while related to views found in Chronicles, these laws are much later than those included in the Pentateuch).

25. Zech. 9:9. A perusal of the Babylonian parallels to this description of the Messiah assembled by S. I. Feigin in the *Schorr Mem. Vol.*, pp. 227–40, shows that Zechariah used an existing idiom for his own purposes. The new meaning of the term, *'ani*, shortly after the destruction of the Temple, is illustrated, particularly, by Deutero-Isaiah's references to "the poor and needy" of whom God says: "I the Lord will answer them" (41:17). This change did not preclude the possibility, however, that once Jewish society became differentiated again after the Restoration, the word began to regain its original meaning, as it did in some later psalms. Cf. H. Birkeland's detailed analysis of *'Ani und 'Anaw in den Psalmen*; and P. A. Munch's "Problem des Reichtums in den Ps. 37, 49, 73," *ZAW*, LV, 36–46. A strong residuum of national-religious connotation, nevertheless, remained in so far as, with the later developments, class distinctions often marked also different attitudes to the foreign cultures steadily penetrating the country. Since the upper classes, even before the Maccabean age, were much more open to external pressures, the poor, pious masses came to be regarded as the mainstay of Judaism.

26. Zech. 13:3. The intriguing problem of "When Did Prophecy Cease?" is analyzed in a succinct Hebrew essay by E. A. Urbach in *Tarbiz*, XVII, 1–11. He points out, in particular, the dichotomy between the feeling, intimated in I Macc. 4:46 and clearly stated in such rabbinic sources as *Seder 'Olam rabbah*, XX–XXI (in Neubauer's *Mediaeval Jewish Chronicles*, II, 51 ff.), and T. Sotah XIII, 2, 318, that "prophecy"

had ceased at the time of Alexander, and the preachment of various prophets under Herod and later, as attested by Josephus. One must bear in mind, however, that Josephus records a period of great upsurge of religious creativity and sectarianism which had followed an era of relative quiet, while the rabbis after 70 were engaged in the arduous task of consolidation and had to stem the irruption of uncontrolled visionary forces. The climate of opinion in the second and third centuries c.e. essentially resembled that of the fifth and fourth centuries b.c.e., under which Old Testament prophecy had gradually withered away. Once again engaged in a deep struggle for survival, Judaism after 70 simply could not indulge in the latitude necessary for the rise of rebellious prophetic spirits. F. M. T. Böhl, on the other hand, overstates the difference between dynamic prophecy and static priesthood not only in Israel, but also in Sumeria and Babylonia. Cf. his otherwise stimulating analysis of "Priester und Prophet," *Nieuwe theologische Studiën*, XXII, 298–313. Cf. also, more generally, J. Hoschander's *Priests and Prophets*; C. W. Reines's *Kohanim u-nebi'im* (Priests and Prophets); and infra, Chap. XII, n. 14.

27. I Chron. 25:1; I Sam. 10:5; Jer. 17:21ff.; II Kings 3:19; Shabbat 13b; Mal. 2:7. For another example, Miriam is called "prophetess" because she takes "a timbrel in her hand" and, together with her associates, performs a ritualistic song and dance (Exod. 15:20–21). Cf. A. Haldar's *Associations of Cult Prophets among the Ancient Semites*; M. H. Segal's "Study in the History of Prophets in Israel" in *Essays Hertz*, Hebrew section, pp. 104 ff.; and E. A. Urbach's "Halakhah and Prophecy" (Hebrew), *Tarbiz*, XVIII, 1–27. Cf. also, more generally, M. Schmidt's dissertation, *Prophet und Tempel*.

28. Ez. 47:22–23; Lev. 24:22; Isa. 56:6–7. There has been no recent study to supersede A. Bertholet's comprehensive, though somewhat colored, analysis of *Die Stellung der Israeliten und der Juden zu den Fremden*. Nor has any good comparative study of both xenophobia and friendliness to strangers among other nations of the ancient Near East come to the writer's attention. Certainly the vast and ever growing source material would make such an investigation, from both the juridical and sociological angles, extremely rewarding.

29. Isa. 51:4 ff.; 53:3 ff., and other passages. The ever-renewed attempt to identify the "Servant of the Lord" with an individual, such as Cyrus, another contemporary of the prophet or the prophet himself, intelligible enough in view of the obvious Christological aspects of these passages, cannot be said to have met with success. The best explanation based on all passages, rather than on unconnected verses, remains that offered by the Septuagint and Rashi (against Saadiah, Ibn Ezra, and others) that the "Servant" is the personification of the Jewish people, or at most a "zwischen eschatologischer Persönlichkeit und Personifikation gleitende Gestalt" (Weber in his *Religionssoziologie*, III, 157 n.). E. Sellin was oversanguine when, in 1937, he believed that scholars had come close to an agreement on "Die Lösung des deuterojesajanischen Gottesknechtsrätsels," *ZAW*, LV, 177–217. In fact, their views are still as divergent as ever. Some of these are well summarized in S. Smith's *Isaiah*, pp. 17 f., to which one may profitably add, in chronological order, K. Dietze's "Ussia, der Knecht Gottes, sein Leben und sein Leiden und seine Bedeutung für den Propheten Jesaja," *Schriften der Bremer Wissenschaftlichen Gesellschaft*, Ser. D, IV, 1–101; K. F. Euler's *Verkündigung vom leidenden Gottesknecht aus Jes. 53 in der griechischen Bibel;* S. Mowinckel's "Neuere Forschungen zu Deuterojesaja, Tritojesaja und dem Äbäd-Jahwä-Problem," *Acta Orientalia*, XVI, 1–40; Johansson's *Parakletoi*, pp. 53 ff.; I. Engnell's "Ebed Yahwe Songs and the Suffering Messiah in 'Deutero-Isaiah,' " *BJRL*, XXXI, 54–95; N. Rabin's "Servant of the Lord" (Hebrew), *Hatekufah*, XXXII–XXXIII, 703–39; C. R. North's *Suffering Servant in Deutero-Isaiah;* N. H. Snaith's "Servant of the Lord in Deutero-

Isaiah," *Studies Robinson*, pp. 187–200; and C. Lindhagen's comprehensive dissertation, *The Servant Motif in the Old Testament*. North and Lindhagen give also extensive up-to-date surveys of the history of Jewish and Christian interpretations. Cf. also N. Hutterer's dissertation on *Die mittelalterlichen jüdischen Kommentare zu den Ebed-JHWH-Liedern des Jesaja;* and H. A. Fischel's briefer study of "Die Deuterojesajanischen Gottesknechtlieder in der jüdischen Auslegung," *HUCA*, XVIII, 53–76.

30. He thus forced the later rabbis to draw a casuistic distinction between the four neighbors. Cf. M. Yebamot VIII, 3; and *infra*, Chaps. XI, n. 32; XIV, n. 17. It must be admitted, however, that the date of the book of Ruth and of the marriage laws reflected therein is debatable. While M. Burrows believes that the latter betray a more ancient situation (cf. *supra*, Chap. III, n. 19), M. David has plausibly restated the case for their postexilic origin in "The Date of the Book of Ruth," *OS*, I, 55–63. Cf. also H. H. Rowley's succinct summary of various other views in "The Marriage of Ruth," *HTR*, XL, p. 78, n. 4.

31. Mal. 1:11; 2:10; Job 12:9. Cf. *supra*, n. 23. Malachi's emphasis on God's fatherhood (here and 1:6) may well have been directed against the foreign cults derided by Jeremiah (2:26–28). On the other hand, the juxtaposition in both passages of God the father, with God the creator and master, was in line with the Israelitic opposition to the surrounding, more pronouncedly tribal, religions which found expression in the practical disappearance, after the tenth century, of *ab* (father) and *ben* (son) compounds from Israelitic names, in contrast to their increased use among Israel's neighbors. Cf. G. E. Wright's "Terminology of Old Testament Religion and Its Significance," *JNES*, I, 404–14. The postexilic emphasis upon the family at first but slightly modified this attitude. Only toward the end of the Second Commonwealth, with the rise of the great syncretistic supertribal deities, Judaism could fully re-emphasize its idea of God's fatherhood. J. Morgenstern seems to go too far, however, in expanding S. H. Blank's suggestion that the phrase "I am the Lord" frequently invoked by Deutero-Isaiah had, despite the use of the Tetragrammaton, lost its meaning as referring to the Jewish national God and that we ought to translate the divine name by "God" rather than by "Yahweh" (*JBL*, LXII, 271 ff.). Cf. Blank's remarks in *HUCA*, XI, 159 ff., and XV, 18 ff. A mere comparison with the author of Job shows that the great exilic visionary need not have used that divine name, unless he wished to. In fact, in both cases it seems forcing a modern distinction upon ancient writers who must have been perfectly convinced of the identity of Israel's God with the universal Deity. The same holds true for many cultic psalms. Ps. 47, in particular, must have been used more than any other as an enthronement psalm for the specific God of Israel, and yet, "there is no passage of more genuine universalism in the whole of the Old Testament" (J. Muilenberg in *JBL*, LXIII, 237). Incidentally, such cultic lyrics shed a remarkable light on the religion of the officiating priests which, at least in theory, hardly differed from that of the prophets. On the significance of the book of Jonah and its sources, cf., especially, A. Feuillet's two essays in *RB*, LIV, 161–86, 340–61.

32. Cf. O. G. von Wesendonk's "Ueber die Verwendung des Aramäischen im Achämenidenreich," *Litterae Orientales*, 49, 1–10; and, more generally, F. Rosenthal's survey of *Die aramaistische Forschung seit Th. Nöldeke's Veröffentlichungen;* H. L. Ginsberg's comments thereon in *JAOS*, LXII, 229–38; and R. A. Bowman's "Arameans, Aramaic and the Bible," *JNES*, VII, 65–90. Cf. also *supra*, Chap. III, n. 7. Under the circumstances it is not surprising that the mutual influences of Parsiism and Judaism, though subject to investigation for many decades, still are largely in the realm of speculation. To mention only a single recent example, F. Treu's "Anklänge iranischer Motive bei Deuterojesaja," *Studia theologica*, II, 79–95, is fairly typical of the dubious

evidence underlying all such reasonings. Much of the literature mentioned in previous notes (particularly *supra*, Chap. IV, n. 1), likewise deals with some aspects of this problem. In view of the prevailing uncertainties, however, it should prove more fruitful for us to discuss these contacts in our treatment of the Sassanian period, during which talmudic Jewry and the followers of Zoroaster again lived side by side for four centuries. Cf. especially, *infra*, Chap. XV, n. 31.

33. Isa. 65:3–5; 66:3, 17. The collaboration of natives, both Judaean and Samaritan, in the rebuilding of the Temple has been stressed, with some exaggeration, by A. C. Welch in his "Share of Northern Israel in the Restoration of the Temple Worship," *ZAW*, XLVIII, 175–87, and *Work of the Chronicler*, pp. 157 f. It is particularly doubtful whether, as he says, the Chronicler belonged to the community which had never been in Exile and whether Neh. 10 represents a pact with this remnant of both Israel and Judah. Be this as it may, the existing social difficulties seem to have already roused Deutero-Isaiah to try "to raise up [*le-haqim*] the land, to cause to inherit the desolate heritages" (49:8). S. Smith (*Isaiah*, p. 70), considers this function one of the major tasks assumed by the prophet even before the Return under Zerubbabel. Prophetic preachment, however, did not stem the further deterioration of the agrarian situation which inspired some of the subsequent reforms undertaken by Ezra and Nehemiah. Cf. H. Schmidt's *Bodenrecht im Verfassungsentwurf Esras*. Cf. also E. Würthwein's analysis of *Der 'Amm ha-'arez im Alten Testament*.

34. The Eshmunazar inscription (*Corpus inscriptionum semiticarum*, ed. by Ernest Renan, *et al.*, 1st ser., I, No. 3, pp. 13 ff.) is quoted here in H. Gressmann's interpretation in his *Altorientalische Texte*, p. 447. In his *Syrien in der Politik der Achämeniden*, p. 46, K. Galling argues that the inscription antedates 400 B.C.E. Even those scholars who date it later (e.g., A. Mentz who, in his *Beiträge*, pp. 39 ff., places it on palaeographic grounds at about 350 B.C.E.; or H. L. Ginsberg who, in his " 'King of Kings' and 'Lord of Kingdoms,' " *AJSL*, LVII, 71 f., follows Clermont-Ganneau and Cooke in dating "the entire family of Eshmunazarid inscriptions" about 300 B.C.E.) do not disagree with respect to the substantial correctness of these political divisions in the country. The latter are also borne out by Pseudo-Scylax and other sources. Cf. also Galling's remarks in *PJB*, XXXIV, 59 ff.

35. The estimates of the imperial revenue are given here on the basis of C. Huart's computations in his *Ancient Persia and Iranian Civilization*, p. 75. On the Persian administrative divisions, cf. O. Leuze's *Satrapieneinteilung in Syrien und im Zweistromlande;* and P. J. Junge's "Satrapie und Natio. Reichsverwaltung und Reichspolitik im Staate Dareios I," *Klio*, XXXIV, 1–55.

On the "Men of the Great Synagogue" cf. H. Englander's essay under this title in *HUCA Jub. Vol.*, pp. 145–69; Tchernowitz's *Toledoth ha-halakah*, III, 60 ff. Their origin is still very obscure. O. Holtzmann's suggestion that Malachi's mention of an agreement signed by those "that feared the Lord" (3:16) refers to the beginnings of this significant institution is very dubious. See his "Prophet Maleachi und der Ursprung des Pharisäerbundes," *AR*, XXIX, 21. Equally improbable is E. Bickermann's suggestion that the proper translation of the term would be something like "Men of the Great Gathering" and that it simply refers to any member of the generation of the Return. Cf. his " 'Viri Magnae Congregationis,' " *RB*, LV, 397–402. His contention, for example, that the later rabbis still knew the real meaning is controverted by his own quotation of the phrase, "generation of the Men of the Great Synagogue" (Gen. r. XXXV, 2, 328 f.) which would be pure tautology. After listing, on the other hand, 52 rabbinic passages referring to the "Men of the Great Synagogue" and most of the modern literature on the subject, L. Finkelstein comes to the conclusion that the term *keneset* here represents a Supreme Court. Cf. his *Ha-*

Perushim ve-Anshe Keneset ha-Gedolah (The Pharisees and the Men of the Great Synagogue), pp. 51 ff. However, the evidence he adduces from I Macc. 14:28 reporting the promulgation of a decree in favor of Simon the Maccabean, "in a great congregation of priests and people and princes of the nation, and of the elders of the country" creates the impression of a great legislative and administrative council rather than of a tribunal. Of course, the division of functions need not have been sharp and, like the later Sanhedrin, the "Great Synagogue" may indeed have combined judicial with administrative authority. If we so broaden the concept of the Council we come very close to the long-accepted interpretation. Cf. *infra*, Chap. VII, n. 16.

CHAPTER VI: EXPANSION OF JUDAISM

1. The excavations of Beth-Zur caused Hugo Willrich even to question whether Simon the Maccabean, and not John Hyrcanus, was the first to strike some of the famous Maccabean coins. Cf. his "Zum Münzwesen der Makkabäer," *ZAW*, LI, 78–79. Simon's numismatic sovereignty has been convincingly reasserted, however, by P. Boneschi in his "Three Coins of Judaea and Phoenicia" (now extant in Rio de Janeiro) in *JAOS*, LXII, 262–66. Cf. also *supra*, Chap. IV, n. 36; G. Hill's "Shekels of the First Revolt of the Jews," *QDAP*, VI, 78–83; and A. Reifenberg's *Ancient Jewish Coins*, pp. 1 ff. Certainly the right of coinage, granted to many municipalities and small vassal states throughout the Hellenistic world, could not properly be withheld from a full-fledged sovereign like Simon. On the other hand, W. F. Albright's hypothesis that the Jews had lost this right under the Seleucids (cf. his "Light on the Jewish State in Persian Times," *BASOR*, 53, p. 22) appears plausible only if one assumes that this withdrawal of a well-established right was part of the centralizing tendencies or a specific anti-Jewish measure of Antiochus Epiphanes. In any case the charter granted to Palestine Jewry by Antiochus III (200–197; *Antt.* XII, 3, 3, 138 ff.) reveals the general tendency to maintain its favorable status. Cf. E. Bickermann's keen analysis of "La Charte séleucide de Jérusalem," *REJ*, C, 4–35; his "Proclamation séleucide relative au temple de Jérusalem," *Syria*, XXV, 67–85; and, more generally, his *Institutions des Séleucides*.

2. The meaning of the name "Maccabee" is still uncertain. It has been suggested, for example, that it was originally Judah's surname, referring to his physical defect. Cf. F. Perles's "Miscellanea," *JQR*, XVII, 404 f. In his "Origin of the Name Maccabee" (*JTS*, XXX, 191–93), A. A. Bevan explains it as a shortened form of *Makabiahu*, meaning "the naming of the Lord." Cf. also, in general, E. Bickermann's *Gott der Makkabäer*, and his *Maccabees*.

3. The fundamental works for Jewish history of the period still are E. Schürer's *Geschichte des jüdischen Volkes im Zeitalter Jesu Christi;* and J. Juster's *Juifs dans l'empire romain*. Very useful are also the briefer studies by A. Schlatter, *Geschichte Israels von Alexander dem Grossen bis Hadrian*, 3d ed.; J. Klausner, *Historiah Yisre'-elit* (Jewish History), and *Historiah shel ha-bayit ha-sheni;* A. [V.] Tcherikover, *Ha-Yehudim ve-ha-Yevanim ba-tekufah ha-hellenistit* (Jews and Greeks in the Hellenistic Period); and W. O. E. Oesterley's *Jews and Judaism during the Greek Period*. For the Jewish religion of the period, cf. the standard works by G. F. Moore, *Judaism in the First Centuries of the Christian Era;* W. Bousset, *Religion des Judentums im späthellenistischen Zeitalter*, 3d ed. (revised and enlarged by H. Gressmann); and S. Schechter, *Some Aspects of Rabbinic Theology*. Cf. also E. Meyer's *Ursprung und Anfänge des Christentums* (especially Vol. II); I. Halevy's incomplete *Dorot harishonim* (Die Geschichte und Literatur Israels); J. Bonsirven's *Judaïsme palestinien au temps de Jésus-Christ, sa théologie;* C. Guignebert's *Jewish World in the Time of Jesus;* A. [V.] Tcherikover's *Ha-Yehudim be-Miṣrayim* (The Jews in Egypt in the Hellenistic-Roman Age in the Light of the Papyri); M. Rostovtzeff's comprehensive *Social and Economic History of the Hellenistic World;* and much of the literature listed by R. Marcus in his "Selected Bibliography (1920–1945) of the Jews in the Hellenistic-Roman Period," *PAAJR*, XVI, 97–181; and *supra*, Chaps. I, n. 1, and II, n. 1.

4. Neh. 11:25–35; I Macc. 5:23, 45. Cf., in particular, S. Klein's *Ereṣ ha-Galil* (Galilee from the Return from Babvlon to the Conclusion of the Talmud), pp. 10 ff. Klein

tries to prove that even before the Maccabean revolt there were many considerable Jewish settlements in the country, which remained for the most part intact even after the evacuation by Simon. However, this forces him to resort to a strained interpretation of the decisive passage in I. Macc. 5:23. Similarly J. M. Grintz's attempt to prove pre-Nehemian Jewish settlements in Samaria, as well as in Galilee and Transjordan, chiefly on the basis of Judith 4:4–6, largely depends on the highly controversial dating of that pseudepigraphic source. Cf. his "Cities of Nabhrakhta" (Hebrew), Zion, XII, 1–16. An extreme stand in the opposite direction is taken by G. Bertram in his lecture on "Der Hellenismus in der Urheimat des Evangeliums," AR, XXXII, 265–81. Bertram decidedly underestimates the stubborn resistance of the Semitic, though pagan, masses in Galilee to the inroads of Hellenism, which alone accounts for the subsequent rapid and thorough absorption of the entire Galilean population by the Jews. Cf. also A. Alt's "Galiläische Probleme, I–VI," PJB, XXXIII–XXXVI; and infra, Chap. XII, n. 43.

Some new light on the still obscure period between Alexander and the Maccabean revolt has been shed by more recent investigations such as A. Momigliano's "Tobiadi nella preistoria del moto maccabaico," Atti della R. Accademia delle scienze di Torino, LXVII, 165–200; F. M. Abel's essays on Alexander in RB, XLIII–XLIV; his "Expedition des Grecs à Pétra en 312 avant J.–C.," RB, XLVI, 373–91, and his "Confins de la Palestine et de l'Egypte sous les Ptolémées," ibid., Vols. XLVIII–XLIX; R. Fruin's "Studies in Jewish History after 333" (Dutch), Nieuw theologisch Tijdschrift, Vols. XXIV–XXV; A. [V.] Tcherikover's "Palestine in the Light of the Zenon Papyri" (Hebrew), Tarbiz, Vols. IV–V, and his "Palestine under the Ptolemies," Mizraim, IV–V, 9–90.

5. Hecataeus cited in Ag. Ap. I, 22.197. J. Jeremias's attempt to reduce the estimated population of first-century Jerusalem to some 25–30,000 is based upon an assumed lower density of the population per square kilometer than is justified in oriental cities then and now and upon the equally unwarranted assumption that but relatively few Jews resided outside the city walls. Cf. his "Einwohnerzahl Jerusalems zur Zeit Jesu," ZDPV, LXVI, 24–31; my remarks in Abhandlungen Chajes, pp. 115 f.; and infra, Chap. XI, n. 16.

6. G. Kittel goes too far, however, in postulating, on the basis of dubious figures recorded in a contemporary description of an anti-Jewish massacre in Minorca (418 C.E.) and a still more questionable computation of that island's general population, that the fifth-century Jewish community amounted to some 8–10 per cent of the inhabitants of Minorca, perhaps of all Spain. Cf. Die historischen Voraussetzungen der jüdischen Rassenmischung, p. 22. But there is no question that the large and affluent communities of the Visigothic and early Arab periods had antecedents going back to the early Roman Empire, perhaps even to the earlier Phoenician-Carthaginian colonies. Cf. infra, n. 13. The literary and epigraphic evidence of ancient Jewish settlements throughout the Mediterranean world has frequently been reviewed. Cf. especially the detailed data supplied in Schürer's Geschichte, III, 1–70; and Juster's Empire romain, I, 179–209. The Jewish communities in all these countries, including Arabia, Abyssinia and the Black Sea region, will be treated by us in various contexts with fuller documentation.

7. Of course, none of the figures here given, whether absolute or relative, are certain. They are based upon scattered documentary evidence, often very dubious in itself. This must be supplemented by a series of hypotheses, which, while separately often questionable, support one another in their convergence. The final result will perhaps be regarded as satisfactory under the circumstances. Certainly the population problem is of too crucial significance for any phase of human history for us to

take the line of least resistance and give up, because of the great inherent difficulties, as does, for instance, in our case, Rostovtzeff in his *Hellenistic World*, II, 1135 ff., 1140 ff. While my hope to present more detailed and definitive conclusions for the period before the second fall of Jerusalem has not yet materialized, I have analyzed many fundamental issues in the aforementioned Hebrew essay on the period of Israelitic monarchy. These considerations, though subject to revision in many details in the light of present-day knowledge, apply with equal force to the Second Commonwealth.

The statistical aspects of the Jewish expansion at this turning point of western history have not escaped the attention of great scholars in recent decades. The important, though brief, investigations of Beloch, Meyer, Harnack, and Juster may be mentioned here. Although more than sixty years old, K. J. Beloch's estimates of *Die Bevölkerung der griechisch-römischen Welt* are still the starting point of all pertinent discussions. If we sum up Beloch's oblique estimates we may gather a total of some 6,000,000 Jews (including 2,000,000 in Palestine) in the early Roman Empire, against a total population of some 60–70,000,000. E. Meyer accepted, on the whole, Beloch's estimates, except for lowering the total population to some 55,000,000 and that of Palestine to 1,500,000. Cf. his remarks in the article "Bevölkerungswesen" in J. Conrad, *et al.*, *Handwörterbuch der Staatswissenschaften*, 3d ed., II, 904 ff. More detailed recent investigations of Roman provinces (e.g., Gaul in Caesar's time and Syria) have shown that Beloch erred rather on the side of excessive conservatism. Cf. E. Cavaignac's *Population et capital dans le monde méditerranéen antique*, p. 152, n. 4; and F. Cumont's "Population of Syria," *JRS*, XXIV, 187–91. Even skeptical Rostovtzeff is prepared to accept for Alexandria a population of 1,000,000 or more, i.e., twice the number suggested by Beloch. See his *Hellenistic World*, pp. 1138 f. On the other hand, A. Segré (in his "Note sull' economia dell' Egitto ellenistico nell' età tolemaica," *Bulletin de la Société royale d'archéologie d'Alexandrie*, n.s. VIII, 267 ff.) discusses only Ptolemaic Egypt, where he estimates a Jewish population of but 100,000, while admitting its large increase in the Roman period. Segré generally voices an exaggerated skepticism with respect to all figures found in the Judeo-Hellenistic sources. Even he admits, however, that before 38 c.e. the Jews constituted not much less than two-fifths of the "Greek" population in Alexandria. Cf. his "Status of the Jews in Hellenistic and Roman Egypt," *JSS*, VI, 385, n. 33. Without committing himself to any figure, A. Tcherikover has shown at least the great spread and relative density of the Jewish population throughout Egypt. See his *Ha-Yehudim be-Miṣrayim*, pp. 23 ff.

As against these estimates, A. Harnack's computation of only 4,000,000 to 4,500,000 Jews in the empire or 7 per cent of the total population (cf. his *Mission and Expansion of Christianity*, 2d ed., I, 3 ff.), is relatively correct with respect to the Diaspora, to which 3,500,000–4,000,000 are assigned. His conclusion, however, that only 700,000 lived in Palestine is substantiated only by the obviously inadequate comparison with the population of 1902, when Harnack first published his work. The population has, indeed, since risen to more than 2,000,000 in western Palestine alone and is rapidly surpassing the figure here given for the entire area including Transjordan. We shall also see that this obvious disproportion between Palestinian and world Jewry was postulated to fit Harnack's theory of the predominantly Jewish springs of early Christian propaganda. The contrast between the recent biological evolution of Transjordan vs. western Palestine should also have warned C. C. McCown against underestimating "The Density of Population in Ancient Palestine" (in *JBL*, LXVI, 425–36) on the basis of the present fertility of the country. Even disregarding the great improvements introduced in certain areas by the Zionist colonization, one must not overlook the ravages of soil erosion and general mismanagement under the declining Roman Empire and thirteen centuries of Muslim misrule. J. Juster (*Empire romain*, I, 209 ff.) goes to the other extreme of estimating Palestinian Jewry as high as 5,000-

000, while assuming only 1,000,000 or 2,000,000 in the Roman Diaspora. He adduces hardly any reasons for these arbitrary figures, which are but slightly supported by S. Klein's somewhat exaggerated estimate of Galilee's population alone at 1,200,000 (*Ereş ha-Galil*, p. 51). J. Klausner, finally, has studied, in particular, the records pertaining to the wars between 63 and 37 B.C.E. and reached the conclusion that "at the end of the Maccabean reign there lived in all of Palestine approximately 3,000,000 Jews, not including half a million Samaritans, Syro-Phoenicians, Arabs and Greeks" ("How Many Jews Will Be Able to Live in Palestine?" *JSS*, XI, 126).

In support of his total, however, Juster first turned attention to Bar-Hebraeus' statement referred to in our text. It is to be found in the *Historia compendiosa dynastiarum* (ed. by E. Pococke, pp. 73, 116; ed. by A. Salhani, p. 115), and refers approximately to the second year of Claudius' reign. Whether or not there is any connection between this census and the enumeration of the Passover lambs by Agrippa I, recorded in Pesaḥim 64b (Josephus in *War* VI, 9, 2.422 ascribes it to the period of Agrippa II; cf. H. Dessau's *Geschichte der römischen Kaiserzeit*, II, Pt. 2, p. 794, n. 3) cannot be ascertained. But Bar-Hebraeus did not confuse this census with one of the Roman citizens in the empire, as timidly suggested by Tcherikover in his *Ha-Yehudim ve-ha-Yevanim*, p. 300, n. 2; and accepted as "proved" by J. Rosenthal in his "Problems in Jewish History in the Period of the Second Temple" (Hebrew), *SH*, X–XI, 320. Bar-Hebraeus probably knew of the census of Roman citizens taken by Claudius in 48 C.E. and recorded by Tacitus in his *Annales*, XI, 25, but he mentioned both an earlier date, appropriately coinciding with the emperor's preoccupation with the Alexandrian-Jewish controversy, and a figure of almost 1,000,000 more than the 5,984,072 recorded by Tacitus. It must be admitted, however, that Bar-Hebraeus may have had before him the higher figures given by Jerome or Sincellus. Cf. J. Jackson's note to his ed. of Tacitus, III, 292, n. 3. We shall see how deeply concerned Claudius was in his early years over the conflict in Alexandria and the effects of the Jewish religious propaganda. At the same time he recognized the political importance of imperial Jewry. He had every reason, therefore, to try to find out how many Jewish subjects he really had—a task which could well be entrusted to officials trained in such detailed and regular enumerations as are attested by a Brussels and other papyri. Cf., e.g., M. Hombert and C. Préaux's "Recherches sur le recensement dans l'Egypte romaine," *Chronique d'Egypte*, XVIII, 291–305. It stands to reason that had Bar-Hebraeus' significant report come to the attention of Beloch and Harnack they would probably have revised their estimates in the light of his figures. At any rate, Harnack's statement that every fourteenth Roman was a Jew, frequently quoted in subsequent literature with some misgivings, appears to be an understatement, rather than an exaggeration. Cf. also J. Ferlet's *Population Problems of the Time of Augustus;* and *infra*, Chap. XIV, n. 4.

The sources regarding the number of Jews outside the empire are even less numerous and less reliable. The figure of 1,000,000 given here for all Babylonia, Persia, Armenia, Arabia, Abyssinia, etc., is undoubtedly too conservative. For the Iranian countries, it is enough to refer to what has been said in the last chapter about the growth of the Diaspora under Persian domination, there being no reason why a steady influx of Jews from Babylonia should not have continued after Alexander.

8. Cf. the comprehensive study of *The Cities of the Eastern Roman Provinces* by A. H. M. Jones. The fact that many of the larger cities sooner or later were overcrowded was stressed almost seventy years ago by R. von Pöhlmann in his *Ueber-völkerung der antiken Grossstädte*. Undoubtedly new arrivals, whether voluntary or forced had to live for a long time in slums and join the ranks of the increasingly large urban proletariat. The role of urbanization, however, in the growing ethnic-religious conflicts and, particularly, in the progressive deterioration of Judeo-Greek relationships, has not yet been elucidated. Cf. also, in general, L. Homo's suggestive observations on "L'Urbanisme dans la Rome impériale," *CRAI*, 1942, pp. 150–54.

9. Cf. W. Dittenberger's *Sylloge inscriptionum graecarum,* 3d ed., III, 372 f., No. 1229. Some seventy years ago L. Herzfeld pointed out that Syrian Jewry had come largely from Babylonia. The centuries of common history under the domination of Chaldaea, Persia, and the Seleucids, and the propinquity of the Jewish mass settlement at the crossroads from the Euphrates Valley to Syria, could not but have a decisive influence. Cf. his *Handelsgeschichte der Juden des Alterthums,* 2d ed., pp. 199 ff., 224. The deportation of 2,000 Jewish families from Mesopotamia and Babylonia to Asia Minor by Antiochus the Great (*Antt.* XII, 3, 4.149) can, notwithstanding Willrich's arguments, hardly be Josephus' pure invention. Cf. *infra,* Chap. VII, n. 9. It may be noted that Hecataeus of Abdera already sought to explain the large-scale migrations of Jews by their vast population increase. Cf. his remarks quoted by Josephus in *Ag. Ap.* I, 22. 183 ff., 194. On the date and authenticity of that source, cf. the opposing views expressed by Hans Lewy in his "Hekataios von Abdera περὶ Ιουδαίων," *ZNW,* XXXI, 117–32; and E. [M.] Stein in his "Pseudo-Hecataeus, His Time and the Bearing of His Book on the Jews and Their Country" (Hebrew), *Siyyon,* VI, 1–11.

10. Cf. H. Ludin-Jansen's "Existait-il à l'époque hellénistique des prédicateurs itinérants juifs?" *RHPR,* XVIII, 242–54, answering the question in the affirmative.

11. Bousset-Gressmann's *Religion des Judentums,* p. 79; Sifre on Deut. 354, ed. by M. Friedmann, fol. 147a (ed. by L. Finkelstein, p. 416). Jewish proselytism in the different stages of the history of the people has long attracted the attention of scholars. Especially fascinating has been the expansive movement preceding, and the reaction following, the rise of Christianity. Cf., for instance, F. M. Derwacter's *Preparing the Way for Paul: the Proselyte Movement in Later Judaism;* and the two complementary studies, *Proselytism in the Talmudic Period* by B. J. Bamberger, and *Jewish Proselyting in the First Five Centuries of the Common Era* by W. G. Braude. Cf. also G. Allon's review of the latter volume in *KS,* XXIII, 37–42.

Most other religions of antiquity were not propagandist creeds. We know nothing of missionary activities of the Egyptians, Babylonians, or Indians except, of course, the automatic pressure exercised by these religions in countries under the domination of their adherents. The attitude of Persians and, later, of some Hellenistic rulers was quite different. C. Clemen's "Missionary Activity in the Non-Christian Religions," *JR,* X, 107–26; and especially A. D. Nock's *Conversion, the Old and New in Religion from Alexander the Great to Augustine of Hippo.*

12. W. W. Fowler's *Social Life at Rome in the Age of Cicero,* p. 519; Josephus' *Ag. Ap.* II, 39.281. Cf. A. J. Festugière's pertinent remarks in his "Fait religieux à l'époque hellénistique," *RB,* LII, 30–44; and more generally J. Hessen's *Platonismus und Prophetismus.* Despite the tenacity of all these local cults—some survivals are noticeable even today (cf. M. P. Nilsson's *Greek Popular Religion*)—they were steadily losing ground. That Judaism not only attracted individual Greeks and Romans, but exercised a direct influence upon the religious concepts of even the most orthodox among them is stressed somewhat exaggeratedly by W. Fink in *Der Einfluss der jüdischen Religion auf die griechisch-römische.* Onomatologically such influence came to the fore not only in the names of Abram and Helkias recorded as members of pagan societies in Ptolemais and Hermopolis Magna (138–37 and 78 B.C.E.)—these may have been Jewish apostates or Palestinian Gentiles—but possibly also in the ever greater spread of theophorous names. Like their Near Eastern neighbors long inured to such names, the Hellenistic Jews now seem to have called themselves with predilection Theodoros, Theophilos, Theodotos, Dositheos, and the like. Rare in classical Greece, these names, particularly Theodoros, now became quite common. Cf. Tcherikover's *Ha-Yehudim be-Miṣrayim,* pp. 11, n. 10, and 12 f.

That, notwithstanding all legitimate reservations, personal names may still be used as a major criterion for the various ethnic (and religious) groups in Hellenistic Egypt has rightly been emphasized again by W. Peremans in "Noms des personnes et nationalité dans l'Egypte ptolemaïque," *Muséon*, LIX, 241–52. Cf. also T. Hopfner's careful analysis of "Gräzisierte, griechisch-ägyptische, bezw. ägyptisch-griechische und hybride theophore Personennamen . . . und ihre religionsgeschichtliche Bedeutung," *Archivum orientale Pragense*, XV, 1–64. On the other hand, the length to which Egyptian, and probably also other Hellenistic Jews went in adopting the names of their neighbors may be seen from the data found in the Jewish quarter of Edfu (Apollinopolis Magna). The long three-page list of names compiled by J. Manteuffel in his "Quelques textes provenants d'Edfou," *Journal of Juristic Papyrology*, III, 114 ff., includes few Jewish or Semitic names. One Jewish family in the days of Vespasian, for instance, consisted of a father called Antonius Rufus and his five sons, Nicon, Theodotos-Niger, Theodoros-Niger, Diophanes, and Ptullis. Cf. also *infra*, n. 29. It is evident that there were many more Jews in the eastern Mediterranean countries than seems indicated by the stray Jewish names recorded in papyri and other accidental sources.

13. Menaḥot 110a. The disappearance of the Phoenicians during the first centuries of the Christian era has long intrigued modern scholars. Following the investigations of Mowers, Winckler, and Landau, N. Slouschz advanced the theory that many of them were absorbed by Diaspora Jewry, particularly in North Africa. See his *Hébraeo-Phéniciens et Judéo-Berbères*, his *Travels in North Africa;* and on the linguisitic interrelations between Neo-Punic and Hebrew, his Hebrew essay in *Leshonenu*, XVI, 3–11. His theories were sustained and amplified at many points by the anthropological investigations of J. J. Williams in his *Hebrewisms of West Africa.* Cf. also M. Delafosse's *Negroes of Africa*. From another point of view, G. Rosen reached even more radical conclusions in his *Juden und Phönizier*. Neither this volume, however, although brought up to date by the editors, nor various other monographs have furnished more than tentative substantiation. Cf. especially P. Monceaux's "Colonies juives dans l'Afrique romaine" (*REJ*, XLIV, 1–28); M. Mieses's "Juifs et les établissements puniques en Afrique du Nord" (*ibid.*, Vols. XCII–IV); and A. H. Krappe's "Chananéens dans l'ancienne Afrique du Nord et en Espagne," *AJSL*, LVII, 229–43. Careful investigations into the ever-increasing epigraphic and archaeological materials are needed before a definitive solution can be found.

Nevertheless it may be asserted that all recent evidence tends to emphasize, rather than to minimize, the interrelations between the two peoples and their religions, which, as we know from Ugarit, had been quite intensive, even in the early period of Israel's settlement in Palestine. True, on the whole, "Phoenicians and Carthaginians knew how to maintain their religion with remarkable tenacity. If in the Graeco-Roman period their deities, too, assumed a Graeco-Roman guise and Baalshamem, the lord of heaven, became known as Zeus or Jupiter, Baal Hammon as Kronos and Saturn, Astarte and Tanit as Aphrodite and Juno, this was merely an external camouflage. The essence of these deities remained Phoenician and Punic" (Eissfeldt in his *Philister und Phönizier*, p. 38). However, the corrosive influences of these syncretistic equations, superimposed upon the loss of political moorings, must, in the long run, have thrown untold numbers of Phoenician and Punic individuals into the arms of either Graeco-Roman paganism or Jewish monotheism. An example of the former in Palestine itself was the "Sidonian" colony of Marissa which, completely Hellenized as early as 250 B.C.E., had merely retained its ancestors' Phoenician names. Cf. Tcherikover's remarks in *Mizraim*, V, 9 ff. But no matter how large the differences between these Sidonians and Jews may have loomed within the confines of Palestine, they paled to insignificance in any distant environment often equally hostile to both.

Incidentally, this success of Jewish propaganda may help explain both the animosity of Tyre and (to a lesser extent) Sidon to the Jews (cf. I Macc. 5:15; Josephus' *War* II, 18, 5.478–79; and *Ag. Ap.* I, 13.70) and the keen interest of the "Africans" in Palestine, discussed by Hans Lewy in his "Rechtsstreit um den Boden Palästinas," *MGWJ*, LXXVII, 89. We may perhaps ascribe to it also the stupendous growth of the Jewish settlement in Cyprus which had long harbored a mixed Graeco-Phoenician population. Cf. A. Reifenberg's data in "Das antike zyprische Judentum und seine Beziehungen zu Palästina," *JPOS*, XII, 209–15; G. Hill's *A History of Cyprus*, I, 241 ff.; and *infra*, Chap. XI, n. 11.

14. Proverbs 8:4. It is remarkable how, without even remotely suggesting anything like the modern documentary hypothesis, the Septuagint clearly distinguished between the term *ger* meaning "immigrant" in J and E, that approximating a "resident alien" in D, and the religious convert of P. Cf. T. J. Meek's "Translation of *Gêr* in the Hexateuch," *JBL*, XLIX, 180. Understandably, it had to coin a new term, *proselytos*, for the latter, thereby adjusting the existing political category of *epelytos* to the ethnic-religious realities in Judaism. Cf. Moore's *Judaism*, III, 107. Cf. also O. Stählin's *Hellenistisch-jüdische Literatur*, p. 539; A. Causse's "Propagande juive et l'hellénisme," *RHPR*, III, 397–414; his "Sagesse et la propagande juive à l'époque perse et hellénistique" in *Werden und Wesen*, ed. by P. Volz *et al.*, pp. 148–54; V. Tcherikover and F. M. Heichelheim's debate on "Jewish Religious Influence in the Adler Papyri?" *HTR*, XXXV, 25–44; *infra*, n. 55; and *supra*, Chap. V, n. 23.

15. Suetonius' *Tiberius*, XXXII, 2; Josephus' *Ag. Ap.*, II, 39. 282; Sifra on Lev. 19:34, ed. by E. H. Weiss, fol. 91a; T. Demai II, 5.47; b. Gittin 57b. There is little doubt that Diaspora Jewry went further than the Palestinian sages in the reinterpretation of the biblical provisions to fit the exigencies of their own environment. On the new meaning of *ger toshab* in rabbinic letters, cf., e.g., R. Meir's view that this term applied to any Gentile abjuring idolatry in the presence of three learned Jews (*haberim;* 'A. Z. 64b). If other rabbis required from resident aliens the observance of all seven Noahide commandments or even imposed upon them all laws except those relating to ritually slaughtered meat, they evidently had in mind Palestinian realities alone. They may also have been affected by the opposition to the "God-fearing" groups which had spread in Palestine after the fall of Jerusalem. R. Meir's opinion was doubtless shared by the Greek-speaking Jewish masses to whom a *ger* of any kind had long become an ethnic-religious "proselyte," rather than a political "alien." This point is too readily overlooked by the formalistic interpretation of rabbinic passages, given, for instance, by E. Schürer in his *Geschichte*, III, 178 ff. Cf. also H. A. Wolfson's *Philo*, II, 370 f.; and *infra*, Chap. XII, n. 28.

16. Strabo quoted in *Antt.* XIV, 7, 2.115. This remark is an integral part of Josephus' quotation from Strabo, concerning the position of the Jews in Cyrenaica in 85 B.C.E. There is no justification for detaching the second sentence and declaring it a gratuitous exclamation of Strabo about the condition in his own, the Augustan age, merely because there is a slight change in the grammatical tenses, as suggested by Bousset-Gressmann (*op. cit.*, p. 67, n. 1). No one is able to tell, however, how many of these Jews in Cyrenaica and elsewhere were Jews, and how many proselytes or "God-fearing." Cf. also K. Friedmann's "Fonti per la storia degli Ebrei di Cirenaica nell' antichità," *Miscellanea di studi ebraici in memoria H. P. Chajes*, pp. 39–55; and his "Condizioni e cultura degli Ebrei di Cirenaica nell' antichità," *GSAI*, n.s. II, 323–34.

17. M. Abot I, 12 (Hillel, transl. by Herford); b. Pesahim 87b (with reference to Hos. 2:25; R. Eleazar is here confirmed by his teacher-colleague R. Johanan who referred to the continuation of the same verse); Mekilta Mishpatim 18 (R. Eliezer, ed.

by Lauterbach, III, 138). Cf. also Moore's *Judaism*, I, 323 ff., III, 107 ff.; I. Lévi's "Proselytisme juif," *REJ*, L–LI; M. Guttmann's *Judentum und seine Umwelt*; and *supra*, n. 11.

The inclusion of the "righteous proselytes" in the thirteenth benediction of the '*Amidah*, today still recited three times daily by every orthodox Jew, seems to have taken place in our period in Palestine. About the original formulation and later changes, cf. I. Elbogen's data in *Der jüdische Gottesdienst in seiner geschichtlichen Entwicklung*, 3d ed., pp. 52, 519; and L. Finkelstein's "Development of the Amidah," *JQR*, XVI, 1–43, 127–70. There is no necessity for assuming that this prayer originated as a counterpart to the prayer directed against the *minim* at the time when the Christian mission began to become unpopular (Finkelstein, *ibid.*, p. 19); that it was introduced by the leaders of Diaspora Jewry (hesitantly suggested by I. Lévi in his "Dix-huit bénédictions et les Psaumes de Salomon," *REJ*, XXXII, 163, n. 1); or that it voiced an indirect protest against the enforced conversion of Idumaeans (V. Aptowitzer in his *Parteipolitik der Hasmonäerzeit*, p. 47). Although during the last decades of national independence there were fewer proselytes in Palestine than in the Diaspora, the Palestinian legislators certainly had the entire Jewish world in view. This is especially true in all matters pertaining to the synagogue, which was primarily an institution of Diaspora Jewry.

18. Philo. *De spec. legibus*, I, 9. 51. Cf. G. La Piana's "Foreign Groups in Rome during the First Centuries of the Empire," *HTR*, XX, 325 f.; and, more generally, S. W. Baron's *Modern Nationalism and Religion*, pp. 7 ff., 275.

19. *Fragments of a Zadokite Work*, ed. by S. Schechter, XIV, 5–6; M. Qiddushin IV, 6; Bikkurim I, 4; J. B. Frey's *Corpus inscriptionum judaicarum*, I, 19 f. (No. 21), 384 (No. 523). The complex legislation concerning priestly marriages with proselytes is discussed by S. Zeitlin and the present writer in *REJ*, CII, 142 f.; CIV, 144. It appears doubtful, however, whether the regulation concerning daily prayers antedates the destruction of the Temple. It bears all the earmarks of the antimissionary reaction which followed the national catastrophes of 70 and 135. Soon, however, a calmer attitude seems to have been regained. At any rate, the Palestinian Talmud invokes against the Mishnah a characteristic utterance of R. Judah that a proselyte *should* say "our fathers" in the similar prayer at the offering of first fruits: "Why? For a father of many nations have I made thee [said God to Abraham while changing his name from Abram to Abraham, Gen. 17:5]. In the past thou wast the father of Aram [*Ab-Ram*], but from now on thou art a father to all nations. R. Joshua ben Levi says the halakhah is in accordance with R. Judah. When a case was brought before R. Abbahu he [too] decided it in accordance with R. Judah" (j. Bikkurim I, 4, 64a). R. Abbahu, especially, must have referred to the daily prayer rather than to that of the first fruits, which could no longer be offered after the destruction of the Temple. Decision and motivation are quoted as authoritative by Maimonides in his commentary on the Mishnah (Bikkurim *loc. cit.*) and in his code (*M.T.*, Bikkurim, IV, 3), and were generally accepted by the medieval rabbis.

20. Philo's *De migratione Abrahami*, XXXVI, 201; *De confusione linguarum*, XXVIII, 146; Origen's *In Ioannem*, II, 25 (*PG*, XIV, 169: ἀνὴρ ὁρῶν θεόν). Cf. E. Stein's "Zur apokryphen Schrift, Gebet Josefs," *MGWJ*, LXXXI, 283, n. 7.

21. Cf. A. Marmorstein's somewhat overconfident remarks on "A Greek Lyric and a Hebrew Prophet," *JQR*, XXXVII, 169–73 (elaborating F. M. Heichelheim's suggestion); and F. Dornseiff's *Echtheitsfragen antik-griechischer Literatur*. The wide, though tenuous range of these early Hebrew-Greek interrelations may be illustrated by G. R. Lewy's attempt to link the figure of Heracles to Sumerian-Babylonian deities and, indirectly, to the biblical Samson. See her "Oriental Origin of Herakles,"

Journal of Hellenic Studies, LIV, 40–53. Cf. also W. Baumgartner's "Israelitisch-griechische Sagenbeziehungen," *Schweizerisches Archiv für Volkskunde*, XLI, 1–29; Salomo Rappaport's "Antikes zur Bibel und Agada," *Festschrift Armand Kaminka*, pp. 71–101; and, more generally, S. Bernfeld's still useful survey of "Jewish Hellenism before the Maccabean Period" (Hebrew), *Hashiloah*, XVI; and R. H. Pfeiffer's "Hebrews and Greeks before Alexander," *JBL*, LVI, 91–101 (expatiating chiefly on Gen. 10:2–5). Some earlier, but still more obscure data are included in K. Schefold's study of "Die Bergvölker, Hellas und Palästina in frühgeschichtlichen Verbindungen," *Schweizer Beiträge zur Allgemeinen Geschichte*, IV, 236–46; and H. J. Kantor's *The Aegean and the Orient in the Second Millennium B.C.*

22. *Ag. Ap.* I, 22. 176 ff.; Clement's *Stromata*, I, 15, 70, 2 (in O. Stählin's ed. II, 44); *Antt.* XI, 8, 3–6. 317–45. The essential historicity, for instance, of Aristotle's meeting with the Jew of Coele-Syria, at that time probably the equivalent of much of the Persian province of 'Abar Nahara which included Palestine (on the subsequent changes in the meaning of this name, cf. E. Bickerman's data in *RB*, LIV, 256–68), has been reaffirmed by E. Silberschlag's analysis of the "Earliest Record of Jews in Asia Minor," *JBL*, LII, 66–77. In his "Aristotle and the Jewish Sage according to Clearchus of Soli," *HTR*, XXXI, 205–35, Hans Lewy merely demolished some imaginary embellishments of Clearchus' story. Cf. also W. Jaeger's "Greeks and Jews," *JR*, XVIII, 127–43. Considering that the Hebrew Wisdom literature, that repository of centuries of general oriental lore, seems to have been especially popular among the Jewish travelers in the Diaspora, even Clearchus' unhistorical hypothesis concerning the Indian origin of the Jewish sage's profound remarks is not quite as fantastic as it first appears.

The more decisive encounter between Alexander the Great and Jewish leaders in Palestine a dozen years later (331) was already in antiquity shrouded in the obscurity of international sagas. Cf. R. Marcus's review of the older literature in his ed. of Josephus, VI, 512 ff. Another, none too successful, attempt to unravel the historic strains was made by J. Gutman in his "Alexander the Great in Palestine" (Hebrew), *Tarbiz*, XI, 271–94. On some of the legends cf. L. Wallach's "Alexander the Great and the Indian Gymnosophists in Hebrew Tradition," *PAAJR*, XI, 47–83; M. Simon's "Alexandre le Grand, juif et chrétien," *RHPR*, XXI, 177–91; and, on the foundation of Alexandria, F. Pfister's *Jüdische Gründungsgeschichte Alexandriens*. On the views held by such Greek writers of the generation after Alexander as Hecataeus of Abdera and Theophrastus, cf. the literature mentioned *supra*, n. 9; and J. Gutman's "Theophrastos on Theosophy in Israel" (Hebrew), *Tarbiz*, XVIII, 157–65.

23. I Macc. 12:7 ff., 19 ff.; *Antt.* XII, 4, 10.226. These and other documents preserved in the books of Maccabees and Josephus have been carefully scrutinized ever since the seventeenth century. For a time the conviction grew that, as elsewhere in antiquity, these letters, decrees, treaties, etc., were, for the most part, political forgeries of the day which misled already such ancient historians as Josephus. The chief modern expounder of this theory was H. Willrich in his *Urkundenfälschung in der hellenistisch-jüdischen Literatur*. With the increase of our knowledge of Graeco-Roman institutions and official style, however, much that had appeared bizarre and inconsequential found reasonable explanation. The "brotherhood" of Jews and Spartans likewise appears less suspicious when we know that, for instance, the people of Tyre also claimed blood relationships with the inhabitants of Delos. Cf. M. S. Ginsburg's "Sparta and Judaea," *Classical Philology*, XXIX, 117–22. Cf. also Bickermann's "Makkabäerbücher" in *PWRE*, XIV, 779–800; his "Ein jüdischer Festbrief vom Jahre 124 v. Chr.," *ZNW*, XXXII, 233–54; A. [V.] Tcherikover's "Documents in II Maccabees" (Hebrew), *Tarbiz*, I, Pt. 1, 31–45; and C. C. Torrey's "Letters Prefixed to Second Maccabees," *JAOS*, LX, 119–50. While Bickerman is still reluctant to acknowledge the genuineness of Areus' letter, E. Meyer (in his *Ursprung*, II, 30) and

V. Ehrenberg (in his article, "Sparta," *PWRE*, 2d ser., III, 1373–1453) declare that, although it cannot be authentic in its present form, it must contain a kernel of truth. Moreover, one must bear in mind that we possess only the Greek translation of a Hebrew or Aramaic translation made by the author of I Maccabees from a Greek original. The form must have suffered considerably through this double rendering. Cf. also P. Churgin's Hebrew essays on I and II Macc., in his *Meḥqarim bitequfat bayit sheni* (Studies in the Times of the Second Temple), pp. 190 ff., 230 ff.

24. *Antt.* XX, 11, 2.263; *Ag. Ap.* I, 9.50. Cf. E. J. Bickerman's "Colophon of the Greek Book of Esther," *JBL*, LXIII, 339–62; J. Freudenthal's *Alexander Polyhistor*, pp. 125 ff.; H. St. J. Thackeray's *Josephus, the Man and the Historian*, pp. 104 ff. It should be noted, however, that the identity of the diplomat Eupolemus and the historian bearing the same name is not altogether certain. A much more generous appreciation of both Josephus' knowledge of Greek and his familiarity with Greek letters is given by Elchanan Stein in his detailed analysis of *De Woordenkeuze in het Bellum Judaicum van Flavius Josephus* (The Choice of Words in Josephus' *War*); and by G. C. Richards in "The Composition of Josephus' Antiquities," *Classical Quarterly*, XXXIII, 36–40. In any case, once he decided to write historical works Josephus closely followed the patterns of Greek historiography. Cf., e.g., S. Ek's "Herodotismen in der jüdischen Archäologie des Josephos," *HVLA*, 1945–46, pp. 27–62 (particularly influenced by Dionysios); H. Sprödowsky's dissertation on *Die Hellenisierung der Geschichte von Joseph in Aegypten bei Flavius Josephus*; P. Collomp's "Place de Josèphe dans la technique de l'historiographie hellénistique," *Etudes historiques de la Faculté des Lettres de Strasbourg*, 1947, pp. 81–92; and, more generally, E. Stein's "De Flavii Josephi arte narrandi," *Eos*, XXXIII, 641–50 (also in Hebrew); I. Heinemann's "Josephus' Method in the Presentation of Jewish Antiquities" (Hebrew), *Zion*, V, 180–203; A. Schalit's introduction to his Hebrew transl. of *Antt.*, pp. xi–lxxii; and the detailed "Critical Notes on Josephus' Antiquities," by G. C. Richards and R. J. H. Shutt in *Classical Quarterly*, XXXI, 170–77, XXXIII, 180–83. One must always bear in mind the possibility of extensive corruptions in Josephus' text. That even the splendid editions by Niese and Thackeray-Marcus may be modified by further discoveries is illustrated by the folio from his *War*, found in a Rainer papyrus in Vienna which has many significant variants. Cf. H. Oellacher's ed. of *Griechische Literarische Papyri*, pp. 61–63 (giving variant readings of *War* II, 20, 6–7, from a papyrus which, the editor claims, is at least seven centuries older than our main Byzantine-medieval tradition).

On the knowledge of Greek in Palestine after the Maccabean age, cf. particularly S. Lieberman's *Greek in Jewish Palestine*; and *Hellenism in Jewish Palestine* (includes on pp. 210 ff. additions and corrections to the former volume). It is evident that if Greek succeeded in penetrating the sacred precincts of the synagogue and the sheltered domain of Jewish law, it played an even greater role in the daily life of the people. Certainly the widespread use of Greek funerary inscriptions in Palestinian Jewish cemeteries was exceeded only by such Hellenistic communities as Alexandria and Rome, but has absolutely no parallel in any medieval or modern Jewish cemetery, until the recent period of Jewish linguistic assimilation. Suffice it to say that not only in coastal Jaffa the ratio of now extant Greek to Hebrew-Aramaic inscriptions is 60:7, but, even in the recently uncovered ancient cemetery of Beth She'arim, the 32 Hebrew-Aramaic epitaphs are vastly outnumbered by the 175 written in Greek. Cf. *Sefer ha-Yishub* (Record of Jewish Settlement . . . in Palestine and Its History from the Destruction of the Second Temple to the Beginning of Modern Colonization), I, pp. xxxix ff., 80 ff., 167 ff., 177 f.; and B. Maisler's *Beth-She'arim*, I. Of course, many Greek, and practically all Latin, inscriptions in Palestine stem from non-Jews. Cf., e.g., the 14 inscriptions on Roman milestones included in the 24 Latin and 2 Greek inscriptions published by M. Avi-Yonah in his "Newly Discovered Latin and Greek Inscriptions," *QDAP*, XII, 84–102. Cf. also, in general, F. M. Abel's

"Hellénisme et orientalisme en Palestine au déclin de la période séleucide," *RB*, LIII, 385–402.

25. Cf. W. F. Albright's "Biblical Fragment from the Maccabean Age: the Nash Papyrus," *JBL*, LVI, 145–76; K. Kohler's "Origin and Composition of the Eighteen Benedictions," *HUCA*, I, 408 ff.; A. Spanier's "Erste Benediktion des Achtzehngebetes," *MGWJ*, LXXXI, 71–76; H. I. Bell and T. C. Skeat's *Fragments of an Unknown Gospel and Other Early Christian Papyri*, pp. 56–60 (the editors mistakenly identified this fragment as a leaf from a Christian liturgical book); J. Wahrhaftig's "Jewish Prayer in a Greek Papyrus," *JTS*, XL, 376–81; A. Marmorstein's "Oldest Form of the Eighteen Benedictions," *JQR*, XXXIV, 137–59; Philo's *De congressu*, VIII, 44. The dating of the Nash papyrus has been discussed again by E. R. Lacheman in his "Matter of Method in Hebrew Paleography," *JQR*, XL, 15–39 (arguing for the second century c.e.) and W. F. Albright in *BASOR*, 115, pp. 14 ff. (defending, with apparent success, its date in the first half of the first century b.c.e.). Cf. also *infra*, n. 37.

26. Nock in "The Vocabulary of the New Testament," *JBL*, LII, 138. Another curious example is offered by the Egyptian-Jewish author of III Macc. Generally writing in ordinary, though somewhat crude and bombastic Greek, he imitated, perhaps unconsciously, the style of the Septuagint, or of the current Jewish liturgy related to it, in the two lengthy prayers which he attributed to the priests Simon and Eleazar (2:1–20; 6:1–15).

The theory of a transcribed Hebrew text underlying the Septuagint, suggested by J. Tychsen nearly two centuries ago (1772), found a persistent recent champion in Franz Wutz. Cf. especially his *Systematische Wege von der Septuaginta zum hebräischen Urtext*. This view has found little acceptance, however, among other scholars. Cf., e.g., C. Heller's *Untersuchungen zur Septuaginta;* H. M. Orlinsky's review of Wutz's volume in *JBL*, LVII, 215–18; his "On the Present State of Proto-Septuagint Studies," *JAOS*, LXI, 81–91; and the literature cited *infra*, n. 37. On the other hand, the difficulties encountered by modern, as well as by these ancient translators of the Old Testament have been illustrated by numerous characteristic examples in two essays by T. J. Meek, in *Religion in Life*, III, 491–506, and *JAOS*, LVIII, 122–29; and in A. Sperber's preliminary studies for "A New Bible Translation" in *Marx Jub. Vol.*, pp. 547–80. Cf. also W. Rosenau's detailed examination of *Hebraisms in the Authorized Version of the Bible;* G. Bertram's "Sprachschatz der Septuaginta und der des hebräischen Alten Testaments," *ZAW*, LVII, 85–101; H. J. Leon's analysis of "The Language of the Greek Inscriptions from the Jewish Catacombs of Rome," *Transactions of the American Philological Association*, LVIII, 210–33; and, more generally, L. Radermacher's "Koine" in *SB* Vienna, CCXXIV, 5, and especially pp. 32 ff.

27. Good surveys of the extensive literature on the subject are to be found in the articles of B. Jacob in *EJ*, II, 956–72; and of I. Heinemann, in *PWRE*, Sup. Vol. V, 3–43. Cf. also the latter's "Ursprung und Wesen des Antisemitismus im Altertum" in *Festgabe zum zehnjährigen Bestehen der Akademie für die Wissenschaft des Judentums*, pp. 76–91; F. Dijkema's *Het anti-semitisme in ouden tijd* (Antisemitism in Ancient Times); N. W. Goldstein's "Cultivated Pagans and Ancient Antisemitism," *JR*, XIX, 346–64; and R. Marcus's "Antisemitism in the Hellenistic-Roman World" in *Essays on Antisemitism*, ed. by K. S. Pinson, 2d ed., pp. 61–78. On the other hand, H. Willrich's *Entstehung des Antisemitismus*, and J. Leipoldt's *Antisemitismus in der alten Welt* are biased political pamphlets, rather than scholarly investigations. Amicable as well as hostile relations are treated by I. Heinemann in his "Attitude of the Ancients toward Judaism" (Hebrew), *Zion*, IV, 269–93, and his shorter English essay in *RR*, IV, 385–400.

The most complete collection of sources is still to be found in T. Reinach's *Textes*.

A more up-to-date compilation, long in preparation by H. Lewy, was interrupted by the compiler's untimely death. Cf. his posthumously published address, "The Period of the Second Temple in the Light of Graeco-Roman Literature" (Hebrew), *Lewy Mem. Vol.*, pp. 1–12. Neither has the widely scattered papyrological material been as yet assembled in one publication, although V. Tcherikover has been working for a number of years on the preparation of such a *Corpus*. Not even the much-debated "Acts of the Heathen Martyrs," containing much antisemitic material, have been made available in a single collection. The editor of the earliest of these texts hitherto published, A. von Premerstein, listed the literature up to 1939 (cf. his *Alexandrinische Geronten vor Kaiser Gaius*), while Tcherikover (in his *Ha-Yehudim be-Miṣrayim*, pp. 158 ff.) has carefully analyzed each document and its bearing on the Jewish question. New materials are constantly turning up, however. Cf., e.g., C. H. Roberts's "Titus and Alexandria," *JRS*, XXXIX, 79–80, which helps fill the long-felt lacuna between Claudius and Trajan; and *infra*, Chap. XIII, n. 25.

On the geographically more diversified epigraphic sources, we now possess a good compilation in J. B. Frey's *Corpus inscriptionum judaicarum*, I, which offers a fairly complete collection of European inscriptions from the third century B.C.E. to the seventh century C.E. It is corrected and supplemented by several reviewers, particularly L. Robert in *REJ*, CI, 73–86 (reprinted with additions in his *Hellenica*, III, 90–108), and A. Farrua in *Epigraphica*, III, 30–46. The inscriptions of Asia and Africa, promised by Frey for the second volume of his *Corpus*, have, owing to the author's demise, not yet appeared. In the meantime the Palestinian inscriptions have largely been republished under the respective areas in *Sefer ha-Yishub*, I. Many had been treated more fully by S. Klein in his *Jüdisch-Palästinisches Corpus Inscriptionum*; J. E. Hondius, *et al.*, in their *Supplementum epigraphicum graecum*, Vol. VIII; and, in regard to Jerusalem alone, by P. Thomsen in *Die lateinischen und griechischen Inschriften der Stadt Jerusalem und ihrer nächsten Umgebung*, supplemented in *ZDPV*, LXIV, 203–56. Further inscriptions of Jewish interest are found in L. Robert's *Hellenica*, I, 18 ff., etc. Cf. *infra*, Chaps. IX, n. 11; XIII, n. 42. However, most of the investigators of extant sources have treated the subject chiefly from the philological and ideological points of view, and have not paid enough attention to *historical* developments in Syria and Rome, two of the three main foci of classical antisemitism. Egypt alone has been the subject of extensive treatment as will be seen in the following notes.

28. Cicero's *Pro Flacco*, XXVIII, 66. In attacking the Jews, Cicero spoke not only as a lawyer defending his client, but also as a politician defending Flaccus and other members of his party, then under attack. Cf. Joh. Lewy's *Ha-Yehudim le-or ha-sifrut ha-romit* (Jews in the Light of Roman Literature); and L. R. Taylor's "Foreign Groups in Roman Politics of the Late Republic," *Hommages à Joseph Bidez*, pp. 323–30.

29. *War* II, 18, 7.488. The relatively fullest information is now available for the Jewish quarter of Apolinopolis Magna (Edfu) which, once briefly described by C. Wessely, yielded in 1937–38 a remarkable collection of papyri. Cf. J. Manteuffel's report in *Fouilles franco-polonaises, Tell Edfou, 1937–38*, ed. by B. Bruyère, *et al.*, I, 145 ff. More recently Manteuffel commented that "it appears that Jews lived in various quarters of the city and that only in the Roman period they were enclosed in the fourth quarter which formed a regular Jewish ghetto." Cf. his remarks in the *Journal of Juristic Papyrology*, III, 109 ff. This formulation is too sharp in so far as it presupposes some kind of legal enforcement of such segregation, for which we have no evidence whatsoever either here or elsewhere in antiquity. The term "ghetto" is here used, therefore, to describe Jewish quarters voluntarily established by Jews, as even most of the medieval ghettoes owed their origin to voluntary segregation rather than legal enforcement. Cf. also my *Jewish Community*, I, 80 f., 85 f., III, 15 n.

14; and Tcherikover's *Ha-Yehudim be-Miṣrayim*, pp. 23, 31 f. On Rome, cf. S. Collon's "Remarques sur les quartiers juifs de la Rome antique," *Mélanges de l'École française à Rome*, LVII, 72–94.

30. Josephus' *War* I, 4, 3.89, etc.; T. Qiddushin V, 4, 342. Ezechielos tried to minimize the hostility of whatever Gentile audience his play might attract by glossing over some of the particularistic emphases in the Passover legislation. But he could not help underscoring the main theme of his drama. Cf. verses 175 ff. of the fragments preserved in Eusebius' *Praeparatio evangelica*, IX, 29 (in E. H. Gifford's English transl. III, 473 f.), and the comments by K. Kuiper in his "Poète juif, Ezéchiel," *REJ*, XLVI, 66; and by J. Wienecke in his edition of *Ezechielis Judaei poetae Alexandrini fabulae quae inscribitur* Ἐξαγωγή *fragmenta*. Cf. also the apologetic explanations of the "Spoils of Egypt" (Exod. 12:35–36) in the Hellenistic and rabbinic literatures briefly analyzed by M. Guttmann in his Hebrew essay in *Festschrift Kaminka*, pp. 1–5; and, on the original biblical narrative, J. Morgenstern's observations on "The Despoiling of the Egyptians," *JBL*, LXVIII, 1–28.

In his "Oldest Midrash," *HTR*, XXXI, 291–317; and his "Pre-Maccabean Documents in the Passover Haggadah," *ibid.*, XXXV, 291–332, XXXVI, 1–38, L. Finkelstein has argued that the early authors of the Passover Haggadah had in many ways tried to meet the sensitivities of their Egyptian overlords. Even those who do not accept this interpretation and, particularly, the dating of many portions of the Haggadah in the third pre-Christian century, will admit that Egypt, the villain in the biblical story, now had to be treated with far greater circumspection by the Pharisaic and rabbinic leaders of Palestine who did not wish to jeopardize the interests of the myriads of their coreligionists living in the neighboring country.

31. *Aegyptische Urkunden . . . Berlin* [B.G.U.], II, No. 511; and U. Wilcken's *Grundzüge und Chrestomatie der Papyruskunde*, I, Pt. 2, pp. 24 ff., No. 14. Unfortunately the meaning of this badly preserved passage is uncertain, and A. von Premerstein suggested an alternative reading, "Thou hast been incited against us by the Jewess, Salome," referring to the well-known granddaughter of Herod. Cf. his *Zu den sogenannten Alexandrinischen Märtyrerakten*, pp. 24 f. Cf. also Tcherikover's *Ha-Yehudim be-Miṣrayim*, p. 162, n. 18. Of course, even in the Ptolemaic period internal political conflicts often inflamed anti-Jewish passions. It is possible that the first, somewhat obscure, Jew-baiting utterance, recorded in an Egyptian papyrus of the second century in connection with alleged misdeeds of a Jewish horse trader (cf. Wilcken's *Grundzüge*, I, Pt. 2, p. 81, No. 57) reflected the animosity created among Cleopatra III's opponents by the queen's numerous Jewish supporters. Cf. F. M. Heichelheim's review of the first ed. of the present work in *Classical Weekly*, XXXI, 155.

Alexandrian and Egyptian antisemitism has been the subject of lengthy debates ever since A. Bludau's *Juden und Judenverfolgungen im alten Alexandria*. Cf., e.g., H. I. Bell's "Anti-Semitism in Alexandria," *JRS*, XXXI, 1–18; and A. Segré's "Antisemitism in Hellenistic Alexandria," *JSS*, VIII, 127–36. With so many of the original sources coming from Alexandria, much of the general literature dealing with classical antisemitism has also been primarily concerned with the situation in the Nile delta. Nevertheless, very much still remains to be explored. Particularly the reaction of Egyptian nationalists to the imperial loyalties of the Jews—even in his attacks on Caligula's intolerant outbursts Philo insisted that the Jews had always been *philokaisares* and called the emperor a "savior" and "benefactor" (*Legatio*, XXXVI, 280) —would deserve a special monograph. That, however submerged, there existed a fairly strong "Egyptian Nationalism under Greek and Roman Rule" is briefly documented by J. G. Milne in *JEA*, XIV, 226–34. Despite W. L. Westermann's spirited defense of the governmental efforts (cf. his "Ptolemies and the Welfare of Their Subjects." *Amer. Historical Review*, XLIII, 270–87), we can deny neither the severe economic hardships of the Egyptian masses nor the widespread social unrest. Both became even more pronounced under Roman rule.

32. In trying to explain the origin of the Jewish Sabbath the Graeco-Roman world resorted to fantastic combinations of that day with both the deity and the planet Saturn. Finally Tacitus gave the reason for Jews serving cold meals on that day as stemming from the "coldness" of that star. Cf. his *Hist.*, V, 2, 4; and, more fully, H. Lewy's "Aethiopier und Juden in der antiken Literatur," *MGWJ*, LXXXI, 65–71. Understandably Tacitus adduced the Jewish year of fallowness as another illustration of proclivity for idleness.

It appears that Jewish (and Christian) persistence in refusing to cremate the bodies of their dead also added the more fuel to the resentment of conservatives, as it seems to have greatly contributed to the gradual adoption of burial by Roman society itself. This, notwithstanding A. D. Nock's arguments in favor of its being but an accidental change in fashion ("Cremation and Burial in the Roman Empire," *HTR*, XXV, 321–59). For Palestine, cf. especially D. Schütz's "Ossuarien in Palästina," *MGWJ*, LXXV, 286–92; and L. H. Vincent's "Sur la date des ossuaires juives," *RB*, XLIII, 564–67. The rabbinic legislation concerning cremation is treated by M. Higger in his *Halakhot ve-aggadot* (Laws and Legends), pp. 161–83. Cf. also my *Jewish Community*, I, 93 f.; the extensive comparative material assembled by A. Parrot in his *Malédictions et violations des tombes;* and *infra*, Chaps. VIII, n. 19; XIV, n. 59.

33. *Ag. Ap.* II, 8.95. The underlying propaganda aims, intimated by Josephus, have been satisfactorily explained by E. Bickermann in his "Ritualmord und Eselskult," *MGWJ*, LXXI, 171–87, 255–64. In regard to ritual murder, Bickermann's conclusion appears fully justified: "Josephus is right, the ritual murder myth was invented by Seleucid propagandists. It was manufactured out of an ethnographic tale concerning the sacrifice of the 'king of the Saturnalia' and of a recurrent motif in the Greek propaganda literature about conspiracy" (p. 187). Cf. also J. P. Waltzing's study of "Le Crime rituel reproché aux chrétiens du IIe siècle," *Bulletin de l'Académie r. de Belgique*, 5th ser., XI, 205–39.

Much less convincing is Bickermann's other argument concerning the allegation of Jewish donkey worship. Cf. Tcherikover's *Ha-Yehudim ve-ha-Yevanim*, p. 370. It is not impossible, however, that the legend originated in Idumaea and found literary formulation in Mnaseas, and that later the donkey became identified with the Egyptian god, Set-Typhon, the identification having been facilitated, perhaps, through the popular etymology of *Jao* as derived from *eio* (donkey) in Egyptian. Finally, Antiochus' publicity agents adduced the testimony of an "eye-witness." To the older literature, quoted by Bickermann, p. 256, add A. Jacoby's study, "Der angebliche Eselskult der Juden und Christen," *AR*, XXV, 265–82; and especially D. Flusser's analysis of " 'Blood Libels' against Jews in the Light of Views Held by the Hellenistic World" (Hebrew), *Lewy Mem. Vol.*, pp. 104–24. On Tacitus, cf. Joh. Lewy's observations in *Ha-Yehudim*, p. 31, n. 26. Cf. also I. Heinemann's "Wer veranlasste den Glaubenszwang der Makkabäerzeit?" *MGWJ*, LXXXII, 145–72; F. M. Abel's "Antiochus Epiphane," *RB*, L, 231–54; *supra*, n. 2; and *infra*, Chap. VII, n. 24.

34. Juvenal's *Satires*, XIV, 103–4; Tacitus' *Hist.*, V, 5; *Greek Anthology*, V, 160 (from Meleager's *Stephanus*). Cf. N. Bentwich's "Of Jews and Hebraism in the Greek Anthology," *JQR*, XXIII, 181–86. Joh. Lewy's overingenious interpretation of Juvenal's verses (*Ha-Yehudim*, pp. 83 f.) as a veiled attack on Jewish proselytism and secret conspiracy does not alter their ordinary meaning. It should be mentioned, on the other hand, that according to Ovid, young Romans often visited synagogues in the presumably not altogether hopeless search for romantic adventures. Cf. his *Ars Amatoria*, I, 75. On the varying Jewish attitudes to endogamy and intermarriage, cf. *infra*, Chap. XIV, n. 17–18.

35. It is very doubtful whether even the singular warning "To beware of the Jews" cited here from a papyrus of 41 C.E. (*Aegyptische Urkunden* [B.G.U.], IV, No. 1079, ll. 24 f.; and U. Wilcken's *Grundzüge*, I, Pt. 2, pp. 84 f., No. 60) had any economic bearing at all. Cf. the purely political explanation suggested by H. Dessau in his *Geschichte*, II, Pt. 2, p. 667, n. 3. Josephus' reference to oppression of ancient Israelites by the Egyptians, "a voluptuous people and slack to labour," because of Egyptian envy of the former's "abundant wealth" (*Antt.* II, 9, 1.201–2) reflected contemporary realities only with respect to the masses of Egyptian villeins. Nor did Tacitus' passing references to *unde auctae Judaeorum res* (*Hist.*, V, 5) and *immensae opulentiae templum* (V, 8) convey more than the fact that Jewish cohesiveness had greatly augmented the resources of the Jewish communal organs. Cf. Joh. Lewy's *Ha-Yehudim*, pp. 39, n. 84; 69, n. 245; and more generally, A.M.A. Hospers-Jansen's detailed Utrecht dissertation on *Tacitus over de Joden*. About Jewish banking in Alexandria, cf. *infra*, Chap. VIII, n. 15–16.

36. The personality of the alleged father of literary antisemitism (his name, Manethon, is explained by Spiegelberg as the equivalent of "the Truth of Thot") has often attracted the attention of scholars. It seems, however, that he was no more anti-Jewish than any average Egyptian of his time. The careful analysis of the Manethon fragments preserved in Josephus by R. Laqueur (in his "Manethon," *PWRE*, XIV, 1060 ff.) uncovered the following three distinctive layers: (1) authentic excerpts from Manethon, which show no anti-Jewish bias; (2) a rationalist criticism by a Hellenist of a later age; (3) amplifications by both Egyptians and Jews, who used the original material to suit their own purposes. The latter are, of course, partly for and partly against the Jews. On the other hand, apparently written as a Ptolemaic counterblast against the propagandistic Seleucid glorification of Babylonia's antiquity by Berossos (cf. W. G. Waddell's introduction to his ed. and transl. of the extant fragments of Manethon pp. ix f.), Manethon's work had to try to whitewash the blemish of the Jewish exodus from Egypt. Cf. also Heinemann's remarks in *PWRE*, Suppl. Vol. V, pp. 26 ff.

37. Cf. Charles T. Fritsch's *Anti-Anthropomorphisms of the Greek Pentateuch;* R. Marcus's review thereof in *RR*, VIII, 389–92, and his "Jewish and Greek Elements in the Septuagint," *Ginzberg Jub. Vol.*, pp. 227–45. Cf. also P. Churgin's comparison of "The Targum and the Septuagint," *AJSL*, L, 41–65. As against the views here expressed G. Bertram's manifold studies concerning the basic difference in approach between the Hebrew and Greek texts have, if one discards their occasional anti-Hebraic animus, merely documented the intrinsic disparity of the Hebrew and Greek idioms as well as of the underlying world outlooks. Only occasionally could these ancient translators coin such new terms as *proselytos*. As a rule they had to adapt words and phrases which had already been filled with Greek, even pagan meanings. Cf. Bertram's "Religiöse Umdeutung altorientalischer Lebensweisheit in der griechischen Uebersetzung des ATs," *ZAW*, LIV, 153–67; and, more generally, his critical review, "Zur Septuaginta-Forschung, I–III" in *Theologische Rundschau*, n.s. III, V, X. Cf. also, from another angle, A. Descamps's "Justice de Dieu dans la Bible grecque," *Studia hellenistica*, V, 69–92.

The study of the Septuagint has entered a new phase in recent years since the discovery of the Chester Beatty and John H. Scheide papyri. Largely dating from the second and third centuries, these documents, covering substantial portions of the Greek Old Testament, have preserved a more ancient form than that long known from the famous Vatican, Alexandrian, and Sinaitic manuscripts. A small fragment of some 45 verses, published by C. H. Roberts (in *BJRL*, XX, 236 ff.) was actually written in the second pre-Christian century, i.e., a relatively short time after the translation itself. It seems to be closer to the Alexandrian text and even, in some respects, to that of the Masora, than to that of the Vatican manuscript, hitherto considered the best. Of later vintage but nevertheless of considerable scholarly interest are also many of the *Dated Greek Minuscule Manuscripts to the Year 1200*, carefully listed by K. and S. Lake. The scholarly editions, long under way in both Cambridge and Göttingen, have been greatly enriched by these new finds. Their excessive adherence to the Vatican manuscript, however, with but a relatively small selection of other readings, still leaves the student in the dark as to the best available variants. Only the book of Joshua found in M. L. Margolis a most careful compiler of all known readings.

Under these circumstances it is not astonishing that the old question as to whether the Septuagint is based upon a single set of translations or is derived from a variety of disparate efforts has remained unresolved. Of course, we know of such independent translations into Greek as were prepared later by Aquila, Theodotion, Symmachus, and others. On the whole problem, cf. P. Kahle's *Cairo Geniza*, pp. 132 ff.; H. M. Orlinsky's remarks in *JAOS*, LXI, 81 ff.; and in H. R. Willoughby's *Study of the Bible*, pp. 144–61; and I. L. Seeligmann's detailed survey of the "Problems and Perspectives in the Modern Investigation of the Septuagint" (Dutch), *JEOL*, VII, 359–90e. Cf., in general, also F. Kenyon's *Our Bible and the Ancient Manuscripts*; P. Katz's *Philo's Bible*, and his "Problem des Urtextes der Septuaginta," *Theologische Zeitschrift*, V, 1–24; and W. F. Howend's chapter in H. W. Robinson's *Bible in Its Ancient and English Versions;* as well as such monographs as A. Sperber's *Septuaginta-Probleme*, I; his "New Testament and Septuagint," *JBL*, LIX, 193–293; A. Allgeier's *Chester-Beatty Papyri zum Pentateuch;* O. Stegmüller's *Berliner Septuagintafragmente;* J. Ziegler's "Studien zur Verwertung der Septuaginta im Zwölfprophetenbuch," *ZAW*, LX 107–31; I. L. Seeligmann's *Septuagint Version of Isaiah* (both of more general interest); E. J. Bickerman's "Some Notes on the Transmission of the Septuagint," *Marx Jub. Vol.*, pp. 149–78; H. M. Orlinsky's "Septuagint and Its Use in Textual Criticism," *BA*, IX, 21–34; D. K. Andrews's "Translation of Aramaic *Dî* in the Greek Bibles," *JBL*, LXVI, 15–51; *supra*, n. 26; and *infra*, Chaps. X, n. 23; XII, n. 19, 20, 35.

38. Cf. Aristobulus' fragments in Eusebius' *Praeparatio evangelica*, VIII, 10; XIII, 12 (in Gifford's transl., III, 406 ff., 718 ff.); *Letter of Aristeas*, 150, 171, 187 ff. An unpublished Bonn dissertation of 1948 by Robert Keller, *De Aristobulo Judeo* may be mentioned here for the benefit of whichever reader may have access to it. Aristeas' (or Pseudo-Aristeas') significant memoir has been ascribed to various periods ranging from 200 B.C.E. to 50 C.E. Among more recent writers R. Tramontano argues for the earliest of these dates in the introduction to his edition and translation of *La Lettera di Aristea a Filocrate;* E. Bickermann prefers the uncertain date of 145–27 in his "Zur Datierung des Ps.-Aristeas," *ZNW*, XXIX, 280–98; while H. G. Meecham in his *Letter of Aristeas*, p. 333, rather timidly suggests about 100 as the relatively safest assumption. There is greater consensus with respect to its author's Egyptian origin. Only M. (E.) Stein suggests, on the basis of very meager evidence, that he was a Palestinian envoy to the court of Alexandria. Cf. Stein's otherwise meritorious analysis of "The Author of the Letter of Aristeas as a Jewish Apologist" (Hebrew), *Zion*, I, 129–47. Cf. also more generally, his Polish article on the "First Hellenistic-Jewish Apologists," *Eos*, XXXVIII, 79–93, 210–23, 470–91.

In his stimulating essay on "The Ideological Background of the 'Letter of Aristeas' " (Hebrew), *Dinaburg Jub. Vol.*, pp. 83–101, A. Tcherikover has marshaled many arguments against the accepted view that the author of that Letter was an apologist to the Gentiles. In his opinion, the small treatise was addressed exclusively to the Jewish audience. This thesis is expanded with reference to the entire body of literature in his "General Observations" (Hebrew) in the *Lewy Mem. Vol.*, pp. 139–60. This "either-or" approach seems to be pushed here to an unjustified extreme, however. The author of the Letter, even if writing for the non-Jewish public, must have known from the experience of his Alexandrian predecessors and contemporaries that few

Gentiles cared to consult their works. Like modern antidefamation, that of the ancients must have served a double purpose of answering anti-Jewish allegations and fortifying the morale of the Jewish people itself. It should also be noted that a crucial document cited in the Letter (22–25) seems to be essentially authentic, notwithstanding W. L. Westermann's legitimate reservations concerning some of its wording. Cf. his "Enslaved Persons Who Are Free," *American Journal of Philology*, LIX, 1–30; and A. Wilhelm's brief analysis, "Zu dem Judenerlasse des Ptolemaios Philadelphos," *Archiv für Papyrus-Forschung*, XIV, 30–35.

39. Cf. J. Wienecke's edition of Ezechielos' *Exagogé;* M. Hadas's "III Maccabees and the Tradition of Patriotic Romance," *Chronique d'Egypte*, XXIV, 104. Wienecke's careful edition, based upon ten manuscripts illustrates the unsatisfactory state of preservation of the few surviving remnants of Hellenistic Jewish letters, other than the Septuagint, Philo, and Josephus. Cf. also M. Freyhan's "Ezechiel, der Tragiker," *JJGL*, XXXI, 46–83.

40. Cf. W. Naumann's *Untersuchungen über den apokryphen Jeremiasbrief;* H. C. Youtie's "Sambathis," *HTR*, XXXVII, 209–18. The remarkable collection of *Sibylline Oracles* is such a maze of Jewish and Christian poems extending over half a millennium beginning with the second pre-Christian century (even the earliest Jewish "prophecies" were subsequently partially rewritten by Christians) that the intensive efforts of modern scholars to unravel the various strains have proved largely unavailing. Certainly the manuscripts dating from the fourteenth century or later, or the few references in the writings of Church Fathers cannot secure full clarity. That is why not only J. Geffcken's textual edition but also his analysis of the *Komposition und Entstehungszeit der Oracula Sibyllina*, though half a century old, have not yet been superseded. Cf. also such more recent studies, as T. Zielinski's *Sibylle;* A. Causse's "Mythe de la Nouvelle Jérusalem du Deutéro-Isaïe à la IIIe Sibylle," *RHPR*, XVIII, 377–414; W. Scott's "Last Sibylline Oracles of Alexandria," *Classical Quarterly*, IX, 144–66, 207–28, X, 7–16; A. Kurfess's "Oracula Sibyllina, I/II," *ZNW*, XL, 151–65 (dating them about 150 c.e.); and B. H. Badt's "On the Fourth Book of the Sibylline Oracles" (Hebrew), *Sinai*, VIII, Nos. 94–95, pp. 30–39. Cf. also the interesting comparative data assembled by A. Peretti in *La Sibilla babilonese nella propaganda ellenistica*.

Many of these Hellenistic-Jewish writings have from ancient times been included, together with similar Palestinian works long extant only in Greek, in *The Apocrypha and Pseudepigrapha of the Old Testament*, the best English translation of which, provided with full critical notes and introductions, still is that edited by R. H. Charles. As a rule citations in our text stem from this translation. A new "American translation" was prepared by E. J. Goodspeed. More inclusive is P. Riessler's German translation of the *Altjüdisches Schrifttum ausserhalb der Bibel*, although designed for popular use its annotation is often excessively brief. A new edition and translation of *The Jewish Apocryphal Literature* is now being prepared by Dropsie College in Philadelphia. Of some projected 30 volumes, thus far only two have appeared, namely: I Macc. and Letter of Aristeas, transl. by S. Tedeschi and M. Hadas, respectively. A comprehensive bibliography is now available in R. H. Pfeiffer's *History of New Testament Times*, which is preëminently an introduction to the apocrypha and pseudepigrapha and, as such, a companion volume to his *Introduction to the Old Testament*. Of the older works, cf. especially E. J. Goodspeed's analytical *Story of the Apocrypha* (somewhat vitiated by his animus against the assumption of Aramaic originals carried over from his New Testament studies); C. C. Torrey's brief introduction to *The Apocryphal Literature;* O. Stählin's aforementioned survey of Hellenistic-Jewish letters as a segment of Greek literature; R. T. Herford's comparative study of the *Talmud and Apocrypha;* R. Marcus's *Law in the Apocrypha;* and A. Cronbach's brief review

of "The Social Ideals of the Apocrypha and the Pseudepigrapha," *HUCA*, XVIII,
119–56. Various specific aspects of that literature will be discussed later on in their
respective contexts.

41. The date of Sirach's Greek translation, long accepted by scholars as of 132,
was revised by U. Wilcken who, on account of the crucial word ἐπὶ, argued in favor
of placing it after the death of Ptolemy Euergetes in 116. Cf. his review of W. Dittenberger's *Orientis graeci Inscriptiones Selectae*, in *Archiv für Papyrus-Forschung*,
III, 321. On the date of the Greek transl. of Esther and the personalities involved in
its transmission to Alexandria, cf. *infra*, Chap. VII, n. 12.

42. Philo the Elder in Eusebius' *Praeparatio evang.*, IX, 20, 24 (in Gifford's transl.,
III, 453, 460 f.); *Wisdom* 10:1 ff. The fact that Philo's description of Joseph's reign
appeared in the fourth, if not the fourteenth, book of his poem (cf. J. Freudenthal's
Alexander Polyhistor, p. 100, note), would seem to indicate that he dealt at great
length with the patriarchal period and that he assigned but little space to the Israelitic
kings. This may be the meaning of the brief passage in Clement's *Stromata*, I, 21,
141, 3 (ed. by Stählin, II, 87), if indeed it refers to our poet. A detailed analysis of the
first two verses in the book of Wisdom's historical sketch is given by A. Dupont-
Sommer in his "Adam, 'Père du Monde' dans la Sagesse de Salomon," *RHR*, CXIX,
182–203. Cf. also *infra*, n. 54.

43. Philo's *De vita Mosis*, II, 25.187; Numenius cited in Clement's *Stromata*, I, 22,
150, 4 (ed. by Stählin, II, 93). On the authenticity of the latter passage, cf. E. Stein's
Alttestamentliche Bibelkritik in der späthellenistischen Literatur, p. 13, n. 28; and
infra, Chap. XII, n. 36. Cf. in general also I. Heinemann's collection of references to
Moses in Graeco-Roman letters in his "Moses," *PWRE*, XVI, 359–75; P. Churgin's
brief sketches of ancient Jewish historical writings in his *Meḥqarim*, pp. 173 ff.; and,
from another angle, S. Belkin's *Alexandrian Halakah in the Apologetic Literature of
the First Century C.E.*

44. Even J. Z. Lauterbach's ingenious explanation of these "Misunderstood Chronological Statements in the Talmudical Literature" (*PAAJR*, V, 77–84), merely shifts
the burden from the tannaitic to the amoraic age. In consonance with his general
views on the early postexilic period, C. C. Torrey speaks of "a faithfully preserved
and consistent (but romancing) scheme of Persian history and chronology . . . which
was current in Jerusalem from (at least) the third century B.C. on and which differed
very widely from the true course of events." Cf. his " 'Medes and Persians,' " *JAOS*,
LXVI, 1–15. This theory, however, presupposes not only a much later dating of the
work of the Chronicler and other biblical writings than we have been able to accept
(cf. *supra*, Chap. IV, n. 4), but also assumes a certain conscious and overt falsification
of known historical and chronological facts which would have to be supported by
overwhelming evidence. Cf. also J. H. Bondi's forced interpretation of "Die Perser
könige der Bibel nach Rabbi Jose," *Jahrbuch der jüdisch-liter. Gesellschaft, Frankfurt*
XVII, 325–34.

45. Hecataeus' *Peri Judaion* in Reinach's *Textes*, p. 20, no. 9. Onias' plea against
the existing improper Jewish "temples" in Egypt, Syria, and Phoenicia and the ensuing mutual ill-will of the various Jewish groups (*Antt.* XIII, 3, 1.62–68) evidently
referred to many differences in ritualistic practice. Unfortunately, apart from some
stray and mostly dubious references in the apocryphal and rabbinic writings, we depend almost wholly on Philo as a source of information. The Alexandrian philosopher
is far from a reliable guide, however. He was neither a Hellenistic jurist, nor a
halakhic sage. His interests were so overwhelmingly philosophic and ethical that
even in a treatise dealing with "special laws" he lacked legal clarity and precision.

Nevertheless he threw out enough hints for us to see that there were considerable differences between the Palestinian halakhah and the customs of his own community. That is why the legal ingredients in his interpretation of Scripture have long intrigued scholars. Cf. especially B. Ritter's *Philo und die Halacha;* G. Allon's "Studies in Philonic Halakah" (Hebrew), *Tarbiz,* Vols. V–VI; and S. Belkin's *Philo and the Oral Law.* Cf. also E. R. Goodenough's review of Belkin's work in *JBL,* LIX, 413–19; and *infra,* Chap. XIV, n. 42.

46. Bousset-Gressmann's *Religion,* p. 438; Philo's *Legum allegoriae,* I, 17.58. Unfortunately biographical data concerning the Jewish sage of Alexandria are extremely meager. Apart from his championship of Jewish rights toward the end of his life we know next to nothing about his participation in public affairs. Cf., however, E. R. Goodenough's *Politics of Philo Judaeus,* pp. 64 ff.

Philo's works in Greek with an English translation by F. H. Colson (and G. H. Whitaker) are available in the Loeb Classical Library, from which most of our citations are given, with occasional minor variations. Cf. also K. Stahlschmidt's "Unbekannte Schrift Philons von Alexandrien (oder eines ihm nahestehenden Verfassers)," *Aegyptus,* XXII, 161–76; and R. Marcus's "Notes on the Armenian Text of Philo's *Questiones in Genesin* Books I–III," *JNES,* VII, 111–15. In addition there have existed through the ages many writings wrongly attributed to Philo. Cf. especially H. Lewy's ed. of *The Pseudo-Philonic De Jona,* I; and G. Kisch's ed. of *Pseudo-Philo's Liber Antiquitatum Biblicarum,* supplemented by his remarks on the first ed. of this work in *Marx Jub. Vol.,* pp. 425–41. A most comprehensive analysis of Philo's teachings is now available in H. A. Wolfson's *Philo.* Of considerable value are also the older treatments (often disagreeing with Wolfson as well as among themselves) by E. Bréhier in his *Idées philosophiques et religieuses de Philon d'Alexandrie,* 2d ed.; I. Heinemann in his *Philons griechische und jüdische Bildung;* E. R. Goodenough in his *By Light, Light;* and M. Stein's Hebrew biography of *Pilon ha-Aleksandroni.* Cf. also Heinemann's judicious critique of the two extremes represented by the latter two volumes in *MGWJ,* LXXXI, 355–67; and of Wolfson's main thesis in his "Philo als Vater der mittelalterlichen Philosophie?" *Theologische Zeitschrift,* VI, 99–116; Goodenough's brief *Introduction to Philo Judaeus;* his critique of "Wolfson's Philo" in *JBL,* LXVII, 87–109; and W. L. Knox's review in *JTS,* XLIX, 210–14. The vast literature on Philo was reviewed by Goodenough and H. L. Goodhard in the "General Bibliography" appended to the former's *Politics;* and, within a briefer compass but with more extensive critical comments, by R. Marcus in his "Recent Literature on Philo (1924–1934)," *Kohut Mem. Vol.,* pp. 463–91. Cf. also more recent monographs such as H. Neumark's *Verwendung griechischer und jüdischer Motive in den Gedanken Philons über die Stellung Gottes zu seinen Freunden;* Albrecht Meyer's *Vorsehungsglaube und Schicksalsidee in ihrem Verhältnis bei Philo von Alexandrien;* M. Pohlenz's "Philon von Alexandreia," *Nachrichten von der Gesellschaft der Wissenschaften zu Göttingen,* 1942, pp. 409–87; and the literature mentioned previously and in the following notes.

47. Philo's *De migratione Abrahami,* XVI, 90. On the "literalists" and other factions in Alexandrian Jewry, cf. Schlatter's *Geschichte,* p. 216 and n. 202; M. J. Shroyer's "Alexandrian Jewish Literalists," *JBL,* LV, 261–84; and Wolfson's *Philo,* I, 56 ff.

48. *Quis rerum divinarum haeres,* LIII, 265. Platonic, Stoic, and Dionysian influences, together with the mystery cults widely practiced before Philo's eyes, helped to fashion the mystic doctrines of the serene thinker. They were much more influential here than any similar notions in the Palestinian pre-Christian gnosis. As to the mystery religions, no less an authority than R. Reitzenstein asserts that "Philo knows all the main teachings of the mystery religions. Indeed, for some (e.g., the idea of renascence) his is the most important testimony. Time and again he speaks their

idioms, and he reveals throughout numerous points of contact with their writings" (*Die hellenistischen Mysterienreligionen*, 2d ed., p. 41). Cf. also the (incomplete) list of terms presumably borrowed by Philo from the mystery cults, given by Bousset-Gressmann (*Religion*, p. 519, n. 3); and particularly Goodenough's *By Light, Light* reaching, in part, the extreme conclusion that "Judaism in the Greek Diaspora did, for at least an important minority, become primarily such a mystery" (p. 5).

This quest for the manifold extra-Jewish sources of Philo's teachings, which allegedly included not only the better known works of the Pythagorean, Platonic, Aristotelian, and Stoic schools but also Egyptian and Persian religious doctrines and practices (Bréhier, Pascher, Reitzenstein and others) or those of the various astral and mystery cults (Cumont, Leisegang and others), has evoked a fully justified reaction. Already W. Völker protested against these extremes, denied that Philo was a mystic altogether and declared that he could be understood only "out of himself." Cf. the critique of earlier writings in his *Fortschritt und Vollendung bei Philo von Alexandrien*, pp. 1 ff. Wolfson has likewise denied any influence of mystery religions on Philo (I, 44 ff.), explaining the various Philonic references to mysteries which should not be communicated to the uninitiated only in terms of the latter's requisite intellectual and moral preparation. In this respect Philo would go no farther than the rabbis in their well-known prohibition of discoursing on the works of creation and the chariot before pupils (at most two or one, respectively), unless they be "wise and able to reason by" themselves (M. Ḥagigah II, 1).

The pendulum seems to have swung too far, however. Greatly hampered as we all are by the nearly total absence of sources, more or less contemporary with Philo—even Plutarch's standard work, *De Iside et Osiride*, was written several decades after Philo's death—one may perhaps subscribe to Goodenough's moderate definition that "from Plato to Proclus, for thoughtful men 'true' mystery was the miraculous elevation of the soul through its assimilation of and by the immaterial, though most men needed the myth and the rite to assist in the great transition" (*Introduction*, p. 184). Philo doubtless considered Jewish rites rather than those of the pagan mystery cults (upon which he often heaped utmost scorn) as a means of such elevation. Circumcision, for one example, appeared to him as a symbol of the "excision of pleasures" and the banishment of "the grievous malady of conceit" (*De spec. leg.*, I, 2.9–10). But he could readily borrow words and concepts from trends of thought closely related to his own (e.g., in the startling allegories concerning Abraham and Isaac in his *Quaestiones . . . in Genesin*, III, 10, 44; IV, 138), without in any way forsaking his deep attachment to Jewish tradition. If Wolfson contends that "the relation of Philo to Greek philosophy is like that of any medieval philosopher, be he Christian or Moslem or Jewish" (I, 45), one must not lose sight of the difference in the two periods. The medieval Jewish philosophers lived at a time when the Jewish tradition had already become definitely formulated in the talmudic literature, itself not insignificantly influenced by the Hellenistic environment. To Christian scholastics, the New Testament and patristic letters, themselves the effect of a synthesis of Jewish and Greek thinking, represented the sources of the "faith," with which they had to try to harmonize the rational doctrines of Greek philosophers. And what would Muslim philosophy have been without this late Judeo-Christian background of Islam and the theological thinking of the Neo-Platonic and Syriac schools of philosophy? Philo's was one of the first endeavors to harmonize two such basically different worlds as that of the Old Testament and of Greek philosophy, drawn but slightly closer by the Septuagint reinterpretation of the former and the manifold "Oriental" adaptations of the latter. He also had to offer a rationale for the usages and outlook of his own community in whose daily life these diverse elements had already become blended into a living entity. Facing a challenge of such magnitude, he was certainly entitled to borrow individual ingredients from any congenial trend within his mental reach, without being too much concerned about their general validity or even mutual consistency. Notwithstanding all such borrowings he, like most of his Diaspora coreligionists, was "externally more Greek than Jewish, but internally more Jewish than Greek" (R. Marcus in *Ginzberg Jub. Vol.*, pp. 244 f.).

It is also worth noting that in H. Leisegang's *Index* to Philo, the Platonic term *enthousiasmos* is listed five times, chiefly in connection with Philo's explanation of Israelitic prophecy, but Hans Lewy has made it plausible that the expression "sober intoxication" (μέθη νεφάλιος; *Quod omnis probus liber*, II. 13) was probably coined by Philo. Cf. Lewy's *Sobria ebrietas*. However, Philo's *logos* idea differs greatly from the rabbinic notion of *shekhinah* or even *memra* (which likewise means "word") freely used in the Palestinian Targum and talmudic literature. Cf. G. H. Box's "Idea of Intermediation in Jewish Theology," *JQR*, XXIII, 103–19; and V. Hamp's analysis of *Der Begriff "Wort" in den aramäischen Bibelübersetzungen*. Incidentally, the "Word" appears in an ancient Sumerian psalm, as pointed out by Marmorstein in his *Old Rabbinic Doctrine of God*, I, 89, and by Dürr in his *Wertung des göttlichen Wortes*, pp. 3 f. Cf. also H. Ringgren's *Word and Wisdom: Study in the Hypostatization of Divine Qualities and Functions in the Ancient Near East.*

49. Philo's *De opificio mundi*, XXIII, 69; XLVI, 134; LXI, 171–72. On the *logos* idea, cf. the very numerous passages listed in Leisegang's *Index*, pp. 500 f. Cf. also *De posteritate Caini*, XLVIII, 167–69. On the meaning of the term *apoios*, cf. Wolfson's *Philo*, II, 101 ff., 115 f., where a strong argument is also advanced (against the views expounded by E. Norden) that Philo originated the doctrine that God is unknowable in his essence as well as unnamable and ineffable. Cf. also H. Jonas's searching analysis of "Problems in Philo's Doctrine of the Knowledge of God" (Hebrew), *Lewy Mem. Vol.*, pp. 65–84 (pointing out the inner contradictions of some teachings and the philosopher's often paradoxical attempts at harmonization); and, from other angles, J. Giblet's "Homme image de Dieu dans les commentaires littéraires de Philon d'Alexandrie," *Studia hellenistica*, V, 93–118; and R. Marcus's survey of the "Divine Names and Attributes in Hellenistic Jewish Literature," *PAAJR*, 1931–32, pp. 43–120.

50. *De spec. leg.*, I, 57.308–9; *De praemiis et poenis*, XXVI, 152; *De virtutibus*, XX, 102, 104. Cf. Wolfson's *Philo*, II, 352 ff., 370, n. 329; and *infra*, n. 55. Curiously, neither the idea of the covenant concluded by God with Israel, nor that of a "new covenant" debated in contemporary Palestinian circles, seems to play any role in Philo's thinking, despite his acceptance of the doctrine of the "merits of the fathers." Perhaps the fact that the Septuagint had watered down the biblical concept of *berit* to a mere contractual relationship (διαθήκη) made Philo unaware of this pillar of Old Testament theology. Cf. Heinemann's *Philons Bildung*, pp. 483 f.

51. Philo's *De vita Mosis*, II, 9.48; C. Siegfried's *Philo von Alexandria als Ausleger des Alten Testaments*, p. 159. Cf. also such a typical Philonic formulation as that "now probably there was an actual man called Samuel; but we conceive of the Samuel of the Scripture, not as a living compound of soul and body, but as a mind which rejoices in the service and worship of God and that only" (*De ebrietate*, XXXVI, 144). That Philo was conscious of his own free scope in interpreting away the literal meaning of biblical passages is best seen in his frequent polemics against the "literalists," who probably included some of his own friends. Cf. *supra*, n. 47. On Philo's much-debated allegorical method, cf. especially E. Stein's *Allegorische Exegese des Philo aus Alexandreia*; his *Philo und der Midrasch*; and, more generally, his *Alttestamentliche Bibelkritik*; S. Belkin's "Problem of Sources of the Exegesis of Philo Alexandrinus" (Hebrew), *Horeb*, IX, 1–20; and I. Heinemann's *Altjüdische Allegoristik*. Heinemann has also pointed out that, while the author of the Wisdom of Solomon was clearly more indebted to the popular Jewish biblical exegesis than to Greek prototypes, there is a clear dichotomy in this respect between Philo's philosophic works and his historical writings or his exposition of Jewish law. Cf. "Synkrisis und

äussere Analogie in der 'Weisheit Salomos,' " *TZ*, IV, 241–51. Cf. also his "Allegorical Method among Hellenistic Jews Other than Philo" (Hebrew), *Lewy Mem. Vol.*, pp. 46–58; and W. Völker's essay cited *infra*, Chap. XII, n. 12.

52. The fact that L. Finkelstein succeeded in answering his query, "Is Philo Mentioned in Rabbinic Literature?" (*JBL*, LIII, 142–49) in the affirmative only by a rather strained interpretation of two tannaitic passages (*Midrash tannaim*, VI, 7, ed. by Hoffmann, p. 27; and T. Yebamot III, 4.244), shows clearly of how little consequence Philo's teachings appeared to the Palestinian Jewish contemporaries and successors of Clement and Origen. On the early medieval period, cf. S. Poznanski's "Philon dans l'ancienne littérature judéo-arabe," *REJ*, L, 10–31; and, by way of contrast, G. Quispel's "Philo und die altchristliche Häresie," *TZ*, V, 429–36. A spirited defense of Philo's allegorical method and its influence on the early Church may be found in H. de Lubac's " 'Typologie' et 'allégorisme,' " *Recherches de science religieuse*, XXXIV, 180–226.

53. Cf. Wisdom, 2:21–3:8; 4:1, 7; 5:15–16; 8:20; IV Macc. 13:15; 15:2 f.; 17:12, 18; 18:23, contrasted with II Macc. 7:3–36, 12:43–45 (especially 7:22–23). Conceivably, however, Jason of Cyrene but naïvely repeated here such scriptural statements as he may have read in Isa. 26:19; Dan. 12:2. Even if he had been a native Hellenistic rather than a Palestinian Jew, which in the absence of all biographical data cannot be ascertained, and hence possibly unfamiliar with Hebrew Scripture, he could have echoed here the pertinent unequivocal passages from the Septuagint. A Greek translation in its early form was doubtless already available to him, as it evidently was to another contemporary, Sirach's grandson. Some of the Sibylline poets likewise betrayed at times their unsophisticated belief in physical resurrection. Cf. their *Oracles* III, 66; IV, 186–90. Cf. also H. Bückers's interpretation of "Das ewige Leben 2 Makk. 7, 36," *Biblica*, XXI, 406–12; A. Dupont-Sommer's notes to his French translation of *Le Quatrième Livre des Machabées*; E. J. Bickerman's "Date of Fourth Maccabees," *Ginzberg Jub. Vol.*, pp. 105–12 (dating it later than most other scholars at about 35 C.E.); and, principally for a later period, H. Dörrie's edition of the ancient Latin version of the *Passio SS. Machabaeorum*.

54. Philo's *Quis rerum divinarum haeres*, LVII, 280–81 (with reference to Gen. 15:15); Wisdom 1:16 ff. Cf. E. R. Goodenough's "Philo on Immortality," *HTR*, XXXIX, 85–108; and A. Dupont-Sommer's affirmative reply to his query, "Les 'Impies' du Livre de la Sagesse sont-ils des Epicuriens?" *RHR*, CXI, 90–109. Less convincing is the latter's astral interpretation of Wisdom 3:7, "And in the time of their visitation they shall shine forth, and like sparks among stubble they shall run to and fro," notwithstanding the various more or less equivocal apocryphal passages quoted by him. Nor is the crucial word, γαλαξίη altogether certain. Cf. his "De l'immortalité astrale dans la 'Sagesse de Salomon' (III, 7)," *Revue des études grecques*, LXII, 80–89. Underlying this interpretation is the assumption that the author of Wisdom shared the belief of some Greek thinkers that the celestial bodies have a soul. But it may be noted that no trace of such astral interpretaion can be found in Philo, despite his apparent acceptance of that underlying belief in *De gigantibus*, II, 8. Cf. Wolfson's *Philo*, I, 363 ff. where, however, the latter passage, like several others, is interpreted to be but a reference to a view not shared by Philo himself. Cf. also R. Schütz's *Idées eschatologiques du livre de la Sagesse*; H. Bückers's *Unsterblichkeitslehre des Weisheitsbuches*; and, more generally, J. Fichtner's "Stellung der Sapientia Salomonis in der Literatur und Geistesgeschichte ihrer Zeit," *ZNW*, XXXVI, 113–31; his detailed commentary on the *Weisheit Salomos*; and P. W. Skehan's "Text and Structure of the Book of Wisdom," *Traditio*, III, 1–12.

The Palestinian belief in resurrection, on the other hand, appears to have had, as we recall, deep roots in Israelitic and even Canaanite history. Cf. the literature listed *supra,* Chap. V, n. 4–5; and *infra,* Chap. IX, n. 47–48; as well as E. Dhorme's "Idée de l'au-delà dans la religion hébraïque," *RHR,* CXXIII, 130 ff. (with special reference to the literature of Wisdom); and L. Finkelstein's "Jewish Doctrine of Human Immortality," *Harvard Divinity School Bulletin,* 1944–45, pp. 5–34.

55. Philo in *De vita Mosis,* II, 7.44; *Quod Deus sit immutabilis,* XXXVI, 176 (cf. Colson and Whitaker's note in their transl. III, 489); Paul in Rom. 2:19. On Philo's messianism, cf. especially his *De praemiis et poenis,* I, 14–20.79–126; and the analyses by F. Gregoire, "Le Messie chez Philon d'Alexandrie," *Ephemerides theologicae lovanienses,* XII, 28–50 (explaining the relative "effacement" of the Messiah in Philo's writings by the philosopher's extreme veneration of Moses); by Wolfson in *Philo,* II, 395 ff.; and in the literature listed *infra,* Chap. X, n. 3.

One must bear in mind, however, that here even more than in many other doctrines Philo's presentation was deeply influenced by his apologetic interests. Cf., in general, E. R. Goodenough's analysis of some of Philo's writings from the standpoint of their purely missionary aim in his "Philo's Exposition of the Law and His *De vita Mosis,*" *HTR,* XXVI, 109–25; and G. Bertram's colored description of "Philo und die jüdische Propaganda in der antiken Welt" in W. Grundmann's *Christentum und Judentum,* pp. 79–105.

56. Pliny's *Historia naturalis,* III, 5.39; Josephus' *War* VI, 5, 4.312. After the catastrophe Josephus explained this oracle to have referred to Vespasian who, while in Palestine, became emperor of Rome. This hindsight was also shared by Tacitus in his *Hist.,* V, 13; and Suetonius in his *Vespasianus,* IV, 5. Cf. also W. Weber's *Josephus und Vespasian,* pp. 42 ff.; and, more generally, H. Fuchs's collection of data on *Der geistige Widerstand gegen Rom in der antiken Welt.*

CHAPTER VII: PALESTINIAN CENTER

1. Cf. Tcherikover's *Ha-Yehudim be-Miṣrayim*, p. 10. This estimate is admittedly tenuous, for inclusion of a papyrus in the field of Jewish interest largely depends on the identification of Jewish names. But the paucity of "Jewish" names in such a distinctly Jewish area as the ghetto of Edfu has underscored the unreliability of this onomatological approach. Cf. *supra*, Chap. VI, n. 12. Tcherikover has, on the whole, played safe, excluding many items considered Jewish by his predecessors. Most of these papyri and potsherds date from the late Ptolemaic and early Roman periods, but even Palestine's obscure pre-Maccabean period has been elucidated, to some extent, by stray items contained in the records of an Egyptian merchant, Zeno, who visited Palestine in 259. As though it still were the early age of a Sinuhe or Wenamon! Cf., in particular, Tcherikover's summaries in *Tarbiz*, IV–V; and in *Mizraim*, IV–V.

2. Dan. 6:11; T. Berakhot III, 16, p. 8. Cf. E. Peterson's "Geschichtliche Bedeutung der jüdischen Gebetsrichtung," *TZ*, III, 1–15. Of a different order was the orientation *within* the Temple which underwent a change from east to west largely in response to the growing appreciation of rain. Cf. P. Romanoff's "Orientation in the Temple and the Jewish Cult" (Hebrew), *Bitzaron*, V, 440–53. Living under the impact of Greek culture, to be sure, Diaspora Jews could not extol the *natural* superiority of Palestine over all other countries, as did many Palestinian preachers with utter abandon. Philo was even ready to echo some of the Greeks' boasts about the extraordinary natural endowment of Hellas. But he and others expatiated on the *historic* importance of the Jewish metropolis. Cf. the passages cited by I. Heinemann in "The Relationship between the Jewish People and Their Land in Hellenistic-Jewish Literature" (Hebrew), *Zion*, XIII–XIV, 1–9.

3. M. Ḥagigah I, 1; b. Sukkah 51b; Ta'anit 28a. Cf. also M. Berakhot IV, 5; and I. Elbogen's brief review of "Die Feier der drei Wahlfahrtsfeste im zweiten Tempel," *Bericht der Hochschule für die Wissenschaft des Judentums in Berlin*, XLVI, 25–46.

4. Philo's *De spec. legibus*, I, 12.69; his *De Providentia* cited by Eusebius in his *Praeparatio*, VIII, 14, 398b (in Gifford's transl. III, 430); Josephus' *War* II, 14, 3.280, VI, 9, 3.422–25; b. Pesaḥim 64b. In his *Jerusalem zur Zeit Jesu* (I, 90–97), J. Jeremias has attempted a new estimate. His figure of 180,000 participants (55,000 Jerusalemites and 125,000 pilgrims) is, however, undoubtedly too low. The basis of his computation was the size of the available space in the Temple. He overlooked, however, the fact stressed in M. Pesaḥim V, 5–7, that the ceremony had to be repeated at least three times for successive groups. Cf. also A. Causse's "Vision de la Nouvelle Jérusalem (Esaïe LX) et la signification sociologique des assemblées de fête et de pèlerinages dans l'Orient sémitique," *Mélanges Dussaud*, II, 739–50; his "Pèlerinage à Jérusalem et la première Pentecôte," *RHPR*, XX, 120–41; and *supra*, Chap. VI, n. 7.

5. *Antt.* XVII, 2, 2.26, XVIII, 9, 1.312–13; Acts 6:9. On Theodotos' long-familiar inscription, cf. E. L. Sukenik's *Ancient Synagogues of Palestine and Greece*, p. 70; and A. Deissmann's *Light from the Ancient East*, p. 440.

6. *Antt.* XIV, 7, 2.110, XVI, 6, 4.167–68; Philo's *De spec. leg.*, I, 14.78. In his "Héliodore au temple du Jérusalem," *Annuaire*, VII, 14, E. Bikerman has questioned the practice of such annual payments or at least their regular collections before the Maccabean age. But this seems to overstrain the *argumentum a silentio* in a period

with such extreme paucity of extant source material. According to A. Schwarz's somewhat dubious estimate the annual surplus of the Temple treasury's revenue from this tax averaged some twenty-three talents of silver. Cf. his "Studien über die Tosifta," *MGWJ*, XXIV, 360, n. 3; and his "Schatzkammer des Tempels in Jerusalem," *ibid.*, LXIII, 234 ff. Very likely the "hall ot reckonings" outside Jerusalem, recorded in several obscure midrashic passages (Lam. r. II, 19 on Lam. 2:15, etc.), also had something to do with this sacred revenue. S. Gandz has plausibly identified this hall with a Hellenistic *logisterion* or bureau of accounting. Cf. his "Hall of Reckoning in Jerusalem," *JQR*, XXXI, 383–404. It may not be too venturesome to suggest that this bureau registered all contributions brought in by foreign delegations during the declining years of the Second Temple. Hence its association in the minds of contemporaries with Jerusalem, as "the joy of the whole earth" (Lam. 2:15). Possibly even before the destruction of the Temple it was removed outside the city limits, reminiscent of the well-known peregrinations of the Sanhedrin (Shabbat 15a, etc.). Having changed both its locale and its function, it was but dimly remembered in subsequent generations. Hence the several confused and contradictory attempts by homilists to explain its connection with the biblical "joy."

7. Cicero's *Pro Flacco;* Josephus' *Antt.* XVI, 6, 4–5.167–70. In this decree Agrippa actually ordered all persons (including Gentiles) guilty of such sacrilege to be delivered to the Jewish authorities even from their places of asylum. If this meant that they were to be executed, Agrippa extended to these Jewish funds the protection granted in Greek law only against thefts committed within a sanctuary. Cf. E. Bickerman's "Warning Inscription of Herod's Temple," *JQR*, XXXVII, 404, n. 89. This interpretation is debatable, but there is no question that, even without the extreme penalty, the Jewish authorities were given great leeway in protecting their collections of half shekels and gifts for Jerusalem. On Apamaea's commercial importance and the influence of its Jewish community as reflected in the local coinage, cf. A. H. M. Jones's *Cities of the Eastern Roman Provinces*, pp. 69 f.; and *infra*, Chap. IX, n. 29.

8. The last twenty-eight high priests who, according to Josephus (*Antt.* XX, 10, 5.250), officiated between Herod's rise to power and the fall of Jerusalem, have been subject to debate ever since ancient times. As in other matters, their names, as recorded by the Jewish historian, do not quite tally with those mentioned, more incidentally, in both the New Testament and the rabbinic literature. On the various explanations hitherto suggested, none of them altogether conclusive, cf. Schürer's *Geschichte*, II, 267 ff.; and G. Hölscher's *Hohenpriesterliste bei Josephus und die evangelische Chronologie*.

9. *Antt.* XII, 3, 3.138 ff., 4.147 ff.; *War* VII, 3, 3.43–45; II Macc. 11:22 ff.; I Macc. 10:25 ff., 13:55 ff. The essential authenticity of Antiochus III's privilege has been convincingly demonstrated by E. Bickermann in his "Charte séleucide de Jérusalem," *REJ*, C, 4–35. Various views on this charter, as well as on Jewish rights under Antiochus' predecessors, are discussed by R. Marcus in Appendixes C and D to his translation of Josephus' *Works*, VII, 737 ff. Objections are frequently raised against the purported existence of significant Jewish communities in northern Syria, including Antioch, at a time when the smallness of Jewish settlements closer to Judaea (Galilee, Transjordan, etc.) enforced their evacuation by the Maccabean warriors. This argument overlooks, however, the main propelling forces in ancient Jewish migrations. Certainly whatever Jewish captives had been carried away by conquerors were more likely to find their way into large cities, however distant, than into neighboring villages. Voluntary *émigrés* must also have preferred settling in large new cities, like Antioch, with populations recruited from many ethnic and religious groups, than among their atavistically hostile more immediate neighbors. The same factors which operated to make Alexandria the largest Jewish community in the world also favored

the early formation of important communities in other metropolitan areas through-out the Near East. On the situation in Palestine at the time of transition from Ptolemaic to Seleucid rule, cf. also E. Täubler's "Jerusalem 201 to 199 B.C.E.," *JQR*, XXXVII, 1–30, 125–37, 249–63 (postulating, on the basis of somewhat dubious passages, the suppression there by Scopas of a Jewish messianic movement).

10. *Antt.* XII, 9, 6.381. Lysias' speech is not mentioned by Jason (or his epitomizer), because he construed the preceding events as having ended in the Syrian general's total defeat (II Macc. 11:6 ff.). But it seems confirmed by the briefer form given to it in I Macc. (6:57 ff.) culminating in Lysias' exhortation to "make peace with them, and with all their nation." The chronology of the Maccabean revolt, here given, follows that of W. Kolbe's *Beiträge zur syrischen und jüdischen Geschichte* and Bickermann's *Gott der Makkabäer*. On the chronological setting of the first two years of Syrian persecution, cf. also E. Cavaignac's "Remarques sur le deuxième Livre des 'Macchabées,' " *RHR*, CXXX, 53 ff.

11. M. Menaḥot XIII, 10; T. XIII, 12–15, 533. Even the Temple tax seems to have been paid by Egyptian Jewry to Jerusalem rather than to Leontopolis, as plausibly argued by Tcherikover (*Ha-Yehudim be-Miṣrayim*, pp. 109 f.) against S. L. Wallace (*Taxation in Egypt from Augustus to Diocletian*, pp. 174 ff.). Fifty-three inscriptions found in Tell al-Yahudia in the district of Heliopolis, once known as the "land of Onias" and occupied by a Jewish military colony, have been published by C. C. Edgar in 1920–22 and republished, with some emendations, by H. Lietzmann in his "Jüdisch-griechische Inschriften aus Tell el Yehudieh," *ZNW*, XXII, 280–88. According to L. Robert's improved reading and interpretation of another inscription, probably dated in the first century C.E., one Abraham served here as πολιταρχῶν (head of a *politeuma*) of the twin communities of Leontopolis and Tell al-Yahudia. See Robert's *Hellenica*, I, 20. Subsequent publications are listed in J. Leibovich's essay in *ASAE*, XLI, 41–51, which includes three new texts from inscribed stelae now in the Cairo museum. Cf. also Count du Mesnil du Buisson's "Temple d'Onias et le camp Hyksos à Tell el-Yahoudiyé," *Bulletin de l'Institut français d'archéologie orientale du Caire*, XXXV, 59–71; and H. Kees's "Ονιου χώρα," *PWRE*, XVIII, Pt. 1, pp. 477–79 (controverting the latter's identification of the *Castra Judaeorum* with the site of the temple by pointing out that there were other Jewish colonies, including a *vicus Judaeorum* and another Tell al-Yahudia, in northeastern Egypt). In his "Relations entre Jérusalem et la Disapora égyptienne au 2e siècle avant J.-C.," *Oud-testamentische Studien*, II, 119–43, M. A. Beck has suggested that the temple of Leontopolis had been built earlier by the Jewish colonists. But this suggestion seems acceptable only in the sense that the Palestinian refugees raised an existing local institution (whether a decayed pagan temple or one used as a synagogue by local Jews) to the status of a temporary central sanctuary. On the other hand, Tcherno-witz's theory that the well-known "pairs" among the Pharisaic leaders served as respective chairmen of councils in Jerusalem and Leontopolis or Alexandria has little to commend itself. Cf. "The Zuggot and the Temple of Onias," *Ginzberg Jub. Vol.*, Hebrew section, pp. 223–47; and his *Toledot ha-halakah*, IV, 165 ff. The rabbinic material on "The Temple of Onias" is fully analyzed by S. A. Hirsch in *Jews' College Jubilee Volume*, pp. 39–80; and by J. Brand in a Hebrew essay in *Yavneh*, I, 76–84. Cf. also I. L. Seeligmann's excursus in his *Septuagint Version of Isaiah*, pp. 91 ff.

12. Schlatter's *Geschichte*, p. 129. E. Bickerman's suggestion (in behalf of S. Lieber-man) that the difficult combination of "priest and levite" in the Greek transl. of Esther be replaced by "priest Levitas," i.e., the name of another Palestinian messenger (cf. "The Colophon of the Greek Book of Esther," *JBL*, LXIII, 348 f.) was rightly rejected by R. Marcus in his "Dositheus, Priest and Levite," *ibid.*, LXIV, 269–71. Whether or not we accept Bickerman's dating of this missive at 78–77 (independently

suggested also by J. Cohen in his *Judaica et Aegyptiaca*, p. 30), rather than 114 (Nöldeke, Jakob, Wendland) or 48–47 (Willrich, Schürer), his conclusion that the festival of Purim had been unknown in Alexandria before that date is extremely dubious. All that Dositheus and his son wished to convey was that "this epistle of Phurim," as "interpreted" by Lysimachus of Jerusalem and including many significant accretions, "was the same" as the canonical book of Esther. There is no more reason for assuming that at that late date Alexandrian Jewry knew nothing about the book of Esther than that it was not used in its present form in Jerusalem in the days of Lysimachus. Precisely because of its liturgical popularity it lent itself admirably to homiletical amplification as in this Greek version or in the Aramaic *Targum sheni*. Cf. M. David's introduction to his critical edition of that Targum. Cf. also *supra*, Chap. IV, n. 8; and E. Stein's "Essai d'adaptation de la fête de Pourim dans l'Alexandrie hellénistique," *REJ*, XCIX, 109–18.

13. III Macc. 7:19; Philo's *De vita Mosis*, II, 7.41–42. The original Hasmonean letter, cited in another missive of 124 (II Macc. 1–2), was written in Hebrew and may or may not have been accompanied by a Greek translation. Cf. Bickerman's arguments in *ZNW*, XXXII, 246, referring to the records of Hebrew-Aramaic writs of divorce in Alexandria and the Hebrew synagogue receipts found in Ptolemaic Egypt. This is also borne out by comparison with the evidently authentic text of a similar epistle, addressed a few decades later by Simon ben Shetah to the Alexandrian community. Cf. j. Hagigah II, 2, 77d; and b. Sotah 47a, Amsterdam edition. To be sure, the crucial citation of the customary Aramaic formula from an Alexandrian writ of divorce (in T. Ketubot IV, 9, 264 f.) may possibly have been due to a retranslation into Aramaic at Hillel's court. Cf. A. Gulak's *Urkundenwesen im Talmud*, pp. 1 ff., 37, 150 f.; S. Belkin's *Alexandrian Halakah*, pp. 49 ff.; and Tcherikover's *Ha-Yehudim be-Miṣrayim*, p. 144 n. 35. However, the Hebrew hymns found among the Oxyrhynchus papyri, dating not later than the second century B.C.E. (cf. A. N. Modona's "Antichissimi papiri ebraici rinvenuti recentemente a Ossirinco," *Aegyptus*, IV, 31–37, 125–31; and H. Loewe's "Petrie Hirschfeld Papyri," *JTS*, XXIV, 126–41), clearly indicate the partial survival of Hebrew in the communal and religious affairs of Egyptian Jewry. Cf. also *supra*, Chap. VI, n. 25; and with respect to the later (fourth-century C.E.) date of one of these Hebrew Oxyrhynchus papyri, P. A. H. de Boer's "Notes" thereon in *Vetus Testamentum*, I, 49–57.

On the date of the original proclamation of Hanukkah (165 or 164) and its oriental background, cf. O. S. Rankin's *Origins of the Festival of Hanukkah* and his "Festival of Hanukkah" in *The Labyrinth*, ed. by S. H. Hooke, pp. 161–209; and S. Zeitlin's "Hanukkah: Its Origin and Its Significance," *JQR*, XXIX, 1–36. In his *Maccabees*, pp. 43 f., Bickerman sees in Judah's "unprecedented" proclamation of this festival, not recorded in Scripture, the influence of an age-old Greek custom. One must bear in mind, however, not only the earlier innovation of the feast of Purim, but also the general Old Testament bent toward placing historical sanctions on old nature festivals. Cf. *supra*, Chap. I, n. 2.

14. T. Nega'im IX, 9, 630; j. Berakhot VII, 2, 11b; M. Q. III, 1, 81d; b. Pesaḥim 53ab. From the text of the Palestinian missive it would seem that Theudas lived before the fall of Jerusalem, perhaps in the days of Caligula, as suggested by Brüll. But rather weighty arguments have been advanced for placing him under the reign of Hadrian. Cf. H. Vogelstein and P. Rieger's *Geschichte der Juden in Rom*. I, 188 f.

15. I Macc. 14:27 ff.; *Antt.* XIII, 6, 7.216. Bickerman explains the awkward style of this compact between Simon and the people through its being extant only in a Greek retranslation from the Hebrew translation, by the author of I Macc., of an original "Greek honorary decree." Cf. *Maccabees*, p. 89. It is very unlikely, however, that Simon, who in order to stimulate the national revival consciously inscribed his

coins in the archaic Hebrew script and adopted the archaic Hebrew title, *nasi* (prince), should have adopted the Greek chancery style for a state paper which represented one of his most traditionally Jewish acts of government. Perhaps some such Greek paraphrase of the original Hebrew inscription, engraved on brass possibly in very much shorter form, was prepared for the documentation of Simon's claim to the ethnarchate of Judaea for use in his negotiations with such foreign countries as Rome. For some reason this paraphrase alone was subsequently available to the court historian who compiled I Macc. Hence also the chronological confusion between the introductory narrative to the decree and the reference therein to the Roman alliance (I Macc. 14:24, 40 f.).

16. There is considerable confusion, in both the original sources and modern literature, concerning the Sanhedrin and its functions. In regard to its presidency, for example, talmudic literature persists in stating that a Pharisaic rabbi was the president (*nasi*) and another the vice president (*ab bet din*, head of the court), whereas the few records in Josephus and the New Testament mention several high priests as chairmen of the body. The various attempts at reconciling these contradictory sources are summarized by Schürer in his *Geschichte*, II, 247 n. 26, and 255 n. 54; Z. Taubes in *Ha-Nasi ba-sanhedrin ha-gedolah* (The President of the Great Sanhedrin); and H. Albeck in his "Sanhedrin and Its President" (Hebrew), *Zion*, VIII, 165–78. S. Zeitlin's contention that, before the fall of Jerusalem, the term Sanhedrin had been used exclusively for a council and not a court of justice has been effectively controverted by H. A. Wolfson and S. B. Hoenig. Cf. in particular, their debate in *JQR*, XXXVI–XXXVII; and Hoenig's earlier Hebrew study on "The End of the Sanhedrin during the Second Commonwealth," *Horeb*, III, 169–75. But there is some merit in Zeitlin's expatiating on a thesis once developed by A. Büchler concerning the existence of two parallel bodies, a purely political council and an academy devoted to religious affairs. Cf. Büchler, *Das Synedrion in Jerusalem und das Grosse Bet Din*, closely followed by J. Z. Lauterbach in his "Sanhedrin," *Jewish Encyclopedia*, XI, 41–44, and essentially repeated also by E. Bickerman in his "Sanhedrin" (Hebrew), *Zion*, III, 356–60. Of course, this division of functions must not be overstressed in a polity like the Second Jewish Commonwealth in which politics and religion were indistinguishably blended. Cf. also Zucker's *Studien*, pp. 54, n. 2, and 92 ff.; H. Tchernowitz's "On the Sanhedrin Leadership" (Hebrew), *Bitzaron*, XIII, 305–16 (essentially repeated in his *Toledot ha-halakah*, IV, 217 ff.); A. Weiss's "Court of Seventy-One," *Ginzberg Jub. Vol.*, Hebrew section, pp. 189–216 (distinguishing between that court and the Sanhedrin although each had the same membership of seventy-one elders); and E. A. (L.) Finkelstein's *Ha-Perushim*, pp. 22 ff. (oversimplifying the problem by relating the titles *nasi* and *ab bet din* in M. Ḥagigah II, 2, etc., only to chairmen of two early Pharisaic courts outside the Sanhedrin).

17. *Antt.* XIII, 9, 1.257–58, 11, 3.318–19; S. Klein's *Ereṣ Yehudah*, pp. 74 ff., 85 ff. The dichotomy in the latter passage of *Antt.* has long been noted. Josephus' main source, Strabo, merely reported, in behalf of Timagenes, who wrote not long after the event, that Aristobulus had "brought over to them [the Jews] a portion of the Iturean nation, whom he joined to them by the bond of circumcision." Unless Josephus had some other source, his own statement that the Hasmonean conqueror had "compelled the inhabitants, if they wished to remain in the country, to be circumcized" is but a gratuitous extension of what he had read. Cf. also Alt's remarks in *PJB*, XXXV, 80 ff.; and *supra*, Chap. VI, n. 4.

18. Cf. *Antt.* XIII, 15, 4.397, XV, 8, 5.292–98; *War* I, 21, 2–10. 403–21. In the well-built Transjordanian city of Gerasa (Jerash), excavated by Anglo-American archaeologists in 1928–34, "Some Early Jewish Architectural Vestiges" had to be laboriously identified by A. H. Detweiler. Cf. his remarks in *BASOR*, 87, pp. 10–17. To be sure,

many buildings were destroyed by the Romans during the Great War, from the effects of which the local Jewish community seems never to have recuperated. Cf. C. H. Kraeling's *Gerasa. City of the Decapolis, passim.* But the extreme paucity of Jewish remains can only be explained by the smallness and relative insignificance of the Jewish settlement there before 66 C.E. Unfortunately S. Klein's plan to devote to the non-Jewish cities a special volume (IV) of his series of studies on Palestine's topography from the return of the Exiles to the end of the talmudic age, was cut short by his premature death. However, much material on them is presented in his two published volumes on Judaea and Galilee. Cf. also O. Eissfeldt's general survey of the *Tempel und. Kulte syrischer Städte in hellenistisch-römischer Zeit;* K. Galling's "Judäa, Galiläa und der Osten im J. 164/3 v. Chr.," *PJB,* XXXVI, 43–77; and, for the later period, D. Krencker and W. Zschietzschmann's *Römische Tempel in Syrien.*

Some confusion in regard to the various Palestinian provinces has arisen on account of the loose usage of the term "Judaea" not only by such outsiders as Strabo or Dio Cassius but also by Josephus. More often than not they mean the whole of Palestine, or at least its Jewish-dominated sections, rather than a specific province. In rabbinic literature, on the other hand, as well as in the New Testament, Yehudah or Judaea is clearly differentiated from Galilee or Transjordan. Cf. the passages quoted by D. Saliternik in his Hebrew transl. of Strabo's *Geographica,* XVI, 2, in the *Qobeṣ* (Journal) of the Jewish Pal. Exploration Society, 1934–35, p. 241, n. 4 (on 756, 21); and E. Levesque in "Le Mot 'Judée' dans le N.T.," *RB,* LII, 104–11.

19. The fact that Herod probably was a descendant of ancient Judaeans intermingled with Edomites (cf. *supra,* n. 17) was, nevertheless, lost on his subjects, to whom he always remained the "Idumaean slave." Rumor had it that his grandfather had been a temple slave of Apollo at Ascalon. It found far greater credence than Nicolaus of Damascus' fabrication of Herod's descent from returning Babylonian exiles. Cf. *Antt.* XIV, 1, 3.8–9, 15, 2.403; and R. Marcus's notes thereon.

20. Originally "scribe" and Pharisee were by no means synonymous. If we may take a clue from Sirach, a warm sympathizer with the Sadducean outlook (39:1–11, with a clear reference to Ezra 7:10), the glorification of these scriptural experts was not limited to any particular faction. Sirach's contemporary Antiochus III included among the tax-exempt officials also "the scribes of the temple [*grammateis tou hierou*]" (*Antt.* XII, 3, 3.142), who, if already embroiled in the Sadducean-Pharisaic controversy, were more apt to belong to the pro-Sadducean group. After the sharp clashes of the Maccabean era, however, the name *sofer* began to connote more and more a person's allegiance to the work of the first scribe, Ezra, whose memory was increasingly associated with the "Men of the Great Synagogue" both in Babylonia and Palestine. Cf. also *supra,* Chap. V, n. 35.

21. *Antt.* XIII, 10, 5–6.288–99. Aptowitzer's attempt (in his *Parteipolitik*) to reconstruct the political conflicts of the Maccabean era from laws preserved in later traditions is certainly justified thus far. As a matter of fact no more far-reaching reorientation in the study of ancient Judaism has taken place in recent years than in the evaluation of Jewish legalism. Led by Herford, Moore, and Billerbeck, Protestant and other investigators of the New Testament era have arrived at a new and more balanced judgment. Old Testament scholars, too, as we have seen, realize more and more clearly that the period of Exile, so harshly denounced as legalistic by the school of Wellhausen, had by no means been a sharp break with the prophetic past. Cf. the literature listed *infra,* Chap. IX, n. 44.

22. Sirach 42:2; I Macc. 1:14–15; II Macc. 4:13; Dio Chrysostom's *Orations,* XXXII, 44. The almost immediate impact of Greek athletics on neighboring Phoenicia is illustrated by the athletic trophies carried away by gymnasts of Byblos and Sidon

little more than half a century after Alexander. Cf. *Inscriptiones graecae*, XI, Pt. 2, No. 203; E. Bikerman's "Sur une inscription grecque de Sidon," *Mélanges Dussaud*, I, 91–99; and, more generally, C. A. Forbes's "Expanded Uses of the Greek Gymnasium," *Classical Philology*, XL, 32–42.

23. These measures of the Syrian administration are far from certain. They depend on the interpretation of the crucial passage relating to Jason's undertaking "to register the Jerusalemites as citizens of Antioch ['Ἀντιοχεῖς ἀναγράψαι]" (II Macc. 4:9). While Bickerman interprets it to reflect merely the formation of a corporate group of Antiochians in Jerusalem (cf. his *Gott der Makkabäer*, p. 59, n. 1), V. Tcherikover has successfully defended the more widely accepted interpretation presented in our text. Cf. his "Antiochia in Jerusalem" (Hebrew), *Tarbiz*, XX, 61–67. Here Tcherikover seeks to establish the following main objectives of Jason's Hellenistic reform: "(1) Official abrogation of the existing constitution based on the law of Moses and the mores of forefathers, and its replacement by the form of government of a Greek *polis*; (2) Giving the city the name of Antioch; (3) Compilation of a list of members of the *demos*, i.e., of the citizenry of the *polis*; (4) Erection of Greek educational institutions as an integral part of the city's political life; and (5) Confirmation of the existing city council (*gerousia*) as the city's chief administrative organ." Even he admits, however, that there is no record of the new *polis* having been granted the usual prerogative of striking her own coins and that no such coins have as yet turned up. On the renaming of Gerasa during that period, cf. C. H. Kraeling's plausible arguments in his *Gerasa*, p. 30.

24. Cf. *Antt.* XII, 5, 5.258; Dan. 11:36 ff. The authenticity of the Samaritan letter to Antiochus has been successfully defended by E. Bikerman in his "Document relatif à la persécution d'Antiochos IV Épiphane," *RHR*, CXV, 188–223. To judge from the fulminations in the book of Daniel, Antiochus pushed his identification with Zeus far beyond any of his predecessors, although the apotheosis of the royal power in Syria seems to have antedated him by a century or more. Cf. U. Wilcken's "Zur Entstehung des hellenistischen Königskultes." *SB* Berlin, 1938, pp. 298–321; and H. Seyrig's "Antiquités syriennes," *Syria*, XX, 296–323. The identification of Antiochus as the object of the apocalyptic author's anger depends, of course, on the dating of the book of Daniel. The regnant critical theory has long placed its final composition at the beginning of the Maccabean revolt (about 165 B.C.E.). However, the opposition not only of traditionalists but also among critical Old Testament students has received weighty support in H. L. Ginsberg's recent *Studies in Daniel*. But even if one accepts an earlier date for the first six chapters, which still is very doubtful, one need not rule out the possibility of later interpolations of such passages as the one quoted here. Cf. also M. J. Gruenthaner's "Four Empires of Daniel, I–II," *CBQ*, VII, 72–82, 201–12; A. Bentzen's "Daniel 6," *Festschrift Bertholet*, pp. 58–64; and on the historical background of "The Theory of the Four Monarchies" J. W. Swain's essay in *Classical Philology*, XXXV, 1–21.

In his desperate need of funds Antiochus did not limit himself to the despoliation of the Temple of Jerusalem. He plundered, for example, also the chief pagan temple in Hierapolis, Syria (notwithstanding the reservations in G. Goossens's *Hierapolis en Syrie*, pp. 196 ff.). On Antiochus' general religious policies and his attempt to unify the Hellenistic world as a barrier against Roman encroachments, without daring to take up the gauntlet thrown him by his personal friend Popolius Laenas, cf. F. Reuter's *Beiträge zur Beurteilung des Königs Antiochos Epiphanes*; F. M. Abel's remarks in *RB*, L, 235 ff.; and J. W. Swain's "Antiochus Epiphanes and Egypt," *Classical Philology*, XXXIX, 73–94.

25. IV Macc. 18:11–15. On the severe trials of Abraham and other great biblical figures, cf. Ginzberg's *Legends, passim;* and such monographs as V. Aptowitzer's *Kain*

und Abel in der Agadah; S. H. Blank's "Death of Zechariah in Rabbinic Literature,"
HUCA, XII–XIII, 327–46; and, more generally, H. A. Fischel's fine analysis of the
interrelated rabbinic ideas concerning the "Martyr and Prophet" in *JQR,* XXXVII,
265–80, 363–86.

26. Josephus' *War* II, 10, 4.197. Cf. also his *Antt.* XVIII, 8, 2.263–64; Philo's *Legatio,*
XXXI, 207–24. The spelling of Modein, rather than the more customary Modiin, is
explained in Klein's *Ereṣ Yehudah,* pp. 57 ff. On the "imperial worship" and the legend
of the Ten Martyrs, cf. *infra,* n. 41; and Chap. XI, n. 9.

27. III Macc. 2:30, 5:8; Philo's *De praemiis et poenis,* XXVIII, 164. On the palinode
to his *Legatio,* cf. *infra,* n. 39. The Philonic statement clearly adumbrates the later
doctrine of the *galut* as a penalty for the Jewish people's sins. One must accordingly
modify I. Heinemann's otherwise enlightening remarks in *Zion,* XIII–XIV, 7. Cf.,
in general, V. Tcherikover's keen analysis of "The Third Book of the Maccabees as
an Historical Source of the Augustan Period" (Hebrew), *Zion,* X, 1–20; and, more
generally, the data cited by P. Churgin in his *Meḥqarim,* pp. 11 ff. Tcherikover's
thesis remains essentially valid, even if one refuses to subscribe to his dating of III
Macc., largely derived from his interpretation of the census (*laographia*) which
plays such a major role in the book. The fact that the Egyptian author had made
use of Greek literary and folkloristic motifs has been made clear with reference
to *Aegyptische Urkunden* (B.G.U.) No. 1211 and the role of elephants on bas
reliefs by J. Moreau in "Le Troisième Livre des Macchabées," *Chronique d'Egypte,*
XVI, 111–22. He also wrote distinctly in the tradition of Greek patriotic romances,
although he obviously diverged "in the absence of two elements essential to Greek
romance, the erotic factor and the personal hero. The hero is patently all Israel"
(M. Hadas, *ibid.,* XXIV, 104). Cf. also Hadas's "Aristeas and III Maccabees," *HTR,*
XLII, 175–84. However, such absorption of Greek culture patterns could well go
together with perfect despair with respect to any satisfactory solution of the Jewish
question in the dispersion. Cf. also, in general, F. M. Abel's detailed commentary on
Les Livres des Maccabées.

28. Josephus' *Ag. Ap.* II, 6.65; and his *War* II, 8, 10.152. On the general relations
between the Jewish ideas of religious martyrdom and the doctrines of messianic redemption, individual resurrection and theodicy, cf. *infra,* Chap. IX, n. 46–48. Christianity inherited from Judaism its general attitude to martyrdom but, having severed
its ties with the Jewish nationality, it could no longer emphasize the idea of a whole
nation suffering death for the preservation of its faith. Being forced to stress individual, rather than group, self-sacrifice, the Church Fathers could readily invoke the
example of the Greek philosophers almost on a par with that of the Jewish martyrs
(Clement, Tertullian, Chrysostom, and others). Cf. Fischel's data in *JQR,* XXXVII,
267 n. 7. Moreover, as M. L. Carlson correctly pointed out, "in apologetic literature,
above all, the Church Fathers seem to have felt that there was a decided advantage to
be gained from refuting pagan opponents with their own arguments and therefore
with their own examples." Cf. her "Pagan Examples of Fortitude in the Latin Christian Apologists," *Classical Philology,* XLIII, 94. However, the Maccabean example,
historical and legendary, outshone most others within the Church and came to play
an important role even in the sociopolitical controversies of modern times. Cf. Bickerman's *Gott der Makkabäer,* pp. 36 ff. Cf. also, from other viewpoints, A. J.
Wensinck's "Oriental Doctrine of the Martyr," reprinted in his posthumous *Semietische
Studien,* pp. 90–113; E. Lohmeyer's "Idee des Martyriums im Judentum und Urchristentum," *Zeitschrift für systematische Theologie,* V, 232–49; H. W. Surkau's *Martyrien
in jüdischer und frühchristlicher Zeit;* and, from other angles, J. Gutman's survey
of the various teachings, reflecting social and religious attitudes concerning "The
Mother and Her Seven Sons in the Aggadah and II and IV Macc." (Hebrew), *Lewy*

Mem. Vol., pp. 25–37; and W. Wichmann's *Leidenstheologie. Eine Form der Leidensdeutung im Spätjudentum.*

29. The impact of martyrology on the minds of early Christians, as well as on those of Jews, forever after can hardly be overestimated. Pharisaic Judaism, soon politically powerless in its own land, and constantly a struggling minority in the dispersion, seized upon the old exilic doctrine of the suffering Messiah-people, to view the entire history of the Jews in the light of an uninterrupted series of persecutions. In several monographs (*The Martyrs;* "Die Verfolgunslogien in formgeschichtlicher und soziologischer Beleuchtung," *ZNW*, XXXIII, 271–89, etc.) D. W. Riddle has analyzed the sociological aspects of the feeling of being a permanently persecuted minority which pervaded the entire early Church. He has shown that the idea of martyrdom had soon become an effective means of "social control." Many of his findings have equal validity with respect to Jews. It mattered little whether or not the asserted persecutions actually occurred. In fact, hardly any serious persecutions of Christians by pagans took place before the third century. The much-debated "Persecution of Domitian," for one example, is borne out by neither literary nor archaeological evidence, according to R. L. P. Milburne's analysis in *Church Quarterly Review*, CXXXIX, 154–64. That the numerous alleged anti-Christian persecutions by Jews also were largely figments of a fertile imagination has been shown by I. Abrahams in his *Studies in Pharisaism and the Gospels*, II, 56–71. Cf. also *infra*, Chap. XII, n. 49. Nevertheless "the martyrologies of the Gospels undertook to do for the disciples what such a missionary as Paul had felt to be indispensable, namely, to prepare the adherents of the Christ cult for persecutions and to regulate in advance their behavior under the pressure of persecutions" (Riddle in *ZNW*, XXXIII, 286). Consciously or unconsciously the talmudic and medieval rabbis, with their unceasing emphasis upon real or imaginary persecutions, likewise helped to strengthen the social control of the community in exile. Cf. also, from another angle, J. Bergmann's "In der Zeit der Religionsnot," *MGWJ*, LXXII, 449–57; and on the influence of this evolution upon the formation and persistence of the "lachrymose conception of Jewish history," *supra*, Chap. I, n. 7; and S. W. Baron's "New Horizons in Jewish History," *Cohen Mem. Vol.*, pp. 337–53.

30. The connection between Ḥanukkah and the Feast of Tabernacles, claimed by the author of II Macc. (1:18), their respective types of illumination, the origin of the requirement that each household display lamps in places visible from the outside, etc., are all historically very obscure. The numerous theories advanced on this score are discussed and largely discarded by Rankin in his aforementioned studies (cf. *supra*, n. 13), but his own explanations are no more tenable. This matter is further complicated by the nearly total absence in talmudic literature of concrete data on the Palestinian observance of this ritual. The few rabbinic references to the lighting of Ḥanukkah candles mostly stem from later Babylonian sages. L. Ginzberg has therefore suggested that the laws of Ḥanukkah were relatively unimportant in Palestine, while in Persian Babylonia they assumed new significance because of the opposition of the Zoroastrian fire worshipers to the kindling of lights. Cf. his *Ginze Schechter*, I, 476. It is likely, however, that the bitterness generated by the later factional controversies over the Maccabeans contributed to that self-imposed silence. In any case, the seemingly nationalistic restoration of the old-type, rather impractical, saucer apparently ended together with the Maccabean regime. Cf. G. E. Wright's concise remarks in his "Lamps, Politics and the Jewish Religion," *BA*, II, 22–24. Only within the Temple precincts were some alterations in the traditional ritual, enacted, obviously for nationalistic reasons, by John Hyrcanus, maintained to the end. Cf. M. Ma'aser sheni V, 15; and Lieberman's interpretation thereof in his *Hellenism*, pp. 139 ff.

31. Reifenberg's *Ancient Jewish Coins,* 2d ed., pp. 39 ff.; and M. Narkis's "Notes on the Coins of the Herodian Dynasty" (Hebrew), *BJPES,* I, Pt. 4, pp. 8–14. "The gradual Hellenization of the Hasmonean family and the Romanization of the Herodian dynasty . . . are vividly portrayed by the types, symbols and inscriptions on the coins," observes P. Romanoff in his "Jewish Symbols on Ancient Jewish Coins," *JQR,* XXXIII, 8, n. 19. Cf. also B. Pick's "Contributions to Palestinian Numismatics," *Numismatic Review,* II, 5–11. Agrippa I also went to the extreme of allowing his family's statues to be erected at his various residences located in his pagan possessions. Cf. *Antt.* XIX, 9, 1.357, and, more generally, A. Reifenberg's *Ancient Hebrew Arts.*

The meaning of *ḥeber* on the early Maccabean coins, like that of the *ḥeber ha-'ir* (the *ḥeber* of the city) mentioned in the Talmud, has long been the subject of endless controversy. Cf. the literature listed in Schürer's *Geschichte,* I, 269, n. 25; and my *Jewish Community,* III, 26, n. 16. Its mention in the *Keret* legend of Ras Shamra seems to have tipped the balance in favor of a collective entity, although the question may still remain open as to whether the term designated primarily the community at large (as seems to be the meaning of the legend on coins), or of one of its organs, a council of elders. In his transl. of *The Legend of King Keret,* B IV: 9–10 (p. 24), H. L. Ginsberg leaves the matter open, but in his comment (p. 37) on A II:87, which he translates "assembled multitude," he questions the relation between the two terms. The meaning "council" seems, in any case, preferable when one speaks of the city *ḥeber.* Some talmudic passages, however, may refer to an individual *ḥaber,* rather than the collective *ḥeber.* Cf. also L. Ginzberg's *Perushim ve-ḥiddushim ba-Yerushalmi* (Commentary on the Palestinian Talmud), III, 411 ff. (favoring the collective meaning); and P. Chertoff's *"Ḥeber ha-'ir* and *'Asara baṭlanim* [The Ten Men of Leisure]," *JQR,* XXXIV, 87–98.

32. Cf. *Antt.* XIX, 7, 3.329, echoing what must have been a widespread grievance among Josephus' coreligionists. The nexus between this liberality and the local antisemitism of the Greek cities, suggested by A. H. M. Jones (in his *Herods of Judaea,* pp. 100 ff.) is somewhat remote. Herod certainly neglected such major foci of ancient antisemitism as Alexandria or Rome. Nor do we see any effects of that liberality in his defense (through Nicolaus) of Jewish rights threatened in the cities of Asia Minor. On the location of the three Greek structures in Jerusalem, cf. Klein's *Ereṣ Yehudah,* p. 87. Herod's successors seem not to have emulated his foreign subsidies, but even they continued to build, within their means, imposing Greek theaters and other structures. For one example, the theater excavated by Michigan archaeologists in the city of Sepphoris seems to have been built or rebuilt by Herod Antipas (4 B.C.E.–39 C.E.). Cf. S. Yeivin's remarks in the *Preliminary Report of the University of Michigan Excavations at Sepphoris, Pal. in 1931,* ed. by L. Waterman, p. 29. One must bear in mind, however, that such "conspicuous consumption" was an outright necessity for any self-respecting vassal prince of the Roman Empire.

33. *Antt.* XIV, 3, 2.41; 13, 1–2.324–29; XVII, 11, 1–2.299–314. In his "Attitude of the Pharisees toward Roman Rule and the Herodian Dynasty" (Hebrew), *Zion,* III, 300–22, G. (A.) Allon argued against regarding the Pharisees as politically disloyal. In his opinion, they merely opposed Jannaeus and the Herodians because they wished to see the Sanhedrin restored to its former position of parity with the high priest. Most of Allon's evidence, however, is derived from much later, often dubious, talmudic sources. Moreover, he had to admit that already in the days of Pompey the Pharisees "knew well that, once Rome had occupied Palestine militarily, she would not give up *her* control of the country" (p. 310). In other words, they merely strove to secure the type of self-government which would be more fitting to their socioreligious program. Such a view does not necessarily controvert the position

taken here. Cf., in particular, the unequivocal statement in *Antt.* XVII, 11, 2.314. Clearly, not all Pharisees were of one mind, and particularly the nondescript mass of their followers must have revealed diverse attitudes in such crucial matters as appreciation or deprecation of the Maccabean dynasty. Cf. Aptowitzer's *Parteipolitik;* his "Hasmonean and Anti-Hasmonean Politics in Halakhah and Aggadah" (Hebrew), *Livre d'hommage S. Poznanski,* pp. 145–69 (includes discussions not repeated in the volume); P. Churgin's *Meḥqarim,* pp. 63 ff.; and *supra,* n. 21, 23. Of course, in addition to these political conflicts, profound economic and social, as well as religious, antagonisms underlay the struggle between Pharisaism and Sadduceeism. Some of these aspects will be more adequately treated in Chap. IX.

34. Josephus' *War* I, 33, 2.650; M. Middot I, 3; b. Menaḥot 98a. That in erecting his golden eagle Herod pursued a similar political purpose and was not merely innocently imitating Greek architectural motifs (cf. Thackeray's note on his ed. of *War, loc. cit.*) is evident from the attack of the two rabbis. Whatever its historical value, the formulation in the Slavonic version of Josephus is likewise revealing. The preamble reads: "For Herod had at that time erected a golden eagle over the great gate at the Temple, in honor of the emperors; and he called it the golden-winged eagle." Cf. the excerpt, *ibid.,* Vol. III, pp. 642 f.

35. Josephus' *War* II, 9, 2–3.169–74; *Antt.* XVIII, 3, 1.55–59, 4, 3.90–95, 5, 3.120–22, XX, 1, 1–2.6–14. The importance of "The Episode of the Roman Standards at Jerusalem" and its likely connection with the sense of eschatological crisis permeating the preachment of John the Baptist have been elucidated by C. H. Kraeling in *HTR,* XXXV, 263–89. There is no reason to doubt the authenticity of Claudius' edict cited in *Antt.* XX, *loc. cit.* The emperor's emphasis on his wish that all subjects observe their national rites is confirmed, rather than controverted, by his action against the Italian Jews. It is certainly in line with his general religious policies. Cf. his biographies by A. Momigliano, pp. 29 ff.; and V. M. Scramuzza, pp. 66, 71 ff., 151 f.

36. Josephus' *War* II, 12, 2.228–31, V, 5, 2.194; *Antt.* XII, 3, 4.145–46. In addition to the two authentic inscriptions, found in 1871 and 1935, respectively (they were first published by C. Clermont-Ganneau in 1872 and by J. H. Iliffe in 1938; cf. the latter's "Θανατὸs Inscription from Herod's Temple," *QDAP,* VI, 1–3), there have appeared also two spurious ones. See Thomsen's remarks in *ZDPV,* LXIV, 248. The uniqueness of this sanction and the impression it must have made on the Romans is well illustrated by the material assembled by E. J. Bickerman in *JQR,* XXXVII, 387–405. The inscription nowhere indicates the need of a trial. In fact, Jewish law allowed lynching in such exceptional cases as when a Jew stole a vessel of libation, uttered magical curses, or was caught cohabiting with a Gentile woman. A still closer parallel was the priest who served in a state of impurity. "His fellow priests do not bring him before the court, but young priests take him out of the compartment and beat his brain out with blocks of wood" (M. Sanhedrin IX, 6). Presumably the Gentile trespasser at the Temple would also be caught *in flagranti* and no trial would produce more decisive evidence. Since the Jews had lost their capital jurisdiction "forty years" before the destruction of the Temple (cf. *infra,* Chap. X, n. 19), the warning would have become quite meaningless, if its execution had depended entirely on the willing coöperation of interested Roman authorities.

37. This execution of the Roman soldier, reported with some relish by Josephus (*War* II, 12, 2.230–31), was secured by popular clamor, evidently without any formal reference to either Jewish or Roman law. The procurator merely yielded to the wish of the populace, as did other Roman officials when they executed slayers of animals held sacred by the Egyptians. On the chronological setting, see M. Aberbach's none-

too-successful attempt to harmonize "The Conflicting Accounts of Josephus and Tacitus Concerning Cumanus' and Felix' Terms of Office," *JQR*, XL, 1–14.

38. *Antt.* XIV, 10, 1.188; XIX, 5, 2–3.280–91. Cf. E. Täubler's detailed analysis in his *Imperium Romanum*, pp. 159 ff. The standard work on the political and legal status of the Jews under the Roman Empire still is that of J. Juster. The use of this extremely valuable work is unfortunately irksome; it has no index, because of the author's premature death in battle (nor has Professor John Maynard's extensive French index, prepared under my direction, appeared in print). In general, Juster has gone too far in stressing the complete equality of rights of the Jews with their neighbors, who were themselves divided into many groups of different status (cf. especially his *Empire romain*, II, 1 ff.). Among more recent discussions of some phases of the problem, cf. the following: D. Askowith's *Toleration of the Jews under Julius Caesar and Augustus;* M. S. Ginsburg's *Rome et la Judée*, pp. 85 ff.; H. Dessau's *Geschichte*, II, 727 ff.; I. Ostersetzer's "On the Legal Status of the Alexandrian Jews in the Roman Period" (Hebrew), *M. Z. Braude Jub. Vol.*, pp. 75–122; A. Segré's "Note sullo *Status civitatis* degli ebrei nell' Egitto tolemaico e imperiale," *Bull. de la Société royale d'archéologie d'Alexandrie*, n.s. VIII, 143–82; his "Status of the Jews in Ptolemaic and Roman Egypt," *JSS*, VI, 375–400; M. Brücklmeier's dissertation, *Beiträge zur rechtlichen Stellung der Juden im römischen Reich;* and Tcherikover's *Ha-Yehudim be-Miṣrayim*, pp. 154 ff. Segré's and Tcherikover's investigations are especially meritorious, inasmuch as they have shown that the "Greek" minority itself was divided in numerous classes (*Astoi*, Alexandrians, etc.), and that consequently *isopoliteia* cannot mean general equality with one particular ethnic majority. Cf. also V. Arangio-Ruiz's review of the various theories in "Intorno agli ἀστοί dell' Egitto greco-romano," *RIDA*, IV, 7–20. In his detailed enumeration of the rights actually enjoyed by the Jews (*Bull.*, pp. 175 ff.), however, Segré comes close to our classification of civil equality as opposed to political equality. Cf. also F. de Visscher's further proofs of the compatibility of allegiance to more than one area in "La Dualité des droits de cité dans le monde romain," *Bulletin de l'Académie r. de Belgique*, 5th ser. XXXIII, 50–59; and, more generally, A. N. Sherwin-White's comprehensive analysis of *The Roman Citizenship*.

In view of the extreme scarcity of authentic material, outside of Josephus, the publication of Claudius' epistle to the city of Alexandria in 41 C.E. by H. I. Bell, in his *Jews and Christians in Egypt*, caused a stir in scholarly circles. Interesting, although sharply contradictory views, were immediately thereafter expressed by such scholars as S. and T. Reinach, H. Willrich, R. Laqueur, M. Engers, and many others. It must be borne in mind, however, that according to Roman usage, such private letters had legal validity only if the emperor expressly stated his wish that this be the case. Claudius' "edict," on the other hand, written in an altogether different vein, was, if authentic, an unimpeachable legal instrument. As to its essential authenticity, cf. Tcherikover's *Ha-Yehudim ve-ha-Yevanim*, pp. 399–407, which is, if anything, over-critical in regard to some allegedly interpolated passages. Cf. also, in general, the interesting, though highly biased article of T. Zielinski, "L'Empereur Claude et l'idée de la domination mondiale des Juifs," *Revue de l'Université de Bruxelles*, XXXII, 128–48; H. Janne's "Un Passage controversé de la lettre de Claude aux Alexandrins," *Revue archéologique*, 5th ser. XXXV, 268–81; and *infra*, Chap. X, n. 40.

39. Philo's *De vita Mosis*, I, 7.34–35. H. A. Wolfson may be right that, in this passage, Philo referred to the contemporary status of his coreligionists in Alexandria but, if he did, he has contributed little to its elucidation. Cf. Wolfson's "Philo on Jewish Citizenship in Alexandria," *JBL*, LXIII, 165–88; and his *Philo*, II, 398 ff. The essential purpose of Philo's *In Flaccum* and *Legatio* is well described in the various subtitles, authentic or spurious, which ancient tradition attributed to them. The

former was supposedly intended as a treatise on the operations of Providence, while the latter forms a part of a lengthy discourse on divine virtues. It may well have ended in the no longer extant *palinode* concerning God's use of Caligula as an instrument of Jewish sufferings in behalf of virtue. Cf., e.g., H. Leisegang's "Philons Schrift über die Gesandtschaft der Alexandrinischen Juden," *JBL*, LVII, 377–405.

40. Tertullian's statement (*De idolatria*, XVII, in *PL*, I, 764) is quoted here in the English transl. given by P. Vinogradoff in *Cambridge Medieval History*, I, 554 f. Cf. also Tertullian's *De corona* [*militis*], XIII (*PL*, II, 117), and other passages. We must bear in mind, however, that this Christian statesman was even less of a Roman patriot than the average Diaspora Jew of his time. On Jews in Roman public service, cf. the stray data assembled by Juster in *Empire romain*, II, 243 ff. The extant sources regrettably are not only for the most part purely legalistic, but also largely date from later periods.

41. Philo's *Legatio* XXIII.157, XL.317, XLV.357; Josephus' *War* II, 10, 4.197; *Ag. Ap.* II, 6.77. On the minor contraditions here, cf. Schürer's *Geschichte*, II, 361 f. Cf. also J. W. Swain's "Gamaliel's Speech and Caligula's Statue," *HTR*, XXXVII, 341–49 (suggesting a rather dubious connection between the speech mentioned in Acts 5:34–39 and the events following the death of Agrippa, the "expulsion" of the Jews from Rome by Claudius and Acts 12). Prayers as well as sacrifices in behalf of, rather than to the king, are recorded also among non-Jews. Cf. the references in C. Roberts, *et al.*, "Gild of Zeus Hypsistos," *HTR*, XXIX, 49. It may be noted, in this connection, that the Jewish form of the daily offering, the *tamid*, had aroused objections on the part of such rationalistic pagans as Theophrastus. Cf. A. D. Nock's "Cult of Heroes," *ibid.*, XXXVII, 162, 174. But this did not prevent Augustus from subsidizing such a daily sacrifice from the imperial treasury. Avilius Flaccus, on the other hand, was not the only high Roman official who, because of his previous friendship with Tiberius, now had to flatter Caligula doubly by forcing the issue of Jewish imperial worship. One Gaius Iulius Asclas, serving in Egypt as "exegetes and strategus," also assumed the title of high priest of Gaius Caesar Augustus Germanicus in deference to the reigning monarch. Cf. H. I. Bell and C. H. Roberts's *Descriptive Catalogue of the Greek Papyri in the Collection of Wilfred Merton*, I, 47 f., No. 11. Cf. also L. Robert's "Culte de Caligula à Milet et la province d'Asie" in his *Hellenica*, VII, 206–38.

On general imperial worship, cf. especially the studies by E. Bickermann, "Die römische Kaiserapotheose," *AR*, XXVII, 1–34; L. R. Taylor, *The Divinity of the Roman Emperor;* K. Scott, *The Imperial Cult under the Flavians;* and, on its historic background, C. W. McEwan's *Oriental Origin of Hellenistic Kingship.* Cf. also K. Scott's delightful illustrations of ancient "Humor at the Expense of the Ruler Cult" in *Classical Philology*, XXVII, 317–28; and *supra*, n. 24, Chaps. III, n. 40, and V, n. 24. The general allegiance of ancient Jews to their respective rulers is apologetically overstressed in H. Loewe's *"Render unto Caesar": Religious and Political Loyalty in Palestine.*

42. Cf. M. 'A.Z. II, 6; j. II, 9.41d; b. 36ab; Josephus' *Life* 13.74. Augustus' pro-Jewish attitude is not controverted by his general emphasis at home upon the cultivation of the ancient Roman faith and his opposition to the upsurge of oriental cults. He was by no means a fanatic. His new western orientation was but a part of his new imperial policy, as is rightly stressed by R. Syme in *The Roman Revolution*, pp. 446 ff. Precisely because of his insistence that the Romans return to their ancient ways, the emperor must have evinced greater sympathy also for his Jewish subjects' strict adherence to their "ancestral laws." Cf. also K. Scott's "Notes on Augustus' Religious Policy," *AR*, XXXV, 121–30; and, more generally, my *Jewish Community*, I, 107 ff.; III, 19 f.

43. Eusebius, *Hist. eccles.*, II, 5.7; Bell's *Jews and Christians*, pp. 25, 29. Cf. also W. A. Heidel's "Why Were the Jews Banished from Italy in 19 A.D.?" *Amer. Journal of Philology*, XLI, 38–47 (implausibly suggesting the association in Tiberius' mind of Jewish religious propaganda exemplified by one Roman lady, Fulvia, with some oriental rites which had led to the religious prostitution of other Roman ladies); C. E. Smith's *Tiberius and the Roman Empire*, pp. 230 ff.; and G. May's "Politique religieuse de l'empereur Claude," *Revue historique de droit français et étranger*, 4th ser., XVII, 1–46.

CHAPTER VIII: SOCIAL TURMOIL

1. Pliny's *Historia naturalis*, XII, 32. 65. The general economic trends of the period are well summarized in the standard works by Rostovtzeff on the Hellenistic world and the Roman Empire, as well as in T. Frank's *Economic Survey of Ancient Rome* and F. M. Heichelheim's *Wirtschaftsgeschichte des Altertums*. Far less satisfactory is our knowledge of Jewish economic history of that period. On the socio-economic developments in Palestine cf. in particular A. Büchler's *Economic Conditions of Judaea after the Destruction of the Second Temple* (also valuable for the preceding period); J. Jeremias's *Jerusalem*; F. C. Grant's *Economic Background of the Gospels*; J. Klausner's *Ha-Bayit ha-sheni bi-gedulato* (The Second Temple in Its Glory), pp. 42 ff.; and S. Yeivin's *Ha-Mishar*. The conditions in the countries of the dispersion are summarized by J. Juster in *Empire romain*, II, 291 ff.; and by A. Tcherikover in his *Ha-Yehudim ve-ha-Yevanim*, pp. 340 ff. Many valuable data culled from talmudic sources are also given in S. Krauss's *Talmudische Archäologie*. Despite these and other publications L. Herzfeld's *Handelsgeschichte der Juden des Alterthums* has not yet been completely superseded. Cf. S. W. Baron's "Levi Herzfeld: the First Jewish Economic Historian" in *Ginzberg Jub. Vol.*, pp. 75–104. Cf. also *infra*, Chap. X, n. 14.

2. Letter of Aristeas, 107, 112; Benzinger's *Hebräische Archäologie*, p. 146; Ketubot 112a; Columella's *De re rustica*, III, 3, 4; Varro's *De re rustica*, I, 44, 1. It must be borne in mind, however, that these talmudic statements belong to the period after the fall of Jerusalem, when Palestinian agriculture was in steady decline. Cf., in general, H. Vogelstein's *Landwirtschaft in Palästina zur Zeit der Mischnah*; S. Krauss's *Talmudische Archäologie*, II, 147 ff.; I. Schur's *Jüdische Erntebräuche im Altertum*; and M. S. Geshuri's "Agriculture in Bible and Talmud" (Hebrew), *Sinai*, I, Pt. 2, pp. 275–92. Comprehensive data on the plants cultivated in ancient Palestine and some socio-economic as well as philological problems connected with them are given in I. Löw's voluminous *Flora der Juden*. It goes without saying that agricultural productivity was enhanced, rather than curtailed, by the growing "Urbanization of Palestine," convincingly demonstrated by A. H. M. Jones in his article in *JRS*, XXI, 78–85. Cf. also *supra*, Chaps. III, n. 14, and VI, n. 8.

3. The liturgical formula (obligatory, according to R. Eliezer, Berakhot 48b) and its Hellenistic background are discussed by J. Weill in his "Notes de littérature judéo-hellénistique," *REJ*, LXXXII, 129 ff. Cf. also the more detailed studies of J. Taglicht, "Dattelpalme in Palästina," *Festschrift Schwarz*, pp. 403–16; S. Klein, "Weinstock, Feigenbaum und Sykomore in Palästina," *ibid.*, pp. 389–402; his "Paper and Paper Industry in Ancient Palestine" (Hebrew) in Yeivin's *Ha-Mishar*, pp. 61–84; N. Wilbush, "On the Olive-Oil Industry in Ancient Times" (Hebrew), *BJPES*, XIII, 24–27 (supplemented *ibid.*, XIV, 43); G. Contenau, "Drogues de Canaan, d'Amurru et jardins botaniques," *Mélanges Dussaud*, I, 11–14; and various monographs by E. and H. Hareubeni.

4. Strabo's *Geographica*, XVI, 2, 41 (763); Pliny's *Historia naturalis*, XII, 54.113. Cf. also Saliternik's comment on the former in *Qobeṣ*, 1934–35, p. 250. This "scorched earth" policy is reflected also in some rabbis' comments on what had, in their opinion, transpired during the Israelitic conquest of Palestine. Cf. Mekilta, Beshallaḥ, I, ed. by Lauterbach, I, 172; Exod. r. XX, 10. Such historical allusions are customary hints to events in the preacher's own period. On the "fat lands of Jericho," cf. Sifre, on Num. 81, ed. by Friedmann fol. 21b. The country's natural shortage of water had to

be made up by extensive irrigation and other investments of capital and labor, which, carried on for countless generations, suffered greatly in periods of war and civil strife. The significance of the water supply was not lost on the people and greatly affected its general outlook, rituals, and customs. Cf. the data assembled by R. Patai in his *Ha-Mayim* (Water: a Study in Palestinian Topography and Folklore in the Biblical and Tannaitic Periods).

5. T. Bikkurim II, 16, 102; b. Pesaḥim 50b; M. B. Q. VII, 7; b. Ḥullin 84a; Cato's *De agri cultura*, I, 7; Varro's *De re rustica*, II, Introduction, 4; III, 3. In his "Défense d'élever du menu bétail en Palestine," *REJ*, LIII, 14–55, S. Krauss contended that the legislation against cattle raising was purely academic. But A. Büchler rightly opposed to this assertion the fact that, during the two or three generations after 70, none of the numerous rabbis and landowners is recorded as an owner of flocks. Cf. his *Economic Conditions*, p. 45. On the other hand, his own explanation of the connection between cattle raising and fruit growing, namely, that goats endangered newly planted trees, is much too mechanical. Certainly, a fence could be erected to keep off the goats! Conditions having changed later, however, the rabbis, too, as we shall see, changed their minds. Cf. also C. Yeo's "Overgrazing of Ranch-Lands in Ancient Italy," *Transactions of the American Philological Association*, LXXIX, 275–307 ("a contributing cause of the decay of a significant portion of ancient Italy"); and, from other angles, J. Aharoni's "Small Cattle in the Bible and Postbiblical Literature" (Hebrew), *Tarbiz*, XI, 56–73; J. N. Epstein's editorial comments thereon, *ibid.*, pp. 123–24; and S. von Bohlen's *Untersuchungen zur Tiermiete und Viehpacht im Altertum* (of interest also to Jewish law). See *infra*, Chap. XIV, n. 38. On the much-debated problem of whether or not the Essenes forbade the consumption of meat altogether, see Schürer's *Geschichte*, II, 664 f.

6. Josephus' *War* III, 10, 8.519–20; j. Pesaḥim IV, 1, 30d; Strabo's *Geographica*, XVI, 2.45 (764). According to Klein's *Ereṣ ha-Galil*, pp. 49 f., Tarichaea was located north of Tiberias. Cf. also the interesting, though brief, "Greek Jewish Inscription of a Fisherman's Family from Jaffa," published with Hebrew annotations by M. Schwabe in *Krauss Jub. Vol.*, pp. 80–86; and, more generally, D. Bohlen's dissertation, *Die Bedeutung der Fischerei für die antike Wirtschaft*; and Rostovtzeff's *Hellenistic World*, II, 1177 ff. Rostovtzeff's remark that "bread and fish, with the addition of olive-oil and wine, formed in ancient times the most substantial parts of the diet of the people, rich and poor," incidentally underscores Palestine's self-sufficiency with respect to all four staple products.

7. Josephus' *Antt.* XIII, 9, 2.261, XIV, 10, 22.249–50; *War* III, 9, 2–4.414–31; I Macc. 14:5, 15:35; Sifre on Deut., 354, ed. by Friedmann, fol. 147a (ed. by Finkelstein, p. 416). Cf. S. Tolkowsky's *Gateway of Palestine: a History of Jaffa*; R. Patai's *Ha-Sappanut ha-'ibrit* (Jewish Seafaring in Ancient Times); more summarily in his English essay in *JQR*, XXXII, 1–26; and, on the general Syrian participation in piratical raids, J. Dobiaš's "Premiers rapports des Romains avec les Parthes," *Archiv orientalni*, III, 247 f. Dobiaš believes that the drive to suppress piracy along the West Asiatic coast, particularly in Syria, was mainly responsible for Pompey's invasion.

8. Cf. j. Yoma V, 3, 42c. Despite Herzfeld's and M. Avi-Yonah's efforts at marshaling the pertinent evidence (cf. especially the latter's "Trade and Industry in Roman and Byzantine Palestine" [Hebrew] in Yeivin's *Ha-Mishar*, pp. 85–112), there is still little proof for any significant participation of the Palestinian Jews in local or international trade before 70. Herzfeld has meritoriously culled from various sources a list of some 78 or 87 domestic and 118 foreign products which appeared in Palestine's international trade (*Handelsgeschichte*, pp. 129 f.). But apart from his main dependence on talmudic sources, for the most part of a later date, he could not produce

any telling testimony that such export and import trade was exclusively or even principally in the hands of Jews. The unnamed later rabbi who explained the grammatically awkward form of the "land of Canaan" (Num. 34:2) by calling it the "land of commerce" (Num. r. XXIII, 10), may have had the contemporary Phoenician or Syrian, rather than Jewish, merchants in mind. On the other hand, the familiarity of the author of the book of Jubilees with the existing trade routes has been postulated, on fairly cogent grounds, by P. Borchardt in "Das Erdbild der Juden nach dem Buche der Jubiläen," *Petermann's geographische Mitteilungen*, LXXI, 244–50; and, from another angle, by G. Hölscher in his *Drei Erdkarten*, pp. 57 ff. Sound geographic knowledge, perhaps likewise based on an existing map of the *oikoumene*, is revealed also by the author of Judith. Cf. F. Stummer's *Geographie des Buches Judith*.

9. Cf. R. P. Blake's note on "The Egyptian Mines on the Sinai Peninsula" in Rostovtzeff's *Hellenistic World*, III, 1633 ff.; Abel's *Géographie*, I, 180 ff.; I. Löw's analysis of the numerous references in Jewish literature to "Copper" (Yiddish) in *Yivo Bleter*, XIII, 537–56; R. J. Forbes's *Bitumen and Petroleum in Antiquity;* his "Zinc and Brass in Antiquity," *JEOL*, VIII, 747–57 (particularly p. 751); and M. Narkiss's study of the metal industry in ancient Palestine in Yeivin's *Ha-Mishar*, pp. 113–25. Because of its rarity, building lumber added to the aforementioned general appreciation of trees.

10. Josephus' *War* V, 8, 1.331; Diocletian's edict, XXVI–XXIX in T. Mommsen's ed., *Der Maximaltarif des Diocletian*, pp. 168 ff. With the latter cf. also j. Qiddushin II, 5, 62c. It should be noted that the edict pays more attention to the price of linens than to that of any other product, devoting to it 248 lines—more than to all other articles of clothing or all foodstuffs combined. This is understandable when one realizes that a garment made of Scythopolis linen could not be paid for even by skilled workers with a whole year's wages. Cf. L. C. West's "Notes on Diocletian's *Edict*," *Classical Philology*, XXXIV, 239–45. Galilee's specialization on the production of linen, as against Judaea's concentration on woolen goods at least in home production, is mentioned, long before Diocletian, in M.B.Q. X, 9. Cf. also, more generally, A. S. Herschberg's study of the weaving industry in the talmudic period in his *Ḥayye ha-tarbut be-Yisrael* (Israel's Cultural Life in the Period of Mishnah and Talmud), Vol. I; and G. A. Faber (pseud.), "Teinturerie et tannage dans l'antiquité," *Cahiers Ciba*, II, 617–57.

11. M. Demai IV, 7, etc. Cf. the first-century Hebrew (not Aramaic) inscriptions, recording names and working days of Palestinian laborers, as analyzed by E. L. Sukenik in his "Cave at Bethpage and Its Inscriptions" (Hebrew), *Tarbiz*, VII, 102–9. Cf. also I. Mendelsohn's "Guilds" in *BASOR*, 80, pp. 19 f.; my *Jewish Community*, I, 364 f.; III, 94, n. 18; and C. Préaux's "À propos des associations dans l'Égypte gréco-romain," *RIDA*, I, 189–98 (with R. Taubenschlag's reservations in the *Journal of Juristic Papyrology*, III, 199–207). On the mention, in an early Zenon papyrus, of two Palestinian employees engaged in the transportation, rather than the sale, of four slave girls, cf. Tcherikover's interpretation in *Tarbiz*, IV, 231 ff. Cf. also *supra*, Chap. III, n. 10; and *infra*, Chap. XIV, n. 35.

12. *Antt.* XV, 11, 2.390; 6.421; T. Me'ilah I, 21, 23, 558; Matt. 21:12. Cf. the brief studies by E. Lambert, "Les Changeurs et la monnai en Palestine du Ier au IIIe siècle de l'ère vulgaire," *REJ*, LI, 217–44; LII, 24–42; and S. Ejges, *Geld im Talmud;* as well as S. W. Baron's "Economic Views of Maimonides" in *Essays on Maimonides*, pp. 188 ff. (money), 199 ff. (banking). Although somewhat modified by the conditions under Islam, Maimonides' doctrines, on the whole, reflect deep-rooted conceptions of rabbinic Judaism, which often go back in unbroken continuity to the Second Commonwealth.

13. *Oxyrhynchus Papyri*, ed. by B. P. Grenfell, *et al.*, IX, No. 1205 (the community paid as much as 14 talents of silver for a mother and two children); Schürer's *Geschichte*, III, 55 f. On Delphi, cf. A. Calderini's *Manomissione e la condizione dei liberti in Grecia*, pp. 408 ff.; and other literature listed by Rostovtzeff in his *Hellenistic World*, III, 1465 f., 1515 f. Additional manumissions of that period which came to light after Calderini's computation seem to mention no Jews at all. By way of contrast, it may be emphasized that Calderini's list includes 38 Syrian slaves, while five additional Syrians (the largest national contingent) manumitted about the middle of the century are mentioned by Rostovtzeff, *loc. cit.* We need not be astonished, therefore, at the extreme paucity of unequivocal references to Jewish slaves in the Egyptian papyri. Cf. L. Fuchs's *Juden Aegyptens*, p. 54; and Tcherikover's *Ha-Yehudim be-Miṣrayim*, pp. 82 ff. Cf. also, in general, the data assembled by Juster in his *Empire romain*, II, 17 f.

14. T. 'Arakhin II, 3–4, 544; Fuchs's *Juden Aegyptens*, p. 49. On the changes in Egyptian viticulture during the Ptolemaic and Roman periods, cf. Rostovtzeff's *Hellenistic World*, II, 1252 f.; and, for the Jewish part therein, the Zenon and other papyri cited by Tcherikover in *Ha-Yehudim be-Miṣrayim*, pp. 70 f. Cf. also N. Aimé-Giron's somewhat dubious identification of the names of Jewish workers in the arsenal of Memphis during the Persian period, mentioned *supra*, Chap. IV, n. 13.

15. A. Calderini's "Censimento topografico delle banche dell' Egitto greco-romano," *Aegyptus*, XVIII, 244–78 (includes 11 entries for Alexandria, 50 for Arsinoe and environs, four with a dozen names for Edfu, etc.); Tcherikover's *Ha-Yehudim be-Miṣrayim*, pp. 78 ff.; E. N. Adler's introduction to his ed. of *The Adler Papyri*, pp. 5 f.; F. M. Heichelheim's and Tcherikover's discussion of the latter in *HTR*, XXXV, 25–44; *The Tebtunis Papyri*, ed. by B. P. Grenfell, *et al.*, III, 315 ff., Nos. 817–18. At times the general rate of interest went up to 48 per cent and more. Cf., e.g., the business letter of the second century C.E. enjoining the recipient, "Collect for interest on each mina four drachmas per month; but do not collect the interest for less than a year." Pap. Merton, No. 23, in H. I. Bell and C. H. Roberts's *Descriptive Catalogue*, I, 85 f.; and more generally, A. Segré's data on "Il Mutuo e il tasso d'interesse nell' Egitto greco-romano," *Atene e Roma*, n.s. V, 119–38. Although no longer up to date, this study reveals how unrealistic in practice was the Jewish prohibition of all interest, or even the later Roman limitation to 12 per cent. Cf. also L. C. West and A. C. Johnson's *Currency in Roman and Byzantine Egypt* which, by supplying data on budgets, accounting methods, etc., sheds interesting light also on similar aspects of Jewish economic life there and in Palestine; and, on possible antecedents in the Persian period, *supra*, Chap. IV, n. 11.

16. Letter of Aristeas, 109; Josephus' *Antt.* XVIII, 6, 3.160. The likelihood that Alexander had a Jewish correspondent or a branch office at Puteoli is enhanced by the recorded existence there of a well-to-do "Jewish colony" already in the days of Caesar. Cf. Josephus' *War* II, 7, 1.104; and, more generally, R. Annecchino's "Pozzuoli antica nei traffici di Roma con l'Oriente," *Atti del IV Congresso Nazionale di Studi Romani*, I, 224–32. Cf. also A. Fuchs's "Marcus Julius Alexander" (Hebrew), *Zion*, XIII–XIV, 10–17. The meaning of the title *alabarch* is still controversial. While in "L'Arabarchès d'Egypte," *Revue archéologique*, 5th ser., VI, 95–103, J. Lesquier, followed by most modern scholars, considered him merely a general tax administrator and chief of customs, Rostovtzeff and C. B. Welles once again suggested a distinction between an Arab chief called "arabarch," who occasionally served as governor-general of southern Egypt, and the "alabarch" who, they believe, was somehow "closely connected with special taxes paid by the Jews." Cf. their "Parchment Contract of Loan from Dura Europus on the Euphrates," *Yale Classical Studies*, II, 49 ff. Apart from its artificiality, this division has little support in the sources, particularly in view

of the continued existence of the alabarchic office long after the decline of Egyptian Jewry after its uprising against Trajan. A tax or customs duty called *alabarchiká* (Emperor Valentinian spoke in Latin of a *vectigal alabarchiae*) was farmed out in 383. The office of *alabarch* is recorded in Antinoupolis as late as 568. It appears, therefore, that at least during the Byzantine period the *alabarch* was "in charge of local customs and presumably of imports and exports from Alexandria." Cf. A. C. Johnson and L. C. West's *Byzantine Egypt*, pp. 298 f. It should be noted that the talmudic term for bankers, *shulḥanim*, like that of their Greek counterparts, the *trapezitai*, evidently arose from the tables used by money changers. Cf. W. L. Westermann's "Warehousing and Trapezite Banking in Antiquity," *Journal of Economic and Business History*, III, 30–54; and, more generally, Heichelheim's *Wirtschaftsgeschichte*, pp. 144 ff., 256 ff., 349 ff., 550 ff., 722 ff.

17. The existence of commercial relations between North African Jewry and Rome, as well as the former's participation in the tremendous *annona* collected by Romans, is further confirmed by the epigraphic references to the synagogues of the "Tripolitans" and of the "Scinians" in the city of Rome, if the identification of *sekenoi* with the inhabitants of Scina in North Africa is to be accepted. Cf. J. B. Frey's *Corpus*, I, p. lxxix. All earlier explanations (cf. G. La Piana's remarks in *HTR*, XX, 357, n. 27) are less plausible. Of course, some of the other Roman synagogues, named after the place of origin of their members, would serve as an indication of similar commercial relations with other lands. Cf., in general, also Juster's *Empire romain*, II, 291 ff.

18. Tacitus' *Hist.*, V, 5; Yoma 18a; Giṭṭin 56a; Sanhedrin 41a; Josephus' *War* VI, 5, 3.293; M. Middot I, 4; II, 3. Cf. P. Roussel's "Nikanor d'Alexandrie et la porte du Temple de Jérusalem," *Revue des études grecques*, XXXVII, 79–82; J. Brand's "Gates of Nikanor" (Hebrew), in *Minḥah li-Yehudah* (J. L. Zlotnik Jubilee Volume), pp. 5–19; and E. L. Sukenik's reinterpretation of a Greek inscription, first published in 1902, in his "Gleanings in Jewish Epigraphy" (Hebrew), *Gulak-Klein Mem. Vol.*, pp. 134 ff. ("the bones of the sons of Nicanor of Alexandria who had made the gates").

19. Strabo's *Geographica*, XVI, 2, 46 (765); Josephus' *Antt.* XVII, 4–5, 3.18–21. Even Horace (in his *Epistles*, II, 2.184) admiringly referred to "Herod's rich palm-groves." Cf. also Jeremias's *Jerusalem*, II, Pt. 2, pp. 31 ff.; H. Willrich's *Haus des Herodes*, pp. 91 ff. In case of need Herod did not hesitate to plunder the ancient tomb of King David, as did also John Hyrcanus before him. Cf. Josephus' *Antt.* VII, 15, 3.393. If none of the other royal tombs of Judah seem to have suffered from similar despoliation, the reason seems to have been simple ignorance of their location which, incidentally, is still debated today. Cf. S. Yeivin's "Sepulchres of the Kings of the House of David," *JNES*, VII, 30–45. We must bear in mind, however, that violation of tombs even by private burglars was sufficiently frequent at that time for Augustus to issue a specific decree against it. On the date of this decree, previously ascribed to Claudius, cf. H. Markowski's detailed analysis, *Diatagma Kaisaros*. Cf. also *supra*, Chap. VI, n. 32, and *infra*, Chaps. IX, n. 23, and XIV, n. 59.

20. Josephus' *Antt.* XVIII, 1, 1.2 ff.; 6, 5.172–73; M. Middot I, 3; Aelius Spartianus' *Pescennius Niger*, VII, 9 in *Scriptores historiae Augustae*, ed. by D. Magie, I, 447. Among recent studies on some of the Roman officials in Syria and Palestine cf. P. Fraccaro's "C. Herennius Capito di Teate," *Athenaeum*, XVIII, 136–44; F. Morison's semipopular study, *And Pilate Said;* and S. J. de Laet's "Successeur de Ponce-Pilate," *Antiquité classique*, VIII, 413–19 (on Marcellus). On the census of Quirinius, which is of particularly great importance for New Testament chronology (Luke 2:1–5), cf. the lengthy excursus in Schürer's *Geschichte*, I, 508 ff.; L. R. Taylor's "Quirinius and the Census of Judaea," *American Journal of Philology*, LIV, 120–33 (affirming its his-

toricity); and S. Accame's "Primo censimento della Giudea," *Rivista di filologia classica*, LXXII–LXXIII, 138–70 (postulating also an earlier census by Herod in 9–8 B.C.E.). It may be noted that popular uprisings, instigated by Roman censuses, occurred also in Spain, Gaul, and Dalmatia.

The important problem of Roman taxation in Palestine (even unfriendly Tacitus intimated that it was a major cause of the Jewish revolt; cf. his *Annales*, XII, 54) has not received due attention from modern scholars. Most of the existing studies are concerned with either such special Jewish taxes as the *fiscus judaicus* or with the terminological, rather than substantive-historical, elucidation of the rabbinic sources. The latter reflect, of course, to a large extent conditions after 70 and under Persia as well as in the Roman Empire. Cf., e.g., L. Goldschmid's "Impôts et droits de douane en Judée sous les Romains," *REJ*, XXXIV, 192–217; and *infra*, n. 32; and Chap. XIII, n. 17–18. A more promising beginning was made by A. Gulak in his "Method of Collecting Roman Taxes in Palestine" (Hebrew), *Magnes Anniv. Book*, pp. 97–104; and "Boulé and Strategia" (Hebrew), *Tarbiz*, XI, 119–22, although his conclusions therefrom concerning the general relations between the Palestinian city and countryside seem rather far-fetched. Cf. also, in general, A. Schalit's *Ha-Mishṭar ha-roma'i be-Ereṣ Yisrael* (The Roman Administration in Palestine); and the literature listed *infra*, Chap. XI, n. 20–21.

21. *Lam. r. Intro.* 17. The same passage is quoted anonymously on verse 3:14: "I am become a derision to all my people." Cf. also the inferences in T. *Shabbat* XII, 16, 128; and b. 113a; and, on the general quality of this type of theatrical performance, the literature cited in L. Robert's "'Ἀρχαιολόγος [The Mime]," *Revue des études grecques*, XLIX, 235–54.

22. Philo's *In Flaccum*, VII, 57 (transl. by Box); *De spec. leg.* II, 17.75; *De virtutibus*, XIV, 82–87. One Ḥananiah, probably a petty Jewish trader, from Alexandria died in Jaffa. See his tombstone inscription in *Sefer ha-Yishub*, I, 80, No. 4. From the days of Philo on, the economic position of Alexandrian Jewry constantly deteriorated. This community, too, never fully recovered from the catastrophic outcome of its uprising under Trajan. While in later centuries it still had some wealthy members, in a decree of 390 included in the Theodosian Code (XIII, 5, 18) the majority was correctly described as *inopes vilibusque commerciis occupati* (poor and engaged in petty trade). Cf. *infra*, Chap. XI, n. 25.

23. *Tebtunis Papyri*, I, 383, No. 86 (cf. the editors' note to line 20); III, Pt. 2, pp. 139 ff., No. 882; Manteuffel's ed. of "Les Papyrus et les Ostraca grecs" in *Fouilles . . . Edfou*, II, 149, Nos. 270, 272; Martial's *Epigrams*, XII, 57.13 ("the Jew taught by his mother to beg"). Cf., however, Reinach's interpretation of the latter passage in his *Textes*, p. 289. Cf. also Joh. Lewy's brief summary of the available data concerning "The Jewish Poor in Ancient Rome" (Hebrew), *Dinaburg Jub. Vol.*, pp. 104–109. On Jewish taxation in Egypt, cf. Tcherikover's *Ha-Yehudim be-Miṣrayim*, pp. 86 ff.; and, more generally, S. L. Wallace's *Taxation*. Curiously, the author of III Macc., although evidently influenced by the book of Esther, did not stress the fiscal usefulness of the king's Jewish subjects. In Esther (10:1), Mordecai appears to have advised the king to replace the loss of 10,000 silver talents promised by Haman, probably from Jewish spoils, by a new tax "upon the land and upon the isles of the sea." (In his "Last Chapter of Esther," *JQR*, XXXVII, 140, D. Daube considers this plea "one of the great political arguments of the author.") But III Macc. 6:22 ff. merely shows that, after his change of heart, the Egyptian king accused his counselors of having secretly devised "things that are unprofitable to the kingdom," because of the Jews' well-attested loyalty to the Crown and their fidelity in guarding the fortresses of the country.

24. M. 'Arakhin VIII, 5; b. Qiddushin 20a (with reference to Deut. 15:16), 69a, etc. Philo was certainly right in contending that "people in this position, though we find them called slaves, are in reality laborers" (De spec. leg., II, 18.81). Cf. also numerous other rabbinic laws and homilies on slavery, both Hebrew and Gentile, summarized in Krauss's Talmudische Archäologie, II, 83 ff.; my Essays on Maimonides, pp. 229 ff. (with a fuller discussion of the socio-economic implications); R. Salomon's Esclavage en droit comparé juif et romain; and supra, Chap. III, n. 12.

25. On the discontinuation of sales of defaulted debtors, cf. A. Gulak's Toledot ha-mishpaṭ be-Yisrael (On the History of Hebrew Law in the Talmudic Period), I, 18 ff., 149 f. J. Jeremias tried to prove the existence of numerous Jewish slaves in Jerusalem before 70 (cf. his Jerusalem, II, Pt. 2, pp. 184 ff.), but his evidence is very dubious. Certainly we hear nothing about slave revolts in Palestine of the kind that terrorized Italy and other lands.

26. Josephus' War IV, 9, 3.508; Giṭṭin 44a, etc. Josephus mentions, however, also 2,000 prisoners, doubtless Jewish for the most part, who, liberated by the Idumaeans, immediately joined Simon (War IV, 6, 1.353). Josephus may have exaggerated here the number of slaves and brigands who had joined Simon son of Giyoras for the benefit of his Graeco-Roman bourgeois readers, whose flesh must have crawled at the mention of these evil men.

27. M. Abot II, 7; Yadaim IV, 7; T. B.B. IV, 7, 403 (elaborated b. 92b-93a); Pes. 113b. On the meaning of the Pharisaic Sadducean controversy with respect to damages, see Finkelstein's Pharisees, I, 283 ff., II, 684 f. His interpretation, however, that the Sadducees, as representatives of the slaveholding upper classes, were interested in establishing the master's responsibility, is inconclusive. One might argue with equal force that a slave-owning class stood to gain much more from the absolution from responsibility, while all other classes would lose their uncollectible claims without any countervailing benefits.

28. M. Yoma III, 11; T. II, 5-6, 183-84; b. 38a. The translation of po'el baṭel by "unemployed worker," given in the text, has been questioned by H. Heinemann in his "Payment of a 'Po'el Baṭel,' " Journal of Jewish Studies, I, 178-81. However, his alternative explanation that it referred to an ordinary worker temporarily idle for reasons beyond his control (e.g., the weather) does not remove the main difficulty of estimating the exact amount of wages due. Even if there was a constant ratio between wages paid during such enforced idleness and regular wages, which is extremely dubious, the amounts doubtless varied greatly by occupation, region, and time. A far greater stability might be expected in the case of wages paid to unemployed laborers of any kind, particularly in periods of mass unemployment. On the ancient Jewish attitude to labor, cf. D. Farbstein's Recht der unfreien und der freien Arbeiter nach jüdisch-talmudischem Recht; H. Z. (W.) Reines's Ha-Po'el bi-zeman ha-miqra, ha-mishnah ve-ha-talmud (The Worker in the Periods of Bible and Talmud); and F. S. Granger's Legal Status of Labour in the New Testament (pointing out that of the 120 passages referring to doulos not one is correctly translated in the Revised Version and quite a few are misrepresented also in the Authorized Version). We may mention here in passing B. I. Nadel's explanation of the "economic significance" of a phrase in one of the well-known Bosporus inscriptions. Nadel believes that it proves the permanent obligation of freedmen to perform certain farm labors in behalf of the Jewish synagogue. Cf. his Russian essay in Vestnik drevnei istorii, 1948, Pt. 1, pp. 203-16. This theory has rightly been rejected by J. Falenciak in the Journal of Juristic Papyrology, III, 196 f. Cf. also infra, Chap. XIV, n. 35.

29. Josephus' *Life* I, 1.1–6 ("pedigree which I cite as I find it recorded in the public registers"); *Antt.* XIV, 1, 3.9 (cf. Marcus's notes thereon); Sirach 7:29–31, 45:6 ff.; Prov. 3:9–10; T. Ḥallah II, 7–10, 99; j. IV, 11, 60b; M. Bikkurim III, 2–3. Not only Josephus but also Philo, though neither priest nor Palestinian, was well informed about this complex system of dues. Cf. especially *Antt.* IV, 4, 4.69–75; and Philo's numerous statements analyzed by Belkin in his *Philo and the Oral Law*, pp. 67 ff. Cf. also Z. Karl's brief analysis of "The Tithe and the Heave-Offering" (Hebrew), *Tarbiz*, XVI, 11–17.

It should be noted, however, that because of legal barriers, even the most unscrupulous high priests seem to have neglected such a major source of revenue as lending Temple funds on interest. Elsewhere, except perhaps in Rome, this was a fairly common practice. Compare B. Bromberg's negative findings concerning "Temple Banking in Rome," *Economic History Review*, X, 128–31, with the positive evidence adduced by A. M. Andreades in his *History of Greek Public Finance*, I, 62, 168, 171, 173 n. 2, 191; and, for Egypt, by C. Préaux in her *Economie royale des Lagides*, pp. 293 ff. Bickerman's strictures (in *Annuaire*, VII, 15 n. 67) are not only in themselves rather dubious, but would merely remove the actual lending operations from the personnel of respective temples to banking intermediaries employed by it. In fact, the Temple of Jerusalem seems not even to have served as an important depositary of private funds. Cf. such sporadic records as II Macc. 3:10–11; and Josephus' *War* VI, 5, 2.282, whereas IV Macc. 4:3, 6–7, rather reflects conditions in Diaspora lands. There also existed a healthy popular distrust in the administration of Temple funds which could legally be used for certain needs of the city of Jerusalem and extralegally were often appropriated by Herod and his successors for other governmental uses. Cf., in general, also A. Büchler's valuable, though somewhat overspeculative monograph, *Die Priester und der Cultus im letzten Jahrzehnt des jerusalemischen Tempels*. A new comprehensive and up-to-date study is clearly indicated.

30. The figure of 18,000 priests and levites as given by J. Jeremias (in his *Jerusalem*, II, Pt. 2, pp. 61 ff.) seems better supported than that of 25,000 suggested by Büchler. Jeremias's deductions therefrom as to the total population of Palestine appear, however, to be erroneous. His argument from the list of those who returned from the Exile (Ezra 2 and Nehemiah 7), with its 10 per cent of priests and levites, defeats itself when one considers that there were only 74 levites (with the singers and porters, 360), along with 4,289 priests. Obviously the population left behind in 586 had a smaller proportion of priests, who were most affected by the deportations, and a larger proportion of levites who, as lower servants of the Temple, were not deemed worthy of Nebukadrezzar's full attention. After Zerubbabel, less than 10 per cent in all belonged to the priestly class. This proportion sank further with each expansive movement, as practically all Jews of the subjected regions eventually joined the Israelites, but not the *kohanim* or levites. The levites again increased relatively by incorporating singers and porters, and perhaps also some lower priests, who performed services similar to theirs. Desecrated priests (*kohanim ḥalalim*), in particular, must have been rather numerous in the periods of intermarriage in the time of Ezra and early Hellenism. Their descendants might have joined the levites at times, while a levite never could become a "priest."

At any rate, after the destruction of the Second Temple, the whole distinction began to become primarily one of prestige. In later days, when social control over the pedigrees weakened, some Jews claimed priestly or levitical descent improperly. In second-century Sepphoris, we hear of *kohanim*, who, originally slaves of priests, succeeded by a subterfuge in insinuating themselves into the revered class (cf. Yebamot 99b, Ketubot 28b, etc.). In the Islamic age, Egyptian and other communities introduced the requirement that any *kohen* or levite, arriving from another city, must produce documentary proof, confirmed by the authorities of his former domicile. That some of these "priests" derived also financial gains from donations, etc., as late as the eleventh century, is demonstrated by the remarkable, delightfully caustic responsum in twenty-four poetic stanzas, written by Hai Gaon to the priests of North Africa and published by B. M. Lewin in *Ginze Kedem*, IV, 51–56, 111. It is possible, on the other hand, that the priests and levites resisted successive waves of conversion to other creeds more effectively than did the majority of "Israelites." Whatever the reason, there are today in world Jewry more Cohens and Levis, under these or other names, than 1 or 2 per cent, the probable proportion of their purported ancestors before 70.

31. *Antt.* XX, 8, 8.180–81; 9, 2.206–7; T. Menaḥot XIII, 18–21, 533; Sifre on Deut. 352, ed. by Friedmann fol. 145a (ed. by Finkelstein, p. 409). On the gradual discontinuation of anointing high priests, cf. Schürer's *Geschichte*, II, 285, n. 26.

32. Cf. J. Jeremias's "Zöllner und Sünder," *ZNW*, XXX, 293–300; A. Bloom's *Lèpre dans l'ancienne Egypte et chez les anciens Hébreux;* and my *Jewish Community*, III, 155, n. 29. On the subsequent changes in tax-collecting methods and the ensuing ambivalence in the rabbinic attitude to the collectors, cf. *infra*, Chaps. XIII, n. 17–18, XIV, n. 26.

33. Cf. Klein's aforementioned Hebrew essay in *Qobeṣ* of the Jewish Palestine Exploration Society, 1934–35, pp. 81–107. Similarly, Philo's remarks (in his *Quaestiones in Genesin*, III, 52; *De spec. leg.* III, 23.131–33; cf. Colson's note in *Works*, VII, 638) must be taken to reflect not contemporary realities, but literary reconstructions aided by the existing Greek institution of asylum.

34. See A. H. M. Jones's *Herods of Judaea*, p. 213. A severe famine in Jerusalem which had allegedly caused many deaths before Queen Helena's intervention is recorded in *Antt.* XX, 2, 5.51, and Acts 11:28. On the inflationary pressures of that period, cf. F. M. Heichelheim's *Wirtschaftliche Schwankungen der Zeit von Alexander bis Augustus;* and G. Mickwitz's "Inflation," *PWRE*, Suppl. Vol. VI, pp. 127–33. The data culled by the present writer from scattered rabbinic sources tentatively bear out the gradual rise in Palestinian prices as well.

35. Following Rostovtzeff's lead, S. Klein made a valiant effort to marshall some of the scattered and tenuous evidence in his "Notes on the History of Large Estates in Palestine" (Hebrew), *BJPES*, I, Pt. 3, pp. 3–9; III, 109–16; and his "Vestiges of Large Estates in the Environs of Lydda" (Hebrew), *Krauss Jub. Vol.*, pp. 69–79. Cf. also J. Herz's "Grossgrundbesitz in Palästina im Zeitalter Jesu," *PJB*, XXIV, 98–113. All these studies, however, are merely a promising beginning, Klein's researches, in particular, being concerned with the topographical, rather than economic, aspects of the recorded large estates.

36. Cf. j. Shabbat XVI, 9, 15d. Because of its importance in the evolution of Pharisaism and the rise of Christianity, the problem of the *'am ha-areṣ*, the permutation of this term's meaning from biblical to talmudic times and the social class it was supposed to define have been subjected to careful scrutiny for many years. Perhaps the best general analysis is still to be found in I. Abrahams's " '*Am ha-'Areç*" in the Appendix to C. G. Montefiore's *Synoptic Gospels*, II, 647–69. Cf. also R. Meyer's more recent sociological analysis, "Der 'Am ha-'Areṣ," *Judaica*, III, 169–99. On the much-debated problem of levitical purity in connection with these "people of the land," especially if they happened to be "priests," cf. A. Büchler's "Schammaiten und die levitische Reinheit des 'Am ha-Areṣ," *Festschrift . . . J. Freimann*, pp. 21–37.

37. Shebuot 39a. Caesar's decree, cited by Josephus (*Antt.* XIV, 10, 6.202 ff.), is somewhat equivocal. The crucial words, "the second year [*etei*]" have been amended on fairly convincing grounds, into "the second month [*meni*]" by T. Reinach (cf. the note to his French transl. of Josephus *ad loc.*). Certainly the latter part of the decree provides for an *annual* payment of a lump sum for the district of Jaffa. One readily understands the popular resentment against Roman tolls in view of their number, size and complex administration. The customs duties alone required a vast and expensive administrative machinery which added very tangible burdens to the population's general tax bill. Cf., e.g., S. J. de Laet's very detailed analysis of the *Portorium*.

38. Cf. Tobit 1:8; M. Ma'aser sheni V, 6, 9–10; and other sources discussed by Schürer in his *Geschichte*, II, 307 n. 22, 4.

39. Cf. the passage from T. Menahot XIII, 22, 533 f., cited *infra*, Chap. X, end. Another significant aspect of the agrarian situation during the Second Commonwealth which has never been fully investigated is that of the various forms of land tenancy. A reëxamination of at least the extant legal material and its bearing on the socioeconomic evolution likewise promises to shed some new light on the growing state of social revolution during the last decades of the Second Commonwealth. The purely juridical, but not the economic, aspects have been analyzed by A. Gulak in his *Le-Heqer toledot ha mishpaṭ ha-'ibri* (On the History of Hebrew Law in the Period of the Talmud), I, 109 ff.

40. Tobit 4:8–9; Emperor Julian's *Epistles*, ed. by Wright, III, 71, n. 22. Other apocryphal and pseudepigraphic passages relating to charities, partly of Diaspora origin, are listed by A. Cronbach in his "Social Ideals of the Apocrypha and the Pseudepigrapha," *HUCA*, XVIII, 119–56. Cf., in general, also my *Jewish Community*, I, 131 f.; III, 25 f.; J. Bergmann's *Ha-Ṣedaqah be-Yisrael* (Charity among Jews: Its History and Institutions); and *infra*, Chap. XIV, n. 45, 49.

41. It must be borne in mind, however, that few, if any, semiproselytes were buried in Jewish cemeteries. Since they usually did not formally join the community for which full conversion was a prerequisite, there was no occasion for them to ask for, nor for the communal leaders to assign to them, resting places in Jewish consecrated grounds. That is why Frey is right in saying that no certain evidence of an ordinary *metuens* having been buried in a Jewish catacomb in Rome has as yet come to light (see his *Corpus*, I, 390). The few references hitherto treated as such, are properly considered doubtful.